Middle School 3-1

학교시험 완벽대비

1학기 전과정

적중 100 plus

영어 기출문제집

중3

동아 | 윤정미

Best Collection

구성과 특징

교과서의 주요 학습 내용을 중심으로 학습 영역별 특성에 맞춰 단계별로 다양한 학습 기회를 제공하여
단원별 학습능력 평가는 물론 중간 및 기말고사 시험 등에 완벽하게 대비할 수 있도록 내용을 구성

Words & Expressions

Step1　Key Words 단원별 핵심 단어 설명 및 풀이
　　　　Key Expression 단원별 핵심 숙어 및 관용어 설명
　　　　Word Power 반대 또는 비슷한 뜻 단어 배우기
　　　　English Dictionary 영어로 배우는 영어 단어

Step2　실력평가 단원별 수시평가 대비 주관식, 객관식 문제풀이

Step3　서술형 대비 학업성취도 및 수행능력평가 대비 서술형 문제풀이

Conversation

Step1　핵심 의사소통 소통에 필요한 주요 표현 방법 요약
　　　　핵심 Check 기본적인 표현 방법 및 활용능력 확인

Step2　대화문 익히기 교과서 대화문 심층 분석 및 확인

Step3　교과서 확인학습 빈칸 채우기를 통한 문장 완성 능력 확인

Step4　기본평가 시험대비 기초 학습 능력 평가

Step5　실력평가 단원별 수시평가 대비 주관식, 객관식 문제풀이

Step6　서술형 대비 학업성취도 및 수행능력평가 대비 서술형 문제풀이

Grammar

Step1　주요 문법 단원별 주요 문법 사항과 예문을 알기 쉽게 설명
　　　　핵심 Check 기본 문법사항에 대한 이해 여부 확인

Step2　기본평가 시험대비 기초 학습 능력 평가

Step3　실력평가 단원별 수시평가 대비 주관식, 객관식 문제풀이

Step4　서술형 대비 학업성취도 및 수행능력평가 대비 서술형 문제풀이

Reading

Step1　구문 분석 단원별로 제시된 문장에 대한 구문별 분석과 내용 설명
　　　　확인문제 문장에 대한 기본적인 이해와 인지능력 확인

Step2　확인학습A 빈칸 채우기를 통한 문장 완성 능력 확인

Step3　확인학습B 제시된 우리말을 영어로 완성하여 작문 능력 키우기

Step4　실력평가 단원별 수시평가 대비 주관식, 객관식 문제풀이

Step5　서술형 대비 학업성취도 및 수행능력평가 대비 서술형 문제풀이
　　　　교과서 구석구석 교과서에 나오는 기타 문장까지 완벽 학습

Composition

|영역별 핵심문제|

단어 및 어휘, 대화문, 문법, 독해 등 각 영역별 기출문제의 출제 유형을 분석하여 실전에 대비하고 연습할 수 있도록 문제를 배열

|단원별 예상문제|

기출문제를 분석한 후 새로운 시험 출제 경향을 더하여 새롭게 출제될 수 있는 문제를 포함하여 시험에 완벽하게 대비할 수 있도록 준비

|서술형 실전 및 창의사고력 문제|

학교 시험에서 점차 늘어나는 서술형 시험에 집중 대비하고 고득점을 취득하는데 만전을 기하기 위한 학습 코너

|단원별 모의고사|

영역별, 단계별 학습을 모두 마친 후 실전 연습을 위한 모의고사

교과서 파헤치기

- **단어Test1~3** 영어 단어 우리말 쓰기, 우리말을 영어 단어로 쓰기, 영영풀이에 해당하는 단어와 우리말 쓰기
- **대화문Test1~2** 대화문 빈칸 완성 및 전체 대화문 쓰기
- **본문Test1~5** 빈칸 완성, 우리말 쓰기, 문장 배열연습, 영어 작문하기 복습 등 단계별 반복 학습을 통해 교과서 지문에 대한 완벽한 습득
- **구석구석지문Test1~2** 지문 빈칸 완성 및 전문 영어로 쓰기

Contents

Lesson 1

Follow Your Dream

의사소통 기능

- 경험 묻고 답하기
  A: Have you ever visited Jeju-do?
  B: Yes, I have. / No, I haven't.

- 희망 표현하기
  I hope you can visit there sometime.

언어 형식

- 접속사 whether/if
  I didn't know **whether I really enjoyed it**.

- to부정사의 형용사적 용법
  I got a chance **to see** the Northern Lights.

Words & Expressions

Key Words

- **achieve**[ətʃíːv] 동 성취하다, 달성하다
- **air pollution** 공기 오염
- **beat**[biːt] 동 (심장이) 고동치다, 뛰다
- **bold**[bould] 형 용감한, 대담한
- **chance**[tʃæns] 명 기회
- **college**[kálidʒ] 명 대학(교)
- **company**[kʌ́mpəni] 명 회사
- **contest**[kántest] 명 대회
- **courage**[kə́ːridʒ] 명 용기
- **decision**[disíʒən] 명 결정, 결심
- **designer**[dizáinər] 명 디자이너
- **engineer**[èndʒiníər] 명 엔지니어, 기술자
- **engineering**[èndʒiníəriŋ] 명 공학 (기술), 엔지니어링
- **enter**[éntər] 동 입장하다, 참가하다
- **environment**[inváiərənmənt] 명 환경, 상황, 분위기
- **follow**[fálou] 동 따르다, 뒤를 잇다
- **goal**[goul] 명 목표
- **graduate**[ɡrǽdʒuət] 동 졸업하다
- **inspire**[inspáiər] 동 영감을 주다, 고무하다
- **lead**[liːd] 동 이끌다
- **local**[lóukəl] 형 (특정) 지역의, 현지의
- **major**[méidʒər] 형 중요한, 주된 명 전공 동 전공하다
- **memorable**[mémərəbl] 형 기억할 만한, 인상적인
- **Northern Lights** 오로라, 북극광
- **part-time**[páːrttaim] 형 시간제 근무의
- **photographer**[fətáɡrəfər] 명 사진사
- **photography**[fətáɡrəfi] 명 사진 촬영술
- **professional**[prəféʃənl] 형 전문적인, (전문) 직업의
- **pursue**[pərsúː] 동 추구하다, 좇다
- **quit**[kwit] 동 (직장·학교 등을) 그만두다, (하던 일을) 그만두다
- **realize**[ríːəlàiz] 동 알다, 깨닫다, 실현하다[달성하다]
- **skill**[skil] 동 기량, 기술
- **stable**[stéibl] 형 안정된, 안정적인
- **succeed**[səksíːd] 동 성공하다
- **surprise**[sərpráiz] 동 놀라다, 놀라게 하다
- **surprisingly**[sərpráiziŋli] 부 놀랍게도
- **train**[trein] 동 (특정 직업을) 훈련하다
- **truly**[vàləntíər] 정말로, 진심으로
- **volunteer**[trúːli] 동 자원하다, 봉사하다
- **whether**[hwéðər] 접 ~인지 아닌지
- **win**[win] 동 (상을) 타다, 이기다

Key Expressions

- **be scared** 두려워하다
- **come true** 실현되다, 사실이 되다
- **decide on** (숙고하여 뭔가를) 고르다, (여러 가지 가능성 가운데) ~으로 결정하다
- **follow one's heart** 기분 내키는 대로 하다
- **for a living** 생계 수단으로
- **for the first time** 처음으로
- **get a job** 직장을 얻다
- **get better** (병이나 상황이) 나아지다
- **go on vacation to** ~로 휴가를 가다
- **in fact** 사실은
- **in one's case** ~의 경우에
- **make a decision** 결정하다
- **not ~ at all** 전혀 ~가 아니다
- **right after** 그 직후, 바로 후
- **take a chance** 기회를 잡다
- **take a picture of** ~의 사진을 찍다
- **trial and error** 시행착오
- **walk across** ~을 걸어서 건너다
- **work at** ~에서 일하다

Word Power

※ 다의어

1. **realize** ① 실감하다, (생생하게) 깨닫다 ② (소망·계획 따위를) 실현하다, 현실화하다

2. **major**

  (1) 형용사: ① (둘 중에서) 큰 쪽의, 과반의, 대부분의 ↔ **minor** ② 주요한, 중요한, 일류의

  (2) 명사: (미국 대학) 전공 과목

  (3) 동사: (미국 대학) 전공하다(in)

※ **make + (주로 목적어로 동사에서 파생한) 명사 = 동사**

- **make an attempt** = **attempt** (시도하다)
- **make a change** = **change** (변경하다)
- **make a choice** = **choose** (선택하다)
- **make a decision** = **decide** (결정하다)
- **make a discovery** = **discover** (발견하다)
- **make an excuse** = **excuse** (변명하다)
- **make haste** = **hasten** (급히 서둘다)
- **make a journey** = **journey** (여행하다)
- **make a request** = **request** (요구[부탁]하다)
- **make a response** = **respond** (응답하다)
- **make a bad start** = **start badly** (출발을 그르치다)
- **make a living** (생계를 꾸려가다)

English Dictionary

- **achieve** 성취하다, 달성하다
  → to gain with effort
  노력하여 얻다

- **beat** (심장이) 고동치다, 뛰다
  → make a regular sound or movement of the heart
  심장이 규칙적인 소리를 내고 움직이다

- **bold** 용감한, 대담한
  → not afraid to do things which involve danger
  위험을 포함하고 있는 것들을 하는 것을 두려워하지 않는

- **courage** 용기
  → the ability to do something that frightens one
  사람을 두렵게 하는 어떤 것을 하는 능력

- **goal** 목표
  → something that you hope to achieve, especially when much time and effort will be needed
  특히 많은 시간과 노력이 필요할 때 당신이 성취하기를 희망하는 어떤 것

- **graduate** 졸업하다
  → to complete your studies successfully and leave your school or university
  학업을 성공적으로 마치고 학교나 대학교를 떠나다

- **inspire** 영감을 주다, 고무하다
  → to make you feel that you want to achieve something or create something
  어떤 것을 성취하거나 만들고 싶게 느끼도록 만들다

- **major** 중요한, 주된; 전공
  → very important, serious, main 매우 중요한, 중대한, 주된

  the main subject that a student is studying at a university or college 학생이 대학에서 공부하는 전공 과목

- **pursue** 추구하다, 추진하다
  → to work hard in order to achieve something
  무언가를 성취하기 위해 열심히 일하다

- **quit** (하던 일을) 그만두다
  → to stop doing something
  어떤 것을 하는 것을 멈추다

- **realize** 실현하다[달성하다]
  → to achieve something that you want
  원하는 어떤 것을 성취하다

- **skill** 기량, 기술
  → an ability to do something very well because you have learned it
  익혀왔기 때문에 어떤 것을 매우 잘하는 능력

- **stable** 안정된, 안정적인
  → staying the same, with no big changes or problems
  큰 변화나 문제없이 그대로 유지되는

- **train** (특정 직업을) 훈련하다
  → to teach someone the skills of a particular job or activity, or to be taught these skills
  특정한 직업이나 활동의 기술을 누군가에게 가르치다 또는 이러한 기술을 배우다

- **trial and error** 시행착오
  → experimenting until a solution is found
  해결책이 발견될 때까지 실험하는

[01~02] 다음 밑줄 친 부분과 바꿔 쓸 수 있는 말을 쓰시오.

01

> You will <u>achieve</u> everything you want if you work hard.

① fail   ② save

③ lose   ④ goal

⑤ accomplish

02

> The recovery of his health enabled him to <u>pursue</u> his study.

① succeed   ② decide

③ bold   ④ chase

⑤ realize

03 다음 〈보기〉의 단어를 사용하여 자연스러운 문장을 만들 수 <u>없는</u> 것은? (단어는 한 번씩만 사용할 것.)

> ┌─ 보기 ┐
> major   bold   cause   environment

① Salt is the major _____ of many health problems.

② Students here do not like to study science and _____ .

③ Now the world may be divided into two _____ camps.

④ We have to protect the _____ from pollution.

⑤ He looks very _____ , but he is very weak on the inside.

04 다음 빈칸에 들어갈 알맞은 말을 고르시오.

> I don't have the authority to _____ on this matter.

① decide   ② win

③ come   ④ get

⑤ take

05 다음 밑줄 친 부분의 의미로 알맞지 <u>않은</u> 것은?

① <u>In my case</u>, having bad grades didn't matter. (제 경우에)

② He believes that one should work hard <u>for a living</u>. (생계를 위해)

③ That does not concern me <u>at all</u>. (모두)

④ The young, <u>in fact</u>, are already living in a new country. (사실은)

⑤ In general, every achievement requires <u>trial and error</u>. (시행착오)

서답형

06 다음 두 문장이 같은 의미가 되도록 빈칸을 채우시오. (주어진 철자로 시작할 것.)

> Most parents want their children to have a secure job.
> = Most parents want their children to have a s_____ job.

07 다음 영영풀이가 나타내는 말은?

> to stop doing something

① achieve   ② pursue

③ quit   ④ graduate

⑤ realize

01 다음 영영풀이에 알맞은 어휘를 〈보기〉에서 찾아 쓰시오.

> ┤ 보기 ├
> major   stable   beat   inspire

(1) staying the same, with no big changes or problems
(2) very important, serious, main
(3) to make you feel that you want to achieve something or create something
(4) make a regular sound or movement of the heart

➡ (1) _____ (2) _____ (3) _____

    (4) _____

02 다음 우리말에 맞게 한 단어를 추가하여 주어진 단어를 알맞게 배열하시오.

(1) 행복하게 살고 싶다면, 기분이 내키는 대로 하여라. (you, your, life, heart, live, want, happy, if, a, to) (if로 시작할 것)

   ➡ _____

(2) 아이들은 시행착오를 통해 컴퓨터 프로그램 사용을 배운다. (programs, children, error, computer, use, learn, and, to, by)

   ➡ _____

    _____

(3) 기회를 봐서 개인 사업이나 해야겠어요. (I, my, chance, business, will, start, own, a, and)

   ➡ _____

    _____

03 다음 빈칸에 적절한 말을 주어진 단어를 이용하여 채우시오.

> I hope your birthday wishes will all _____! (true)

04 다음 짝지어진 두 단어의 관계가 같도록 빈칸에 알맞은 말을 주어진 철자로 시작하여 쓰시오.

(1) major : minor = fail : s_____
(2) encourage : inspire = aim : g_____

05 다음 우리말에 맞도록 빈칸에 알맞은 말을 쓰시오.

(1) 그는 생계를 위해 전국을 돌아다녀야만 했다.
   → He was forced to travel around the whole country for a _____.
(2) 한국인들은 처음 만났을 때 서로 머리 숙여 인사한다.
   → Koreans bow to each other when they meet _____ the first time.
(3) 당신을 모욕할 생각은 전혀 없었다.
   → I did not intend to insult you at _____.
(4) 머리가 복잡할 때는 결정하지 마라.
   → Don't _____ a decision when you can't think straight.

Conversation

1 경험 묻고 답하기

> **A** Have you ever visited Jeju-do? 제주도에 가 본 적 있어요?
>
> **B** Yes, I have. / No, I haven't. 네. 가 봤어요. / 아니오. 가 본 적 없어요.

- 'Have you ever+과거분사 ~?'는 '~을 해 본 적 있어요?'라는 의미로 경험을 물을 때 사용하는 표현이다. 경험한 횟수를 물을 때는 'How often have you+과거분사 ~?'를 써서 나타낸다. ever는 '한 번이라도'의 뜻으로 강조의 의미이며, 생략해도 된다.

- 질문의 대답으로 경험이 있으면(긍정) 'Yes, I have.'로, 경험이 없으면(부정) 'No, I haven't.'로 대답하거나 never를 써서 '한 번도 ~한 적이 없다'라고 강조하여 말할 수 있다.

  - Have you ever thought about becoming a teacher? 선생님이 될 생각을 해 본 적 있어요?
  - How often have you been to the Grand Park? 대공원에는 얼마나 자주 가 보셨습니까?
  - I have never regretted being a teacher. 나는 교사가 된 것을 후회한 적이 없다.

- 상대방에게 같은 질문을 하고 싶으면 'Have you?'라고 간단하게 질문할 수 있다.

- 경험을 나타낼 때는 다음과 같은 부사(구)를 함께 쓰는 경우가 많다.

> ever(지금까지, 여태껏), never(~한 적 없는), once(한 번), twice(두 번),
> 숫자+times(~번), often(자주), before(이전에)

유사 표현

- Do you have any experience in this field? 이 분야에 경험은 있습니까?
- Have you had any musical experience before? 당신은 전에 악기를 다룬 경험이 있나요?

핵심 Check

1. 우리말과 일치하도록 주어진 단어를 배열하여 문장을 쓰시오.

   다른 나라에 가 본 적 있니? (another, have, visited, ever, country, you, ?)

   ➡ _____

2. 다음 문장과 같은 의미가 되도록 주어진 단어를 이용하여 쓰시오.

   Have you ever visited Paris?

   ➡ _____ (be)

2 희망 표현하기

• **I hope you can visit there sometime.** 나는 언젠가 네가 거기에 가 볼 수 있기를 바라.

■ 희망을 표현할 때는 '~하기를 바라, ~하면 좋겠어'라는 뜻의 'I hope (that)+주어(+can/will)+동사 ~.' 또는 'I hope to+동사원형 ~.'의 표현을 사용하여 말할 수 있다. 시간을 나타내는 부사 soon, someday, sometime 등을 문장 끝에 붙이기도 한다.

  • I hope you like it here. 이곳을 좋아하셨으면 좋겠어요.
  • I hope to visit that city again. 나는 그 도시를 한 번 더 방문하고 싶다.

■ 유사 표현으로는 'I wish ~', 'I pray ~', 'I expect ~', 'I want to+동사원형 ~' 'I'd like to+동사원형 ~' 등이 있다.

희망 표현하기

  • I pray you will not hate me. 나는 당신이 나를 미워하지 않기를 바랍니다.
  • I wish I could speak English well. 나는 영어를 잘하기를 바라.
  • I expect you will pass the test next year. 내년에는 네가 그 시험에 합격하길 기대해.
  • I want to thank you from the bottom of my heart. 진심으로 감사드리고 싶군요.

희망 묻기

  • What is your wish for the New Year? 당신의 새해 소원은 무엇인가요?
  • What do you want to do tonight? 오늘밤 뭐 하고 싶어?
  • What do you hope for? 희망이 뭡니까?

핵심 Check

3. 밑줄 친 우리말과 일치하도록 주어진 단어를 배열하여 문장을 만드시오.

A: Have you ever had Spanish food before?

B: No, I haven't. Have you tried it?

A: Yes, I have. 네가 언젠가 그것을 먹어 보길 바라. (try, sometime, I, you, can, it, hope) It's really good.

➡ _____

🎙 **Listen and Talk A 1**

> G: ❶Have you ever had Spanish food before?
>
> B: ❷No, I haven't. Have you tried ❸it?
>
> G: ❷Yes, I have. ❹I hope you can try ❸it sometime. ❸It's really good.
>
> B: ❺I will. ❻For now, I'll just buy this Spanish ❼recipe book.

G: 스페인 요리를 먹어 본 적 있니?

B: 아니, 없어. 너는 먹어 본 적이 있니?

G: 응, 있어. 네가 언젠가 그것을 먹어 보길 바라. 정말 맛있거든.

B: 그럴게. 우선 이 스페인 요리책을 사야겠어.

❶ 'Have you ever+과거분사 ~?'는 '~을 해 본 적 있어요?'라는 의미로 경험을 물을 때 사용하는 표현이다. ever는 '한 번이라도'의 뜻으로 강조의 의미이며, 생략해도 된다.
❷ 질문의 대답으로 경험이 있으면(긍정) 'Yes, I have.'로, 경험이 없으면(부정) 'No, I haven't.'로 대답하거나 never를 써서 '한 번도 ~한 적이 없다'라고 강조하여 말할 수 있다.
❸ it은 Spanish food를 받는 인칭대명사이다.
❹ 'I hope (that)+주어+(can/will)+동사 ~.' 또는 'I hope to+동사원형 ~.'은 '~하기를 바라, ~하면 좋겠어.'라는 뜻으로 희망을 표현할 때 쓰는 말이다.
❺ I will. 다음에는 'try Spanish food sometime'이 생략되어 있다.　　❻ For now: 우선은, 현재로는　　❼ recipe: (요리의) 조리법

Check(√) True or False

(1) The girl has never had Spanish food before.　　T ☐ F ☐

(2) The boy will try Spanish food sometime.　　T ☐ F ☐

🎙 **Listen and Talk C**

> B: I really liked your book ❶about training dogs.
>
> W: Thank you. Do you like dogs?
>
> B: Yes, I do. I love all ❷kinds of animals.
>
> W: ❸Have you ever thought of becoming an animal doctor?
>
> B: Yes, I have. I really want to become an animal doctor.
>
> W: What ❹are you doing to achieve your goal?
>
> B: I'm doing volunteer work at the local animal house.
>
> W: ❺That's good. What else are you doing?
>
> B: I'm also watching a lot of TV shows about animals.
>
> W: You're doing great! ❻I hope you become a good animal doctor someday.
>
> B: Thank you.

B: 개를 훈련하는 것에 관한 당신의 책이 저는 정말 좋았어요.

W: 고마워요. 개를 좋아해요?

B: 네, 저는 모든 종류의 동물을 매우 좋아해요.

W: 수의사가 되는 것을 생각해 본 적 있어요?

B: 네, 있어요. 저는 수의사가 정말 되고 싶어요.

W: 목표를 이루기 위해 무엇을 하고 있나요?

B: 지역 동물의 집(동물 보호소)에서 자원봉사를 하고 있어요.

W: 좋군요. 또 무엇을 하고 있나요?

B: 동물에 관한 TV 쇼도 많이 보고 있어요.

W: 매우 잘하고 있어요! 언젠가 좋은 수의사가 되기를 바랄게요.

B: 감사합니다.

❶ about은 '~에 관한'의 뜻으로 on으로 바꿔 쓸 수 있다.　　❷ kind는 '종류'를 뜻하는 명사로 사용되었다.
❸ 경험을 물을 때 사용하는 표현이다.　　❹ 현재 하고 있는 것을 묻기 위해 현재진행시제를 사용했다.
❺ That은 'doing volunteer work at the local animal house'를 가리킨다.　　❻ 희망을 표현할 때 쓰는 말이다.

Check(√) True or False

(3) The woman wants to be an animal doctor.　　T ☐ F ☐

(4) The boy is watching a lot of TV shows about animals.　　T ☐ F ☐

Listen and Talk A 2

B: ❶Have you ever visited another country?
G: No, I haven't. ❷Have you?
B: Yes, ❸I've been to France. ❹I hope you can travel ❺to ❻another country sometime.
G: Yes, I really want ❼to visit Canada. Look! This book ❽about Canada ❾looks very interesting.

❶ 경험을 묻는 표현이다.
❷ 뒤에 'ever visited another country'가 생략되어 있다.
❸ 'have been to'로 '갔다 온' 경험을 나타내고 있다. 'have gone to'는 '가버리고 여기 없다'라는 결과를 나타내므로 그 차이에 유의한다.
❹ 희망을 나타내는 표현이다. 'I wish ~', 'I pray ~', 'I expect ~', 'I want to+동사원형 ~', 'I'd like to+동사원형 ~' 등으로 표현할 수도 있다.
❺ '~로 여행하다'라는 것을 나타내기 위해 전치사 to를 붙였다.
❻ another 다음에는 단수 명사가 이어진다. other 다음에는 보통 복수 명사가 나온다.
❼ to부정사가 목적으로 사용되었다.
❽ about은 '~에 관한'의 뜻으로 on으로 바꿔 쓸 수 있다.
❾ 'look+형용사'로 interestingly로 쓰지 않도록 주의한다.

Listen and Talk A 3

G: You ❶should read this book about the moon. ❷It's really interesting.
B: I know. I've ❸already read ❷it.
G: ❹You ❺did? ❻How about the movie? Have you also seen the movie about the book?
B: No, ❼I haven't.
G: Well, ❽it's ❾even better than the book. I hope you can see the movie ❿soon.

❶ should는 '권유, 권고'의 의미로 쓰였다.
❷ 두 개의 It과 it 모두 'this book about the moon'을 가리킨다.
❸ already는 '이미, 벌써'라는 뜻으로 완료시제에서 '완료'를 나타내는 문장과 많이 쓰인다.
❹ 구어체에서 평서문의 어순으로 쓰고 끝을 올려서 말하여 의문문을 대신한다.
❺ read it을 대신하는 대동사이다.
❻ 'How about ~?'은 '~은 어때?'라는 뜻으로 'What about ~?'으로 바꿔 쓸 수 있다.
❼ 뒤에 'seen the movie about the book'이 생략되어 있다.
❽ it은 'the movie about the book'을 가리킨다.
❾ even은 비교급을 강조하는 부사로 'much, far, a lot, still' 등으로 바꿔 쓸 수 있다.
❿ soon은 '곧'이라는 의미로 희망을 표현할 때, 종종 시간을 나타내는 부사 soon, someday, sometime 등을 문장 끝에 붙이기도 한다.

Listen and Talk A 4

G: ❶I'm going to buy this CD. I love ❷ listening to piano music.
B: Me, ❸too. I also enjoy ❹playing the piano.
G: Really? So ❺you can play the piano?
B: Yes. How about you?

G: Well, I've never learned ❻how to play.
B: It's fun. I hope you'll have a chance ❼to learn.

❶ 'be going to'로 미래를 나타내고 있다.
❷ love의 목적으로 'to listen'으로 쓸 수도 있다.
❸ 긍정의 의미로 too를 쓰고 있다.
❹ enjoy의 목적어로 쓰인 동명사이다.
❺ 구어체에서 평서문의 어순으로 쓰고 끝을 올려서 말하여 의문문을 대신한다.
❻ '의문사+to부정사'로 목적으로 쓰이고 있다.
❼ 'a chance'를 수식하는 to부정사(형용사적 용법)이다.

Review 1

G: Mike, ❶have you ❷tried Bulgogi ❸before?
B: No, ❹I haven't.
G: ❺How about Bibimbap? Have you tried ❻ that?
B: Yes, I've eaten ❼it ❽once. ❼It was really delicious.

❶ 경험을 묻는 표현이다.
❷ try는 '먹어 보다'라는 의미로 쓰였다.
❸ ago를 쓰지 않는다는 것에 주의한다.
❹ 뒤에 'tried Bulgogi before'가 생략되어 있다.
❺ 'How about Bibimbap?'은 '비빔밥은 어때?'라는 뜻으로 'What about Bibimbap?', 'What do you say to Bibimbap?' 등으로 바꿔 쓸 수 있다.
❻ that은 Bibimbap을 가리킨다.
❼ it과 It은 Bibimbap을 가리킨다.
❽ once는 '한 번'이라는 뜻으로 '경험'을 나타내는 완료시제 문장과 자주 쓰인다.

Review 2

G: My favorite book is *Charlie and the Chocolate Factory*. ❶Have you read ❷it, Peter?
B: No, ❸I haven't, but I've seen the movie. ❹ How about you, Yubin? Have you seen the movie, too?
G: Yes, ❺I have. But I like the book ❻more. ❼I hope you can read it ❽sometime.
B: OK, ❾I will.

❶ 경험을 묻는 표현이다.
❷ it은 'Charlie and the Chocolate Factory'라는 책을 가리킨다.
❸ 뒤에 'read it'이 생략되어 있다.
❹ 상대방은 어떤지를 묻는 표현이다.
❺ 뒤에 'seen the movie'가 생략되어 있다.
❻ 책과 영화, 두 개를 비교하고 있는 것이므로 비교급을 사용했다.
❼ 희망을 나타내는 표현이다. 'I wish ~', 'I pray ~', 'I expect ~', 'I want to+동사원형 ~', 'I'd like to+동사원형 ~' 등으로 표현할 수도 있다.
❽ sometime은 '언젠가'라는 의미로 희망을 표현할 때, 종종 시간을 나타내는 부사 soon, someday, sometime 등을 문장 끝에 붙이기도 한다.
❾ 뒤에 'read it sometime'이 생략되어 있다.

다음 우리말과 일치하도록 빈칸에 알맞은 말을 쓰시오.

Listen and Talk A 1

G: _____ you ever had _____ food _____?

B: No, I _____. Have you _____ _____?

G: Yes, I _____. _____ _____ you _____ try it _____. It's really good.

B: I _____. _____ _____, I'll just buy this _____ _____ book.

G: 스페인 요리를 먹어 본 적 있니?
B: 아니, 없어. 너는 먹어 본 적이 있니?
G: 응, 있어. 네가 언젠가 그것을 먹어 보길 바라. 정말 맛있거든.
B: 그럴게. 우선 이 스페인 요리 책을 사야겠어.

Listen and Talk A 2

B: Have you _____ visited _____ country?

G: No, I _____. _____ you?

B: Yes, _____ _____ _____ France. _____ _____ you _____ travel _____ another _____ _____.

G: Yes, I really want _____ _____ Canada. Look! This book about Canada looks very _____.

B: 다른 나라에 가 본 적이 있니?
G: 아니, 없어. 너는 가 본 적이 있니?
B: 응, 난 프랑스에 가 본 적이 있어. 네가 언젠가 다른 나라를 여행해 보기를 바라.
G: 응. 난 캐나다에 정말 가고 싶어. 봐! 캐나다에 관한 이 책은 정말 흥미로워 보인다.

Listen and Talk A 3

G: You _____ read this book about the moon. It's really interesting.

B: I know. I've _____ read _____.

G: You _____? _____ _____ the movie? _____ _____ also seen the movie about the book?

B: No, I _____.

G: Well, it's _____ _____ _____ the book. _____ you can see the movie _____.

G: 달에 관한 이 책을 꼭 읽어 봐. 그것은 정말 흥미로워.
B: 알고 있어. 나 이미 그것을 읽은 적이 있어.
G: 그랬니? 영화는? 그 책에 관한 영화도 본 적이 있니?
B: 아니, 없어.
G: 음, 그것은 책보다도 더 재미있어. 네가 그 영화를 곧 볼 수 있기를 바랄게.

Listen and Talk A 4

G: I'm going to buy this CD. I love _____ to piano music.

B: Me, _____. I also enjoy _____ _____ piano.

G: Really? So you _____ _____ _____ piano?

B: Yes. _____ _____ _____?

G: Well, I've _____ learned _____ _____.

B: It's _____. _____ _____ you'll have a chance _____ _____.

G: 난 이 CD를 살 거야. 난 피아노 음악을 듣는 것을 좋아해.
B: 나도. 난 피아노 치는 것도 즐겨서 해.
G: 정말? 넌 피아노를 칠 수 있니?
B: 응. 너는 어때?
G: 음, 난 피아노 치는 법을 배운 적이 없어.
B: 그것은 재미있어. 너도 배울 기회가 있길 바랄게.

Listen and Talk C

B: I really liked your book _____ _____ dogs.

W: Thank you. Do you like dogs?

B: Yes, I _____. I love all _____ of animals.

W: _____ you _____ thought of _____ an animal doctor?

B: Yes, I _____. I really want _____ _____ an animal doctor.

W: W h a t _____ _____ _____ _____ _____ y o u r _____?

B: I'm _____ volunteer work at the local animal house.

W: That's good. What _____ are you doing?

B: I'm _____ _____ a lot of TV shows about animals.

W: You're doing _____! _____ _____ you become a good animal doctor _____.

B: Thank you.

B: 개를 훈련하는 것에 관한 당신의 책이 저는 정말 좋았어요.
W: 고마워요. 개를 좋아해요?
B: 네, 저는 모든 종류의 동물을 매우 좋아해요.
W: 수의사가 되는 것을 생각해 본 적 있어요?
B: 네, 있어요. 저는 수의사가 정말 되고 싶어요.
W: 목표를 이루기 위해 무엇을 하고 있나요?
B: 지역 동물의 집(동물 보호소)에서 자원봉사를 하고 있어요.
W: 좋군요. 또 무엇을 하고 있나요?
B: 동물에 관한 TV 쇼도 많이 보고 있어요.
W: 매우 잘하고 있어요! 언젠가 좋은 수의사가 되기를 바랄게요.
B: 감사합니다.

Review 1

G: Mike, _____ you _____ Bulgogi _____?

B: No, I _____.

G: _____ _____ Bibimbap? _____ you _____ that?

B: Yes, I've eaten it _____. It was really delicious.

G: Mike, 불고기를 먹어 본 적이 있니?
B: 아니, 없어.
G: 비빔밥은? 먹어 본 적이 있니?
B: 응, 한번 먹어 본 적이 있어. 그것은 정말 맛있었어.

Review 2

G: My favorite book is *Charlie and the Chocolate Factory*. _____ you read _____, Peter?

B: No, I _____, but I've seen the movie. _____ _____ you, Yubin? _____ you seen the movie, _____?

G: Yes, I _____. But I like the book _____. _____ _____ you can read it _____.

B: OK, I _____.

G: 내가 가장 좋아하는 책은 "찰리와 초콜릿 공장"이야. Peter, 그것을 읽어 본 적이 있니?
B: 아니, 읽은 적은 없지만 영화를 본 적은 있어. 유빈아, 넌 어때? 영화도 본 적이 있니?
G: 응, 있어. 그렇지만 난 책을 더 좋아해. 난 네가 언젠가 그 책을 읽을 수 있기를 바라.
B: 알겠어, 읽어 볼게.

01 다음 대화의 순서를 바르게 배열하시오.

> (A) I hope I can visit there again.
> (B) Yes, I have. The island is beautiful.
> (C) Have you ever visited Jeju-do?

➡ _____

[02~03] 다음 대화를 읽고 물음에 답하시오.

B: _____(A)_____ (ever, have, country, visit, another)
G: No, I haven't. Have you?
B: Yes, I've been to France. I hope ___(B)___ you can travel to another country sometime.
G: Yes, I really want to visit Canada. Look! This book about Canada looks very interesting.

02 주어진 어휘를 이용하여 문맥에 맞게 빈칸 (A)에 알맞은 말을 쓰시오.

➡ _____

03 빈칸 (B)에 알맞은 말을 고르시오.

① that   ② what   ③ which
④ who   ⑤ if

[04~05] 다음 밑줄 친 우리말을 주어진 단어를 이용해 영작하시오.

04

> A: <u>나는 네가 그 책을 언젠가 읽어 보기를 바라.</u> (hope, sometime)
> B: Yes, I will.

➡ _____ (8 words)

05

> A: <u>영국에 얼마나 자주 가 보셨나요?</u> (be, have)
> B: Three times.

➡ _____ (7 words)

01 다음 중 짝지어진 대화가 어색한 것은?

① A: Have you ever had Spanish food before?

　B: No, I haven't. Have you tried it?

② A: I've been to France. I hope you can travel to another country sometime.

　B: I really want to visit Canada.

③ A: You should read this book about the moon. It's really interesting.

　B: I know. I've already read it.

④ A: I have tried Indian curry.

　B: I hope you can visit an Indian curry restaurant.

⑤ A: I really liked your book about training dogs.

　B: Thank you. Do you like dogs?

[02~04] 다음 대화를 읽고 물음에 답하시오.

B: I really liked your book about training dogs.

W: Thank you. Do you like dogs?

B: Yes, I do. I love all kinds of animals. (①)

W: Have you ever thought of becoming an animal doctor? (②)

B: Yes, I have. I really want to become an animal doctor. (③)

W: What are you doing to ___(A)___ your goal? (④)

B: I'm doing volunteer work at the local animal house.

W: (⑤) What else are you doing?

B: I'm also watching a lot of TV shows about animals.

W: You're doing great! (B)언젠가 좋은 수의사가 되기를 바랄게요. (hope, someday, animal, become, good)

B: Thank you.

02 위 대화의 ①~⑤ 중 주어진 문장이 들어갈 알맞은 곳은?

That's good.

①　　　②　　　③　　　④　　　⑤

03 빈칸 (A)에 알맞은 말을 고르시오.

① reject　　　② achieve

③ decide　　　④ pass

⑤ succeed

서답형

04 밑줄 친 (B)의 우리말에 맞게 주어진 어휘를 이용하여 영작하시오.

➡ _____

　_____

[05~06] 다음 대화를 읽고 물음에 답하시오.

G: _____(A)_____

B: No, I haven't. Have you tried it?

G: Yes, I have. I hope you can try it sometime. It's really good.

B: I will. (B)우선 I'll just buy this Spanish recipe book.

05 위 대화의 빈칸 (A)에 들어갈 말로 알맞은 것은?

① Do you want to have Spanish food?

② How about ordering Spanish food?

③ Did you have Spanish food before?

④ Have you ever had Spanish food before?

⑤ Why didn't you have Spanish food before?

06 밑줄 친 (B)의 우리말을 두 단어로 쓰시오.

➡ _____

07 다음 대화의 밑줄 친 부분의 의도로 알맞은 것은?

> B: <u>Have you ever visited another country?</u>
> G: No, I haven't. Have you?
> B: Yes, I've been to France. I hope you can travel to another country sometime.
> G: Yes, I really want to visit Canada. Look! This book about Canada looks very interesting.

① 궁금증 표현하기 ② 유감 표현하기
③ 격려하기 ④ 희망 표현하기
⑤ 경험 묻기

[08~09] 다음 대화를 읽고 물음에 답하시오.

> A: _____(A)_____
> B: I make clothes.
> A: Did you finish making my clothes?
> B: Yes. After a lot of (B)<u>시행착오</u>, I made the most beautiful clothes. Which do you prefer?
> A: I like both. I can't (C)<u>결정하다</u>.

08 위 대화의 빈칸 (A)에 알맞은 것은?

① What are you doing?
② What do you do for a living?
③ Do you make clothes?
④ Why do you make clothes?
⑤ How do you make clothes?

09 위 대화의 밑줄 친 우리말 (B)와 (C)를 각각 3 단어로 쓰시오.

➡ (B) _____ (C) _____

10 주어진 글에 이어 대화가 자연스럽게 연결되도록 (A)~(D) 를 순서대로 가장 적절하게 배열한 것은?

> You should read this book about the moon. It's really interesting.

> (A) You did? How about the movie? Have you also seen the movie about the book?
> (B) No, I haven't.
> (C) I know. I've already read it.
> (D) Well, it's even better than the book. I hope you can see the movie soon.

① (B) – (A) – (C) – (D)
② (B) – (C) – (A) – (D)
③ (C) – (A) – (B) – (D)
④ (C) – (B) – (A) – (D)
⑤ (C) – (D) – (B) – (A)

[11~12] 다음 대화를 읽고 물음에 답하시오.

> G: Mike, have you tried Bulgogi before?
> B: No, I haven't.
> G: (a)<u>How about Bibimbap?</u> Have you tried that?
> B: Yes, _____(A)_____ It was really delicious.

11 위 대화의 빈칸 (A)에 '한 번 먹어 보았다.'는 경험을 말하는 문장을 쓰시오.

➡ _____

12 밑줄 친 (a)와 같은 뜻이 되도록 다음 문장의 빈칸에 알맞은 말을 쓰시오.

➡ _____ about Bibimbap?

[01~03] 다음 대화를 읽고 물음에 답하시오.

G: My favorite book is *Charlie and the Chocolate Factory*. Have you read it, Peter?

B: No, I haven't, but I've seen the movie. How about you, Yubin? _____(A)_____, too?

G: Yes, I have. But I like the book more. I hope you can read it sometimes.

B: OK, I will.

01 빈칸 (A)에 '그 영화를 보았는지' 경험을 묻는 말을 쓰시오. (5 단어)

➡ _____

02 Which does Yubin like better, the book or the movie?

➡ _____

03 What have both Peter and Yubin done?

➡ _____

[04~06] 다음 대화를 읽고 물음에 답하시오.

B: I really liked your book about training dogs.

W: Thank you. Do you like dogs?

B: Yes, I do. I love all kinds of animals.

W: (A)수의사가 되는 것을 생각해 본 적 있어요?

B: Yes, I have. I really want to become an animal doctor.

W: What are you doing to achieve your goal?

B: I'm doing volunteer work at the local animal house.

W: That's good. What else are you doing?

B: I'm also watching a lot of TV shows about animals.

W: You're doing great! _____(B)_____ (hope, animal doctor, someday)

B: Thank you.

04 현재완료시제를 이용하여 밑줄 친 (A)의 우리말을 9 단어로 영작하시오.

➡ _____

_____

05 주어진 어휘를 이용하여 빈칸 (B)에 알맞은 말을 9 단어로 쓰시오.

➡ _____

_____

06 What is tho boy doing to achieve his goal?

➡ _____

_____

[07~08] 다음 대화를 읽고 물음에 답하시오.

G: You _____(A)_____. (this book, the moon, read, about) It's really interesting.

B: I know. I've already read it.

G: You did? How about the movie? Have you also seen the movie about the book?

B: No, I haven't.

G: Well, it's ___(B)___ better than the book. I hope you can see the movie soon.

07 주어진 어휘에 한 단어를 추가하여 빈칸 (A)에 권고하는 말을 쓰시오.

➡ _____

08 빈칸 (B)에 강조하는 말을 3개 이상 쓰시오.

➡ _____

Grammar

① 접속사 whether/if

> • I didn't know **whether** I really enjoyed it. 난 내가 그것을 정말로 좋아하는지는 알 수가 없었어요.
> • She's not sure **if** she can do it. 그녀는 자신이 그것을 할 수 있을지 확신할 수 없다.

■ whether와 if는 '~인지 아닌지'의 뜻을 갖는 명사절을 이끄는 접속사로 'whether+주어+동사'의 어순으로 쓰인다. 보통 ask, be not sure, find out, know, see, tell, wonder 등의 동사 뒤에 whether[if]절이 목적어로서 나온다.

> • The man **asked whether[if]** he could borrow the woman's calculator.
> 남자는 여자의 계산기를 빌릴 수 있는지 물어봤다.
> • I **wonder whether[if]** Mom is home now. 나는 엄마가 지금 집에 계신지 궁금하다.

■ whether와 if는 보통 다음과 같은 차이가 있다.

(1) whether는 문두에서 주절을 이끌 수 있지만 if는 그럴 수 없다.
> • **Whether** he will carry out his plan (or not) is not confirmed.
> 그가 자기의 계획을 실행할지는 확인되지 않는다.

(2) whether는 전치사의 목적어가 되는 명사절을 이끌 수 있지만 if는 그럴 수 없다.
> • Keep track of **whether** the screensaver has become active (or not).
> 화면 보호기가 활성화됐는지 여부를 추적하세요.

(3) whether는 to부정사와 붙여 쓸 수 있지만 if는 그럴 수 없다.
> • He seemed to try to decide **whether to say** something or not.
> 그는 뭔가를 말할지 말지 결정하려고 애쓰는 듯 보였다.

(4) 'whether or not'은 쓸 수 있지만 if는 그럴 수 없다. 단, 'or not'을 따로 뒤에 쓸 수는 있다.
> • I don't know **whether or not** it was true. 나는 그것이 사실이었는지 아닌지 모른다.
> • I don't know **whether[if]** he'll be promoted or not. 나는 그가 승진할지 여부를 모른다.

(5) whether는 주격 보어가 되는 명사절에 쓸 수 있지만 if는 그럴 수 없다.
> • The question is **whether** he is ready for it. 문제는 그가 그것에 대해 준비가 되었느냐는 것이다.

cf. whether[if]로 시작하는 명사절은 의문사 없는 의문문이 간접의문문이 된 구조이다. 'whether[if]+주어+동사'의 어순으로 쓴다.

> • Do you know? + Does she have any personal problems?
> → Do you know **whether[if]** she has any personal problems?
> 당신은 그녀에게 개인적인 문제들이 있는지 여부를 알고 있습니까?

핵심 Check

1. 다음 괄호 안에서 알맞은 말을 고르시오.

(1) The manager couldn't tell (if / that) the customers needed anything.

(2) Anna asked her brother (that / whether) he believed the story.

② to부정사의 형용사적 용법

- I got a chance **to see** the Northern Lights. 나는 오로라를 볼 수 있는 기회가 있었죠.
- Here's some advice **to help** them. 여기 그들을 도울 몇 가지 충고가 있습니다.

■ to부정사는 명사 뒤에서 명사를 꾸밀 수 있다.(형용사적 용법) : 문맥에 따라 '~한, ~하는, ~할'로 과거, 현재, 미래 의미 등으로 해석 가능한데, '~할'의 뜻으로 주로 쓰인다.
- Junko Tabei is the first woman **to climb** Mt. Everest. Junko Tabei는 에베레스트산을 오른 최초의 여성이다. 〈과거: ~한〉
- A firefighter is a person **to protect** life and property. 소방관은 생명과 재산을 보호하는 사람이다. 〈현재: ~하는〉
- Wilber needs some food **to eat**. Wilber는 먹을 음식을 좀 필요로 한다. 〈미래: ~할〉

■ to부정사의 형용사적 용법에서도 for+목적격의 '의미상 주어'를 쓸 수 있다.
- It is an easy problem **to solve**. 그것은 해결하기 쉬운 문제이다. 〈일반인〉
- It is an easy problem **for her to solve**. 그것은 그녀가 해결하기 쉬운 문제이다. 〈특정인〉

■ '-thing, -body, -one'으로 끝나는 대명사를 to부정사가 뒤에서 수식한다.
- The runners need **something to drink**. 그 주자들은 마실 어떤 것이 필요하다.
- Becky is looking for **somebody to turn to**. Becky는 의지할 어떤 사람을 찾고 있다.
- Is there **anyone to stop** him from hurting himself? 그가 스스로를 괴롭히지 않도록 막아줄 누군가가 있을까요?

■ to부정사의 형용사적 용법에서는 동사 뒤의 '전치사'에 유의하여 의미를 이해해야 한다.
- I have something **to write**. 나는 쓸 어떤 것이 있다. 〈직접적인 글쓰기의 소재〉
- I have something **to write about**. 나는 그것에 관해 쓸 어떤 것이 있다. 〈간접적인 소재〉
- I have something **to write on**. 나는 그 위에 쓸 어떤 것이 있다. 〈종이나 흑판 같은, 글씨를 그 위에 쓸 어떤 것〉
- I have something **to write with**. 나는 가지고 쓸 어떤 것이 있다. 〈연필이나 붓과 같은 글씨를 쓰기 위한 도구로서의 어떤 것〉
- I need some **money to buy**. (X) → 돈이 사는 것이 아니라, 돈을 갖고 내가 구매
- I need some **money to buy with**. (○) 나는 구매를 위해 돈이 좀 필요하다.
- The lonely child needs **games to play**. (○) → 플레이할 게임들
- The lonely child needs **friends to play with**. (○) → (같이) 놀 친구들

핵심 Check

2. 다음 괄호 안에서 알맞은 말을 고르시오.
 (1) Please give him something (drinking / to drink).
 (2) It is time for them (to leave / leaving).
 (3) The baby needs a spoon (to eat / to eat with).

01 다음 빈칸에 들어갈 말로 알맞은 것은?

> I brought some books _____ on the train.

① read ② reads ③ to read
④ have read ⑤ reading

02 다음 각 문장의 빈칸에 공통으로 들어갈 말로 알맞은 것은? (대 · 소문자 구분 없음)

> • She asked me _____ I found the solution to the issue.
> • _____ it will snow tomorrow or not matters to those climbers.
> • I often wonder _____ or not the man can smile.

① if ② that ③ what
④ whether ⑤ which

03 다음 중 밑줄 친 부분의 쓰임이 〈보기〉와 같은 것을 고르시오.

┌─ 보기 ┤
> She wasn't sure if she could take the test.

① You will be sick if you keep eating junk food.
② They won't miss the bus if they leave now.
③ She can play with her friends if she finishes her homework.
④ All of them wanted to know if it was true.
⑤ Let's take a taxi if you are too tired.

04 다음 우리말에 맞게 주어진 어휘를 바르게 배열하시오.

(1) 그들은 뜨거운 마실 것을 원한다. (hot, want, to, they, drink, something)
➡ _____

(2) Paula는 대화할 누군가가 필요하다. (talk, needs, Paula, someone, with, to)
➡ _____

(3) 논의할 주제들이 거의 없다. (issues, to, are, there, few, discuss)
➡ _____

1 다음 중 어법상 <u>어색한</u> 것은?

① I wonder if she knows about my broken finger.

② I wonder if she knows about my broken finger or not.

③ I wonder whether she knows about my broken finger or not.

④ I wonder if or not she knows about my broken finger.

⑤ I wonder whether or not she knows about my broken finger.

2 다음 중 어법상 바르지 <u>않은</u> 것은?

① Bring me two pieces of paper to write on.

② Finally we bought a small apartment to live in.

③ Sally ordered something not to drink too cold.

④ Johnson bought the armchair to take a rest in.

⑤ She prepared five pencils to write with.

3 다음 각 문장의 밑줄 친 to부정사가 '형용사적 용법'으로 쓰인 것을 <u>모두</u> 고르시오.

ⓐ It is not always good for your health <u>to eat</u> vegetables.

ⓑ Grace needed some books <u>to read</u> while she was waiting for her mom.

ⓒ Timothy promised <u>to get</u> strong after the brain surgery.

ⓓ All of my friends gathered together <u>to celebrate</u> my baby's first birthday party.

ⓔ Sean visited Harvard University <u>to suggest</u> collaborative research.

ⓕ Michael didn't have a chance <u>to watch</u> the movie with Kathy.

ⓖ My mom was disappointed <u>to find</u> me spend my monthly allowances in just a week.

4 다음 우리말을 어법상 알맞게 영작한 것을 고르시오.

> 그녀는 내게 콘서트에 가길 원하는지 물었다.

① She wanted to ask me to go to the concert with her.

② She asked that I would like to go to the concert.

③ She asked me that I would go to the concert.

④ She asked me if I wanted to go to the concert.

⑤ She asked me whether I wanted to have the concert to go.

5 주어진 문장의 <u>틀린</u> 부분을 찾아, 올바르게 고친 것을 고르시오.

> I wasn't sure that I could succeed in taking pictures for a living.

① I wasn't sure what I could succeed in taking pictures for a living.

② I wasn't sure that if I could succeed in taking pictures for a living.

③ I wasn't sure whether or not I could succeed in taking pictures for a living.

④ I wasn't sure even if I could succeed in taking pictures for a living or not.

⑤ I wasn't sure what if I could succeed in taking pictures for a living.

06 다음 중 우리말을 바르게 영작한 것은?

① 나는 나의 프로젝트를 끝낼 시간이 충분하다.
→ I have enough time to finish my project on.

② 그녀에게 먹을 것이 좀 있을까요?
→ Does she eat anything to have?

③ 그 여우는 할 게 아무 것도 없었다.
→ The fox had to do nothing.

④ Mary는 같이 춤출 친구들이 없다.
→ Mary doesn't have any friends to dance with.

⑤ 볼 만한 흥미로운 것이 있습니까?
→ Do you have anything interested to watch?

07 다음 밑줄 친 @∼ⓕ 중 to부정사의 형용사적 용법으로만 묶은 것은?

- My daughters agreed @to learn baking cookies during the winter vacation.
- The great artist had no brush ⓑto paint with when young.
- The schedule of my boss is ⓒto leave for the airport after lunch.
- Think about what you like ⓓto do.
- I chose ⓔto major in engineering.
- Here's my advice ⓕto help you.

① @, ⓑ   ② @, ⓒ   ③ ⓒ, ⓔ
④ ⓑ, ⓕ   ⑤ ⓓ, ⓕ

08 다음 문장의 빈칸에 들어갈 알맞은 말은?

Kevin forgot to bring the money _____.

① to eat out his wife for dinner
② to take dinner with his wife out
③ out to take his wife for dinner
④ to take his wife out for dinner with
⑤ for taking his wife out paid for

09 다음 밑줄 친 부분 중 어법상 옳은 것은?

① She has no time to sleep today.
② Judy has no friends to play.
③ I needed a bag to put those things.
④ There were many places to go during my business trip.
⑤ I have many clips to show you them.

10 다음 빈칸에 들어갈 말로 알맞은 것은?

_____ the student can get the perfect scores doesn't matter. How hard she prepared for the test is even more important.

① Though   ② As
③ If   ④ Whether
⑤ Whatever

11 다음 각 @, ⓑ 문장들 중 밑줄 친 부분의 쓰임이 서로 같은 것끼리 짝지어진 것은?

① @ He went to Iceland to take pictures of the Northern Lights.
   ⓑ I quit my job and decided to take pictures for a living.

② @ She grew up to be a scientist.
   ⓑ It is essential for the beginners to use the introduction manual.

③ @ There was no chair for the old lady to sit on.
   ⓑ The country has a lot of social issues to handle.

④ @ To be your assistant is exciting.
   ⓑ Einstein lived to be 76 years old.

⑤ @ They brought me something soft to chew.
   ⓑ Kevin is old enough to do his homework for himself.

12 밑줄 친 부분 중 어법상 어색한 것은?

① Isabelle was so sad. She never had <u>any</u> friends to help her.

② I'm hungry to death. I must buy <u>something to eat great</u>.

③ Please listen carefully. The principal has <u>some stories to announce you</u>.

④ Kathy has lots of things to complete. She has <u>no time to waste</u>.

⑤ You need <u>the sunglasses to wear</u> at the beach.

13 다음 중 밑줄 친 if의 쓰임이 나머지 넷과 다른 것은?

① I want to know <u>if</u> my own fashion brand will succeed.

② Has she decided <u>if</u> she is going to study abroad or get married?

③ Listen to your inner voice <u>if</u> you want to focus on yourself.

④ I'm wondering <u>if</u> Mike could help the people in need.

⑤ I'm not sure <u>if</u> Chris will come to the meeting.

서답형

14 다음 Amy의 일기를 읽고, <보기>와 같이 빈칸에 알맞은 문장을 일기 순서대로 영작해서 써 넣으시오. (whether는 사용 금지)

My Diary
• Can I get an A in the exam?
• Does Peter like me?
• Can I become a teacher?
• Did Sally run in the marathon?

┤ 보기 ├
• She wonders if she can get an A in the exam.

(1) She's not sure _____.

(2) She wants to know _____

_____.

(3) She is wondering _____

_____.

15 밑줄 친 if의 쓰임이 나머지 넷과 다른 것은?

① Tell her <u>if</u> he will come or not.

② I want to know <u>if</u> you can help me.

③ I wonder <u>if</u> she ate breakfast today.

④ Let's swim <u>if</u> it is fine this evening.

⑤ I doubt <u>if</u> he deserves the prize.

[16~17] 주어진 우리말에 맞게 어법상 가장 적절한 문장을 고르시오.

16

여러분이 꿈을 찾고 실현할 수 있도록 도와줄 몇 가지 조언이 여기 있다.

① Here are some advices to help you to find and realized your dream.

② Here are some advice you help to find and realize your dream.

③ Here's some advice to help you find and realize your dream.

④ Here's some advice help you to find and to realize your dream.

⑤ Here some advice is to find you help and realize your dream.

17

내가 정말로 엔지니어라는 일을 즐기는지 알 수 없었다.

① I didn't know that I really enjoyed the engineering job.

② I didn't know if or not I really enjoy and like the job of engineer.

③ I didn't know what if I enjoyed really in the field of engineering.

④ I didn't know whether an engineer really enjoyed me and happy.

⑤ I didn't know whether I really enjoyed the job of engineer.

01 다음 우리말과 일치하도록 괄호 안에 주어진 어구를 바르게 배열하여 문장을 완성하시오.

(1) 그녀는 그녀에게 중국어를 가르쳐 줄 누군가를 필요로 한다.

→ She _____.

(to, her, Chinese, somebody, needs, teach)

(2) Alex는 자기가 시험에 통과할 수 있을지 확신하지 못하고 있었다.

→ Alex _____

_____.

(sure, pass, was, he, the test, not, could, whether)

(3) 나는 오로라(북극광)를 볼 기회를 얻었다.

→ I _____.

(the Northern Lights, see, got, to, chance, a)

(4) Mike는 부근에 버스 정류장이 있는지 그 소녀에게 물어보고 있다.

→ Mike is asking _____

_____.

(nearby, if, the girl, is, there, a bus stop)

02 다음 일과표를 보고, 괄호 안의 단어와 to부정사의 형용사적 용법을 활용하여, 내용과 어법에 맞게 〈보기〉와 같이 문장을 완성하시오.

┤ 보기 ├

(have, eat, bread, at)

Santa has bread to eat at 9:00.

(1) Santa _____.

(need, train, deer, at)

(2) There are _____.

(for, toy, choose, Santa, at)

(3) Santa has _____.

(pack, gift, at, many)

03 다음 그림을 보고 〈보기〉에 주어진 동사들 중에서 골라 어법상 알맞게 빈칸을 완성하시오.

┤ 보기 ├

play   know   drink

	(1) Ben wanted to go far, so he needed something cold _____ _____.
	(2) Shasha is so lonely. She needs a friend _____ _____.
	(3) Here are last year's sales figures for you _____ _____.

04 다음 문장에서 어법상 어색한 것을 바르게 고쳐 다시 쓰시오.

(1) I asked Peter what he would join our research team or not.

➡ _____

_____

(2) She couldn't judge if to accept the job offer or not.

➡ _____

_____

(3) If you follow your heart or not matters in your life.

➡ _____

_____

(4) I wasn't sure that I could succeed but I decided to try.

➡ _____

_____

(5) All my classmates are wondering if it snows tomorrow.

➡ _____

_____

(6) I won first prize, which gave me a chance thinking about my life.

➡ _____

_____

(7) There is a hammer to nail.

➡ _____

_____

05 괄호 안에 주어진 단어와 글자 수 조건을 활용하여, 다음 우리말을 영작하시오.

(1) 나는 당신이 프로젝트를 하도록 도와줄 많은 친구들이 있다. (with, many, help, have, the project, 10 단어)

➡ _____

(2) William은 Emma와 그 뮤지컬을 볼 기회를 놓쳤다. (a chance, with, miss, see, 10 단어)

➡ _____

_____

(3) 당신의 꿈을 이루기 위해 해야 할 많은 것들이 있습니다. (to, there, things, realize, dream, 10 단어)

➡ _____

_____

(4) Jim이 그 다친 고양이를 구해 줄 충분한 시간이 있을까요? (save, enough, injured, have, cat, 10 단어)

➡ _____

_____

06 다음 〈보기〉와 같이 두 문장을 한 문장으로 쓸 때 빈칸에 알맞은 말을 쓰시오.

┌─ 보기 ─┐
• Tom has many friends. He'll support them.
→ Tom has many friends to support.
└─────┘

(1) I need a bed. My parents will sleep on it.
→ I need _____ .

(2) Bring us a piece of paper. She will sign on it.
→ Bring us _____ .

(3) Lena gave her son some money. He will buy the shoes with the money.
→ Lena gave _____

_____ .

07 다음 각 문장에서 어법상 어색한 부분을 찾아 한 단어만 고치거나 추가하시오.

(1) If Mary likes flowers or not is very important to Jordan.

_____ ➡ _____

(2) I want to know that you can help me with the project.

_____ ➡ _____

(3) In London, there are many fancy restaurants for us to eat.

_____ ➡ _____

(4) Do you have anything to write? Such as a pencil or a fountain pen.

_____ ➡ _____

Reading

Find a Dream and Live It!

Hello, everyone. My name is David Parker, and I'm a photographer.
_{강연자의 이름 / 강연자의 직업}

Today, I'm going to tell you how I found my dream and realized it.
_{간접의문문(의문사+주어+동사)}

I hope my story can inspire you.
_{hope 뒤에 명사절을 이끄는 접속사 that 생략}

When I was young, I loved stars. I also liked taking pictures.
_{~할 때(접속사) / = to take}

However, I never thought these things could lead to a job. In fact,
_{'별을 사랑한 것'과 '사진 찍는 것을 좋아한 것' / 사실은, 사실상}

I didn't have a dream at all.
_{not과 함께 쓰여 '전혀 ~가 아니다'}

When I had to decide on a major in college, I chose engineering.
_{had to+동사원형: ~해야 했다 / (숙고하여 뭔가를) 고르다}

Being an engineer looked OK. After college, I got a job at an
_{동명사구 주어: '엔지니어가 되는 것' / 감각동사 look+형용사: ~해 보이다 / get a job: 직장을 얻다}

engineering company. It was a stable job, but I didn't know whether I
_{접속사 whether는 명사절을 이끌어 '~인지 아닌지'라는 의미를 나타내며, if로 바꿔 쓸 수 있다.}

really enjoyed it.
_{a job at an engineering company}

Everything changed when I went on vacation to Iceland one winter.
_{go on vacation to: ~로 휴가를 가다}

There I got a chance to see the Northern Lights! The lights were
_{to부정사의 형용사적 용법 / = the Northern Lights}

amazing, and I took many pictures of the dancing lights in the sky. For
_{빛이 커튼 모양으로 넘실거리는 모습을 은유적으로 표현한 것}

the first time in many years, I could feel my heart beating fast.
_{지각동사(feel)+목적어+~ing/동사원형}

---

realize 실현하다

inspire 영감을 주다, 고무하다

lead 이끌다

major 전공; 전공하다

engineering 공학(기술)

stable 안정된, 안정적인

chance 기회

beat (심장이) 고동치다, 뛰다

확인문제

● 다음 문장이 본문의 내용과 일치하면 T, 일치하지 않으면 F를 쓰시오.

1 David Parker is a photographer. ☐

2 When young, David Parker had a dream to be a photographer. ☐

3 When David Parker had to decide on a major in college, he chose engineering. ☐

4 After college, David Parker got an unstable job at an engineering company. ☐

5 One winter, David Parker got a chance to see the Northern Lights in Iceland. ☐

6 David Parker drew many pictures of the dancing lights in the sky. ☐

After I came back, I entered a photo contest with the pictures I took
entered into(×)

in Iceland. Surprisingly, I won first prize, and this gave me a chance
사진 경연 대회에서 1등상을 받은 것

to think about my life. I realized that taking pictures made me happy.
to부정사의 형용사적 용법   동명사구 주어: 사진을 찍는 것   happily(×)

Suddenly, I wanted to become a good photographer, so I started

to learn more about photography. After years of trial and error, I got
= learning

better, and I began to do some part-time work as a photographer.
= doing   ~로서(자격을 나타내는 전치사)

Then one day, I made a bold decision. I quit my job and decided to
뒤따르는 문장, 즉 직장을 그만두고 생계를 위해서 사진작가가 되기로 결심한 것

take pictures for a living. I wasn't sure if I could succeed, but I decided
if는 명사절을 이끌어 '~인지 아닌지'라는 의미를 나타내며, whether로 바꿔 쓸 수 있다.

to try. I really wanted to do something that made me happy. Now, I'm
trying(×)   주격 관계대명사   happily(×)

a professional photographer, and I'm happy.
⋯ amateur(비전문가, 아마추어)

surrisingly 놀랍게도
trial and error 시행착오
make a decision 결정하다
bold 용감한, 대담한
quit (학교, 직장 등을) 그만두다
for a living 생계 수단으로
professional 전문적인, (전문) 직업의

📎 **확인문제**

● 다음 문장이 본문의 내용과 일치하면 T, 일치하지 않으면 F를 쓰시오.

1 The writer entered a photo contest and won first prize. ☐

2 The writer realized that taking pictures was boring. ☐

3 The writer started to learn more about photography. ☐

4 After years of trial and error, the writer began to do full-time work as a photographer. ☐

5 One day, the writer made a bold decision, quit the job and decided to take pictures for a living. ☐

6 Now, the writer is an amateur photographer. ☐

So do you want to find a dream and realize it? Here's some advice
to부정사의 명사적 용법   = to realize

to help you.
to부정사의 형용사적 용법

First, follow your heart. Think about what you like to do and
마음   간접의문문(의문사+주어+동사)

what makes you happy. In my case, it was taking pictures of stars.
간접의문문(의문사+주어+동사)   = what I liked to do and what made me happy

Second, work hard. Pursuing a dream is not easy. I became a
동명사 주어(추구하는 것) = To pursue

photographer through hard work.
열심히 노력해서

Third, be bold. You need courage to make decisions that will change
to부정사의 부사적 용법(목적)   주격 관계대명사

your life. I was afraid but I took a chance.
take a chance: 기회를 잡다

I truly hope you can find a dream, pursue it, and live it!
= a dream   = a dream

pursue 추구하다, 밀고 나가다

case 경우, 사정

courage 용기

📎 **확인문제**

● 다음 문장이 본문의 내용과 일치하면 T, 일치하지 <u>않으면</u> F를 쓰시오.

1   The first advice of the writer is to follow your heart. ☐

2   What made the writer happy was to draw pictures of stars. ☐

3   It is not easy to pursue a dream. ☐

4   The writer became a photographer without difficulty. ☐

5   You need courage to make decisions that will change your life. ☐

6   Many worries prevented the writer from taking a chance. ☐

우리말을 참고하여 빈칸에 알맞은 말을 쓰시오.

1 Find a _____ and _____ It!

2 _____, everyone.

3 My name is David Parker, and I'm _____ _____.

4 Today, I'm going to tell you _____ _____ _____ my dream and _____ it.

5 I hope my story can _____ _____.

6 _____ _____, I loved stars.

7 I also liked _____ _____.

8 However, I never thought these things could _____ _____ _____ _____.

9 _____ _____, I didn't have a dream _____ _____.

10 When I had to _____ _____ a major in college, I chose engineering.

11 Being an engineer _____ _____.

12 After college, I got a job at _____ _____ _____.

13 It was a _____ job, but I didn't know _____ I really enjoyed it.

1 꿈을 찾고 실현하세요!

2 여러분, 안녕하세요.

3 나의 이름은 David Parker이고, 나는 사진작가입니다.

4 오늘 나는 어떻게 내가 꿈을 찾아서 실현했는지 이야기하려고 해요.

5 나의 이야기가 여러분에게 영감을 주기를 바라요.

6 나는 어렸을 때 별을 사랑했어요.

7 나는 또한 사진 찍는 것을 좋아했어요.

8 하지만 나는 이것들이 직업과 연관될 수 있다고 전혀 생각하지 못했어요.

9 사실 나는 아예 꿈이 없었어요.

10 내가 대학에서 전공을 정해야 했을 때, 나는 공학을 선택했어요.

11 엔지니어가 되는 것이 괜찮아 보였거든요.

12 대학 졸업 후 저는 엔지니어링 회사에 취직했어요.

13 그것은 안정적인 직업이었지만, 난 내가 그 일을 정말로 좋아하는지는 알 수가 없었어요.

14 Everything changed when I _____ _____ _____ to Iceland one winter.

15 There I _____ _____ _____ to see the Northern Lights!

16 The lights were _____, and I _____ _____ _____ of the _____ _____ in the sky.

17 _____ _____ _____ _____ in many years, I could feel my heart _____ _____.

18 After I came back, I _____ a photo contest with _____ _____ _____ _____ in Iceland.

19 Surprisingly, I _____ _____ _____, and this gave me a chance to think about my life.

20 I realized that taking pictures _____ _____ _____.

21 Suddenly, I wanted to become a good photographer, so I started to _____ _____ _____ _____.

22 After years of _____ _____ _____, I got better, and I began to do some _____ _____ as a photographer.

23 Then one day, I made a _____ _____.

24 I quit my job and decided to take pictures _____ _____ _____.

25 I _____ _____ _____ I could succeed, but I decided to try.

14 어느 겨울, 내가 아이슬란드로 휴가를 갔을 때 모든 것이 바뀌었어요.

15 그곳에서 나는 오로라를 볼 수 있는 기회가 있었죠.

16 빛들은 경이로웠고 나는 하늘에서 춤추는 빛들의 사진을 많이 찍었어요.

17 수년 만에 처음으로 나는 심장이 빠르게 뛰고 있는 것을 느낄 수 있었어요.

18 나는 돌아와서 아이슬란드에서 찍은 사진으로 사진 경연 대회에 참가했어요.

19 놀랍게도 나는 1등상을 받았고, 이 일은 나에게 인생을 생각해 볼 기회를 주었어요.

20 나는 사진 찍는 것이 나를 행복하게 한다는 것을 깨달았어요.

21 갑자기 나는 좋은 사진작가가 되고 싶어서 사진 촬영 기술에 대해 더 배우기 시작했어요.

22 몇 년의 시행착오 끝에 나는 더 나아졌고 사진작가로 시간제 근무일을 하기 시작했어요.

23 그러던 어느 날 나는 대담한 결심을 했어요.

24 나는 직장을 그만 두고 생계 수단으로 사진을 찍기로 했어요.

25 나는 내가 성공할 수 있을지 확신하지 못했지만 시도해 보기로 결심했어요.

26 I really wanted to do _____ _____ made me happy.

27 Now, I'm a _____ _____, and I'm happy.

28 So do you want to _____ _____ _____ and _____ _____?

29 Here's _____ _____ to help you.

30 First, _____ _____ _____.

31 Think about what you like to do and _____ _____ _____ _____.

32 In my case, it was _____ _____ _____ _____.

33 Second, _____ _____.

34 _____ a dream is not easy.

35 I became a photographer _____ _____ _____.

36 Third, _____ _____.

37 You need _____ to _____ _____ that will change your life.

38 I was afraid but I _____ _____ _____.

39 I _____ _____ you can find a dream, pursue it, and live it!

26 나는 나를 행복하게 만드는 무언가를 정말로 하고 싶었어요.

27 지금, 나는 전문 사진작가이고, 나는 행복합니다.

28 그렇다면 여러분은 꿈을 찾아 실현하고 싶은가요?

29 여기 여러분을 도와줄 몇 가지 조언이 있습니다.

30 첫째, 여러분의 마음을 따르세요.

31 여러분이 무엇을 하고 싶고 여러분을 행복하게 하는 것이 무엇인지 생각해 보세요.

32 나의 경우에 그것은 별 사진을 찍는 거였어요.

33 둘째, 열심히 노력하세요.

34 꿈을 추구하는 것은 쉽지 않아요.

35 나는 열심히 노력해 사진작가가 되었어요.

36 셋째, 대담해지세요.

37 여러분의 인생을 바꿀 결정을 하기 위해서는 용기가 필요합니다.

38 나는 두려웠지만 기회를 잡았어요.

39 나는 여러분이 꿈을 찾고, 꿈을 추구하고, 꿈을 실현하길 진심으로 바랍니다!

● 우리말을 참고하여 본문을 영작하시오.

1 꿈을 찾고 실현하세요!

➡ _____

2 여러분, 안녕하세요.

➡ _____

3 나의 이름은 David Parker이고, 나는 사진작가입니다.

➡ _____

4 오늘 나는 어떻게 내가 꿈을 찾아서 실현했는지 이야기하려고 해요.

➡ _____

5 나의 이야기가 여러분에게 영감을 주기를 바라요.

➡ _____

6 나는 어렸을 때 별을 사랑했어요.

➡ _____

7 나는 또한 사진 찍는 것을 좋아했어요.

➡ _____

8 하지만 나는 이것들이 직업과 연관될 수 있다고 전혀 생각하지 못했어요.

➡ _____

9 사실 나는 아예 꿈이 없었어요.

➡ _____

10 내가 대학에서 전공을 정해야 했을 때, 나는 공학을 선택했어요.

➡ _____

11 엔지니어가 되는 것이 괜찮아 보였거든요.

➡ _____

12 대학 졸업 후 저는 엔지니어링 회사에 취직했어요.

➡ _____

13 그것은 안정적인 직업이었지만, 난 내가 그 일을 정말로 좋아하는지 알 수가 없었어요.

➡ _____

14 어느 겨울, 내가 아이슬란드로 휴가를 갔을 때 모든 것이 바뀌었어요.

➡ _____

15 그곳에서 나는 오로라를 볼 수 있는 기회가 있었죠.

➡ _____

16 빛들은 경이로웠고 나는 하늘에서 춤추는 빛들의 사진을 많이 찍었어요.

➡ _____

17 수년 만에 처음으로 나는 심장이 빠르게 뛰고 있는 것을 느낄 수 있었어요.

➡ _____

18 나는 돌아와서 아이슬란드에서 찍은 사진으로 사진 경연 대회에 참가했어요.

➡ _____

19 놀랍게도 나는 1등상을 받았고, 이 일은 나에게 인생을 생각해 볼 기회를 주었어요.

➡ _____

20 나는 사진 찍는 것이 나를 행복하게 한다는 것을 깨달았어요.

➡ _____

21 갑자기 나는 좋은 사진작가가 되고 싶어서 사진 촬영 기술에 대해 더 배우기 시작했어요.

➡ _____

22 몇 년의 시행착오 끝에 나는 더 나아졌고 사진작가로 시간제 근무일을 하기 시작했어요.

➡ _____

23 그러던 어느 날 나는 대담한 결심을 했어요.

➡ _____

24 나는 직장을 그만 두고 생계 수단으로 사진을 찍기로 했어요.

➡ _____

25 나는 내가 성공할 수 있을지 확신하지 못했지만 시도해 보기로 결심했어요.

➡ _____

26 나는 나를 행복하게 만드는 무언가를 정말로 하고 싶었어요.

➡ _____

27 지금, 나는 전문 사진작가이고, 나는 행복합니다.

➡ _____

28 그렇다면 여러분은 꿈을 찾아 실현하고 싶은가요?

➡ _____

29 여기 여러분을 도와줄 몇 가지 조언이 있습니다.

➡ _____

30 첫째, 여러분의 마음을 따르세요.

➡ _____

31 여러분이 무엇을 하고 싶고 여러분을 행복하게 하는 것이 무엇인지 생각해 보세요.

➡ _____

32 나의 경우에 그것은 별 사진을 찍는 거였어요.

➡ _____

33 둘째, 열심히 노력하세요.

➡ _____

34 꿈을 추구하는 것은 쉽지 않아요.

➡ _____

35 나는 열심히 노력해 사진작가가 되었어요.

➡ _____

36 셋째, 대담해지세요.

➡ _____

37 여러분의 인생을 바꿀 결정을 하기 위해서는 용기가 필요합니다.

➡ _____

38 나는 두려웠지만 기회를 잡았어요.

➡ _____

39 나는 여러분이 꿈을 찾고, 꿈을 추구하고, 꿈을 실현하길 진심으로 바랍니다!

➡ _____

[01~04] 다음 글을 읽고 물음에 답하시오.

Hello, everyone. My name is David Parker, and I'm a photographer. Today, I'm going to tell you how I found my dream and realized it. I hope my story can inspire you.

When I was young, I loved stars. I also liked taking pictures. However, I never thought these things could lead ___ⓐ___ a job. In fact, I didn't have a dream at all.

When I had to decide ___ⓑ___ a major in college, I chose engineering. Being an engineer looked OK. After college, I got a job at an engineering company. It was a stable job, but I didn't know whether I really enjoyed it.

Everything changed when I went on vacation to Iceland one winter. There I got a chance to see the Northern Lights! The lights were amazing, and I took many pictures of the dancing lights in the sky. ⓒ<u>For the first time in many years, I could feel my heart beating fast.</u>

01 위 글의 빈칸 ⓐ와 ⓑ에 들어갈 전치사가 바르게 짝지어진 것은?

	ⓐ	ⓑ			ⓐ	ⓑ
①	to – on		②	in – for
③	in – on		④	at – in
⑤	to – in			

02 위 글의 종류로 알맞은 것을 고르시오.

① discussion　　② lecture
③ commercial　　④ conversation
⑤ advertisement

03 위 글의 밑줄 친 ⓒ에서 알 수 있는 David Parker의 심경으로 가장 알맞은 것을 고르시오.

① embarrassed　　② frightened
③ excited　　④ annoyed
⑤ relieved

04 According to the passage, which is NOT true?

① David Parker is a photographer.
② When young, David Parker loved stars.
③ David Parker majored in engineering.
④ David Parker got a chance to see the Northern Lights in Iceland.
⑤ David Parker drew many pictures of the dancing lights in the sky.

[05~07] 다음 글을 읽고 물음에 답하시오.

After I came back, I entered a photo contest with the pictures I took in Iceland. Surprisingly, I won first prize, and ⓐ<u>this</u> gave me a chance to think about my life. I realized that taking pictures made me happy. ⓑ<u>Suddenly</u>, I wanted to become a good photographer, so I started to learn more about photography. After years of trial and error, I got better, and I began to do some part-time work as a photographer.

Then one day, I made a bold decision. I quit my job and decided to take pictures for a living. I wasn't sure if I could succeed, but I decided to try. I really wanted to do something ⓒ<u>that</u> made me happy. Now, I'm a professional photographer, and I'm happy.

05 위 글의 밑줄 친 ⓐthis가 가리키는 내용을 본문에서 찾아 쓰시오.

➡ _____

06 위 글의 밑줄 친 ⓑSuddenly와 바꿔 쓸 수 있는 말을 <u>모두</u> 고르시오.

① In haste
② All of a sudden
③ Rapidly
④ Gradually
⑤ All at once

07 아래 <보기>에서 위 글의 밑줄 친 ⓒthat과 문법적 쓰임이 같은 것의 개수를 고르시오.

> ┤ 보기 ├
> ① Who was the first man that came here?
> ② This is the watch that I bought yesterday.
> ③ Is this the farm that they spoke of?
> ④ The actress hid the fact that she was married.
> ⑤ There's a man that wants to see you.

① 1개 ② 2개 ③ 3개 ④ 4개 ⑤ 5개

[08~10] 다음 글을 읽고 물음에 답하시오.

When I was young, I loved stars. I also liked taking pictures. ___ⓐ___, I never thought these things could lead to a job. In fact, I didn't have a dream at all.

When I had to decide on a major in college, I chose engineering. ⓑBeing an engineer looked OK. After college, I got a job at an engineering company. It was a stable job, but ⓒ난 내가 그 일을 정말로 좋아하는지는 알 수가 없었어요.

08 위 글의 빈칸 ⓐ에 들어갈 알맞은 말을 고르시오.

① Therefore
② However
③ Moreover
④ For example
⑤ In other words

09 위 글의 밑줄 친 ⓑBeing과 문법적 쓰임이 같은 것을 <u>모두</u> 고르시오.

① He was fond of taking pictures.
② He was wasting his time on something else.
③ He didn't mind choosing engineering.
④ His dream was having a stable job.
⑤ He was working for an engineering company.

서답형

10 위 글의 밑줄 친 ⓒ의 우리말에 맞게 주어진 어휘를 이용하여 8 단어로 영작하시오.

> whether, enjoyed

➡ _____

[11~14] 다음 글을 읽고 물음에 답하시오.

So do you want to find a dream and realize it? Here's ⓐsome advice to help you.

First, follow your heart. Think about what you like to do and what makes you happy. In my case, it was ⓑtaking pictures of stars.

Second, work hard. Pursuing a dream is not easy. I became a photographer through hard work.

Third, be bold. You need courage to make decisions that will change your life. I was afraid but I took a chance.

I truly hope you can find a dream, pursue it, and live it!   <I: David Parker>

11 위 글의 밑줄 친 ⓐsome advice에 해당하지 <u>않는</u> 것을 고르시오.

① Follow your heart.
② Think about what you like to do and what makes you happy.
③ Take pictures of stars.
④ Work hard.
⑤ Be bold.

12 위 글의 밑줄 친 ⓑtaking과 문법적 쓰임이 같은 것을 모두 고르시오.

① His hobby is taking pictures.
② I saw him taking pictures.
③ Do you know the boy taking pictures there?
④ She is good at taking pictures.
⑤ When I saw him, he was taking pictures.

13 위 글의 제목으로 알맞은 것을 고르시오.

① It Is Important to Follow Your Heart
② Tips for Taking Pictures of Stars
③ Difficulty of Pursuing a Dream
④ You Need Courage to Change Your Life
⑤ How to Find a Dream and Realize It

서답형

14 본문의 내용과 일치하도록 다음 빈칸 (A)~(C)에 알맞은 단어를 쓰시오.

What David liked to do was (A)_____
_____ of stars. So, he worked hard to become (B)_____ _____. He needed (C)_____ to make decisions that would change his life and he took a chance.

[15~17] 다음 글을 읽고 물음에 답하시오.

When I was young, I loved stars. I also liked taking pictures. (①) However, I never thought these things could lead to a job. ⓐIn fact, I didn't have a dream at all. (②)

When I had to decide on a major in college, I chose engineering. (③) Being an engineer looked OK. (④) It was a stable job, but I didn't know whether I really enjoyed it. (⑤)

Everything changed when I went on vacation to Iceland one winter. There I got a chance ⓑto see the Northern Lights! The lights were amazing, and I took many pictures of the dancing lights in the sky. For the first time in many years, I could feel my heart beating fast.

15 위 글의 흐름으로 보아, 주어진 문장이 들어가기에 가장 적절한 곳은?

After college, I got a job at an engineering company.

① ② ③ ④ ⑤

16 위 글의 밑줄 친 ⓐIn fact와 바꿔 쓸 수 있는 말을 모두 고르시오.

① Exactly ② Actually
③ Especially ④ In particular
⑤ As a matter of fact

17 아래 〈보기〉에서 위 글의 밑줄 친 ⓑto see와 to부정사의 용법이 같은 것의 개수를 고르시오.

┤ 보기 ├
① His dream was to see the Northern Lights.
② He had the fortune to see the Northern Lights.
③ He was excited to see the Northern Lights.
④ Isn't it exciting to see the Northern Lights?
⑤ It is high time to see the Northern Lights.

① 1개 ② 2개 ③ 3개 ④ 4개 ⑤ 5개

[18~20] 다음 글을 읽고 물음에 답하시오.

Hello, everyone. My name is David Parker, and I'm a photographer. Today, I'm going to tell you how I found my dream and realized ①it. I hope my story can inspire you.

When I was young, I loved stars. I also liked taking pictures. However, I never thought ②these things could lead to a job. In fact, I didn't have a dream ⓐat all.

When I had to decide on a major in college, I chose engineering. Being an engineer looked OK. After college, I got a job at an engineering company. ③It was a stable job, but I didn't know whether I really enjoyed ④it.

Everything changed when I went on vacation to Iceland one winter. ⑤There I got a chance to see the Northern Lights! The lights were amazing, and I took many pictures of the dancing lights in the sky. For the first time in many years, I could feel my heart beating fast.

18 위 글의 밑줄 친 ①~⑤가 가리키는 것에 대한 설명으로 옳지 않은 것을 고르시오.

① my dream
② the love for stars and a fondness for taking pictures
③ a job at an engineering company
④ a stable job
⑤ In Iceland

19 위 글의 밑줄 친 ⓐat all과 바꿔 쓸 수 있는 말을 고르시오.

① anyway   ② at least
③ in the least   ④ somehow
⑤ somewhat

20 위 글을 읽고 대답할 수 없는 것을 고르시오.

① What is David Parker's job?
② How did David Parker realize his dream?
③ In college, what did David Parker major in?
④ Where did David Parker see the Northern Lights?
⑤ What did David Parker do when he saw the Northern Lights?

[21~24] 다음 글을 읽고 물음에 답하시오.

After I came back, I (A)[entered / entered into] a photo contest with the pictures I took in Iceland. Surprisingly, I won first prize, and this gave me a chance to think about my life. I realized that ①taking pictures made me happy. Suddenly, I wanted ②to become a good photographer, so I started ③to learn more about photography. After years of trial and error, I got better, and I began ④to do some part-time work as a photographer.

Then one day, I made a bold decision. I quit my job and decided to take pictures for a living. I wasn't sure (B)[if / that] I could succeed, but I decided ⑤to try. I really wanted to do something that made me happy. Now, I'm a(n) (C)[amateur / professional] photographer, and I'm happy.

<I: David Parker>

서답형

21 위 글의 괄호 (A)~(C)에서 문맥이나 어법상 알맞은 낱말을 골라 쓰시오.

➡ (A) _____ (B) _____ (C) _____

22 밑줄 친 ①~⑤ 중에서 to부정사와 동명사 형태로 둘 다 쓸 수 있는 것을 <u>모두</u> 고르시오.

①   ②   ③   ④   ⑤

서답형

23 Why did David Parker start to learn more about photography? Fill in the blanks with suitable words.

> Because he wanted to become _____ _____.

중요

24 위 글에 어울리는 속담으로 가장 알맞은 것을 고르시오.

① A stitch in time saves nine.
② Where there is a will, there is a way.
③ Look before you leap.
④ Too many cooks spoil the broth.
⑤ Two heads are better than one.

[25~28] 다음 글을 읽고 물음에 답하시오.

So do you want to find a dream and realize it? Here's some advice to help you.

First, follow your heart. (A)여러분이 무엇을 하고 싶고 여러분을 행복하게 하는 것이 무엇인지 생각해 보세요. In my case, it was taking pictures of stars.

Second, work hard. Pursuing a dream is not easy. I became a photographer through hard work.

Third, be ⓐ . (B)You need courage to make decisions that will change your life. I was afraid but I took a chance.

I truly hope you can find a dream, pursue it, and live it!   <I: David Parker>

25 위 글의 빈칸 ⓐ에 들어갈 알맞은 말을 고르시오.

① calm   ② patient
③ generous   ④ bold
⑤ considerate

서답형

26 위 글의 밑줄 친 (A)의 우리말에 맞게 주어진 어휘를 알맞게 배열하시오.

> you / what / to / think / about / makes / you / do / and / happy / like / what / .

➡ _____

_____

중요

27 다음 중 위 글의 내용을 올바르게 이해하지 <u>못한</u> 사람을 고르시오.

① 수진: 꿈을 찾아 실현하려면 먼저 자신의 마음을 따라야 해.
② 진경: David를 행복하게 해준 것은 별 사진을 찍는 것이었어.
③ 영미: 꿈을 추구하는 것은 쉽지 않기 때문에 열심히 노력해야 해.
④ 형준: 인생을 바꿀 결정을 하기 위해서는 대담함보다는 지혜가 필요해.
⑤ 나리: David는 두려웠지만 기회를 잡았어.

서답형

28 위 글의 밑줄 친 (B)를 다음과 같이 바꿔 쓸 때 빈칸에 들어갈 알맞은 단어를 쓰시오.

➡ You need courage _____ _____

_____ you _____ make decisions that will change your life.

[01~03] 다음 글을 읽고 물음에 답하시오.

After I came back, I entered a photo contest with the pictures I took in Iceland. Surprisingly, I won first prize, and this gave me a chance to think about my life. I realized that taking pictures made me happy. Suddenly, I wanted to become a good photographer, so I started to learn more about ⓐ_____. After years of trial and error, I got better, and I began to do some part-time work as a photographer.

Then one day, ⓑI made a bold decision. I quit my job and decided to take pictures for a living. I wasn't sure if I could succeed, but I decided to try. ⓒ나는 나를 행복하게 만드는 무언가를 정말로 하고 싶었어요. Now, I'm a professional photographer, and I'm happy.

<I: David Parker>

01 본문의 단어를 변형하여 위 글의 빈칸 ⓐ에 들어갈 알맞은 단어를 쓰시오.

➡ _____

02 다음 빈칸 (A)와 (B)에 알맞은 단어를 넣어 밑줄 친 ⓑ에 대한 설명을 완성하시오.

It means that he decided (A)_____ _____ his job and to take pictures (B)_____ _____.

03 위 글의 밑줄 친 ⓒ의 우리말에 맞게 주어진 어휘를 알맞게 배열하시오.

me / wanted / that / something / I / made / happy / to do / really / .

➡ _____

[04~06] 다음 글을 읽고 물음에 답하시오.

So do you want to find a dream and realize it? Here's ⓐsome advice to help you.

First, follow your heart. Think about what you like to do and what makes you happy. In my case, it was taking pictures of stars.

Second, work hard. Pursuing a dream is not easy. I became a photographer through hard work.

Third, be bold. You need courage to make decisions that will change your life. I was afraid but I took a chance.

I truly hope you can find a dream, pursue it, and live it!

04 위 글의 밑줄 친 ⓐsome advice 세 가지를 우리말로 쓰시오.

➡ (1) _____
  (2) _____
  (3) _____

05 본문의 내용과 일치하도록 다음 빈칸 (A)~(C)에 알맞은 단어를 쓰시오.

To follow (A)_____ _____, you need to think about (B)_____ you like to do and (C)_____ makes you happy.

06 What is needed to make decisions that will change your life? Fill in the blank with a suitable word.

I need _____.

[07~10] 다음 글을 읽고 물음에 답하시오.

Hello, everyone. My name is David Parker, and I'm a photographer. ⓐToday, I'm going to tell you the way how I found my dream and realized it. I hope my story can (A)[discourage / inspire] you.

When I was young, I loved stars. I also liked taking pictures. However, I never thought these things could lead to a job. In fact, I didn't have a dream at all.

When I had to decide on a ___ⓑ___ in college, I chose engineering. Being an engineer looked OK. After college, I got a job at an engineering company. It was a stable job, but I didn't know whether I really enjoyed it.

Everything changed when I went on vacation to Iceland one winter. There I got a chance to see the Northern Lights! The lights were (B)[amazing / amazed], and I took many pictures of the dancing lights in the sky. For the first time in many years, I could feel my heart (C)[beating / beaten] fast.

07 위 글의 밑줄 친 ⓐ에서 어법상 틀린 부분을 찾아 고치시오.

_____ ➡ _____

08 주어진 영영풀이를 참고하여 빈칸 ⓑ에 철자 m으로 시작하는 단어를 쓰시오.

the main subject that a student is studying at a university or college

➡ _____

09 위 글의 괄호 (A)~(C)에서 문맥이나 어법상 알맞은 낱말을 골라 쓰시오.

➡ (A) _____ (B) _____ (C) _____

10 When did David Parker feel his heart beating fast? Fill in the blanks (A) and (B) with suitable words.

One winter when he saw the (A)_____ _____ in Iceland and (B)_____ _____ _____ of the dancing lights in the sky, he felt his heart beating fast.

[11~13] 다음 글을 읽고 물음에 답하시오.

When I had to decide on a major in college, I chose engineering. ⓐBeing an engineer looked OK. After college, I got a job at an engineering company. ⓑIt was an unstable job, but I didn't know whether I really enjoyed it.

Everything changed when I went on vacation to Iceland one winter. There I got a chance to see the Northern Lights! The lights were amazing, and I took many pictures of ⓒthe dancing lights in the sky. For the first time in many years, I could feel my heart beating fast.

11 위 글의 밑줄 친 ⓐ를 다음과 같이 바꿔 쓸 때 빈칸에 들어갈 알맞은 단어를 쓰시오.

➡ _____ looked OK to be an engineer.

12 위 글의 밑줄 친 ⓑ에서 흐름상 어색한 부분을 찾아 고치시오.

_____ ➡ _____

13 위 글의 밑줄 친 ⓒ가 가리키는 것을 본문에서 찾아 쓰시오.

➡ _____

교과서

구석구석

Team Project Step 3

We respect Dr. Park Byeong-seon. She was a historian. We chose her because she spent her whole life searching for Korean national treasures abroad.

spend+돈, 노력, 시간 등+동명사: ~하는 데 …를 보내다   aboard (×)

구문해설 · respect: 존경하다 · historian: 역사학자 · national treasure: 국보

우리는 박병선 박사님을 존경합니다. 그녀는 역사가였습니다. 우리가 그녀를 고른 이유는 그녀가 해외에 있는 한국의 문화 유산을 찾는 데 일생을 보냈기 때문입니다.

After You Read B

David Parker's Advice

1. Follow your heart. Think about what you like to do and what makes you happy.

간접의문문(의문사+주어+동사)   간접의문문(의문사+주어+동사)

2. Work hard. Pursuing a dream is not easy.

동명사 주어   동명사 주어는 단수 취급

3. Be bold. You need courage to make decisions that will change your life.

to부정사의 부사적 용법(목적)   = which

구문해설 · follow: ~을 따르다 · pursue: 추구하다 · bold: 대담한 · courage: 용기

David Parker의 조언

1. 여러분의 마음을 따르세요. 여러분이 무엇을 하고 싶고 여러분을 행복하게 하는 것이 무엇인지 생각해 보세요.

2. 열심히 노력하세요. 꿈을 추구하는 것은 쉽지 않아요.

3. 대담해지세요. 여러분의 인생을 바꿀 결정을 하기 위해서는 용기가 필요합니다.

Think and Write

My dream is to become a famous fashion designer. There are many things

보어 '되는 것': to부정사의 명사적 용법   복수

to do to realize my dream. First, I'll go to design school and study fashion

형용사(~할) 부사적 용법(~하기 위해)   go와 병렬 구조

design. Then, after I graduate, I'll work at a fashion company. When I'm 30, I'll

'시간'의 부사절(will graduate ×)   '시간'의 부사절-현재시제로 표현

start my own brand. When I'm 35, I'll hold my first fashion show. I hope my

hope 뒤에 that 생략

dream will come true.

미래시제 명사절 will(○)

구문해설 · realize: 실현하다 · hold a fashion show: 패션쇼를 주최하다

내 꿈은 유명한 패션디자이너가 되는 것이다. 내 꿈을 실현시키기 위해서는 해야 할 일들이 많이 있다. 우선, 나는 디자인 스쿨에 진학해서 패션 디자인을 공부할 것이다. 그러고 나서, 졸업을 한 후에는 패션 회사에서 일할 것이다. 서른 살에는 나만의 상표를 시작할 것이다. 서른다섯 살이 되면, 첫 번째 패션쇼를 주최할 것이다. 나는 내 꿈이 실현되기를 희망한다.

Words & Expressions

1 〈보기〉의 밑줄 친 어휘와 같은 의미로 쓰인 것을 고르시오.

> ┤ 보기 ├
>
> She never <u>realized</u> her ambition of becoming a professional singer.

① I didn't <u>realize</u> that he was so ill.

② His dream of going abroad was finally <u>realized</u>.

③ The situation was more complicated than they had at first <u>realized</u>.

④ He <u>realized</u> that he was in danger.

⑤ These details help to <u>realize</u> the scene.

2 다음 짝지어진 두 단어의 관계가 같도록 빈칸에 알맞은 말을 주어진 철자로 시작하여 쓰시오.

> enter : come in = bravery : c_____

3 다음 영영풀이에 해당하는 단어를 주어진 철자로 시작하여 빈칸에 쓰고, 알맞은 것을 골라 문장을 완성하시오.

> • p_____ : to work hard in order to achieve something
>
> • a_____ : to gain with effort

(1) She wishes to _____ a medical career.

(2) It takes time to _____ an important goal.

4 다음 빈칸에 공통으로 들어갈 말을 쓰시오.

> • Ask them what they do _____ a living and if they like it.
>
> • A hurricane hit the city _____ the first time in 26 years!

Conversation

5 다음 중 짝지어진 대화가 <u>어색한</u> 것은?

① A: Hello! Nice to meet you. What's your major?

　B: Hi. I'm studying engineering.

② A: Have you also seen the movie about the book?

　B: No, I haven't.

③ A: I can't walk across this bridge. I'm scared.

　B: This bridge is very stable. You just need courage!

④ A: Have you ever visited Jeju-do?

　B: No, but the island is beautiful. I hope you can visit there sometime.

⑤ A: I heard that you were a professional soccer player.

　B: Yes, I was, but I quit playing last year.

6 다음 대화의 밑줄 친 우리말에 맞게 주어진 단어를 이용하여 영어로 쓰시오.

> A: <u>Canada에 가 본 적 있어요?</u> (be, ever)
>
> B: Yes, I have. I saw a beautiful view from the mountains.
>
> A: Oh, I see. Please sign here.

➡ _____

07 주어진 문장 앞에 이어질 대화의 순서로 알맞은 것은?

(A) Yes. After a lot of trial and error, I made the most beautiful clothes. Which do you prefer?
(B) Did you finish making my clothes?
(C) What do you do for a living?
(D) I make clothes.

I like both. I can't make a decision.

① (B) – (A) – (C) – (D)
② (B) – (C) – (A) – (D)
③ (C) – (B) – (D) – (A)
④ (C) – (D) – (B) – (A)
⑤ (D) – (B) – (C) – (A)

[08~10] 다음 대화를 읽고 물음에 답하시오.

G: I'm going to buy this CD. I love listening to piano music.
B: Me, too. I also enjoy (A)[playing / to play] the piano.
G: Really? So you can play the piano?
B: Yes. _____ⓐ_____
G: Well, I've never learned (B)[how / what] to play.
B: It's fun. I hope you'll have a chance (C)[to learn / learning].

08 위 대화의 빈칸 ⓐ에 들어갈 말로 나머지 넷과 의미가 다른 것은?

① How about you?
② What about you?
③ And you?
④ Can you play the piano, too?
⑤ Why don't you play the piano?

09 위 대화의 괄호 (A)~(C)에서 적절한 것을 골라 쓰시오.

➡ (A) _____ (B) _____ (C) _____

10 What does the boy want the girl to do? Answer in English with a full sentence.

➡ _____

_____

[11~13] 다음 대화를 읽고 물음에 답하시오.

B: Have you ever visited other country? (①)
G: No, I haven't. Have you? (②)
B: Yes, I've been to France. (③) I hope you can travel to another country sometime. (④)
G: (⑤) Look! This book about Canada looks very interesting.

11 ①~⑤ 중 주어진 문장이 들어갈 곳은?

Yes, I really want to visit Canada.

①   ②   ③   ④   ⑤

12 Does the boy have the experience of visiting another country? If so, where? Answer in English with a full sentence.

➡ _____

13 위 대화에서 어법상 어색한 것을 하나 찾아 바르게 고치시오.

_____ ➡ _____

Grammar

14 다음 그림을 보고 괄호 안의 단어를 배열하여 빈칸을 알맞게 채우시오.

➡ Jenny can't decide _____

_____ the piano.

(she, whether, should, playing, practice, or, running)

15 다음 〈보기〉에 나온 전치사들 중에서 알맞은 것을 골라 문장을 완성하시오. (중복 사용, 또는 복수 정답 가능)

┌─ 보기 ├─
with	in	on	about
of	to	for	at
└────

(1) Please get the old lady a stick to walk _____.

(2) Mr. Parker needs someone to talk _____.

(3) Daddy bought a chair to sit _____.

(4) The farmer had no basket to carry the oranges _____.

(5) Would you bring me a few pieces of paper to write _____?

(6) There are many brushes to draw _____.

(7) I need just a friend to play _____.

(8) The young girl from the organization has some issues to speak _____.

(9) Amy's friend has no money to buy the luxury bag _____.

(10) She has shown something for you to get interested _____.

16 다음 중 밑줄 친 'if'의 의미가 나머지 넷과 다른 것으로 묶인 것은?

┌──────
ㄱ If it snows this weekend, we will go skiing with Sam's family.
ㄴ Do you know if he's sick today?
ㄷ I wonder if the experiment will fail.
ㄹ If you can dream it, you can do it.
ㅁ Mike isn't sure if he has his passport with him.
ㅂ Harry is asking the woman if she can help him.
└──────

① ㄱ, ㄷ   ② ㄱ, ㄹ   ③ ㄴ, ㄹ

④ ㄹ, ㅁ   ⑤ ㄷ, ㄹ

17 다음 Barbie의 내일 일정표를 보고, 〈보기〉에서 알맞은 단어를 각각 하나씩 선택하여 빈칸에 어법상 알맞은 형태로 넣으시오.

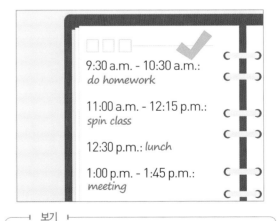

┌─ 보기 ├─
| take | do | attend | eat |
└────

Barbie has a few things _____ tomorrow. After doing homework, she has a spin class _____ at 11:00. A half hour after noon, she needs something _____. She has a meeting _____ at 1:00 p.m.

18 주어진 문장을 읽고, 그 내용을 간접의문을 사용하여 바꿨을 때, 다음 중 바르게 된 것은?

> Alex thinks to himself, "Am I going in the right direction to the Gate 4?"

① Alex isn't sure if it is to go in the right direction to the Gate 4.

② Alex isn't sure where I am going in the right direction to the Gate 4.

③ Alex isn't sure that is he going in the right direction to the Gate 4.

④ Alex isn't sure if he is going in the right direction to the Gate 4.

⑤ Alex isn't sure where is he going in the right direction to the Gate 4.

19 다음 〈보기〉와 같이 if를 사용하여, 주어진 문장을 완성하시오.

> ┤ 보기 ├
>
> Should I wear a jacket?
>
> → I'm not sure if I should wear a jacket.

(1) Will he come back home?

　　→ I wonder _____ .

(2) Did he have lunch?

　　→ I want to know _____ .

Reading

[20~21] 다음 글을 읽고 물음에 답하시오.

　When I was young, I loved stars. I also liked taking pictures. However, I never thought these things could lead to a job. ___ⓐ___, I didn't have a dream at all.

　When I had to decide on a major in college, I chose engineering. Being an engineer looked OK. After college, I got a job at an engineering company. ⓑIt was a stable job, but I didn't know whether I really enjoyed it.

20 위 글의 빈칸 ⓐ에 들어갈 알맞은 말을 고르시오.

① Similarly　　　② That is

③ For instance　　④ In fact

⑤ By contrast

21 위 글의 밑줄 친 ⓑ를 다음과 같이 바꿔 쓸 때 빈칸에 들어갈 알맞은 한 단어를 쓰시오.

➡ _____ it was a stable job, I didn't know whether I really enjoyed it.

[22~24] 다음 글을 읽고 물음에 답하시오.

　After I came back, I entered a photo contest with the pictures I took in Iceland. Surprisingly, I won first prize, and this gave me a chance to think about my life. I realized that taking pictures made me happy. Suddenly, I wanted to become a good photographer, so I started to learn more about photography. After years of trial and error, I got better, and I began to do some part-time work ⓐas a photographer.

　Then one day, I made a bold decision. I quit my job and decided to take pictures for a living. I wasn't sure if I could succeed, but I decided to try. I really wanted to do something that made me happy. Now, I'm a professional photographer, and I'm happy.

<I: David Parker>

22 위 글의 밑줄 친 ⓐas와 같은 의미로 쓰인 것을 고르시오.

① Take as much as you want.

② She cares for the old as a social worker.

③ Do as I do.

④ Some animals, as the fox and the squirrel, have bushy tails.

⑤ As it was getting dark, we soon turned back.

23 According to the passage, which is NOT true?

① Taking pictures made David Parker happy.

② David Parker started to learn more about photography as he wanted to become a good photographer.

③ David Parker quit his job and decided to take pictures for a living.

④ David Parker was sure that he could succeed.

⑤ Now, David Parker is a professional photographer, and he is happy.

24 본문의 내용과 일치하도록 다음 빈칸 (A)와 (B)에 알맞은 단어를 쓰시오.

> David Parker won (A)_____ _____ in a photo contest, and taking this opportunity he learned more about (B)_____ to become a good photographer.

[25~26] 다음 글을 읽고 물음에 답하시오.

So do you want to find a dream and realize it? Here's some advice to help you.

First, follow your heart. Think about what you like to do and what makes you happy. In my case, ⓐit was taking pictures of stars.

Second, work hard. Pursuing a dream is not. I became a photographer through hard work.

Third, be bold. You need courage to make decisions that will change your life. I was afraid but ⓑ나는 기회를 잡았어요.

I truly hope you can find a dream, pursue it, and live it!

25 다음 빈칸 (A)와 (B)에 알맞은 단어를 넣어 위 글의 밑줄 친 ⓐit이 가리키는 것을 완성하시오.

> what I liked (A)_____ _____ and what made me (B)_____

26 위 글의 밑줄 친 ⓑ의 우리말에 맞게 take를 변형하여 4 단어로 영작하시오.

➡ _____

[27~29] 모둠의 롤 모델에 관한 다음 글을 읽고 물음에 답하시오.

We respect Dr. Park Byeong-seon. She was a historian. We chose her because she spent her whole life ___ⓐ___ for Korean national treasures abroad.

27 위 글의 빈칸 ⓐ에 search를 알맞은 형태로 쓰시오.

➡ _____

28 위 글의 종류로 알맞은 것을 고르시오.

① article   ② book report
③ introduction   ④ biography
⑤ review

29 위 글을 읽고 알 수 없는 것을 고르시오.

① Whom do they respect?

② What was Dr. Park Byeong-seon's job?

③ Why did they choose Dr. Park Byeong-seon?

④ What was Dr. Park Byeong-seon's achievement?

⑤ What made Dr. Park Byeong-seon search for Korean national treasures abroad?

출제율 100%

01 다음 밑줄 친 부분의 의미로 알맞지 않은 것을 고르시오.

① She made her decision to marry him on love, not money. (결정, 결심)
② It is important to train children to be polite. (훈련시키다)
③ Don't try to make an excuse next time. (호소하다)
④ He should be back right after lunch. (그 직후, 바로 후)
⑤ Several staff members volunteered for early retirement. (자원했다)

출제율 90%

02 다음 빈칸에 공통으로 들어갈 알맞은 말을 쓰시오.

- In her twenties, she began to write her _____ novels.
- My parents pushed me to _____ in medicine.

출제율 95%

03 다음 주어진 우리말에 맞게 빈칸을 채우시오. (철자가 주어진 경우 주어진 철자로 시작할 것.)

(1) 기억에 남는 공연이 있습니까?
　➡ Is there a m_____ performance for you?
(2) 당신은 전문 곡예사가 되었을 것입니다.
　➡ You would be a p_____ juggler.
(3) 제 영어 실력이 빨리 늘면 좋겠어요.
　➡ I hope my English will g_____ better soon.

출제율 90%

04 (A)~(C)의 빈칸에 공통으로 들어갈 말을 쓰시오.

(A) I like travelling by _____.
(B) Truths require a _____ of ideas placed in order.
(C) These girls are being _____ed as nurses.

[05~07] 다음 대화를 읽고 물음에 답하시오.

B: I really liked your book about training dogs.
W: Thank you. Do you like dogs?
B: Yes, I do. I love all kinds of animals.
W: Have you ever thought of becoming an animal doctor?
B: Yes, I have. I really want to become an animal doctor.
W: What are you doing to achieve your goal?
B: I'm doing volunteer work at the local animal house.
(A) You're doing great! I hope you become a good animal doctor someday.
(B) I'm also watching a lot of TV shows about animals.
(C) That's good. What else are you doing?
(D) Thank you.

출제율 100%

05 위 대화의 (A)~(D)를 문맥에 맞게 자연스럽게 배열하시오.

➡ _____

출제율 95%

06 밑줄 친 That이 가리키는 것을 우리말로 쓰시오.

➡ _____

출제율 100%

7 위 대화의 내용과 일치하지 <u>않는</u> 것을 고르시오.

① B는 W의 책을 읽었다.
② B는 동물을 매우 좋아한다.
③ B는 수의사가 되고 싶어한다.
④ W는 지역 동물의 집에서 자원봉사를 하고 있다.
⑤ W는 B가 좋은 수의사가 되기를 바란다.

[08~09] 다음 대화를 읽고 물음에 답하시오.

G: Have you ever had Spanish food before?
B: No, I (a)<u>haven't</u>. Have you tried it?
G: Yes, I (b)<u>have</u>. I hope you can try it sometime. It's really good.
B: I will. For now, I'll just buy this Spanish ____(A)____ book.

출제율 95%

8 다음 영영풀이를 참고하여 위 대화의 빈칸 (A)에 알맞은 말을 쓰시오.

> a list of ingredients and a set of instructions that tell you how to cook something

➡ _____

출제율 90%

9 위 대화의 밑줄 친 (a)와 (b) 다음에 생략된 말을 쓰시오.

➡ (a) _____ (b) _____

출제율 90%

10 다음 중 밑줄 친 부분의 쓰임이 나머지 넷과 <u>다른</u> 것은?

① People have to go through trial and error <u>to be</u> an expert.
② Elsa had a lot of dresses <u>to wear</u>.
③ Olaf brought them something <u>to eat</u>.
④ Anna didn't have a chance <u>to watch</u> the movie.
⑤ Steven had enough time <u>to finish</u> his project.

출제율 90%

11 〈보기〉의 단어들 중에서 하나씩 각각 골라 다음 각 빈칸에 넣을 때, 나머지 넷과 성격이 <u>다른</u> 하나는?

> ┤ 보기 ├
> teach   sleep   read   sing   do

① She is so busy that she has no time _____ these days.
② There are many things _____ to realize your dream.
③ I have many books _____ seriously.
④ Susan needs somebody _____ her cooking.
⑤ He watched TV, with his mom _____ in the kitchen.

출제율 100%

12 다음 중 어법상 올바른 문장을 <u>모두</u> 고르면? (정답 2개)

① Robert couldn't tell if she was lying or telling the truth.
② Sue is wondering if or not there is a pizza store at the airport.
③ I want to know if it is fine tomorrow.
④ Sarah isn't sure whether Chris will come to the party last Saturday.
⑤ Paul asked me whether Sophia liked the flowers.

출제율 95%

13 다음 빈칸 ⓐ, ⓑ, ⓒ에 공통으로 들어갈 말로 가장 적절한 것은?

> • Taylor wanted to know ___ⓐ___ he could help her with the project.
> • You can do it ___ⓑ___ you can dream it.
> • Michelle is asking the girl ___ⓒ___ there is a train station nearby.

① when   ② that   ③ how
④ if   ⑤ whether

14 다음 그림을 보고 우리말에 맞게 괄호 안의 어구를 활용하여 영작하시오. [출제율 95%]

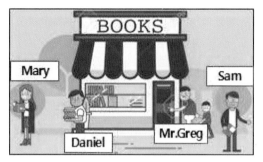

(1) Mary는 서점 앞에서 Betty를 만날 약속을 했다. (meet, in front of, make an appointment, the bookstore)

➡ _____

_____

(2) Daniel은 도서관에 반납할 몇 권의 책들이 있다. (to the library, return, have, several)

➡ _____

_____

(3) Greg씨는 읽을 교육 잡지 몇 권을 살 것이다. (read, educational magazine, buy, some)

➡ _____

_____

(4) Sam은 평론할 소설책을 들고 있다. (hold, review, a novel, is)

➡ _____

_____

[15~17] 다음 글을 읽고 물음에 답하시오.

When I had to ⓐdecide on a ⓑmajor in college, I chose engineering. ⓒBeing an engineer looked like OK. After college, I got a job at an engineering company. It was a stable job, but I didn't know whether I really enjoyed it.

15 위 글의 밑줄 친 ⓐdecide와 바꿔 쓸 수 있는 말을 쓰시오. [출제율 90%]

➡ _____

16 위 글의 밑줄 친 ⓑmajor와 같은 의미로 쓰인 것을 고르시오. [출제율 100%]

① We have encountered major problems.
② He's a major in the US army.
③ Her major is French.
④ She spent the major part of her income on shopping.
⑤ Did he major in mathematics?

17 위 글의 밑줄 친 ⓒ에서 어법상 틀린 부분을 찾아 고치시오. [출제율 95%]

_____ ➡ _____

[18~20] 다음 글을 읽고 물음에 답하시오.

After I came back, I entered a photo contest with the pictures I took in Iceland. Surprisingly, I won first prize, and this gave me a chance to think about my life. I realized that taking pictures made me happy. Suddenly, I wanted to become a good photographer, so I started to learn more about photography. After years of ⓐ시행착오, I got better, and I began to do some part-time work as a photographer.

Then one day, I made a bold decision. I quit my job and decided to take pictures for a living. I wasn't sure ⓑif I could succeed, but I decided to try. I really wanted to do something that made me happy. Now, I'm a professional photographer, and I'm happy.

18 위 글의 밑줄 친 ⓐ의 우리말에 맞게 3 단어로 영작하시오. [출제율 95%]

➡ _____

19 위 글의 밑줄 친 ⓑif와 같은 의미로 쓰인 것을 모두 고르시오.

① Give him this note if you see him.
② Ask him if it is true.
③ You can stay for the weekend if you like.
④ Do you know if he's married?
⑤ Do you mind if I open the sindow?

20 위 글의 주제로 알맞은 것을 고르시오.

① Have the pleasure of entering a photo contest.
② Be happy by doing what makes you happy.
③ Find your hidden talent.
④ Be aware of the danger of making a bold decision.
⑤ Look before you leap as it's better safe than sorry.

[21~22] 다음 글을 읽고 물음에 답하시오.

So do you want to find a dream and realize it? Here's some advice to help you.

First, follow your heart. Think about what you like to do and what makes you happy. In my case, it was taking pictures of stars.

Second, work hard. Pursuing a dream is not easy. I became a photographer through hard work.

Third, be bold. You need courage to make decisions that will change your life. I was afraid but I took a chance.

I truly hope you can find a dream, pursue it, and ⓐlive it!   <I: David Parker>

21 위 글의 밑줄 친 ⓐlive it과 바꿔 쓸 수 있는 말을 본문에서 찾아 쓰시오.

➡ _____

22 According to the passage, which is NOT true?

① David Parker gives some advice about finding a dream and realizing it.
② Taking pictures of stars made David Parker happy.
③ It is not easy to pursue a dream.
④ Boldness is not necessary to make decisions that will change your life.
⑤ David Parker truly hopes the audience can find a dream, pursue it, and live it.

[23~25] 다음 글을 읽고 물음에 답하시오.

My dream is to become a famous fashion designer. There are many things to do to realize my dream. First, I'll go to design school and study fashion design. Then, (A)after I graduate, I'll work at a fashion company. When I'm 30, I'll start my own brand. When I'm 35, I'll hold my first fashion show. I hope my dream will ____ⓐ____.

23 위 글의 빈칸 ⓐ에 들어갈 알맞은 말을 두 단어로 쓰시오.

➡ _____ 또는 _____

24 밑줄 친 (A)를 다음과 같이 바꿔 쓸 때 빈칸에 들어갈 알맞은 한 단어를 쓰시오.

➡ after _____

25 Which question CANNOT be answered after reading the passage?

① What is the writer's dream?
② What will the writer major in?
③ Where does the writer hope to work?
④ What is the name of the writer's brand?
⑤ When does the writer plan to hold his or her first fashion show?

[01~03] 다음 대화를 읽고 물음에 답하시오.

G: My favorite book is *Charlie and the Chocolate Factory*. Have you read it, Peter?

B: No, (a)I haven't, but I've seen the movie. How about you, Yubin? Have you seen the movie, too?

G: _____(A)_____ But I like the book more. I hope you can read it sometimes.

B: OK, I will.

01 빈칸 (A)에 알맞은 말을 쓰시오. (3 단어)

➡ _____

02 밑줄 친 (a)를 주어진 단어로 시작하여 바꿔 쓰시오. (총 10 단어)

➡ though _____

_____ .

03 위 대화에서 어색한 어휘를 하나 찾아 바르게 고치시오.

_____ ➡ _____

04 다음 각 문장을 읽고, 괄호 안에 주어진 동사와 if를 이용한 간접의문문을 사용하여 같은 내용이 되도록 만드시오.

(1) Laura said to me, "Do you love me?" (ask)

➡ _____

(2) Parker thought to himself, "Do I really enjoy the job?" (be sure)

➡ _____

(3) James mumbles to himself, "Can I pass the test?" (wonder) *mumble: 중얼거리다

➡ _____

05 다음 우리말에 맞게 괄호 안의 어구를 알맞게 배열하시오.

(1) 엄마는 아기를 배달하는 황새 이야기를 Dave 가 믿는지 궁금해 한다. (the story, Mom, delivering, if, the stork, wonders, Dave, of, believes, the baby)

➡ _____

(2) Dave는 아기가 태어나는 어떤 다른 방법이 있는지 엄마에게 물어본다. (for, Dave, the baby, if, any other way, to be born, asks, there, Mom, is)

➡ _____

_____

06 다음 중에서 틀린 문장을 찾아 번호를 쓰고, 바르게 고쳐 문장을 다시 쓰시오.

① Parker didn't know if watching stars and taking pictures could lead to a job.

② He got a chance to see the Northern Lights in Iceland.

③ His camera had a flash taking a picture of the Aurora.

④ Parker wondered if he really enjoyed the job of engineer.

⑤ He has courage to make decisions that will change his life.

➡ _____

_____

07 다음 우리말과 일치하도록 괄호 안에 주어진 단어들을 배열할 때 네 번째와 일곱 번째로 올 단어를 쓰시오.

> John은 가지고 쓸 연필이 전혀 없다.
> (write, any, John, with, doesn't, pencils, have, to)

➡ _____

[08~10] 다음 글을 읽고 물음에 답하시오.

When I was young, I loved stars. I also liked taking pictures. However, ⓐ나는 이것들이 직업과 연관될 수 있다고 전혀 생각하지 못했어요. In fact, I didn't have a dream at all.

When I had to decide on a major in college, I chose engineering. Being an engineer looked OK. After college, I got a job at an engineering company. ⓑIt was a stable job, but I didn't know that I really enjoyed it.

Everything changed when I went on vacation to Iceland one winter. There I got a chance to see the Northern Lights! The lights were amazing, and I took many pictures of the dancing lights in the sky. For the first time in many years, I could feel my heart beating fast. <I: David Parker>

08 위 글의 밑줄 친 ⓐ의 우리말에 맞게 한 단어를 보충하여, 주어진 어휘를 알맞게 배열하시오.

> thought / I / lead / these things / a job / never / could

➡ _____

09 위 글의 밑줄 친 ⓑ에서 어법상 틀린 부분을 찾아 고치시오.

_____ ➡ _____

10 본문의 내용과 일치하도록 다음 빈칸 (A)와 (B)에 들어갈 알맞은 단어를 본문에서 찾아 쓰시오. (필요한 경우 변형 가능.)

> David Parker was (A)_____ at the Northern Lights and took many pictures of them, which made him feel his fast heart beat (B)_____ _____ _____ _____ in many years.

[11~13] 다음 글을 읽고 물음에 답하시오.

So do you want to find a dream and realize ⓐit? (A)[Here's / Here're] some advice to help you.

First, follow your heart. Think about what you like to do and what makes you happy. In my case, it was taking pictures of stars.

Second, work (B)[hard / hardly]. Pursuing a dream is not easy. I became a photographer (C)[though / through] hard work.

Third, be bold. You need courage to make decisions that will change your life. I was afraid but I took a (A)chance.

I truly hope you can find a dream, pursue ⓑit, and live ⓒit!

11 위 글의 밑줄 친 ⓐit, ⓑit, ⓒit이 공통으로 가리키는 것을 본문에서 찾아 쓰시오.

➡ _____

12 위 글의 괄호 (A)~(C)에서 문맥이나 어법상 알맞은 낱말을 골라 쓰시오.

➡ (A)_____ (B)_____ (C)_____

13 위 글의 밑줄 친 (A)chance와 바꿔 쓸 수 있는 단어를 철자 r로 시작하여 쓰시오.

➡ _____

01 괄호 안의 어휘를 이용하여 다음 대화의 빈칸에 경험을 묻는 질문을 쓰시오.

> A: _____
> B: No, I haven't. Have you?
> A: Yes, I have. It was really delicious.
> (eat Bulgogi, have Bibimbap, try Samgyupsal)

(1) _____
(2) _____
(3) _____

02 어떤 선택을 할지 고민하는 사람의 마음을 표현하는 문장을, 〈보기〉와 같이 if 또는 whether를 사용하여 자유롭게 영작하시오.

> ┤ 보기 ├
> I'm not sure if I should choose Tom or David.

(1) I can't decide _____.
(2) I was wondering _____.
(3) I want to know _____.

03 다음 내용을 바탕으로 꿈을 이루기 위한 자신의 계획을 설명하는 글을 쓰시오.

> My Dream: a famous fashion designer
> Age 20: go to design school
> Age 25: work at a fashion company
> Age 30: start my own brand
> Age 35: hold my first fashion show

> My dream is to become (A)_____. There are many things to do to realize my dream. First, I'll go to design school and study (B)_____. Then, after I graduate, I'll work at (C)_____. When I'm 30, I'll start (D)_____. When I'm 35, I'll hold (E)_____. I hope my dream will come true.

단원별 모의고사

1 〈보기〉의 밑줄 친 어휘와 같은 의미로 쓰인 것을 고르시오.

> ┤ 보기 ├
> (1) My heart <u>beat</u> fast with joy.
> (2) He <u>beat</u> me at chess.

① Somebody was <u>beating</u> at the door.
② My pulse <u>beats</u> fast.
③ Someone was <u>beating</u> a drum.
④ This type of music has a strong <u>beat</u> to it.
⑤ Our team <u>beat</u> theirs by a huge score.

➡ (1) _____ (2) _____

[02~03] 다음 영영풀이에 해당하는 어휘를 주어진 철자로 시작하여 쓰시오.

2
> c_____ : the ability to do something that frightens one

3
> g_____ : something that you hope to achieve, especially when much time and effort will be needed

4 빈칸에 공통으로 들어갈 말을 쓰시오.

> • Air _____ is a major environmental problem.
> • I'm sure that water _____ is bad for animals.

➡ _____

5 다음 밑줄 친 부분의 뜻이 <u>잘못된</u> 것은?

① <u>For now</u>, Charlie and the kittens are great friends. (현재로는, 당분간은)
② Raise my salary, and I'll work <u>even</u> harder. (훨씬)
③ I don't know how many boys will <u>volunteer</u> to help with this. (자원하다, 봉사하다)
④ He asked me to visit him <u>sometime</u>. (언젠가)
⑤ Have you <u>tried</u> this new coffee? It's very good. (노력하다)

6 다음 중 짝지어진 대화가 <u>어색한</u> 것은?

① A: I'm not feeling well. I think I have a cold.
  B: That's too bad. I hope you feel better soon.
② A: You should read this book about the moon. It's really interesting.
  B: I don't know. I've already read it.
③ A: You can play the piano?
  B: Yes. How about you?
④ A: Have you ever been to Canada?
  B: Yes, I have. I saw a beautiful view from the mountains.
⑤ A: I hope you can read it sometime.
  B: OK, I will.

[07~09] 다음 대화를 읽고 물음에 답하시오.

B: I really liked your book about ⓐ<u>training</u> dogs.
W: Thank you. Do you like dogs?
B: Yes, I do. I love all ⓑ<u>kinds</u> of animals. (①)
W: Have you ever thought of ⓒ<u>becoming</u> an animal doctor? (②)

B: Yes, I have. (③)

W: What are you doing ⓓto achieve your goal? (④)

B: I'm doing volunteer work at the local animal house. (⑤)

W: That's good. What ⓔother are you doing?

B: I'm also watching a lot of TV shows about animals.

W: You're doing great! I hope you become a good animal doctor someday.

B: Thank you.

07 ①~⑤ 중 주어진 문장이 들어갈 곳은?

> I really want to become an animal doctor.

①　②　③　④　⑤

08 ⓐ~ⓔ 중 어법상 어색한 것은?

① ⓐ　② ⓑ　③ ⓒ　④ ⓓ　⑤ ⓔ

09 위 대화를 읽고 답할 수 없는 질문을 고르시오.

① What is the woman doing to achieve her goal?

② What does the boy want to be?

③ What does the woman wish the boy to be?

④ Is the boy doing well to achieve his goal?

⑤ Why is the boy watching a lot of TV shows about animals?

[10~12] 다음 대화를 읽고 물음에 답하시오.

G: I'm going to buy this CD. I love to listen to piano music.

B: Me, too. I also enjoy playing the piano.

G: Really? So you can play the piano?

B: Yes. _____(A)

G: Well, I've never learned how to play.

B: It's fun. I hope you'll have a chance (a)to learn.

10 위 대화의 빈칸 (A)에 알맞은 말을 3 단어로 쓰시오.

➡ _____

11 위 대화의 밑줄 친 (a)to learn과 쓰임이 같은 것을 고르시오.

① He went to France last year to learn French.

② Mom asked me to learn how to play the piano.

③ To learn English is not so difficult for children.

④ It's time to learn our history.

⑤ Korean is a beautiful language and easy to learn.

12 Why is the girl going to buy the CD? Answer in English with a full sentence. (9 words)

➡ _____

13 다음 중 밑줄 친 부분의 쓰임이 나머지 넷과 다른 것은?

① Kate received something exciting to watch.

② Alison doesn't have enough time to sleep.

③ Kayne has a good assistant to help him.

④ Thames participated in the meeting to catch up-to-date information.

⑤ There are a lot of organizations to support senior citizens.

14 다음 〈보기〉의 밑줄 친 부분과 쓰임이 다른 하나는?

> ┌─ 보기 ─┐
> I wonder if my son ate lunch today.

① He wasn't sure if she saw him or not.

② I won't join the meeting if he shows up today.

③ They wonder if the contest was held in 1997 or in 1998.

④ I'm not sure if he will come here tomorrow or not.

⑤ Emma asked her sisters if the dress would fit her.

15 다음 중 어법상 <u>어색한</u> 것을 <u>모두</u> 고르면?

① There is a remote controller to watch TV.

② I saw a lot of people reading books.

③ Do they need something eating?

④ She wants a piece of paper to write.

⑤ It's time to say goodbye to her.

16 다음 상황과 각 인물의 생각을 기록한 〈보기〉를 보고, 내용에 맞게 빈칸에 알맞은 말을 쓰시오. (단, whether와 or not 사용 금지)

〈상황 설명〉
은행 강도 3명이 Dave, Lily, Sean이 근무하는 은행을 점거했다. 강도 A가 바닥에 넘어진 Sean을 내려다보고 있다. 강도 B가 Dave에게 총을 겨누며 놀란 표정을 짓고 있다. 강도 C가 Lily에게 총을 겨누고 있다.

┌─ 보기 ─
Lily: Am I going to be all right?
Dave: Can I move my toes?
Robber A: Did he fall by mistake?
Sean: Will anyone come to save me?
Robber B: Is the man my friend, Dave?
Robber C: Should I shoot her?

(1) Lily isn't sure _____.
(2) Dave wonders _____.

(3) Robber A doubts _____.
(4) Sean wants to know _____
_____.
(5) Robber B wonders _____
_____.
(6) Robber C can't decide _____
_____.

17 다음 중에서 <u>틀린</u> 문장을 찾아 번호를 쓰고, 바르게 고쳐 문장을 다시 쓰시오.

① Are there any good places to visit?

② Does he have any plans to achieve?

③ Sally bought sunglasses to put on.

④ Give your daughter a spoon to eat.

⑤ Pedro has many pens to write with.

➡ _____

[18~19] 다음 글을 읽고 물음에 답하시오.

When I had to decide on a major in college, I chose engineering. Being an engineer looked OK. After college, I got a job at an engineering company. It was a stable job, but @I didn't know whether I really enjoyed it.

Everything changed when I went on vacation to Iceland one winter. There I got a chance to see the Northern Lights! The lights were amazing, and I took many pictures of the dancing lights in the sky. For the first time in many years, I could feel my heart ⓑbeating fast.

18 위 글의 밑줄 친 ⓐ와 바꿔 쓸 수 있는 말을 <u>모두</u> 고르시오.

① I didn't know whether or not I really enjoyed it.
② I didn't know if I really enjoyed it.
③ I didn't know that I really enjoyed it.
④ I didn't know whether I really enjoyed it or not.
⑤ I didn't know if or not I really enjoyed it.

19 아래 〈보기〉에서 위 글의 밑줄 친 ⓑbeating과 문법적 쓰임이 <u>다른</u> 것의 개수를 고르시오.

┌─ 보기 ┌
① The sound of rain <u>beating</u> the window woke me up.
② My dream is <u>beating</u> him at chess.
③ Somebody was <u>beating</u> at the door.
④ <u>Beating</u> a drum is very interesting.
⑤ Look at the waves <u>beating</u> the shore.
└

① 1개　② 2개　③ 3개　④ 4개　⑤ 5개

[20~21] 다음 글을 읽고 물음에 답하시오.

Suddenly, I wanted to become a good photographer, so I started to learn more about photography. (①) After years of trial and error, I got better, and I began to do some part-time work as a photographer. (②)
Then one day, I made a bold decision. (③) I wasn't sure if I could succeed, but I decided to try. (④) ⓐI really wanted to do something that made me happily. (⑤) Now, I'm a professional photographer, and I'm happy.

20 위 글의 흐름으로 보아, 주어진 문장이 들어가기에 가장 적절한 곳은?

I quit my job and decided to take pictures for a living.

①　　②　　③　　④　　⑤

21 위 글의 밑줄 친 ⓐ에서 어법상 <u>틀린</u> 부분을 찾아 고치시오.

_____ ➡ _____

[22~23] 다음 글을 읽고 물음에 답하시오.

So do you want to find a dream and realize it? Here's some advice to help you.
First, follow your heart. Think about what you like to do and what makes you happy. In my case, it was taking pictures of stars.
Second, work hard. Pursuing a dream is not easy. I became a photographer through hard work.
Third, be bold. You need courage to make decisions that will change your life. I was afraid but I took a chance.
I truly hope you can find a dream, pursue it, and live it!

22 위 글의 세 번째 조언과 어울리는 속담으로 가장 알맞은 것을 고르시오.

① Birds of a feather flock together.
② Nothing ventured, nothing gained.
③ It never rains but it pours.
④ Practice makes perfect.
⑤ A watched pot never boils.

23 Which question CANNOT be answered after reading the passage?

① To follow your heart, what do you have to do?
② Is pursuing a dream easy?
③ How did the writer become a photographer?
④ How long did it take for the writer to become a photographer?
⑤ To make decisions that will change your life, what do you need?

Lesson 2

Food for the Heart

🎙 의사소통 기능

- 음식 주문하기 1
  A: What would you like to order?
  B: I'd like to order two hot dogs.

- 음식 주문하기 2
  A: Is it for here or to go?
  B: It's for here, please. / It's to go, please.

🎙 언어 형식

- 사역동사의 목적격보어 – 원형부정사
  It **makes you feel** good when you are sad, angry, or stressed out.

- 접속사 so that
  My father made me a bowl of chicken soup **so that** I could get well.

Words & Expressions

Key Words

- **add**[æd] 동 더하다
- **audience**[ɔ́ːdiəns] 명 청중, 관중
- **bake**[beik] 동 굽다
- **beat**[biːt] 동 두드리다, 휘젓다, 섞다
- **bowl**[boul] 명 사발
- **cassava**[kəsáːvə] 명 (열대 지방의) 카사바
- **chip**[tʃip] 명 조각, 감자튀김
- **clearly**[klíərli] 부 분명하게
- **comfort**[kʌ́mfərt] 명 위로, 위안
- **cool**[kuːl] 동 차게 하다
- **crisp**[krisp] 형 바삭바삭한
- **differ**[dífər] 동 다르다
- **disappear**[dìsəpíər] 동 사라지다
- **dish**[diʃ] 명 음식
- **especially**[ispéʃəli] 부 특히
- **favorite**[féivərit] 형 좋아하는
- **fix**[fiks] 동 수리하다
- **flour**[fláuər] 명 밀가루
- **fortunately**[fɔ́ːrtʃənətli] 부 다행스럽게도
- **guide**[gaid] 명 안내원
- **include**[inklúːd] 동 포함시키다
- **international**[ìntərnǽʃənəl] 형 국제적인
- **Italian**[itǽljən] 이탈리아의
- **laptop**[lǽptap] 명 휴대용 컴퓨터
- **madeleine**[mǽdəlin] 명 마들렌(작은 카스텔라의 일종)
- **maybe**[méibiː] 부 아마도
- **melt**[melt] 동 녹이다
- **mix**[miks] 동 섞다, 혼합하다
- **mixture**[míkstʃər] 명 혼합물, 반죽
- **moment**[móumənt] 명 순간
- **mushroom**[mʌ́ʃruːm] 명 버섯
- **nap**[næp] 명 낮잠
- **once**[wʌns] 부 한 번
- **order**[ɔ́ːrdər] 동 주문하다 명 주문
- **peel**[piːl] 명 껍질 동 껍질을 벗기다[깎다]
- **pour**[pɔːr] 동 쏟아 붓다
- **quantity**[kwántəti] 명 양, 수량, 분량
- **recently**[ríːsntli] 부 최근에
- **recipe**[résəpi] 명 조리법
- **satisfy**[sǽtisfài] 동 만족하게 하다
- **seashell**[síːʃel] 명 조개껍데기, 조가비
- **share**[ʃɛər] 동 공유하다
- **snack**[snæk] 명 간식
- **special**[spéʃəl] 형 특별한
- **stay**[stei] 동 머무르다
- **stomach**[stʌ́mək] 명 위, 복부, 배
- **suddenly**[sʌ́dnli] 부 갑자기
- **taste**[teist] 동 맛이 나다
- **tasty**[téisti] 형 맛있는
- **vegetable**[védʒətəbl] 명 채소
- **warm**[wɔːrm] 동 따뜻하게 하다 형 따뜻한
- **while**[hwail] 접 ~하는 동안

Key Expressions

- **a bowl of ~** ~ 한 그릇
- **around the world** 전 세계에서
- **be filled with ~** ~로 가득 차다
- **break down** 고장 나다
- **catch a cold** 감기에 걸리다
- **come right out of ~** ~에서 바로 나오다
- **comfort food** 위안을 주는 음식
- **do one's best** 최선을 다하다
- **every time ~** ~할 때마다
- **feel better** 기분이 나아지다, 기분이 좋아지다
- **For here or to go?** 여기에서 드시겠어요, 아니면 가져가 시겠어요?
- **get well** 회복하다
- **look like ~** ~처럼 보이다
- **not only A but (also) B** A 뿐만 아니라 B도
- **similar to ~** ~과 비슷한
- **so that 주어 can ~** ~하기 위하여
- **stressed out** 스트레스로 지친
- **take an order** 주문을 받다
- **think of ~** ~에 대하여 생각하다
- **would like to ~** ~하기를 원하다

Word Power

※ 서로 비슷한 뜻을 가진 어휘

☐ **audience** 청중, 관중 : **spectator** 구경꾼

☐ **comfort** 위로, 위안 : **consolation** 위로, 위안

☐ **especially** 특히 : **specially** 특별히

☐ **maybe** 아마도 : **perhaps** 아마도

☐ **suddenly** 갑자기 : **abruptly** 갑자기

☐ **differ** 다르다 : **vary** 다르다

☐ **fix** 수리하다 : **repair** 수리하다

☐ **mix** 섞다, 혼합하다 : **mingle** 섞다

※ 서로 반대의 뜻을 가진 어휘

☐ **add** 더하다 ↔ **subtract** 빼다

☐ **comfort** 위로, 위안 ↔ **discomfort** 불쾌, 불안

☐ **melt** 녹이다 ↔ **freeze** 얼리다

☐ **appear** 나타나다 ↔ **disappear** 사라지다

☐ **fortunately** 다행스럽게 ↔ **unfortunately** 불행하게도

☐ **warm** 따뜻하게 하다 ↔ **cool** 차게 하다

※ 명사 – 형용사(명사+y)

☐ **taste** 맛 – **tasty** 맛있는

☐ **rain** 비 – **rainy** 비 내리는

☐ **sleep** 잠 – **sleepy** 졸리는

☐ **salt** 소금 – **salty** 짠

☐ **snow** 눈 – **snowy** 눈이 내리는

☐ **health** 건강 – **healthy** 건강한

English Dictionary

☐ **audience** 청중, 관중
→ the group of people watching or listening to a play, film or public meeting
연극, 영화 또는 공적인 회의 등을 보거나 듣는 사람들의 무리

☐ **bake** 굽다
→ to cook something using dry heat, in an oven
오븐에서 건열을 이용하여 음식을 조리하다

☐ **beat** 휘젓다, 섞다
→ to mix things together quickly with a fork or special kitchen machine
포크나 주방 기계로 신속하게 함께 섞다

☐ **bowl** 사발
→ a wide round container that is open at the top
위가 열린 넓고 둥근 그릇

☐ **comfort** 위로, 위안, 편안
→ a feeling of being relaxed
편안한 느낌

☐ **disappear** 사라지다
→ to become impossible to see or find
보거나 찾을 수 없게 되다

☐ **fix** 수리하다
→ to repair something that is broken
고장 난 것을 고치다

☐ **flour** 밀가루
→ a powder used for making bread and cakes
빵과 케이크를 만드는 데 사용되는 가루

☐ **melt** 녹이다
→ to become liquid
액체가 되도록 하다

☐ **order** 주문하다
→ to ask for food or a drink in a restaurant
식당에서 음식이나 음료를 요구하다

☐ **peel** 껍질
→ the skin of a fruit or vegetable
과일이나 채소의 껍질

☐ **recipe** 조리법
→ a set of instructions for cooking a particular type of food
특정한 음식을 요리하기 위한 일련의 설명서

☐ **satisfy** 만족하게 하다
→ to make someone feel happy, by doing what he or she wants
누군가가 원하는 것을 함으로써 행복하게 느끼도록 만들다

☐ **snack** 간식
→ a small amount of food that is eaten between main meals
주된 식사 사이에 먹는 소량의 음식

01 다음 빈칸에 들어갈 알맞은 말을 고르시오.

> After lunch, I felt very tired and sleepy, so I took a _____.

① cold   ② comfort
③ dish   ④ food
⑤ nap

02 다음 빈칸에 공통으로 들어갈 말로 알맞은 것은?

> • People like to live in _____.
> • I wanted to _____ him over his terrible loss.

① comfort   ② enjoy
③ peel   ④ fortune
⑤ differ

03 다음 〈보기〉의 단어를 사용하여 자연스러운 문장을 만들 수 없는 것은?

> ┤ 보기 ├
> crisp include audience fix

① Service enterprises _____ many types of businesses.
② Maybe you'll receive lots of letters from our _____.
③ I spread butter on a _____ piece of toast.
④ On a hot day, sunlight is usually enough to _____ chocolate.
⑤ The man is all thumbs and can never _____ things.

04 다음 짝지어진 단어의 관계가 같도록 빈칸에 알맞은 말은?

> differ – vary : fix – _____

① mind   ② pour
③ mix   ④ repair
⑤ melt

05 다음 중 밑줄 친 부분의 의미로 알맞지 않은 것은?

① A flea market is <u>similar to</u> a yard sale, only bigger. (~과 비슷한)
② By the end of the semester I was totally <u>stressed out</u>. (스트레스로 지친)
③ <u>Every time</u> I looked at him, he was yawning. (항상)
④ I wanted to know what you <u>think of</u> her music. (~에 대하여 생각하다)
⑤ They say you'll <u>get well</u> soon after the treatment. (회복하다)

06 다음 대화의 빈칸에 알맞은 말이 바르게 짝지어진 것을 고르시오.

> A: Hello, welcome to Happy Burger. May I _____ your order?
> B: I would like to _____ an order for three doughnuts.

① take – place
② take – ask
③ get – ask
④ make – place
⑤ make – take

01 다음 영영풀이에 알맞은 어휘를 〈보기〉에서 찾아 쓰시오.

┌─ 보기 ─┐
snack   comfort   recipe   flour
└────────┘

(1) a feeling of being relaxed

(2) a small amount of food that is eaten between main meals

(3) a set of instructions for cooking a particular type of food

(4) a powder used for making bread and cakes

➡ (1) _____ (2) _____ (3) _____
   (4) _____

02 다음 우리말에 맞도록 빈칸에 알맞은 말을 쓰시오.

(1) 요가를 연습하는 것은 사람들이 기분이 더 나아지는 데 실제로 도움이 된다.
   → Practicing yoga actually helps people _____ better.

(2) 이것을 여기에서 드시겠어요, 아니면 가져가시겠어요?
   → Do you want this for here or _____? (two words)

(3) 그는 가난할 뿐만 아니라 게으르다.
   → He is not only poor _____ lazy.

(4) 어제 길 한가운데서 차가 고장났어.
   → The car _____ down in the middle of the road yesterday.

03 다음 짝지어진 두 단어의 관계가 같도록 빈칸에 알맞은 말을 주어진 철자로 시작하여 쓰시오.

(1) add : addition = differ : d_____

(2) beauty : beautiful = health : h_____

04 밑줄 친 부분과 바꿔 쓸 수 있는 말을 주어진 철자로 시작하여 쓰시오.

┌─────────────────────────────┐
│ When she won a gold medal, she found │
│ contentment at last.   │
└─────────────────────────────┘

➡ s_____

05 다음 우리말에 맞게 한 단어를 추가하여 주어진 단어를 알맞게 배열하시오.

(1) 그 양동이는 모래와 더러운 것들로 가득 차 있다. (the bucket, is, sand, things, filled, dirty, and)
   ➡ _____
      _____

(2) 웨이트리스가 주문을 받으러 우리 식탁으로 왔다. (a waitress, the table, our order, came, to, to)
   ➡ _____
      _____

(3) 그 토마토는 내 정원에서 바로 나온 겁니다! (my own garden, right, the tomatoes, come, out)
   ➡ _____
      _____

Conversation

1 음식 주문하기 1

A What would you like to order? 무엇을 주문하시겠습니까?

B I'd like to order two hot dogs. 핫도그 두 개 주문할게요.

- 주문을 받을 때는 'What would you like to order?(무엇을 주문하시겠습니까?)', 'May I take your order?', 'Are you ready to order?(주문하시겠습니까?)'와 같은 질문에 이어서 'I want to order ~', 'I'd like to order ~.', 'I'd like ~.(~를 주문하겠습니다.)', 'I'll have ~.' 또는 'Can/Could I get ~?(~이 됩니까?)'라고 주문한다.

- 음식을 주문할 때 사용하는 'have', 'get'의 의미는 '먹다'이다. 주문하고자 하는 음식의 종류와 수량을 제시한다. 간단하게 음식의 종류와 수량을 제시하고 'please'를 붙이기도 한다. 'I want ~.'라고 할 수도 있지만, 보통 무작정 요구하는 것처럼 들리지 않고 대화의 흐름을 이어가기 위하여 'I'd like to ~.'라고 하거나 'Can I get ~?'라고 한다.

  • I'd like to order a supreme pizza to go. 수프림 피자 하나 포장해서 주세요.

  • I want a tuna salad sandwich. 참치 샐러드 샌드위치 주세요.

- '주문하다'는 'order', 'place an order' 등을 쓰고, '주문을 받다'는 'take an order'라고 한다.

음식 주문하기

  • I'd like to have ~.

  • I'll have ~.

  • Can I get ~, please?

  • May I have ~, please?

  • Can I order ~?

핵심 Check

1. 다음 우리말과 일치하도록 빈칸에 알맞은 말을 쓰시오.

   A: Hello. (A)_____? (무엇을 주문하시겠습니까?)

   B: (B)_____. (핫도그 두 개를 주문하고 싶어요.)

   A: Would you like anything to drink?

   B: Yes, one orange juice, please.

② 음식 주문하기 2

A Is it for here or to go? 여기에서 드시겠어요, 아니면 가져가시겠어요?

B It's for here, please. 여기에서 먹을게요. / It's to go, please. 가지고 갈게요.

■ 음식을 주문 받을 때 음식을 정하고 나면 음식 가격을 계산하기 전에 보통 'For here or to go?(여기에서 드시겠어요, 아니면 가져가시겠어요?)'라고 묻는 경우가 많다. 매장에서 음식을 먹고 싶다면, 'For here.', 'It's for here, please.' 또는 'For here, please.'라고 말한다. 가지고 가는 경우 'It's to go, please.(가지고 갈 겁니다.)'라고 한다.

■ 매장 밖으로 음식을 들고 나가는 것을 to go 또는 take out이라고 한다. to go는 보통 음료와 음식 모두 (또는 우리가 먹는 모든 것들)에 쓰이고, take out은 주로 음식에 쓰인다.

　• Do you want this for here or to go? 여기에서 드시겠어요, 아니면 가져가시겠어요?

■ 음식을 주문한 후 다음과 같은 표현을 쓸 수 있다.

'여기서 먹는다./가지고 간다.'의 여러 가지 표현

　• For here. 여기에서 먹겠습니다.

　• It's for here, please.

　• For here, please.

　• It's to go, please. 가지고 갈 겁니다.

　• Can I get this to go? 가지고 갈 수 있을까요?

　• I'd like the ~, to go please.

핵심 Check

2. 다음 대화를 자연스러운 순서로 배열하시오.

　A: Welcome to Dessert World. May I take your order?

　B: Yes, please. I'd like to order two doughnuts.

　A: Would you like anything to drink?

　(A) For here, please.

　(B) Is it for here or to go?

　(C) Yes, one orange juice, please.

　➡

교과서 대화문 익히기

Listen and Talk A 1

W: Welcome to Italian Food. ❶What would you like to order?

B: ❷I want to order a mushroom pizza.

W: Will ❸that be all?

B: Yes.

W: ❹Is the order for here or to go?

B: ❺For here, please.

W: Italian Food에 오신 것을 환영합니다. 무엇을 주문하시겠어요?
B: 버섯 피자를 먹으려고요.
W: 그것이 전부인가요?
B: 네.
W: 여기에서 드시겠어요, 아니면 가져가시겠어요?
B: 여기에서 먹을게요.

❶ 무엇을 주문할 것인지 묻는 표현이다.
❷ 질문의 대답으로 어떤 것을 주문하겠다고 할 때 사용하는 표현이다.
❸ that은 a mushroom pizza를 받는 대명사이다.
❹ '여기에서 드실 건가요 아니면 가져가실 건가요?'라고 묻는 것이다.
❺ 여기에서 먹겠다는 의미이다.

Check(√) True or False

(1) The boy is visiting an Italian restaurant. T ☐ F ☐

(2) The woman is placing an order. T ☐ F ☐

Listen and Talk C

M: Welcome to Sandwich Place. ❶What would you like to order?

G: I'd like to ❷have a hamburger, and she'll have a chicken sandwich.

M: Would you like ❸anything else?

G: One salad, please.

M: OK, then will ❹that be all?

G: No, I'd like to order two bottles of water.

M: Is it for here or to go?

G: It's for here, please.

M: The total ❺comes to 12 dollars.

G: OK. ❻Here you are.

M: Sandwich Place에 오신 것을 환영합니다. 무엇을 주문하시겠어요?
G: 저는 햄버거 하나를 먹고 싶고, 이 아이는 치킨 샌드위치를 먹을 거예요.
M: 더 필요한 것은 없으세요?
G: 샐러드 하나 주세요.
M: 알겠습니다. 그럼 그것이 다인가요?
G: 아니요, 물 두 병 주세요.
M: 여기에서 드시겠어요, 아니면 가져가시겠어요?
G: 여기에서 먹을게요.
M: 모두 12 달러입니다.
G: 네, 여기 있어요.

❶ 'May I take your order?', 'Are you ready to order?' 등으로 바꿔 쓸 수 있다.
❷ have는 '먹다'라는 의미로 사용되었다.
❸ -thing으로 끝난 대명사를 else가 뒤에서 수식하고 있다.
❹ that은 지금까지 주문한 것을 가리킨다.
❺ 'comes to'는 다음에 명사가 나와서 '합계 ~이 되다'를 의미한다.
❻ '여기 있습니다.'라는 뜻으로 물건을 건네주면서 쓰는 표현이다.

Check(√) True or False

(3) The girl will take out her order. T ☐ F ☐

(4) The man seems to be a customer. T ☐ F ☐

Listen and Talk A 2

> W: Hello. ❶Are you ready to order?
> B: Yes, please. ❷I'd like a piece of cake.
> W: What ❸kind of cake would you like?
> B: Chocolate cake, please.
> W: ❹For here or to go?
> B: ❺To go, please. Thank you.

❶ 주문하겠는지 묻는 표현으로 'May I take your order?', 'What would you like to order?' 등으로 바꿔 쓸 수 있다.
❷ 주문할 때 쓰는 표현이다. 'I'd like to order ~.', 'I want ~.', 'I want to order ~.', 'I'll have ~.' 또는 'Can/Could I get ~?' 등으로도 말할 수 있다.
❸ kind는 '종류'를 뜻하는 명사로 사용되었다.
❹ 앞에 'Is it(= your order)'이 생략되어 있다.
❺ 음식을 가져가겠다는 의미이다.

Listen and Talk A 3

> W: Hello. ❶What would you like to order?
> B: ❷I'd like to order Manduguk.
> W: Would you like ❸anything to drink?
> B: Yes, ❹one bottle of water, please.
> W: ❺Is it for here or to go?
> B: ❻It's to go, please.

❶ 무엇을 주문할지 묻는 표현이다.
❷ 주문할 때 쓰는 표현이다.
❸ 'to drink'는 anything을 수식하는 to부정사의 형용사적 용법이다.
❹ 물질명사의 수량을 나타내는 표현으로 '수량+단위명사+of+물질명사'의 순서로 쓴다.
❺ 매장에서 먹을지 아니면 가져갈지를 묻는 표현이다.
❻ '가져가겠다.'라는 뜻으로 'to go'는 'take out'을 의미한다.

Listen and Talk A 4

> W: Hello. ❶What would you like to order?
> B: ❷I want a hot dog and one milk, please.
> W: ❸Would you like anything ❹else?
> B: No, thank you.
> W: Will it be for here or to go?
> B: To go, please. Thank you.

❶ 무엇을 주문할지 묻는 표현이다.
❷ 주문할 때 쓰는 표현이다. 물질명사에 부정관사 a와 수량을 나타내는 one을 붙인 것은 '제품 하나'를 나타내는 것이다. one 대신 a를 써도 좋다.
❸ 추가 주문 여부를 묻는 표현이다.
❹ else는 '그 밖에' 정도의 의미로 anything을 뒤에서 수식하고 있다.

Listen and Talk B

> A: Hello. ❶What would you like to order?
> B: ❷I'd like to order ❸two hot dogs.

> A: Would you like ❹anything to drink?
> B: Yes, one orange juice, please.
> A: Is it for here or to go?
> B: It's for here, please. / B: It's to go, please.

❶ 주문 받을 때 쓰는 표현으로 'May I take your order?', 'Are you ready to order?' 등으로 바꿔 쓸 수 있다.
❷ I'd like to = I would like to = I want to
❸ 물질명사에 수량을 나타내는 two를 붙인 것은 '제품 두 개'를 나타내는 것이다.
❹ 'to drink'는 anything을 수식하는 to부정사의 형용사적 용법이다.

Review 1

> M: Hello. ❶Are you ready to order?
> G: Yes, please. ❷I'd like ❸a chicken salad.
> M: Will that be all?
> G: Yes.
> M: For here or to go?
> G: To go, please.

❶ be ready to: ~할 준비가 되다
❷ 주문할 때 쓰는 표현으로 'I'd like ~.', 'I want ~.', 'I want to order ~.', 'I'll have ~.' 또는 'Can/Could I get ~?' 등으로 바꿔 쓸 수 있다.
❸ '제품 하나'를 나타내기 위해 물질명사 앞에 부정관사를 붙인 것이다.

Review 2

> W: Hello. What would you like to order?
> B: I'd like to order a sandwich.
> W: Would you like ❶anything to drink?
> B: Yes. ❷One milk, please.
> W: ❸Will that be all?
> B: Yes. Thank you.

❶ 'to drink'는 to부정사의 형용사적 용법으로 anything을 수식하고 있다.
❷ 제품 하나를 나타내는 One이다.
❸ 주문이 끝났는지, 더 주문할 것은 없는지 묻는 것이다.

Review 3

> W: Hello. What would you like to order?
> B: ❶I want Gimchi Gimbap, please.
> W: ❷Would you like anything else?
> B: No, thank you.
> W: ❸Is it for here or to go?
> B: To go, please.

❶ 주문할 때 쓰는 표현으로 'I want to order ~.', 'I'd like ~.', 'I'd like to order ~.', 'I'll have ~.' 또는 'Can/Could I get ~?' 등으로 바꿔 쓸 수 있다.
❷ 'Would you like ~?'는 '~을 원합니까?'라는 의미이다.
❸ '여기에서 드실 건가요 아니면 가져가실 건가요?'라고 묻는 표현이다. 'Is it'을 생략해서 쓰기도 한다.

다음 우리말과 일치하도록 빈칸에 알맞은 말을 쓰시오.

Listen and Talk A 1

W: _____ _____ Italian Food. _____ would you like _____ order?

B: I _____ to order a mushroom pizza.

W: Will _____ be all?

B: Yes.

W: Is the order _____ here or _____ go?

B: _____ here, please.

해석

W: Italian Food에 오신 것을 환영합니다. 무엇을 주문하시겠어요?
B: 버섯 피자를 먹으려고요.
W: 그것이 전부인가요?
B: 네.
W: 여기에서 드시겠어요, 아니면 가져가시겠어요?
B: 여기에서 먹을게요.

Listen and Talk A 2

W: Hello. Are you _____ _____ order?

B: Yes, please. I'd _____ a _____ of cake.

W: What kind of cake would you _____?

B: Chocolate cake, please.

W: For _____ or to _____?

B: To _____, please. Thank you.

W: 안녕하세요, 주문하시겠어요?
B: 네, 케이크 한 조각 주세요.
W: 어떤 종류의 케이크로 드시겠어요?
B: 초콜릿 케이크로 주세요.
W: 여기에서 드시겠어요, 아니면 가져가시겠어요?
B: 가져갈게요. 감사합니다.

Listen and Talk A 3

W: Hello. _____ would you like to _____?

B: I'd _____ _____ _____ Manduguk.

W: Would you like _____ _____ drink?

B: Yes, _____ _____ water, please.

W: Is it _____ _____ or _____ _____?

B: It's _____ _____, please.

W: 안녕하세요, 무엇을 주문하시겠어요?
B: 만둣국 주세요.
W: 마실 것을 주문하시겠어요?
B: 네, 물 한 병 주세요.
W: 여기에서 드시겠어요, 아니면 가져가시겠어요?
B: 가져갈게요.

Listen and Talk A 4

W: Hello. What _____ you _____ _____ _____?

B: I _____ a hot dog and _____ milk, please.

W: Would you like _____ _____?

B: No, thank you.

W: Will _____ be for here or _____ _____?

B: _____ _____, please. Thank you.

W: 안녕하세요, 무엇을 주문하시겠어요?
B: 핫도그와 우유 하나 주세요.
W: 더 필요한 것은 없으세요?
B: 없어요.
W: 여기에서 드시겠어요, 아니면 가져가시겠어요?
B: 가져갈게요. 감사합니다.

Listen and Talk B

A: Hello. _____ _____ _____ _____ _____ _____?
B: _____ _____ _____ _____ two hot dogs.
A: Would you like _____ _____ _____?
B: Yes, _____ orange juice, please.
A: _____ _____ for here or to go?
B: It's _____ _____, please. / B: It's _____ _____, please.

Listen and Talk C

M: _____ _____ Sandwich Place. _____ would you like to order?
G: I'd like to _____ _____ hamburger, and she'll have _____ chicken sandwich.
M: Would you like _____ _____?
G: One salad, please.
M: OK, then _____ _____ be all?
G: No, I'd like to _____ _____ _____ of water.
M: _____ _____ _____ or _____ _____?
G: It's _____ _____, please.
M: The total _____ _____ 12 dollars.
G: OK. _____ you _____.

Review

(1) M: Hello. _____ you _____ _____ order?
    G: Yes, please. I'd like a chicken salad.
    M: Will that _____ _____?
    G: Yes.
    M: _____ _____ or to go?
    G: _____ _____, please.

(2) W: Hello. What _____ you _____ _____ order?
    B: I'd like _____ _____ a sandwich.
    W: Would you like _____ _____ _____?
    B: Yes. One milk, please.
    W: Will that be all?
    B: Yes. Thank you.

(3) W: H e l l o. _____ _____ _____ _____ _____ _____?
    B: I _____ Gimchi Gimbap, please.
    W: Would you like _____ _____?
    B: No, thank you.
    W: Is it for here or _____ _____?
    B: _____ _____, please.

A: 안녕하세요, 주문하시겠어요?
B: 핫도그 두 개 주세요.
A: 음료를 주문하시겠어요?
B: 네, 오렌지 주스 하나 주세요.
A: 여기에서 드시겠어요, 아니면 가져가시겠어요?
B: 여기에서 먹을게요. / B: 가져갈게요.

M: Sandwich Place에 오신 것을 환영합니다. 무엇을 주문하시겠어요?
G: 저는 햄버거 하나를 먹고 싶고, 이 아이는 치킨 샌드위치를 먹을 거예요.
M: 더 필요한 것은 없으세요?
G: 샐러드 하나 주세요.
M: 알겠습니다. 그럼 그것이 다인가요?
G: 아니요, 물 두 병 주세요.
M: 여기에서 드시겠어요, 아니면 가져 가시겠어요?
G: 여기에서 먹을게요.
M: 모두 12 달러입니다.
G: 네, 여기 있어요.

(1) M: 안녕하세요, 주문하시겠어요?
    G: 네, 치킨 샐러드 하나 주세요.
    M: 그것이 다인가요?
    G: 네.
    M: 여기에서 드시겠어요, 아니면 가져가시겠어요?
    G: 가져갈게요.

(2) W: 안녕하세요, 무엇을 주문하시겠어요?
    B: 샌드위치 하나 주세요.
    W: 마실 것 주문하시겠어요?
    B: 네, 우유 하나 주세요.
    W: 그것이 다인가요?
    B: 네, 고맙습니다.

(3) W: 안녕하세요, 무엇을 주문하시겠어요?
    B: 김치 김밥 주세요.
    W: 더 필요하신 것은 없으세요?
    B: 없어요.
    W: 여기에서 드시겠어요, 아니면 가져가시겠어요?
    B: 가져갈게요.

01 다음 우리말에 해당하는 영어 문장을 쓰시오.

> A: Hello. What would you like to order?
> B: I'd like to order two hot dogs.
> A: Would you like anything to drink?
> B: Yes, one orange juice, please.
> A: 여기에서 드시겠어요, 아니면 가져가시겠어요? (7 단어)
> B: It's for here, please.

➡ _____

02 다음 대화의 빈칸에 들어갈 말로 알맞은 것은?

> W: Is it for here or to go?
> B: _____, please.

① I can make it here
② You'd have it here
③ Don't forget to take it out
④ It's to go
⑤ I want to go to the restaurant

03 다음 대화의 빈칸에 들어갈 말로 어색한 것은?

> W: Hello. _____
> B: I'd like to order Manduguk.

① What would you like to order?
② May I take your order?
③ What did you order?
④ Can I have your order?
⑤ Are you ready to order?

04 다음 밑줄 친 우리말을 주어진 단어를 이용해 영작하시오.

> M: What would you like to order?
> G: 햄버거 하나 주세요. (to는 사용하지 말 것. want, hamburger)

➡ _____

01 다음 중 짝지어진 대화가 <u>어색한</u> 것은?

① A: Welcome to Italian Food. What would you like to order?
　 B: I want to order a mushroom pizza.

② A: What kind of cake would you like?
　 B: Chocolate cake, please.

③ A: Is it for here or to go?
　 B: It's to go, please.

④ A: OK, then will that be all?
　 B: Yes, I'd like to order two bottles of water.

⑤ A: Would you like anything else?
　 B: No, thank you.

[02~04] 다음 대화를 읽고 물음에 답하시오.

M: Welcome to Sandwich Place. (a)<u>무엇을 주문하시겠어요?</u>

G: I'd like to have a hamburger, and she'll have a chicken sandwich.

M: Would you like anything else?

G: One salad, please.

M: OK, then will that be all?

G: No, I'd like to order two bottles of water.

M: Is it ＿＿＿＿＿＿(A)＿＿＿＿＿＿ ?

G: It's for here, please.

M: The total comes to 12 dollars.

G: OK. Here you are.

02 빈칸 (A)에 알맞은 말을 고르시오.

① for both of you only
② for here or to go
③ enough for you
④ cheap for you
⑤ enough for two persons

서답형
03 밑줄 친 (a)의 우리말에 맞게 주어진 어휘를 이용하여 영작하시오.

> you, what, would, order

➡ ＿＿＿＿＿＿＿＿＿＿＿＿＿＿＿

04 위 대화의 내용과 일치하지 <u>않는</u> 것은?

① The man seems to be a waiter.
② The man wants to take an order.
③ The girl will pay 12 dollars.
④ The girl will have a hamburger.
⑤ The girl will take out her food.

[05~06] 다음 대화를 읽고 물음에 답하시오.

W: Welcome to Italian Food. What would you like to order?

B: ＿＿＿＿＿＿(A)＿＿＿＿＿＿

W: Will that be all?

B: Yes.

W: Is the order for here or ＿＿(B)＿＿ ?

B: For here, please.

05 위 대화의 빈칸 (A)에 들어갈 말로 알맞지 <u>않은</u> 것은?

① Why don't you order a mushroom pizza?
② Can I get a mushroom pizza?
③ I'd like to order a mushroom pizza.
④ I want a mushroom pizza.
⑤ I want to order a mushroom pizza.

서답형
06 위 대화의 빈칸 (B)에 들어갈 말로 알맞은 말을 쓰시오.

➡ ＿＿＿＿＿＿＿＿＿＿＿＿＿

07 주어진 문장 사이에 이어 대화가 자연스럽게 연결되도록 (A)~(D)를 순서대로 가장 적절하게 배열한 것은?

> W: Hello. Are you ready to order?
> (A) Chocolate cake, please.
> (B) Yes, please. I'd like a piece of cake.
> (C) For here or to go?
> (D) What kind of cake would you like?
> B: To go, please. Thank you.

① (B) – (A) – (C) – (D)
② (B) – (C) – (A) – (D)
③ (B) – (D) – (A) – (C)
④ (C) – (B) – (A) – (D)
⑤ (C) – (D) – (B) – (A)

[08~09] 다음 대화를 읽고 물음에 답하시오.

> W: Hello. _____(A)_____ (would, like, order)
> B: I'd like to order Manduguk.
> W: _____(B)_____
> B: Yes, one bottle of water, please.
> W: Is it for here or to go?
> B: It's to go, please.

서답형

08 위 대화의 빈칸 (A)에 알맞은 말을 주어진 어휘를 이용하여 쓰시오.

➡ _____

09 위 대화의 빈칸 (B)에 알맞은 말은?

① Which one do you like to drink, this one or that one?
② Why don't you try one bottle of water?
③ What do you like to drink?
④ Would you like anything to drink?
⑤ Did you try one bottle of water?

10 다음 대화의 밑줄 친 부분의 의도로 알맞은 것은?

> W: Hello. <u>What would you like to order?</u>
> B: I want a hot dog and one milk, please.
> W: Would you like anything else?
> B: No, thank you.

① 음식 주문받기　　② 경험 묻기
③ 음식 주문하기　　④ 조언 구하기
⑤ 설명 요청하기

[11~13] 다음 대화를 읽고 물음에 답하시오.

> A: Hello. What would you like to order?
> B: I'd like to order two hot dogs.
> A: Would you like anything (a)<u>to drink</u>?
> B: Yes, one orange juice, please.
> A: (b)<u>여기에서 드시겠어요, 아니면 가져가시겠어요?</u>
>   (it, for, to)
> B: It's for here, please.

11 밑줄 친 (a)to drink와 같은 용법으로 쓰인 것을 고르시오.

① I want some water <u>to drink</u>.
② His failure caused him <u>to drink</u>.
③ It's dangerous <u>to drink</u> and drive.
④ The water from the well isn't fit <u>to drink</u>.
⑤ People come here <u>to drink</u> coffee.

서답형

12 밑줄 친 우리말 (b)를 주어진 어휘를 이용하여 7 단어로 �시오.

➡ _____

13 위 대화의 내용과 일치하지 <u>않는</u> 것을 고르시오.

① A는 주문을 받고자 한다.
② B는 핫도그를 주문하려고 한다.
③ A는 마실 것을 주문할지 묻는다.
④ B는 오렌지 주스를 주문한다.
⑤ B는 주문한 것을 가져갈 것이다.

[01~03] 다음 대화를 읽고 물음에 답하시오.

M: Welcome to Sandwich Place. What would you like to order?

G: I'd like to have a hamburger, and she'll have a chicken sandwich.

M: _____(A)_____

G: One salad, please.

M: OK, then will that be all?

G: No, I'd like to order two bottles of water.

M: Is it for here or to go?

G: It's for here, please.

M: _____(B)_____

G: OK. Here you are.

01 빈칸 (A)에 would와 like를 이용하여 '다른 어떤 것을 원하는지' 묻는 말을 쓰시오. (5 단어)

　➡ _____

02 빈칸 (B)에 come을 이용하여 '총 12달러'라는 의미가 되도록 쓰시오. (6 단어)

　➡ _____

03 What food did the girl order?

　➡ _____
　　 _____

[04~05] 다음 대화를 읽고 물음에 답하시오.

A: Welcome to Dessert World. _____(A)_____ (may, your order)

B: Yes, please. I'd _____(B)_____ to order two doughnuts.

A: Would you _____(C)_____ anything to drink?

B: Yes, one orange juice, please.

A: Is it for here or to go?

B: For here, please.

04 괄호 안에 주어진 어휘를 이용하여 빈칸 (A)에 알맞은 말을 5 단어로 쓰시오.

　➡ _____

05 빈칸 (B)와 (C)에 공통으로 들어갈 말을 쓰시오.

　➡ _____

[06~07] 다음 대화를 읽고 물음에 답하시오.

Thank you for your help, but you look stressed out. What's wrong?

(A) This is for you. It's filled with food.

(B) My family has nothing to eat.

(C) Thanks. Wow! (a)It (food, also, only, has, but, not) gold.

06 주어진 문장 다음에 (A)~(C)를 알맞은 순서로 배열하시오.

　➡ _____

07 밑줄 친 (a)의 괄호 안에 주어진 어휘를 알맞은 순서로 배열하시오.

　➡ _____

08 다음 대화의 밑줄 친 문장과 같은 의미의 문장을 3개 이상 쓰시오.

W: What would you like to order?

B: I want Gimchi Gimbap, please.

　➡ _____
　　 _____
　　 _____

Grammar

교과서

1 사역동사 have/make/let – 5형식 문장

- It **makes you feel** good when you are sad, angry, or stressed out.
  당신이 슬프거나, 화나거나, 스트레스로 녹초가 되었을 때, 그것은 당신이 기분 좋게 느끼도록 만들어 준다.

- Sad movies always **make me cry**. 슬픈 영화는 언제나 나를 울게 한다.

- 일반적으로 주어가 목적어에게 어떤 동작을 하도록 '시키는' 동사로 이루어진 5형식 문장에서, 목적보어는 to부정사 형태를 취한다. 대표적으로 advise, allow, cause, enable, encourage, expect, force, get, order, persuade, want 등은 5형식 동사들이다.
  - The teacher **told the kids to be** quiet. 선생님이 아이들에게 조용히 하라고 말했다.
  - Mr. Smith doesn't **allow people to smoke** in his home.
    Smith 씨는 자신의 집에서 사람들이 흡연하도록 허락하지 않는다.

- have, make, let 등이 5형식 문장을 이끌어 '시키다'의 의미로 쓰일 때, 이를 사역동사라고 부르고, 목적보어 자리에 to부정사가 아닌 동사원형(원형부정사)을 쓴다. 지각동사(see, hear, watch, listen to, feel, notice 등)도 목적보어 자리에 to부정사를 쓰지 않고 원형부정사 또는 현재분사를 쓴다.
  - They **made him wait** for a week. 그들은 그가 1주일을 기다리도록 했다.
  - Mom **had my brother clean** his room. 엄마는 형이 자기 방을 청소하도록 했다.
  - Sally **let her sister wear** the dress. Sally는 언니가 그 드레스를 입게 (허락)해 줬다.
  - I **saw Charlie dance[dancing]** in the street. 나는 Charlie가 거리에서 춤추는 것을 보았다.

- help의 목적보어는 to부정사 또는 원형부정사 둘 다 가능하다.
  - She **helped me (to) wash** the cats. 그녀는 내가 그 고양이들을 씻기는 것을 도왔다.

- 사역[지각]동사가 있는 5형식 문장을 수동태로 전환할 때에는 원형부정사를 to부정사로 바꾼다. have와 let은 수동태가 될 때, 유사한 의미의 다른 동사로 바꿔야 한다.
  - He **was made to wait** for a week (by them). 그는 (그들에 의해서) 1주일을 기다리게 되었다.
  - Charlie **was seen to dance** in the street (by me). Charlie는 거리에서 춤추는 것이 (나에 의해) 목격되었다.
  - Mom **had** Tom **clean** his room. → Tom **was asked to clean** his room by Mom.
  - Sally **let** her sister **wear** the dress. → Sally's sister **was allowed to wear** the dress by Sally.

핵심 Check

1. 다음 괄호 안에서 알맞은 말을 고르시오.
  (1) My brother let me (use / to use) his laptop.
  (2) Eating chocolate makes me (felt / feel) good.

2 '목적'을 나타내는 so that

- My father made me a bowl of chicken soup **so that** I **could** get well.
  아버지는 내가 회복할 수 있도록 치킨수프 한 그릇을 만들어 주셨다.

- He studies much harder than before **so that** he **can** make his dream come true. 그는 전보다 훨씬 더 열심히 공부해서 그의 꿈을 이루고자 한다.

■ so that은 '~하기 위해', '~하고자', '~하도록'의 의미로 '목적'이나 '의도'를 나타낸다. 일반적으로 '주절 +so that+주어+can/may/will(조동사)+동사원형 ~'의 구조로 쓰인다.

- The woman ate hot potato soup **so that** it **could** warm her body.
  그 여자는 몸을 따뜻하도록 하기 위해 뜨거운 감자 수프를 먹었다.

- John did his best **so that** his team **would** win. John은 그의 팀이 승리하도록 최선을 다했다.

■ so that은 다양한 표현들로 같은 의미를 나타낼 수 있다.

- The girl practiced hard **so that** she **could be** a singer. 그 소녀는 가수가 되기 위해 열심히 연습했다.
  = The girl practiced hard **in order that** she **could be** a singer.
  = The girl practiced hard **to be** a singer. 〈to부정사의 부사적 용법 – 목적〉
  = The girl practiced hard **so as to be** a singer.
  = The girl practiced hard **in order to be** a singer.

- Paul hurried **so that he wouldn't miss** the meeting. Paul은 회의를 놓치지 않기 위해 서둘렀다.
  = Paul hurried **in order that he wouldn't miss** the meeting.
  = Paul hurried **(in order) not to miss** the meeting.
  = Paul hurried **so as not to miss** the meeting.

■ so that이 '결과'의 의미를 갖는 접속사로 쓰이기도 한다. 보통 so that 앞에 쉼표가 온다.

- The girl practiced hard, **so that** she **became** a world famous singer.
  그 소녀는 열심히 연습을 했고, 결국 세계적으로 유명한 가수가 되었다.

■ so ~ that 사이에 형용사나 부사가 오는 경우, 의미가 완전히 달라져서, '너무 ~해서 결국 …하다'로 '원 인'과 '결과'를 나타내는 상관접속사가 된다.

- The man was **so sad that** he cried all day. 그 남자는 너무나 슬퍼 하루 종일 울었다.

- It was **so dark that** she could see nothing. 너무 어두워서 그녀는 아무것도 볼 수 없었다.

핵심 Check

2. 다음 괄호 안에서 알맞은 말을 고르시오.

(1) She went to Hawaii so (that / what) she could meet her friend.

(2) He runs every morning in (so / order) to lose some weight.

(3) Turn on the light (such that / so that) I can read the letter.

01 다음 빈칸에 들어갈 말로 알맞은 것은?

> Comic movies always make me _____.

① laugh   ② to laugh   ③ laughed
④ laughing   ⑤ to laughing

02 다음 각 문장의 빈칸에 공통으로 들어갈 말로 알맞은 것은?

> • Please turn the volume down _____ that the baby won't wake up.
> • Brian quit his job _____ as not to overwork himself.
> • Those problems were _____ easy that the boy could answer them.

① such   ② enough   ③ quite
④ so   ⑤ too

03 다음 중 밑줄 친 부분의 쓰임이 다른 하나를 고르시오.

① I eat the cassava chips so <u>that</u> I could remove my stress.
② Mina ran in order <u>that</u> she could meet her boyfriend earlier.
③ Please speak clearer so <u>that</u> everyone could understand you.
④ Betty was so nervous <u>that</u> she could hardly stand.
⑤ He jogs every morning in order <u>that</u> he will stay fit.

04 다음 우리말에 맞게 주어진 어휘를 바르게 배열하시오.

(1) 제 첫사랑 이야기를 말씀드리겠습니다.

   (you, tell, love, about, me, story, my, let, first)

   ➡ _____

(2) Mike의 아버지는 그에게 방을 청소하도록 시켰다.

   (clean, him, Mike's father, the room, made)

   ➡ _____

(3) 엄마가 누나에게 집에 오는 길에 두부를 사오도록 시켰다.

   (my sister, her way, my mom, buy, home, tofu, had, on)

   ➡ _____

1 다음 중 어법상 어색한 것은?

① My father let her eating the soup.
② The lady had the birds sing outside.
③ The heavy rain made me feel gloomy.
④ The burger made the old lady think of her homeland.
⑤ My mom had my brother fix her laptop.

[2~ 3] 다음 우리말을 어법상 알맞게 영작한 것을 고르시오.

2
> 위로 음식은 당신이 기분 좋게 느끼도록 만들어 주는 음식이다.

① Comfort food is that makes you feel good.
② Comfort food is food what makes you feel good.
③ Comfort food is food that makes you to feel good.
④ Comfort food is food that makes you feel good.
⑤ Comfort food is food that make you felt good.

3
> 나는 몸이 따뜻해지도록 그 뜨거운 수프를 먹었다.

① I ate the hot soup enough so what it could warm my body.
② I ate the hot soup so that I could warm it.
③ I ate the hot soup so to warm my body.
④ I ate the hot soup so that could warm my body.
⑤ I ate the hot soup so that it could warm my body.

4 다음 중 어법상 옳은 것은?

① Emma woke up early so that her not be late for the meeting.
② The crow was so happiness that it was able to fly up higher.
③ Lucas took a taxi in order that he could be there on time.
④ She has been saving money for 3 years so to buy her own house.
⑤ I took my umbrella in order for my mother could use it.

5 다음 중 밑줄 친 부분의 쓰임이 〈보기〉와 같은 것끼리 짝지어진 것은?

┌─ 보기 ├─
What food makes you think of happy time?
└────

ⓐ My mom makes my brother clean his room.
ⓑ My teacher told us not to make a noise in class.
ⓒ The man made us kites.
ⓓ The director always makes sad movies.
ⓔ I made my sister wear my new T-shirt.

① ⓐ, ⓑ   ② ⓐ, ⓔ   ③ ⓑ, ⓒ, ⓓ
④ ⓑ, ⓓ   ⑤ ⓐ, ⓒ, ⓔ

6 다음 문장의 빈칸 (A), (B), (C)에 들어갈 말로 가장 적절한 것은?

• Let him (A) home now. (go)
• What made you (B) sad? (look)
• Mike helped us (C) the street. (clean)

	(A)	(B)	(C)
①	go	looked	clean
②	go	look	to clean
③	go	to look	clean
④	going	look	to clean
⑤	going	look	cleaning

07 다음 두 문장의 의미가 같도록 바꿔 쓸 때 적절하지 <u>않은</u> 것은?

① John did his best so that his team could win.
 = John did his best in order that his team could win.

② Jackson exercised regularly in order to stay healthy.
 = Jackson exercised regularly so that he could stay healthy.

③ Jane walks fast so that she won't be late for church.
 = Jane walks fast not to be late for church.

④ I eat the chips so that I can feel good again.
 = I eat the chips to feel good again.

⑤ She left early to meet him first.
 = She left early, so she could meet him first.

08 다음 중 밑줄 친 부분의 쓰임이 〈보기〉와 같은 것을 <u>모두</u> 고르시오.

┌─── 보기 ───
Madeleines <u>make</u> me think of my grandma.
└───────────

① Let's see what comfort foods people <u>make</u>.
② What <u>made</u> you think so?
③ Director Bong <u>made</u> many great films.
④ Isabella <u>made</u> up her mind to join us.
⑤ What time will Robert <u>make</u> it?
⑥ The boss <u>made</u> them clean the toilets.
⑦ Eating spicy foods <u>makes</u> me feel bad.
⑧ The musical <u>made</u> by the company let all of us feel happy.
⑨ My father <u>made</u> me a bowl of chicken soup.
⑩ My grandma <u>made</u> me share her recipe.

09 다음 중 의미가 나머지 넷과 <u>다른</u> 하나는?

① I'm saving money to travel to Europe.
② I'm saving money in order to travel to Europe.
③ I'm saving money in order that I can travel to Europe.
④ I'm saving so much money that I can travel to Europe.
⑤ I'm saving money so as to travel to Europe.

10 다음 문장의 빈칸 (A), (B)에 들어갈 말로 가장 적절한 것은?

┌─────────────────────────┐
│ My computer broke down, and it made │
│ me feel ___(A)___ . My mom had my dad │
│ ___(B)___ my computer and my brother let │
│ me ___(C)___ his laptop. │
└─────────────────────────┘

	(A)	(B)	(C)
①	worried	fix	use
②	worry	fixes	used
③	worried	fix	using
④	worry	fixed	use
⑤	worrying	to fix	using

11 다음 문장의 밑줄 친 so that의 쓰임이 흐름상 어색한 것은?

① The Brazilian girl ate the hot potato soup <u>so that</u> it could warm her body.
② Mason's aunt made some cookies <u>so that</u> they can eat them together.
③ The tour guide walked faster <u>so that</u> every schedule can be completed.
④ Jacob failed the test <u>so that</u> he had studied harder than ever before.
⑤ Amelia spoke clearly <u>so that</u> all the audience could understand her.

[12~13] 다음 중 어법상 옳은 문장을 고르시오.

12
① His jokes always make me to laugh.
② I had my brother fixes the car.
③ Let him going home now.
④ The art teacher had us to paint the gate.
⑤ Mom had Mijin water the plants.

13 중요
① I went to bed early so as to get up early in the morning.
② John helped his sister in order to that she might finish her project in time.
③ I practiced yoga hard in order to be stay healthy.
④ Melt the butter so that in order to mix.
⑤ I study English so hard that to go to London.

[14~15] 주어진 우리말에 맞게 어법상 가장 적절한 문장을 고르시오.

14
마들렌 냄새는 그녀가 할머니에 대해 생각하도록 만들어 준다.

① The smell of madeleines make her think of her grandmother.
② The smell of madeleines make her to think of her grandmother.
③ The smell of madeleines makes her think of her grandmother.
④ The smell of madeleines makes her to think of her grandmother.
⑤ The smell of madeleines make her thinking of her grandmother.

15
여러분이 마들렌을 만들 수 있도록, 저의 요리법을 공유해 드릴게요.

① Let me to share my recipe that you can make madeleines.
② Let my share be your recipe so that we can make madeleines.
③ Let me share my recipe so as you can make madeleines.
④ Let me share my recipe so that you can make madeleines.
⑤ Let me sharing my recipe so that you can be make madeleines.

서답형
16 다음 괄호 안에 주어진 단어를 바르게 배열하여 빈칸을 완성하시오.

(1) Speak clearly _____
_____.(that, you, so, we, may, understand)
(2) He worked hard _____
_____.(he, in, a, make, living, order, that, might)
(3) Ryan covered his test _____
_____. (that, cheat, Daniel, not, so, could)
(4) Sumin studied _____
_____. (Harvard University, order, could, in, that, she, harder, enter)

01 다음 우리말과 일치하도록 괄호 안에 주어진 어구를 바르게 배열하여 문장을 완성하시오.

(1) 야구 경기를 보기 위해서 우리는 TV를 켰다.
→ We turned on TV _____
_____ a baseball game.
(that, watch, order, we, in, could)

(2) 무슨 음식이 당신에게 행복한 순간을 생각나게 만들어 줍니까?
→ _____ happy
moments? (you, food, makes, of, what, think)

(3) 그 여행 가이드는 모든 사람이 그를 따라오도록 천천히 걸었다.
→ The tour guide walked _____
_____. (everybody, so, follow, slowly, could, him, that)

(4) 카사바칩을 먹는 바삭한 소리는 내 기분을 더 좋게 만들었다.
→ The crisp sound of _____
_____. (made, better, cassava chips, eating, feel, me)

02 다음 〈보기〉와 같이 두 문장이 같은 의미가 되도록 주어진 단어를 활용하여 다시 쓰시오.

┌─ 보기 ─┐
Don't stop me from sharing my madeleine recipe. (let)
→ Let me share my madeleine recipe.
└────────┘

(1) Hanna often feels happy when she eats chocolate cookies. (make, often)

➡ _____

_____

(2) The doctor advised me to wear the mask. (have)

➡ _____

_____

(3) Whenever I see sad movies, I can't help crying. (make, always)

➡ _____

_____

(4) I asked Mom if I could play computer games and she allowed it. (let)

➡ _____

_____

03 다음 Sophie네 4 남매가 각자 일을 하고 있는 그림을 보고, 〈보기〉의 단어를 이용하여 문장을 완성하시오.

┌─ 보기 ─┐
water   clean   sweep   take out
└────────┘

(1) Mom made Sophie _____ her room.
(2) Mom got Tim _____ the garbage.
(3) Mom had Joy _____ the plants.
(4) Mom let Aron _____ the floor.

04 다음 문장에서 어법상 어색한 것을 바르게 고쳐 다시 쓰시오.

(1) Write down the addresses so as that you won't forget them.

➡ _____

_____

(2) Please wake me up so order that I won't be late for school.

➡ _____

_____

(3) I'm saving money so which I can travel to Europe.

⇒ _____

_____

(4) Comfort food can make you to think of happy moments from the past.

⇒ _____

_____

(5) My father made me a bowl of chicken soup in order to me get well.

⇒ _____

_____

(6) The scary dog made the delivery man ran away.

⇒ _____

_____

05 괄호 안에 주어진 어구를 활용하여, 다음 우리말을 영작하시오.

(1) 당신이 마들렌을 만들 수 있기 위해서는 밀가루와 설탕이 필요하다. (that, so, flour, can, madeleines, need, 11 단어)

⇒ _____

_____

(2) 내 컴퓨터가 고장 났고, 그것은 나를 걱정하도록 만들었다. (made, broke down, worried, which, feel, 9 단어)

⇒ _____

_____

(3) 버터를 녹이고, 그것이 식도록 하세요. (cool, the butter, let, melt, 7 단어)

⇒ _____

_____

(4) 나는 건강하도록 매일 운동합니다. (can, every day, exercise, healthy, be, so that, 10 단어)

⇒ _____

_____

06 다음 〈보기〉의 문장과 같은 뜻이 되도록 각 괄호 안에 주어진 조건에 맞게 빈칸을 채우시오.

┤ 보기 ├

Jane is walking fast so that she won't be late for school.

(1) Jane is walking fast _____ for school. (to부정사 부사적 용법 활용, 4 단어)

(2) Jane is walking fast _____ for school. (so as 활용, 6 단어)

(3) Jane is walking fast _____ she won't be late for school. (in 활용, 3 단어)

07 다음 각 문장에서 어법상 어색한 부분을 찾아 한 단어만 수정, 삭제 또는 추가하시오. (단, 문장의 본동사는 수정하지 말 것.)

(1) Mom made me to eat the chicken soup.

_____ ⇒ _____

(2) Have you seen the girl to eat the chips?

_____ ⇒ _____

(3) Sad dramas always make me cried.

_____ ⇒ _____

(4) She helped me wore my new dress.

_____ ⇒ _____

(5) Dad allowed me use his computer.

_____ ⇒ _____

(6) The teacher had us to clean the classroom.

_____ ⇒ _____

(7) She asked me help with the homework.

_____ ⇒ _____

(8) The government let him to leave the country.

_____ ⇒ _____

Reading

Letters from Our Readers: My Comfort Food

Comfort food is food that makes you feel good when you are sad,
주격 관계대명사. 앞의 food 수식   make(사역동사)+목적어+목적격보어(동사원형)

angry, or stressed out. It can also make you think of happy moments
Comfort food   make(사역동사)+목적어+목적격보어(동사원형)

from the past. It satisfies not only the stomach but also the heart.
not only A but (also) B = B as well as A: A뿐만 아니라 B도

Comfort foods differ around the world. Let's see what comfort foods
세계적으로   Let's see 뒤에 간접의문문(의문사+주어+동사)이 이어짐.

our international readers enjoy.

Jessica from USA

My comfort food is chicken soup. In the USA, people eat this soup

when they have a cold. When I was a small child, I caught a very
catch[have, get] a cold: 감기에 걸리다

bad cold. My father made me a bowl of chicken soup so that I could
make+간접목적어+직접목적어: ~에게 …을 만들어 주다   so that+

get well. The hot soup warmed my body, and I slowly started to feel
주어+can[may] ~: ~하도록(목적). get well = recover = restore one's health: 병이 나아지다   = started feeling

better. It was also very tasty. Now, when I catch a cold, I eat chicken
'A bowl of chicken soup' 또는 'The hot soup'

soup.

---

comfort 위로, 위안

stressed out 스트레스로 지친

satisfy 만족하게 하다

differ 다르다

not only ~ but also … ~뿐만 아니
라 …도

stomach 위, 복부, 배

international 국제적인

warm 따뜻하게 하다

tasty 맛있는

확인문제

● 다음 문장이 본문의 내용과 일치하면 T, 일치하지 않으면 F를 쓰시오.

1 Comfort food makes you feel good when you are sad, angry, or stressed out. ☐

2 Comfort food satisfies the heart, not the stomach. ☐

3 Comfort foods differ around the world. ☐

4 Jessica's father's comfort food is chicken soup. ☐

5 In the USA, people eat chicken soup when they catch a cold. ☐

6 Now, when Jessica's father catches a cold, he eats chicken soup. ☐

Maria from Brazil

In Brazil, there are many dishes that are made with cassava, a vegetable similar to a potato. I love cassava chips the most. Once when I had a bad day at school and felt stressed out, my best friend bought me a bag of cassava chips. When I started to eat the chips, my stress suddenly disappeared. The crisp sound of eating chips made me feel better. Now, every time I'm stressed out, I eat cassava chips. Then I feel good again!

Simon from France

I have many comfort foods, but I love madeleines the most. A madeleine is a small cake that looks like a sea shell. People in France enjoy madeleines as an afternoon snack. My grandmother always makes madeleines for me when I visit her. They taste best when they come right out of the oven. Then the kitchen is filled with a sweet smell. I especially like eating her orange madeleines with a cup of tea. Every time I see or smell madeleines, I think of my grandmother.

cassava 카사바
similar to ~과 비슷한
disappear 사라지다
crisp 바삭바삭한
every time ~할 때마다
madeleine 마들렌(작은 카스텔라의 일종)
out of ~ 밖으로, ~에서
be filled with ~로 가득 차다
smell 냄새
especially 특히

 확인문제

● 다음 문장이 본문의 내용과 일치하면 T, 일치하지 않으면 F를 쓰시오.

1 Cassava is a vegetable which is similar to a potato. ☐

2 Once when Maria had a bad day at school and felt stressed out, her mother bought her a bag of cassava chips. ☐

3 The crisp sound of eating cassava chips made Maria feel better. ☐

4 People in France enjoy madeleines as a morning snack. ☐

5 Madeleines taste best when they come right out of the oven. ☐

6 Whenever Simon makes or eats madeleines, he thinks of his grandmother. ☐

Let me share my grandmother's special recipe with you so that you
let(사역동사)+목적어+목적격보어(동사원형)   so that+

can make orange madeleines, too. Maybe madeleines will become a
주어+can[may] ~: ~하도록(목적)

comfort food for you!

recipe 요리법

flour 밀가루

peel 껍질

bowl 그릇

beat 때리다, 휘젓다

mixture 혼합물, 반죽

bake 굽다

Grandma's Special Recipe: Orange Madeleines

You need: 1 cup of flour, 2/3 cup of sugar, 2 eggs, some orange peel,

1/4 cup of butter, 1/8 teaspoon of salt

1. Melt the butter and let it cool.
명령문으로 동사 Melt와 let이 and로 연결   let(사역동사)+목적어+목적격보어(동사원형)

2. Put the eggs, sugar, and salt in a bowl and beat.
                    sugar와 salt: 물질명사로 단수 형태로 씀.

3. Add the flour to the bowl and mix.
   add A to B: B에 A를 더하다   동사 Add와 mix가 and로 연결됨.

4. Add the butter and orange peel to the mixture and mix.
            add A to B: B에 A를 더하다   동사 Add와 mix가 and로 연결됨.

5. Pour the mixture into the madeleine pan.
   pour A into B: A를 B에 붓다

6. Bake in the oven for 10 to 15 minutes.
                      10분에서 15분 동안

 확인문제

- 다음 문장이 본문의 내용과 일치하면 T, 일치하지 않으면 F를 쓰시오.

1 To make orange madeleines, you need 1 cup of flour, 2/3 cup of sugar, 2 eggs, some orange peel, 1/4 cup of butter, and 1/8 teaspoon of salt. ☐

2 To make orange madeleines, you need to melt the butter and let it hot first. ☐

3 After melting the butter, you need to put the eggs, sugar, and salt in a bowl and beat. ☐

4 You need to add the flour to the bowl and boil. ☐

5 Before you bake the madeleines in the oven, you need to pour the mixture into the madeleine pan. ☐

6 You need to bake the madeleines in the oven for 10 to 20 minutes. ☐

우리말을 참고하여 빈칸에 알맞은 말을 쓰시오.

1 Letters from Our Readers: My _____ _____

2 Comfort food is food that makes you _____ _____ when you are sad, angry, or _____ _____.

3 It can also make you _____ _____ happy moments _____ _____ _____.

4 It satisfies _____ _____ the stomach _____ _____ the heart.

5 Comfort foods _____ around the world.

6 Let's see _____ _____ _____ our international readers enjoy.

7 Jessica _____ USA

8 My comfort food is _____ _____.

9 In the USA, people eat this soup when they _____ _____ _____.

10 When I was a small child, I caught _____ _____ _____.

11 My father made me a bowl of chicken soup _____ _____ I _____ get well.

12 The hot soup _____ my body, and I slowly started to _____ _____.

13 It was also _____ _____.

14 Now, when I _____ _____ _____, I eat chicken soup.

1 우리의 독자들로부터 온 편지: 나에게 위안이 되는 음식

2 comfort food는 여러분이 슬프거나 화가 나거나 스트레스를 받을 때 기분을 좋게 해 주는 음식이다.

3 그것은 또한 여러분에게 과거의 행복한 순간들을 생각나게 할 수 있다.

4 그것은 위뿐만 아니라 마음도 충족해 준다.

5 comfort food는 전 세계적으로 다양하다.

6 세계 여러 나라의 우리 독자들은 어떤 comfort food를 즐기는지 알아보자.

7 미국에 사는 Jessica

8 나의 comfort food는 치킨 수프야.

9 미국에서는 사람들이 감기에 걸릴 때 이 수프를 먹어.

10 나는 어린아이였을 때 매우 심한 감기에 걸렸어.

11 아빠는 내가 나을 수 있도록 치킨 수프 한 그릇을 만들어 주셨어.

12 그 뜨거운 수프는 내 몸을 따뜻하게 했고, 나는 서서히 나아지기 시작했어.

13 그것은 매우 맛있기도 했어.

14 지금도 나는 감기에 걸리면 치킨 수프를 먹어.

15 Maria _____ Brazil

16 In Brazil, there are many dishes that _____ _____ _____ cassava, a vegetable _____ _____ a potato.

17 I love cassava chips _____ _____.

18 _____ when I _____ _____ _____ _____ at school and felt stressed out, my best friend bought me _____ _____ _____ cassava chips.

19 When I started to eat the chips, my stress _____ _____.

20 The _____ _____ of eating chips _____ _____ _____ better.

21 Now, _____ _____ I'm stressed out, I eat cassava chips.

22 Then I _____ _____ again!

23 Simon _____ France

24 I have many _____ _____, but I love madeleines the most.

25 A madeleine is a small cake that _____ _____ a sea shell.

26 People in France enjoy madeleines _____ _____ _____ _____.

27 My grandmother always _____ madeleines _____ me when I visit her.

28 They taste best when they come _____ _____ _____ the oven.

15 브라질에 사는 Maria

16 브라질에는 감자와 비슷한 채소 인 카사바로 만든 요리가 많아.

17 나는 카사바 칩을 좋아해.

18 한번은 내가 학교에서 안 좋은 일이 있고 스트레스를 받았을 때, 나의 가장 친한 친구가 나에 게 카사바 칩 한 봉지를 사 줬 어.

19 그 칩을 먹기 시작했을 때, 내 스트레스가 갑자기 사라졌어.

20 칩을 먹을 때 나는 바삭한 소리 가 내 기분을 더 좋게 만들었어.

21 지금도 나는 스트레스를 받을 때마다 카사바 칩을 먹어.

22 그러면 나는 기분이 다시 좋아 져!

23 프랑스에 사는 Simon

24 나는 comfort food가 많아, 하 지만 가장 좋아하는 것은 마들 렌이야.

25 마들렌은 조개처럼 생긴 작은 케이크야.

26 프랑스 사람들은 오후 간식으로 마들렌을 즐겨 먹어.

27 우리 할머니는 내가 찾아뵐 때 는 항상 마들렌을 만들어 주셔.

28 마들렌은 오븐에서 막 나올 때 가장 맛있어.

29 Then the kitchen _____ _____ _____ a sweet smell.

30 I _____ like eating her orange madeleines _____ a cup of tea.

31 _____ _____ I see or smell madeleines, I think of my grandmother.

32 _____ _____ _____ my grandmother's special recipe with you _____ _____ you _____ _____ orange madeleines, too.

33 Maybe madeleines will _____ _____ _____ _____ for you!

34 Grandma's _____ _____ : Orange Madeleines

35 You need: 1 cup of _____, 2/3 cup of sugar, 2 eggs, some orange peel, 1/4 cup of butter, 1/8 teaspoon of salt

36 1. _____ the butter and _____ it _____.

37 2. _____ the eggs, sugar, and salt in a bowl and _____.

38 3. _____ the flour _____ the bowl and mix.

39 4. Add the butter and _____ _____ to the _____ and mix.

40 5. _____ the mixture _____ the madeleine pan.

41 6. _____ in the oven for 10 _____ 15 minutes.

29 그러면 부엌은 달콤한 냄새로 가득 차.

30 나는 특히 차 한 잔과 함께 오렌지 마들렌을 먹는 것을 좋아해.

31 마들렌을 보거나 냄새 맡을 때마다 나는 할머니가 생각나.

32 너희들도 오렌지 마들렌을 만들 수 있도록 우리 할머니의 특별한 요리법을 공유할게.

33 아마도 마들렌이 너희에게도 comfort food가 될 거야!

34 할머니의 특별한 요리법: 오렌지 마들렌

35 재료: 밀가루 1컵, 설탕 2/3컵, 달걀 2개, 오렌지 껍질 조금, 버터 1/4컵, 소금 1/8티스푼

36 1. 버터를 녹여서 식힌다.

37 2. 달걀, 설탕, 소금을 그릇에 넣고 휘젓는다.

38 3. 그릇에 밀가루를 넣고 섞는다.

39 4. 반죽에 버터와 오렌지 껍질을 넣고 섞는다.

40 5. 반죽을 마들렌 팬에 붓는다.

41 6. 오븐에서 10분에서 15분 동안 굽는다.

● 우리말을 참고하여 본문을 영작하시오.

1 우리의 독자들로부터 온 편지: 나에게 위안이 되는 음식

➡ _____

2 comfort food는 여러분이 슬프거나 화가 나거나 스트레스를 받을 때 기분을 좋게 해 주는 음식이다.

➡ _____

3 그것은 또한 여러분에게 과거의 행복한 순간들을 생각나게 할 수 있다.

➡ _____

4 그것은 위뿐만 아니라 마음도 충족해 준다.

➡ _____

5 comfort food는 전 세계적으로 다양하다.

➡ _____

6 세계 여러 나라의 우리 독자들은 어떤 comfort food를 즐기는지 알아보자.

➡ _____

7 미국에 사는 Jessica

➡ _____

8 나의 comfort food는 치킨 수프야.

➡ _____

9 미국에서는 사람들이 감기에 걸릴 때 이 수프를 먹어.

➡ _____

10 나는 어린아이였을 때 매우 심한 감기에 걸렸어.

➡ _____

11 아빠는 내가 나을 수 있도록 치킨 수프 한 그릇을 만들어 주셨어.

➡ _____

12 그 뜨거운 수프는 내 몸을 따뜻하게 했고, 나는 서서히 나아지기 시작했어.

➡ _____

13 그것은 매우 맛있기도 했어.

➡ _____

14 지금도 나는 감기에 걸리면 치킨 수프를 먹어.

➡ _____

15 브라질에 사는 Maria

➡ _____

16 브라질에는 감자와 비슷한 채소인 카사바로 만든 요리가 많아.

➡ _____

17 나는 카사바 칩을 좋아해.

➡ _____

18 한번은 내가 학교에서 안 좋은 일이 있고 스트레스를 받았을 때, 나의 가장 친한 친구가 나에게

카사바 칩 한 봉지를 사 줬어.

➡ _____

_____

19 그 칩을 먹기 시작했을 때, 내 스트레스가 갑자기 사라졌어.

➡ _____

20 칩을 먹을 때 나는 바삭한 소리가 내 기분을 더 좋게 만들었어.

➡ _____

21 지금도 나는 스트레스를 받을 때마다 카사바 칩을 먹어.

➡ _____

22 그러면 나는 기분이 다시 좋아져!

➡ _____

23 프랑스에 사는 Simon

➡ _____

24 나는 comfort food가 많아, 하지만 가장 좋아하는 것은 마들렌이야.

➡ _____

25 마들렌은 조개처럼 생긴 작은 케이크야.

➡ _____

26 프랑스 사람들은 오후 간식으로 마들렌을 즐겨 먹어.

➡ _____

27 우리 할머니는 내가 찾아뵐 때는 항상 마들렌을 만들어 주셔.

➡ _____

28 마들렌은 오븐에서 막 나올 때 가장 맛있어.

➡ _____

29 그러면 부엌은 달콤한 냄새로 가득 차.

➡ _____

30 나는 특히 차 한 잔과 함께 오렌지 마들렌을 먹는 것을 좋아해.

➡ _____

31 마들렌을 보거나 냄새 맡을 때마다 나는 할머니가 생각나.

➡ _____

32 너희들도 오렌지 마들렌을 만들 수 있도록 우리 할머니의 특별한 요리법을 공유할게.

➡ _____

33 아마도 마들렌이 너희에게도 comfort food가 될 거야!

➡ _____

34 할머니의 특별한 요리법: 오렌지 마들렌

➡ _____

35 재료: 밀가루 1컵, 설탕 2/3컵, 달걀 2개, 오렌지 껍질 조금, 버터 1/4컵, 소금 1/8티스푼

➡ _____

36 1. 버터를 녹여서 식힌다.

➡ _____

37 2. 달걀, 설탕, 소금을 그릇에 넣고 휘젓는다.

➡ _____

38 3. 그릇에 밀가루를 넣고 섞는다.

➡ _____

39 4. 반죽에 버터와 오렌지 껍질을 넣고 섞는다.

➡ _____

40 5. 반죽을 마들렌 팬에 붓는다.

➡ _____

41 6. 오븐에서 10분에서 15분 동안 굽는다.

➡ _____

[01~03] 다음 글을 읽고 물음에 답하시오.

Comfort food is food that makes you feel good when you are sad, angry, or stressed out. It can also ___ⓐ___ you think of happy moments from the past. It satisfies not only the stomach but also the heart. Comfort foods differ around the world. Let's see what comfort foods our international readers enjoy.

 01 위 글의 빈칸 ⓐ에 들어갈 수 없는 단어를 모두 고르시오.

① allow
② make
③ let
④ help
⑤ get

 02 위 글의 뒤에 올 내용으로 가장 알맞은 것을 고르시오.

① the definition of comfort food
② how to reduce the excessive stress
③ comfort foods that international readers enjoy
④ how to choose healthy food
⑤ popular local foods of the world

03 According to the passage, which is NOT true?

① By eating comfort food, you can feel good.
② Comfort food can be a way to ease your sadness.
③ Comfort food satisfies your stomach.
④ Comfort food satisfies your heart, too.
⑤ Comfort foods of the world are similar to each other.

[04~06] 다음 글을 읽고 물음에 답하시오.

Maria from Brazil

In Brazil, there are many ⓐdishes that are made with cassava, a vegetable similar to a potato. (①) I love cassava chips the most. (②) Once when I had a bad day at school and felt stressed out, my best friend bought me a bag of cassava chips. (③) The crisp sound of eating chips made me feel better. (④) Now, every time I'm stressed out, I eat cassava chips. (⑤) Then I feel good again!

04 위 글의 흐름으로 보아, 주어진 문장이 들어가기에 가장 적절한 곳은?

When I started to eat the chips, my stress suddenly disappeared.

①   ②   ③   ④   ⑤

05 위 글의 밑줄 친 ⓐdishes와 같은 의미로 쓰인 것을 고르시오.

① I'll do the dishes.
② She is looking for serving dishes.
③ My mom always dishes the dinner up.
④ He likes to eat Chinese dishes.
⑤ Tom dishes out leaflets to passers-by.

서답형

06 다음 빈칸에 알맞은 단어를 넣어 Maria가 카사바 칩을 좋아하게 된 계기를 완성하시오. (3 단어)

Maria got to like cassava chips when her stress suddenly disappeared while she was eating a bag of cassava chips that _____ _____ _____ bought her.

[07~09] 다음 글을 읽고 물음에 답하시오.

Grandma's Special ____(A)____ : Orange Madeleines

You need: 1 cup of flour, 2/3 cup of sugar, 2 eggs, some orange peel, 1/4 cup of butter, 1/8 teaspoon of salt

1. ____ⓐ____ the butter and let it cool.

2. ____ⓑ____ the eggs, sugar, and salt in a bowl and beat.

3. ____ⓒ____ the flour to the bowl and mix.

4. Add the butter and orange peel to (A)the mixture and mix.

5. ____ⓓ____ the mixture into the madeleine pan.

6. ____ⓔ____ in the oven for 10 to 15 minutes.

서답형

07 주어진 영영풀이를 참고하여 빈칸 (A)에 철자 R로 시작하는 단어를 쓰시오.

> a list of ingredients and a set of instructions that tell you how to cook something

➡ _____

08 위 글의 빈칸 ⓐ~ⓔ에 들어갈 수 없는 단어를 고르시오.

① Put ② Add ③ Pour
④ Melt ⑤ Fry

중요

09 Choose the ingredient that is not needed to make orange madeleines.

① butter ② orange ③ sugar
④ flour ⑤ salt

[10~12] 다음 글을 읽고 물음에 답하시오.

Jessica from USA

My comfort food is chicken soup. In the USA, people eat this soup when they have a cold. When I was a small child, I caught a very bad cold. My father made me a bowl of chicken soup so that I could ⓐget well. The hot soup warmed my body, and I slowly started to feel better. It was also very tasty. Now, when I catch a cold, I eat chicken soup.

10 위 글의 밑줄 친 ⓐget well과 바꿔 쓸 수 있는 말을 모두 고르시오.

① grow up ② recover
③ get on ④ get worse
⑤ restore my health

서답형

11 다음 문장에서 위 글의 내용과 다른 부분을 찾아서 고치시오.

> The chicken soup that Jessica's father made for her when she caught a very bad cold was not tasty, but she slowly started to feel better.

➡ _____

중요

12 Which question CANNOT be answered after reading the passage?

① What is Jessica's comfort food?
② In the USA, what do people eat when they have a cold?
③ Who made Jessica a bowl of chicken soup when she had a bad cold?
④ What did Jessica's mother make for her when she had a bad cold?
⑤ At present, what does Jessica eat when she catches a cold?

[13~15] 다음 글을 읽고 물음에 답하시오.

Simon from France

I have many comfort foods, but I love madeleines the most. A madeleine is a small cake ___ⓐ___ looks like a sea shell. People in France enjoy madeleines as an afternoon snack. My grandmother always makes madeleines for me when I visit her. ⓑThey taste best when they come right out of the oven. Then the kitchen is filled with a sweet smell. I especially like eating her orange madeleines with a cup of tea. Every time I see or smell madeleines, I think of my grandmother.

Let me share my grandmother's special recipe with you ⓒso that you can make orange madeleines, too. Maybe madeleines will become a comfort food for you!

13 위 글의 빈칸 ⓐ에 들어갈 알맞은 말을 고르시오. (2개)

① what　　　　② that
③ where　　　④ who
⑤ which

서답형

14 위 글의 밑줄 친 ⓑThey가 가리키는 것을 본문에서 찾아 쓰시오.

➡ _____

15 위 글의 밑줄 친 ⓒ와 바꿔 쓸 수 있는 말로 옳지 않은 것을 고르시오.

① in order that you can make orange madeleines
② so that you may make orange madeleines
③ in order for you to make orange madeleines
④ in order that you may make orange madeleines
⑤ for me to make orange madeleines

[16~19] 다음 글을 읽고 물음에 답하시오.

Grandma's Special Recipe: Orange Madeleines

ⓐ**You need:** 1 cup of flour, 2/3 cup of sugar, 2 eggs, some orange peel, 1/4 cup of butter, 1/8 teaspoon of salt

1. Melt the butter and let it cool.
(a) Add the flour to the bowl and mix.
(b) Pour the mixture into the madeleine pan.
(c) Put the eggs, sugar, and salt in a bowl and beat.
(d) Add the butter and orange peel to the mixture and mix.
6. Bake in the oven ⓑ10분에서 15분 동안.

서답형

16 마들렌 조리법의 순서에 맞도록 위 글의 (a)~(d)를 알맞게 배열하시오.

➡ _____

서답형

17 위 글의 밑줄 친 ⓐYou need를 한 단어로 바꿔 쓰시오.

➡ _____

서답형

18 위 글의 밑줄 친 ⓑ의 우리말에 맞게 5 단어로 영작하시오.

➡ _____

19 Which question CANNOT be answered after reading the passage?

① What are the ingredients that are needed to make orange madeleines?
② What do you need to do first to make orange madeleines?
③ After adding the flour to the bowl and mixing, what do you need to do?
④ How long do you need to bake the mixture in the oven?
⑤ To what temperature do you need to heat the oven?

[20~22] 다음 글을 읽고 물음에 답하시오.

Maria from Brazil

In Brazil, there are many dishes that are made ____ⓐ____ cassava, a vegetable similar ____ⓑ____ a potato. I love cassava chips the most. Once when I had a bad day at school and felt stressed out, my best friend bought me a bag of cassava chips. ⓒWhen I started to eat the chips, my stress was suddenly disappeared. ⓓ칩을 먹을 때 나는 바삭한 소리가 내 기분을 더 좋게 만들었어. Now, every time I'm stressed out, I eat cassava chips. Then I feel good again!

20 위 글의 빈칸 ⓐ와 ⓑ에 들어갈 전치사가 바르게 짝지어진 것은?

	ⓐ	ⓑ		ⓐ	ⓑ
①	with	– at	②	by	– in
③	of	– at	④	with	– to
⑤	by	– to			

서답형

21 위 글의 밑줄 친 ⓒ에서 어법상 틀린 부분을 찾아 고치시오.

_____ ➡ _____

서답형

22 위 글의 밑줄 친 ⓓ의 우리말에 맞게 주어진 어휘를 이용하여 10 단어로 영작하시오.

> crisp, of, made

➡ _____

_____

[23~25] 다음 글을 읽고 물음에 답하시오.

Jessica from USA

My comfort food is chicken soup. In the USA, people eat this soup when they ____ⓐ____ a cold. When I was a small child, I caught a very bad cold. My father made me a bowl of chicken soup (A)내가 나을 수 있도록. The hot soup warmed my body, and I slowly started to feel better. It was also very tasty. Now, when I ____ⓑ____ a cold, I eat chicken soup.

중요

23 위 글의 빈칸 ⓐ와 ⓑ에 공통으로 들어갈 수 있는 단어를 모두 고르시오.

① get ② bring
③ catch ④ have
⑤ keep

서답형

24 위 글의 밑줄 친 (A)의 우리말에 맞게 6 단어로 영작하시오.

➡ _____ 또는

_____

서답형

25 What did Jessica's father make for Jessica when she caught a very bad cold? Answer in English in a full sentence. (8 words)

➡ _____

[26~28] 다음 글을 읽고 물음에 답하시오.

Comfort food is food ⓐthat makes you feel good when you are sad, angry, or (A)[stressing / stressed] out. It can also make you (B)[think / thinking] of happy moments from the past. It satisfies not only the stomach but also the heart. Comfort foods differ (C)[around / from] the world. Let's see what comfort foods our international readers enjoy.

26 위 글의 괄호 (A)~(C)에서 문맥이나 어법상 알맞은 낱말을 골라 쓰시오.

➡ (A) _____ (B) _____ (C) _____

27 위 글의 밑줄 친 ⓐthat과 문법적 쓰임이 같은 것을 모두 고르시오.

① I know the very person that will do the job quickly.
② The climate of this country is like that of Italy.
③ The woman isn't that rich.
④ These are the books that I bought yesterday.
⑤ What's that over there?

28 본문의 내용과 일치하도록 다음 빈칸 (A)와 (B)에 알맞은 단어를 쓰시오.

> Comfort foods satisfy not only your hunger but your (A)_____ as well, and they (B)_____ around the world.

[29~31] 다음 글을 읽고 물음에 답하시오.

Simon from France

I have many comfort foods, but I love madeleines the most. A madeleine is a small cake that looks like a sea shell. People in France enjoy madeleines as an afternoon snack. ⓐMy grandmother always makes madeleines for me when I visit her. They taste best when they come right out of the oven. Then the kitchen is filled with a sweet smell. I especially like eating her orange madeleines with a cup of tea. Every time I see or smell madeleines, I think of my grandmother.

Let me share my grandmother's special recipe with you so that you can make orange madeleines, too. Maybe madeleines will become a comfort food for you!

29 위 글의 제목으로 알맞은 것을 고르시오.

① There Are Many Comfort Foods
② What Is a Madeleine?
③ When Does Madeleine Taste Best?
④ What Is Simon's Comfort Food?
⑤ Grandma's Special Recipe for Orange Madeleines

30 위 글의 밑줄 친 ⓐ를 4형식 문장으로 고치시오.

➡ _____

31 Which question CANNOT be answered after reading the passage?

① What comfort food does Simon love the most?
② What does a madeleine look like?
③ When do people in France enjoy madeleines?
④ With what does Simon especially like eating his grandma's orange madeleines?
⑤ What is Simon's grandmother's special recipe for madeleines?

[01~03] 다음 글을 읽고 물음에 답하시오.

Simon from France

I have many comfort foods, but I love madeleines the most. A madeleine is a small cake that looks like a sea shell. People in France enjoy madeleines as an afternoon snack. My grandmother always makes madeleines for me when I visit her. They taste best when they come right out of the oven. Then the kitchen is filled with a sweet smell. I especially like eating her orange madeleines with a cup of tea. ⓐ<u>마들렌을 보거나 냄새 맡을 때마다 나는 할머니가 생각나.</u>

01 When Simon visits his grandmother, what does she always make for him? Answer in English in a full sentence. (6 words)

➡ _____

 위 글의 밑줄 친 ⓐ의 우리말에 맞게 주어진 어휘를 알맞게 배열하시오.

my grandmother / madeleines / I / think / I / of / every time / see or smell / ,

➡ _____

_____

03 본문의 내용과 일치하도록 다음 빈칸 (A)와 (B)에 알맞은 단어를 쓰시오.

A madeleine is a small cake with an appearance that is very similar to (A)_____ _____ _____, and the French enjoy it as (B)_____ _____ _____.

04 다음 빈칸 (A)와 (B)에 알맞은 단어를 넣어, 그림 (1)과 (2)에 대한 설명을 완성하시오.

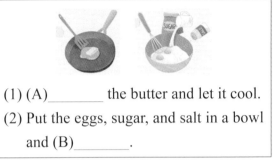

(1) (A)_____ the butter and let it cool.
(2) Put the eggs, sugar, and salt in a bowl and (B)_____.

[05~07] 다음 글을 읽고 물음에 답하시오.

Comfort food is food that makes you feel good when you are sad, angry, or stressed out. It can also make you think of happy moments from the past. (A)<u>It satisfies not only the stomach but also the heart.</u> Comfort foods differ around the world. Let's see
_____ ⓐ _____.

05 위 글의 빈칸 ⓐ에 다음 문장을 알맞은 형태로 쓰시오.

What comfort foods do our international readers enjoy?

➡ _____

06 위 글의 밑줄 친 (A)를 as well as를 사용하여 고치시오.

➡ _____

07 본문의 내용과 일치하도록 다음 빈칸 (A)와 (B)에 들어갈 알맞은 단어를 본문에서 찾아 쓰시오.

Comfort food can satisfy (A)_____ _____ because it makes you not only feel good when you are sad, angry, or stressed out but also think of (B)_____ _____ from the past.

[08~10] 다음 글을 읽고 물음에 답하시오.

Jessica from USA

My comfort food is chicken soup. In the USA, people eat this soup when they have a cold. When I was a small child, I caught a very bad cold. ⓐMy father made me a bowl of chicken soup so that I could get well. The hot soup warmed my body, and I slowly started to feel better. ⓑIt was also very tasty. Now, when I catch a cold, I eat chicken soup.

08 위 글의 밑줄 친 ⓐ를 다음과 같이 바꿔 쓸 때 빈칸에 들어갈 알맞은 말을 다섯 단어로 쓰시오.

➡ My father made me a bowl of chicken soup _____.

09 위 글의 밑줄 친 ⓑIt이 가리키는 것을 본문에서 찾아 쓰시오.

➡ _____

10 다음 빈칸 (A)와 (B)에 본문에 있는 알맞은 단어를 넣어 Jessica의 comfort food에 대한 소개를 완성하시오.

(A)_____ _____ is Jessica's comfort food. When she catches a cold, she eats chicken soup because the hot soup warms her body, and she slowly starts to (B)_____ _____.

[11~13] 다음 글을 읽고 물음에 답하시오.

Maria from Brazil

In Brazil, there are many dishes that are made with cassava, a vegetable similar to a potato. I love cassava chips the most. Once when I had a bad day at school and felt stressed out, my best friend bought me a bag of cassava chips. When I started to eat the chips, my stress suddenly disappeared. The crisp sound of eating chips made me feel better. Now, every time I'm stressed out, I eat cassava chips. Then I feel good again!

11 다음 문장에서 위 글의 내용과 다른 부분을 찾아서 고치시오.

Once when Maria had a bad day at school and felt stressed out, she bought a bag of cassava chips.

_____ ➡ _____

12 다음 빈칸 (A)와 (B)에 알맞은 단어를 넣어 cassava에 대한 소개를 완성하시오.

Cassava is a vegetable which is similar to (A)_____ _____ and there are many (B)_____ that are made with cassava in Brazil.

13 How could Maria get rid of her stress when she had a bad day at school and felt stressed out? Fill in the blanks (A) and (B) with suitable words.

She could do so by eating a bag of cassava chips that her best friend (A)_____ her. When she started eating the chips, her stress suddenly disappeared and the crisp sound of eating chips enabled her to feel (B)_____.

구석구석

Listen and Talk D

I like Italian food, so I'd like to go to Taste of Italy. At the restaurant, I'd like
= I want to   장소 앞에 붙이는 전치사
to order a potato pizza. For a drink, I'd like to order an orange Juice.
[관련] ~에 관해서는   (물질명사에 붙여서) ~로 만든 것(하나): 1개의

구문해설 • order: 주문하다

After You Read A

Q: What is your comfort food?

Jessica, USA

When I caught a very bad cold, my father made me a bowl of chicken soup.
make+간접목적어+직접목적어: ~에게 …을 만들어 주다
The hot soup warmed my body, and I slowly started to feel better.

Maria, Brazil

When I felt stressed out, my best friend bought me a bag of cassava chips.
buy+간접목적어+직접목적어: ~에게 …을 사 주다
When I ate the chips, my stress disappeared. The crisp sound of eating chips
전치사 of의 목적어로 동명사
made me feel better.
made(사역동사)+목적어+목적격보어(동사원형)

Simon, France

My grandmother makes madeleines for me when I visit her. I especially like
= makes me madeleines
eating her orange madeleines with tea. Every time I see or smell madeleines, I
eating은 동명사로 like의 목적어   = Whenever
think of her.

구문해설 • comfort: 위로, 위안 • stressed out: 스트레스로 지친 • cassava: 카사바
• disappear: 사라지다 • crisp: 바삭바삭한 • madeleine: 마들렌(작은 카스텔라의 일종)

Think and Write Step 2

My Comfort Food

My comfort food is chocolate. I usually eat it when I feel bad. Recently, I
빈도부사(일반동사 앞, be동사 뒤)   2형식V+형용사 보어(badly(×))
didn't do well on a test and got stressed out. I went to the store and bought
good(×)   과거분사 형태에 유의
some chocolate. After eating the sweet chocolate, I felt better. Eating chocolate
some+불가산명사   전치사+동명사   2형식 V+형용사 동명사(주어)
makes me feel good.
make+목적어+원형부정사

구문해설 • comfort food: 위로 음식 • recently: 최근에 • get stressed out: 스트레스를 받다

해석

나는 이탈리아 음식을 좋아해서 Taste of Italy에 가고 싶어. 그 식당에서 나는 감자 피자를 주문하고 싶어. 음료로 오렌지 주스를 주문하고 싶어.

Q: 너의 comfort food는 무엇이니?

Jessica, 미국

내가 매우 심한 감기에 걸렸을 때, 아빠는 내게 치킨 수프 한 그릇을 만들어 주셨어. 그 뜨거운 수프는 내 몸을 따뜻하게 했고, 나는 서서히 나아지기 시작했어.

Maria, 브라질

내가 스트레스를 받았을 때, 나의 가장 친한 친구가 카사바 칩 한 봉지를 내게 사 줬어. 칩을 먹자 내 스트레스가 사라졌어. 칩을 먹을 때 나는 바삭하는 소리가 내 기분을 더 좋게 만들었어.

Simon, 프랑스

우리 할머니는 내가 찾아뵐 때 마들렌을 만들어 주셔. 나는 특히 차와 함께 할머니의 오렌지 마들렌을 먹는 것을 좋아해. 마들렌을 보거나 냄새를 맡을 때마다 할머니를 떠올려.

나의 comfort food

나의 comfort food는 초콜릿이다. 나는 보통 그것을 기분이 좋지 않을 때 먹는다. 최근에 나는 시험을 잘 보지 못해서 스트레스를 받았다. 나는 가게에 가서 초콜릿을 샀다. 달콤한 초콜릿을 먹고 난 후, 나는 기분이 좋아졌다. 초콜릿을 먹는 것은 나를 기분 좋게 한다.

Words & Expressions

1 〈보기〉의 밑줄 친 어휘와 같은 의미로 쓰인 것을 고르시오.

> **보기**
>
> Put the eggs, sugar, and salt in a bowl and beat.

① I will beat around the bush no longer.
② Beat the eggs and add to the rest of the ingredients.
③ Hailstones beat against the window.
④ His heart missed a beat when he saw her.
⑤ It seems that Japan will never beat Korea.

2 다음 빈칸에 알맞은 말을 쓰시오.

> His job is not only interesting but very well-paid _____ _____.

3 다음 영영풀이에 해당하는 단어를 주어진 철자로 시작하여 빈칸에 쓰고, 알맞은 것을 골라 문장을 완성하시오.

> • d_____ : to become impossible to see or find
> • m_____ : to become liquid

(1) Few are suggesting that the PC is going to _____.
(2) The ice began to _____ down since the beginning of summer.

4 괄호 안에 주어진 어휘를 이용하여 빈칸에 알맞게 쓰시오.

> • The cake is always sweet and _____.
>   (taste)
> • I must have eaten something too _____ for lunch. (salt)

5 다음 대화의 빈칸 (A)~(C)에 알맞은 말을 쓰시오.

> A: Thank you for your help, but you look stressed out. What's wrong?
> B: My family has nothing to eat.
> A: This is for you. It's filled (A)_____ food.
> B: Thanks. Wow! It has (B)_____ only food (C)_____ also gold.

Conversation

6 다음 중 짝지어진 대화가 어색한 것은?

① A: Welcome to Dessert World. May I take your order?
  B: Yes, please. I'd like to order two doughnuts.
② A: Is it for here or to go?
  B: For here, please.
③ A: Are you ready to order?
  B: Yes. I'd like a chicken salad.
④ A: Would you like anything else?
  B: No, you're welcome.
⑤ A: Will that be all?
  B: Yes.

[07~08] 다음 대화를 읽고 물음에 답하시오.

W: Hello. What would you like to order?
(A) 그것이 다인가요? (will, all, that)
(B) Would you like anything to drink?
(C) Yes. One milk, please.
(D) I'd like to order a sandwich.
B: Yes. Thank you.

07 주어진 문장 사이에 들어갈 대화의 순서로 알맞은 것은?

① (B) – (A) – (C) – (D)
② (B) – (C) – (A) – (D)
③ (C) – (B) – (D) – (A)
④ (C) – (D) – (B) – (A)
⑤ (D) – (B) – (C) – (A)

08 위 대화의 밑줄 친 우리말에 맞게 주어진 단어를 이용하여 영어로 쓰시오.

➡ _____

[09~10] 다음 대화를 읽고 물음에 답하시오.

W: Hello. What would you like (A)[to order / ordering]?
B: I want Gimchi Gimbap, please.
W: Would you like anything else?
B: No, thank you.
W: Is it for here or (B)[go / to go]?
B: _____(a)_____, please.

09 위 대화의 빈칸 (a)에 다음 문장과 같은 의미의 말을 쓰시오.

┌─────────────────────────────┐
│ I will take it out   │
└─────────────────────────────┘

➡ _____

10 위 대화의 괄호 (A)~(B)에서 적절한 것을 골라 쓰시오.

➡ (A) _____ (B) _____

[11~12] 다음 대화를 읽고 물음에 답하시오.

A: Welcome to Dessert World. May I take your order?
B: Yes, please. (①)
A: (②) Would you like anything to drink?
B: (③) Yes, one orange juice, please.
A: (④) Is it for here or to go?
B: (⑤) For here, please.

11 ①~⑤ 중 주어진 문장이 들어갈 곳은?

┌─────────────────────────────┐
│ I'd like to order two doughnuts. │
└─────────────────────────────┘

①   ②   ③   ④   ⑤

12 What did B order? Answer in English with a full sentence.

➡ _____

Grammar

[13~14] 다음 대화를 참고하여 아래 문장을 완성하시오.

13
┌─────────────────────────────────────┐
│ William: Henry, can John and I join your │
│   reading club?   │
│ Henry: Of course, you can!   │
└─────────────────────────────────────┘

➡ Henry let John and _____

_____.

14

> Teacher: Liz, why did you mess up with the math quiz for the final exam? Have you forgotten to review the math textbook?
>
> Elizabeth: Sorry for that. I'll do sometime soon by this weekend.
>
> Teacher: I'd like you to do it now.

➡ Elizabeth's teacher had her _____ _____.

15 다음 괄호 안에서 어법상 알맞은 것을 고르시오.

(1) Samantha won't make her kids (dance / to dance) at the street stage.

(2) David's father wanted him (go / to go) fishing with him.

(3) No one expected the ballerina (perform / to perform) at such a high level.

(4) The king didn't let Elsa (come / to come) out of the castle.

(5) Anna asked Elsa (open / to open) the door to play together.

(6) Kristoph heard her (singing / to sing) in the snow storm.

(7) Elsa doesn't let Olaf (melt / melting) away at the sunlight.

16 다음 중 어법상 어색한 문장을 고르시오.

① You need rice and water so that you can make *Juk*, the Korean porridge.

② I study English so as to travel abroad.

③ Samuel practiced hard so that for him to win the game.

④ Dylan got up early so as not to miss the train.

⑤ Let me share my secret so that you can succeed like me.

17 다음 중 어법상 올바른 문장을 고르시오. (정답 2개)

① Maria helped her mother make the cassava chips.

② Simon's boss let him working overnight.

③ My father don't let me go out with my boyfriend.

④ My mom had my brother to bring the madeleines to the guests.

⑤ Action movies always make me feel excited and thrilled.

[18~19] 다음 괄호 안의 단어를 배열하여 빈칸을 알맞게 채우시오.

18 Jim put on his headphones _____ _____ by his parents.

(scolded, he, avoid, being, that, could, so)

19 We learn Chinese letters _____ _____.

(we, language, that, understand, can, so, better, our)

20 다음 두 문장의 의미가 같도록 바꿔 쓸 때 적절하지 않은 것은?

① Grace eats the chips so that she can feel good again.
= Grace eats the chips so as to feel good again.

② Leo could make orange madeleines since he practiced hard.
= Leo practiced so hard that he could make orange madeleines.

③ Jane's father made a bowl of chicken soup so that she could get well.
= Jane's father made a bowl of chicken soup so as to get well.

④ Dad makes pizza in order for me to eat.
= Dad makes pizza so that I can eat it.

⑤ Adam studied really hard in order to pass the exam.
= Adam studied really hard so that he could pass the exam.

Reading

[21~22] 다음 글을 읽고 물음에 답하시오.

Comfort food is food that makes you feel good when you are sad, angry, or stressed out. It can also make you think of happy moments from the past. ⓐIt satisfies not only the stomach but also the heart. Comfort foods differ around the world. Let's see what comfort foods our international readers enjoy.

21 위 글의 밑줄 친 ⓐIt이 가리키는 것을 본문에서 찾아 쓰시오.

➡ _____

22 위 글의 주제로 알맞은 것을 고르시오.

① What makes you feel sad or angry?
② What do you do when you are stressed out?
③ Comfort food is good for your health.
④ Comfort food feeds the heart.
⑤ Comfort foods differ around the world.

[23~25] 다음 글을 읽고 물음에 답하시오.

Maria from Brazil

In Brazil, there are many dishes that are made with cassava, a vegetable similar to a potato. I love cassava chips the most. Once when I had a bad day at school and felt stressed out, my best friend bought me a bag of cassava chips. When I started to eat the chips, my stress suddenly disappeared. The crisp sound of ⓐeating chips made me feel better. Now, ⓑevery time I'm stressed out, I eat cassava chips. Then I feel good again!

23 아래 〈보기〉에서 위 글의 밑줄 친 ⓐeating과 문법적 쓰임이 같은 것의 개수를 고르시오.

─┤ 보기 ├─

① It is important to brush your teeth after eating chips.
② My bad habit is eating chips late at night.
③ I don't mind eating chips before dinner.
④ Eating chips is not always good.
⑤ When I met him, he was eating chips.

① 1개 ② 2개 ③ 3개 ④ 4개 ⑤ 5개

24 위 글의 밑줄 친 ⓑ를 다음과 같이 바꿔 쓸 때 빈칸에 들어갈 알맞은 단어를 쓰시오.

➡ _____ I'm stressed out, I eat cassava chips

= _____ _____ I'm stressed out, I eat cassava chips

= _____ I'm stressed out, I _____ eat cassava chips

25 According to the passage, which is NOT true?

① There are many dishes made with cassava in Brazil.

② Cassava is a vegetable similar to a potato.

③ Maria's favorite snack is cassava chips.

④ Maria once got rid of her stress by eating a bag of cassava chips.

⑤ The crisp sound of eating cassava chips made Maria feel nervous.

[26~28] 다음 글을 읽고 물음에 답하시오.

Simon from France

I have many comfort foods, but I love madeleines the most. A madeleine is a small cake that looks like a sea shell. (①) People in France enjoy madeleines ___ⓐ___ an afternoon snack. (②) My grandmother always makes madeleines for me when I visit her. (③) Then the kitchen is filled with a sweet smell. (④) I especially like eating her orange madeleines with a cup of tea. (⑤) Every time I see or smell madeleines, I think of my grandmother.

26 위 글의 빈칸 ⓐ에 들어갈 알맞은 말을 고르시오.

① to   ② on   ③ in
④ at   ⑤ as

27 위 글의 흐름으로 보아, 주어진 문장이 들어가기에 가장 적절한 곳은?

They taste best when they come right out of the oven.

①   ②   ③   ④   ⑤

28 다음 문장에서 위 글의 내용과 다른 부분을 찾아서 고치시오.

A madeleine is a side dish that people in France enjoy.

_____ ➡ _____

[29~30] 다음 글을 읽고 물음에 답하시오.

My Comfort Food

My comfort food is chocolate. I usually eat it when I feel bad. Recently, I didn't do well on a test and got stressed out. I went to the store and bought some chocolate. After eating the sweet chocolate, I felt better. Eating chocolate makes me feel good.

29 위 글의 종류로 알맞은 것을 고르시오.

① article   ② essay
③ book report   ④ review
⑤ summary

30 위 글을 읽고 대답할 수 없는 질문을 고르시오.

① What is the writer's comfort food?

② When does the writer usually eat the comfort food?

③ Recently, why did the writer get stressed out?

④ When the writer got stressed out, what did the writer do?

⑤ How often does the writer buy the comfort food?

출제율 95%

01 다음 밑줄 친 부분의 의미로 알맞지 <u>않은</u> 것을 고르시오.

① His speech moved the <u>audience</u> to tears.
(청중, 관중)

② Can you state it a bit more <u>clearly</u> for me, please? (분명하게)

③ You can start <u>taking orders</u> now. (주문하다)

④ Customs <u>differ</u> from country to country.
(다르다)

⑤ Can you clear a space <u>so that</u> this boy can sit down, please? (~하기 위하여)

출제율 90%

02 다음 빈칸에 공통으로 들어갈 알맞은 말을 쓰시오.

> • She is not only tough _____ also very sweet.
> • He is not a teacher _____ a doctor.

출제율 95%

03 다음 주어진 우리말에 맞게 빈칸을 채우시오. (철자가 주어진 경우 주어진 철자로 시작할 것)

(1) 사람들은 스트레스로 지쳐 있을 때 보통 부드러운 음악을 듣는 것을 좋아한다.
➡ When people are s_____ _____, they usually like to listen to soft music.

(2) 너의 의견은 나의 의견과 비슷하다.
➡ Your opinion is s_____ to mine.

(3) 그녀의 서재는 책으로 가득하다.
➡ Her study is _____ with books.

출제율 100%

04 다음 중 동사의 형용사형이 <u>잘못된</u> 것은?

① rain – rainy

② fog – fogy

③ sleep – sleepy

④ taste – tasty

⑤ snow – snowy

[05~07] 다음 대화를 읽고 물음에 답하시오.

M: Welcome to Sandwich Place. What would you like to order?
(A) OK, then will that be all?
(B) I'd like to have a hamburger, and she'll have a chicken sandwich.
(C) One salad, please.
(D) Would you like anything else?
G: No, (a)물 두 병 주세요.
M: Is it for here or to go?
G: It's for here, please.
M: The total comes to 12 dollars.
G: OK. Here you are.

출제율 95%

05 위 대화의 (A)~(D)를 문맥에 맞게 자연스럽게 배열하시오.

➡ _____

출제율 100%

06 위 대화를 읽고 대답할 수 <u>없는</u> 질문을 고르시오.

① Is the man a customer?

② What does the girl order?

③ With whom does the girl make a visit to the restaurant?

④ Will the girl take out her order?

⑤ How much does the girl have to pay?

07 밑줄 친 (a)의 우리말을 like를 포함하여 8 단어로 영작하시오.

➡ _____

[08~09] 다음 대화를 읽고 물음에 답하시오.

A: Hello. What would you like to ___(A)___ ?
B: I'd like to ___(A)___ two hot dogs.
A: _____(B)_____
B: Yes, one orange juice, please.
A: Is it for here or to go?
B: It's to go, please.

08 다음 영영풀이를 참고하여 위 대화의 빈칸 (A)에 알맞은 말을 쓰시오.

> to ask for food or a drink in a restaurant

➡ _____

09 위 대화의 빈칸 (B)에 다음 문장과 같은 의미의 문장을 like를 이용하여 쓰시오.

> Will you order anything to drink?

➡ _____

_____

10 다음 중 어법상 어색한 문장을 고르시오.

① Dad helped me to do the dishes.
② Nobody can make the baby stop crying.
③ I heard Michael to read the novel.
④ They advised him not to smoke again.
⑤ The world famous Korean singer IU had her fans freely take pictures of her.

11 다음 각 빈칸에 공통으로 들어갈 단어 중 나머지 넷과 성격이 다른 하나는?

① My grandma was _____ busy that she couldn't share the recipe.
② Riley ran fast _____ that she wouldn't miss the appointment.
③ The guide spoke much louder _____ that the elder lady could understand.
④ Sam's kids woke up early _____ that they could meet Santa Clause.
⑤ Melt the butter _____ that you could make some mixture.

12 다음 David의 에세이를 읽고 글의 내용을 요약하는 문장을 〈조건〉에 따라 어법에 맞게 영작하시오.

David's Comfort Food

My comfort food is chocolate. I usually eat it when I feel bad. Recently, I didn't do well on a test and got stressed out. I went to the store and bought some chocolate. After eating the sweet chocolate, I felt better.

┤ 조건 ├

1. David, make 외에는 본문에 나온 단어만 활용할 것.
2. 동명사, 현재시제를 사용할 것.
3. 총 6단어로 영작할 것.

➡ _____

13 다음 우리말에 맞게 괄호 안의 단어를 활용하여 영작하시오. (동사는 어법에 맞게 변형 가능)

(1) Damon은 Morgan이 대본을 확인하게 했다.
(check, had, the script)

➡ _____

(2) Damon이 "준비됐는지 알려주세요."라고 외쳤다. (know, me, ready, if, shout, you're, let)

➡ _____

(3) Andy는 배우들이 계속 서 있도록 했다.
(keep, make, the actors, stand)

➡ _____

(4) Mary는 Scarlet이 자신의 연기에 집중하도록 도와줬다. (focus, her acting, help, on)

➡ _____

(5) Fred의 재산이 Damon이 영화에 합류하도록 결심하게 만들었다. (decide, the movie, wealth, make, join, Fred's, to)

➡ _____

14 다음 중 밑줄 친 부분의 쓰임이 나머지 넷과 다른 것은?

① I turned off the light, so that my sister slept well.

② April ran to the station so that she wouldn't miss the subway.

③ I'm going to give you my number so that you can call me anytime.

④ The student answered loudly so that the teacher could hear him well.

⑤ James did his best so that his class could win the song contest.

[15~16] 다음 글을 읽고 물음에 답하시오.

Jessica (A)[for / from] USA

My comfort food is chicken soup. In the USA, people eat this soup when they have a cold. When I was a small child, I caught a very bad cold. My father made me a bowl of chicken soup so that I could get well. The hot soup warmed my body, and I slowly started to feel (B)[better / worse]. It was also very (C)[taste / tasty]. Now, when I catch a cold, I eat chicken soup.

15 위 글의 괄호 (A)~(C)에서 문맥이나 어법상 알맞은 낱말을 골라 쓰시오.

➡ (A) _____ (B) _____ (C) _____

16 According to the passage, which is NOT true?

① Jessica's comfort food is chicken soup.

② Americans eat chicken soup when they catch a cold.

③ Jessica's mother made her chicken soup when Jessica had a very bad cold.

④ The hot chicken soup warmed Jessica's body.

⑤ At present, when Jessica has a cold, she eats chicken soup.

[17~19] 다음 글을 읽고 물음에 답하시오.

Grandma's Special Recipe: Orange Madeleines
You need: 1 cup of flour, ⓐ2/3 cup of sugar, 2 eggs, some orange peel, ⓑ1/4 cup of butter, ⓒ1/8 teaspoon of salt

1. Melt the butter and let ⓓit cool.
2. Put the eggs, sugar, and salt in a bowl and beat.

3. Add the flour to the bowl and mix.

4. Add the butter and orange peel to ⓔthe mixture and mix.

5. Pour the mixture into the madeleine pan.

6. Bake in the oven for 10 to 15 minutes.

출제율 90%

17 위 글의 밑줄 친 ⓐ2/3, ⓑ1/4, ⓒ1/8을 읽는 법을 영어로 쓰시오.

➡ ⓐ _____ ⓑ _____ ⓒ _____

출제율 95%

18 위 글의 밑줄 친 ⓓit이 가리키는 것을 본문에서 찾아 쓰시오.

➡ _____

출제율 100%

19 다음 중 위 글의 밑줄 친 ⓔthe mixture에 들어간 재료가 아닌 것을 고르시오.

① salt   ② eggs   ③ butter
④ flour   ⑤ sugar

[20~21] 다음 글을 읽고 물음에 답하시오.

Maria from Brazil

ⓐIn Brazil, there are many dishes that is made with cassava, a vegetable similar to a potato. I love cassava chips the most. ⓑOnce when I had a bad day at school and felt stressed out, my best friend bought me a bag of cassava chips. When I started to eat the chips, my stress suddenly disappeared. The crisp sound of eating chips made me feel better. Now, every time I'm stressed out, I eat cassava chips. Then I feel good again!

출제율 95%

20 위 글의 밑줄 친 ⓐ에서 어법상 틀린 부분을 찾아 고치시오.

_____ ➡ _____

출제율 100%

21 위 글의 밑줄 친 ⓑOnce와 의미가 같지 않은 것을 고르시오.

① Once there lived an old man in a village.
② She was once very miserable.
③ There was once a giant in the forest.
④ Once you hesitate, you are lost.
⑤ This book was famous once, but nobody reads it today.

[22~24] 다음 글을 읽고 물음에 답하시오.

Simon from France

I have many comfort foods, but I love madeleines the most. ⓐ마들렌은 조개처럼 생긴 작은 케이크야.(that, like) People in France enjoy madeleines as an afternoon snack. ⓑMy grandmother always makes madeleines for me when I visit to her. They taste best when they come ⓒright out of the oven. Then the kitchen is filled with a sweet smell. I especially like eating her orange madeleines with a cup of tea. Every time I see or smell madeleines, I think of my grandmother.

출제율 90%

22 밑줄 친 ⓐ의 우리말에 맞게 주어진 어휘를 이용하여 12 단어로 영작하시오.

➡ _____

출제율 90%

23 밑줄 친 ⓑ에서 어법상 틀린 부분을 찾아 고치시오.

_____ ➡ _____

출제율 95%

24 밑줄 친 ⓒright과 같은 의미로 쓰인 것은?

① Stop playing right now.
② Keep on the right side of the road.
③ Always do what is right.
④ She had every right to be angry.
⑤ He's the right man for the job.

[01~03] 다음 대화를 읽고 물음에 답하시오.

A: Thank you for your help, but you look _____(A)_____. What's wrong?

B: My family has nothing (a)to eat.

A: This is for you. It (b)is filled with food.

B: Thanks. Wow! It has not only food but also gold.

01 다음 영영풀이에 해당하는 말을 빈칸 (A)에 s로 시작하여 쓰시오. (2 words)

> very tense and anxious because of difficulties in lives

➡ _____

02 위 대화의 밑줄 친 (a)to eat과 같은 쓰임을 이용하여 다음 우리말을 영작하시오.

> 그는 엄마와 함께 살 집을 한 채 샀다. (10 단어)

➡ _____

03 위 대화의 밑줄 친 (b)is filled with와 같은 뜻의 말을 3 단어로 쓰시오.

➡ _____

[04~05] 다음 중에서 틀린 문장을 찾아 기호를 쓰고, 바르게 고쳐 문장을 다시 쓰시오.

04 ① We saved lots of money so that we could take a long vacation.

② He tried his best in order that he could win the race.

③ Speak very clearly in that they can understand you.

④ He is so wise that everyone respects him.

⑤ She was so careful that she wouldn't drop the egg.

➡ _____
_____

05 ① The club members have the strongest passion. This club makes students practice their English.

② It was so windy yesterday. The wind made the picture fall on the floor.

③ Bora's family had a big garden. Her mother had Bora water the flowers.

④ There was a big fire, so the officers made let everyone leave.

⑤ He is very stubborn. Nothing will make him change his mind.

➡ _____
_____

06 다음 우리말로 제시한 세 문장을 영작할 때, <보기>의 단어들을 사용하여 빈칸에 알맞게 써 넣으시오. (중복 사용 불가)

> ┤ 보기 ├
> could / wear / in order to / let / so that / it / cool / my sister / give / her body

(1) 그녀는 몸을 식힐 수 있도록 찬 커피를 주문했다.

➡ She ordered cold coffee _____
_____ .

(2) 나는 언니가 내 새로운 치마를 입도록 해줬다.

➡ I _____ my new skirt.

(3) 그는 할머니께 드리기 위해서 마들렌을 만들었다.

➡ He made madeleines _____
them to his grandmother.

Maria from Brazil

ⓐIn Brazil, there are many dishes that are made with cassava, a vegetable similar to a potato. I love cassava chips the most. Once when I had a bad day at school and felt stressed out, my best friend bought me a bag of cassava chips. When I started to eat the chips, my stress suddenly disappeared. ⓑThe crisp sound of eating chips made me feel better. Now, every time I'm stressed out, I eat cassava chips. Then I feel good again!

07 위 글의 밑줄 친 ⓐ에서 생략할 수 있는 단어를 쓰시오.

➡ _____

08 위 글의 밑줄 친 ⓑ를 다음과 같이 바꿔 쓸 때 빈칸에 들어 갈 알맞은 말을 두 단어로 쓰시오.

➡ _____ _____ the crisp sound of eating chips, I could feel better.

09 다음 빈칸 (A)와 (B)에 본문에 있는 알맞은 단어를 넣어 Maria의 comfort food에 대한 소개를 완성하시오.

(A)_____ _____ are Maria's comfort food. Her stress suddenly disappears and she feels good again when she eats cassava chips. In addition, the (B)_____ _____ of eating chips makes her feel better.

[10~12] 다음 글을 읽고 물음에 답하시오.

Simon from France

I have many comfort foods, but I love madeleines the most. A madeleine is a small cake that (A)[looks / looks like] a sea shell. People in France enjoy madeleines as an afternoon snack. My grandmother always makes madeleines for me when I visit her. They (B)[taste / taste like] best when they come right out of the oven. ⓐThen the kitchen is filled with a sweet smell. I especially like eating her orange madeleines with a cup of tea. Every time I see or smell madeleines, I think of my grandmother.

Let me (C)[share / to share] my grandmother's special recipe with you so that you can make orange madeleines, too. Maybe madeleines will become a comfort food for you!

10 위 글의 괄호 (A)~(C)에서 문맥이나 어법상 알맞은 낱말을 골라 쓰시오.

➡ (A)_____ (B)_____ (C)_____

11 위 글의 밑줄 친 ⓐThen이 가리키는 내용을 본문에서 찾아 쓰시오.

➡ _____

12 When does Simon think of his grandmother? Answer in English in a full sentence. (11 words)

➡ _____

_____

창의사고력 서술형 문제

01 괄호 안의 어휘를 이용하여 다음 대화의 빈칸에 음식을 주문받는 문장을 쓰시오.

> A: _____
>
> B: I'd like to order Bibimbap.
>
> ((1) would, (2) ready, (3) take)

(1) _____

(2) _____

(3) _____

02 다음 그림을 보고, 사역동사 have, make, let을 활용하여, 상황에 맞게 자유롭게 영작하시오.

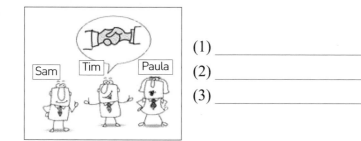

(1) _____

(2) _____

(3) _____

03 다음 내용을 바탕으로 자신에게 위안이 되는 음식을 소개하는 에세이를 쓰시오.

> 1. Q: What is your comfort food?
>   A: It is chocolate.
> 2. Q: When do you usually eat your comfort food?
>   A: I usually eat chocolate when I feel bad.
> 3. Q: Do you have any special stories about your comfort food?
>   A: Recently, I didn't do well on a test and got stressed out. I went to the store and bought some chocolate. After eating the sweet chocolate, I felt better.

> **My Comfort Food**
>
> My comfort food is (A)_____. I usually eat it when I (B)_____.
> Recently, I (C)_____ on a test and got stressed out. I went to the store and
> bought (D)_____. After eating the sweet chocolate, I (E)_____.
> Eating chocolate makes me feel good.

단원별 모의고사

1 다음 짝지어진 단어의 관계가 같도록 빈칸에 알맞은 말을 쓰시오.

> appear – disappear : comfort – _____

[02~03] 다음 영영풀이에 해당하는 어휘를 주어진 철자로 시작하여 쓰시오.

2
> f_____ : to repair something that is broken

3
> b_____ : to mix things together quickly with a fork or special kitchen machine

4 다음 빈칸에 공통으로 들어갈 말을 고르시오.

> • Excuse me, can you _____ our order now?
> • I usually _____ a nap in the afternoon.

① take ② make ③ get
④ turn ⑤ have

5 다음 문장의 밑줄 친 부분과 의미가 가장 가까운 것을 고르시오.

> These fans have been quite popular among tourists lately.

① suddenly ② fortunately
③ clearly ④ especially
⑤ recently

6 다음 영영풀이가 나타내는 말은?

> to cook something using dry heat, in an oven

① bowl ② beat ③ bake
④ order ⑤ include

7 두 문장이 같은 의미가 되도록 빈칸을 채우시오. (주어진 철자로 시작할 것)

> Beat the flour and milk together.
> = S_____ the flour and milk together.

[08~10] 다음 대화를 읽고 물음에 답하시오.

> A: Welcome to ___(A)___ World. May I ⓐplace your order?
> B: Yes, please. I'd like to ⓑorder two doughnuts.
> A: Would you like anything ⓒto drink?
> B: Yes, ⓓone orange juice, please.
> A: Is it for here or ⓔto go?
> B: For here, please.

8 다음 영영풀이에 해당하는 어휘를 빈칸 (A)에 쓰시오.

> something sweet, such as fruit or a pudding, that you eat at the end of a meal

➡ _____

9 위 대화의 내용과 일치하는 것을 고르시오.

① A is a guest to the restaurant.
② B is taking orders.
③ A likes to drink orange juice.
④ B buys doughnuts and an orange juice.
⑤ B will take out her order.

10 밑줄 친 ⓐ~ⓔ 중 어색한 것은?

① ⓐ   ② ⓑ   ③ ⓒ   ④ ⓓ   ⑤ ⓔ

[11~12] 다음 대화를 읽고 물음에 답하시오.

M: Welcome to Sandwich Place. What would you like to order?

G: I'd like to have a hamburger, and she'll have a chicken sandwich.

M: Would you like anything else?

G: One salad, please.

M: OK, then will that be all?

G: Yes, I'd like to order two bottles of water.

M: Is it for here or to go?

G: (A)여기에서 먹을게요, please.

M: The total comes to 12 dollars.

G: OK. Here you are.

11 위 대화의 밑줄 친 (A)의 우리말을 3 단어로 쓰시오.

➡ _____

12 위 대화의 흐름상 어색한 것을 하나 찾아 바르게 고치시오.

_____ ➡ _____

13 다음 주어진 우리말을 바르게 영작한 것은?

> Sean은 시험에 합격하기 위해 열심히 공부했다.

① Sean studied so hard what he passed the test.

② Sean studied so hard that he passed the test.

③ Sean studied hard so that he could pass the test.

④ Sean passed the test so that he could study hard.

⑤ Sean passed the test in order to study hard.

14 다음 중 밑줄 친 부분의 쓰임이 다른 하나는?

① The smell of baking cookies makes me feel good.

② Her father made Cindy a bowl of hot potato soup.

③ The teacher made us write down the list of our comfort food.

④ The recipe will make you cook madeleines like an expert chef.

⑤ The sad movie about mother's love made the audience cry.

15 다음 그림을 보고, 〈보기〉에서 알맞은 단어를 하나씩 선택하여 ⓐ~ⓔ의 빈칸에 어법상 알맞은 형태로 써 넣고, (A)에는 〈보기〉에 없는 단어 두 개를 써 넣으시오.

> ┤ 보기 ├
> feel   allow   stay   use   play

My teacher ⓐ_____ us ⓑ_____ the gym when the exam was over. Sam and I ⓒ_____ table tennis (A)_____ we could ⓓ_____ healthy. Exercise made us ⓔ_____ good.

16 다음 문장의 빈칸 (가)~(라)에 들어갈 말을 〈보기〉에서 골라 순서대로 나열한 것은?

- Willy would like to share his grandma's recipe ___(가)___ .
- My girlfriend often eats cassava chips when stressed out ___(나)___ .
- Mr. Trump paid all his debts ___(다)___ .
- Carla took a taxi to the theater ___(라)___ .

┤ 보기 ├
(A) so that he wouldn't go to prison
(B) so that she could watch the musical
(C) so that others can make madeleines
(D) so that she can feel better again

① (A) – (B) – (C) – (D)
② (A) – (C) – (D) – (B)
③ (B) – (D) – (A) – (C)
④ (C) – (A) – (B) – (D)
⑤ (C) – (D) – (A) – (B)

17 다음 그림을 보고, 내용에 맞게 〈보기〉에서 필요한 표현을 찾아 빈칸에 넣으시오. (단, 동사 형태는 변형 가능.)

┤ 보기 ├
- put the can into the recycle bin
- sweep the playground
- pick up a can
- throw away an empty bottle
- sort the garbage

(1) The teacher made Tim _____ _____ .
(2) The teacher asked Dave _____ _____ .
(3) The teacher _____ .
(4) The teacher got Brad _____ _____ .
(5) Lena helped Brad _____ _____ .

[18~19] 다음 글을 읽고 물음에 답하시오.

ⓐcomfort food는 여러분이 슬프거나 화가 나거나 스트레스를 받을 때 기분을 좋게 해 주는 음식이다. It can also make you think of happy moments from the past. It satisfies not only the stomach but also the heart. Comfort foods differ around the world. Let's see what comfort foods our international readers enjoy.

18 위 글의 밑줄 친 ⓐ의 우리말에 맞게 주어진 어휘를 알맞게 배열하시오.

are / when / is / good / that / feel / you / food / you / sad, angry, or stressed out / comfort food / makes

➡ _____

19 다음 문장에서 위 글의 내용과 <u>다른</u> 부분을 as well as를 써서 올바르게 고쳐 쓰시오..

Comfort food satisfies the heart, not the stomach.

➡ _____

[20~22] 다음 글을 읽고 물음에 답하시오.

Maria from Brazil

In Brazil, there are many dishes that are made with cassava, a vegetable ⓐsimilar to a potato. I love cassava chips the most. Once when I had a bad day at school and felt stressed out, ⓑmy best friend bought me a bag of cassava chips. When I started to eat the chips, my stress suddenly disappeared. The crisp sound of eating chips made me feel better. Now, every time I'm stressed out, I eat cassava chips. Then I feel good again!

20 위 글의 밑줄 친 ⓐsimilar 앞에 생략된 단어를 쓰시오. (2 단어)

➡ _____

21 위 글의 밑줄 친 ⓑ를 3형식 문장으로 고치시오.

➡ _____

_____

22 위 글의 제목으로 알맞은 것을 고르시오.

① What Is Cassava?
② What Is Maria's Comfort Food?
③ What Made Maria Feel Stressed Out?
④ A Present from Maria's Best Friend
⑤ The Crisp Sound of Eating Chips

[23~25] 다음 글을 읽고 물음에 답하시오.

Simon from France

I have many comfort foods, but I love madeleines the most. A madeleine is a small cake that looks like a sea shell. People in France enjoy madeleines as an afternoon snack. My grandmother always makes madeleines ___ⓐ___ me when I visit her. They taste best when they come right out of the oven. Then the kitchen (A)is filled with a sweet smell. I especially like eating her orange madeleines with a cup of tea. Every time I see or smell madeleines, I think of my grandmother.

Let me share my grandmother's special recipe ___ⓑ___ you so that you can make orange madeleines, too. Maybe madeleines will become a comfort food for you!

23 위 글의 빈칸 ⓐ와 ⓑ에 들어갈 전치사가 바르게 짝지어진 것은?

    ⓐ   ⓑ   ⓐ   ⓑ
① to – with   ② in – to
③ to – for   ④ for – with
⑤ for – to

24 위 글의 밑줄 친 (A)is filled with와 바꿔 쓸 수 있는 말을 쓰시오. (3 단어)

➡ _____

25 According to the passage, which is NOT true?

① Simon's favorite comfort food is madeleines.
② A madeleine looks like a sea shell.
③ Madeleines taste best right before they come out of the oven.
④ Simon especially likes to eat his grandma's orange madeleines with a cup of tea.
⑤ Whenever Simon sees or smells madeleines, he thinks of his grandmother.

Lesson 3

Stories of English Words and Expressions

🌱 의사소통 기능

- 설명 요청하기
  A: What does that mean?
  B: It means "It's raining a lot."

- 반복 설명 요청하기
  Can you say that again?

🌱 언어 형식

- '계속적 용법'의 관계대명사
  The word *shampoo* comes from the Hindi word
  chāmpo, **which** means "to press."

- It is[was] ~ that 가주어, 진주어 구문
  It is interesting **that** the idea of using the word
  robot didn't come from Karel Čapek himself.

Words & Expressions

Key Words

- **advanced** [ədvǽnst] 형 진보한, 발전된
- **anger** [ǽŋɡər] 동 화나게 하다
- **borrow** [bárou] 동 빌리다
- **British** [brítiʃ] 형 영국인의
- **cause** [kɔːz] 동 초래하다 명 원인
- **century** [séntʃəri] 명 세기, 100년
- **civilization** [sìvəlizéiʃən] 명 문명
- **contact** [kántækt] 명 접촉
- **create** [kriéit] 동 창조하다
- **culture** [kʌ́ltʃər] 명 문화
- **decide** [disáid] 동 결심하다
- **design** [dizáin] 동 설계하다
- **example** [iɡzǽmpl] 명 사례
- **experience** [ikspíəriəns] 동 경험하다
- **explorer** [iksplɔ́ːrər] 명 탐험가
- **expression** [ikspréʃən] 명 표현
- **factory** [fǽktəri] 명 공장
- **flood** [flʌd] 명 홍수
- **German** [dʒə́ːrmən] 명 독일어
- **hurricane** [hə́ːrəkèin] 명 허리케인
- **include** [inklúːd] 동 포함하다
- **introduce** [intrədjúːs] 동 소개하다
- **invent** [invént] 동 발명하다
- **judge** [dʒʌdʒ] 명 재판관, 판사 동 재판하다
- **justice** [dʒʌ́stis] 명 정의
- **law** [lɔː] 명 법
- **language** [lǽŋɡwidʒ] 명 언어
- **massage** [məsáːʒ] 명 마사지, 안마
- **Mayan** [máːjən] 형 마야 사람의
- **mean** [miːn] 동 의미하다
- **meaning** [míːniŋ] 명 의미
- **myth** [miθ] 명 신화
- **nervous** [nə́ːrvəs] 형 불안한
- **origin** [ɔ́ːrədʒin] 명 기원, 유래
- **originally** [ərídʒənəli] 부 원래, 본래
- **originate** [ərídʒənèit] 동 유래하다
- **present** [préznt] 형 현재의
- **press** [pres] 동 누르다
- **produce** [prədjúːs] 동 생산하다
- **science fiction** 공상과학
- **shampoo** [ʃæmpúː] 명 샴푸
- **shortly** [ʃɔ́ːrtli] 부 곧, 즉시
- **slave** [sleiv] 명 노예
- **slice** [slais] 명 얇게 썬 조각; 한 조각
- **soap** [soup] 명 비누
- **special** [spéʃəl] 형 특별한
- **Spanish** [spǽniʃ] 형 스페인의
- **storm** [stɔːrm] 명 폭풍
- **suggest** [səɡdʒést] 동 제안하다
- **tool** [tuːl] 명 도구
- **trader** [tréidər] 명 상인, 거래자
- **universe** [júːnəvə̀ːrs] 명 우주, 은하계
- **weather** [wéðər] 명 날씨
- **yoga** [jóuɡə] 명 요가

Key Expressions

- **be in hot water** 곤경에 처하다
- **be late for ~** ~에 지각하다
- **be made into ~** ~로 만들어지다
- **break a leg** 행운을 빌다
- **call ~ after ...** ...을 본떠 ~의 이름을 부르다
- **come from ~** ~에서 오다, 유래하다
- **cup of tea** [부정어와 함께; one's ~] 기호[취미]에 맞는 사람[물건]
- **It's a piece of cake.** 그것은 식은 죽 먹기이다.
- **keep in touch** 연락하다
- **keep one's fingers crossed** 행운을 빌다
- **look like ~** ~처럼 보이다
- **Lunch is on me.** 점심은 제가 사겠습니다.
- **make a long face** 우울한 얼굴을 하다
- **not ~ at all** 전혀 ~가 아니다
- **originate from** ~에서 비롯되다
- **pass through** 거쳐 지나가다
- **pick up ~** ~을 익히게 되다
- **pig out** 돼지 같이 먹다
- **pull one's leg** 놀리다
- **rain cats and dogs** 비가 세차게 내리다
- **see eye to eye** 의견을 같이하다
- **under the weather** 몸이 안 좋은
- **watch out** 조심하다

Word Power

※ 서로 비슷한 뜻을 가진 어휘

- □ **borrow** 빌리다 : **rent** 임대하다
- □ **trader** 상인, 거래자 : **merchant** 상인
- □ **tool** 도구 : **device** 장치
- □ **design** 설계하다 : **devise** 고안하다

- □ **example** 사례 : **instance** 사례
- □ **origin** 기원 : **source** 근원
- □ **present** 현재의 : **current** 현재의
- □ **decide** 결심하다 : **determine** 결정하다

※ 서로 반대의 뜻을 가진 어휘

- □ **borrow** 빌리다 ↔ **lend** 빌려주다
- □ **produce** 생산하다 ↔ **consume** 소비하다

- □ **include** 포함하다 ↔ **exclude** 제외하다
- □ **special** 특별한 ↔ **general** 일반적인

※ 동사 – 명사

- □ **decide** 결심하다 – **decision** 결심
- □ **introduce** 소개하다 – **introduction** 소개
- □ **originate** 유래하다 – **origination** 유래
- □ **suggest** 제안하다 – **suggestion** 제안

- □ **express** 표현하다 – **expression** 표현
- □ **produce** 생산하다 – **production** 생산
- □ **create** 창조하다 – **creation** 창조
- □ **invent** 발명하다 – **invention** 발명

※ 나라 이름 – 형용사/언어

- □ **Spain** 스페인 – **Spanish** 스페인어
- □ **Germany** 독일 – **German** 독일어

- □ **Italy** 이탈리아 – **Italian** 이탈리아어
- □ **Korea** 한국 – **Korean** 한국어

English Dictionary

- □ **anger** 화나게 하다
  → to make someone angry 다른 사람을 화나게 만들다
- □ **borrow** 빌리다
  → to use something that belongs to someone else and that you must give back to them later
  누군가에게 속한 것을 사용하고 나중에 되돌려 주어야만 하다
- □ **century** 세기, 100년
  → a period of a hundred years 백년의 기간
- □ **contact** 접촉
  → communication between people, countries either by talking or writing
  말이나 글로 사람이나 나라 간의 의사소통
- □ **civilization** 문명
  → a society that is well organized and developed
  잘 정돈되고 발전된 사회
- □ **expression** 표현
  → something you say, write, or do that shows what you think or feel 생각과 감정을 보여주는 말, 글, 행동
- □ **flood** 홍수
  → a lot of water that covers land that is usually dry
  평상시 마른 땅을 뒤덮는 많은 물

- □ **originally** 원래
  → in the beginning, before other things happened
  처음에, 다른 일이 일어나기 전에
- □ **present** 현재의
  → happening or existing now 지금 일어나거나 존재하는
- □ **shortly** 곧, 즉시
  → in a short time; soon 짧은 시간에, 곧
- □ **slave** 노예
  → someone who is owned by another person and works for them for no money
  돈을 받지 않고 다른 사람에게 소유되어 그들을 위하여 일하는 사람
- □ **suggest** 제안하다
  → to tell someone you think he or she should do something 무엇을 해야 하는지를 누군가에게 말하다
- □ **trader** 무역업자
  → someone who buys and sells goods
  상품을 사고파는 사람
- □ **universe** 우주, 은하계
  → all of space, including all the stars and planets
  항성과 행성을 포함한 모든 공간

01 다음 짝지어진 단어의 관계가 같도록 빈칸에 알맞은 말은?

> source – origin : determine – _____

① present   ② cause
③ judge   ④ produce
⑤ decide

서답형
02 다음 주어진 영어 설명에 맞게 빈칸에 알맞은 말을 쓰시오.

> He presented a new concept of the beginning of the _____.

> <영어 설명> all of space, including all the stars and planets

➡ _____

03 다음 〈보기〉의 단어를 사용하여 자연스러운 문장을 만들 수 없는 것은?

> ┌─ 보기 ─┐
> justice   suggest   civilization   present

① Our _____ situation is difficult, but we'll do our best.
② My teacher _____ed that we should read newspapers every day.
③ If you want to be a good judge, be in _____ to a person!
④ The Inca Empire was a very developed _____.
⑤ Like any great _____ or legend, the question still remains.

04 다음 빈칸에 들어갈 알맞은 말을 고르시오.

> The _____ of the hamburger is uncertain.

① origin   ② contact
③ flood   ④ expression
⑤ soap

중요
05 다음 중 밑줄 친 부분의 의미가 잘못된 것은?

① The movie's title originated from a Latin expression. (~에서 비롯되었다)
② I want to keep in touch with you but I don't know how. (연락하다)
③ I think I can introduce some new companies to you. (소개하다)
④ We don't produce the model any longer. (파괴하다)
⑤ They called their first daughter after her grandmother. (…을 본떠 ~의 이름을 불렀다)

06 다음 빈칸에 알맞은 말이 바르게 짝지어진 것을 고르시오.

> • Horror movies are just not my cup of _____.
> • The actor told me to break a _____.

① tea – leg
② tea – arm
③ cake – leg
④ cake – arm
⑤ coffee – foot

01 다음 영영풀이에 알맞은 어휘를 〈보기〉에서 찾아 쓰시오.

보기
suggest   slave   borrow   flood

(1) a lot of water that covers land that is usually dry

(2) someone who is owned by another person and works for them for no money

(3) to tell someone you think he or she should do something

(4) to use something that belongs to someone else and that you must give back to them later

➡ (1) _____ (2) _____ (3) _____
　(4) _____

02 다음 짝지어진 두 단어의 관계가 같도록 빈칸에 알맞은 말을 쓰시오.

(1) China : Chinese = Italy : _____

(2) decide : decision = suggest : _____

03 다음 우리말에 맞도록 빈칸에 알맞은 말을 쓰시오.

(1) 요새 건강이 안 좋으시다니 안타깝네요.
　→ I'm sorry to hear that you've been under the _____ lately.

(2) 나는 너를 안 믿으니까 나를 그만 놀리시지.
　→ I don't believe you, so stop _____ my leg.

(3) 그녀는 언어를 정말 쉽게 습득한다.
　→ She _____ up languages really easily.

(4) 우리는 여기에 머무르지 않고 지나갈 것입니다.
　→ We're not staying here, we're just _____ through.

04 다음 우리말에 맞게 한 단어를 추가하여 주어진 단어를 알맞게 배열하시오.

(1) 그 학생의 버릇없음에 선생님은 화가 났다.
(rudeness, the teacher, the student's, angered, by)
➡ _____
_____

(2) 문화 차이를 경험한 적이 있나요?
(differences, you, experienced, cultural, ever)
➡ _____
_____

(3) 컴퓨터를 켜고 싶다면, 이 빨간 버튼을 누르세요. (the computer, button, you, this, turn, press, want, red, if, to)
➡ _____
_____

(4) 그는 법학 대학원을 들어가기 위한 시험을 통과했다. (the exam, he, school, entering, passed, a, for)
➡ _____
_____

Conversation

① 설명 요청하기

A What does that mean? 그게 무슨 뜻이니?

B It means "It's raining a lot." 그것은 "비가 아주 많이 내린다."라는 뜻이야.

■ 상대방이 한 말의 의미를 설명해 달라고 요청할 때 쓰는 표현은 "What does that mean?(그것이 무슨 뜻입니까?)", "What do you mean by that?(그것이 무슨 뜻이니?)", "What is the meaning of that?(그것의 의미가 무엇이니?)" 등이 있다. that은 상대방이 말한 내용을 언급하는 대명사이고, by that은 "그 말로써, 그것으로"라는 뜻으로, 직역하면 "그 말로써 너는 무엇을 의미하니?"라는 뜻이다.

■ 상대방에게 설명을 요청할 때는 "설명하다, 말하다"의 의미를 가지는 동사 explain, tell이나 give information, be specific 등의 표현을 사용하여 "Could you explain the meaning of it?", "Could you tell me more about them?" 등의 표현을 사용하기도 한다. Could 대신 Would, Can, Will 등을 사용할 수 있고, "Do you mind if I ask you to explain ~?"이라고 말할 수도 있다.

■ 상대방의 말을 알아듣지 못했을 때는 "I'm not following you.(잘 못 알아듣겠습니다.)", "I don't get it.(제대로 이해를 못하겠어요.)" 등의 표현을 사용하여 상대방이 다시 설명을 하도록 요청할 수도 있다.

설명 요청하기

• What does that mean? 그게 무슨 뜻이죠?

• What do you mean by that? 그게 무슨 말이야?

• Could you give me more information? 좀 더 정보를 주시겠습니까?

• Can you explain more in detail? 좀 더 자세히 설명해 주시겠습니까?

• Could you be more specific? 좀 더 구체적으로 말해 주시겠습니까?

• What is the meaning of that exactly? 정확하게 그게 무슨 뜻입니까?

• Could you explain what it means? 그게 무엇을 의미하는지 설명 좀 해 주시겠습니까?

핵심 Check

1. 다음 우리말과 일치하도록 주어진 어휘를 이용하여 빈칸에 알맞은 말을 쓰시오.

A: It's raining cats and dogs.

B: Excuse me, but can you please say that again?

A: I said, "It's raining cats and dogs."

B: _____? (그게 무슨 뜻이니?) (what, mean)

A: It means "It's raining a lot."

② 반복 설명 요청하기

• **Can you say that again?** 다시 한 번 말해 줄래?

■ 상대방의 말을 잘 듣지 못했거나, 이해하지 못해서 다시 한 번 반복해서 말해줄 것을 요청하고 싶을 때 "Can you (please) say that again?(다시 한 번 말씀해 주시겠습니까?)" 또는 "Excuse me(, but I'm not following you)?(죄송하지만 잘 못 알아들었어요.)" "Can you repeat that?", "What did you say?" 등을 사용한다. 이렇게 요청받고 반복해서 말해 줄 때는 "I said "~.(저는 ~라고 말했습니다.)" 라는 표현을 사용한다.

■ 일상적으로 부담 없이 상대방에게 반복을 요청하는 표현은 "What?(뭐라고 하셨죠?)" "What did you say?(뭐라고 말씀하셨는지요?)", "(I beg your) Pardon?(다시 한 번 말씀해 주시겠습니까?)" "Excuse me?(실례지만 잘 못 알아들었습니다.)" 등이 있는데 이런 표현은 의문의 뜻으로 억양을 올려서 말한다.

■ 좀 더 공손해야 할 필요가 있을 때는 "(Sorry, I'm afraid) I don't know what you mean[meant]." "Will you say that again, please? (다시 한 번 말씀해 주시겠어요?)"와 같은 표현을 쓰거나 아주 격식을 갖출 필요가 있을 때는 "I am afraid I am not quite clear what you mean by that.(죄송합니다만, 말씀하신 내용이 명확하게 이해가 되지 않습니다.)"라고 말하고 다시 이야기해 달라고 말하거나, "I didn't quite follow what you said, please repeat it.(말씀하신 것을 잘 알아듣지 못했는데, 다시 한 번 말씀해 주세요.)"라고 한다.

설명 요청하기

• Can you please say that again? 다시 한 번 말씀해 주시겠습니까?

• Will you say that again, please? 다시 한 번 말씀해 주시겠어요?

• Excuse me, but I'm not following you. 죄송하지만 잘 못 알아들었어요.

• Pardon? / Pardon me? 잘 못 알아들었습니다. / 뭐라고요?

• I beg your pardon? 다시 한 번 말씀해 주시겠어요?

• Sorry? 뭐라고 하셨는지요?　　　　• Excuse me? 잘 못 알아들었습니다.

• I didn't quite follow what you said. 말씀하신 것을 잘 알아듣지 못했습니다.

핵심 Check

2. 주어진 문장 다음에 이어질 (A)~(D)를 바르게 배열하시오.

　A: I'm under the weather.

　(A) It means "I don't feel well."　　　(B) I said, "I'm under the weather."

　(C) What do you mean by that?　　　(D) Excuse me, but I'm not following you.

　➡ _____

Listen and Talk A 1

> G: Look. ❶It's raining cats and dogs.
>
> B: Raining cats and dogs? ❷What does that mean?
>
> G: It means "It's raining ❸a lot."
>
> B: Oh. Don't worry. I have an umbrella in my backpack.

G: 봐. 고양이와 개처럼 비가 내려.

B: 고양이와 개처럼 비가 내린다고? 그게 무슨 뜻이니?

G: 그것은 "비가 아주 많이 내린다."라는 뜻이야.

B: 오, 걱정 마. 내 배낭에 우산이 있어.

❶ 'rain cats and dogs'는 '비가 많이 온다'라는 뜻이다.
❷ 상대방이 한 말의 의미를 설명해 달라고 요청할 때 쓰는 표현이다. "What do you mean by that?", "What is the meaning of that?" 등으로 바꿔 쓸 수 있다.
❸ 'a lot'은 부사구로 사용되었다.

Check(√) True or False

(1) The boy knew the meaning of "raining cats and dogs."　　　　T ☐ F ☐

(2) The girl is explaining the meaning of "raining cats and dogs."　　T ☐ F ☐

 Listen and Talk C

> G: Thank you for everything, Jiho. ❶I had a great time in Korea.
>
> B: My pleasure. Please ❷come visit me again, Lucy.
>
> G: I'd love to, but before I do, I'd like to invite you to visit me in London.
>
> B: Thanks. Anyway, it's too bad that you can't come to my soccer game tomorrow.
>
> G: I'm sorry that I can't stay longer. I'll ❸keep my fingers crossed for you.
>
> B: ❹Excuse me, but can you please say that again?
>
> G: I said, "I'll keep my fingers crossed for you." It means "I wish you good luck."
>
> B: Oh. Thanks. Have a nice trip.
>
> G: Thanks. I'll ❺keep in touch.

G: 지호야, 모든 게 고마웠어. 한국에서 정말 좋은 시간을 보냈어.

B: 천만에. 다음에 또 와줘, Lucy.

G: 그러고 싶지만, 그 전에 난 런던으로 널 초대하고 싶어.

B: 고마워. 어쨌든, 내일 네가 내 축구 시합에 올 수 없어서 너무 안타깝다.

G: 나도 더 오래 머물 수 없어서 유감이야. 너를 위해 내 손가락을 교차할게.

B: 미안한데, 다시 한 번 말해 줄래?

G: 나는 "너를 위해 내 손가락을 교차할게."라고 말했어. 그것은 "행운을 빌게."라는 뜻이야.

B: 아, 고마워. 즐거운 여행이 되길 바랄게.

G: 고마워. 연락할게.

❶ 'have a good[great] time'은 '좋은[재미있는] 시간을 보내다'라는 의미이다.
❷ 'come visit'은 'come and visit' 또는 'come to visit'으로도 쓸 수 있다.
❸ 'keep one's fingers crossed'는 '행운을 빌다'라는 뜻이다.
❹ 반복해서 설명해 줄 것을 요청하는 표현이다.
❺ 'keep in touch'는 '연락하다'를 의미한다.

Check(√) True or False

(3) Lucy is leaving for London.　　　　　　　　　　　　　　　T ☐ F ☐

(4) Jiho is glad that Lucy will come to his soccer game.　　　　　T ☐ F ☐

Listen and Talk A 2

G: ❶This juice is on me, Suho.

B: Excuse me? ❷Can you say that again?

G: I said, "This juice is on me." It means "I'll pay for the juice."

B: Oh. Thanks a lot.

G: ❸You're welcome.

G: 수호야, 이 주스는 내 위에 있어.

B: 뭐라고 했어? 다시 한 번 말해 줄래?

G: "이 주스는 내 위에 있어."라고 했어. 그것은 "내가 그 주스를 낼게."라는 뜻이야.

B: 오. 정말 고마워.

G: 천만에.

❶ '~ is on me.'는 '~은 내가 내겠다.'라는 의미이다.
❷ 반복해서 설명해 줄 것을 요청할 때 쓰는 표현이다. 'Pardon me?', 'Can you repeat that?', 'What did you say?' 등으로 바꿔 쓸 수 있다.
❸ '천만에요.'라는 뜻으로 'Don't mention it.', 'Not at all.', 'No problem.', 'My pleasure.' 등으로도 말할 수 있다.

Check(√) True or False

(5) The girl will pay for Suho's juice.   T ☐ F ☐

(6) Suho wants to buy the juice for the girl.   T ☐ F ☐

Listen and Talk A 3

B: Everything ❶looks delicious.

G: Yes. ❷Would you like some of my spaghetti?

B: No, thanks. Spaghetti is ❸not my cup of tea.

G: ❹Not your cup of tea? What does that mean?

B: It means "I don't like ❺something."

G: Oh, ❻I see. You don't like spaghetti.

B: 모든 것이 맛있어 보여.

G: 응. 내 스파게티 좀 먹을래?

B: 괜찮아. 스파게티는 나의 차 한 잔이 아니야.

G: 네 차 한 잔이 아니라고? 그게 무슨 뜻이니?

B: 그것은 "난 무언가를 좋아하지 않아."라는 뜻이야.

G: 오, 알겠어. 넌 스파게티를 좋아하지 않는구나.

❶ look+형용사: ~하게 보이다
❷ 'Would you like ~?'는 'Do you want ~?'와 같은 의미로 공손히 말할 때 쓰는 표현이다.
❸ 'not my cup of tea'는 '좋아하지 않는 것[사람]'이라는 뜻이다.
❹ 끝을 올려 읽어서 의문문 대용으로 사용한다.
❺ 부정문이지만 'something'이 사용됐음에 주의한다.
❻ '알겠다.'라는 뜻이다.

Check(√) True or False

(7) The boy doesn't like spaghetti.   T ☐ F ☐

(8) The girl will drink a cup of tea.   T ☐ F ☐

Listen and Talk A 4

G: I feel ❶under the weather.

B: Excuse me, but ❷can you please say that again?

G: I said, "I feel under the weather." It means "I don't feel well." I think I ❸have a cold.

B: Oh. ❹Why don't you buy some medicine before you get on the plane? You can get medicine at the store over there.

G: I guess ❺I should.

❶ 'under the weather'는 '몸이 안 좋은'이라는 의미이다.
❷ 반복해서 설명해 줄 것을 요청할 때 쓰는 표현이다.
❸ have a cold = catch a cold: 감기에 걸리다
❹ 'Why don't you ~?'는 '권유'하는 표현으로 'How about ~?', 'What about ~?', 'What do you say to ~?' 등으로 바꿔 쓸 수 있다. 'Why don't we ~'는 '제안'할 때 쓰는 것이므로 서로 혼동하지 않도록 주의한다.
❺ 뒤에 'get medicine at the store'가 생략되어 있다.

 Listen and Talk B

M: ❶Break a leg.

W: ❷Excuse me, but can you please say that again?

M: I said, "Break a leg."

W: ❸What does that mean?

M: It means "Good luck."

❶ '행운을 빈다.'라는 뜻이다.
❷ 반복해서 말해 줄 것을 요청할 때 쓰는 표현이다.
❸ 상대방이 한 말의 의미를 설명해 달라고 요청할 때 쓰는 표현이다.

 Review 1

G: ❶I'll keep my fingers crossed for you.

B: ❷I'm sorry, but can you please say that again?

G: I said, "I'll keep my fingers crossed for you." It means "I wish you good luck."

❶ 'keep one's fingers crossed'는 '행운을 빌다'라는 뜻이다.
❷ 반복해서 설명해 줄 것을 요청할 때 쓰는 표현이다.

 Review 2

W: ❶I feel under the weather.

M: Excuse me, but can you please say that again?

W: I said, "I feel under the weather."

M: ❷What does that mean?

W: It means "I don't feel well." I think I have a cold.

M: Oh. ❸Why don't you buy some medicine? You can get medicine at the store over there.

W: OK, I will.

❶ 'under the weather'는 '몸이 안 좋은'이라는 의미이다.
❷ 상대방이 한 말의 의미를 설명해 달라고 요청할 때 쓰는 표현이다.
❸ Why don't you ~?'는 '권유'하는 표현이다.

 Review 3

M: Look. It's raining cats and dogs.

W: ❶Can you say that again?

M: It's raining cats and dogs.

W: What does ❷that mean?

M: It means "It's raining a lot."

❶ 반복해서 말해 줄 것을 요청하고 있다.
❷ that은 'It's raining cats and dogs.'를 받고 있다.

 Review 4

G: ❶This pizza is on me, Suho.

B: ❷What does that mean?

G: It means "I'll ❸pay for the pizza."

❶ 피자 값을 자기가 지불하겠다는 표현이다.
❷ 상대방이 한 말의 의미를 설명해 달라고 요청할 때 쓰는 표현이다.
❸ 'pay for'는 '~에 대한 값을 지불하다'라는 뜻이다.

다음 우리말과 일치하도록 빈칸에 알맞은 말을 쓰시오.

Listen and Talk A 1

G: Look. It's raining _____ _____ _____.

B: Raining _____ _____ _____? What does _____ _____?

G: It _____ "It's raining _____ _____."

B: Oh. Don't _____. I have an umbrella in my backpack.

G: 봐. 고양이와 개처럼 비가 내려.
B: 고양이와 개처럼 비가 내린다고? 그게 무슨 뜻이니?
G: 그것은 "비가 아주 많이 내린다."라는 뜻이야.
B: 오, 걱정 마. 내 배낭에 우산이 있어.

Listen and Talk A 2

G: This juice is _____ _____, Suho.

B: _____ _____? _____ you _____ _____ again?

G: I said, "This juice is _____ _____." It means "I'll _____ _____ the juice."

B: Oh. Thanks _____ _____.

G: _____ _____.

G: 수호야, 이 주스는 내 위에 있어.
B: 뭐라고 했어? 다시 한 번 말해 줄래?
G: "이 주스는 내 위에 있어."라고 했어. 그것은 "내가 그 주스를 낼게."라는 뜻이야.
B: 오, 정말 고마워.
G: 천만에.

Listen and Talk A 3

B: Everything looks _____.

G: Yes. _____ you _____ _____ _____ of my spaghetti?

B: No, thanks. Spaghetti is _____ my cup of _____.

G: _____ your cup of _____? What does that mean?

B: It means "I _____ _____ _____."

G: Oh, I _____. You don't like spaghetti.

B: 모든 것이 맛있어 보여.
G: 응. 내 스파게티 좀 먹을래?
B: 괜찮아. 스파게티는 나의 차 한 잔이 아니야.
G: 네 차 한 잔이 아니라고? 그게 무슨 뜻이니?
B: 그것은 "난 무언가를 좋아하지 않아."라는 뜻이야.
G: 오, 알겠어. 넌 스파게티를 좋아하지 않는구나.

Listen and Talk A 4

G: I feel _____ _____ _____.

B: _____ _____, but _____ you please _____ _____ _____?

G: I said, "I feel _____ _____ _____." It means "I _____ _____." I think I have a cold.

B: Oh. _____ _____ _____ buy some medicine before you _____ on the plane? You can _____ medicine at the store over there.

G: I guess I _____.

G: 난 날씨 아래 있는 기분이야.
B: 미안하지만 다시 한 번 말해 줄래?
G: "나는 날씨 아래 있는 기분이야."라고 말했어. 그것은 "몸이 좋지 않다."라는 뜻이야. 난 감기에 걸린 것 같아.
B: 오, 비행기 타기 전에 약을 좀 사는 게 어때? 저기에 있는 가게에서 약을 살 수 있어.
G: 그래야겠다.

Listen and Talk B 1

A: Don't _____ _____ _____ _____.

B: _____ _____, but _____ _____ _____ _____ _____ _____?

A: I said, "Don't _____ _____ _____ _____."

B: _____ _____ _____ _____ _____?

A: It means "Don't _____ _____."

Listen and Talk B 2

M: _____ _____ _____ _____.

W: _____ _____, but _____ _____ _____ _____?

M: I said, "_____ _____ _____."

W: _____ _____ _____ _____?

M: It means "_____ _____."

Listen and Talk B 3

M: I feel _____ _____ _____.

W: _____ _____, but _____ _____ _____ _____?

M: I said, "I feel _____ _____ _____."

W: _____ _____ _____ _____?

M: It means "I don't feel well."

Listen and Talk C

G: Thank you for everything, Jiho. I _____ _____ in Korea.

B: _____ _____. Please _____ _____ me again, Lucy.

G: I'd _____ _____, but before I do, I'd _____ _____ you to visit me in London.

B: Thanks. Anyway, _____'s too bad _____ you can't _____ to my soccer game tomorrow.

G: I'm sorry that I can't stay _____. I'll _____ _____ _____ for you.

B: _____ _____, but _____ please _____ _____?

G: I said, "I'll _____ _____ _____ for you." It means "I _____ _____ _____ _____ _____."

B: Oh. Thanks. _____ a nice _____.

G: Thanks. I'll _____ _____ _____.

해석

A: 얼굴을 길쭉하게 만들지 마.
B: 미안하지만 다시 한 번 말해 줄래?
A: "얼굴을 길쭉하게 만들지 마."라고 했어.
B: 그게 무슨 뜻이니?
A: 그것은 "슬퍼하지 마."라는 뜻이야.

M: 다리를 부러뜨려.
W: 미안하지만 다시 한 번 말해 줄래?
M: "다리를 부러뜨려."라고 했어.
W: 그게 무슨 뜻이니?
M: 그것은 "행운을 빌어."라는 뜻이야.

M: 나는 날씨 아래 있는 기분이야.
W: 미안하지만 다시 한 번 말해 줄래?
M: "나는 날씨 아래 있는 기분이야."라고 했어.
W: 그게 무슨 뜻이니?
M: 그것은 "난 몸이 좋지 않아."라는 뜻이야.

G: 지호야, 모든 게 고마웠어. 한국에서 정말 좋은 시간을 보냈어.
B: 천만에. 다음에 또 와줘, Lucy.
G: 그러고 싶지만, 그 전에 난 런던으로 널 초대하고 싶어.
B: 고마워. 어쨌든, 내일 네가 내 축구 시합에 올 수 없어서 너무 안타깝다.
G: 나도 더 오래 머물 수 없어서 유감이야. 너를 위해 내 손가락을 교차할게.
B: 미안한데, 다시 한 번 말해 줄래?
G: 나는 "너를 위해 내 손가락을 교차할게."라고 말했어. 그것은 "행운을 빌게."라는 뜻이야.
B: 아, 고마워. 즐거운 여행이 되길 바랄게.
G: 고마워. 연락할게.

해석

Review 1

G: I'll _____ _____ _____ _____ for you.

B: I'm sorry, but _____ _____ _____ _____ _____ _____?

G: I said, "I'll _____ _____ _____ _____ for you." It means "I _____ _____ _____ _____."

G: 너를 위해 내 손가락을 교차할게.
B: 미안하지만 다시 한 번 말해 줄래?
G: "너를 위해 내 손가락을 교차할게." 라고 했어. 그것은 "행운을 빌게."라 는 뜻이야.

Review 2

W: I _____ _____ _____ _____.

M: Excuse me, but _____ _____ _____ _____ _____?

W: I said, "I _____ _____ _____ _____ _____."

M: _____ _____ _____ _____?

W: It means "I _____ _____ _____." I think I have a cold.

M: Oh. _____ _____ _____ _____ some medicine? You can get medicine at the store over there.

W: OK, I _____.

W: 저는 날씨 아래에 있는 기분이에요.
M: 죄송한데, 다시 한 번 말해 주시겠어 요?
W: "저는 날씨 아래에 있는 기분이에 요."라고 말했어요.
M: 그게 무슨 뜻인가요?
W: 그것은 "몸이 좋지 않다."라는 뜻이 에요. 감기에 걸린 것 같아요.
M: 오. 약을 좀 사는 게 어때요? 저기에 있는 가게에서 약을 살 수 있어요.
W: 네, 그럴게요.

Review 3

M: Look. It's raining _____ _____ _____.

W: _____ _____ _____ _____ _____ _____?

M: It's raining _____ _____ _____.

W: _____ _____ _____ _____ _____?

M: It means "It's raining _____ _____."

M: 봐요. 고양이와 개처럼 비가 내리네 요.
W: 다시 한 번 말해 주시겠어요?
M: 고양이와 개처럼 비가 내려요.
W: 그게 무슨 뜻인가요?
M: 그것은 "비가 아주 많이 내린다."라 는 뜻이에요.

Review 4

G: This pizza _____ _____ _____, Suho.

B: _____ _____ _____ _____ _____?

G: It means "I'll _____ _____ the pizza."

G: 수호야, 이 피자는 내 위에 있어.
B: 그게 무슨 뜻이니?
G: 그것은 "피자는 내가 살게."라는 뜻 이야.

01 다음 빈칸 (A)에 알맞은 문장을 쓰시오.

> M: Look. _____ (A)
>
> W: Can you say that again?
>
> M: _____ (A)
>
> W: What does that mean?
>
> M: It means "It's raining a lot."

➡ _____

02 다음 밑줄 친 우리말에 해당하는 영어 문장을 고르시오.

> G: Look. It's raining cats and dogs.
>
> B: Raining cats and dogs? 그게 무슨 뜻이니?
>
> G: It means "It's raining a lot."
>
> B: Oh. Don't worry. I have an umbrella in my backpack.

① Can you say that again?   ② Is it on me?
③ Do you feel under the weather?   ④ What does that mean?
⑤ Are you pulling my leg?

03 다음 대화의 빈칸에 들어갈 말로 어색한 것은?

> G: This juice is on me, Suho.
>
> B: Excuse me? Can you say that again?
>
> G: I said, "This juice is on me." It means "I'll pay for the juice."
>
> B: Oh. Thanks a lot.
>
> G: _____

① You're welcome.   ② Don't mention it.
③ That's alright.   ④ My pleasure.
⑤ Not at all.

04 다음 밑줄 친 우리말을 주어진 단어를 이용해 영작하시오.

> A: You look tired today.
>
> B: 다시 한 번 말해 줄래? (say, can, that, 5 단어)

➡ _____

중요
01 다음 중 짝지어진 대화가 <u>어색한</u> 것은?

① A: I'll keep my fingers crossed for you.
   B: I'm sorry, but can you please say that again?
② A: What does that mean?
   B: It means "It's raining a lot."
③ A: Excuse me, but can you please say that again?
   B: I said, "I feel under the weather."
④ A: What does that mean?
   B: I said, "It's raining cats and dogs."
⑤ A: Have a nice trip.
   B: Thanks. I'll keep in touch.

[02~05] 다음 대화를 읽고 물음에 답하시오.

B: Everything looks delicious.
G: Yes. Would you like some of my spaghetti?
B: _____(A)_____ Spaghetti is not my cup of tea.
G: Not your cup of tea? (a)그게 무슨 뜻이니?
B: It means "_____(B)_____"
G: Oh, I see. You don't like spaghetti.

02 빈칸 (A)에 알맞은 말을 고르시오.

① Why not?
② No, thanks.
③ I had enough.
④ Thanks a lot.
⑤ You're welcome.

서답형
03 위 대화의 빈칸 (B)에 들어갈 말로 알맞을 쓰시오.

➡ _____

서답형
04 밑줄 친 (a)의 우리말에 맞게 that을 이용하여 영작하시오.

➡ _____

중요
05 위 대화의 내용과 일치하는 것은?

① The girl and the boy meet for the first time.
② The boy is having spaghetti.
③ The boy likes spaghetti a lot.
④ The girl knows the meaning of 'not my cup of tea.'
⑤ The girl understands what the boy means.

[06~07] 다음 대화를 읽고 물음에 답하시오.

A: Don't make a long face.
B: _____(A)_____
A: I said, "Don't make a long face."
B: What does that mean?
A: It means "_____(B)_____"

06 위 대화의 빈칸 (A)에 들어갈 말로 알맞은 것은?

① I want to make a long face.
② I don't want to make a long face.
③ Do I make a long face?
④ Do you want me to make a long face?
⑤ Excuse me, but can you please say that again?

서답형
07 위 대화의 빈칸 (B)에 들어갈 알맞은 말을 쓰시오. (3 words)

➡ _____

08 주어진 문장 사이에 대화가 자연스럽게 연결되도록 (A)~(D)를 순서대로 적절하게 배열한 것은?

> W: I feel under the weather.
> M: Excuse me, but can you please say that again?
> (A) It means "I don't feel well." I think I have a cold.
> (B) What does that mean?
> (C) I said, "I feel under the weather."
> (D) Oh. Why don't you buy some medicine? You can get medicine at the store over there.
> W: OK, I will.

① (B) – (A) – (C) – (D)
② (B) – (C) – (A) – (D)
③ (C) – (B) – (A) – (D)
④ (C) – (B) – (D) – (A)
⑤ (C) – (D) – (B) – (A)

[09~12] 다음 대화를 읽고 물음에 답하시오.

G: Thank you for everything, Jiho. I had a great time in Korea.
B: _____(A)_____ Please come visit me again, Lucy.
G: I'd love to, but before I do, I'd like to invite you to visit me in London.
B: Thanks. Anyway, it's too bad that you can't come to my soccer game tomorrow.
G: I'm sorry that I can't stay longer. I'll keep my fingers crossed for you.
B: Excuse me, but _____(B)_____? (can, please, that)
G: I said, "I'll keep my fingers crossed for you." It means "(a)행운을 빌게.(wish, good)"
B: Oh. Thanks. Have a nice trip.
G: Thanks. _____(C)_____

09 위 대화의 빈칸 (A)에 알맞지 <u>않은</u> 말은?

① You're welcome.
② Don't mention it.
③ My pleasure.
④ You can say that again.
⑤ Not at all.

서답형

10 위 대화의 빈칸 (B)에 알맞은 말을 주어진 어휘를 이용하여 쓰시오.

➡ _____

11 위 대화의 빈칸 (C)에 가장 알맞은 말은?

① Welcome!
② I'll keep in touch.
③ Would you like anything else?
④ Don't feel under the weather.
⑤ You can come again.

서답형

12 위 대화의 밑줄 친 우리말 (a)에 맞게 주어진 어휘를 이용하여 5단어로 쓰시오.

➡ _____

13 다음 대화의 밑줄 친 부분의 의도로 알맞은 것은?

> G: I'll keep my fingers crossed for you.
> B: <u>I'm sorry, but can you please say that again?</u>
> G: I said, "I'll keep my fingers crossed for you." It means "I wish you good luck."

① 희망 표현하기   ② 경험 묻기
③ 경험 답하기   ④ 설명 요청하기
⑤ 다시 말해 달라고 요청하기

[01~03] 다음 대화를 읽고 물음에 답하시오.

G: Thank you for everything, Jiho. I had a great time in Korea.

B: My pleasure. (a)다음에 또 와줘(please, me, visit), Lucy.

G: I'd love to, but before I do, I'd like to invite you to visit me in London.

B: Thanks. Anyway, it's too bad that you can't come to my soccer game tomorrow.

(A) Oh. Thanks. Have a nice trip.

(B) Excuse me, but can you please say that again?

(C) I said, "I'll keep my fingers crossed for you." It means "I wish you good luck."

(D) I'm sorry that I can't stay longer. I'll keep my fingers crossed for you.

G: Thanks. I'll keep in touch.

01 위 대화의 (A)~(D)를 알맞은 순서로 배열하시오.

➡ _____

02 괄호 안에 주어진 어휘를 이용하여 밑줄 친 우리말 (a)에 맞게 5 단어로 쓰시오.

➡ _____

03 Why can't Lucy go to Jiho's soccer game tomorrow? Use the phrase 'It's because'.

➡ _____
_____

[04~06] 다음 대화를 읽고 물음에 답하시오.

G: I feel under the weather.

B: Excuse me, but can you please say that again?

G: I said, "I feel under the weather." It means "_____(A)_____" I think I have a cold.

B: Oh. Why don't you buy some medicine before you get on the plane? You can get medicine at the store over there.

G: I guess I should.

04 위 대화의 빈칸 (A)에 알맞은 말을 쓰시오. (well을 포함해서 4 단어)

➡ _____

05 Why does the girl feel under the weather?

➡ _____

06 Where do you guess they are now?

➡ _____

[07~08] 다음 대화를 읽고 물음에 답하시오.

G: _____(A)_____, Suho.

B: What does that mean?

G: It means "I'll pay ___(B)___ the pizza."

07 위 대화의 빈칸 (A)에 알맞은 말을 5 단어로 쓰시오.

➡ _____

08 위 대화의 빈칸 (B)에 알맞은 전치사를 쓰시오.

➡ _____

Grammar

1 '계속적 용법'의 관계대명사 which / who

• This book is about King Sejong, **who** invented Hangeul.
이 책은 세종대왕에 관한 것이고, 그는 한글을 창제했다.

■ 계속적 용법은, 형태상으로 콤마(,)를 쓰며, 관계대명사가 받는 '선행사의 범위'가 다르다.

• I want to see *the Mona Lisa* **which** Leonardo da Vinci painted. – 콤마(×),
다빈치가 그린 모나리자를 보고 싶다.(다른 사람이 그린 모나리자도 있을 수 있음) → 제한적 용법

• I want to see *the Mona Lisa*, **which** Leonardo da Vinci painted. – 콤마(○),
모나리자라는 작품을 보고 싶고(유일한 작품), 그것을 다빈치가 그렸다. → 계속적 용법

■ 계속적 용법의 관계대명사는 '접속사+대명사'로 전환 가능하다. (and, but, for, though 등)

• She bought a laptop, **which** was broken.

= She bought a laptop, **but it** was broken. 그녀는 노트북 한 대를 구매했지만, 그것은 고장 났다.

cf. She bought a laptop **which** was broken. 제한적 – 그녀는 고장 난 노트북 한 대를 구매했다.

• The Louvre has thousands of works of art, most of **which** were stolen.

= The Louvre has thousands of works of art, and most of them were stolen.
Louvre 박물관은 수천 점의 예술 작품이 있는데, 그것들 대부분은 훔친 것이다.

■ 선행사는 앞에 나온 명사, 대명사 뿐만 아니라, 구, 절, 앞 문장 전체 등이 모두 가능하다.

• Some animals can use tools, **which** I feel amazed at.

= Some animals can use tools, and I feel amazed at that. 어떤 동물들은 도구를 사용할 수 있고, 나는 그것을 놀랍다고 느낀다. → 선행사는 앞 문장 전체(어떤 동물들이 도구를 사용할 수 있다는 것)이며, '접속사 and와 대명사 it/that'으로 받을 수 있다.

• It is good for the young not to give up their dream, **which** a few think to be natural.

= It is good for the young not to give up their dream, though a few think it to be natural.
청년들이 자신들의 꿈을 포기하지 않는 것은 좋은 일이다. 비록 몇몇 소수는 그것[꿈을 포기하는 것]을 당연하다고 생각하지만. → 선행사는 준동사구(to give up their dream)이며, 문맥상 '접속사 though와 대명사 it'으로 받을 수 있다.

■ that, what은 계속적 용법으로 쓸 수 없고, '전치사+관계대명사'는 관계부사로 바꿀 수 있다.

• They bought the farm, **which** goats lived in. 그들은 그 농장을 구매했는데, 염소들이 그곳에서 살았다.

= They bought the farm, **in which** goats lived. (= , where)

핵심 Check

1. 다음 괄호 안에서 알맞은 단어를 고르시오.

(1) I visited the British Museum, (that / which) is in London.

(2) Chris only blames his colleagues, (which / who) makes his boss angry.

2 It is[was] ~ that 주어+동사 (가주어 it – 진주어 that 절)

- **It** is interesting **that** the idea of using the word *robot* didn't come from Karel Capek himself. robot이라는 단어를 사용하려는 생각이 Karel Capek 자신에게서 나오지 않은 것은 흥미롭다.

- **It** is true **that** he was the first president of the club.
  그가 그 클럽의 첫 번째 회장이었다는 것은 사실이다.

- 접속사 that이 명사절로서 문장의 주어 역할을 할 때, 이렇게 절로 표현된 긴 주어 부분을 뒤로 보내 짧은 형식상 주어로 대체하는 것을 가주어 It이라 부르며, 뒤로 보내진 that 명사절을 진주어라고 한다. 'It+be동사+[형용사/명사]+that+완전한 절'의 형태를 취한다.

  - **It** is interesting **that** some animals can use tools. 어떤 동물들이 도구를 쓸 수 있다는 것은 흥미롭다.
  - **It** was shocking **that** he lost the race. 그가 경주에서 졌다는 것은 충격적이었다.

- 목적절로 쓰인 that절을 수동태로 바꿀 때에도, 가주어–진주어 형식으로 표현한다.

  - People believe **that** Koreans are very diligent. 사람들은 한국인들이 매우 근면하다고 생각한다.

    → **It is believed that** Koreans are very diligent. 이 경우 that절 안의 주어를 앞으로 보내서 문장 전체의 주어로 변환시키면 to부정사를 활용해서 단문으로 표현 가능하다.

    → Koreans **are believed to be** very diligent.

- to부정사(구) 또는 의문사절도 진주어가 될 수 있다. 동명사(구)는 흔하지 않지만, 쓸 때도 있다.

  - **It** is good for you **to exercise every day**. 당신이 매일 운동하는 것은 좋다.
  - **It** is a mystery **why he left us**. 왜 그가 우리를 떠났는지는 미스테리이다.
  - **It** is no use **crying over spilt coke**. 엎질러진 콜라를 보며 우는 것은 소용 없다.

- It ~ that 강조구문과 가주어–진주어 구문은 구조로 쉽게 구분할 수 있다.

  - It ~ that 사이에 부사(구/절)이 쓰이면, 무조건 강조구문이다.
  - 강조구문에서는 It ~ that 사이에 주로 명사 또는 부사(구/절)이 쓰이고, 가주어–진주어 구문에서는 It ~ that 사이에 주로 형용사/분사 그리고 일부 명사가 쓰인다.
  - 강조구문에서 It ~ that 사이에 명사가 쓰이면, that절 뒤는 불완전한데, 가주어–진주어 구문에서는 언제나 접속사 that 뒤가 완전한 절이다.
  - 강조구문의 that은 강조 대상에 따라 who, which 등으로 대체 가능하지만, 가주어–진주어 구문의 접속사 that은 다른 단어로 대체 불가능하다.

핵심 Check

2. 다음 괄호 안에서 알맞은 단어를 고르시오.

(1) It is true (if / that) some birds can't fly.

(2) It is thought (that / when) Mom fell in love with Daddy 20 years ago.

Grammar 시험대비 기본평가

Step2

01 다음 문장에서 어법상 어색한 단어를 한 개씩만 찾아 고치시오.

(1) He suggested *roboti*, that means "slave workers" in Czech.

_____ ➡ _____

(2) British traders experienced a bath in India, which they introduced it to Britain in the 18th century.

_____ ➡ _____ , _____ ➡ _____

(3) Huracán is one of the gods in Maya, which created humans.

_____ ➡ _____

(4) This is Gimchi, and which is a traditional Korean food.

_____ ➡ _____ , _____ ➡ _____

02 다음 중 밑줄 친 단어의 쓰임이 다른 하나는?

① It is interesting <u>that</u> many birds can use tools.
② It was strange <u>that</u> the man was waiting for the boss.
③ It is worth reading <u>that</u> book written by Arthur Conan Doyle.
④ It was shocking <u>that</u> Mike wrote that musical at 12.
⑤ It is not surprising <u>that</u> she spent all of her money.

03 다음 빈칸에 들어갈 말로 알맞은 것은?

This is *Sunflowers*, _____ Vincent van Gogh painted.

① and   ② which   ③ that
④ who   ⑤ what

04 다음 밑줄 친 that절을 진주어로 하는, 수동태로 바꿔 다시 쓰시오.

People think <u>that the origin of the first hamburger is not clear.</u>

➡ _____

01 다음 중 어법상 어색한 것을 모두 골라 기호를 쓰고 알맞게 고치시오.

> ⓐ I want to visit the Louvre, which have about four hundred thousand works of art.
> ⓑ She read about the origin of the word of *shampoo*, who means "pressing something".
> ⓒ A cook in Texas placed a Hamburg-style cheese between two slices of bread, which people started to call such food a hamburger.
> ⓓ The flood destroyed the village, which was shocking to people there.
> ⓔ The play *R.U.R* was written by a Czech writer, which was not a famous author then.

➡ _____

_____

02 다음 중 밑줄 친 부분의 쓰임이 나머지와 다른 것은?

① It is interesting <u>that</u> he originally called the machines *labori*.
② It is Sophia <u>that</u> made such a bad decision.
③ It was true <u>that</u> he was not creative.
④ It is clear <u>that</u> they are still alive.
⑤ It was a mistake <u>that</u> he pushed me.

서답형
03 다음 대화의 문맥에 맞게 가주어-진주어와 괄호 속 단어를 사용하여 영작하시오. (현재시제로 9 단어로 쓸 것.)

> Sam: Did Mat cheat on the exam?
> Jonathan: Yes, _____. (true)

➡ _____

04 다음 중 어법상 어색한 문장은?

① I don't know where my review is, which I put in the drawer yesterday.
② Yewon helped the old man carry the baggage, who had trouble walking fast.
③ The little girl was playing the piano enthusiastically, which was so moving.
④ Robert had his laptop fixed by the mechanic, who cost him 200 dollars.
⑤ There was a car accident, which killed three people.

05 다음 우리말과 의미가 같도록 주어진 단어를 배열할 때 여섯 번째로 오는 것은?

> robot이라는 단어를 사용하려는 생각이 작가 자신에게서 나온 게 아니었다는 것이 흥미롭다.
> (the idea of, interesting, didn't come, using, it is, that, the word *robot*, himself, from the author).

① the word *robot* ② using
③ the idea of ④ didn't come
⑤ that

[06~07] 다음 중 'that'의 쓰임이 나머지 넷과 다른 것은?

06 ① It is clear <u>that</u> Sejong invented Hangeul.
② It was strange <u>that</u> the police were waiting for her.
③ It is mysterious <u>that</u> Susan doesn't remember me.
④ It was certain <u>that</u> Mary fell in love with the professor at a glance.
⑤ It was a dress <u>that</u> her aunt made Kathy for the Academy Awards.

07

① It was half an hour ago that the train left for Daegu.

② It was at Thomas' house that the party was held.

③ It is playing the cello that Phoebe often enjoys after her dinner.

④ It is surprising to her that her son got promoted to the CEO of the company.

⑤ It was Comet Halley that crossed the night sky yesterday.

서답형

08 다음 우리말을 〈조건〉에 맞게 영작하시오.

> 내 친구들은 Jasmine을 아는데, 그녀에 의해 풀리지 않는 수학 문제들은 없다.

├── 조건 ───
1. can't, math problems, no, solved를 활용할 것.
2. 계속적 용법의 관계대명사 who와 제한적 용법의 관계대명사 that을 반드시 사용할 것.
3. 수동태 표현을 반드시 사용하여 총 13단어로 영작할 것.

➡ _____

_____

09 다음 중 어법상 어색한 문장은?

① People called the food Sandwich, which was named after the Earl Sandwich.

② She said, "I'll keep my fingers crossed", which means "good luck."

③ King Sejong created Hangeul, which is one of the most scientific writing systems.

④ Chris loves Japchae, which is a healthy and tasty Korean food.

⑤ Sunny was born in 1988, which the Olymic games were held in Seoul.

10 다음 문장의 빈칸 (A)~(C)에 들어갈 말로 가장 적절한 것은?

> • The volunteers visited a girl in Buenos Aires, ___(A)___ grew up to be a world famous actress this year.
> • The computer had a button, ___(B)___ let it save electricity when not in use.
> • That was 1517, ___(C)___ the first Spanish contact with the Mayan civilization occurred.

	(A)	(B)	(C)
①	which	which	which
②	who	that	when
③	which	that	which
④	who	who	which
⑤	who	which	when

서답형

11 다음 주어진 문장의 진주어를 that절로 전환하여 같은 의미의 문장으로 바꾸시오.

> It is important for them to learn many words of foreign origin.

➡ _____

_____

12 다음 중 어법상 옳은 문장은?

① It snowed heavily yesterday, that made Brian stay all day long.

② The novels, which Kate borrowed from a neighbor, were so interesting.

③ The writer passed away this morning, who was shocking to me.

④ There was a figure on his desk, of which was made of plastic.

⑤ Koro is a Japanese actor, who often come to Seoul to eat *Bulgogi*.

13 다음 주어진 단어를 모두 배열하여 대화를 완성하시오. (단, 계속적 용법의 관계대명사를 반드시 추가할 것.)

> Becky: I heard that you're traveling to England. Where would you like to go and where is it?
>
> Shanon: _____
>
> (visit, to, in, want, the British Museum, I, is, London)

➡ _____

14 다음 중 밑줄 친 that을 다른 단어로 대체하여 바꿔 쓸 수 있는 문장은?

① It was a mistake that he left his bag at the subway.
② It is no wonder that the clerk was fired for being rude to anyone.
③ It was shocking that the AI machine composed such a great music.
④ It was at the cafeteria that my uncle made pizza for 5 years.
⑤ It is a good luck that I know the man offering me the job opportunity.

15 다음 중 어법상 올바른 문장의 개수는?

> ⓐ Maria saw the kids singing on the street, that made her join them.
> ⓑ Nolan told his brother to wash his shirt, which were dirty with paint marks.
> ⓒ It was surprising which his girlfriend took Michael to the CEO's office.

> ⓓ The young student helped the hurt dog to cross the street, who was so impressive.
> ⓔ Bob met the man living upstairs, and who was the one making a huge noise last night.
> ⓕ It was impossible that all the prisoners escaped from the jail overnight.

① 1개 ② 2개 ③ 3개 ④ 4개 ⑤ 5개

16 다음 우리말에 맞게 괄호 안의 단어를 배열하시오. (단, 괄호에 없는, 필요한 두 단어는 직접 써 넣으시오.)

> 그 피자가 Jane에 의해 만들어졌다는 것은 놀라운데, Jane은 이제 겨우 7살이다.
> (the pizza, is only, surprising, by, was made, it is, 7, Jane / 추가 단어 포함 총 14 단어)

➡ _____

_____

17 다음 중 어법상 어색한 문장을 고르면? (3개)

① I read a book about Thomas Edison, who was a great inventor.
② Sarah was found alive, that made all of us relieved.
③ Yulgok was proud of his mother, which was good at writing and painting.
④ It is true that the doctor devoted her life to helping poor people.
⑤ It was impressive that Chris made at the convention.

01 다음 영화의 장면과 그 내용을 설명하는 글을 읽고, 괄호 안에 주어진 단어들을 알맞게 배열하여 요약문을 완성하시오.

Coco, the great grandmother of Miguel, was too old to remember even the names of her family members. One day, while Miguel was singing the song of her childhood, Coco sang along with it. People were amazed at the scene.
→ It is (anything, can't, along, that, who, remember, an old lady, amazing, sings) with her childhood song.

➡ It is _____

_____ with

her childhood song.

02 다음 문장을 관계대명사의 계속적 용법을 이용하여 한 문장으로 만드시오.

(1) • Mom said, "I feel under the weather."
   • It means "I don't feel well."

   ➡ _____

   _____

(2) • Emma is a coffee trader.
   • She buys and sells coffee.

   ➡ _____

   _____

(3) • I learned the expression, "This is on me."
   • That refers to "I'll pay for this."

   ➡ _____

   _____

03 다음 각 문장에서 어법상 어색한 부분을 찾아 바르게 고치시오.

(1) It's impossible of her to do those things all by herself.

   _____ ➡ _____

(2) It was foolish for him to spend all the money given by winning the lottery.

   _____ ➡ _____

(3) It is surprising what the celebrity is waiting for my sister.

   _____ ➡ _____

(4) It is safe of Kate to fasten the seatbelt when her son drives her car.

   _____ ➡ _____

(5) It is excited that I will move to Jeju island.

   _____ ➡ _____

04 다음 우리말에 맞게 괄호 안의 단어를 활용하여 영작하시오.

비버와 같은 몇몇 동물들이 도구를 사용할 수 있다는 것은 흥미롭다.
(animals, beavers, tools, some, such as, can, interesting 사용, 가주어-진주어 형식, 총 12단어)

➡ _____

_____

05 다음 각 문장에서 어법상 어색한 부분을 한 곳씩 찾아 고치시오.

(1) The police officers don't examine all the suspects, but which is a routine.

➡ _____

(2) A cook placed a Hamburg-style steak between two slices of bread, which people started to call such food a hamburger.

➡ _____

(3) Linda broke her arms practicing the yoga movement, who was very important to her.

➡ _____

(4) King Sejong finished working of inventing Hangeul, that made him so happy.

➡ _____

(5) This is the movie *Avatar*, it was popular around the world.

➡ _____

06 다음 그림을 보고, 우리말에 맞게 괄호 안의 단어를 배열하여 영작하되, 한 단어의 형태만 바꾸시오. (대·소문자와는 무관)

많은 영어 단어들이 다른 여러 민족들로부터 왔다는 것은 사실이다.

(words, is, different, came, true, it, English, that, people, many, from)

➡ _____

_____

07 다음 〈보기〉와 같이 두 문장이 같은 의미가 되도록, '접속사+대명사'는 관계대명사로, 관계대명사는 '접속사+대명사'로 바꿔 문장을 다시 쓰시오.

┤ 보기 ├

There are many English words about music and they come from Italia.

→ There are many English words about music, which come from Italia.

(1) Robot comes from *roboti* and it means 'slave workers' in Czech.

➡ _____

(2) Most people in the temple stop working every three hours, and they pray to their god.

➡ _____

(3) Hamburger comes from Hamburg and it is the second-largest city in Germany.

➡ _____

(4) Amy uses shampoo every day to wash her dog, but he doesn't like it.

➡ _____

(5) Wendy received a massage from her aunt, which didn't make her feel better.

➡ _____

(6) The castle looked quite modern, which was built in the 8th century.

➡ _____

_____

(7) Maria loves Spanish food, but actually it is not Spanish but Mayan.

➡ _____

Reading

English Words of Foreign Origin

English has often borrowed words from other cultures or languages. Here are some examples with interesting stories.

shampoo

The word *shampoo* comes from the Hindi word *chāmpo*, which means "to press." In India, the word was used for a head massage. British traders in India experienced a bath with a head massage and introduced it to Britain in the 18th century.

The meaning of the word *shampoo* changed a few times after it first entered English around 1762. In the 19th century, *shampoo* got its present meaning of "washing the hair." Shortly after that, the word began to be also used for a special soap for the hair.

robot

The word *robot* comes from the play *R.U.R.*, which was written in 1920 by a Czech writer Karel Čapek. In the play, robots are machines that look like humans. They are designed to work for humans and are produced in a factory.

It is interesting that the idea of using the word *robot* didn't come from Karel Čapek himself. He originally called the machines in his play *labori* from the Latin word for "work." However, his brother suggested *roboti*, which means "slave workers" in Czech. Karel Čapek liked the idea and decided to use the word *roboti*. In 1938, the play was made into a science fiction show on television in Britain.

shampoo 샴푸	
press 누르다	
massage 마사지, 안마	
British 영국인의	
trader 상인, 거래자	
century 세기, 100년	
present 현재의	
soap 비누	
originally 원래, 본래	
suggest 제안하다	
slave 노예	

확인문제

● 다음 문장이 본문의 내용과 일치하면 T, 일치하지 않으면 F를 쓰시오.

1 English has often borrowed words from other cultures or languages. ☐

2 The Hindi word *chāmpo* means "to wash the hair." ☐

3 In India, *chāmpo* was used for a head massage. ☐

4 The word *robot* comes from the movie *R.U.R.* ☐

5 Karel Čapek originally called the machines in his play *labori*. ☐

hurricane

The word *hurricane* comes from the Spanish word *huracán*, which originates from the name of a Mayan god. In the Mayan creation myth, Huracán is the weather god of wind, storm, and fire, and he is one of the three gods who created humans. However, the first humans angered the gods, so Huracán caused a great flood.

The first Spanish contact with the Mayan civilization was in 1517. Spanish explorers who were passing through the Caribbean experienced a hurricane and picked up the word for it from the people in the area. In English, one of the early uses of *hurricane* was in a play by Shakespeare in 1608.

hamburger

The word *hamburger* originally comes from Hamburg, Germany's second-largest city. *Hamburger* means "people or things from Hamburg" in German.

The origin of the first hamburger is not clear. However, it is believed that the hamburger was invented in a small town in Texas, USA, sometime between 1885 and 1904. A cook placed a Hamburg-style steak between two slices of bread, and people started to call such food a hamburger.

hurricane 허리케인
originate from ~에서 비롯되다
Mayan 마야 사람의
flood 홍수
Spanish 스페인의
contact 접촉
civilization 문명
pass through ~을 거쳐 지나가다
pick up ~을 익히게 되다
origin 기원, 유래
slice 얇게 썬 조각, 한 조각

확인문제

● 다음 문장이 본문의 내용과 일치하면 T, 일치하지 <u>않으면</u> F를 쓰시오.

1 The word *hurricane* comes from the Spanish word *huracán*. ☐

2 The Spanish word *huracán* originates from the name of a Spanish god. ☐

3 The first Spanish contact with the Mayan civilization was in 1517. ☐

4 The word *hamburger* originally comes from Hamburg, Germany's third-largest city. ☐

5 *Hamburger* means "people or things from Hamburg" in German. ☐

6 The origin of the first hamburger is clear. ☐

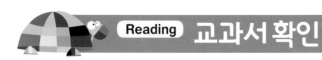

● 우리말을 참고하여 빈칸에 알맞은 말을 쓰시오.

1 **English Words of** _____ _____

2 English has often _____ _____ from _____ _____ or languages.

3 Here are some examples _____ _____ _____.

shampoo

4 The word *shampoo* comes _____ the Hindi word *chāmpo*, which means "_____ _____."

5 In India, the word _____ _____ for a head massage.

6 British traders in India experienced a bath _____ _____ _____ _____ and introduced it to Britain in the 18th century.

7 The meaning of the word *shampoo* changed _____ _____ after it first _____ English around 1762.

8 In the 19th century, *shampoo* got its _____ meaning of "_____ _____ _____."

9 _____ _____ _____, the word began _____ _____ _____ _____ for a special soap for the hair.

robot

10 The word *robot* comes from the play *R.U.R.*, which _____ _____ in 1920 by a Czech writer Karel Čapek.

11 In the play, robots are machines that _____ _____ humans.

12 They _____ _____ to work for humans and _____ _____ in a factory.

13 It is interesting that _____ _____ _____ _____ the word *robot* didn't come from Karel Čapek _____.

14 He originally called the machines in his play *labori* _____ the Latin word _____ "work."

1	외국어에서 유래된 영어 단어
2	영어는 종종 다른 문화나 언어에서 단어를 빌려왔다.
3	여기 재미있는 이야기가 있는 몇 개의 예가 있다.

샴푸

4	*shampoo*라는 단어는 힌디어 *chāmpo*에서 왔고, '누르다'라는 의미이다.
5	인도에서 그 단어는 머리 마사지라는 의미로 쓰였다.
6	인도에 있는 영국 상인들은 머리 마사지를 함께하는 목욕을 경험했고 마사지를 18세기에 영국에 소개했다.
7	*shampoo*라는 단어의 의미는 그 단어가 1762년쯤 영어에 처음으로 들어온 이후 몇 번 바뀌었다.
8	19세기에, *shampoo*는 '머리 감기'라는 현재의 의미를 갖게 되었다.
9	그 후 얼마 지나지 않아, 그 단어는 머리에 사용하는 특별한 비누에도 쓰이기 시작했다.

로봇

10	*robot*이라는 단어는 "*R.U.R.*"에서 왔는데, 그 연극은 1920년 체코의 작가 Karel Čapek에 의해 쓰였다.
11	그 연극에서 로봇은 인간처럼 생긴 기계이다.
12	그들은 인간을 위해 일하도록 설계되고, 공장에서 생산된다.
13	*robot*이라는 단어를 사용하려는 생각이 Karel Čapek 자신에게서 나온 게 아니었다는 것이 흥미롭다.
14	그는 원래 자신의 연극에서 그 기계들을 '일'을 의미하는 라틴어에서 온 *labori*라고 불렀다.

15 _____, his brother suggested *roboti*, which means "slave workers" _____ _____.

16 Karel Čapek liked the idea and decided _____ _____ the word *roboti*.

17 In 1938, the play _____ _____ _____ a science fiction show on television in Britain.

hurricane

18 The word *hurricane* comes from the Spanish word *huracán*, which _____ _____ the name of a Mayan god.

19 In the Mayan _____ _____, Huracán is the weather god of wind, storm, and fire, and he is one of the three _____ who _____ humans.

20 However, the first humans _____ the gods, _____ Huracán _____ a great flood.

21 The first _____ _____ _____ the Mayan civilization was in 1517.

22 Spanish explorers who were _____ _____ the Caribbean experienced a hurricane and _____ _____ the word _____ _____ from the people in the area.

23 _____ _____, one of the early _____ of *hurricane* was in a play _____ Shakespeare in 1608.

hamburger

24 The word *hamburger* _____ comes from Hamburg, Germany's _____ city.

25 *Hamburger* means "people or things from Hamburg" _____ _____.

26 The origin of the first hamburger _____ _____ _____.

27 However, _____ _____ _____ _____ the hamburger was invented in a small town in Texas, USA, sometime _____ 1885 _____ 1904.

28 A cook _____ a _____ steak between _____ _____, and people started to call _____ _____ a hamburger.

15 하지만, 그의 형이 *roboti*를 제안했는데, *roboti*는 체코어로 '노예 근로자들'을 의미한다.

16 Karel Čapek은 그 아이디어가 마음에 들어 *roboti*라는 단어를 사용하기로 결정했다.

17 1938년에 그 연극은 영국 TV에서 공상 과학물로 만들어졌다.

태풍

18 *hurricane*이라는 단어는 스페인어 단어 *huracán*에서 왔고, 그것은 마야 신의 이름에서 유래한다.

19 마야의 창조 신화에서, Huracán은 바람, 폭풍우, 그리고 불에 관한 날씨의 신이며, 그는 인간을 창조한 세 명의 신들 중 한 명이다.

20 하지만, 최초의 인간들이 신들을 화나게 해서 Huracán은 거대한 홍수를 일으켰다.

21 스페인이 마야 문명과 했던 첫 접촉은 1517년이었다.

22 카리브 제도를 지나던 스페인 탐험가들이 허리케인을 겪었고, 그 지역 사람들로부터 그것을 의미하는 단어를 듣게 되었다.

23 영어에서 일찍이 *hurricane*을 사용한 것 중 하나는 1608년 셰익스피어에 의한 희곡에서였다.

햄버거

24 *hamburger*라는 단어는 원래 독일에서 두 번째로 큰 도시인 함부르크에서 왔다.

25 *hamburger*는 독일어로 '함부르크 출신의 사람 또는 사물'을 의미한다.

26 최초의 햄버거의 기원은 분명하지 않다.

27 하지만 햄버거는 1885년에서 1904년 사이의 언젠가 미국 텍사스에 있는 작은 마을에서 발명되었다고 믿어진다.

28 한 요리사가 빵 두 조각 사이에 함부르크 스타일의 스테이크를 넣었고, 사람들은 그런 음식을 햄버거라고 부르기 시작했다.

● 우리말을 참고하여 본문을 영작하시오.

1 외국어에서 유래된 영어 단어

➡ _____

2 영어는 종종 다른 문화나 언어에서 단어를 빌려왔다.

➡ _____

3 여기 재미있는 이야기가 있는 몇 개의 예가 있다.

➡ _____

shampoo 샴푸

4 shampoo라는 단어는 힌디어 *chāmpo*에서 왔고, '누르다'라는 의미이다.

➡ _____

5 인도에서 그 단어는 머리 마사지라는 의미로 쓰였다.

➡ _____

6 인도에 있는 영국 상인들은 머리 마사지를 함께하는 목욕을 경험했고 마사지를 18세기에
영국에 소개했다.

➡ _____

_____

7 *shampoo*라는 단어의 의미는 그 단어가 1762년쯤 영어에 처음으로 들어온 이후 몇 번 바뀌었다.

➡ _____

8 19세기에, *shampoo*는 '머리 감기'라는 현재의 의미를 갖게 되었다.

➡ _____

9 그 후 얼마 지나지 않아, 그 단어는 머리에 사용하는 특별한 비누에도 쓰이기 시작했다.

➡ _____

robot 로봇

10 robot이라는 단어는 "*R.U.R.*"에서 왔는데, 그 연극은 1920년 체코의 작가 Karel Čapek에 의해 쓰였다.

➡ _____

11 그 연극에서 로봇은 인간처럼 생긴 기계이다.

➡ _____

12 그들은 인간을 위해 일하도록 설계되고, 공장에서 생산된다.

➡ _____

13 robot이라는 단어를 사용하려는 생각이 Karel Čapek 자신에게서 나온 게 아니었다는 것이 흥미롭다.

➡ _____

14 그는 원래 자신의 연극에서 그 기계들을 '일'을 의미하는 라틴어에서 온 *labori*라고 불렀다.

➡ _____

15 하지만, 그의 형이 roboti를 제안했는데, *roboti*는 체코어로 '노예 근로자들'을 의미한다.

➡ _____

16 Karel Čapek은 그 아이디어가 마음에 들어 *roboti*라는 단어를 사용하기로 결정했다.

➡ _____

17 1938년에 그 연극은 영국 TV에서 공상 과학물로 만들어졌다.

➡ _____

hurricane 태풍

18 hurricane이라는 단어는 스페인어 단어 *huracán*에서 왔고, 그것은 마야 신의 이름에서 유래한다.

➡ _____

19 마야의 창조 신화에서, Huracán은 바람, 폭풍우, 그리고 불에 관한 날씨의 신이며, 그는 인간을 창조한 세 명의 신들 중 한 명이다.

➡ _____

_____

20 하지만, 최초의 인간들이 신들을 화나게 해서 Huracán은 거대한 홍수를 일으켰다.

➡ _____

21 스페인이 마야 문명과 했던 첫 접촉은 1517년이었다.

➡ _____

22 카리브 제도를 지나던 스페인 탐험가들이 허리케인을 겪었고, 그 지역 사람들로부터 그것을 의미하는 단어를 듣게 되었다.

➡ _____

_____

23 영어에서 일찍이 *hurricane*을 사용한 것 중 하나는 1608년 셰익스피어의 희곡에서였다.

➡ _____

hamburger 햄버거

24 *hamburger*라는 단어는 원래 독일에서 두 번째로 큰 도시인 함부르크에서 왔다.

➡ _____

25 *hamburger*는 독일어로 '함부르크 출신의 사람 또는 사물'을 의미한다.

➡ _____

26 최초의 햄버거의 기원은 분명하지 않다.

➡ _____

27 하지만 햄버거는 1885년에서 1904년 사이의 언젠가 미국 텍사스에 있는 작은 마을에서 발명되었다고 믿어진다.

➡ _____

_____

28 한 요리사가 빵 두 조각 사이에 함부르크 스타일의 스테이크를 넣었고, 사람들은 그런 음식을 햄버거라고 부르기 시작했다.

➡ _____

_____

[01~03] 다음 글을 읽고 물음에 답하시오.

English has often borrowed words from other cultures or languages. Here are some examples with interesting stories.

shampoo

The word *shampoo* comes ____ⓐ____ the Hindi word *chāmpo*, (A)which means "to press." In India, the word was used for a head massage. British traders in India experienced a bath with a head massage and introduced it ____ⓑ____ Britain in the 18th century.

The meaning of the word *shampoo* changed a few times after it first entered English around 1762. In the 19th century, *shampoo* got its present meaning of "washing the hair." Shortly after that, the word began to be also used for a special soap for the hair.

01 위 글의 빈칸 ⓐ와 ⓑ에 들어갈 전치사가 바르게 짝지어진 것은?

	ⓐ	ⓑ		ⓐ	ⓑ
①	for	to	②	from	on
③	in	at	④	for	on
⑤	from	to			

서답형

02 위 글의 밑줄 친 (A)which를 대명사를 포함하여 두 단어로 바꿔 쓰시오.

➡ _____

중요

03 According to the passage, which is NOT true?

① English has many words that it lent to other cultures or languages.

② The word *shampoo* originates in the Hindi word *chāmpo*.

③ In India, the word *chāmpo* was used for a head massage.

④ The word *shampoo* first entered English around 1762.

⑤ Shortly after getting its present meaning of "washing the hair," the word *shampoo* began to be also used for a special soap for the hair.

[04~05] 다음 글을 읽고 물음에 답하시오.

hamburger

The word *hamburger* originally comes from Hamburg, Germany's second-largest city. *Hamburger* means "people or things from Hamburg" in German.

The origin of the first hamburger is not clear. However, it is believed that the hamburger was invented in a small town in Texas, USA, sometime between 1885 and 1904. A cook placed a Hamburg-style steak between two ____ⓐ____ of bread, and people started to call such food a hamburger.

04 위 글의 빈칸 ⓐ에 들어갈 알맞은 말을 고르시오.

① sheets ② lumps ③ bars
④ slices ⑤ pounds

서답형

05 위 글의 내용과 일치하도록 다음 빈칸 (A)와 (B)에 알맞은 단어를 쓰시오.

(A)_____ is the name of Germany's second-largest city and the word (B)_____ means "people or things from (C)_____" in German.

[06~08] 다음 글을 읽고 물음에 답하시오.

robot

The word *robot* comes from the play *R.U.R.*, which was written in 1920 by a Czech writer Karel Čapek. In the play, ⓐ로봇은 인간처럼 생긴 기계이다. They are designed to work for humans and are produced in a factory.

ⓑIt is interesting that the idea of using the word *robot* didn't come from Karel Čapek himself. He originally called the machines in his play *labori* from the Latin word for "work." However, his brother suggested *roboti*, which means "slave workers" in Czech. Karel Čapek liked the idea and decided to use the word *roboti*. In 1938, the play was made into a science fiction show on television in Britain.

서답형

06 위 글의 밑줄 친 ⓐ의 우리말에 맞게 주어진 어휘를 이용하여 7 단어로 영작하시오.

that, like

➡ _____

07 위 글의 밑줄 친 ⓑ와 문법적 쓰임이 같은 것을 고르시오.

① I make it a rule to jog after dinner.
② How's it going with you?
③ It was three weeks later that he heard the news.
④ Look! It's going up that tree.
⑤ It will be difficult for him to come so early.

서답형

08 What were the machines that looked like humans called in the play *R.U.R.*? Answer in English in a full sentence. (4 words)

➡ _____

[09~11] 다음 글을 읽고 물음에 답하시오.

hurricane

The word *hurricane* comes from the Spanish word *huracán*, which originates from the name of a Mayan god. ①In the Mayan creation myth, Huracán is the weather god of wind, storm, and fire, and he is one of the three gods who created humans. ②Every year the hurricane damages many areas near the Caribbean. ③However, the first humans angered the gods, so Huracán caused a great flood.

④The first Spanish contact with the Mayan civilization was in 1517. ⑤Spanish explorers who were passing through the Caribbean experienced a hurricane and picked up the word for it from the people in ⓐthe area. In English, one of the early uses of *hurricane* was in a play by Shakespeare in 1608.

중요

09 위 글의 ①~⑤ 중에서 전체 흐름과 관계 없는 문장은?

①   ②   ③   ④   ⑤

서답형

10 위 글의 내용과 일치하도록 다음 빈칸 (A)와 (B)에 알맞은 단어를 쓰시오.

According to the Mayan creation myth, Huracán, who is the (A)_____ god and one of the three gods who created humans, caused a (B)_____ _____ as the first humans angered the gods.

서답형

11 위 글의 밑줄 친 ⓐthe area가 가리키는 것을 본문에서 찾아 쓰시오.

➡ _____

[12~14] 다음 글을 읽고 물음에 답하시오.

English ⓐhas often borrowed words from other cultures or languages. Here are some examples with interesting stories.

shampoo

The word *shampoo* comes from the Hindi word *chāmpo*, which means "to press." In India, ⓑthe word was used for a head massage. British traders in India experienced a bath with a head massage and introduced it to Britain in the 18th century.

The meaning of the word shampoo changed a few times after it first entered English around 1762. In the 19th century, *shampoo* got its present meaning of "washing the hair." Shortly after that, the word began to be also used for a special soap for the hair.

12 위 글의 밑줄 친 ⓐ와 현재완료의 용법이 같은 것을 모두 고르시오.

① He has gone to Paris.
② Have you ever been to Jeju Island?
③ I have lived in Seoul for 10 years.
④ She has already finished dinner.
⑤ How many times have you seen it?

13 위 글의 밑줄 친 ⓑthe word가 가리키는 것을 본문에서 찾아 쓰시오.

➡ _____

14 위 글의 제목으로 알맞은 것을 고르시오.

① The Influence of Other Cultures or Languages
② Do You Know the Behind Stories of Various Cultures?
③ Let Me Tell You the Interesting Story of the Word *Shampoo*

④ How about a Bath with a Head Massage?
⑤ Wow! This is a Really Special Soap for the Hair!

[15~17] 다음 글을 읽고 물음에 답하시오.

robot

The word *robot* comes from the play *R.U.R.*, which was written in 1920 by a Czech writer Karel Čapek. In the play, robots are machines that look like humans. They are designed to work for humans and are produced in a factory.

It is interesting that the idea (A)of using the word *robot* didn't come from Karel Čapek himself. He originally called the machines in his play *labori* from the Latin word ____ⓐ____ "work." However, his brother suggested *roboti*, which means "slave workers" ____ⓑ____ Czech. Karel Čapek liked the idea and decided to use the word *roboti*. In 1938, the play was made into a science fiction show on television in Britain.

15 위 글의 빈칸 ⓐ와 ⓑ에 들어갈 전치사가 바르게 짝지어진 것은?

	ⓐ	ⓑ		ⓐ	ⓑ
①	in	from	②	for	in
③	for	from	④	in	at
⑤	on	in			

16 위 글의 밑줄 친 (A)of와 문법적 쓰임이 같은 것을 고르시오.

① I didn't know the fact of your meeting him.
② He is a man of ability.
③ Look at the house built of brick.
④ He was robbed of his money on his way home.
⑤ She comes of a good family.

위 글을 읽고 *labori*에 대해 알 수 <u>없는</u> 것을 고르시오.

① Where was the word *labori* used?
② What did the word *labori* indicate?
③ Who used the word *labori*?
④ How long was the word *labori* used?
⑤ What does the word *labori* mean in Latin?

[18~20] 다음 글을 읽고 물음에 답하시오.

hurricane

The word *hurricane* comes from the Spanish word *huracán*, ①which originates from the name of a Mayan god. In the Mayan creation myth, Huracán is the weather god of wind, storm, and fire, and ②he is one of the three gods who created humans. However, the first humans angered ③the gods, (A)[as / so] Huracán caused a great flood.

The first Spanish contact with the Mayan civilization was in 1517. Spanish explorers who (B)[was / were] passing through the Caribbean experienced a hurricane and picked up ④the word for ⑤it from the people in the area. In English, one of the early uses of *hurricane* (C)[was / were] in a play by Shakespeare in 1608.

서답형

18 What's the origin of the Spanish word *huracán*? Answer in English in a full sentence. (7 words)

➡ _____

서답형

19 위 글의 괄호 (A)~(C)에서 문맥이나 어법상 알맞은 낱말을 골라 쓰시오.

➡ (A) _____ (B) _____ (C) _____

20 다음 중 위 글의 밑줄 친 ①~⑤가 가리키는 것에 대한 설명이 옳지 <u>않은</u> 것을 고르시오.

① the Spanish word *huracán*
② a Mayan god Huracán
③ the three gods who created humans
④ *huracán*
⑤ the Caribbean

[21~22] 다음 글을 읽고 물음에 답하시오.

hamburger

The word *hamburger* originally comes from Hamburg, ⓐ<u>독일에서 두 번째로 큰 도시</u>. *Hamburger* means "people or things from Hamburg" in German.

The origin of the first hamburger is not clear. However, it is believed that the hamburger was invented in a small town in Texas, USA, sometime between 1885 and 1904. A cook placed a Hamburg-style steak between two slices of bread, and people started to call such food a hamburger.

서답형

21 위 글의 밑줄 친 ⓐ의 우리말에 맞게 3 단어로 영작하시오.

➡ _____

22 위 글의 주제로 알맞은 것을 고르시오.

① the origin of the word *hamburger* and the first hamburger
② to introduce the place where a hamburger was invented
③ to introduce the time when a hamburger was invented
④ to introduce the creativity of a cook
⑤ the popularity of a hamburger in America

[01~03] 다음 글을 읽고 물음에 답하시오.

hurricane

The word *hurricane* comes from the ⓐ_____ word *huracán*, which originates from the name of a Mayan god. In the Mayan creation myth, Huracán is the weather god of wind, storm, and fire, and he is one of the three gods who created humans. However, the first humans angered the gods, so Huracán caused a great flood.

The first ⓑ_____ contact with the Mayan civilization was in 1517. ⓒ_____ explorers who were passing through the Caribbean experienced a hurricane and picked up the word for it from the people in the area. In English, ⓓ일찍이 *hurricane*을 사용한 것 중 하나는 was in a play by Shakespeare in 1608.

01 위 글의 빈칸 ⓐ~ⓒ에 공통으로 들어갈 Spain의 알맞은 형태를 쓰시오.

➡ _____

02 위 글의 밑줄 친 ⓓ의 우리말에 맞게 주어진 어휘를 이용하여 7 단어로 영작하시오.

early

➡ _____

03 다음 빈칸 (A)~(C)에 알맞은 단어를 넣어 마야어, 스페인어, 영어에서 쓰이는 huracán이라는 단어와 관련된 내용을 완성하시오.

(1) In Mayan: (A)_____, a Mayan god, is the weather god in the Mayan creation myth.

(2) In Spanish: The Spanish word (B)_____ was picked up by Spanish explorers from the people in the Caribbean for the hurricane they experienced while passing through the area.

(3) In English: The word (C)_____ comes from the word *huracán*, and in 1608, the word *hurricane* was used by Shakespeare in his play.

04 다음 글을 읽고 주어진 글의 빈칸 (A)와 (B)에 알맞은 단어를 넣어 햄버거의 발명에 대한 소개를 완성하시오.

hamburger

The word *hamburger* originally comes from Hamburg, Germany's second-largest city. *Hamburger* means "people or things from Hamburg" in German.

The origin of the first hamburger is not clear. However, it is believed that the hamburger was invented in a small town in Texas, USA, sometime between 1885 and 1904. A cook placed a Hamburg-style steak between two slices of bread, and people started to call such food a hamburger.

A cook in a small town in Texas, USA, invented the (A)_____ _____ sometime between 1885 and 1904 by placing a (B)_____ _____ between two slices of bread.

[05~07] 다음 글을 읽고 물음에 답하시오.

English has often (A)[borrowed / lent] words from other cultures or languages. Here are some examples with interesting stories.

shampoo

The word *shampoo* comes from the Hindi word *chāmpo*, which means "to press." In India, the word was used for a head (B)[massage / message]. British traders in India experienced a bath with a head massage and introduced it to Britain in the 18th century.

The meaning of the word *shampoo* changed a few (C)[hours / times] after it first entered English around 1762. In the 19th century, *shampoo* got its present meaning of "washing the hair." Shortly after that, the word began to be also used for a special soap for the hair.

05 위 글의 괄호 (A)~(C)에서 문맥상 알맞은 낱말을 골라 쓰시오.

➡ (A) _____ (B) _____ (C) _____

06 다음 문장에서 위 글의 내용과 다른 부분을 찾아서 고치시오.

> The meaning of the word *shampoo* did not change at all after it first entered English around 1762.

_____ ➡ _____

07 위 글의 내용과 일치하도록 다음 빈칸 (A)와 (B)에 알맞은 단어를 쓰시오.

> The Hindi word *chāmpo* means "(A)_____ _____," and in India, people used the word for a (B)_____ _____.

[08~10] 다음 글을 읽고 물음에 답하시오.

robot

The word *robot* comes from the play *R.U.R.*, ⓐwhich was written in 1920 by a Czech writer Karel Čapek. In the play, robots are machines that look like humans. They are designed to work for humans and are produced in a factory.

It is interesting that ⓑthe idea of using the word *robot* didn't come from Karel Čapek himself. He originally called the machines in his play *labori* from the Latin word for "work." However, his brother suggested *roboti*, which means "slave workers" in Czech. Karel Čapek liked the idea and decided to use the word *roboti*. In 1938, the play was made into a science fiction show on television in Britain.

08 위 글의 밑줄 친 ⓐ를 능동태로 고치시오.

➡ _____

09 위 글의 밑줄 친 ⓑthe idea가 가리키는 것을 본문에서 찾아 쓰시오.

➡ _____

10 다음 빈칸 (A)~(C)에 알맞은 단어를 넣어 *robot*이라는 단어가 생기게 된 과정을 완성하시오.

> (1) In 1920, in the play *R.U.R.*, a Czech writer Karel Čapek called the machines that looked like humans (A)_____.
> (2) Karel's brother suggested using the word (B)_____ instead of *labori*.
> (3) In 1938, the play *R.U.R.* was made into a (C)_____ _____ _____ on television in Britain.

After You Read A

Online Dictionary

English words from other cultures or languages

shampoo: It comes from the Hindi word *chāmpo*, which means "to press."
= originates from = and it

robot: It comes from *roboti*, which means "slave workers" in Czech.
체코어로

hurricane: It comes from Spanish word, *huracán*, which originates from the
that(×) = comes from
name of a Mayan god.
Maya의 형용사

hamburger: It comes from Hamburg, the second-largest city in Germany.
Hamburg와 the second-largest city in Germany는 동격 관계

구문해설 • from: (출처, 기원) ~에서 온 • press: 누르다 • slave: 노예 • hurricane: 허리케인
• Spanish: 스페인의 • originate from: ~에서 비롯되다 • Mayan: 마야 사람의

Around the World

1. Many English words about law come from French. Examples include words
~에서 오다 France의 형용사/언어 ··exclude
like judge and justice.
전치사(= such as)

2. There are many English words about music that come from Italian. For
주격 관계대명사
example, piano and violin come from Italian.
Italy의 형용사/언어

3. Many English words for vegetables come from Spanish. For example,
Spain의 형용사/언어 = for instance
tomato comes from *tomate* and potato comes from *patata* in Spanish.

구문해설 • include: 포함하다 • judge: 판사 • justice: 정의

Think and Write Step 2

The Origin of the Word *Sandwich*

The word *sandwich* comes from John Montagu, who was the 4th Earl of
관계대명사 계속적 용법(= and he)
Sandwich. He enjoyed eating meat between two slices of bread because he
enjoy+동명사 목적어 빵(물질명사)은 slice 등의 단위로 수를 셈
could play a card game while he was eating. People thought that it was a great
(= playing a card game while eating)
idea and began to call such food a sandwich after him.
= began calling 전치사+대명사 목적격

구문해설 • origin: 기원 • earl: 백작 • slice: (얇은) 조각
• call A after B: B의 이름을 따서 A를 부르다

해석

온라인 사전

다른 문화나 언어에서 온 영어 단어들

샴푸: 그것은 힌디어 *chāmpo*에서 왔는데, '누르다'를 의미한다.

로봇: 그것은 *roboti*에서 왔는데, *roboti*는 체코어로 '노예 근로자들'을 의미한다.

허리케인: 그것은 스페인어 *huracán*에서 왔는데, 마야 신의 이름에서 유래된다.

햄버거: 그것은 독일에서 두 번째로 큰 도시인 함부르크에서 왔다.

1. 법에 관한 많은 영어 단어들은 프랑스어에서 왔다. judge(판사)와 justice(정의)와 같은 단어들을 예로 들 수 있다.
2. 이탈리아어에서 온 음악에 관한 많은 영어 단어들이 있다. 예를 들어, piano(피아노)와 violin(바이올린) 등이 있다.
3. 채소에 관한 많은 영어 단어들은 스페인어에서 왔다. 예를 들어, tomato(토마토)는 *tomate*에서 왔고, potato(감자)는 *patata*에서 왔다.

단어 sandwich의 유래

단어 sandwich는 John Montagu에게서 유래했는데, 그는 샌드위치 백작 4세였다. 그는 먹는 동안에 카드 게임을 할 수 있었기 때문에 빵 두 조각 사이에 고기를 끼워서 먹는 것을 즐겼다. 사람들은 그것을 좋은 생각이라고 여겼고, 그의 이름을 따서 그런 음식을 샌드위치라고 부르기 시작했다.

영역별 핵심문제

---

1 〈보기〉의 밑줄 친 어휘와 같은 의미로 쓰이지 <u>않은</u> 것을 고르시오.

┌─ 보기 ─┐

Did you know that the word *tea* <u>originates</u> from Chinese?

① When did the idea <u>originate</u> in your mind?
② Where did this wonderful tradition <u>originate</u>?
③ Yoga <u>originated</u> from India.
④ Many of the sandstorms <u>originate</u> in Mongolia.
⑤ From which country does spam mail <u>originate</u>?

2 다음 대화의 빈칸에 〈영영풀이〉에 해당하는 단어를 쓰시오.

A: This cake is so delicious.
B: I _____ _____ tips from this book and made it.

<영영풀이> to learn a new skill or start a habit without intending to

➡ _____

3 괄호 안에 주어진 어휘를 이용하여 빈칸에 알맞게 쓰시오.

• The _____ directly bought goods from producers. (trade)
• My family _____ comes from Mexico. (origin)

4 다음 영영풀이에 해당하는 단어를 주어진 철자로 시작하여 빈칸에 쓰고, 알맞은 것을 골라 문장을 완성하시오.

• l_____ : a system of rules that a society or government develops in order to deal with crime etc.
• o_____ : the beginning, cause, or source of something

(1) All men are equal in the eye of the _____.
(2) The _____ of the rings of Saturn is still unknown.

5 다음 대화의 빈칸 (A)~(C)에 알맞은 말을 쓰시오.

A: Where are you from?
B: I'm from Vietnam. I'm (A)_____.
C: I'm from France. I'm (B)_____.
D: I'm from Ireland. I'm (C)_____.

[06~07] 다음 대화를 읽고 물음에 답하시오.

B: Everything looks delicious.
(A) It means "I don't like something."
(B) No, thanks. Spaghetti is not my cup of tea.
(C) Not your cup of tea? What does that mean?
(D) Yes. (a)Would you like some of my spaghetti?
G: Oh, I see. You don't like spaghetti.

06 주어진 두 문장 사이에 이어질 대화의 순서로 알맞은 것은?

① (B) – (A) – (C) – (D)
② (C) – (B) – (A) – (D)
③ (C) – (B) – (D) – (A)
④ (D) – (B) – (A) – (C)
⑤ (D) – (B) – (C) – (A)

07 위 대화의 밑줄 친 (a)와 같은 뜻의 문장을 괄호 안에 주어진 어휘를 이용하여 영어로 쓰시오.

➡ _____

(will, have)

➡ _____

(do, want)

08 다음 중 짝지어진 대화가 <u>어색한</u> 것은?

① A: It means "I don't like something."
　 B: Oh, I see. You don't like spaghetti.
② A: I feel under the weather.
　 B: Excuse me, but can you please say that again?
③ A: Oh. Why don't you buy some medicine before you get on the plane? You can get medicine at the store over there.
　 B: I guess you should.
④ A: I said, "Break a leg."
　 B: What does that mean?
⑤ A: Thank you for everything, Jiho. I had a great time in Korea.
　 B: My pleasure. Please come visit me again, Lucy.

[09~10] 다음 대화를 읽고 물음에 답하시오.

G: Look. It's raining cats and dogs.
B: Raining cats and dogs? What does that mean?

G: It means "_____(A)_____"
B: Oh. Don't worry. I have an umbrella in my backpack.

09 위 대화의 빈칸 (A)에 알맞은 말을 쓰시오. (4 words)

➡ _____

10 Why does the boy tell the girl not to worry? (8 words)

➡ _____

[11~13] 다음 대화를 읽고 물음에 답하시오.

G: This juice is on me, Suho. (①)
B: Excuse me? (②) Can you say that again? (③)
G: I said, "This juice is on me." (④)
B: (⑤) Oh. Thanks a lot.
G: You're welcome.

11 ①~⑤ 중 주어진 문장이 들어갈 곳은?

It means "I'll pay for the juice."

①　　　②　　　③　　　④　　　⑤

12 Who will pay for the juice? Answer in English with a full sentence.

➡ _____

13 위 대화의 내용과 일치하는 것은?

① 수호는 'This juice is on me.'의 의미를 알고 있었다.
② 수호는 미안해하고 있다.
③ 수호는 주스를 소녀에게 쏟았다.
④ 그들은 주스를 마셨다.
⑤ 그들은 서로 환영하고 있다.

14 다음 중 어법상 올바른 문장은?

① My grandmother had four sons, that all became businessmen.

② Jenny likes the cell phone what Peter got her from Paris.

③ The one in the middle of the picture is Eddy, which is the most famous scientist in his country.

④ A word derived from a person's name is sandwich, which was the name of the 4th Earl of Sandwich.

⑤ The word *shampoo*, what is commonly used when washing hair, is from the Hindi word *chāmpo*.

15 다음 중 우리말을 영작한 것이 <u>어색한</u> 것을 고르면?

① 누가 최초의 햄버거를 만들었는지는 확실하지 않다.
→ It is not clear that who made the first hamburger.

② 그 단어를 쓰는 아이디어가 작가의 동생으로부터 왔다는 것은 흥미롭다.
→ It is interesting that the idea of using the word came from the author's brother.

③ 그 단어가 마사지를 의미하는 것은 놀랍다.
→ It is amazing that the word means a massage.

④ 영어 단어의 70%가 다른 언어에서 유래했다는 것은 사실이다.
→ It is true that 70 percent of English words come from other languages.

⑤ 내가 그녀를 기다리는 것은 낯설다.
→ It is strange that I'm waiting for her.

[16~17] 주어진 우리말을 알맞게 영작할 때 어법상 옳은 문장을 고르시오.

16
> George는 Sarah가 내게서 빌린 펜과 똑같은 펜을 가지고 있다.

① George has a pen, and it is the same as the one what Sarah borrowed from me.

② George has a pen, which is the same as the one which Sarah borrowed it from me.

③ George has a pen which the same as the one that Sarah borrowed from me.

④ George has a pen, which is the same as what Sarah borrowed from me.

⑤ George has a pen, and which is the same as the one that Sarah borrowed from me.

17
> 그 백작이 포커를 좋아한다는 것은 그의 많은 친구들이 다 알고 있다.

① The earl likes poker, and all of whose many friends know it.

② The earl likes poker, which all of his many friends know it.

③ The earl likes poker, which all of his many friends know.

④ All of his many friends know which the earl likes poker.

⑤ The earl has many friends, all of whom knows he likes poker.

18 다음 중 밑줄 친 that의 쓰임이 나머지와 다른 하나는?

① It was a pizza that my family often ordered through the app.

② It is very strange that Susan forgot my name.

③ It was not surprising that he spent all the money fixing his computer.

④ It is true that he became rich by marrying the girl.

⑤ It is a bad idea that we should throw the garbage away into the river.

19 다음 중 밑줄 친 부분의 쓰임이 〈보기〉와 같지 않은 것은?

┌─ 보기 ┐
Minjoo worked out harder despite her injury, which worsened her health.
└───────┘

① Yewon tried to stay awake during the boring lecture, which didn't work.

② Susan doesn't remember her daughter, which is so strange.

③ Mom ordered beef for me, which was not a usual thing.

④ We saw the crows use tools, which was quite interesting.

⑤ The princess had difficulty choosing which prince she would marry.

20 다음 주어진 세 문장을 관계대명사의 계속적 용법과 제한적 용법을 활용하여, 〈조건〉에 맞게 한 문장으로 표현하시오.

• My father made a family motto.
• The motto would remind us the love between family members.
• The love between family members had never been thought of before.

┌─ 조건 ┐
that과 which를 반드시 사용할 것. 본문에 있는 표현만을 활용할 것. (변형 불가)
└───────┘

➡ _____

_____

_____

21 다음 중 어법상 어색한 문장은?

① Many people lost their houses, which was because of the flood.

② Martha saw the map of Washington, which would be her second home.

③ The Mayan civilization, which is in Central America, was very advanced.

④ He is a tea trader, who buy and sell tea around the world.

⑤ Did you throw away my sandwich, which I brought home four days ago?

▶ **Reading**

[22~24] 다음 글을 읽고 물음에 답하시오.

shampoo

The word *shampoo* comes from the Hindi word *chāmpo*, ①which means "to press." In India, the word ⓐ _____ for a head massage. British traders in India experienced a bath with a head massage and introduced ②it to Britain in the 18th century.

The meaning of the word *shampoo* changed a few times after it first entered English around 1762. In the 19th century, *shampoo* got its present meaning of "washing the hair." ③ Shortly after that, ④the word began ⑤to be also used for a special soap for the hair.

22 위 글의 빈칸 ⓐ에 use를 알맞은 형태로 쓰시오.

➡ _____

23 다음 중 위 글의 밑줄 친 ①~⑤에 대한 설명을 바르게 하지 못한 사람을 고르시오.

① 지연: which는 계속적 용법의 관계대명사이기 때문에 that으로 바꿔 쓸 수 없어.

② 민호: it은 바로 앞에 나온 a bath with a head massage를 가리키는 거야.

③ 규빈: Shortly는 '간단히'라는 뜻이야.

④ 재성: the word는 shampoo를 가리키는 거야.

⑤ 덕수: 그 단어는 머리에 사용하는 특별한 비누에도 쓰이기 시작했다고 해야 하므로 to부정사의 수동태로 쓰는 것이 옳아.

24 위 글의 주제로 알맞은 것을 고르시오.

① the meaning of the word *chāmpo*

② the origin and the meaning of the word *shampoo*

③ the experience of a bath with a head massage in India

④ the explanation of the time when the word *shampoo* entered English

⑤ the research on the special soap for the hair

[25~27] 다음 글을 읽고 물음에 답하시오.

robot

The word *robot* comes from the play *R.U.R.*, which was written in 1920 by a Czech writer Karel Čapek. In the play, robots are machines that look like humans. They are designed to work for humans and are produced in a factory.

It is (A)[interesting / interested] that the idea of using the word *robot* didn't come from Karel Čapek ⓐhimself. He originally called the machines in his play *labori* from the Latin word for "work." However, his brother suggested *roboti*, which means "slave workers" in Czech. Karel Čapek liked the idea and decided (B)[using / to use] the word *roboti*. In 1938, the play was made (C)[by / into] a science fiction show on television in Britain.

25 위 글의 괄호 (A)~(C)에서 어법상 알맞은 낱말을 골라 쓰시오.

➡ (A) _____ (B) _____ (C) _____

26 위 글의 밑줄 친 ⓐhimself와 문법적 쓰임이 같은 것을 고르시오.

① He went there by himself.

② He killed himself.

③ He himself made it.

④ He seated himself on the chair.

⑤ He made it for himself.

27 According to the passage, which is NOT true?

① A Czech writer Karel Čapek wrote the play *R.U.R.* in 1920.

② In the play *R.U.R.*, robots are machines that look like humans.

③ In his play *R.U.R.*, Karel Čapek originally called the machines *labori*.

④ Karel's brother suggested *roboti*, which means "work" in Latin.

⑤ The play *R.U.R.* was made into a science fiction show on television in Britain in 1938.

출제율 95%

01 다음 중 짝지어진 단어의 관계가 나머지와 다른 것은?

① trader – merchant
② include – exclude
③ present – current
④ suggest – propose
⑤ design – devise

출제율 95%

02 다음 중 밑줄 친 부분의 의미로 알맞지 않은 것은?

① He stole a car and is in hot water with the law. (곤경에 처하다)
② My mom made all the things I loved, so I pigged out. (돼지 같이 먹었다)
③ I've heard the course was a piece of cake. (힘든 일)
④ I'll keep my fingers crossed for your new business. (행운을 빌다)
⑤ They do not see eye to eye with each other. (의견을 같이하다)

출제율 90%

03 다음 빈칸에 공통으로 들어갈 알맞은 말을 쓰시오.

• We _____d difficult times because of the flood.
• Hemingway later wrote about his _____ in Italy.

출제율 100%

04 다음 주어진 우리말에 맞게 빈칸을 채우시오. (철자가 주어진 경우 주어진 철자로 시작할 것)

(1) 나는 피자 한 조각을 먹고 싶다.
➡ I would like to have a s_____ of pizza.

(2) Lincoln은 미국의 노예를 해방하는 것을 도왔다.
➡ Lincoln helped set _____ in the US free.

(3) 홍수로 건물들이 파괴되었다.
➡ The _____ destroyed the buildings.

[05~07] 다음 대화를 읽고 물음에 답하시오.

G: I feel under the weather.
B: Excuse me, but can you please say that again?
G: I said, "I feel under the weather." It means "I don't feel well." I think I have a cold.
B: Oh. _____ (A) _____ some medicine before you ___ (B) ___ on the plane? You can ___ (C) ___ medicine at the store over there.
G: I guess I should.

출제율 90%

05 위 대화의 빈칸 (A)에 '사는 게 어때'라는 의미의 말을 쓰시오. (4 단어)

➡ _____

출제율 95%

06 위 대화의 빈칸 (B)와 (C)에 공통으로 들어갈 알맞은 말을 쓰시오.

➡ _____

7 위 대화를 읽고 대답할 수 <u>없는</u> 질문을 고르시오.

① Why does the girl feel under the weather?

② What does the boy ask the girl to say again?

③ What does the boy suggest to the girl?

④ What will the girl do after getting on the plane?

⑤ Where are the boy and the girl now?

[08~09] 다음 대화의 빈칸 (A)에 알맞은 말을 쓰시오.

8

A: I'm in hot water.

B: Can you please say that again?

A: I said, "I'm in hot water."

B: What does that mean?

A: It means "_____(A)_____" (3 words)

➡ _____

9

A: I'm in hot water. We pigged out.

B: Can you please say that again?

A: I said, "We pigged out."

B: What does that mean?

A: It means "_____(A)_____" (4 words)

➡ _____

10 다음 중 어법상 <u>어색한</u> 문장은?

① There are some English words, which originate from other cultures.

② The rabbit provided Alice with some pizza, which made her small.

③ Genie was reading a book about Rome, which she visited last year.

④ Mike had his phone stolen, which his mother bought it for him as a graduation gift.

⑤ This is Makgully, which is a traditional Korean drink.

11 다음 각 문장에 사용된 어법 사항을 〈보기〉에서 골라 기호를 괄호 안에 쓰시오.

┌─ 보기 ─

ⓐ It(가주어) ~ that(진주어) 구문 문장

ⓑ It ~ that 강조 구문 문장

(1) It is Mona Lisa that Leonardo da Vinci painted in 1503. (_____)

(2) Is it possible that Hangeul was invented by the King's warm heart? (_____)

(3) It was by her sacrifice that all the villagers got happy. (_____)

(4) It is wonderful that Peter will get a scholarship. (_____)

(5) It is only when you work hard that you experience the real success. (_____)

12 다음 중 밑줄 친 관계대명사가 가리키는 것으로 바르지 <u>않은</u> 것은?

① The actor remembered the band's title song, <u>which</u> was related to the first love.

(→ the band's title song)

② Maria became the manager of the restaurant, <u>which</u> was her first work place.

(→ the restaurant)

③ They should have taken the subway line 2, <u>which</u> runs through Seoul City.

(→ the subway line 2)

④ Seohyeon is a student at Balsan middle school, <u>which</u> is situated in Ilsan.

(→ Balsan middle school)

⑤ Jim is not afraid of fire, <u>which</u> enabled him to be a fire fighter.

(→ fire)

13 다음 그림을 보고, 우리말에 맞게 괄호 안의 단어를 배열하되, 어법에 맞게 한 단어만 추가하여 영작하시오.

당나귀가 자기의 주인을 속인 것은 어리석었다.
(the donkey, foolish, deceive, was, master, to, its, it)

➡ _____

[14~16] 다음 글을 읽고 물음에 답하시오.

hamburger

The word *hamburger* originally comes from Hamburg, Germany's second-largest city. *Hamburger* means "people or things from Hamburg" in German.

The origin of the first hamburger is not clear. However, it is believed that the hamburger was invented in a small town in Texas, USA, sometime between 1885 and 1904. A cook placed a Hamburg-style steak between two slices of bread, and people started to call ⓐ <u>such food</u> a hamburger.

14 위 글의 밑줄 친 ⓐsuch food가 가리키는 것을 우리말로 쓰시오.

➡ _____

15 According to the passage, which is NOT true?

① The word *hamburger* originally comes from Hamburg.

② Hamburg is Germany's second-largest city.

③ "People or things from Hamburg" can be called *hamburger* in German.

④ The origin of the first hamburger is clear.

⑤ People believe that the hamburger was invented in a small town in Texas, USA, sometime between 1885 and 1904.

16 Why did people start to call a food made by placing a Hamburg-style steak between two slices of bread a hamburger? Fill in the blanks (A) and (B) with suitable words.

It's because *hamburger* means "people or things from (A)_____" in German and this food was made by placing a (B)_____ steak between two slices of bread.

[17~19] 다음 글을 읽고 물음에 답하시오.

robot

The word *robot* comes from the play *R.U.R.*, which was written in 1920 by a Czech writer Karel Čapek. In the play, robots are machines (A)<u>that</u> look like humans. They ___ⓐ___ to work for humans and ___ⓑ___ in a factory.

It is interesting (B)<u>that</u> the idea of using the word robot didn't come from Karel Čapek himself. He originally called the machines in his play *labori* from the Latin word for "work." However, his brother suggested *roboti*, which means "slave workers" in Czech. Karel Čapek liked the idea and decided to use the word *roboti*. In 1938, the play was made into a science fiction show on television in Britain.

17 위 글의 빈칸 ⓐ와 ⓑ에 design과 produce를 각각 알맞은 형태로 쓰시오.

➡ ⓐ _____ ⓑ _____

18 다음 〈보기〉 중에서 위 글의 밑줄 친 (A)that, (B)that과 문법적 쓰임이 같은 것을 각각 고르시오.

┌ 보기 ┐
① She said that she was tired.
② It's the best novel that I've ever read.
③ This is the house that the poet was born in.
④ The trouble is that we are short of money.
⑤ Is this the letter that came yesterday?

➡ (A)that과 같은 것: _____
   (B)that과 같은 것: _____

19 본문의 내용과 일치하도록 다음 빈칸 (A)와 (B)에 알맞은 단어를 쓰시오.

In the play *R.U.R.*, the machines that looked like humans were originally called (A)_____, which was changed into (B)_____.

[20~22] 다음 글을 읽고 물음에 답하시오.

shampoo

The word *shampoo* ⓐcomes from the Hindi word *chāmpo*, which means "to press." (①) British traders in India experienced a bath with a head massage and introduced ⓑit to Britain in the 18th century. (②)

The meaning of the word *shampoo* changed a few times after it first entered English around 1762. (③) In the 19th century, shampoo got its present meaning of "washing the hair." (④) Shortly after that, the word began to be also used for a special soap for the hair. (⑤)

20 위 글의 흐름으로 보아, 주어진 문장이 들어가기에 가장 적절한 곳은?

In India, the word was used for a head massage.

①   ②   ③   ④   ⑤

21 위 글의 밑줄 친 ⓐcomes from과 바꿔 쓸 수 있는 말을 모두 고르시오.

① happens   ② originates in
③ occurs to   ④ comes up with
⑤ originates from

22 위 글의 밑줄 친 ⓑit이 가리키는 것을 본문에서 찾아 쓰시오.

➡ _____ _____

[23~24] 다음 글을 읽고 물음에 답하시오.

The Origin of the Word *Sandwich*

The word *sandwich* comes from John Montagu, who was the 4th Earl of Sandwich. He enjoyed eating meat between two slices of bread because he could play a card game while he was eating. People thought that it was a great idea, and began to call such food a sandwich ⓐ_____ him.

23 위 글의 빈칸 ⓐ에 들어갈 알맞은 전치사를 고르시오.

① to   ② after   ③ for
④ as   ⑤ into

24 위 글의 내용과 일치하도록 다음 빈칸 (A)와 (B)에 알맞은 단어를 쓰시오.

The word *sandwich* comes from the 4th Earl of Sandwich because he enjoyed eating meat (A)_____ _____ _____ _____ _____ in order to play (B)_____ _____ _____ while eating.

[01~03] 다음 대화를 읽고 물음에 답하시오.

G: Thank you for everything, Jiho. I had a great time in Korea.

B: My pleasure. Please come visit me again, Lucy.

G: I'd love to, but before I do, I'd like to invite you to visit me in London.

B: Thanks. Anyway, it's too bad that you can't come to my soccer game tomorrow.

G: I'm sorry that I can't stay longer. I'll keep my fingers crossed for you.

B: _____(A)_____, but can you please say that again?

G: I said, "I'll keep my fingers crossed for you." It means "I wish you good luck."

B: Oh. Thanks. Have a nice trip.

G: Thanks. I'll keep in touch.

01 다음 영영풀이에 해당하는 말을 빈칸 (A)에 쓰시오.

> This is used before you do or say something that might annoy somebody.

➡ _____

02 Where does Lucy invite Jiho?

➡ _____

03 What is Jiho doing at the airport? Use the word, 'off.' (5 words)

➡ _____

04 다음 대화를 읽고, 빈칸에 들어갈 알맞은 말을 괄호 안에 주어진 어휘를 이용하여 쓰시오. (필요할 경우 변형 가능.)

> Jiho: It's too bad that you can't come to my soccer game tomorrow.
>
> Lucy: I'm sorry that I can't stay longer. I'll keep my fingers crossed for you.
>
> Jiho: Wait. Mom, can you please explain that expression to me?
>
> Mom: She said, "I'll keep my fingers crossed for you," _____, Jiho. (you, mean, luck, which, good, wish, she)
>
> Jiho: Oh, thanks, Mom. Thanks, Lucy. Have a nice trip.

➡ _____

05 다음 그림을 보고, 괄호 안에 주어진 단어를 활용하여 밑줄 친 우리말에 맞게 영작하시오. (단, 반드시 가주어-진주어 표현을 써야 함.)

> The origin of the first hamburger is not clear. However, 햄버거는 미국 텍사스에 있는 작은 마을에서 발명되었다고 믿어진다. A cook placed a Hamburg-style steak between two slices of bread, and people started to call such food a hamburger.
> (in a small town / invent / believe / in Texas, USA / that / is / was / 총 15 단어)

➡ _____

shampoo

The word *shampoo* comes from the Hindi word *chāmpo*, which means "to press." In India, the word was used for a head massage. British traders in India experienced a bath with a head massage and introduced it to Britain in the 18th century.

ⓐThe meaning of the word *shampoo* changed a few times after it first entered into English around 1762. In the 19th century, *shampoo* got its present meaning of "washing the hair." Shortly after that, the word began to be also used for a special soap for the hair.

06 위 글의 밑줄 친 ⓐ에서 어법상 틀린 부분을 찾아 고치시오.

_____ ➡ _____

07 In India, what word did people use for a head massage? Fill in the blanks with suitable words.

➡ They used _____ _____ _____ for a head massage.

08 다음 빈칸 (A)~(C)에 알맞은 단어를 넣어 *shampoo*라는 단어가 현재의 의미를 가지게 된 과정을 완성하시오.

> (1) In the 18th century, British traders who experienced a bath with (A)_____ _____ _____(*chāmpo*) in India introduced it to Britain.
>
> (2) In the 19th century, *shampoo* got its present meaning of "(B)_____ _____ _____."
>
> (3) Shortly after that, the word began to be also used for (C)_____ _____ _____ _____ _____.

robot

The word *robot* comes from the play *R.U.R.*, which was written in 1920 by a Czech writer Karel Čapek. In the play, robots are machines that look like humans. They are designed to work for humans and are produced in a factory.

It is interesting that the idea of using the word *robot* didn't come from Karel Čapek himself. He originally called the machines in his play *labori* from the Latin word for "work." However, his brother suggested *roboti*, which means "slave workers" in Czech. Karel Čapek liked the idea and decided to use the word *roboti*. In 1938, the play was made into a science fiction show on television in Britain.

09 다음 문장에서 위 글의 내용과 다른 부분을 찾아서 고치시오. (두 군데)

> In the play *R.U.R.*, Karel Čapek called the machines that looked like humans *roboti*, but his brother suggested calling them *labori*.

➡ _____, _____

10 위 글의 내용과 일치하도록 다음 빈칸 (A)와 (B)에 알맞은 단어를 쓰시오.

> *Labori* means "work" in (A)_____, and *roboti* means "(B)_____ _____" in Czech.

01 (A)와 (B)의 표현을 이용하여 〈보기〉와 같이 다음 대화의 빈칸에 알맞은 말을 쓰시오.

> Do you know what the expression "_____" means?
> It means "_____."

보기

> Do you know what the expression "I feel under the weather" means?
> It means "I don't feel well."
> (A) I feel under the weather. / He hit the ceiling again. / He pulled my leg. / It's a piece of cake.
> (B) feel well / angry again / make fun of / very easy

(1) _____

(2) _____

(3) _____

02 다음 대화를 바탕으로 단어 sandwich의 유래를 설명하는 글을 쓰시오.

> A: Who's that man?
> B: He's John Montagu, the 4th Earl of Sandwich.
> A: What's he eating?
> B: He's eating meat between two slices of bread. I think he's enjoying it.
> A: What a great idea! That way, he can play a card game while he's eating.
> B: Yes. Let's call such food a sandwich after him.

> **The Origin of the Word *Sandwich***
> The word *sandwich* comes from John Montagu, who was (A)_____. He enjoyed eating meat (B)_____ because he could (C)_____ while he was (D)_____. People thought that it was a great idea, and began to call such food (E)_____ after him.

단원별 모의고사

01 다음 짝지어진 단어의 관계가 같도록 빈칸에 알맞은 말을 쓰시오.

> special – general : lend – _____

02 주어진 영어 설명에 맞게 문장의 빈칸에 알맞은 말을 쓰시오.

> The castle was built in the middle of the 8th _____.

> <영어 설명> a period of a hundred years

➡ _____

03 다음 빈칸에 알맞은 말로 짝지어진 것을 고르시오.

> • There is no _____ against loving her.
> • He sent her roses as an _____ of his love.

① rare – invention
② row – creation
③ raw – depression
④ low – impression
⑤ law – expression

[04~05] 다음 영영풀이에 해당하는 어휘를 주어진 철자로 시작하여 쓰시오.

04
> c_____ : to make something happen

05
> p_____ : to push something strongly

06 다음 영영풀이를 참고하여 빈칸에 알맞은 말을 쓰시오.

> a society that is well organized and developed

> The Orient closed the door against to Western _____.

07 다음 빈칸에 알맞은 말이 바르게 짝지어진 것은?

> • I _____ yoga twice a week.
> • I _____ up some useful English expressions from this book.

① do – picked
② make – made
③ get – pressed
④ take – meant
⑤ have – included

[08~10] 다음 대화를 읽고 물음에 답하시오.

G: I feel under the __(A)__ .
B: ⓐI'm sorry, but can you please say that again?
G: I said, "I feel under the __(A)__ ."
B: What does that mean?
G: It means "I don't feel well." I think I ⓑcatch a cold.
B: Oh. Why don't you ⓒpurchase some medicine. You can ⓓdose medicine at the store over there.
G: OK, I ⓔwill.

08 다음 영영풀이에 해당하는 어휘를 빈칸 (A)에 쓰시오.

> the condition of the atmosphere in one area at a particular time

➡ _____

09 밑줄 친 ⓐ~ⓔ 중 어색한 것은?

① ⓐ ② ⓑ ③ ⓒ ④ ⓓ ⑤ ⓔ

10 What does the boy suggest to the girl? (9 words)

➡ _____

[11~13] 다음 대화를 읽고 물음에 답하시오.

G: Thank you for everything, Jiho. I had a great time in Korea.
B: My pleasure. Please come visit me again, Lucy.
G: I'd love to, but before I do, I'd like to invite you to visit me in London.
B: Thanks. Anyway, it's too bad that you can't come to my soccer game tomorrow.
G: I'm sorry that I can't stay longer. I'll keep my fingers crossed for you.
B: Excuse me, but can you please say that again?
G: I said, "I'll keep my fingers crossed for you." It means "I wish you good luck."
B: Oh. Thanks. _____ (A)
G: Thanks. I'll keep in touch.

11 위 대화의 빈칸 (A)에 알맞은 말을 4 단어로 쓰시오.

➡ _____

12 What does Jiho ask Lucy to do? (8 words)

➡ _____

13 What does Lucy ask Jiho to do? (8 words)

➡ _____

14 다음 우리말에 맞게 괄호 안에 주어진 어구를 배열하시오.

(1) 여우는 그 포도들을 먹으려고 애썼지만, 그것들은 너무 높이 있었다.
(the fox, were, which, to eat, tried, too, the grapes, high)

➡ _____
_____

(2) 그 포도들은 여우가 닿기에는 너무 높이 있어서, 여우는 그것들이 맛이 시큼할 거라고 여겼다.
(the grapes, the fox, were, considered, so, sour, high, for, who, them)

➡ _____
_____

15 다음 밑줄 친 부분과 어법상 쓰임이 같은 것은?

Miranda said the pizza was on her, which means she would pay for the pizza.

① Hurricane was named by Spanish explorers, who were passing by the sea.
② The farmers figured out which products they would sell.
③ This is the play in which the word *robot* first showed up.
④ What Jenny eats doesn't bother me but the way in which she eats it annoys me.
⑤ If the accident happened to you, which do you choose to save?

16 다음 내용을 읽고, 질문에 대한 답을 조건에 맞게 영작하시오.

> • I watched *Frozen 2* with my friends.
> • The movie is the second episode of *Frozen*.
> • Taeyeon sang its Korean version OST.
> • As a huge fan of hers, I was surprised with the fact that she joined the movie.

(1) What did I watch and what is it specifically? ('계속적' 용법의 관계대명사 which와 the movie, episode를 반드시 사용할 것, 총 12 단어 - 영화 제목은 1 단어로 취급)

　➡ _____

　_____

(2) What did you think of the fact that Taeyeon sang the OST? (sang, Korean version OST, surprising, its, Taeyeon을 반드시 사용할 것, 가주어-진주어 구문으로 영작할 것, 총 10 단어)

　➡ _____

　_____

17 다음 밑줄 친 부분의 쓰임이 <u>다른</u> 하나를 고르면?

① It is believed <u>that</u> she created them.

② It wasn't true <u>that</u> he was a genius.

③ It seemed <u>that</u> she hated the boss.

④ It was my fault <u>that</u> the baby got burnt.

⑤ It was Peter <u>that</u> cheated on her.

18 다음 우리말을 주어진 어구를 활용하여 조건에 맞게 영작하시오. (어형 변화 가능)

(1) 그 문어 미술가는 손이 많은데, 그것이 한꺼번에 그림을 그리는 데 도움이 된다.

(help, at, the octopus artist, many hands, has, her, once, draw, which 활용, 총 12 단어)

　➡ _____

　_____

(2) 음악 천재들 중 하나가 바로 모차르트인데, 그는 여덟 살에 교향곡을 작곡했다.

(the musical geniuses, the age, one of, is, Mozart, a symphony, eight, at, of, write, who 활용, 총 16 단어)

　➡ _____

　_____

[19~21] 다음 글을 읽고 물음에 답하시오.

shampoo

　The word *shampoo* comes from the Hindi word *chāmpo*, which means "to press." In India, the word was used for a head massage. British traders in India experienced a bath with a head massage and introduced it to Britain in the 18th century.

　The meaning of the word *shampoo* changed a few times after it first entered English ⓐ <u>around</u> 1762. In the 19th century, *shampoo* got its present meaning of "washing the hair." Shortly after that, the word began to be also used for a special soap for the hair.

19 Who introduced a bath with a head massage to Britain in the 18th century? Fill in the blanks with suitable words.

> _____ _____ who experienced a bath with a head massage in India introduced it to Britain in the 18th century.

20 위 글의 밑줄 친 ⓐaround와 같은 의미로 쓰인 것을 고르시오.

① I heard laughter all around.
② Our house is just around the corner.
③ He arrived around five o'clock.
④ We were all running around trying to get ready in time.
⑤ The house was built around a central courtyard.

21 위 글의 내용과 일치하도록 다음 빈칸 (A)와 (B)에 알맞은 단어를 쓰시오.

> The original meaning of the word *shampoo* was "to press," but since the 19th century, it has been used not only for "(A)_____ _____ _____" but also for "(B)_____ _____ _____ for the hair."

[22~23] 다음 글을 읽고 물음에 답하시오.

robot

The word *robot* comes from the play *R.U.R.*, which was written in 1920 by a Czech writer Karel Čapek. (①) In the play, robots are machines that look like humans. (②) They are designed ⓐto work for humans and are produced in a factory. (③) It is interesting that the idea of using the word *robot* didn't come from Karel Čapek himself. (④) However, his brother suggested *roboti*, which means "slave workers" in Czech. (⑤) Karel Čapek liked the idea and decided to use the word *roboti*. In 1938, the play was made into a science fiction show on television in Britain.

22 위 글의 흐름으로 보아, 주어진 문장이 들어가기에 가장 적절한 곳은?

> He originally called the machines in his play *labori* from the Latin word for "work."

①　　　②　　　③　　　④　　　⑤

23 아래 〈보기〉에서 위 글의 밑줄 친 ⓐto work와 to부정사의 용법이 다른 것의 개수를 고르시오.

┌─ 보기 ─┐
① It's possible for robots to work without stopping.
② My hope is to work for Apple Inc.
③ He must be tired to work till late at night.
④ Is it normal to work 60 hours a week?
⑤ I was glad to work with her as a team.

① 1개　② 2개　③ 3개　④ 4개　⑤ 5개

[24~25] 다음 글을 읽고 물음에 답하시오.

hurricane

The word *hurricane* comes from the Spanish word *huracán*, which originates from the name of a Mayan god. In the Mayan creation myth, Huracán is the weather god of wind, storm, and fire, and he is one of the three gods who created humans. However, the first humans angered the gods, so Huracán caused a great flood.

The first Spanish contact with the Mayan civilization was in 1517. Spanish explorers who were passing through the Caribbean experienced a hurricane and picked up the word for it from the people in the area. In English, one of the early uses of *hurricane* was in a play by Shakespeare in 1608.

24 위 글의 제목으로 알맞은 것을 고르시오.

① Have You Heard of the Mayan Creation Myth?
② The Origin of the Word *Hurricane*
③ The Anger of the Three Gods
④ The Spanish Contact with the Mayan Civilization
⑤ The Hurricane in the Caribbean

25 According to the passage, which is NOT true?

① The word *hurricane* originates from the Spanish word *huracán*.
② The Spanish word *huracán* comes from the name of a Mayan god.
③ In the Mayan creation myth, Huracán is the weather god and caused a great earthquake.

④ In 1517, the first Spanish contact with the Mayan civilization was established.
⑤ In English, Shakespeare used the word *hurricane* in his play in 1608.

[26~27] 다음 글을 읽고 물음에 답하시오.

1. Many English words about ⓐlaw come from French. Examples ⓑexclude words like judge and justice.
2. There are many English words about ⓒmusic that come from Italian. For example, piano and violin come from Italian.
3. Many English words for ⓓvegetables come from Spanish. ⓔFor example, tomato comes from *tomate* and potato comes from *patata* in Spanish.

26 위 글의 밑줄 친 ⓐ~ⓔ에서 문맥상 낱말의 쓰임이 적절하지 <u>않은</u> 것을 찾아 알맞게 고치시오.

_____ ➡ _____

27 다음 빈칸에 알맞은 단어를 넣어 위 글에 대한 소개를 완성하시오.

The contents of the text above are about some English words of foreign _____.

[28~29] 다음 글을 읽고 물음에 답하시오.

hurricane

The word *hurricane* comes from the Spanish word *huracán*, which originates from the name of a Mayan god. In the Mayan creation myth, Huracán is the weather god of wind, storm, and fire, and he is one of the three gods who created humans. ___ⓐ___, the first humans angered the gods, so Huracán caused a great flood.

The first Spanish contact with the Mayan civilization was in 1517. Spanish explorers who were passing through the Caribbean experienced a hurricane and picked up the word for it from the people in the area. In English, one of the early uses of *hurricane* was in a play by Shakespeare in 1608.

28 위 글의 빈칸 ⓐ에 들어갈 알맞은 말을 고르시오.

① Moreover   ② However
③ Therefore   ④ For example
⑤ Similarly

29 다음 빈칸 (A)~(C)에 알맞은 단어를 넣어 huracán이라는 단어가 스페인어에 들어오게 된 과정을 완성하시오.

(1) In the (A)_____ creation myth, Huracán, the weather god, caused a great flood as the first humans angered the gods who were their creators.
(2) In 1517, the explorers from Spain experienced (B)_____ _____ while passing through the Caribbean and (C)_____ _____ the word for it from the people in the area.

[30~31] 다음 글을 읽고 물음에 답하시오.

Online ___ⓐ___

English words from other cultures or languages

shampoo: It ⓑ<u>comes from</u> the Hindi word *chāmpo*, which means "to press."

robot: It comes from *roboti*, which means "slave workers" in Czech.

hurricane: It comes from Spanish word, *huracán*, which originates from the name of a Mayan god.

hamburger: It comes from Hamburg, the second-largest city in Germany.

30 위 글의 빈칸 ⓐ에 들어갈 알맞은 단어를 쓰시오.

➡ _____

31 위 글의 밑줄 친 ⓑ<u>comes from</u>과 바꿔 쓸 수 있는 말을 본문에서 찾아 쓰시오.

➡ _____

Lesson

4

Be a Smart Spender

 의사소통 기능

- 교환 요청하기
  I'd like to exchange this bag.

- 환불 요청하기
  I'd like to get a refund for this bag.

 언어 형식

- 현재완료진행형
  I think you**'ve been spending** too much.

- 의문사+to부정사
  I don't know **how to solve** this problem.

Words & Expressions

Key Words

- **advice** [ædváis] 명 충고
- **allowance** [əláuəns] 명 용돈
- **already** [ɔːlrédi] 부 이미, 벌써
- **although** [ɔːlðóu] 접 비록 ~이지만
- **balance** [bǽləns] 명 균형, 통장의 잔액
- **budget** [bʌ́dʒit] 명 예산
- **by** [bai] 전 ~쯤에는, ~가 되었을 때
- **case** [keis] 명 사례, 경우
- **charity** [tʃǽrəti] 명 자선 단체
- **comfortable** [kʌ́mfərtəbl] 형 편안한
- **correct** [kərékt] 동 바로 잡다
- **couch** [kautʃ] 명 소파
- **divide** [diváid] 동 나누다
- **donate** [dóuneit] 동 기부하다
- **effort** [éfərt] 명 노력
- **exchange** [ikstʃéindʒ] 명 교환 동 교환하다
- **gift** [gift] 명 선물
- **however** [hauévər] 부 그러나
- **instead** [instéd] 부 그 대신에
- **item** [áitəm] 명 물품
- **lastly** [lǽstli] 부 마지막으로
- **loose** [luːs] 형 헐렁한, 느슨한
- **majority** [mədʒɔ́ːrəti] 명 대다수
- **manage** [mǽnidʒ] 동 관리하다
- **medicine** [médəsn] 명 의약품
- **native** [néitiv] 명 원주민
- **paper money** 지폐
- **pocket money** 용돈
- **price** [prais] 명 가격, 가치
- **rainy** [réini] 형 비가 내리는
- **receipt** [risíːt] 명 영수증
- **receive** [risíːv] 동 받다
- **recently** [ríːsntli] 부 최근에
- **refund** [rífʌnd] 명 환불 동 환불받다
- **remaining** [riméiniŋ] 형 남아 있는
- **result** [rizʌ́lt] 명 결과
- **return** [ritə́ːrn] 동 반품하다
- **save** [seiv] 동 저축하다, 구하다
- **survey** [sərvéi] 명 설문조사
- **tight** [tait] 형 빠듯한, 꽉 조이는[딱 붙는]
- **weekly** [wíːkli] 형 매주의, 주간의 부 매주
- **while** [hwail] 접 ~하는 동안, ~하는 반면에
- **work** [wəːrk] 동 작동하다
- **worry** [wə́ːri] 명 걱정 동 걱정하다

Key Expressions

- **be gone** 사라지다, 없어지다
- **carry around** 가지고 다니다
- **change one's mind** 마음을 바꾸다
- **for example** 예를 들면
- **get an exchange** 교환받다
- **get a refund** 환불받다
- **go camping** 캠핑하러 가다
- **have difficulty (in) -ing** ~하는 데 어려움을 겪다
- **have money back** 돈을 돌려받다
- **Here you are.** 여기 있습니다.
- **Let's see.** 어디 보자. (무엇인가 생각하면서 하는 말)
- **look for** ~을 찾다
- **make a budget plan** 예산 계획을 세우다
- **on sale** 할인 중인, 판매되는
- **on the spot** 그 자리에서, 현장에서
- **right away** 즉시
- **spending habit** 소비 습관
- **take care of** ~을 돌보다, ~을 처리하다
- **take effort** 노력을 필요로 하다
- **use up** 다 쓰다, 완전히 소모하다
- **would like to** ~하기를 원하다, ~을 좋아하다

Word Power

※ 서로 비슷한 뜻을 가진 어휘

- □ **case** 사례, 경우 : **example** 사례
- □ **paper money** 지폐 : **bill** 지폐
- □ **recently** 최근에 : **lately** 최근에

- □ **lastly** 마지막으로 : **finally** 마지막으로
- □ **pocket money** 용돈 : **allowance** 용돈
- □ **result** 결과 : **outcome** 결과

※ 서로 반대의 뜻을 가진 어휘

- □ **easy** 쉬운 ↔ **difficult** 어려운
- □ **loose** 헐렁한 ↔ **tight** 꽉 조이는[딱 붙는]
- □ **smart** 현명한 ↔ **foolish** 어리석은

- □ **expensive** 값비싼 ↔ **cheap** 값싼
- □ **same** 같은 ↔ **different** 다른
- □ **true** 진실인 ↔ **false** 거짓인

※ 동사 – 명사

- □ **advise** 충고하다 – **advice** 충고
- □ **divide** 나누다 – **division** 나누기

- □ **correct** 바로 잡다 – **correction** 수정
- □ **donate** 기부하다 – **donation** 기부

English Dictionary

- □ **advice** 충고
  - → an opinion you give someone about what they should do 누군가에게 무엇을 해야 할지 말해 주는 의견
- □ **allowance** 용돈
  - → money given by parents to a child regularly that the child can spend 부모에 의해 아이에게 규칙적으로 주어지는 아이가 쓸 수 있는 돈
- □ **balance** 잔액
  - → the amount of money that you have in your bank account 통장에 남아 있는 금액
- □ **budget** 예산
  - → an amount money that a person or company can spend 개인이나 회사가 쓸 수 있는 금액
- □ **charity** 자선 단체
  - → an organization that gives money, goods, or help to people who are poor, sick, etc. 가난하거나 아픈 사람에게 돈, 물품 또는 도움을 주는 단체
- □ **correct** 바로 잡다
  - → to make something right or to make it work the way it should 무엇인가를 제대로 되도록 하거나 원래의 방식대로 작동하게 만들다
- □ **couch** 소파
  - → a comfortable piece of furniture big enough for two or three people to sit on 두, 세 사람이 앉을 만큼 충분히 크고 편안한 가구
- □ **donate** 기부하다
  - → to give money to a group that needs help 도움이 필요한 단체에 돈을 주다
- □ **effort** 노력
  - → hard work that you do when you are trying to achieve something 어떤 것을 이루려고 애쓸 때 하는 힘든 일
- □ **exchange** 교환
  - → the act of giving someone something and receiving something else from them 누군가에게 무엇인가를 주고 그들로부터 다른 어떤 것을 받는 행위
- □ **loose** 느슨한
  - → not firmly fastened in place 단단히 제자리에 고정되어 있지 않은
- □ **majority** 대다수
  - → most of the people or things in a group 한 그룹 내의 대부분의 사람이나 물건
- □ **medicine** 의약품
  - → a substance used for treating illness 질병을 치료하기 위하여 사용되는 물질
- □ **native** 원주민
  - → a person who was born in a particular place 특정한 장소에서 태어난 사람
- □ **receipt** 영수증
  - → a piece of paper that shows you have paid for something 어떤 것의 대가를 지불했음을 보여주는 종이 조각
- □ **refund** 환불
  - → a sum of money which is returned to you 반환되는 돈의 총액
- □ **remaining** 남아 있는
  - → left over after a part has been taken, used, or lost 일부가 제거되거나 사용되거나 분실된 후에 남아 있는

01 다음 짝지어진 단어의 관계가 같도록 빈칸에 알맞은 말은?

> easy – difficult : true – _____

① happy   ② convenient
③ hard   ④ proud
⑤ false

서답형

02 주어진 영어 설명에 맞게 문장의 빈칸에 알맞은 말을 쓰시오.

> Only a small portion of the _____ is spent on books.

> <영어 설명> an amount money that a person or company can spend

➡ _____

03 밑줄 친 부분의 의미로 알맞지 <u>않은</u> 것은?

① He took a look at the car and decided to buy it <u>on the spot</u>. (즉석에서)
② There is no chance that he will <u>change his mind</u>. (결정하다)
③ I have a few things I have to <u>take care of</u>. (처리하다)
④ I'm <u>having difficulties</u> understanding your point about needing to finish the production by this week. (이해하는 데 어려움을 겪다)
⑤ I'm trying to <u>get a refund</u> for this ticket. (환불받다)

04 다음 빈칸에 들어갈 알맞은 말을 고르시오.

> I bought something 20 days ago, but I don't have the _____.

① receipt   ② refund
③ price   ④ couch
⑤ majority

중요

05 다음 〈보기〉의 단어를 사용하여 자연스러운 문장을 만들 수 <u>없는</u> 것은? (대 · 소문자 무시)

> ┤ 보기 ├
> loose   donate   result   refund

① They will announce the _____ of the vote tonight.
② The clerk is going to _____ my money.
③ These pants are a little _____ for me.
④ _____ to preserve the peace have failed.
⑤ He _____d money to the school in Africa.

06 다음 빈칸에 알맞은 말이 바르게 짝지어진 것을 고르시오.

> • The shirts are on _____ at up to 40 percent off.
> • It will _____ time and effort.

① expansion – take
② expansion – need
③ sale – take
④ sale – hide
⑤ increase – need

01 다음 영영풀이에 알맞은 어휘를 〈보기〉에서 찾아 쓰시오.

┌─ 보기 ─┐
majority remaining correct effort
└──────┘

(1) to make something right or to make it work the way it should
(2) hard work that you do when you are trying to achieve something
(3) left over after a part has been taken, used, or lost
(4) most of the people or things in a group

➡ (1) _____ (2) _____ (3) _____
   (4) _____

02 다음 짝지어진 두 단어의 관계가 같도록 빈칸에 알맞은 말을 쓰시오.

(1) same : different = _____ : tight
(2) donate : donation = advise : _____

03 다음 우리말에 맞도록 빈칸에 알맞은 말을 쓰시오. (철자가 주어진 경우 그 철자로 시작할 것.)

(1) 사람들은 해변을 깨끗하게 하기 위해 노력했다.
→ People made an _____ to clean the beach.
(2) 그들은 이번 주에 일정이 빠듯하다.
→ They have a t_____ schedule this week.

(3) 그 가수는 그의 팬들로부터 많은 선물을 받았다.
→ The singer r_____ lots of gifts from his fans.
(4) 나와 우리 가족은 크리스마스에 서로 선물을 교환한다.
→ My family and I _____ presents on Christmas.

04 우리말에 맞게 한 단어를 추가하여 주어진 단어를 알맞게 배열하시오.

(1) Mike는 그의 새로운 카메라를 사용하는 데 어려움이 있다. (Mike, his, camera, difficulty, has, new)
➡ _____
_____

(2) 나는 모자를 사기 위해 용돈을 모았다. (buy, I, saved, my, have, to, a hat)
➡ _____

(3) Justin은 즉석에서 기타 연주를 했다. (Justin, guitar, the, the, played, on)
➡ _____

(4) 인터넷으로 당신의 통장 잔고를 확인하기는 쉽다. (the Internet, is, check, easy, bank, your, balance, on, to)
➡ _____
_____

Conversation

교과서

1 교환 요청하기

- **I'd like to exchange this bag.** 이 가방을 교환하고 싶습니다.

■ 구입한 물건을 교환해야 할 때는 'exchange(교환; 교환하다)'를 사용한다. 자신이 산 물건을 교환해 달라는 말은 'I would like to exchange this.' 또는 'Can I exchange this?', 'I would like to get an exchange.'라고 한다.

■ 교환을 요청할 때는 'I'd like to exchange … for ~.' 또는 'Can I exchange … for ~?'라고 말한다. 교환할 특정 물건이 있는 경우에는 exchange 뒤에 교환하고 싶은 자신의 물건을, for 뒤에 교환 받고 싶은 새로운 특정 물건을 넣어서 말한다.

- A: Can I exchange this bag for that hat? 이 가방을 저 모자로 교환할 수 있나요?
  B: Sure. 물론이죠.

교환 요청하기

- I would like to exchange this. 이것을 교환하고 싶습니다.
- Can I exchange this? 이것을 교환할 수 있나요?
- I would like to get an exchange. 교환하고 싶어요.
- Why don't we get an exchange? 교환하는 것이 어때요?
- I would like to exchange A for B. A를 B로 교환하고 싶어요.
- Can I exchange A for B? A를 B로 교환할 수 있나요?

핵심 Check

1. 다음 대화의 빈칸에 들어갈 말로 알맞은 것을 고르시오.

A: Hello. Are you looking for anything special?

B: No, I'm not. _____ It's too small.

A: Sure. What size would you like?

B: Large, please.

① I would like to buy this T-shirt.
② I hope you would like this T-shirt.
③ Did you sell this T-shirt here?
④ I'd like to exchange this T-shirt.
⑤ Can I get a refund for this T-shirt?

② 환불 요청하기

• **I'd like to get a refund for this bag.** 이 가방을 환불받고 싶습니다.

■ 구입한 물건을 반품하고, 환불을 요청할 때는 보통 'return(반품)'이나 'refund(환불)'를 사용한다. 환불을 위하여 반품을 할 때는 'I would like to return ~.'이라고 한다. 반품하고 물건의 환불을 요청할 때는 'I would like to return this for refund.'라고 한다.

■ 환불을 요청하는 영어 표현은 'I'd like to get a refund for ~.'라고 말하거나 'Can I get a refund for ~?'라고 말할 수 있다. 같은 의미로 'Can I have money back?'이라고 물을 수도 있다. 전액 환불을 강조하는 경우에는 'a full refund'라고 하기도 한다.

• A: I'd like to get a refund for this bag. 이 가방을 환불받고 싶어요.

B: I'm sorry, you can't. 죄송하지만 안 됩니다.

환불 요청하기

• I'd like a refund. 환불을 원합니다.

• I'd like my money back. 돈을 돌려주시기 바랍니다.

• I'd like to get a refund. 환불 받고 싶습니다.

• Can I get a refund for ~? ~에 대해서 환불 받을 수 있을까요?

• Can I have my money back? 돈을 돌려받을 수 있을까요?

• Is it possible to get a refund for ~? ~에 대하여 환불을 받을 수 있습니까?

핵심 Check

2. 다음 우리말 의미와 같도록 주어진 어구를 바르게 배열하여 문장을 완성하시오.

저는 이 가방을 환불받고 싶습니다. (I'd, get, like, a refund, for, this bag, to)

➡ _____

3. 다음 대화의 빈칸에 들어갈 말로 알맞은 것을 고르시오.

A: Hello. May I help you?

B: Yes, please. I'd like to get a refund for this watch.

A: OK. Was there anything wrong with it?

B: _____ Can I get my money back?

A: OK. I'll take care of it right away.

① Yes, it was really interesting.　② Yes, the watch was very good.

③ No, I just changed my mind.　④ No, I want to get the one over there.

⑤ I'd like to exchange this for that one.

Listen and Talk A 1

W: Hello. ❶May I help you?

B: Yes, please. ❷I'd like to get a refund for this watch.

W: OK. Was there ❸anything wrong with it?

B: No, I just changed my mind. Can I ❹get my money back?

W: OK. I'll take care of it right away.

W: 안녕하세요. 무엇을 도와드릴까요?
B: 네. 이 손목시계를 환불받고 싶어서요.
W: 알겠습니다. 시계에 무슨 문제가 있었나요?
B: 아니요. 그냥 마음이 바뀌었어요. 돈을 돌려받을 수 있을까요?
W: 네. 지금 바로 처리해드리겠습니다.

❶ '도와드릴까요?'라는 의미로 상대방에게 도움을 제공하겠다는 뜻을 나타내는 표현이다.
❷ 환불을 요청할 때 쓰는 표현이다.
❸ wrong이 anything을 뒤에서 수식하고 있다.
❹ 'get my money back'은 '돈을 돌려받다'라는 뜻이다.

Check(√) True or False

(1) The boy wants to get a refund for a watch. T ☐ F ☐

(2) Something was wrong with the watch. T ☐ F ☐

Listen and Talk C

M: Hello. May I help you?

G: Yes, please. ❶I'd like to get a refund for this cap.

M: Do you have the receipt?

G: No, I don't. I received ❷it as a gift.

M: If you don't have the receipt, then, ❸it's not possible to get a refund.

G: I see. Then, can I ❹exchange it for something else?

M: Yes, you can. What would you like to get?

G: I want to get this blue bag.

M: ❺Let me see .... The price is the same, so you can just take it.

G: Thank you.

M: 안녕하세요. 도와드릴까요?
G: 네. 이 모자를 환불받고 싶어요.
M: 영수증을 가지고 있나요?
G: 아니요. 선물로 받았어요.
M: 영수증이 없으면, 환불은 가능하지 않아요.
G: 알겠어요. 그럼, 다른 것으로 교환할 수 있나요?
M: 네, 가능해요. 어떤 것을 원하시나요?
G: 이 파란색 가방을 갖고 싶어요.
M: 한번 볼게요…. 가격이 같으니까 그것을 가져가셔도 돼요.
G: 고맙습니다.

❶ 'I'd like to'는 'I want to'와 같은 의미이다. 'get a refund for ~'는 '~에 대해 환불받다'라는 뜻이다.
❷ 'it'은 'this cap'을 가리킨다.
❸ 'it'은 가주어이고 'to get a refund'는 진주어이다.
❹ exchange A for B: A를 B로 바꾸다
❺ 'Let me see'는 '글쎄, 어디 보자' 정도의 뜻으로 무엇인가 생각하면서 하는 말이다.

Check(√) True or False

(3) The girl received the cap as a gift. T ☐ F ☐

(4) The man lets the girl get a refund for the cap. T ☐ F ☐

Listen and Talk A 2

W: Hello. ❶Do you need some help?

B: Yes. ❷I'd like to return this smartphone case.

W: ❸Let's see. Do you have the receipt with you?

B: Here it is. I bought ❹it three days ago.

W: Oh, then ❺it's possible.

W: 안녕하세요. 도움이 필요하신가요?

B: 네. 이 스마트폰 케이스를 환불받고 싶어요.

W: 잠시만요. 영수증을 가지고 계시나요?

B: 여기 있습니다. 3일 전에 구매했어요.

W: 아, 그렇다면 가능합니다.

❶ 'May[Can] I help you?'와 같은 의미이다.
❷ 환불을 요청하는 말로 쓰였으며 return은 '반환하다'라는 의미이다.
❸ 'Let's see.'는 '어디 보자.' 정도의 뜻으로 생각을 하거나 무엇을 기억하려 하면서 하는 말이다.
❹ it은 'the smartphone case'를 가리킨다.
❺ it은 'to return the smartphone case'를 가리킨다.

Check(√) True or False

(5) The boy wants to return the smartphone case. T☐ F☐

(6) The woman says that he cannot return the smartphone case. T☐ F☐

Listen and Talk A 3

W: Hello. ❶Are you looking for anything special?

B: No, ❷I'm not. ❸I'd like to exchange this T-shirt. It's too small.

W: Sure. ❹What size would you like?

B: Large, please.

W: ❺Here you are.

B: Thank you.

W: 안녕하세요. 특별히 찾으시는 것 있으세요?

B: 아니요. 저는 이 티셔츠를 교환하고 싶어서요. 너무 작아요.

W: 네. 어떤 사이즈를 원하세요?

B: Large 사이즈요.

W: 여기 있습니다.

B: 감사합니다.

❶ 보통 점원이 손님을 응대하면서 하는 말이다. anything을 special이 뒤에서 수식하고 있다.
❷ 'Are you ~?'로 물었으므로 'I'm not.'으로 답한다. don't를 쓰면 안 되는 것에 유의한다.
❸ 교환을 요청하는 표현이다.
❹ What size would you like?: 'What size do you want?'를 보다 공손하게 표현하고 있다.
❺ 'Here you are.'는 '여기 있습니다.'라는 의미이다.

Check(√) True or False

(7) The boy is looking for something special. T☐ F☐

(8) The boy wants a large size. T☐ F☐

Listen and Talk A 4

W: Hello. ❶What can I do for you?

B: ❷Can I ❸exchange this black umbrella for a different color?

W: Sure. ❹What color would you like?

B: ❺I'd like a yellow ❻one, please.

W: OK. Here you are.

❶ 'May I help you?', 'Can I help you?' 또는 'Do you need some help?'와 바꿔 쓸 수 있는 표현이다.
❷ Can은 '허가'의 의미로 쓰였다.
❸ 'exchange A for B'는 'A를 B로 바꾸다'라는 의미이다.
❹ What은 의문형용사로 color를 수식하고 있다.
❺ 'I'd like ~'는 'I want ~'를 보다 공손하게 표현하고 있다.
❻ one은 부정대명사로 umbrella를 받고 있다.

Listen and Talk B 1

A: Hello. May I help you?

B: Yes, please. ❶I'd like to exchange this bag.

A: ❷Sure. What would you like to exchange it for?

B: ❸I'd like to exchange it for a cap.

A: OK.

❶ 교환을 요청하는 표현으로 뒤에 'for something else' 따위가 생략되어 있다.
❷ 긍정의 답으로 'OK.'라고 할 수도 있다.
❸ 'I want to exchange it for a cap.'과 바꿔 쓸 수 있다.

Listen and Talk B 2

A: Hello. May I help you?

B: Yes, please. ❶I'd like to get a refund for this bag.

A: Sure. Do you have the receipt?

B: Yes, ❷I do. ❸Here it is.

❶ 환불을 요청하는 표현이다.
❷ do는 'have the receipt'를 대신하는 대동사이다.
❸ 'Here it is.'는 '여기 있습니다.'라는 의미이다.

Review 1

W: Hello. May I help you?

B: Yes, please. ❶I'd like to return this baseball glove.

W: OK. Was there anything wrong with ❷it?

B: No, I just changed my mind. ❸Can I have my money back?

W: OK. ❹Here's your money.

❶ '반품하고 싶다'는 표현이며 return은 '반환하다'라는 의미이다.
❷ it은 'the baseball glove'를 가리킨다.
❸ 'Can I get my money back?'으로 쓸 수도 있다.
❹ 'Here it is.'나 'Here you are.'로 바꿔 쓸 수 있다.

Review 2

M: Hello. Can I help you?

W: Yes, please. I'd like to exchange this yellow T-shirt. It's ❶too small for me.

M: Sure. ❷What size would you like to exchange it for?

W: Medium size, please. Oh! Can I have ❸it in red?

M: OK. ❹Here you are.

❶ too는 small을 수식하는 부사이다.
❷ 'exchange A for B'는 'A를 B로 바꾸다'라는 의미이다.
❸ it은 'the medium size T-shirt'를 가리킨다.
❹ 'Here it is.'로 바꿔 쓸 수 있다.

Review 3

M: Hello. May I help you?

G: Yes, please. Can I get a refund for this hat?

M: ❶I'm afraid you can't.

G: Then, can I exchange this hat for the gloves ❷over there?

M: Yes, you ❸can.

❶ 'I'm afraid ~'는 유감스러운 내용을 말할 때 예의상 덧붙이는 표현으로 '~할 것 같다, (유감이지만) ~이다' 정도의 뜻이다.
❷ over there: 저기에
❸ can 뒤에는 'exchange the hat for the gloves'가 생략되어 있다.

Review 4

A: Hello. May I help you?

B: ❶I'd like to get a refund for this cap.

A: Sure. Do you have the receipt?

B: Yes, I do. ❷Here it is.

❶ 환불을 요청하는 말이다.
❷ 'Here it is.'는 '여기 있습니다.'라는 의미이다

다음 우리말과 일치하도록 빈칸에 알맞은 말을 쓰시오.

Listen and Talk A 1

W: Hello. May I _____ _____?

B: Yes, please. I'd like to get a _____ for this watch.

W: OK. Was there anything _____ with it?

B: No, I just changed my mind. Can I _____ my money _____?

W: OK. I'll _____ _____ _____ it right away.

해석

W: 안녕하세요. 무엇을 도와드릴까요?

B: 네, 이 손목시계를 환불받고 싶어서요.

W: 알겠습니다. 시계에 무슨 문제가 있었나요?

B: 아니요, 그냥 마음이 바뀌었어요. 돈을 돌려받을 수 있을까요?

W: 네. 지금 바로 처리해드리겠습니다.

Listen and Talk A 2

W: Hello. Do you _____ _____ _____?

B: Yes. I'd like to _____ this smartphone case.

W: _____ _____. Do you have the _____ with you?

B: _____ _____ _____. I bought _____ three days ago.

W: Oh, then _____ _____.

W: 안녕하세요. 도움이 필요하신가요?

B: 네. 이 스마트폰 케이스를 환불받고 싶어요.

W: 어디 봅시다. 영수증을 가지고 계시나요?

B: 여기 있습니다. 3일 전에 구매했어요.

W: 아, 그렇다면 가능합니다.

Listen and Talk A 3

W: Hello. Are you _____ _____ anything _____?

B: No, I'm not. I'd like to _____ this T-shirt. It's too small.

W: Sure. What size _____ _____ _____?

B: Large, please.

W: _____ _____ _____.

B: Thank you.

W: 안녕하세요. 특별히 찾으시는 것 있으세요?

B: 아니요. 저는 이 티셔츠를 교환하고 싶어서요. 너무 작아요.

W: 네. 어떤 사이즈를 원하세요?

B: 큰 사이즈로 주세요.

W: 여기 있습니다.

B: 감사합니다.

Listen and Talk A 4

W: Hello. _____ can I _____ _____ _____ _____?

B: Can I exchange this black umbrella _____ a different color?

W: Sure. _____ color _____ you _____?

B: _____ _____ a yellow _____, please.

W: OK. _____ _____ _____.

W: 안녕하세요. 무엇을 도와드릴까요?

B: 이 검은색 우산을 다른 색으로 교환할 수 있을까요?

W: 물론이죠. 어떤 색을 원하세요?

B: 저는 노란색을 원해요.

W: 알겠습니다. 여기 있습니다.

해석

Listen and Talk B 1

A: Hello. _____ _____ _____ _____?
B: Yes, please. _____ _____ _____ exchange this bag.
A: Sure. _____ would you like to exchange _____ _____?
B: I'd like to exchange _____ _____ a cap.
A: OK.

A: 안녕하세요. 무엇을 도와드릴까요?
B: 네. 이 가방을 교환하고 싶어요.
A: 네. 무엇으로 교환하고 싶으세요?
B: 저는 모자로 교환하고 싶어요.
A: 알겠습니다.

Listen and Talk B 2

A: Hello. _____ _____ help you?
B: Yes, please. I'd like to _____ _____ _____ _____ this bag.
A: Sure. Do you have the _____?
B: Yes, I _____. _____ _____ _____.

A: 안녕하세요. 무엇을 도와드릴까요?
B: 네. 이 가방을 환불받고 싶어요.
A: 물론이죠. 영수증을 가지고 계시나요?
B: 네. 여기 있습니다.

Listen and Talk C

M: Hello. _____ _____ _____ _____ _____?
G: Yes, please. I'd like to _____ _____ _____ _____ this cap.
M: Do you have the _____?
G: No, I _____. I received _____ _____ a gift.
M: If you don't have the receipt, then, _____ not possible _____ _____ a refund.
G: _____ _____. Then, can I _____ it _____ _____ _____?
M: Yes, you _____. What _____ _____ _____ _____?
G: I _____ _____ _____ this blue bag.
M: _____ _____ _____ _____ .... The price is the same, so you can just _____ _____.
G: Thank you.

M: 안녕하세요. 도와드릴까요?
G: 네. 이 모자를 환불받고 싶어요.
M: 영수증을 가지고 있나요?
G: 아니요. 선물로 받았어요.
M: 영수증이 없으면, 환불은 가능하지 않아요.
G: 알겠어요. 그럼, 다른 것으로 교환할 수 있나요?
M: 네, 가능해요. 어떤 것을 원하시나요?
G: 이 파란색 가방을 갖고 싶어요.
M: 한번 볼게요…. 가격이 같으니까 그것을 가져가셔도 돼요.
G: 고맙습니다.

Listen and Talk D

G: I bought this red skirt last week. I like the skirt, but my sister says that the color doesn't _____ _____ _____ me. I wonder _____ I should _____ _____ _____ a different color.
B: It's _____ _____ you but I think it's fine.

G: 나는 지난주에 이 빨간색 치마를 샀어. 나는 치마가 마음에 드는데 내 여동생은 색깔이 나에게 잘 어울리지 않는대. 이걸 다른 색으로 교환을 해야 할지 고민이야.
B: 네가 하고 싶은 대로 하렴, 하지만 내 생각엔 괜찮은 것 같아.

Talk and Play

A: _____ _____ . I'd like to _____ this T-shirt _____ these pants.
B: OK. Is there _____ _____ with it?
A: I don't like the color.
B: I see.

A: _____ _____ . I'd like to _____ _____ _____ _____ this cap.
B: OK. Is there _____ _____ with it?
A: I don't like the color.
B: I see.

A: 실례합니다. 이 티셔츠를 이 바지로 교환하고 싶어요.
B: 네. 티셔츠에 무슨 문제가 있나요?
A: 색이 마음에 들지 않아요.
B: 알겠습니다.

A: 실례합니다. 저는 이 모자를 환불받고 싶어요.
B: 네. 모자에 무슨 문제가 있나요?
A: 색이 마음에 들지 않아요.
B: 알겠습니다.

Review 1

W: Hello. _____ _____ _____ _____ ?
B: Yes, please. _____ _____ _____ _____ this baseball glove.
W: OK. Was there _____ _____ _____ it?
B: No, I just changed my mind. Can I _____ my money _____ ?
W: OK. _____ _____ _____ .

W: 안녕하세요. 무엇을 도와드릴까요?
B: 네. 이 야구 글러브를 환불받고 싶어서요.
W: 알겠어요. 그것에 무슨 문제가 있었나요?
B: 아니요. 그냥 마음이 바뀌었어요. 제 돈을 돌려받을 수 있을까요?
W: 네. 여기 있습니다.

Review 2

M: Hello. _____ _____ _____ _____ ?
W: Yes, please. _____ _____ _____ _____ this yellow T-shirt. It's too small for me.
M: Sure. What size _____ _____ _____ _____ _____ _____ ?
W: Medium size, please. Oh! Can I _____ _____ _____ red?
M: OK. _____ _____ _____ .

M: 안녕하세요. 무엇을 도와드릴까요?
W: 네. 이 노란색 티셔츠를 교환하고 싶어요. 저에게는 너무 작네요.
M: 네. 어떤 사이즈로 교환하고 싶으신가요?
W: 중간 사이즈로 주세요. 오! 빨간색 티셔츠로 바꿀 수 있을까요?
M: 네. 여기 있습니다.

Review 3

M: Hello. May I help you?
G: Yes, please. Can I _____ _____ _____ _____ this hat?
M: I'm _____ _____ _____ .
G: Then, can I _____ this hat _____ the gloves over there?
M: Yes, you _____ .

M: 안녕하세요. 무엇을 도와드릴까요?
G: 네. 이 모자를 환불받을 수 있을까요?
M: 죄송하지만 안 됩니다.
G: 그렇다면 이 모자를 저기에 있는 장갑으로 교환할 수 있을까요?
M: 네. 가능합니다.

Review 4

A: Hello. May I help you?
B: I'd like to _____ _____ _____ _____ this cap.
A: Sure. Do you have the _____ ?
B: Yes, I _____ . _____ _____ _____ .

A: 안녕하세요. 무엇을 도와드릴까요?
B: 네. 이 모자를 환불받고 싶어요.
A: 물론이죠. 영수증을 가지고 계시나요?
B: 네. 여기 있습니다.

01 다음 빈칸 (A)에 알맞은 문장은?

> W: Hello. May I help you?
> B: Yes, please. _____ (A) _____
> W: OK. Was there anything wrong with it?
> B: No, I just changed my mind. Can I get my money back?
> W: OK. I'll take care of it right away.

① What would you like?
② I would like to get an exchange.
③ I'd like to get a refund for this watch.
④ Can I exchange it for something else?
⑤ Can I exchange this?

02 주어진 어휘를 이용하여 밑줄 친 우리말을 영작하시오.

> B: Excause me. I'd like to return this baseball glove.
> W: OK. Was there anything wrong with it?
> B: No, I just changed my mind. <u>제 돈을 돌려받을 수 있을까요?</u>
> W: OK. Here's your money.

➡ _____ (can, have, my)

[03~04] 다음 대화를 읽고 물음에 답하시오.

> W: Hello. (A)<u>Do you need some help?</u>
> B: Yes. I'd like to return this smartphone case.
> W: Let's see. Do you have the __(a)__ with you?
> B: Here it is. I bought it three days ago.
> W: Oh, then it's possible.

03 다음 영영풀이를 참고하여 대화의 빈칸 (a)에 알맞은 말은?

> a piece of paper that shows you have paid for something

① return   ② refund   ③ receipt   ④ exchange   ⑤ allowance

04 May를 이용하여 밑줄 친 (A)와 같은 뜻의 말을 4 단어 쓰시오.

➡ _____

01 다음 중 짝지어진 대화가 어색한 것은?

① A: Hello. May I help you?
　B: Yes, please.
② A: Can I have it in red?
　B: OK. Here you are.
③ A: I'd like to get a refund for this cap.
　B: Sure.
④ A: Do you have the receipt?
　B: I'd like to exchange this T-shirt.
⑤ A: What would you like?
　B: I'd like the blue tie.

[02~05] 다음 대화를 읽고 물음에 답하시오.

M: Hello. _____(A)_____

G: Yes, please. I'd like to get a refund for this cap.

M: Do you have the receipt?

G: No, I don't. I received it as a gift.

M: If you don't have the receipt, then, (a)환불은 가능하지 않아요(it, get, refund).

G: I see. Then, _____(B)_____?

M: Yes, you can. What would you like to get?

G: I want to get this blue bag.

M: Let me see .... The price is the same, so you can just take it.

G: Thank you.

02 빈칸 (A)에 알맞은 말을 고르시오.

① What has brought you here?
② Do I know you?
③ May I help you?
④ Why do you like it?
⑤ Can it be all right?

서답형

03 위 대화의 빈칸 (B)에 들어갈 알맞은 말을 주어진 어휘를 배열하여 쓰시오.

(I, it, something, exchange, can, else, for)

➡ _____

서답형

04 밑줄 친 (a)의 우리말에 맞게 주어진 어휘를 이용하여 영작하시오.

➡ _____

05 소녀에 관한 위 대화의 내용과 일치하는 것은?

① The girl wants to give a refund for the cap.
② The girl gave the cap as a gift.
③ The girl has the receipt.
④ The girl will receive her money back.
⑤ The girl can take a blue bag.

[06~07] 다음 대화를 읽고 물음에 답하시오.

W: Hello. Are you looking for (a)[something / anything] special?

B: No, (b)[I'm not / I don't]. I'd like to (c)[change / exchange] this T-shirt. It's too small.

W: Sure. What size would you like?

B: Large, please.

W: _____(A)_____

B: Thank you.

06 위 대화의 빈칸 (A)에 들어갈 말로 알맞은 것을 모두 고르시오.

① Here they go.
② Here it is.
③ Excuse me, but can you repeat that again?
④ Here you are.
⑤ Enjoy them, please.

07 위 대화의 괄호 (a)~(c)에서 알맞은 것을 골라 바르게 짝지은 것은?

	(a)	(b)	(c)
①	anything	I'm not	exchange
②	anything	I don't	exchange
③	anything	I'm not	change
④	something	I don't	exchange
⑤	something	I'm not	change

08 주어진 문장 다음에 대화가 자연스럽게 연결되도록 (A)~(D)를 순서대로 가장 적절하게 배열한 것은?

> M: Hello. Can I help you?
>
> (A) Medium size, please. Oh! Can I have it in red?
>
> (B) Yes, please. I'd like to exchange this yellow T-shirt. It's too small for me.
>
> (C) Sure. What size would you like to exchange it for?
>
> (D) OK. Here you are.

① (B) – (A) – (C) – (D)
② (B) – (C) – (A) – (D)
③ (B) – (C) – (D) – (A)
④ (C) – (B) – (D) – (A)
⑤ (C) – (D) – (B) – (A)

[09~10] 다음 대화를 읽고 물음에 답하시오.

> A: Hello. May I help you?
> B: Yes, please. _____ (A) _____
> A: Sure. What would you like to exchange it ___(B)___?
> B: I'd like to exchange it ___(B)___ a cap.
> A: OK.

09 위 대화의 빈칸 (A)에 알맞은 말은?

① Do you have a cap?
② I want to have my money back.
③ I'd like to exchange this bag.
④ Where can I get an exchange?
⑤ How can I find the way to the shop?

10 위 대화의 빈칸 (B)에 공통으로 들어갈 알맞은 말은?

① with   ② at   ③ on
④ for   ⑤ by

11 다음 대화의 밑줄 친 부분의 의도로 가장 적절한 것은?

> A: Hello. May I help you?
> B: Yes, please. I'd like to get a refund for this bag.
> A: Sure. Do you have the receipt?
> B: Yes, I do. Here it is.

① 권유하기   ② 희망 표현하기
③ 교환 요청하기   ④ 설명 요청하기
⑤ 환불 요청하기

[12~13] 다음 대화를 읽고 물음에 답하시오.

> W: Hello. What can I do for you?
> B: Can I exchange this black umbrella for a different color?
> W: Sure. What color would you like?
> B: I'd like a yellow (A)one, please.
> W: OK. Here you are.

서답형

12 What does the boy want?

➡ _____

_____

서답형

13 밑줄 친 (A)one이 가리키는 것을 쓰시오.

➡ _____

[01~05] 다음 대화를 읽고 물음에 답하시오.

M: Hello. May I help you?

G: Yes, please. (a)I'd like to get a refund for this cap.

M: Do you have the receipt?

G: No, I don't. I received it as a gift.

M: (b)영수증이 없으면, 환불은 가능하지 않아요. (it, refund, possible, get, then, if)

(A) I want to get this blue bag.

(B) Let me see .... The price is the same, so you can just take it.

(C) Yes, you can. What would you like to get?

(D) I see. Then, can I exchange it for something else?

G: Thank you.

중요

01 위 대화의 (A)~(D)를 알맞은 순서로 배열하시오.

➡ _____

02 괄호 안에 주어진 어휘를 이용하여 밑줄 친 (a)를 12 단어로 쓰시오.

➡ _____

(it, possible)

고난이도

03 Why can't the girl get a refund for the cap? Use the phrase 'It's because' and 'since.'

➡ _____
_____

04 What does the girl finally get?

➡ _____

고난이도

05 괄호 안에 주어진 어휘를 이용하여 밑줄 친 우리말 (b)에 맞게 14 단어로 쓰시오.

➡ _____
_____

[06~08] 다음 대화를 읽고 물음에 답하시오.

W: Hello. (a)특별히 찾으시는 것 있으세요? (look)

B: No, I'm not. I'd like to exchange this T-shirt. It's too small.

W: Sure. What size would you like?

B: Large, please.

W: _____ (A) _____

B: Thank you.

중요

06 위 대화의 빈칸 (A)에 알맞은 말을 you를 포함하여 3 단어로 쓰시오.

➡ _____

07 Why does the boy want to exchange the T-shirt? Use the phrase 'It's because'.

➡ _____

중요

08 괄호 안에 주어진 어휘를 이용하여 밑줄 친 우리말 (a)에 맞게 6 단어로 쓰시오.

➡ _____

고난이도

09 다음 대화의 빈칸에 주어진 〈영영풀이〉에 해당하는 어휘를 쓰시오.

A: Hello. May I help you?

B: Yes, please. I'd like to get a _____ for this watch.

a sum of money which is returned to you

➡ _____

Grammar

① 현재완료진행시제

> • My aunts **have been watching** TV for two hours. 내 이모들은 두 시간 동안 TV를 보고 있다.
> • He **has been feeling** sick since yesterday. 그는 어제부터 몸이 좋지 않다.

■ 과거에 시작한 일이 현재까지 계속 진행되고 있는 경우를 나타낼 때 사용한다.

- Carter **has been teaching** English since 2010. Carter는 2010년부터 영어를 가르쳐 오고 있다.
- The Typhoon **has been heading** to Japan since last week. 태풍이 지난주부터 일본을 향해 가고 있다.

■ 현재완료의 '계속' 용법과 유사하다. 현재완료진행은 '상태'가 아닌, '동작'을 나타낸다.

- Linda and Jane **have known** each other since their childhood. Linda와 Jane은 어린 시절부터 서로 알고 지내 왔다. (상태의 계속 – 현재완료진행 불가)
- Linda and Jane **have been reading** books for three hours. Linda와 Jane은 세 시간 동안 책을 읽어 왔다. (동작의 계속 – 현재완료진행 가능)

■ 현재완료진행형과 자주 쓰는 부사구는 'for(~ 동안)'와 'since(~ 이후로)'이다.

- Miranda **has been studying** in Paris **since** last year. Miranda는 작년부터 파리에서 공부하고 있다.
- Mom and Dad **have been talking** on my future plan **for** three hours. 엄마와 아빠가 내 미래 계획에 대해 세 시간 동안 얘기하고 있다.

■ 현재완료진행형은 의미상 두 문장으로 나누어 쓸 수 있다. (과거의 시작+현재의 진행형)

- The teachers **have been doing** volunteer work since 2002.
  → The teachers **began** to do volunteer work **in 2002**. (과거형)
     + They're **still** doing it. (현재진행형)

■ 현재완료시제는 과거에서 현재까지 동작의 완료, 경험, 결과, 계속을 의미한다.

- Leon **hasn't completed** his application form yet. Leon은 아직 그의 지원서 작성을 완료하지 못했다. 〈완료〉
- **Has** she ever **been** to the Dessert Fair? 그녀가 디저트 박람회에 가 본 적이 있나요? 〈경험〉
- Tom **has lost** his wallet. Tom은 그의 지갑을 잃어버렸다. 〈결과–현재 없음〉
- The Smiths **have lived** in Seoul for 30 years. Smith씨 가족은 30년간 서울에서 살아 왔다. 〈계속〉

핵심 Check

1. 다음 괄호 안에서 알맞은 단어를 고르시오.

(1) It has been raining cats and dogs (for / since) last September.

(2) Marie has been learning Spanish (for / since) almost two years.

② 의문사 + to부정사

• Sarah didn't know **what to do**. Sarah는 무엇을 해야 할지 몰랐다.

• I asked him **where to go** shopping. 나는 그에게 어디로 쇼핑을 가야 할지 물어봤다.

■ '의문사 + to부정사'는 명사구로서 주로 목적어 역할을 한다.

- I don't know **how to make** shikhye. 나는 어떻게 식혜를 만드는지 모른다.
- Let me know **when to press** the button. 언제 버튼을 눌러야 할지 알려 주세요.

■ 의문대명사는 내용상 to부정사의 목적어 역할을 한다.

- She wants to find out **whom to ask** for help. 그녀는 누구에게 도움을 청할지 알고 싶다.
- Mike hasn't decided **which to buy**. Mike는 어느 것을 살지 결정하지 못했다.
- Mom doesn't know **what to say**. 엄마는 무슨 말을 할지 모른다.

■ 의문부사 뒤에는 to부정사의 목적어가 나오며, 'why + to부정사' 형태는 쓸 수 없다.

- The signal tells **when to push the button**. 그 신호는 언제 버튼을 누를지 말해준다.
- Let me know **where to drop you off**. 당신을 어디에 내려줄지 알려 주세요.
- David told me **how to persuade consumers** to buy the products. David는 나에게 어떻게 소비자를 설득해서 제품을 사게 할지 말해줬다.

■ 의문형용사 which와 what은 수식받는 명사를 뒤에 쓴 후에 to부정사가 온다.

- She didn't decide **which dress to put on**. 그녀는 어느 드레스를 입을지 결정하지 못했다.
- Robert wanted to know **what route to take** so that he could arrive as soon as possible. Robert는 가능한 한 빨리 도착할 수 있도록 어떤 경로를 택해야 할지 알고 싶었다.

■ '의문사 + to부정사'는 '의문사+주어+should[can]+동사원형'으로 바꿀 수 있다.

- She didn't know **how to stop buying** unnecessary things.
  = She didn't know **how she could stop buying** unnecessary things. 그녀는 필요하지 않은 물건을 사는 것을 어떻게 멈출지 알지 못했다.
- Can you tell him **when to turn left**?
  = Can you tell him **when he should turn left**? 언제 좌회전해야 할지 그에게 말해 줄 수 있나요?

핵심 Check

2. 다음 우리말에 맞게 주어진 단어를 배열하시오.

(1) 점심으로 무엇을 먹을지 결정합시다. (decide, eat, let's, to, lunch, for, what)

➡ _____

(2) 그녀는 자전거를 어떻게 탈지 모른다. (how, she, a bike, know, to, doesn't, ride)

➡ _____

01 다음 두 문장의 뜻이 같게 빈칸을 채우시오.

(1) Tell her where she should go.

→ Tell her _____ _____ _____.

(2) Sam didn't know which book he should choose.

→ Sam didn't know _____ _____ _____ _____.

(3) George hasn't decided what he should buy for her.

→ George hasn't decided _____ _____ _____ _____

_____.

(4) Let me know how to get to the bus station.

→ Let me know _____ _____ _____ _____ _____

the bus station.

02 다음 우리말에 맞게 주어진 단어를 바르게 배열하시오. (필요하면 어형을 바꿀 것.)

(1) Marie는 네 시간 동안 컴퓨터 게임을 하고 있다. (Marie, four hours, have been, games, play, for, computer)

➡ _____

(2) Susan과 그녀의 친구들은 두 시간 동안 드라마를 시청하고 있다. (a drama, for, have been, and, Susan, watch, two hours, her friends)

➡ _____

03 다음 우리말에 맞게 빈칸에 알맞은 단어를 쓰시오.

이 노트북을 사용하는 법을 알려 주세요.

➡ Let me know _____ _____ _____ this lap top.

= Let me know _____ _____ _____ _____ this lap top.

04 다음 중 어법상 바르지 <u>않은</u> 것은?

① My friends have been watching movies for three hours.

② They have been knowing each other since last year.

③ Squirrels have been digging the hole to spend winter.

④ Amy has been using her smartphone for a day.

⑤ Mark has been shouting since 10 minutes ago.

01 다음 빈칸에 알맞은 것은?

> Lynn began composing a song three weeks ago, and she is still composing it now.
> = Lynn _____ a song since three weeks ago.

① has composing
② has begun composing
③ has been composing
④ has been beginning composing
⑤ has been composed

서답형

02 다음 두 문장을 한 문장으로 표현할 때, 빈칸에 들어갈 알맞은 말을 쓰시오.

> • Riley started to solve the puzzle yesterday.
> • She's still solving the puzzle now.

➡ R i l e y _____ _____
_____ yesterday.

서답형

03 다음 예시와 같이 두 문장을 '의문사+to부정사'를 활용해 한 문장으로 만들 때, 빈칸에 알맞은 말을 넣으시오.

> The girl was wondering. What should she see in London?
> → The girl was wondering what to see in London.

(1) Let the guests know. When should they visit the palace?
　　→ Let the guests know _____
　　_____.

(2) Elsa hasn't decided. Which color should she use to describe the scenery?
　　→ Elsa hasn't decided _____
　　to describe the scenery.

04 다음 대화의 빈칸 (A), (B), (C)에 들어갈 말로 가장 적절한 것은?

> (1) A: Could you tell me ___(A)___ buy?
> 　　B: I think the large one is better.
> (2) A: Do you know ___(B)___ fix the bike?
> 　　B: Sorry, I don't know a thing about it.
> (3) A: I wonder ___(C)___ stay in Paris.
> 　　B: How about a guest house?

	(A)	(B)	(C)
①	which to	how to	where to
②	which to	how to	what to
③	which to	when to	how to
④	where to	what to	how to
⑤	where to	how to	what to

서답형

05 다음 문장에서 어법상 틀린 부분을 한군데 찾아 바르게 고쳐 쓰시오.

> He asked me that to buy for his wife.

_____ ➡ _____

06 다음 주어진 문장과 의미가 같은 것은?

> The participants haven't decided what to eat for dinner.

① The participants haven't decided what they were eating for dinner.
② The participants haven't decided what they should eat for dinner.
③ The participants haven't decided what did they eat for dinner.
④ The participants haven't decided what they ate for dinner.
⑤ The participants haven't decided what eating for dinner.

07 다음 괄호 안의 어휘들을 활용하여, 총 8단어로 우리말을 영작할 때 5번째로 들어갈 단어는?

> 언제 회의를 시작할지 그녀에게 알려 주세요.
> (when, the, meeting, let, know, to)

① her   ② the   ③ to
④ start   ⑤ when

08 다음 우리말을 바르게 영작한 것은?

① 우리는 경주를 세 번 방문했다.
→ We have visiting Gyoungju three times.
② 영화 기생충을 본 적이 있습니까?
→ Have you ever see the movie *Parasite*?
③ 그들은 부산에서 15년 동안 살고 있다.
→ They have been living in Busan for 15 years.
④ 그녀는 3시간 동안 책을 읽고 있다.
→ She has been reading a book since three hours.
⑤ Minsu는 전에 이탈리아 음식을 먹어 본 적이 있다.
→ Minsu has been eating Italian food before.

09 다음 중 어법상 어색한 문장은?

① Has she told her husband what to buy for their parents?
② Does Michael know which to fix the oven?
③ After graduating from college, I couldn't decide what to do.
④ Ask the girl waiting for 3 hours which dress to buy.
⑤ I don't know where to go.

10 다음 중 어법상 옳은 것은?

① The lady has sitting next to the tree since this morning.
② The boy has been riding a bike for over 2 hours.
③ The owner of the shop has been having so much money.
④ Sandra has been losing her first job.
⑤ I have been made a cookie with no one helping me.

서답형

11 다음 대화의 밑줄 친 ⓐ~ⓔ 중 흐름상 어색한 것을 찾아 기호를 쓰고, 고치시오.

> A: ⓐHave you decided what to buy for your daughter's birthday present?
> B: ⓑI can't figure out what I should buy. How about making chocolate cookies?
> A: Wow, that's a great idea. ⓒDo you know how to make them?
> B: ⓓYes, but I don't know when to make the cookies.
> A: How about Peter's office? ⓔLet me ask him when we can use the place.

_____ ➡ _____

12 다음 중 밑줄 친 부분의 쓰임이 〈보기〉와 같은 것은?

> ┤ 보기 ├
> Yumi <u>has been</u> to New York before.

① Emma's kids <u>have gone</u> to Egypt.
② Daniel <u>has not finished</u> his homework yet.
③ <u>Have</u> you and your family <u>lived</u> in Seoul since 1999?
④ Bob <u>has lost</u> all his money in gambling.
⑤ Park <u>has been elected</u> mayor twice.

13 다음 〈보기〉에서 어법상 옳은 문장은 <u>모두</u> 몇 개인가?

> ┤ 보기 ├
>
> a. Mom doesn't know what should say to her.
> b. Would you tell me why to come here?
> c. We don't know who to elect as chairman.
> d. They wondered where to going.
> e. Noah didn't know when to breathe while doing the swimming moves.
> f. Elephants know how to draw the flower.

① 1개   ② 2개   ③ 3개   ④ 4개   ⑤ 5개

14 다음 문장의 빈칸에 들어갈 말로 가장 알맞은 것은?

> The Amazon rainforest _____ for weeks due to a 'record number of fires' since September 12.

① burned   ② is burning
③ was burning   ④ has been burnt
⑤ has been burning

서답형
15 다음 〈보기〉에서 알맞은 동사를 한 번씩만 선택하여, 현재완료진행형으로 빈칸을 채워 문장을 완성하시오.

> ┤ 보기 ├
>
> learn   paint   listen   take   travel

(1) The youth expedition _____ in China since last Spring.

(2) Miranda _____ a foreign language for 5 years.

(3) The patient _____ the pill since she left the hospital last year.

(4) The driver _____ to the traffic radio program for 2 weeks.

(5) The students from the art high school _____ the village walls.

16 다음 문장의 빈칸에 들어갈 수 <u>없는</u> 것을 고르시오.

> The crowds in the square have been dancing to the K-pop _____.

① all this afternoon   ② since 2 o'clock
③ up to now   ④ for an hour
⑤ until 15 minutes ago

서답형
17 다음 우리말과 일치하도록 빈칸에 들어갈 알맞은 단어를 쓰시오.

(1) Vecky는 그녀의 생일 파티에 누구를 초대할지 결정하지 못했다.
→ Vecky hasn't decided _____ _____ _____ to her birthday party.

(2) 저희 레스토랑에 언제 방문할지 알려 주세요.
→ Let us know _____ _____ _____ our restaurant.

(3) 그녀에게 상황이 더 악화되기 전에 언제 멈출지 말하시오.
→ Tell her _____ _____ _____ before things get any worse.

(4) Mary는 성공하기 위해 누구를 만날지 고민 중이다.
→ Mary is wondering _____ _____ _____ in order to succeed.

(5) 나는 두 가지 중에서 어떤 방법을 선택해야 할지 알아낼 수가 없었다.
→ I couldn't figure out _____ _____ _____ _____ between the two.

(6) Kelly는 왕궁에서 무슨 드레스를 입어야 할지 전혀 알 수 없었다.
→ Kelly had no idea _____ _____ _____ _____ in the palace.

01 각 괄호 안의 어구를 바르게 배열하여, 우리말을 영작하시오.

(1) 주자들은 8시간이 넘도록 체육관에서 계속 운동을 하고 있다.

(out / working / in / eight hours / the gym / been / for / the runners / over / have).

➡ _____

_____

(2) Grace는 점심을 먹고 나서 30분간 계속 껌을 씹고 있는 중이다.

(has / after / a gum / been / Grace / chewing / 30 minutes / lunch / for).

➡ _____

_____

(3) Patrick은 컴퓨터를 처음 산 이후, 계속 온라인으로 작곡을 하고 있다.

(he / Patrick / since / has / composing / first / online / been / a computer / bought).

➡ _____

_____

02 다음 그림을 보고, 우리말에 맞게 빈칸을 채우되, 괄호 안의 어휘를 이용하시오.

Roy has been wondering _____ and _____ _____ _____ between the two beverages.

(Roy는 두 음료 중에서 어느 것을, 그리고 어떻게 마실지 고민하고 있는 중이다.)

03 다음에 주어진 각각의 두 문장을 현재완료진행시제를 이용하여, 한 문장으로 쓰시오. 단, 반드시 전치사 for를 사용할 것.

(1) • Oliver started writing an email at 7:00 a.m. this morning.
• He keeps writing the email until noon.
→ Oliver _____

_____ .

(2) • Sam began to learn Chinese in May 2017 for the first time in her life.
• As of May 2019, he is still learning Chinese as usual.
→ Sam _____

_____ .

(3) • Mr. Yu started to practice playing the cello 4 months ago.
• He is still practicing these days.
→ Mr. Yu _____

_____ .

04 다음 〈보기〉의 단어들을 활용하여 우리말에 맞게 영작하시오. (단, '의문사+to부정사' 형태를 반드시 사용할 것.)

보기
tell, teach, piano, use, play, laptop

(1) Mason은 나에게 내 노트북을 사용하는 방법을 말해 주었다.

➡ _____

(2) 피아노를 어떻게 연주하는지 제게 가르쳐 주실 수 있나요?

➡ _____

05 다음 두 문장의 뜻이 자연스럽게 이어지도록 〈보기〉에서 필요한 단어를 선택하여, 조건에 맞게 빈칸을 완성하시오.

┌─ 보기 ┐
how	tell	play
which	know	read
when	teach	park my car
where	decide	visit

┌─ 조건 ┐
1. 각 단어는 한 번씩만 사용할 것.
2. 주어진 단어를 사용하여 완전한 문장을 만들되, '의문사+to부정사'를 포함할 것.
3. 문맥상 필요한 단어는 추가할 것.

(1) • I want to read both of the novels.
    • I can't _____.
(2) • We don't know what time we should visit your office.
    • Please _____.
(3) • Is there a parking place?
    • I don't _____.
(4) • She wants to be a famous violinist.
    • Can you _____?

06 다음 현재완료진행형 문장을 두 문장으로 나눌 때 빈칸에 적절한 단어를 쓰시오.

(1) Shane has been looking after his mom for three years.
  ➡ • Shane began to _____ _____ _____ _____.
    • Shane is still _____ _____ his mom.

(2) I have been watching birds for an hour.
  ➡ • I started to _____ _____ _____ _____ _____.
    • I'm still _____ _____.

07 다음 세 문장을 〈조건〉에 맞게 한 문장으로 다시 쓰시오.

• Emma, Aiden's daughter, brought home her homework five hours ago.
• As soon as she arrived home, Emma asked her father to do her homework and Aiden started instead of his daughter.
• He is still doing her homework.

┌─ 조건 ┐
• 현재 Aiden의 상태를 현재완료진행형의 완전한 영어 문장으로 쓸 것.
• 접속사, 연결어, since 등은 사용하지 말 것.
• for / daughter's / Aiden을 반드시 포함하되, 총 10 단어를 초과하지 않을 것.

➡ _____

08 다음 그림을 보고, 우리말에 맞게 빈칸을 채우되, 괄호 안의 어휘를 이용하시오.

Minju: Hey, Greg! Have you decided
(A) _____ _____ _____ _____? (join, club, 어느 클럽에 가입할지)
Greg: Not yet. I don't even know
(B) _____ _____ _____. (apply, 어디로 신청할지)
Minju: It is the student council office.
Greg: Let me know (C)_____ _____ _____ _____. (will, 네가 언제 신청할지)

Ask Dr. Money

The Green Middle School Times

Teens' Spending Habits

How smart are you with your money? These are the results of a survey of 100 students at Green Middle School.

We first asked students "Are you smart with your money?" As Graph 1 shows, 70% answered "No" while 30% answered "Yes." We then asked the students who answered "No" what their biggest money worry is. As Graph 2 shows, 60% think they don't have enough allowance while 28% think they have difficulty saving money. Lastly, 12% said they spent money on things they didn't need.

Our survey shows that the majority of students think they are not smart with their money. Managing money is not easy, and becoming a smart spender takes effort.

habit 습관
result 결과
worry 걱정, 걱정거리
allowance 용돈
have difficulty -ing ~하는 데 어려움을 겪다
save 저축하다
majority 대다수
effort 노력

확인문제

● 다음 문장이 본문의 내용과 일치하면 T, 일치하지 않으면 F를 쓰시오.

1 The Green Middle School Times first asked students "Are you smart with your money?" ☐

2 70% of the students answered "Yes" while 30% answered "No." ☐

3 60% of the students who answered "No" think they don't have enough allowance. ☐

4 28% of the students who answered "No" said they spent money on things they didn't need. ☐

5 The majority of students think they are not smart with their money. ☐

6 Managing money is not difficult. ☐

Do you have any money worries? Let's talk with Dr. Money.
주로 부정문이나 의문문에서 쓰이며 '약간의, 좀'이라는 의미

Q I'm Jason. I get a weekly allowance, but I never have enough. By
전치사 by+시간: ~쯤에는, ~까지는

Thursday, all of my money is gone. I don't know how to solve this
be gone: 사라지고 없다   how+to부정사: ~하는 방법, 어떻게 ~하는지

problem.

A Hi, I'm Dr. Money. Let's look at your spending diary. You used up

most of your money at the beginning of the week. Here's my tip. Don't
~의 대부분   부정명령문

carry around all of your weekly allowance. Divide the money into
divide A into B: A를 B로 나누다

days. Then carry only the money you need for each day.
money와 you 사이에 목적격 관계대명사 that 생략.

Q Hello, Dr. Money. I'm Steve. I have difficulty saving money. For
have difficulty[trouble/a hard time/a problem] ~ing: ~하는 데 어려움을 겪다

example, I've been saving to go to my favorite singer's concert for the
현재완료진행시제로 과거부터 현재까지 돈을 저 to go ~: to부정사의 부사적 용법(목적)
축해 오고 있다는 의미. 현재완료진행은 현재완료
(have+과거분사)보다 진행의 의미가 더 확실한 표현
last two months. However, I still don't have enough money. I don't

know what to do.
의문사+to부정사(what to do): 목적어 역할을 하고 있음. 무엇을 해야 할지

weekly 매주의

solve 해결하다

use up ~을 다 쓰다

tip 조언

carry around ~을 가지고 다니다

divide 나누다

for example 예를 들면

📎 확인문제

● 다음 문장이 본문의 내용과 일치하면 T, 일치하지 않으면 F를 쓰시오.

1 Jason gets a weekly allowance, but he never has enough. ☐

2 By Tuesday, all of Jason's money is gone. ☐

3 Dr. Money advises Jason not to carry around all of his weekly allowance. ☐

4 Dr. Money advises Jason to divide the money into weeks. ☐

5 Steve has difficulty saving money. ☐

6 Steve has been saving to go to his favorite singer's concert for the last three

months. ☐

A Let's see. In the last few weeks, you spent 80% of your allowance
어디 보자.

and only saved 20%. I think you've been spending too much.
현재완료진행시제는 과거부터 현재까지 어떤 행동이 지속된다는 의미.

To save money, you need to have a tighter budget. For example, you
to부정사의 부사적 용법(목적): 돈을 모으기 위해서

can follow the 50%-40%-10% rule. Save 50%, spend 40%, and donate
동사원형으로 시작하는 명령문. Save ~, spend ~, and donate의 동사가 병렬을 이룸.

the remaining 10% to charity. By following the rule, you can manage
by ~ing: ~함으로써

your money better. Then you can save money faster to buy the ticket.

Q I'm Minji. I like to buy things on sale. If something's on sale, I
on sale: 할인 중인   if: '만약 ~라면'의 뜻으로 조건을 나타내는 접속사

buy it although I don't need it. Last week, I bought two T-shirts on
although+절(주어 +동사): 비록 ~일지라도(접속사)

sale, but I already have many.
= many T-shirts

A Buying things on sale is good if you buy things you need.
동명사(주어)

In your case, the problem is that you buy things you don't even need.
in your case: 너의 경우에는   that 이하: 보어 역할을 하는 명사절   things 뒤에 목적격 관계대명사 생략

Here's some advice. Before you buy something, ask yourself, "Do I
Here is ~: ~가 여기 있다. 주어인 some advice와 동사 is가 도치됨. advice: 셀 수 없는 명사이므로, 단수 동사 is 사용. advices(×)

really need this?" Also, before you go shopping, make a shopping list.

Don't buy items that aren't on the list even if they're on sale. Then you
주격 관계대명사   even if+주어+동사: they: items that aren't on the list
~라고 할지라도(접속사)

won't buy things on the spot.
즉각, 즉석에서

balance 잔액

tight 빠듯한

budget 예산

rule 법칙

donate 기부하다

remaining 남아 있는

charity 자선 단체

on sale 할인 중인

item 품목, 물건

on the spot 즉각, 즉석에서

📎 **확인문제**

● 다음 문장이 본문의 내용과 일치하면 T, 일치하지 <u>않으면</u> F를 쓰시오.

1   To save money, Steve needs to have a tighter budget. ☐

2   The 50%-40%-10% rule means spending 50%, saving 40%, and donating the remaining 10% to charity. ☐

3   Minji likes to buy things on sale. ☐

4   If Minji needs something, she buys it though it's not on sale. ☐

5   In Minji's case, the problem is that she buys things she doesn't even need. ☐

6   Though the items aren't on the list, Minji must buy them if they're on sale. ☐

● 우리말을 참고하여 빈칸에 알맞은 말을 쓰시오.

1 _____ **Dr. Money**

2 **The Green Middle School** _____

3 **Teens'** _____ _____

4 _____ _____ are you with your money?

5 These are the results of _____ _____ of 100 students at Green Middle School.

6 We first asked students "Are you _____ _____ your money?"

7 _____ Graph 1 shows, 70% answered "No" _____ 30% answered "Yes."

8 We then asked the students who answered "No" what their _____ _____ _____ is.

9 _____ Graph 2 shows, 60% think they don't have _____ _____ while 28% think they _____ _____ _____ money.

10 _____, 12% said they _____ money _____ things they didn't need.

11 Our survey shows that _____ _____ of students think they are not _____ _____ their money.

12 _____ money is not easy, and _____ a smart spender takes effort.

13 Do you have any _____ _____ ?

14 Let's _____ _____ Dr. Money.

15 _____ Jason.

1 Dr. Money에게 물어보세요.

2 그린 중학교 타임스

3 10대들의 소비 습관

4 당신은 돈에 관해 얼마나 현명한가?

5 이것은 Green 중학교 학생 100명의 설문 조사 결과이다.

6 우리는 먼저 학생들에게 "당신은 돈에 관하여 현명한가?"라고 물었다.

7 그래프 1이 보여 주듯이, 30%가 "예"라고 대답한 반면 70%가 "아니요"라고 답했다.

8 그 다음 우리는 "아니요"라고 대답한 학생들에게 그들의 돈에 대한 가장 큰 고민이 무엇인지 물었다.

9 그래프 2가 보여주듯이 28%가 자신들이 돈을 모으는 것에 어려움이 있다고 생각하는 반면, 60%는 충분한 용돈을 받지 못한다고 생각한다.

10 마지막으로, 12%는 필요하지 않은 것에 돈을 소비했다고 말했다.

11 우리의 설문 조사는 대다수의 학생들이 자신들이 돈에 관련하여 현명하지 못하다고 생각한다는 것을 보여준다.

12 돈을 관리하는 것은 쉽지 않고 현명한 소비자가 되는 것에는 노력이 필요하다.

13 여러분은 돈과 관련된 걱정거리가 있는가?

14 Dr. Money와 이야기해 보자.

15 저는 Jason이에요.

16 I get a _____ _____, but I never have _____.

17 By Thursday, all of my money _____ _____.

18 I don't know _____ _____ _____ this problem.

19 Hi, _____ Dr. Money.

20 Let's look at your _____ _____.

21 You _____ _____ most of your money _____ _____ _____ of the week.

22 Here's _____ _____.

23 Don't _____ _____ all of your weekly allowance.

24 _____ the money _____ days.

25 Then _____ only the money you need _____ _____ _____.

26 _____, Dr. Money.

27 _____ Steve.

28 I _____ _____ _____ money.

29 For example, _____ _____ _____ to go to my favorite singer's concert _____ _____ _____ _____ _____.

30 _____, I _____ _____ have enough money.

31 I don't know _____ _____ _____.

32 _____ _____.

33 _____ _____ _____ _____ _____ weeks, you spent 80% of your allowance and only saved 20%.

34 I think _____ _____ _____ too much.

16 저는 매주 용돈을 받지만, 절대로 충분하지 않아요.

17 목요일쯤이면 용돈이 모두 사라져요.

18 이 문제를 해결할 방법을 모르겠어요.

19 안녕하세요, Dr. Money입니다.

20 용돈 기입장을 한번 봅시다.

21 주의 초반에 용돈의 대부분을 다 썼군요.

22 이게 내 조언이에요.

23 일주일 용돈 전부를 가지고 다니지 마세요.

24 용돈을 하루 단위로 나누세요.

25 그리고 하루에 필요한 돈만 들고 다니세요.

26 안녕하세요, Dr. Money.

27 저는 Steve예요.

28 저는 돈을 모으기가 어려워요.

29 예를 들면, 저는 좋아하는 가수의 콘서트에 가려고 지난 두 달 동안 돈을 저축해 오고 있어요.

30 하지만 저는 여전히 충분한 돈을 가지고 있지 않아요.

31 어떻게 해야 할지 모르겠어요.

32 어디 봅시다.

33 지난 몇 주에 용돈의 80%를 사용하고 20%만을 저축했군요.

34 나는 Steve가 돈을 너무 많이 써 왔다고 생각해요.

35 To save money, you need to _____ _____ _____ _____.

36 For example, you can follow _____ _____ _____.

37 Save 50%, spend 40%, and _____ _____ _____ 10% to charity.

38 _____ _____ the rule, you can _____ your money _____.

39 Then you can save money _____ _____ _____ the ticket.

40 _____ Minji.

41 I like to buy things _____ _____.

42 If something's on sale, I buy it _____ I don't need it.

43 Last week, I bought two T-shirts on sale, but I _____ _____ many.

44 Buying things on sale is good if you buy _____ _____ _____.

45 _____ _____ _____, the problem is that you buy things you _____ _____ _____.

46 _____ some advice.

47 Before you buy something, _____ _____, "Do I really need this?"

48 Also, before you _____ _____, make a shopping list.

49 Don't buy items that aren't _____ _____ _____ even if they're on sale.

50 Then you won't buy things _____ _____ _____.

35 돈을 모으기 위해서, 더 빠듯한 예산을 세우는 것이 필요해요.

36 예를 들어, Steve는 50%-40%-10%의 규칙을 따를 수 있어요.

37 50%를 저축하고, 40%를 쓰고, 남아 있는 10%를 자선 단체에 기부하세요.

38 이 규칙을 따름으로써 돈을 더 잘 관리할 수 있어요.

39 그러면 그 티켓을 사기 위해 돈을 더 빨리 모을 수 있답니다.

40 저는 민지입니다.

41 저는 할인 판매하는 물건을 사는 것을 좋아해요.

42 어떤 물건이 할인 판매를 하면 저는 그것이 필요하지 않더라도 사요.

43 지난주에는 할인 판매하는 티셔츠 두 장을 샀지만 이미 많이 가지고 있었어요.

44 민지가 필요한 물건을 산다면 할인 판매하는 물건을 사는 것은 좋습니다.

45 민지의 경우에, 문제점은 필요하지 않은 물건도 산다는 거예요.

46 여기 몇 가지 조언이 있어요.

47 민지는 무언가를 사기 전에 "이것이 정말 필요한가?"라고 스스로에게 물어보세요.

48 또한 쇼핑하러 가기 전에 쇼핑 목록을 만드세요.

49 만약 물건들이 할인 판매 중이라고 해도 목록에 없는 물건들은 사지 마세요.

50 그러면 즉석에서 물건을 사지 않게 될 거예요.

● 우리말을 참고하여 본문을 영작하시오.

1 Dr. Money에게 물어보세요.

➡ _____

2 그린 중학교 타임스

➡ _____

3 10대들의 소비 습관

➡ _____

4 당신은 돈에 관해 얼마나 현명한가?

➡ _____

5 이것은 Green 중학교 학생 100명의 설문 조사 결과이다.

➡ _____

6 우리는 먼저 학생들에게 "당신은 돈에 관하여 현명한가?"라고 물었다.

➡ _____

7 그래프 1이 보여 주듯이, 30%가 "예"라고 대답한 반면 70%가 "아니요"라고 답했다.

➡ _____

8 그 다음 우리는 "아니요"라고 대답한 학생들에게 그들의 돈에 대한 가장 큰 고민이 무엇인지 물었다.

➡ _____

9 그래프 2가 보여주듯이 28%가 자신들이 돈을 모으는 것에 어려움이 있다고 생각하는 반면,
60%는 충분한 용돈을 받지 못한다고 생각한다.

➡ _____

_____

10 마지막으로, 12%는 필요하지 않은 것에 돈을 소비했다고 말했다.

➡ _____

11 우리의 설문 조사는 대다수의 학생들이 자신들이 돈에 관련하여 현명하지 못하다고 생각한다는
것을 보여준다.

➡ _____

12 돈을 관리하는 것은 쉽지 않고 현명한 소비자가 되는 것에는 노력이 필요하다.

➡ _____

13 여러분은 돈과 관련된 걱정거리가 있는가?

➡ _____

14 Dr. Money와 이야기해 보자.

➡ _____

15 저는 Jason이에요.

➡ _____

16 저는 매주 용돈을 받지만, 절대로 충분하지 않아요.

➡ _____

17 목요일쯤이면 용돈이 모두 사라져요.

➡ _____

18 이 문제를 해결할 방법을 모르겠어요.

➡ _____

19 안녕하세요, Dr. Money입니다.

➡ _____

20 용돈 기입장을 한번 봅시다.

➡ _____

21 주의 초반에 용돈의 대부분을 다 썼군요.

➡ _____

22 이게 내 조언이에요.

➡ _____

23 일주일 용돈 전부를 가지고 다니지 마세요.

➡ _____

24 용돈을 하루 단위로 나누세요.

➡ _____

25 그리고 하루에 필요한 돈만 들고 다니세요.

➡ _____

26 안녕하세요, Dr. Money.

➡ _____

27 저는 Steve예요.

➡ _____

28 저는 돈을 모으기가 어려워요.

➡ _____

29 예를 들면, 저는 좋아하는 가수의 콘서트에 가려고 지난 두 달 동안 돈을 저축해 오고 있어요.

➡ _____

30 하지만 저는 여전히 충분한 돈을 가지고 있지 않아요.

➡ _____

31 어떻게 해야 할지 모르겠어요.

➡ _____

32 어디 봅시다.

➡ _____

33 지난 몇 주에 용돈의 80%를 사용하고 20%만을 저축했군요.

➡ _____

34 나는 Steve가 돈을 너무 많이 써 왔다고 생각해요.

➡ _____

35 돈을 모으기 위해서, 더 빠듯한 예산을 세우는 것이 필요해요.

➡ _____

36 예를 들어, Steve는 50%-40%-10%의 규칙을 따를 수 있어요.

➡ _____

37 50%를 저축하고, 40%를 쓰고, 남아 있는 10%를 자선 단체에 기부하세요.

➡ _____

38 이 규칙을 따름으로써 돈을 더 잘 관리할 수 있어요.

➡ _____

39 그러면 그 티켓을 사기 위해 돈을 더 빨리 모을 수 있답니다.

➡ _____

40 저는 민지입니다.

➡ _____

41 저는 할인 판매하는 물건을 사는 것을 좋아해요.

➡ _____

42 어떤 물건이 할인 판매를 하면 저는 그것이 필요하지 않더라도 사요.

➡ _____

43 지난주에는 할인 판매하는 티셔츠 두 장을 샀지만 이미 많이 가지고 있었어요.

➡ _____

44 민지가 필요한 물건을 산다면 할인 판매하는 물건을 사는 것은 좋습니다.

➡ _____

45 민지의 경우에, 문제점은 필요하지 않은 물건도 산다는 거예요.

➡ _____

46 여기 몇 가지 조언이 있어요.

➡ _____

47 민지는 무언가를 사기 전에 "이것이 정말 필요한가?"라고 스스로에게 물어보세요.

➡ _____

48 또한 쇼핑하러 가기 전에 쇼핑 목록을 만드세요.

➡ _____

49 만약 물건들이 할인 판매 중이라고 해도 목록에 없는 물건들은 사지 마세요.

➡ _____

50 그러면 즉석에서 물건을 사지 않게 될 거예요.

➡ _____

[01~03] 다음 글을 읽고 물음에 답하시오.

The Green Middle School Times
Teens' Spending Habits

How smart are you ____ⓐ____ your money? These are the results of a survey of 100 students at Green Middle School.

We first asked students "Are you smart ____ⓐ____ your money?" As Graph 1 shows, 70% answered "No" while 30% answered "Yes." We then asked the students who answered "No" what their biggest money worry is. As Graph 2 shows, 60% think they don't have enough allowance while 28% think they have difficulty saving money. Lastly, 12% said they spent money ____ⓑ____ things they didn't need.

01 위 글의 빈칸 ⓐ와 ⓑ에 들어갈 전치사가 바르게 짝지어진 것은?

	ⓐ	ⓑ		ⓐ	ⓑ
①	from	–	on	②	with	–	to
③	from	–	at	④	for	–	to
⑤	with	–	on			

02 위 글의 종류로 알맞은 것을 고르시오.

① essay
② article
③ summary
④ review
⑤ book report

서답형

03 How many students answered the first question in the negative? Fill in the blank with a suitable word.

_____ students did so.

[04~06] 다음 글을 읽고 물음에 답하시오.

Q Hello, Dr. Money. I'm Steve. I have difficulty saving money. ____ⓐ____, I've been saving to go to my favorite singer's concert for the last two months. However, I still don't have enough money. I don't know what to do.
A Let's see. In the last few weeks, you spent 80% of your allowance and only saved 20%. I think you've been spending too much. To save money, you need to have a tighter budget. For example, you can follow ⓑthe 50%-40%-10% rule. Save 50%, spend 40%, and donate the remaining 10% to charity. By following the rule, you can manage your money better. Then you can save money faster to buy the ticket.

04 위 글의 빈칸 ⓐ에 들어갈 알맞은 말을 고르시오.

① For example
② In addition
③ Therefore
④ However
⑤ That is

서답형

05 위 글의 밑줄 친 ⓑ가 의미하는 것을 우리말로 쓰시오.

➡ _____

_____

서답형

06 본문의 내용과 일치하도록 다음 빈칸 (A)와 (B)에 알맞은 단어를 쓰시오.

> Dr. Money advises Steve to increase savings ratio from (A)_____% to (B)_____% of his allowance.
>
> *savings ratio: 저축률

[07~09] 다음 글을 읽고 물음에 답하시오.

Do you have any money worries? Let's talk with Dr. Money.

Q I'm Jason. I get a weekly allowance, but I never have enough. By Thursday, all of my money is gone. I don't know how to solve this problem.

A Hi, I'm Dr. Money. (①) Let's look at your spending diary. (②) You used up most of your money at the beginning of the week. (③) Here's my tip. (④) Divide the money into days. (⑤) Then carry only the money you need for each day.

07 위 글의 흐름으로 보아, 주어진 문장이 들어가기에 가장 적절한 곳은?

> Don't carry around all of your weekly allowance.

①   ②   ③   ④   ⑤

08 위 글의 제목으로 알맞은 것을 고르시오.

① By Thursday, I'm Broke!
② Never Have Enough Allowance? Divide It into Days!
③ Let's Look at Your Spending Diary
④ How about Asking for More Allowance?
⑤ How to Save Your Allowance

09 According to the passage, which is NOT true?

① Jason gets a weekly allowance, but he thinks he never has enough.
② By Tuesday, all of Jason's money is gone.
③ Dr. Money found out Jason used up most of his money at the beginning of the week.
④ Dr. Money advised Jason not to carry around all of his weekly allowance.
⑤ Dr. Money advised Jason to divide the money into days and carry only the money he needs for each day.

10 주어진 글 다음에 이어질 글의 순서로 가장 적절한 것은?

How smart are you with your money? These are the results of a survey of 100 students at Green Middle School.

(A) We then asked the students who answered "No" what their biggest money worry is.

(B) We first asked students "Are you smart with your money?" As Graph 1 shows, 70% answered "No" while 30% answered "Yes."

(C) As Graph 2 shows, 60% think they don't have enough allowance while 28% think they have difficulty saving money. Lastly, 12% said they spent money on things they didn't need.

① (A) – (C) – (B)   ② (B) – (A) – (C)
③ (B) – (C) – (A)   ④ (C) – (A) – (B)
⑤ (C) – (B) – (A)

[11~12] 다음 글을 읽고 물음에 답하시오.

The Green Middle School Times
Teens' Spending Habits

How smart are you with your money? These are the results of a survey of 100 students at Green Middle School.

We first asked students "Are you smart with your money?" ⓐAs Graph 1 shows, 70% answered "No" while 30% answered "Yes." We then asked the students who answered

"No" what their biggest money worry is. As Graph 2 shows, 60% think they don't have enough allowance while 28% think they have difficulty saving money. Lastly, 12% said they spent money on things they didn't need.

11 위 글의 밑줄 친 @As와 문법적 쓰임 및 뜻이 같은 것을 고르시오.

① As it was getting dark, we soon turned back.
② He treats me as a child.
③ As rust eats iron, so care eats the heart.
④ As spring comes, the birds move northward.
⑤ I love you as much as I love her.

서답형
12 본문의 내용과 일치하도록 다음 빈칸에 알맞은 숫자를 영어로 쓰시오.

> The percent of the students who think they don't have enough allowance is _____ times as large as that of the students who said they spent money on things they didn't need.

[13~16] 다음 글을 읽고 물음에 답하시오.

A Let's see. In the last few weeks, you spent 80% of your allowance and only saved 20%. I think you've been spending too much. To save money, you need to have ___@___. For example, you can follow the 50%-40%-10% rule. Save 50%, spend 40%, and donate the remaining 10% to charity. By following the rule, you can manage your money better. Then you can save money faster to buy the ticket.

13 위 글의 빈칸 @에 들어갈 알맞은 말을 고르시오.

① a looser budget   ② a tighter deposit
③ a looser plan   ④ a tighter budget
⑤ a tighter payment

14 위 글의 주제로 알맞은 것을 고르시오.

① the easier way to save money
② to follow the 50%-40%-10% rule in order to save money
③ various reasons to save money
④ enough allowance to buy the ticket
⑤ the difficulty of saving money by following the 50%-40%-10% rule

15 다음 중 Dr. Money의 조언과 어울리지 않는 속담을 고르시오.

① Every little helps.
② Little drops of water make the mighty ocean.
③ Penny-wise and pound-foolish.
④ Many a little makes a mickle.
⑤ Little brooks make great rivers.

서답형
16 본문의 내용과 일치하도록 다음 빈칸 (A)와 (B)에 알맞은 단어를 쓰시오.

> Dr. Money advises Steve to cut back on spending from (A)_____% to (B)_____% of his allowance.
>
> *cut back on: ~을 줄이다

Reading **209**

[17~19] 다음 글을 읽고 물음에 답하시오.

Q I'm Minji. I like to buy things on sale. If something's on sale, I buy it although I don't need it. Last week, I bought two T-shirts on sale, but I already have many.

A Buying things on sale is good if you buy things you need. In your case, the problem is that you buy things you don't even need. Here's some advice. Before you buy something, ask ⓐyourself, "Do I really need this?" Also, before you go shopping, make a shopping list. Don't buy items that aren't on the list even if ⓑthey're on sale. Then you won't buy things on the spot.

17 위 글의 밑줄 친 ⓐyourself와 문법적 쓰임이 같은 것을 모두 고르시오.

① You must love yourself.
② I heard that you yourself made it.
③ Can you imagine yourself as a fish?
④ You must do it yourself.
⑤ You must be proud of yourself.

서답형
18 위 글의 밑줄 친 ⓑthey가 가리키는 것을 본문에서 찾아 쓰시오.

➡ _____

서답형
19 다음 빈칸 (A)와 (B)에 알맞은 단어를 넣어 민지의 돈에 대한 고민과 A의 조언을 완성하시오.

> Minji's Worry: If something's (A)_____ _____, I buy it although I don't need it. Last week, I bought two T-shirts on sale, but I already have many.
> The Advice: Make (B)_____ _____ _____ before you go shopping. Don't buy items that aren't on the list.

[20~22] 다음 글을 읽고 물음에 답하시오.

Do you have any money worries? Let's talk with Dr. Money.

Q I'm Jason. I get a weekly allowance, but I never have enough. By Thursday, all of my money (A)[is disappeared / is gone]. I don't know how to solve ⓐthis problem.

A Hi, I'm Dr. Money. Let's look at your spending diary. You used up (B)[almost / most] of your money at the beginning of the week. Here's my tip. Don't carry around all of your weekly allowance. (C)[Add / Divide] the money into days. Then carry only the money you need for each day.

20 위 글의 괄호 (A)~(C)에서 문맥이나 어법상 알맞은 낱말을 골라 쓰시오.

➡ (A) _____ (B) _____ (C) _____

서답형
21 위 글의 밑줄 친 ⓐthis problem이 가리키는 것을 본문에서 찾아 쓰시오.

➡ _____

중요
22 다음 중 위 글의 내용을 바르게 이해하지 못한 사람을 고르시오.

① 경미: Jason gets an allowance once a week.
② 성민: But he uses up the money by Thursday.
③ 규식: The problem is that though he knows what he should do, he doesn't practice it.
④ 나영: Dr. Money advises him not to carry around all of his weekly allowance.
⑤ 덕수: Dr. Money tells him to carry only the money he needs for each day.

[23~25] 다음 글을 읽고 물음에 답하시오.

The Green Middle School Times
Teens' Spending Habits

How smart are you with your money? These are the results of a survey of 100 students at Green Middle School.

We first asked students "Are you smart with your money?" As Graph 1 shows, ⓐ70% answered "No" while 30% answered "Yes." We then asked the students who answered "No" what their biggest money worry is. ⓑ <u>As Graph 2 shows, 60% thinks they don't have enough allowance while 28% thinks they have difficulty saving money.</u> Lastly, 12% said they spent money on things they didn't need.

23 위 글의 밑줄 친 ⓐ를 다음과 같이 바꿔 쓸 때 빈칸에 들어갈 알맞은 말을 두 단어로 쓰시오.

➡ 70% answered "in _____ _____" while 30% answered "in the affirmative."

24 위 글의 밑줄 친 ⓑ에서 어법상 틀린 부분을 찾아 고치시오. (두 군데)

_____ ➡ _____

_____ ➡ _____

25 According to the passage, which is NOT true?

① The text above shows the results of a survey of 100 students at Green Middle School.

② 30 students answered they were smart with their money.

③ The biggest money worry of three-fifths of the students who answered "No" is that they don't have enough allowance.

④ More than one third of the students who answered "No" have difficulty saving money.

⑤ 12% of the students who answered "No" said they spent money on things they didn't need.

[26~28] 다음 글을 읽고 물음에 답하시오.

The Green Middle School Times
Teens' Spending Habits

How smart are you with your money? These are the ①results of a survey of 100 students at Green Middle School.

We first asked ⓐstudents "Are you smart with your money?" As Graph 1 shows, 70% answered "No" ②while 30% answered "Yes." We then asked the students who answered "No" what ⓑtheir biggest money worry is. As Graph 2 shows, ⓒ60% think they don't have enough ③allowance while 28% think they have difficulty ④saving money. ⑤ Lastly, 12% said they spent money on things they didn't need.

26 위 글의 밑줄 친 ①~⑤와 바꿔 쓸 수 있는 말로 옳지 않은 것을 고르시오.

① outcomes   ② whereas

③ pocket money   ④ rescuing

⑤ Finally

27 위 글의 밑줄 친 ⓐstudents와 ⓑtheir가 가리키는 것을 각각 본문에서 찾아 쓰시오.

➡ ⓐ _____

ⓑ _____

28 위 글의 밑줄 친 ⓒ60%를 분수로 표현하여 읽는 법을 영어로 쓰시오.

➡ _____

[01~04] 다음 글을 읽고 물음에 답하시오.

The Green Middle School Times
Teens' Spending Habits

How smart are you with your money? These are the results of a survey of 100 students at Green Middle School.

We first asked students "Are you smart with your money?" (A)[As / Since] Graph 1 shows, 70% answered "No" while 30% answered "Yes." We then asked the students (B)[what / who] answered "No" what their biggest money worry is. As Graph 2 shows, 60% think they don't have enough allowance while 28% think they have ⓐdifficulty saving money. (C)[At last / Lastly], 12% said they spent money on things they didn't need.

01 위 글의 괄호 (A)~(C)에서 문맥이나 어법상 알맞은 낱말을 골라 쓰시오.

➡ (A) _____ (B) _____ (C) _____

02 위 글의 밑줄 친 ⓐdifficulty와 바꿔 쓸 수 있는 말을 쓰시오.

➡ _____

03 How many students think they don't have enough allowance? Fill in the blank with a suitable word.

_____ students do so.

04 위 글의 내용을 다음과 같이 정리하고자 한다. 빈칸 (A)와 (B)에 들어갈 알맞은 말을 본문의 단어를 이용하여 쓰시오.

70 students among 100 students at Green Middle School don't spend money in a (A)_____ way, and they have (B)_____ _____ like not having enough allowance, having difficulty saving money and spending money on things they don't need.

[05~07] 다음 글을 읽고 물음에 답하시오.

Do you have any money worries? Let's talk with Dr. Money.

🇶 I'm Jason. I get a weekly allowance, but I never have enough. By Thursday, all of my money is gone. ⓐI don't know how to solve this problem.

🇦 Hi, I'm Dr. Money. Let's look at your spending diary. You used up most of your money at the beginning of the week. Here's my tip. Don't carry around all of your weekly allowance. Divide the money into days. ⓑ그리고 하루에 필요한 돈만 들고 다니세요.

05 위 글의 밑줄 친 ⓐ를 다음과 같이 바꿔 쓸 때 빈칸에 들어갈 알맞은 말을 두 단어로 쓰시오.

➡ I don't know how _____ _____ solve this problem.

06 위 글의 밑줄 친 ⓑ의 우리말에 맞게 주어진 어휘를 알맞게 배열하시오.

each day / you / the money / then / only / for / carry / need

➡ _____

07 다음 빈칸 (A)와 (B)에 알맞은 단어를 넣어 Jason의 돈에 대한 고민과 Dr. Money의 조언을 완성하시오.

Jason's Worry: I get an allowance, but I (A)_____ _____ _____. By Thursday, all of my money is gone.

Dr. Money's Advice: Don't carry around all of weekly allowance. (B)_____ the money into days and take only one day's portion with you.

*one day's portion: 하루치

[08~09] 다음 글을 읽고 물음에 답하시오.

A Let's see. In the last few weeks, you spent 80% of your allowance and only saved 20%. I think you've been spending too much. ⓐ 돈을 모으기 위해서, 더 빠듯한 예산을 세우는 것이 필요해요. For example, you can follow the 50%-40%-10% rule. Save 50%, spend 40%, and donate the remaining 10% to charity. By following the rule, you can manage your money better. Then you can save money faster to buy the ticket. <you: Steve>

08 위 글의 밑줄 친 ⓐ의 우리말에 맞게 주어진 어휘를 이용하여 10 단어로 영작하시오.

save, have, tighter

➡ _____

또는 _____

09 Steve의 일주일 용돈이 만원인 경우, 다음 빈칸 ①~⑥에 들어갈 알맞은 숫자를 쓰시오.

	지난 몇 주의 예산	충고 내용
save	①_____원	②_____원
spend	③_____원	④_____원
donate	⑤_____원	⑥_____원

[10~11] 다음 글을 읽고 물음에 답하시오.

A Buying things on sale is good if you buy things you need. In your case, the problem is that you buy things you don't even need. Here's some advice. Before you buy something, ask yourself, "Do I really need this?" Also, before you go shopping, make a shopping list. Don't buy items that aren't on the list even if they're on sale. Then you won't buy things on the spot.. <you: Minji>

10 What does Minji have to do? Fill in the blanks (A) and (B) with suitable words.

➡ (1) Before she buys something: She has to (A)_____ _____, "Do I really need this?"

(2) Before she goes shopping: She has to (B)_____ _____ _____ list.

11 위 글의 내용과 일치하도록 아래 문장의 괄호 (A)~(C)에서 각각 알맞은 낱말을 고르시오.

Minji (A)[should / should not] buy an item (B)[if / even if] it is on sale (C)[if / though] it is not on her shopping list.

➡ (A) _____ (B) _____ (C) _____

After You Read C

Teens' Money Worries and Dr. Money's Advice

Jason's Worry: I get an allowance, but I never have enough. By Thursday, all
전치사 by+시간: ~쯤에는, ~까지는

of my money is gone.
be gone: 사라지고 없다

Dr. Money's Advice: Don't carry around all of weekly allowance. Divide the
divide A into B: A를 B로 나누다

money into days and carry only the money you need for each day.
money와 you 사이에 목적격 관계대명사 생략.

구문해설 • worry: 걱정거리 • allowance: 용돈 • weekly: 매주의 • divide: 나누다

십대들의 돈과 관련된 걱정거리와 **Dr. Money**의 조언

Jason의 걱정거리: 저는 매주 용돈을 받지만, 절대로 충분하지 않아요. 목요일쯤이면 용돈이 모두 사라져요.

Dr. Money의 조언: 일주일 용돈 전부를 가지고 다니지 마세요. 용돈을 하루 단위로 나누고 하루에 필요한 돈만 들고 다니세요.

Language in Use A

1. The computer I bought on sale was very cheap.
computer와 I 사이에 목적격 관계대명사 that[which] 생략

2. It is foolish to go camping during the rainy season.
가주어 ⋯ smart 진주어   during 다음에는 기간을 나타내는 명사가 온다.

3. My jeans are too tight, so I am going to exchange them for a bigger size.
부사(너무) 결과를 나타내는 절을 이끄는 접속사   exchange A for B: A를 B로 교환하다

구문해설 • on sale: 할인 중인, 판매되는 • go camping: 캠핑을 가다 • rainy season: 우기

1. 할인 중에 산 컴퓨터는 매우 값이 쌌다.

2. 우기에 캠핑을 가는 것은 어리석다.

3. 내 청바지가 너무 꽉 끼여서 나는 그것을 더 큰 사이즈로 교환할 것이다.

Think and Write

My money problem is that I buy things on the spot. One time, I bought a
접속사(명사절)-보어 역할   전치사+명사

smartphone case because it looked nice. However, I found out that I already
접속사(부사절)-이유   2형식 동사+형용사   접속사(명사절)-목적어 역할

had three cases at home. I don't know how to stop buying things on the spot.
의문사+to부정사(명사구) stop+동명사 목적어(~하는 것을 멈추다)

구문해설 • on the spot: 즉석에서, 현장에서 • find out: 알게 되다, 알아내다

나의 돈과 관련된 고민은 즉석에서 물건을 산다는 것이다. 한번은, 나는 스마트폰 케이스가 좋아 보여서 그것을 샀다. 하지만, 집에 와서는 내가 이미 케이스를 세 개 갖고 있다는 것을 발견했다. 나는 즉석에서 물건을 사는 것을 어떻게 멈출 수 있는지 모르겠다.

1 〈보기〉의 밑줄 친 어휘와 같은 의미로 쓰이지 <u>않은</u> 것을 고르시오.

> ┤ 보기 ├
>
> As we look deeply within, we understand our perfect <u>balance</u>.

① You can check your bank <u>balance</u> on the Internet.
② You need to try to keep a <u>balance</u> between work and play.
③ Athletes need a good sense of <u>balance</u>.
④ At that moment he lost his <u>balance</u> and fell.
⑤ The impact of the blow knocked Jack off <u>balance</u>.

2 다음 영영풀이에 해당하는 단어를 주어진 철자로 시작하여 빈칸에 쓰고, 알맞은 것을 골라 문장을 완성하시오.

> • c_____ : an organization that gives money or help to people who need it
> • e_____ : the act of giving someone something and receiving something else from them

(1) He founded the _____ in memory of his late wife.
(2) The _____ of prisoners took place this morning.

3 다음 대화의 빈칸에 〈영영풀이〉에 해당하는 단어를 쓰시오.

> A: How much are these apples?
> B: They're _____ , so they're very cheap now.

> <영영풀이> being offered at a reduced price

➡ _____

4 괄호 안에 주어진 어휘를 이용하여 빈칸에 알맞게 쓰시오.

> • I'll let you be a big _____ next time. (spend)
> • I receive an _____ from my parents. (allow)

5 다음 빈칸 (A)~(C)에 알맞은 말을 쓰시오. (주어진 철자로 시작하여 쓸 것.)

> • I want her to eat these and fall asleep. But I'm having so much (A)d_____ selling them.
> • I think it is (B)f_____ to buy such a trash.
> • These shoes are much too (C)t_____, so I am going to exchange them for a bigger size.

Conversation

[06~08] 다음 대화를 읽고 물음에 답하시오.

(A) OK. Was there anything wrong with it?
(B) Yes, please. (a)I'd like to return this baseball glove.
(C) No, I just changed my mind. Can I have my money back?
(D) Hello. May I help you?
W: OK. (b)Here's your money.

06 주어진 문장 앞에 나올 대화의 순서로 알맞은 것은?

① (B) – (A) – (C) – (D)
② (C) – (B) – (A) – (D)
③ (D) – (A) – (C) – (B)
④ (D) – (B) – (A) – (C)
⑤ (D) – (B) – (C) – (A)

07 위 대화의 밑줄 친 (a)와 같은 뜻의 문장을 괄호 안에 주어진 어휘를 이용하여 쓰시오.

➡ _____

(a refund, get, like to)

08 위 대화의 밑줄 친 (b)와 같은 뜻의 문장을 3 단어로 두 개를 쓰시오.

➡ _____, _____

09 다음 중 짝지어진 대화가 <u>어색한</u> 것은?

① A: Can I help you?
   B: Yes. I'd like to exchange this yellow T-shirt. It's too small for me.
② A: Can I get a refund for this hat?
   B: I'm afraid you can.

③ A: Can I exchange this necktie for the gloves over there?
   B: Sure. What would you like?
④ A: I'd like to get a refund for this T-shirt.
   B: I'm afraid you can't return it.
⑤ A: Was there anything wrong with it?
   B: No, I just changed my mind.

[10~13] 다음 대화를 읽고 물음에 답하시오.

B: _____ (A) _____ I'd like to exchange this T-shirt for these pants.
W: OK. (B)티셔츠에 무슨 문제가 있나요? (there, wrong, it)
B: I don't like the color.
W: I see.

10 주어진 〈영영풀이〉를 참고하여 위 대화의 빈칸 (A)에 알맞은 말을 쓰시오.

〈영영풀이〉
This expression is used
(1) before you do or say something that might annoy somebody, or to get somebody's attention
(2) when you are leaving the room for a short time

➡ _____

11 Why does the boy want to exchange the T-shirt?

➡ _____

12 밑줄 친 (B)의 우리말을 영작하시오.

➡ _____

13 위 대화의 내용과 일치하는 것은?

① 소년은 티셔츠를 맘에 들어 하고 있다.
② 소년은 환불을 요청하고 있다.
③ 여자는 교환을 거절하고 있다.
④ 여자는 티셔츠의 문제를 이미 알고 있었다.
⑤ 소년과 여자는 상점에서 대화를 나누고 있다.

Grammar

14 다음 중 어법상 올바른 문장은?

① Sophia didn't know why to fish the small octopus.
② Robert couldn't decide when they to do next.
③ Don't ask the people where to wait for the singer.
④ I don't even know where to starting.
⑤ They learned how they should using the photocopier.

15 다음 두 문장을 현재완료진행시제를 이용하여 한 문장으로 만드시오.

> • Isabelle began to study wild animals in Africa 11 years ago.
> • She is still studying them now.

➡ Isabelle _____

_____ .

16 다음 주어진 문장의 밑줄 친 부분과 의미가 같은 것은?

> Sir, let me know when to start training.

① I will let you know when you should start training
② please let me know when you started training

③ I know when I should start training
④ tell me when I should start training
⑤ you told me when I should start training

17 다음 Emily에 대한 우리말에 맞게 〈보기〉에서 적절한 단어를 선택하여 빈칸에 채우시오. (동사는 변형 가능)

> Emily는 처음 배우가 된 이래로 최고의 배우가 되기 위해 노력해 오고 있다.

┤ 보기 ├
for / before / since / until / to
take / solve / try / have / be / show

> Emily (A)____ ____ ____
> ____ ____ the best actress
> (B)____ she first became an actress.

18 Which of the followings are NOT grammatically correct? Choose all.

① Susan's grandfather has ever played basketball before.
② Morris has been running for an hour.
③ I have been fell in love with the ants.
④ The auditorium has been feeling too hot.
⑤ Amber has been driving for 5 years since she got the license.

19 다음 그림을 보고 괄호 안의 단어를 활용해서 어법에 맞게 빈칸에 채우시오.

(1)

➡ Junsu _____

in the flower garden for an hour since lunch time. (take, be, himself, picture)

(2)

➡ Youngsu _____

in the woods for half an hour since 3 o'clock. (watch, be, bird)

20 다음 우리말을 영작할 때 빈칸 ⓐ에 들어갈 단어로 가장 적절한 것은?

언제 떠날지 그녀가 알게 해주세요.
= Let ( ) ( ) ( ) (ⓐ) ( ).

① to   ② her   ③ know
④ leave   ⑤ when

21 다음 대화의 빈칸에 들어갈 말로 알맞은 것은?

A: _____
B: The yellow one smells much better.

① Tell me what shape to choose.
② Do you know how to smell the perfume?
③ Don't you know where to go?
④ I wonder when to visit Rainbow town.
⑤ Can you tell me which to buy?

22 다음 밑줄 친 부분 중 어법상 어색한 것을 고르시오.

① James <u>has been taking</u> care of his sister's little kids since last week.
② Anna <u>has been making</u> the chocolate candies until now.
③ William <u>has been owning</u> the building since he was born.

④ Bentley <u>has been studying</u> the 3-D printing technology for his mom.
⑤ Lucas' relatives <u>have been living</u> in Suwon for four years.

Reading

[23~25] 다음 글을 읽고 물음에 답하시오.

Teens' Spending Habits

Are you smart with your money?

No 70%   Yes 30%   *total: 100 students

What is your biggest money worry?

1 I don't have enough allowance.
2 I have difficulty saving money.
3 I spend money on things I don't need.

0%   12%   28%   60%

Our survey shows that the majority of students think they are not smart with their money. Managing money is not easy, and ⓐ <u>becoming</u> a smart spender takes effort.

23 위 글의 밑줄 친 ⓐbecoming과 문법적 쓰임이 같은 것을 <u>모두</u> 고르시오.

① Tom's hobby is <u>writing</u> poems.
② <u>Writing</u> poems makes your mind flexible.
③ Where is Tom <u>writing</u> poems?
④ Do you know the man <u>writing</u> poems on the bench?
⑤ Who is good at <u>writing</u> poems?

24 What percent of the students have difficulty saving money? Fill in the blank with a suitable word.

_____ percent of the students do so.

25 위 글을 읽고 대답할 수 <u>없는</u> 질문을 고르시오.

① How many students are smart spenders?

② How many students aren't smart with their money?

③ What do the majority of students think about their spending habits?

④ On average, how much do the students get for allowance in a week?

⑤ Can you become a smart spender without any effort?

[26~28] 다음 글을 읽고 물음에 답하시오.

Do you have any money worries? Let's talk with Dr. Money.

Q I'm Jason. I get a weekly allowance, but I never have enough. ⓐ Thursday, all of my money is gone. I don't know how to solve this problem.

A Hi, I'm Dr. Money. Let's look at your spending diary. You used up most of your money ⓑ the beginning of the week. Here's my tip. Don't carry around all of your weekly allowance. ⓒ용돈을 하루 단위로 나누세요. Then carry only the money you need for each day.

26 위 글의 빈칸 ⓐ와 ⓑ에 들어갈 전치사가 바르게 짝지어진 것은?

ⓐ ⓑ   ⓐ ⓑ

① On – for   ② In – at

③ By – at   ④ On – in

⑤ By – for

27 위 글의 밑줄 친 ⓒ의 우리말에 맞게 5 단어로 영작하시오.

➡ _____

28 How often does Jason get an allowance? Fill in the blank with a suitable word.

He gets an allowance _____ a week.

[29~32] 다음 글을 읽고 물음에 답하시오.

Q I'm Minji. I like to buy things on sale. If something's on sale, I buy (A)<u>it</u> although I don't need it. Last week, I bought two T-shirts on sale, but I already have many.

A Buying things on sale is good if you buy things you need. In your case, the problem is that you buy things you don't even need. (B)<u>Here's some advice.</u> Before you buy something, ask yourself, "Do I really need this?" Also, before you go ⓐ_____, make a shopping list. Don't buy items that aren't on the list even if they're on sale. Then you won't buy things on the spot.

29 위 글의 빈칸 ⓐ에 shop을 알맞은 형태로 쓰시오.

➡ _____

30 위 글의 밑줄 친 (A)it이 가리키는 것을 본문의 단어를 변형하여 쓰시오. (관계대명사 포함 5글자)

➡ _____

31 위 글의 밑줄 친 문장 (B)를 advice 대신 tip을 이용하여 고치시오.

➡ _____

32 What's the reason Minji is not a smart spender though she buys things on sale? Answer in English beginning with "Because". (8 words)

➡ _____

01 다음 중 짝지어진 단어의 관계가 나머지와 <u>다른</u> 것은?

① recently – lately
② divide – combine
③ pocket money – allowance
④ result – outcome
⑤ paper money – bill

02 밑줄 친 부분의 의미로 알맞지 <u>않은</u> 것은?

① We make the <u>medicines</u> that help doctors keep you healthy. (의약품)
② The machine <u>works</u> on its own. (작동하다)
③ It was the first <u>case</u> of mad cow disease in the U.S. (사례)
④ Too many coins are too heavy to <u>carry around</u>. (넣어 두다)
⑤ I found out the money <u>was gone</u> after they left. (사라지다, 없어지다)

03 다음 빈칸에 공통으로 들어갈 알맞은 말을 쓰시오.

- If it fails, you can have the money _____.
- What time did you get _____ last night?

04 다음 주어진 우리말에 맞게 빈칸을 채우시오. (주어진 철자로 시작할 것)

(1) 그 가방이 낡긴 했지만, 나는 디자인이 마음에 든다.
➡ A_____ the bag is old, I like the bag's design.

(2) 이 지역의 원주민 사진이 이 책에 있다.
➡ There is a picture of a n_____ of this area in this book.

(3) 난 최근에 체중이 늘었다.
➡ I've gained weight r_____.

[05~06] 다음 대화를 읽고 물음에 답하시오.

M: Hello. May I help you?
G: Yes, please. _____(A)_____
M: I'm afraid you can't.
G: (B)Then, can I exchange this hat for the gloves over there?
M: Yes, you can.

05 위 대화의 빈칸 (A)에 들어갈 말로 알맞은 것을 고르시오.

① Do you sell this hat here?
② I want to buy this hat.
③ Can I get this hat?
④ Can I get a refund for this hat?
⑤ Is it possible to exchange this hat?

06 위 대화의 (B)Then을 if를 포함한 절로 바꿔 쓰시오. (9 words)

➡ _____

[07~08] 다음 대화를 읽고 물음에 답하시오.

G: I bought this red skirt last week. I like the skirt, but my sister says that the color doesn't look good on me. I wonder ____(A)____ I should exchange it for a different color.

B: It's up to you but I think it's fine.

_{출제율 90%}

07 위 대화의 빈칸 (A)에 들어갈 알맞은 말을 쓰시오.

➡ _____

_{출제율 95%}

08 Why does the girl think about exchanging what she bought?

➡ _____
_____

[09~10] 다음 대화를 읽고 물음에 답하시오.

W: Hello. Do you need some help?

B: Yes. (①) I'd like to return this smartphone case.

W: (②) Do you have the receipt with you?

B: Here it is. (③) I bought it three days ago. (④)

W: Oh, then it's possible. (⑤)

_{출제율 95%}

09 (①)~(⑤) 중 주어진 문장이 들어갈 곳은?

Let's see.

①   ②   ③   ④   ⑤

_{출제율 100%}

10 위 대화를 읽고 대답할 수 없는 질문을 고르시오.

① When did the boy buy the smartphone case?

② What does the boy need?

③ Why does the boy want to return the smartphone case?

④ Does the boy have the receipt with him?

⑤ Does the woman allow B to return the smartphone case?

_{출제율 90%}

11 What is the purpose of the boy's visiting the store? Answer by using 'to infinitive.'

➡ _____

_{출제율 100%}

12 다음 문장의 빈칸 (A), (B), (C)에 들어갈 말로 가장 적절한 것은?

- Miranda isn't sure ____(A)____ to stay in Rome during her business trip.
- The boy showed the foreigner ____(B)____ to get to the Big Ben.
- The little girl didn't know ____(C)____ to do with the boys, so she went out.

	(A)	(B)	(C)
①	which	how	where
②	which	when	where
③	where	how	what
④	where	when	what
⑤	when	how	how

_{출제율 95%}

13 다음 중 어법상 어색한 것을 고르시오.

① They have been watching her sing and dance on TV since this evening.

② What have you been trying to looking for in those caves?

③ Ken has been reading books for 45 minutes.

④ My daughters have been playing the trumpet recently.

⑤ Trump's sons have been playing poker during the summer vacation.

출제율 100%

14 다음 중 빈칸에 들어갈 의문사의 종류가 나머지 셋과 다른 두 개를 고르시오.

① Billy wanted to know _____ to wear to the party.

② The little children didn't know _____ to play basketball on the court.

③ The homeless man didn't know _____ to beg for money, for he was first in that town.

④ Amy hasn't decided _____ to buy with her money.

⑤ Scarlet wanted to know _____ to meet her friends.

출제율 95%

15 다음 각 문장에서 어법상 어색한 부분을 골라 고치시오.

ⓐ The oil prices have been risen steadily for 2 years.

ⓑ The coach showed me what to swim in the deep sea.

ⓒ She wanted to know which to eat noodles as she had never used chopsticks.

ⓓ They have been shouting for help since 15 minutes.

ⓔ Sarah has been having the dress since she was a very little kid.

➡ ⓐ _____ ⓑ _____

   ⓒ _____ ⓓ _____

   ⓔ _____

[16~18] 다음 글을 읽고 물음에 답하시오.

The Green Middle School Times
Teens' Spending Habits

How smart are you with your money? These are the results of a survey of 100 students at Green Middle School.

We first asked students "Are you smart with your money?" As Graph 1 shows, 70% answered "No" (A)while 30% answered "Yes." We then asked the students who answered "No" what their biggest money worry is. As Graph 2 shows, 60% think they don't have enough _____ⓐ_____ while 28% think they have difficulty saving money. Lastly, 12% said they spent money on things they didn't need.

출제율 90%

16 주어진 영영풀이를 참고하여 빈칸 ⓐ에 철자 a로 시작하는 단어를 쓰시오.

money that is given to someone, usually on a regular basis, in order to help them pay for the things that they need

➡ _____

출제율 95%

17 위 글의 밑줄 친 (A)while과 같은 의미로 쓰인 것을 고르시오.

① While you are eating, you shouldn't speak.

② Did anyone call while I was away?

③ Strike while the iron is hot.

④ While there is life, there is hope.

⑤ I've read fifty pages, while he's read only twenty.

출제율 90%

18 다음 문장에서 위 글의 내용과 다른 부분을 찾아서 고치시오.

More than ten students said they spent money on things they didn't need.

_____ ➡ _____

[19~21] 다음 글을 읽고 물음에 답하시오.

Q Hello, Dr. Money. I'm Steve. I have difficulty saving money. For example, ⓐ <u>I've been saving</u> to go to my favorite singer's concert for the last two months. However, I still don't have enough money. I don't know what to do.

A Let's see. In the last few weeks, you spent 80% of your allowance and only saved 20%. (①) I think you've been spending too much. (②) For example, you can follow the 50%-40%-10% rule. (③) Save 50%, spend 40%, and donate the remaining 10% to charity. (④) By following the rule, you can manage your money better. (⑤) Then you can save money faster to buy the ticket.

출제율 95%

19 위 글의 흐름으로 보아, 주어진 문장이 들어가기에 가장 적절한 곳은?

> To save money, you need to have a tighter budget.

①   ②   ③   ④   ⑤

출제율 90%

20 위 글의 밑줄 친 ⓐ와 현재완료의 용법이 같은 것을 <u>모두</u> 고르시오.

① I <u>have been</u> to England before.
② They <u>have watched</u> TV since this morning.
③ I <u>have lost</u> my cell phone.
④ <u>Have</u> you <u>finished</u> your lunch yet?
⑤ How long <u>has</u> she <u>played</u> it?

출제율 100%

21 Which question CANNOT be answered after reading the passage?

① Why has Steve been saving for the last two months?
② Does Steve have enough money to go to his favorite singer's concert?
③ On what did Steve spend 80% of his allowance?
④ What does Steve need to do to save money?
⑤ What advice does Dr. Money give to Steve?

[22~23] 다음 글을 읽고 물음에 답하시오.

My money problem is that I buy things on the spot. One time, I bought a smartphone case because it looked nice. However, I found out that I already had three cases at home. ⓐ <u>I don't know how to stop to buy things on the spot.</u>

출제율 90%

22 위 글의 밑줄 친 ⓐ에서 어법상 <u>틀린</u> 부분을 찾아 고치시오.

_____ ➡ _____

출제율 95%

23 위 글의 내용과 일치하도록 다음 빈칸에 알맞은 단어를 고르시오.

> The writer wants to get some advice on the problem of his or her _____ habit.

① saving   ② spending
③ earning   ④ speaking
⑤ donating

[01~03] 다음 대화를 읽고 물음에 답하시오.

M: Hello. May I help you?

G: Yes, please. I'd like to get a refund for this cap.

M: Do you have the receipt?

G: No, I don't. I ___(A)___ it as a gift.

M: If you don't have the receipt, then, it's not possible to get a refund.

G: I see. Then, can I exchange it for something else?

M: Yes, you can. What would you like to get?

G: I want to get this blue bag.

M: Let me see .... The price is the same, so you can just take it.

G: Thank you.

01 다음 영영풀이에 해당하는 말을 빈칸 (A)에 과거형으로 쓰시오.

> to get something after someone gives it to you or sends it to you

➡ _____

02 What does the girl take instead of the cap?

➡ _____

03 How come the girl is able to get the blue bag? Use the word, 'because' and 'that.' (15 words)

➡ _____
_____

04 다음 우리말과 같은 뜻이 되도록 주어진 단어들을 사용하여 제시된 글자 수에 맞게 영작하시오. (단어 변형 불가하며 숫자는 영어로만 쓰시오.)

(1) Brian이 9시 이후로 무엇을 보고 있는 중이니? (been, o'clock, watching, what, since, 총 8 단어)

➡ _____

(2) 그녀는 인천의 한 중학교에서 프랑스어를 5년간 가르쳐 왔다. (been, teaching, for, French, Incheon, middle, in, 총 14 단어)

➡ _____
_____

05 다음 〈보기〉와 같이 두 문장이 같은 의미가 되도록 빈칸에 알맞은 말을 쓰시오.

> ┤ 보기 ├
> I wonder when to turn right.
> → I wonder when I should turn right.

(1) Ted is wondering what to do next.
→ Ted is wondering _____
_____.

(2) Ms. Rose doesn't know how to get to the subway station.
→ Ms. Rose doesn't know _____
_____.

(3) Ann told Mike where to park his luxury car.
→ Ann told Mike _____
_____.

(4) The baby girl wanted to know how to move the toy.
→ The baby girl wanted to know _____
_____.

[06~08] 다음 글을 읽고 물음에 답하시오.

Are you smart with your money?

*total: 100 students

What is your biggest money worry?

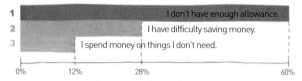

ⓐOur survey shows that the minority of students think they are not smart with their money. ⓑManaging money is not easy, and becoming a smart spender takes effort.

06 위 글의 밑줄 친 ⓐ에서 흐름상 어색한 부분을 찾아 고치시오.

_____ ➡ _____

07 위 글의 밑줄 친 ⓑ를 to부정사를 사용하여 고칠 때, 빈칸에 들어갈 알맞은 말을 쓰시오.

➡ _____ is not easy to manage money

08 What percent of the students spend money on things they don't need? Fill in the blank with a suitable word.

_____ percent of the students do so.

[09~11] 다음 글을 읽고 물음에 답하시오.

Ｑ Hello, Dr. Money. I'm Steve. I have difficulty saving money. For example, I've been saving to go to my favorite singer's concert for the last two months. However, ⓐ 저는 여전히 충분한 돈을 가지고 있지 않아요. I don't know what to do.

Ａ Let's see. In the last few weeks, you spent 80% of your allowance and only saved 20%. ⓑI think you've been saving too much. To save money, you need to have a tighter budget. For example, you can follow the 50%-40%-10% rule. Save 50%, spend 40%, and donate the remaining 10% to charity. By following the rule, you can manage your money better. Then you can save money faster to buy the ticket.

09 위 글의 밑줄 친 ⓐ의 우리말에 맞게 한 단어를 보충하여, 주어진 어휘를 알맞게 배열하시오.

enough / have / I / money / don't

➡ _____

10 위 글의 밑줄 친 ⓑ에서 흐름상 어색한 부분을 찾아 고치시오. (위 글에 나오는 동사를 변형하여 쓸 것.)

_____ ➡ _____

11 다음 빈칸 (A)와 (B)에 알맞은 단어를 넣어 Steve의 돈에 대한 고민과 Dr. Money의 조언을 완성하시오.

Steve's Worry: I have difficulty (A)_____ _____ to go to my favorite singer's concert. I need to save more money.
Dr. Money's Advice: You need to have a tighter budget. Follow the (B)_____ rule. Save 50%, spend 40%, and donate the remaining 10% to charity.

01 주어진 표현을 이용하여 〈보기〉와 같이 다음 대화의 빈칸에 알맞은 말을 쓰시오.

> possible, get a refund for / OK, get a refund for

> A: _____ this skirt?
> B: Sure. Was there anything wrong with it?

> ┌─ 보기 ─┐
> A: Can I get a refund for this bag?
> B: OK. Was there anything wrong with it?

02 다음 정보를 읽고, 주인공 Esther 또는 Alex를 주어로 하는 현재완료진행형 문장을 두 개 이상 쓰시오. (인칭과 시제 등에 유의하여 활용할 것.)

> • Alex started to teach English to the middle school students 15 years ago.
> • Alex began to teach his students how to solve the cube puzzle 5 years ago.
> • Esther, one of Alex's students, first learned to solve the cube puzzle last year when she entered the middle school.
> • He is still teaching the middle school students English and the way of solving the cube puzzle until now.
> • Esther is still learning to solve the cube puzzle.
> • Esther is still learning English from Alex.

03 다음 내용을 바탕으로 자신의 소비 습관의 문제점에 관한 조언을 구하는 글을 쓰시오.

> **My Spending Habits**
> • my money problem: I buy things on the spot.
> • episode showing my problem: I once bought a smartphone case because it looked nice. However, I found out that I already had three cases at home.

> My (A)_____ is that I buy things (B)_____. I once bought a smartphone case because it looked (C)_____. However, I found out that I already (D)_____ at home. I don't know how to stop buying things on the spot.

단원별 모의고사

1 다음 짝지어진 단어의 관계가 같도록 빈칸에 알맞은 말을 쓰시오. (주어진 철자로 시작할 것)

> lastly – finally : result – o_____

[02~03] 주어진 영어 설명에 알맞은 어휘를 빈칸에 쓰시오.

2

> Listen to the _____ of your father and mother.

> <영어 설명> an opinion you give someone about what they should do

➡ _____

3

> She saved up all her _____ and bought a laptop computer.

> <영어 설명> money given by parents to a child regularly that the child can spend

➡ _____

4 다음 빈칸에 알맞은 말로 짝지어진 것을 고르시오.

> • Ice cream is on _____ for half price.
> • Jack drank the _____ juice.

① refund – waiting
② refund – remaining
③ sale – waiting
④ sale – remaining
⑤ return – staying

[05~06] 다음 영영풀이를 참고하여 빈칸에 알맞은 말을 쓰시오.

5

> the state or situation of having a problem

> I had _____ in communicating in English.

6

> in the exact place where something is happening

> He took a look at the car and decided to buy it _____ .

[07~08] 다음 대화를 읽고 물음에 답하시오.

M: Hello. ⓐMay I help you?
G: Yes, please. Can I get ⓑa refund for this hat?
M: _____ (A)
G: Then, can I ⓒchange this hat ⓓfor the gloves over there?
M: Yes, you ⓔcan.

7 위 대화의 빈칸 (A)에 들어갈 말로 알맞은 것을 고르시오.

① Yes, you can.
② Why not?
③ Do you want to return the hat?
④ We can give customers some discount.
⑤ I'm afraid you can't.

8 위 대화의 밑줄 친 ⓐ~ⓔ 중 어색한 것은?

① ⓐ　② ⓑ　③ ⓒ　④ ⓓ　⑤ ⓔ

[09~11] 다음 대화를 읽고 물음에 답하시오.

M: Hello. May I help you?

G: Yes, please. I'd like to get a refund for this cap. (①)

M: Do you have the receipt?

G: No, I don't. I received it ___(A)___ a gift.

M: If you don't have the receipt, then, it's not possible to get a refund. (②)

G: I see. Then, can I exchange it for something else? (③)

M: Yes, you can. (④)

G: I want to get this blue bag.

M: Let me see .... (B)가격이 같으니까 그것을 가져 가셔도 돼요. (just, the price, same, take, so) (⑤)

G: Thank you.

09 (①)~(⑤) 중 주어진 문장이 들어갈 곳은?

> What would you like to get?

①   ②   ③   ④   ⑤

10 위 대화의 빈칸 (A)에 알맞은 말을 1 단어로 쓰시오.

➡ _____

11 위 대화의 밑줄 친 우리말 (B)에 맞게 주어진 어휘를 이용하여 11 단어로 쓰시오.

➡ _____

12 다음 그림을 보고 괄호 안의 단어를 활용해서 우리말에 맞게 빈칸을 채우시오.

(1) 원님이 농부에게 그 초대형 당근을 어떻게 처리할지 물어보고 있다.

➡ The governor is asking the farmer _____ _____ _____ the super big carrot. (handle)

(2) 5분 전부터 나의 개가 내 성적표를 물어 뜯고 있는 중이다.

➡ My dog _____ _____ my report card since 5 minutes ago. (bite)

(3) 그 강아지는 어느 발을 내밀지 고민 중이다.

➡ The puppy is wondering _____ _____ _____ _____. (put out)

13 다음 밑줄 친 부분 중 어법상 어색한 것을 고르시오.

① Timothy wants to know where to buy his new coat.

② The couple decided when to leave for Hawaii.

③ The old pilot almost forgot how to fly.

④ Could you please tell her what to use the monitoring system?

⑤ The girl asked Charlie how to open the box.

14 다음 세 문장을 주어진 〈조건〉에 맞게 한 문장으로 쓰시오.

> ┤ 조건 ├
> • 현재완료진행시제를 사용할 것.
> • 분사가 명사의 뒤에서 수식할 것.
> • for를 반드시 사용할 것.
> • 10 단어를 넘지 않을 것.

(1) • John started to watch the flims last Saturday.
　• Bong directed the films.
　• It's Tuesday today and John is still watching them.
　= John _____
　_____ days.

(2) • Daisy started working at a store last week.
　• Butler owns the store.
　• Daisy is still working there.
　= Daisy _____
　_____ a week.

15 우리말과 일치하도록 괄호 안의 단어를 바르게 배열하시오.

(1) Wilson은 오늘 아침부터 복사기를 어떻게 수리하는지 배우고 있다.
(photocopier, to, Wilson, fix, has, since, how, been, morning, learning, the, this)
➡ _____
_____

(2) Susan의 친구들이 3시간 동안 저 무거운 가방들을 옮겨 주고 있다.
(three, bags, friends, hours, carrying, been, heavy, for, Susan's, those, have)
➡ _____
_____

16 다음 중 밑줄 친 부분의 쓰임이 〈보기〉와 다른 것은?

> ┤ 보기 ├
> The people have lived in this city of New-Town since early 1990s.

① Thomas' uncle has kept the machine working since he first operated it.
② Dave has finished checking all the rooms in his building.
③ Sean has stayed in Paris since he went there to study painting 2 years ago.
④ The girls have known each other since they're born at the same hospital.
⑤ It has been quite chilly these days.

17 다음 우리말을 아래의 어휘들을 배열하여 영작하되 현재완료진행시제로 쓰시오.

> Jack은 지난달 이후로 백화점에서 일하고 있다.
> (working / Jack / last month / the department store / has / since / been / at).

➡ _____
_____

[18~19] 다음 글을 읽고 물음에 답하시오.

Ⓐ Buying things on sale is good if you buy things you need. (①) Here's some advice. (②) Before you buy something, ask yourself, "Do I really need this?" (③) Also, before you go shopping, make a shopping list. (④) ⓐDon't buy items that isn't on the list even if they're on sale. (⑤) Then you won't buy things on the spot.

18 위 글의 흐름으로 보아, 주어진 문장이 들어가기에 가장 적절한 곳은?

> In your case, the problem is that you buy things you don't even need.

①   ②   ③   ④   ⑤

19 위 글의 밑줄 친 ⓐ에서 어법상 틀린 부분을 찾아 고치시오.

_____ ➡ _____

[20~22] 다음 글을 읽고 물음에 답하시오.

The Green Middle School Times
Teens' Spending Habits

 How smart are you with your money? These are the results of a survey of 100 students at Green Middle School.

 We first asked students "Are you smart with your money?" As Graph 1 shows, 70% answered "No" while 30% answered "Yes." We then asked the students who answered "No" ⓐ그들의 돈에 대한 가장 큰 고민이 무엇인지. As Graph 2 shows, 60% think they don't have enough allowance while 28% think they have difficulty saving money. Lastly, 12% said they spent money on things they didn't need.

20 위 글의 밑줄 친 ⓐ의 우리말에 맞게 주어진 어휘를 알맞게 배열하시오.

> money / their / is / biggest / what / worry

➡ _____

21 According to the survey, are the majority of students smart spenders? Answer in English in a full sentence. (3 words)

➡ _____

22 본문의 내용과 일치하도록 다음 빈칸에 들어갈 알맞은 분수를 고르시오.

> The percent of the students who spent money on things they didn't need is _____ _____ of the percent of the students who think they don't have enough allowance.

① one third   ② two-thirds
③ one fourth   ④ three-fourths
⑤ one fifth

[23~25] 다음 글을 읽고 물음에 답하시오.

Q Hello, Dr. Money. I'm Steve. I have difficulty ①saving money. For example, I've been ②saving to go to my favorite singer's concert for the last two months. ___ⓐ___, I still don't have enough money. I don't know what to do.

A Let's see. In the last few weeks, you spent 80% of your allowance and only saved 20%. I think you've been ③spending too much. To save money, you need to have a tighter budget. For example, you can follow the 50%-40%-10% rule. Save 50%, spend 40%, and donate the ④remained 10% to charity. By ⑤following the rule, you can manage your money better. Then you can save money faster to buy the ticket.

23 위 글의 빈칸 @에 들어갈 알맞은 말을 고르시오.

① In addition
② However
③ Thus
④ For example
⑤ Similarly

24 위 글의 밑줄 친 ①~⑤ 중 어법상 <u>틀린</u> 것을 찾아 고치시오.

_____ ➡ _____

25 According to the passage, which is NOT true?

① It is not easy for Steve to save money to go to his favorite singer's concert.
② In the last few weeks, Steve spent four-fifths of his allowance.
③ In the last few weeks, Steve only saved one fifth of his allowance.
④ To save money, Steve needs to follow the 50%-40%-10% rule.
⑤ The 50%-40%-10% rule means spending 50%, saving 40%, and donating the remaining 10% to charity.

[26~28] 다음 글을 읽고 물음에 답하시오.

Q I'm Minji. I like to buy things on sale. If something's on sale, I buy it (A)[although / in spite of] I don't need it. Last week, I bought two T-shirts on sale, but I already have many.

A Buying things on sale is good if you buy things you need. In your case, the problem is that you buy things you don't even need. Here's some (B)[advice / advices]. Before you buy something, ask yourself, "Do I really need this?" Also, before you go shopping, make a shopping list. Don't buy items that aren't on the list (C)[as if / even if] they're on sale. Then you won't buy things @즉석에서.

26 위 글의 괄호 (A)~(C)에서 문맥이나 어법상 알맞은 낱말을 골라 쓰시오.

➡ (A) _____ (B) _____ (C) _____

27 위 글의 밑줄 친 @의 우리말에 맞게 3 단어로 영작하시오.

➡ _____

28 다음 중 민지에 대한 설명이 옳지 <u>않은</u> 것을 고르시오.

① Minji likes to buy things on sale.
② Minji buys something if it's on sale though she doesn't need it.
③ Minji is a smart spender as she always buys things on sale.
④ Minji should ask herself, "Do I really need this?" before she buys something.
⑤ Minji should make a shopping list before she goes shopping.

MEMO

중간+기말 plus⁺

적중100

영어 기출문제집

영어 중 **3**

동아 | 윤정미

Best Collection

내용문의 중등영어발전소 적중100 편집부 TEL 070-7707-0457
인터넷 서비스 www.jj100.co.kr

INSIGHT
on the textbook

교과서 파헤치기

영어 기출 문제집

적중 100 plus
1학기 전과정

영어 중 3

동아 | 윤정미

INSIGHT
on the textbook

교과서 파헤치기

※ 다음 영어를 우리말로 쓰시오.

01 engineering _____

02 graduate _____

03 bold _____

04 chance _____

05 realize _____

06 goal _____

07 enter _____

08 follow _____

09 achieve _____

10 beat _____

11 part-time _____

12 environment _____

13 quit _____

14 volunteer _____

15 company _____

16 train _____

17 whether _____

18 college _____

19 air pollution _____

20 stable _____

21 win _____

22 pursue _____

23 decision _____

24 engineer _____

25 succeed _____

26 inspire _____

27 memorable _____

28 professional _____

29 lead _____

30 major _____

31 local _____

32 courage _____

33 photography _____

34 surprisingly _____

35 in fact _____

36 get better _____

37 for a living _____

38 come true _____

39 in one's case _____

40 not ~ at all _____

41 for the first time _____

42 follow one's heart _____

43 make a decision _____

단어 Test

※ 다음 우리말을 영어로 쓰시오.

01 대학(교)

02 결정, 결심

03 따르다, 뒤를 잇다

04 목표

05 용기

06 놀랍게도

07 성취하다, 달성하다

08 (심장이) 고동치다, 뛰다

09 용감한, 대담한

10 환경, 상황, 분위기

11 기회

12 성공하다

13 전문적인, (전문) 직업의

14 자원하다, 봉사하다

15 회사

16 공기 오염

17 ~인지 아닌지

18 추구하다, 좇다

19 엔지니어, 기술자

20 (상을) 타다, 이기다

21 졸업하다

22 영감을 주다, 고무하다

23 (특정) 지역의, 현지의

24 중요한, 주된; 전공, 전공하다

25 시간제 근무의

26 이끌다

27 기억할 만한, 인상적인

28 사진 촬영술

29 (직장·학교 등을) 그만두다

30 알다, 깨닫다, 실현하다

31 안정된, 안정적인

32 공학 (기술), 엔지니어링

33 (특정 직업을) 훈련하다

34 디자이너

35 전혀 ~가 아니다

36 사실은

37 (숙고하여 뭔가를) 고르다

38 결정하다

39 실현되다, 사실이 되다

40 기회를 잡다

41 (병이나 상황이) 나아지다

42 ~의 경우에

43 처음으로

※ 다음 영영풀이에 알맞은 단어를 <보기>에서 골라 쓴 후, 우리말 뜻을 쓰시오.

1 _____ : to gain with effort: _____

2 _____ : to stop doing something: _____

3 _____ : competition in which people try to win something: _____

4 _____ : not afraid to do things which involve danger: _____

5 _____ : the main subject that a student is studying at a university or college: _____

6 _____ : make a regular sound or movement of the heart: _____

7 _____ : staying the same, with no big changes or problems: _____

8 _____ : to achieve something that you want: _____

9 _____ : to complete your studies successfully and leave your school or university: _____

10 _____ : something that you hope to achieve, especially when much time and effort will be needed: _____

11 _____ : to make you feel that you want to achieve something or create something: _____

12 _____ : to work hard in order to achieve something: _____

13 _____ : to teach someone the skills of a particular job or activity, or to be taught these skills: _____

14 _____ : not afraid to do things which involve danger: _____

15 _____ : experimenting until a solution is found: _____

16 _____ : a person whose job is to decide how things such as clothes, furniture, tools, etc. will look or work by making drawings, plans, or patterns: _____

보기			
designer	goal	bold	quit
contest	pursue	realize	beat
major	graduate	trial and error	achieve
courage	inspire	stable	train

※ 다음 우리말과 일치하도록 빈칸에 알맞은 말을 쓰시오.

Listen and Talk A 1

G: _____ you ever _____ _____ food _____?

B: No, I _____. _____ you _____ _____?

G: Yes, I _____. _____ _____ you _____ try it _____.
It's really good.

B: I _____. _____ _____, I'll just buy this _____ _____
book.

Listen and Talk A 2

B: _____ you _____ _____ _____ country?

G: No, I _____. _____ you?

B: Yes, _____ _____ _____ France. _____ _____ you
_____ travel _____ _____ _____ _____.

G: Yes, I really want _____ _____ Canada. Look! This book about
Canada _____ very _____.

Listen and Talk A 3

G: You _____ read this book about the moon. It's really interesting.

B: I know. I've _____ _____ _____.

G: You _____? _____ _____ the movie? _____ _____
_____ _____ the movie about the book?

B: No, I _____.

G: Well, it's _____ _____ _____ the book. _____ _____
you can see the movie _____.

Listen and Talk A 4

G: I'm going to buy this CD. I love _____ _____ piano music.

B: Me, _____. I also _____ _____ _____ piano.

G: Really? So you _____ _____ _____ piano?

B: Yes. _____ _____ _____ _____?

G: Well, I've _____ _____ _____ _____ _____ _____.

B: It's _____. _____ _____ you'll have a _____ _____
_____.

G: 난 이 CD를 살 거야. 난 피아노 음악을 듣는 것을 좋아해.
B: 나도. 난 피아노 치는 것도 즐겨서 해.
G: 정말? 넌 피아노를 칠 수 있니?
B: 응. 너는 어때?
G: 음, 난 피아노 치는 법을 배운 적이 없어.
B: 그것은 재미있어. 너도 배울 기회가 있길 바랄게.

Listen and Talk C

B: I really liked your book _____ _____ dogs.

W: Thank you. Do you like dogs?

B: Yes, I _____. I love _____ _____ _____ animals.

W: _____ you _____ _____ of _____ an animal doctor?

B: Yes, I _____. I really want _____ _____ an animal doctor.

W: W h a t _____ _____ _____ _____ _____ y o u r _____?

B: I'm _____ _____ _____ at the local animal house.

W: That's good. What _____ are you _____?

B: I'm _____ _____ a lot of TV shows about animals.

W: You're doing _____! _____ _____ you become a good animal doctor _____.

B: Thank you.

Review 1

G: Mike, _____ you _____ Bulgogi _____?

B: No, I _____.

G: _____ _____ Bibimbap? _____ you _____ that?

B: Yes, I've _____ it _____. It was really _____.

Review 2

G: My _____ book is *Charlie and the Chocolate Factory*. _____ you _____ _____, Peter?

B: No, I _____, but I've _____ the movie. _____ you, Yubin? _____ you _____ the movie, _____?

G: Yes, I _____. But I like the book _____. _____ you can read it _____.

B: OK, I _____.

B: 개를 훈련하는 것에 관한 당신의 책이 저는 정말 좋았어요.
W: 고마워요. 개를 좋아해요?
B: 네, 저는 모든 종류의 동물을 매우 좋아해요.
W: 수의사가 되는 것을 생각해 본 적 있어요?
B: 네, 있어요. 저는 수의사가 정말 되고 싶어요.
W: 목표를 이루기 위해 무엇을 하고 있나요?
B: 지역 동물의 집(동물 보호소)에서 자원봉사를 하고 있어요.
W: 좋군요. 또 무엇을 하고 있나요?
B: 동물에 관한 TV 쇼도 많이 보고 있어요.
W: 매우 잘하고 있어요! 언젠가 좋은 수의사가 되기를 바랄게요.
B: 감사합니다.

G: Mike, 불고기를 먹어 본 적이 있니?
B: 아니, 없어.
G: 비빔밥은? 먹어 본 적이 있니?
B: 응, 한번 먹어 본 적이 있어. 그것은 정말 맛있었어.

G: 내가 가장 좋아하는 책은 "찰리와 초콜릿 공장"이야. Peter, 그것을 읽어 본 적이 있니?
B: 아니, 읽은 적은 없지만 영화를 본 적은 있어. 유빈아, 넌 어때? 영화도 본 적이 있니?
G: 응, 있어, 그렇지만 난 책을 더 좋아해. 난 네가 언젠가 그 책을 읽을 수 있기를 바라.
B: 알겠어, 읽어 볼게.

Step2

※ 다음 우리말에 맞도록 대화를 영어로 쓰시오.

Listen and Talk A 1

G: _____

B: _____

G: _____

B: _____

G: 스페인 요리를 먹어 본 적 있니?
B: 아니, 없어. 너는 먹어 본 적이 있니?
G: 응, 있어. 네가 언젠가 그것을 먹어 보길 바라. 정말 맛있거든.
B: 그럴게. 우선 이 스페인 요리 책을 사야겠어.

Listen and Talk A 2

B: _____

G: _____

B: _____

G: _____

B: 다른 나라에 가 본 적이 있니?
G: 아니, 없어. 너는 가 본 적이 있니?
B: 응, 난 프랑스에 가 본 적이 있어. 네가 언젠가 다른 나라를 여행해 보기를 바라.
G: 응. 난 캐나다에 정말 가고 싶어. 봐! 캐나다에 관한 이 책은 정말 흥미로워 보인다.

Listen and Talk A 3

G: _____

B: _____

G: _____

B: _____

G: _____

G: 달에 관한 이 책을 꼭 읽어 봐. 그것은 정말 흥미로워.
B: 알고 있어. 나 이미 그것을 읽은 적이 있어.
G: 그랬니? 영화는? 그 책에 관한 영화도 본 적이 있니?
B: 아니, 없어.
G: 음, 그것은 책보다도 더 재미있어. 네가 그 영화를 곧 볼 수 있기를 바랄게.

Listen and Talk A 4

G: _____

B: _____

G: _____

B: _____

G: _____

B: _____

G: 난 이 CD를 살 거야. 난 피아노 음악을 듣는 것을 좋아해.
B: 나도. 난 피아노 치는 것도 즐겨서 해.
G: 정말? 넌 피아노를 칠 수 있니?
B: 응. 너는 어때?
G: 음, 난 피아노 치는 법을 배운 적이 없어.
B: 그것은 재미있어. 너도 배울 기회가 있길 바랄게.

Listen and Talk C

B: _____

W: _____

B: _____

W: _____

B: _____

W: _____

B: _____

W: _____

B: _____

W: _____

B: _____

B: 개를 훈련하는 것에 관한 당신의 책이 저는 정말 좋았어요.
W: 고마워요. 개를 좋아해요?
B: 네, 저는 모든 종류의 동물을 매우 좋아해요.
W: 수의사가 되는 것을 생각해 본 적 있어요?
B: 네, 있어요. 저는 수의사가 정말 되고 싶어요.
W: 목표를 이루기 위해 무엇을 하고 있나요?
B: 지역 동물의 집(동물 보호소)에서 자원봉사를 하고 있어요.
W: 좋군요. 또 무엇을 하고 있나요?
B: 동물에 관한 TV 쇼도 많이 보고 있어요.
W: 매우 잘하고 있어요! 언젠가 좋은 수의사가 되기를 바랄게요.
B: 감사합니다.

Review 1

G: _____

B: _____

G: _____

B: _____

G: Mike, 불고기를 먹어 본 적이 있니?
B: 아니, 없어.
G: 비빔밥은? 먹어 본 적이 있니?
B: 응, 한번 먹어 본 적이 있어. 그것은 정말 맛있었어.

Review 2

G: _____

B: _____

G: _____

B: _____

G: 내가 가장 좋아하는 책은 "찰리와 초콜릿 공장"이야. Peter, 그것을 읽어 본 적이 있니?
B: 아니, 읽은 적은 없지만 영화를 본 적은 있어. 유빈아, 넌 어때? 영화도 본 적이 있니?
G: 응, 있어, 그렇지만 난 책을 더 좋아해. 난 네가 언젠가 그 책을 읽을 수 있기를 바라.
B: 알겠어, 읽어 볼게.

※ 다음 우리말과 일치하도록 빈칸에 알맞은 것을 골라 쓰시오.

1 _____ a _____ and _____ It!

A. Dream   B. Live   C. Find

2 _____, _____.

A. everyone   B. hello

3 _____ _____ is David Parker, and _____ a _____.

A. I'm   B. name   C. photographer   D. my

4 Today, I'm _____ to tell you _____ I _____ my dream and _____ it.

A. found   B. going   C. realized   D. how

5 I _____ my story can _____ _____.

A. inspire   B. hope   C. you

6 _____ _____ _____ _____, I loved stars.

A. young   B. I   C. when   D. was

7 I _____ liked _____ _____.

A. taking   B. also   C. pictures

8 However, I _____ _____ these things could _____ _____ a job.

A. thought   B. to   C. never   D. lead

9 _____ _____, I didn't have a dream _____ _____.

A. at   B. fact   C. all   D. in

10 When I had to _____ a major in college, I _____ _____.

A. on   B. chose   C. decide   D. engineering

11 _____ an engineer _____ _____.

A. looked   B. being   C. OK

12 After _____, I got a _____ at an _____ _____.

A. company   B. job   C. college   D. engineering

13 It was a _____ job, _____ I didn't know _____ I really _____ it.

A. but   B. enjoyed   C. whether   D. stable

1 꿈을 찾고 실현하세요!

2 여러분, 안녕하세요.

3 나의 이름은 David Parker이고, 나는 사진작가입니다.

4 오늘 나는 어떻게 내가 꿈을 찾아서 실현했는지 이야기하려고 해요.

5 나의 이야기가 여러분에게 영감을 주기를 바라요.

6 나는 어렸을 때 별을 사랑했어요.

7 나는 또한 사진 찍는 것을 좋아했어요.

8 하지만 나는 이것들이 직업과 연관될 수 있다고 전혀 생각하지 못했어요.

9 사실 나는 아예 꿈이 없었어요.

10 내가 대학에서 전공을 정해야 했을 때, 나는 공학을 선택했어요.

11 엔지니어가 되는 것이 괜찮아 보였거든요.

12 대학 졸업 후 저는 엔지니어링 회사에 취직했어요.

13 그것은 안정적인 직업이었지만, 난 내가 그 일을 정말로 좋아하는지는 알 수가 없었어요.

14 Everything _____ when I _____ _____ _____ to Iceland one winter.

    A. went   B. changed   C. vacation   D. on

15 There I _____ a _____ to _____ the Northern Lights!

    A. chance   B. got   C. see

16 The lights were _____, and I _____ many _____ of the dancing _____ in the sky.

    A. lights   B. amazing   C. pictures   D. took

17 _____ the first time in many _____, I could feel my heart _____ _____.

    A. beating   B. for   C. fast   D. years

18 After I came _____, I _____ a photo contest _____ the pictures I _____ in Iceland.

    A. took   B. entered   C. with   D. back

19 Surprisingly, I _____ first _____, and this gave me a _____ to _____ about my life.

    A. prize   B. think   C. won   D. chance

20 I _____ that taking pictures _____ _____ _____.

    A. made   B. happy   C. realized   D. me

21 Suddenly, I wanted to _____ a good photographer, _____ I started to _____ _____ about photography.

    A. more   B. become   C. learn   D. so

22 After years of _____ and _____, I got _____, and I began to do some _____ work as a photographer.

    A. error   B. better   C. part-time   D. trial

23 Then _____ day, I _____ a _____ _____.

    A. bold   B. one   C. decision   D. made

24 I _____ my job and _____ to take pictures _____ a _____.

    A. living   B. quit   C. for   D. decided

25 I _____ _____ if I could _____, but I decided to _____.

    A. try   B. sure   C. succeed   D. wasn't

14 어느 겨울, 내가 아이슬란드로 휴가를 갔을 때 모든 것이 바뀌었어요.

15 그곳에서 나는 오로라를 볼 수 있는 기회가 있었죠.

16 빛들은 경이로웠고 나는 하늘에서 춤추는 빛들의 사진을 많이 찍었어요.

17 수년 만에 처음으로 나는 심장이 빠르게 뛰고 있는 것을 느낄 수 있었어요.

18 나는 돌아와서 아이슬란드에서 찍은 사진으로 사진 경연 대회에 참가했어요.

19 놀랍게도 나는 1등상을 받았고, 이 일은 나에게 인생을 생각해 볼 기회를 주었어요.

20 나는 사진 찍는 것이 나를 행복하게 한다는 것을 깨달았어요.

21 갑자기 나는 좋은 사진작가가 되고 싶어서 사진 촬영 기술에 대해 더 배우기 시작했어요.

22 몇 년의 시행착오 끝에 나는 더 나아졌고 사진작가로 시간제 근무일을 하기 시작했어요.

23 그러던 어느 날 나는 대담한 결심을 했어요.

24 나는 직장을 그만 두고 생계 수단으로 사진을 찍기로 했어요.

25 나는 내가 성공할 수 있을지 확신하지 못했지만 시도해 보기로 결심했어요.

26 I really wanted to do _____ _____ _____ me _____.

    A. made   B. something   C. happy   D. that

27 Now, I'm a _____ _____, and I'm _____.

    A. happy   B. photographer C. professional

28 So do you want to _____ a _____ and _____?

    A. it   B. find   C. realize   D. dream

29 Here's _____ _____ _____ you.

    A. help   B. some   C. to   D. advice

30 First, _____ _____ _____.

    A. heart   B. follow   C. your

31 Think about what you like to do and _____ _____ _____ _____.

    A. what   B. happy   C. makes   D. you

32 In my _____, it was _____ pictures of _____.

    A. case   B. taking   C. stars

33 Second, _____ _____.

    A. hard   B. work

34 _____ a _____ is not _____.

    A. easy   B. pursuing   C. dream

35 I became a photographer _____ _____ _____.

    A. work   B. through   C. hard

36 Third, _____ _____.

    A. bold   B. be

37 You need _____ to _____ _____ that will change your _____.

    A. life   B. make   C. courage   D. decisions

38 I was _____ _____ I _____ a _____.

    A. chance   B. took   C. but   D. afraid

39 I _____ _____ you can _____ a dream, _____ it, and live it!

    A. pursue   B. hope   C. truly   D. find

---

26 나는 나를 행복하게 만드는 무언가를 정말로 하고 싶었어요.

27 지금. 나는 전문 사진작가이고, 나는 행복합니다.

28 그렇다면 여러분은 꿈을 찾아 실현하고 싶은가요?

29 여기 여러분을 도와줄 몇 가지 조언이 있습니다.

30 첫째, 여러분의 마음을 따르세요.

31 여러분이 무엇을 하고 싶고 여러분을 행복하게 하는 것이 무엇인지 생각해 보세요.

32 나의 경우에 그것은 별 사진을 찍는 거였어요.

33 둘째. 열심히 노력하세요.

34 꿈을 추구하는 것은 쉽지 않아요.

35 나는 열심히 노력해 사진작가가 되었어요.

36 셋째. 대담해지세요.

37 여러분의 인생을 바꿀 결정을 하기 위해서는 용기가 필요합니다.

38 나는 두려웠지만 기회를 잡았어요.

39 나는 여러분이 꿈을 찾고. 꿈을 추구하고. 꿈을 실현하길 진심으로 바랍니다!

※ 다음 우리말과 일치하도록 빈칸에 알맞은 것을 골라 쓰시오.

1 _____ a _____ and _____ It!

2 _____, everyone.

3 My name is David Parker, and I'm _____ _____.

4 Today, I'm _____ _____ tell you _____ _____ _____ my dream and _____ it.

5 I _____ my story can _____ _____.

6 _____ _____ _____ _____, I loved stars.

7 I also _____ _____ _____.

8 However, I _____ _____ these things could _____ _____ _____ _____.

9 _____ _____, I didn't have a dream _____ _____.

10 When I had to _____ _____ a major in _____, I chose _____.

11 _____ an engineer _____ _____.

12 _____ _____, I got a job at _____ _____ _____.

13 It was a _____ job, but I didn't know _____ I really enjoyed it.

---

1 꿈을 찾고 실현하세요!

2 여러분, 안녕하세요.

3 나의 이름은 David Parker이고, 나는 사진작가입니다.

4 오늘 나는 어떻게 내가 꿈을 찾아서 실현했는지 이야기하려고 해요.

5 나의 이야기가 여러분에게 영감을 주기를 바라요.

6 나는 어렸을 때 별을 사랑했어요.

7 나는 또한 사진 찍는 것을 좋아했어요.

8 하지만 나는 이것들이 직업과 연관될 수 있다고 전혀 생각하지 못했어요.

9 사실 나는 아예 꿈이 없었어요.

10 내가 대학에서 전공을 정해야 했을 때, 나는 공학을 선택했어요.

11 엔지니어가 되는 것이 괜찮아 보였거든요.

12 대학 졸업 후 저는 엔지니어링 회사에 취직했어요.

13 그것은 안정적인 직업이었지만, 난 내가 그 일을 정말로 좋아하는지는 알 수가 없었어요.

14 Everything changed _____ I _____ _____ _____ to Iceland one winter.

15 There I _____ _____ _____ to see the Northern Lights!

16 The lights were _____, and I _____ _____ _____ of the _____ _____ in the sky.

17 _____ _____ _____ _____ in many _____, I could feel my heart _____ _____.

18 After I _____ _____, I _____ a photo contest with _____ _____ _____ _____ in Iceland.

19 Surprisingly, I _____ _____ _____, and this gave me a _____ _____ _____ about my life.

20 I _____ that taking pictures _____ _____ _____.

21 _____, I wanted to become a good photographer, so I started to _____ _____ _____ _____.

22 After years of _____ _____ _____, I _____ _____, and I began to do some _____ _____ as a photographer.

23 Then _____ _____, I made a _____ _____.

24 I quit my job and _____ _____ take pictures _____ _____.

25 I _____ _____ _____ I could _____, but I decided _____ _____.

14 어느 겨울, 내가 아이슬란드로 휴가를 갔을 때 모든 것이 바뀌었어요.

15 그곳에서 나는 오로라를 볼 수 있는 기회가 있었죠.

16 빛들은 경이로웠고 나는 하늘에서 춤추는 빛들의 사진을 많이 찍었어요.

17 수년 만에 처음으로 나는 심장이 빠르게 뛰고 있는 것을 느낄 수 있었어요.

18 나는 돌아와서 아이슬란드에서 찍은 사진으로 사진 경연 대회에 참가했어요.

19 놀랍게도 나는 1등상을 받았고, 이 일은 나에게 인생을 생각해 볼 기회를 주었어요.

20 나는 사진 찍는 것이 나를 행복하게 한다는 것을 깨달았어요.

21 갑자기 나는 좋은 사진작가가 되고 싶어서 사진 촬영 기술에 대해 더 배우기 시작했어요.

22 몇 년의 시행착오 끝에 나는 더 나아졌고 사진작가로 시간제 근무일을 하기 시작했어요.

23 그러던 어느 날 나는 대담한 결심을 했어요.

24 나는 직장을 그만 두고 생계 수단으로 사진을 찍기로 했어요.

25 나는 내가 성공할 수 있을지 확신하지 못했지만 시도해 보기로 결심했어요.

26 I really wanted to do _____ _____ made me _____.

27 Now, I'm a _____ _____, and I'm happy.

28 So do you want to _____ _____ _____ and _____ _____?

29 Here's _____ _____ _____ _____ you.

30 First, _____ _____ _____.

31 Think about what you like to do and _____ _____ _____ _____.

32 In my _____, it was _____ _____ _____ _____.

33 Second, _____ _____.

34 _____ a dream is not _____.

35 I became a photographer _____ _____ _____.

36 Third, _____ _____.

37 You need _____ to _____ _____ that will change your _____.

38 I was _____ but I _____ _____ _____.

39 I _____ _____ you can find a dream, pursue it, and live it!

26 나는 나를 행복하게 만드는 무언가를 정말로 하고 싶었어요.

27 지금, 나는 전문 사진작가이고, 나는 행복합니다.

28 그렇다면 여러분은 꿈을 찾아 실현하고 싶은가요?

29 여기 여러분을 도와줄 몇 가지 조언이 있습니다.

30 첫째, 여러분의 마음을 따르세요.

31 여러분이 무엇을 하고 싶고 여러분을 행복하게 하는 것이 무엇인지 생각해 보세요.

32 나의 경우에 그것은 별 사진을 찍는 거였어요.

33 둘째, 열심히 노력하세요.

34 꿈을 추구하는 것은 쉽지 않아요.

35 나는 열심히 노력해 사진작가가 되었어요.

36 셋째, 대담해지세요.

37 여러분의 인생을 바꿀 결정을 하기 위해서는 용기가 필요합니다.

38 나는 두려웠지만 기회를 잡았어요.

39 나는 여러분이 꿈을 찾고, 꿈을 추구하고, 꿈을 실현하길 진심으로 바랍니다!

※ 다음 문장을 우리말로 쓰시오.

1 ▶ Find a Dream and Live It!

➡ _____

2 ▶ Hello, everyone.

➡ _____

3 ▶ My name is David Parker, and I'm a photographer.

➡ _____

4 ▶ Today, I'm going to tell you how I found my dream and realized it.

➡ _____

5 ▶ I hope my story can inspire you.

➡ _____

6 ▶ When I was young, I loved stars.

➡ _____

7 ▶ I also liked taking pictures.

➡ _____

8 ▶ However, I never thought these things could lead to a job.

➡ _____

9 ▶ In fact, I didn't have a dream at all.

➡ _____

10 ▶ When I had to decide on a major in college, I chose engineering.

➡ _____

11 ▶ Being an engineer looked OK.

➡ _____

12 ▶ After college, I got a job at an engineering company.

➡ _____

13 ▶ It was a stable job, but I didn't know whether I really enjoyed it.

➡ _____

14 ▸ Everything changed when I went on vacation to Iceland one winter.

➡ _____

15 ▸ There I got a chance to see the Northern Lights!

➡ _____

16 ▸ The lights were amazing, and I took many pictures of the dancing lights in the sky.

➡ _____

17 ▸ For the first time in many years, I could feel my heart beating fast.

➡ _____

18 ▸ After I came back, I entered a photo contest with the pictures I took in Iceland.

➡ _____

19 ▸ Surprisingly, I won first prize, and this gave me a chance to think about my life.

➡ _____

20 ▸ I realized that taking pictures made me happy.

➡ _____

21 ▸ Suddenly, I wanted to become a good photographer, so I started to learn more about photography.

➡ _____

22 ▸ After years of trial and error, I got better, and I began to do some part-time work as a photographer.

➡ _____

23 ▸ Then one day, I made a bold decision.

➡ _____

24 ▸ I quit my job and decided to take pictures for a living.

➡ _____

25 ▸ I wasn't sure if I could succeed, but I decided to try.

➡ _____

26 ▸ I really wanted to do something that made me happy.

➡ _____

27 Now, I'm a professional photographer, and I'm happy.

➡ _____

28 So do you want to find a dream and realize it?

➡ _____

29 Here's some advice to help you.

➡ _____

30 First, follow your heart.

➡ _____

31 Think about what you like to do and what makes you happy.

➡ _____

32 In my case, it was taking pictures of stars.

➡ _____

33 Second, work hard.

➡ _____

34 Pursuing a dream is not easy.

➡ _____

35 I became a photographer through hard work.

➡ _____

36 Third, be bold.

➡ _____

37 You need courage to make decisions that will change your life.

➡ _____

38 I was afraid but I took a chance.

➡ _____

39 I truly hope you can find a dream, pursue it, and live it!

➡ _____

※ 다음 괄호 안의 단어들을 우리말에 맞도록 바르게 배열하시오.

1 ▷ (a / Find / and / Dream / It! / Live)

➡ _____

2 ▷ (everyone. / hello,)

➡ _____

3 ▷ (name / my / is / Parker, / David / and / a / I'm / photographer.)

➡ _____

4 ▷ (I'm / today, / going / tell / to / how / you / found / I / dream / my / and / it. / realized)

➡ _____

5 ▷ (hope / I / story / my / inspire / can / you.)

➡ _____

6 ▷ (I / when / young, / was / loved / I / stars.)

➡ _____

7 ▷ (also / I / taking / liked / pictures.)

➡ _____

8 ▷ (however, / never / I / thought / things / these / lead / could / a / job. / to)

➡ _____

9 ▷ (fact, / in / didn't / I / have / dream / a / all. / at)

➡ _____

10 ▷ (I / when / had / decide / to / on / major / in / a / college, / chose / I / engineering.)

➡ _____

11 ▷ (an / being / looked / engineer / OK.)

➡ _____

12 ▷ (college, / after / got / I / job / a / an / at / company. / engineering)

➡ _____

13 ▷ (was / it / stable / a / job, / I / but / know / didn't / I / whether / really / it. / enjoyed)

➡ _____

1 꿈을 찾고 실현하세요!

2 여러분, 안녕하세요.

3 나의 이름은 David Parker이고, 나는 사진작가입니다.

4 오늘 나는 어떻게 내가 꿈을 찾아서 실현했는지 이야기하려고 해요.

5 나의 이야기가 여러분에게 영감을 주기를 바라요.

6 나는 어렸을 때 별을 사랑했어요.

7 나는 또한 사진 찍는 것을 좋아했어요.

8 하지만 나는 이것들이 직업과 연관될 수 있다고 전혀 생각하지 못했어요.

9 사실 나는 아예 꿈이 없었어요.

10 내가 대학에서 전공을 정해야 했을 때, 나는 공학을 선택했어요.

11 엔지니어가 되는 것이 괜찮아 보였거든요.

12 대학 졸업 후 저는 엔지니어링 회사에 취직했어요.

13 그것은 안정적인 직업이었지만, 난 내가 그 일을 정말로 좋아하는지는 알 수가 없었어요.

14 (changed / everything / I / when / on / went / to / vacation / one / Iceland / winter.)

➡ _____

15 (I / there / got / chance / a / see / to / Northern / the / Lights!)

➡ _____

16 (lights / the / amazing, / were / and / took / I / pictures / many / the / of / dancing / in / lights / sky. / the)

➡ _____

17 (the / for / time / first / many / years, / in / could / I / my / feel / beating / heart / fast.)

➡ _____

18 (I / after / back, / came / entered / I / a / contest / photo / with / pictures / the / I / in / took / Iceland.)

➡ _____

19 (I / surprisingly, / first / won / prize, / this / and / me / gave / a / to / chance / think / about / life. / my)

➡ _____

20 (realized / I / taking / that / made / pictures / happy. / me)

➡ _____

21 (I / suddenly, / to / wanted / become / good / a / photographer, / I / so / to / started / learn / about / more / photography.)

➡ _____

22 (years / after / trial / of / error, / and / got / I / better, / and / began / I / do / to / part-time / some / work / a / as / photographer.)

➡ _____

23 (one / then / day, / made / I / bold / decision. / a)

➡ _____

24 (quit / I / job / my / and / to / decided / take / for / pictures / living. / a)

➡ _____

25 (wasn't / I / sure / I / if / succeed, / could / I / but / to / decided / try.)

➡ _____

14 어느 겨울, 내가 아이슬란드로 휴가를 갔을 때 모든 것이 바뀌었어요.

15 그곳에서 나는 오로라를 볼 수 있는 기회가 있었죠.

16 빛들은 경이로웠고 나는 하늘에서 춤추는 빛들의 사진을 많이 찍었어요.

17 수년 만에 처음으로 나는 심장이 빠르게 뛰고 있는 것을 느낄 수 있었어요.

18 나는 돌아와서 아이슬란드에서 찍은 사진으로 사진 경연 대회에 참가했어요.

19 놀랍게도 나는 1등상을 받았고, 이 일은 나에게 인생을 생각해 볼 기회를 주었어요.

20 나는 사진 찍는 것이 나를 행복하게 한다는 것을 깨달았어요.

21 갑자기 나는 좋은 사진작가가 되고 싶어서 사진 촬영 기술에 대해 더 배우기 시작했어요.

22 몇 년의 시행착오 끝에 나는 더 나아졌고 사진작가로 시간제 근무일을 하기 시작했어요.

23 그러던 어느 날 나는 대담한 결심을 했어요.

24 나는 직장을 그만 두고 생계 수단으로 사진을 찍기로 했어요.

25 나는 내가 성공할 수 있을지 확신하지 못했지만 시도해 보기로 결심했어요.

26 (really / I / to / wanted / something / do / made / that / happy. / me)

➡ _____

27 (I'm / now, / professional / a / photographer, / I'm / and / happy.)

➡ _____

28 (do / so / want / you / find / to / a / and / dream / it? / realize)

➡ _____

29 (some / here's / to / advice / you. / help)

➡ _____

30 (follow / first, / heart. / your)

➡ _____

31 (about / think / you / what / to / like / do / and / makes / what / happy. / you)

➡ _____

32 (my / in / case, / was / it / pictures / taking / stars. / of)

➡ _____

33 (second, / hard. / work)

➡ _____

34 (a / pursuing / dream / not / is / easy.)

➡ _____

35 (became / I / photographer / a / hard / through / work.)

➡ _____

36 (be / third, / bold.)

➡ _____

37 (need / you / to / courage / make / that / decisions / will / your / change / life.)

➡ _____

38 (was / I / but / afraid / took / I / chance. / a)

➡ _____

39 (truly / I / you / hope / find / can / dream, / a / it, / pursue / live / it! / and)

➡ _____

---

26 나는 나를 행복하게 만드는 무언가를 정말로 하고 싶었어요.

27 지금, 나는 전문 사진작가이고, 나는 행복합니다.

28 그렇다면 여러분은 꿈을 찾아 실현하고 싶은가요?

29 여기 여러분을 도와줄 몇 가지 조언이 있습니다.

30 첫째, 여러분의 마음을 따르세요.

31 여러분이 무엇을 하고 싶고 여러분을 행복하게 하는 것이 무엇인지 생각해 보세요.

32 나의 경우에 그것은 별 사진을 찍는 거였어요.

33 둘째, 열심히 노력하세요.

34 꿈을 추구하는 것은 쉽지 않아요.

35 나는 열심히 노력해 사진작가가 되었어요.

36 셋째, 대담해지세요.

37 여러분의 인생을 바꿀 결정을 하기 위해서는 용기가 필요합니다.

38 나는 두려웠지만 기회를 잡았어요.

39 나는 여러분이 꿈을 찾고, 꿈을 추구하고, 꿈을 실현하길 진심으로 바랍니다!

※ 다음 우리말을 영어로 쓰시오.

1 ▸ 꿈을 찾고 실현하세요!

➡ _____

2 ▸ 여러분, 안녕하세요.

➡ _____

3 ▸ 나의 이름은 David Parker이고, 나는 사진작가입니다.

➡ _____

4 ▸ 오늘 나는 어떻게 내가 꿈을 찾아서 실현했는지 이야기하려고 해요.

➡ _____

5 ▸ 나의 이야기가 여러분에게 영감을 주기를 바라요.

➡ _____

6 ▸ 나는 어렸을 때 별을 사랑했어요.

➡ _____

7 ▸ 나는 또한 사진 찍는 것을 좋아했어요.

➡ _____

8 ▸ 하지만 나는 이것들이 직업과 연관될 수 있다고 전혀 생각하지 못했어요.

➡ _____

9 ▸ 사실 나는 아예 꿈이 없었어요.

➡ _____

10 ▸ 내가 대학에서 전공을 정해야 했을 때, 나는 공학을 선택했어요.

➡ _____

11 ▸ 엔지니어가 되는 것이 괜찮아 보였거든요.

➡ _____

12 ▸ 대학 졸업 후 저는 엔지니어링 회사에 취직했어요.

➡ _____

13 ▸ 그것은 안정적인 직업이었지만, 난 내가 그 일을 정말로 좋아하는지는 알 수가 없었어요.

➡ _____

14 어느 겨울, 내가 아이슬란드로 휴가를 갔을 때 모든 것이 바뀌었어요.

➡ _____

15 그곳에서 나는 오로라를 볼 수 있는 기회가 있었죠.

➡ _____

16 빛들은 경이로웠고 나는 하늘에서 춤추는 빛들의 사진을 많이 찍었어요.

➡ _____

17 수년 만에 처음으로 나는 심장이 빠르게 뛰고 있는 것을 느낄 수 있었어요.

➡ _____

18 나는 돌아와서 아이슬란드에서 찍은 사진으로 사진 경연 대회에 참가했어요.

➡ _____

19 놀랍게도 나는 1등상을 받았고, 이 일은 나에게 인생을 생각해 볼 기회를 주었어요.

➡ _____

20 나는 사진 찍는 것이 나를 행복하게 한다는 것을 깨달았어요.

➡ _____

21 갑자기 나는 좋은 사진작가가 되고 싶어서 사진 촬영 기술에 대해 더 배우기 시작했어요.

➡ _____

22 몇 년의 시행착오 끝에 나는 더 나아졌고 사진작가로 시간제 근무일을 하기 시작했어요.

➡ _____

23 그러던 어느 날 나는 대담한 결심을 했어요.

➡ _____

24 나는 직장을 그만 두고 생계 수단으로 사진을 찍기로 했어요.

➡ _____

25 나는 내가 성공할 수 있을지 확신하지 못했지만 시도해 보기로 결심했어요.

➡ _____

26 나는 나를 행복하게 만드는 무언가를 정말로 하고 싶었어요.

➡ _____

27 지금, 나는 전문 사진작가이고, 나는 행복합니다.

➡ _____

28 그렇다면 여러분은 꿈을 찾아 실현하고 싶은가요?

➡ _____

29 여기 여러분을 도와줄 몇 가지 조언이 있습니다.

➡ _____

30 첫째, 여러분의 마음을 따르세요.

➡ _____

31 여러분이 무엇을 하고 싶고 여러분을 행복하게 하는 것이 무엇인지 생각해 보세요.

➡ _____

32 나의 경우에 그것은 별 사진을 찍는 거였어요.

➡ _____

33 둘째, 열심히 노력하세요.

➡ _____

34 꿈을 추구하는 것은 쉽지 않아요.

➡ _____

35 나는 열심히 노력해 사진작가가 되었어요.

➡ _____

36 셋째, 대담해지세요.

➡ _____

37 여러분의 인생을 바꿀 결정을 하기 위해서는 용기가 필요합니다.

➡ _____

38 나는 두려웠지만 기회를 잡았어요.

➡ _____

39 나는 여러분이 꿈을 찾고, 꿈을 추구하고, 꿈을 실현하길 진심으로 바랍니다!

➡ _____

※ 다음 우리말과 일치하도록 빈칸에 알맞은 말을 쓰시오.

Team Project Step 3

1. We _____ Dr. Park Byeong-seon.

2. She was _____ _____.

3. We _____ her because she _____ _____ _____ _____ _____ for Korean national treasures _____.

1. 우리는 박병선 박사님을 존경합니다.
2. 그녀는 역사학자였습니다.
3. 우리가 그녀를 고른 이유는 그녀가 해외에 있는 한국의 문화 유산을 찾는 데 일생을 보냈기 때문입니다.

After You Read B

1. David Parker's _____

2. 1. _____ your _____.

3. Think about _____ _____ _____ _____ _____ and _____ _____ _____.

4. 2. Work _____.

5. _____ a dream _____ not easy.

6. 3. Be _____.

7. You need _____ _____ _____ _____ that will change your life.

1. David Parker의 조언
2. 1. 여러분의 마음을 따르세요.
3. 여러분이 무엇을 하고 싶고 여러분을 행복하게 하는 것이 무엇인지 생각해 보세요.
4. 2. 열심히 노력하세요.
5. 꿈을 추구하는 것은 쉽지 않아요.
6. 3. 대담해지세요.
7. 여러분의 인생을 바꿀 결정을 하기 위해서는 용기가 필요합니다.

Think and Write

1. My dream is _____.

2. There _____ many things _____ _____ _____ _____ _____.

3. First, I'll go to _____ _____ and _____ _____ _____.

4. Then, _____ _____ _____, I'll _____ _____ a fashion company.

5. _____ I'm 30, I'll start my _____ _____.

6. When I'm 35, I'll _____ _____ _____ _____ _____ _____.

7. I _____ my dream _____ _____ _____.

1. 내 꿈은 유명한 패션디자이너가 되는 것이다.
2. 내 꿈을 실현시키기 위해서는 해야 할 일들이 많이 있다.
3. 우선, 나는 디자인 스쿨에 진학해서 패션 디자인을 공부할 것이다.
4. 그리고 나서, 졸업을 한 후에는 패션 회사에서 일할 것이다.
5. 서른 살에는 나만의 상표를 시작할 것이다.
6. 서른다섯 살이 되면, 첫 번째 패션쇼를 주최할 것이다.
7. 나는 내 꿈이 실현되기를 희망한다.

※ 다음 우리말을 영어로 쓰시오.

Team Project Step 3

1. 우리는 박병선 박사님을 존경합니다.
   ➡ _____

2. 그녀는 역사학자였습니다.
   ➡ _____

3. 우리가 그녀를 고른 이유는 그녀가 해외에 있는 한국의 문화 유산을 찾는 데 일생을 보냈기 때문입니다.
   ➡ _____

After You Read B

1. David Parker의 조언
   ➡ _____

2. 1. 여러분의 마음을 따르세요.
   ➡ _____

3. 여러분이 무엇을 하고 싶고 여러분을 행복하게 하는 것이 무엇인지 생각해 보세요.
   ➡ _____

4. 2. 열심히 노력하세요.
   ➡ _____

5. 꿈을 추구하는 것은 쉽지 않아요.
   ➡ _____

6. 3. 대담해지세요.
   ➡ _____

7. 여러분의 인생을 바꿀 결정을 하기 위해서는 용기가 필요합니다.
   ➡ _____

Think and Write

1. 내 꿈은 유명한 패션디자이너가 되는 것이다.
   ➡ _____

2. 내 꿈을 실현시키기 위해서는 해야 할 일들이 많이 있다.
   ➡ _____

3. 우선, 나는 디자인 스쿨에 진학해서 패션 디자인을 공부할 것이다.
   ➡ _____

4. 그러고 나서, 졸업을 한 후에는 패션 회사에서 일할 것이다.
   ➡ _____

5. 서른 살에는 나만의 상표를 시작할 것이다.
   ➡ _____

6. 서른다섯 살이 되면, 첫 번째 패션쇼를 주최할 것이다.
   ➡ _____

7. 나는 내 꿈이 실현되기를 희망한다.
   ➡ _____

※ 다음 영어를 우리말로 쓰시오.

01	fix
02	suddenly
03	crisp
04	differ
05	fortunately
06	include
07	add
08	audience
09	bowl
10	tasty
11	disappear
12	maybe
13	especially
14	moment
15	nap
16	once
17	clearly
18	comfort
19	mix
20	cool
21	order

22	mushroom
23	stomach
24	peel
25	recipe
26	satisfy
27	pour
28	mixture
29	quantity
30	recently
31	while
32	melt
33	flour
34	warm
35	a bowl of ~
36	similar to ~
37	break down
38	get well
39	so that 주어 can ~
40	be filled with ~
41	feel better
42	would like to ~
43	not only A but (also) B

※ 다음 우리말을 영어로 쓰시오.

01 더하다	22 순간	
02 아마도	23 한 번	
03 청중, 관중	24 바삭바삭한	
04 사발	25 주문하다; 주문	
05 섞다, 혼합하다	26 포함시키다	
06 위로, 위안	27 위, 복부, 배	
07 다르다	28 껍질	
08 녹이다	29 조리법	
09 버섯	30 만족하게 하다	
10 차게 하다	31 맛이 나다	
11 낮잠	32 쏟아 붓다	
12 두드리다, 휘젓다, 섞다	33 양, 수량, 분량	
13 사라지다	34 최근에	
14 특히	35 회복하다	
15 맛있는	36 ~로 가득 차다	
16 수리하다	37 주문을 받다	
17 밀가루	38 ~과 비슷한	
18 혼합물, 반죽	39 최선을 다하다	
19 다행스럽게도	40 스트레스로 지친	
20 휴대용 컴퓨터	41 ~하기 위하여	
21 갑자기	42 고장 나다	
	43 A 뿐만 아니라 B도	

※ 다음 영영풀이에 알맞은 단어를 <보기>에서 골라 쓴 후, 우리말 뜻을 쓰시오.

1 _____ : to become liquid: _____

2 _____ : a feeling of being relaxed: _____

3 _____ : the skin of a fruit or vegetable: _____

4 _____ : to repair something that is broken: _____

5 _____ : dry, hard, and easily broken: _____

6 _____ : to cook something using dry heat, in an oven: _____

7 _____ : a small computer that can work with a battery and be easily carried:
_____

8 _____ : to become impossible to see or find: _____

9 _____ : a wide round container that is open at the top: _____

10 _____ : a set of instructions for cooking a particular type of food: _____

11 _____ : to ask for food or a drink in a restaurant: _____

12 _____ : a powder used for making bread and cakes: _____

13 _____ : a small amount of food that is eaten between main meals: _____

14 _____ : to mix things together quickly with a fork or special kitchen machine:
_____

15 _____ : to make someone feel happy, by doing what he or she wants: _____

16 _____ : the group of people watching or listening to a play, film or public meeting:
_____

보기			
satisfy	snack	laptop	bake
comfort	bowl	crisp	melt
disappear	recipe	audience	peel
beat	flour	fix	order

※ 다음 우리말과 일치하도록 빈칸에 알맞은 말을 쓰시오.

Listen and Talk A 1

W: _____ _____ Italian Food. _____ would you like _____ order?

B: I _____ _____ _____ a mushroom pizza.

W: Will _____ be _____?

B: Yes.

W: Is the order _____ _____ or _____ _____?

B: _____ _____, please.

W: Italian Food에 오신 것을 환영합니다. 무엇을 주문하시겠어요?
B: 버섯 피자를 먹으려고요.
W: 그것이 전부인가요?
B: 네.
W: 여기에서 드시겠어요, 아니면 가져가시겠어요?
B: 여기에서 먹을게요.

Listen and Talk A 2

W: Hello. Are you _____ _____ _____?

B: Yes, please. I'd _____ a _____ of _____.

W: _____ _____ of cake would you _____?

B: Chocolate cake, please.

W: For _____ or to _____?

B: To _____, please. Thank you.

W: 안녕하세요, 주문하시겠어요?
B: 네, 케이크 한 조각 주세요.
W: 어떤 종류의 케이크로 드시겠어요?
B: 초콜릿 케이크로 주세요.
W: 여기에서 드시겠어요, 아니면 가져가시겠어요?
B: 가져갈게요. 감사합니다.

Listen and Talk A 3

W: Hello. _____ would you _____ _____ _____?

B: I'd _____ _____ _____ Manduguk.

W: Would you like _____ _____ _____?

B: Yes, _____ _____ _____ water, please.

W: Is it _____ _____ or _____ _____?

B: It's _____ _____, please.

W: 안녕하세요, 무엇을 주문하시겠어요?
B: 만둣국 주세요.
W: 마실 것을 주문하시겠어요?
B: 네, 물 한 병 주세요.
W: 여기에서 드시겠어요, 아니면 가져가시겠어요?
B: 가져갈게요.

Listen and Talk A 4

W: Hello. What _____ you _____ _____ _____?

B: I _____ a hot dog and _____ milk, please.

W: _____ you _____ _____?

B: No, thank you.

W: Will _____ be for here or _____ _____?

B: _____ _____, please. Thank you.

W: 안녕하세요, 무엇을 주문하시겠어요?
B: 핫도그와 우유 하나 주세요.
W: 더 필요한 것은 없으세요?
B: 없어요.
W: 여기에서 드시겠어요, 아니면 가져가시겠어요?
B: 가져갈게요. 감사합니다.

Listen and Talk B

A: Hello. _____ _____ _____ _____ _____ _____ _____ _____?

B: _____ _____ _____ _____ two hot dogs.

A: Would you like _____ _____ _____?

B: Yes, _____ orange juice, please.

A: _____ _____ for here or _____ _____?

B: It's _____ _____, please. / B: It's _____ _____, please.

A: 안녕하세요, 주문하시겠어요?
B: 핫도그 두 개 주세요.
A: 음료를 주문하시겠어요?
B: 네, 오렌지 주스 하나 주세요.
A: 여기에서 드시겠어요, 아니면 가져가시겠어요?
B: 여기에서 먹을게요. / B: 가져갈게요.

Listen and Talk C

M: _____ _____ Sandwich Place. _____ would you _____ _____ _____?

G: I'd like to _____ _____ hamburger, and she'll have _____ chicken sandwich.

M: Would you like _____ _____?

G: One salad, please.

M: OK, then _____ _____ be all?

G: No, I'd like to _____ _____ _____ _____ water.

M: _____ _____ _____ _____ or _____ _____?

G: It's _____ _____, please.

M: The total _____ _____ 12 dollars.

G: OK. _____ you _____.

M: Sandwich Place에 오신 것을 환영합니다. 무엇을 주문하시겠어요?
G: 저는 햄버거 하나를 먹고 싶고, 이 아이는 치킨 샌드위치를 먹을 거예요.
M: 더 필요한 것은 없으세요?
G: 샐러드 하나 주세요.
M: 알겠습니다. 그럼 그것이 다인가요?
G: 아니요, 물 두 병 주세요.
M: 여기에서 드시겠어요, 아니면 가져가시겠어요?
G: 여기에서 먹을게요.
M: 모두 12 달러입니다.
G: 네, 여기 있어요.

Review

(1) M: Hello. _____ you _____ _____ order?
G: Yes, please. I'd _____ a chicken salad.
M: Will that _____ _____?
G: Yes.
M: _____ _____ or to go?
G: _____ _____, please.

(2) W: Hello. What _____ you _____ _____ order?
B: I'd _____ _____ _____ a sandwich.
W: Would you like _____ _____ _____?
B: Yes. One milk, please.
W: Will that _____ _____?
B: Yes. Thank you.

(3) W: Hello. _____ _____ _____ _____ _____ _____ _____ _____ _____?
B: I _____ Gimchi Gimbap, please.
W: _____ you _____ _____ _____?
B: No, thank you.
W: Is it _____ _____ or _____ _____?
B: _____ _____, please.

(1) M: 안녕하세요, 주문하시겠어요?
G: 네, 치킨 샐러드 하나 주세요.
M: 그것이 다인가요?
G: 네.
M: 여기에서 드시겠어요, 아니면 가져가시겠어요?
G: 가져갈게요.

(2) W: 안녕하세요, 무엇을 주문하시겠어요?
B: 샌드위치 하나 주세요.
W: 마실 것 주문하시겠어요?
B: 네, 우유 하나 주세요.
W: 그것이 다인가요?
B: 네, 고맙습니다.

(3) W: 안녕하세요, 무엇을 주문하시겠어요?
B: 김치 김밥 주세요.
W: 더 필요하신 것은 없으세요?
B: 없어요.
W: 여기에서 드시겠어요, 아니면 가져가시겠어요?
B: 가져갈게요.

※ 다음 우리말에 맞도록 대화를 영어로 쓰시오.

Listen and Talk A 1

W: _____

B: _____

W: _____

B: _____

W: _____

B: _____

W: Italian Food에 오신 것을 환영합니다. 무엇을 주문하시겠어요?
B: 버섯 피자를 먹으려고요.
W: 그것이 전부인가요?
B: 네.
W: 여기에서 드시겠어요, 아니면 가져가시겠어요?
B: 여기에서 먹을게요.

Listen and Talk A 2

W: _____

B: _____

W: _____

B: _____

W: _____

B: _____

W: 안녕하세요, 주문하시겠어요?
B: 네, 케이크 한 조각 주세요.
W: 어떤 종류의 케이크로 드시겠어요?
B: 초콜릿 케이크로 주세요.
W: 여기에서 드시겠어요, 아니면 가져가시겠어요?
B: 가져갈게요. 감사합니다.

Listen and Talk A 3

W: _____

B: _____

W: _____

B: _____

W: _____

B: _____

W: 안녕하세요, 무엇을 주문하시겠어요?
B: 만둣국 주세요.
W: 마실 것을 주문하시겠어요?
B: 네, 물 한 병 주세요.
W: 여기에서 드시겠어요, 아니면 가져가시겠어요?
B: 가져갈게요.

Listen and Talk A 4

W: _____

B: _____

W: _____

B: _____

W: _____

B: _____

W: 안녕하세요, 무엇을 주문하시겠어요?
B: 핫도그와 우유 하나 주세요.
W: 더 필요한 것은 없으세요?
B: 없어요.
W: 여기에서 드시겠어요, 아니면 가져가시겠어요?
B: 가져갈게요. 감사합니다.

Listen and Talk B

A: _____

B: _____

A: _____

B: _____

A: _____

B: _____

Listen and Talk C

M: _____

G: _____

M: _____

G: _____

M: _____

G: _____

M: _____

G: _____

M: _____

G: _____

Review

(1) M: _____

   G: _____

   M: _____

   G: _____

   M: _____

   G: _____

(2) W: _____

   B: _____

   W: _____

   B: _____

   W: _____

   B: _____

(3) W: _____

   B: _____

   W: _____

   B: _____

   W: _____

   B: _____

A: 안녕하세요, 주문하시겠어요?

B: 핫도그 두 개 주세요.

A: 음료를 주문하시겠어요?

B: 네, 오렌지 주스 하나 주세요.

A: 여기에서 드시겠어요, 아니면 가져가시겠어요?

B: 여기에서 먹을게요. / B: 가져갈게요.

M: Sandwich Place에 오신 것을 환영합니다. 무엇을 주문하시겠어요?

G: 저는 햄버거 하나를 먹고 싶고, 이 아이는 치킨 샌드위치를 먹을 거예요.

M: 더 필요한 것은 없으세요?

G: 샐러드 하나 주세요.

M: 알겠습니다. 그럼 그것이 다인가요?

G: 아니요, 물 두 병 주세요.

M: 여기에서 드시겠어요, 아니면 가져가시겠어요?

G: 여기에서 먹을게요.

M: 모두 12 달러입니다.

G: 네, 여기 있어요.

(1) M: 안녕하세요, 주문하시겠어요?

   G: 네, 치킨 샐러드 하나 주세요.

   M: 그것이 다인가요?

   G: 네.

   M: 여기에서 드시겠어요, 아니면 가져가시겠어요?

   G: 가져갈게요.

(2) W: 안녕하세요, 무엇을 주문하시겠어요?

   B: 샌드위치 하나 주세요.

   W: 마실 것 주문하시겠어요?

   B: 네, 우유 하나 주세요.

   W: 그것이 다인가요?

   B: 네, 고맙습니다.

(3) W: 안녕하세요, 무엇을 주문하시겠어요?

   B: 김치 김밥 주세요.

   W: 더 필요하신 것은 없으세요?

   B: 없어요.

   W: 여기에서 드시겠어요, 아니면 가져가시겠어요?

   B: 가져갈게요.

※ 다음 우리말과 일치하도록 빈칸에 알맞은 것을 골라 쓰시오.

1 _____ from Our _____ : My _____ Food

A. Readers   B. Letters   C. Comfort

2 Comfort food is food that makes you _____ _____ when you are sad, angry, or _____ _____.

A. stressed   B. good   C. out   D. feel

3 It can also _____ you _____ of happy _____ from the _____.

A. think   B. past   C. make   D. moments

4 It satisfies _____ _____ the stomach _____ _____ the heart.

A. but   B. not   C. also   D. only

5 Comfort foods _____ _____ the world.

A. around   B. differ

6 _____ see _____ comfort foods our _____ _____ enjoy.

A. readers   B. what   C. let's   D. international

7 Jessica _____ _____

A. USA   B. from

8 _____ comfort food is _____ _____.

A. soup   B. my   C. chicken

9 In the USA, people eat this soup _____ they _____ a _____.

A. cold   B. when   C. have

10 When I was a small child, I _____ a very _____.

A. cold   B. caught   C. bad

11 My father made me a _____ of chicken soup _____ I _____ get well.

A. could   B. so   C. bowl   D. that

12 The hot soup _____ my body, and I _____ started to _____.

A. better   B. warmed   C. feel   D. slowly

13 It was _____ _____ _____.

A. tasty   B. very   C. also

14 Now, when I _____ a _____, I eat chicken _____.

A. cold   B. catch   C. soup

1 우리의 독자들로부터 온 편지: 나에게 위안이 되는 음식

2 comfort food는 여러분이 슬프거나 화가 나거나 스트레스를 받을 때 기분을 좋게 해 주는 음식이다.

3 그것은 또한 여러분에게 과거의 행복한 순간들을 생각나게 할 수 있다.

4 그것은 위뿐만 아니라 마음도 충족해 준다.

5 comfort food는 전 세계적으로 다양하다.

6 세계 여러 나라의 우리 독자들은 어떤 comfort food를 즐기는지 알아보자.

7 미국에 사는 Jessica

8 나의 comfort food는 치킨 수프야.

9 미국에서는 사람들이 감기에 걸릴 때 이 수프를 먹어.

10 나는 어린아이였을 때 매우 심한 감기에 걸렸어.

11 아빠는 내가 나을 수 있도록 치킨 수프 한 그릇을 만들어 주셨어.

12 그 뜨거운 수프는 내 몸을 따뜻하게 했고, 나는 서서히 나아지기 시작했어.

13 그것은 매우 맛있기도 했어.

14 지금도 나는 감기에 걸리면 치킨 수프를 먹어.

15 Maria _____ _____

    A. Brazil   B. from

16 In Brazil, there are many dishes that are _____ _____ cassava, a vegetable _____ _____ a potato.

    A. with   B. similar   C. to   D. made

17 I love cassava _____ _____ _____.

    A. most   B. the   C. chips

18 _____ when I had a _____ day at school and felt _____ out, my best friend bought me a _____ of cassava chips.

    A. bag   B. once   C. stressed   D. bad

19 _____ I _____ to eat the chips, my stress _____ _____.

    A. disappeared   B. when   C. suddenly   D. started

20 The _____ _____ of eating chips _____ me better.

    A. made   B. sound   C. feel   D. crisp

21 Now, _____ _____ I'm _____ _____, I eat cassava chips.

    A. out   B. time   C. every   D. stressed

22 _____ I _____ _____ again!

    A. feel   B. then   C. good

23 Simon _____ _____

    A. France   B. from

24 I _____ _____ comfort foods, _____ I love madeleines the _____.

    A. most   B. but   C. many   D. have

25 A madeleine is a small cake that _____ _____ a _____.

    A. like   B. shell   C. looks   D. sea

26 People _____ France enjoy madeleines _____ an _____.

    A. as   B. in   C. afternoon   D. snack

27 My grandmother always _____ madeleines _____ me _____ I _____ her.

    A. for   B. visit   C. makes   D. when

28 They _____ best when they come _____ of the _____.

    A. oven   B. right   C. taste   D. out

15 브라질에 사는 Maria

16 브라질에는 감자와 비슷한 채소인 카사바로 만든 요리가 많아.

17 나는 카사바 칩을 좋아해.

18 한번은 내가 학교에서 안 좋은 일이 있고 스트레스를 받았을 때, 나의 가장 친한 친구가 나에게 카사바 칩 한 봉지를 사 줬어.

19 그 칩을 먹기 시작했을 때, 내 스트레스가 갑자기 사라졌어.

20 칩을 먹을 때 나는 바삭한 소리가 내 기분을 더 좋게 만들었어.

21 지금도 나는 스트레스를 받을 때마다 카사바 칩을 먹어.

22 그러면 나는 기분이 다시 좋아져!

23 프랑스에 사는 Simon

24 나는 comfort food가 많아, 하지만 가장 좋아하는 것은 마들렌이야.

25 마들렌은 조개처럼 생긴 작은 케이크야.

26 프랑스 사람들은 오후 간식으로 마들렌을 즐겨 먹어.

27 우리 할머니는 내가 찾아뵐 때는 항상 마들렌을 만들어 주셔.

28 마들렌은 오븐에서 막 나올 때 가장 맛있어.

29 Then the kitchen is _____ _____ a sweet _____.

A. with　　　　B. smell　　　　C. filled

30 I _____ like _____ her orange madeleines _____ a cup of tea.

A. eating　　　　B. with　　　　C. especially

31 _____ _____ I see or smell madeleines, I _____ _____ my grandmother.

A. think　　　　B. time　　　　C. every　　　　D. of

32 _____ me _____ my grandmother's special recipe with you _____ _____ you can make orange madeleines, too.

A. that　　　　B. share　　　　C. let　　　　D. so

33 _____ madeleines will _____ a comfort food _____ you!

A. become　　　　B. for　　　　C. maybe

34 _____ _____ _____: Orange Madeleines

A. Recipe　　　　B. Grandma's　　　　C. Special

35 You need: 1 cup of _____, 2/3 cup of sugar, 2 eggs, some orange _____, 1/4 cup of butter, 1/8 teaspoon of _____

A. peel　　　　B. flour　　　　C. salt

36 1. _____ the butter and _____ it _____.

A. let　　　　B. melt　　　　C. cool

37 2. _____ the eggs, sugar, and salt in a _____ and _____.

A. bowl　　　　B. beat　　　　C. put

38 3. _____ the flour _____ the bowl and _____.

A. mix　　　　B. to　　　　C. add

39 4. _____ the butter and orange _____ to the _____ and _____.

A. peel　　　　B. mix　　　　C. add　　　　D. mixture

40 5. _____ the _____ _____ the madeleine pan.

A. mixture　　　　B. into　　　　C. pour

41 6. _____ in the oven _____ 10 _____ 15 minutes.

A. to　　　　B. bake　　　　C. for

---

29 그러면 부엌은 달콤한 냄새로 가득 차.

30 나는 특히 차 한 잔과 함께 오렌지 마들렌을 먹는 것을 좋아해.

31 마들렌을 보거나 냄새 맡을 때마다 나는 할머니가 생각나.

32 너희들도 오렌지 마들렌을 만들 수 있도록 우리 할머니의 특별한 요리법을 공유할게.

33 아마도 마들렌이 너희에게도 comfort food가 될 거야!

34 할머니의 특별한 요리법: 오렌지 마들렌

35 재료: 밀가루 1컵, 설탕 2/3컵, 달걀 2개, 오렌지 껍질 조금, 버터 1/4컵, 소금 1/8티스푼

36 1. 버터를 녹여서 식힌다.

37 2. 달걀, 설탕, 소금을 그릇에 넣고 휘젓는다.

38 3. 그릇에 밀가루를 넣고 섞는다.

39 4. 반죽에 버터와 오렌지 껍질을 넣고 섞는다.

40 5. 반죽을 마들렌 팬에 붓는다.

41 6. 오븐에서 10분에서 15분 동안 굽는다.

※ 다음 우리말과 일치하도록 빈칸에 알맞은 것을 골라 쓰시오.

1 _____ from Our _____ : My _____ _____

2 Comfort food is food that _____ _____ _____ _____ when you are sad, angry, or _____ _____ .

3 It _____ _____ make you _____ _____ happy moments _____ _____ _____ .

4 It satisfies _____ _____ the stomach _____ _____ the heart.

5 Comfort foods _____ _____ the world.

6 _____ see _____ _____ _____ our international readers enjoy.

7 Jessica _____ _____

8 My comfort food is _____ _____ .

9 In the USA, people eat this soup _____ they _____ _____ _____ .

10 When I was a small child, I _____ _____ _____ _____ _____ .

11 My father made me _____ _____ _____ chicken soup _____ _____ I _____ _____ _____ .

12 The hot soup _____ my body, and I slowly started to _____ _____ .

13 It was also _____ _____ .

14 Now, when I _____ _____ _____ , I eat chicken soup.

1 우리의 독자들로부터 온 편지: 나에게 위안이 되는 음식

2 comfort food는 여러분이 슬프 거나 화가 나거나 스트레스를 받을 때 기분을 좋게 해 주는 음 식이다.

3 그것은 또한 여러분에게 과거의 행복한 순간들을 생각나게 할 수 있다.

4 그것은 위뿐만 아니라 마음도 충족해 준다.

5 comfort food는 전 세계적으로 다양하다.

6 세계 여러 나라의 우리 독자들 은 어떤 comfort food를 즐기는 지 알아보자.

7 미국에 사는 Jessica

8 나의 comfort food는 치킨 수프야

9 미국에서는 사람들이 감기에 걸 릴 때 이 수프를 먹어.

10 나는 어린아이였을 때 매우 심 한 감기에 걸렸어.

11 아빠는 내가 나을 수 있도록 치킨 수프 한 그릇을 만들어 주셨어.

12 그 뜨거운 수프는 내 몸을 따뜻 하게 했고, 나는 서서히 나아지 기 시작했어.

13 그것은 매우 맛있기도 했어.

14 지금도 나는 감기에 걸리면 치 킨 수프를 먹어.

15 Maria _____ _____

16 In Brazil, _____ _____ many dishes that _____ _____
_____ cassava, a vegetable _____ _____ a potato.

17 I love cassava chips _____ _____ .

18 _____ when I _____ _____ _____ _____ at school
and felt _____ _____ , my best friend bought me _____
_____ _____ cassava chips.

19 When I started to eat the chips, my stress _____ _____ .

20 The _____ _____ _____ _____ chips _____ _____
_____ better.

21 Now, _____ _____ I'm _____ _____ , I eat cassava
chips.

22 Then I _____ _____ again!

23 Simon _____ France

24 I have many _____ _____ , but I love madeleines _____
_____ .

25 A madeleine is a small cake that _____ _____ a _____
_____ .

26 People in France enjoy madeleines _____ _____ _____
_____ .

27 My grandmother _____ _____ madeleines _____ me
when I visit her.

28 They taste best when they come _____ _____ _____ the
oven.

---

15 브라질에 사는 Maria

16 브라질에는 감자와 비슷한 채소
인 카사바로 만든 요리가 많아.

17 나는 카사바 칩을 좋아해.

18 한번은 내가 학교에서 안 좋은
일이 있고 스트레스를 받았을
때, 나의 가장 친한 친구가 나에
게 카사바 칩 한 봉지를 사 줬어.

19 그 칩을 먹기 시작했을 때, 내
스트레스가 갑자기 사라졌어.

20 칩을 먹을 때 나는 바삭한 소리
가 내 기분을 더 좋게 만들었어.

21 지금도 나는 스트레스를 받을
때마다 카사바 칩을 먹어.

22 그러면 나는 기분이 다시 좋아져!

23 프랑스에 사는 Simon

24 나는 comfort food가 많아, 하
지만 가장 좋아하는 것은 마들
렌이야.

25 마들렌은 조개처럼 생긴 작은
케이크야.

26 프랑스 사람들은 오후 간식으로
마들렌을 즐겨 먹어.

27 우리 할머니는 내가 찾아뵐 때
는 항상 마들렌을 만들어 주셔.

28 마들렌은 오븐에서 막 나올 때
가장 맛있어.

29 Then the kitchen _____ _____ _____ a sweet _____.

30 I _____ _____ _____ her orange madeleines _____ a cup of tea.

31 _____ _____ I see or smell madeleines, I _____ _____ my grandmother.

32 _____ _____ _____ my grandmother's special recipe with you _____ _____ you _____ _____ orange madeleines, too.

33 Maybe madeleines will _____ _____ _____ for you!

34 Grandma's _____ _____ : Orange Madeleines

35 You need: 1 cup of _____ , 2/3 cup of sugar, 2 eggs, some orange _____ , 1/4 _____ _____ butter, 1/8 teaspoon of salt

36 1. _____ the butter and _____ it _____ .

37 2. _____ the eggs, sugar, and salt in a _____ and _____ .

38 3. _____ the flour _____ the bowl and _____ .

39 4. _____ the butter and _____ _____ to the _____ and mix.

40 5. _____ the mixture _____ the madeleine pan.

41 6. _____ in the oven _____ 10 _____ 15 _____ .

29 그러면 부엌은 달콤한 냄새로 가득 차.

30 나는 특히 차 한 잔과 함께 오렌지 마들렌을 먹는 것을 좋아해.

31 마들렌을 보거나 냄새 맡을 때마다 나는 할머니가 생각나.

32 너희들도 오렌지 마들렌을 만들 수 있도록 우리 할머니의 특별한 요리법을 공유할게.

33 아마도 마들렌이 너희에게도 comfort food가 될 거야!

34 할머니의 특별한 요리법: 오렌지 마들렌

35 재료: 밀가루 1컵, 설탕 2/3컵, 달걀 2개, 오렌지 껍질 조금, 버터 1/4컵, 소금 1/8티스푼

36 1. 버터를 녹여서 식힌다.

37 2. 달걀, 설탕, 소금을 그릇에 넣고 휘젓는다.

38 3. 그릇에 밀가루를 넣고 섞는다.

39 4. 반죽에 버터와 오렌지 껍질을 넣고 섞는다.

40 5. 반죽을 마들렌 팬에 붓는다.

41 6. 오븐에서 10분에서 15분 동안 굽는다.

※ 다음 문장을 우리말로 쓰시오.

1   Letters from Our Readers: My Comfort Food

➡ _____

2   Comfort food is food that makes you feel good when you are sad, angry, or stressed out.

➡ _____

3   It can also make you think of happy moments from the past.

➡ _____

4   It satisfies not only the stomach but also the heart.

➡ _____

5   Comfort foods differ around the world.

➡ _____

6   Let's see what comfort foods our international readers enjoy.

➡ _____

7   Jessica from USA

➡ _____

8   My comfort food is chicken soup.

➡ _____

9   In the USA, people eat this soup when they have a cold.

➡ _____

10   When I was a small child, I caught a very bad cold.

➡ _____

11   My father made me a bowl of chicken soup so that I could get well.

➡ _____

12   The hot soup warmed my body, and I slowly started to feel better.

➡ _____

13   It was also very tasty.

➡ _____

14   Now, when I catch a cold, I eat chicken soup.

➡ _____

15 Maria from Brazil

➡ _____

16 In Brazil, there are many dishes that are made with cassava, a vegetable similar to a potato.

➡ _____

17 I love cassava chips the most.

➡ _____

18 Once when I had a bad day at school and felt stressed out, my best friend bought me a bag of cassava chips.

➡ _____

_____

19 When I started to eat the chips, my stress suddenly disappeared.

➡ _____

20 The crisp sound of eating chips made me feel better.

➡ _____

21 Now, every time I'm stressed out, I eat cassava chips.

➡ _____

22 Then I feel good again!

➡ _____

23 Simon from France

➡ _____

24 I have many comfort foods, but I love madeleines the most.

➡ _____

25 A madeleine is a small cake that looks like a sea shell.

➡ _____

26 People in France enjoy madeleines as an afternoon snack.

➡ _____

27 My grandmother always makes madeleines for me when I visit her.

➡ _____

28 They taste best when they come right out of the oven.

➡ _____

29 Then the kitchen is filled with a sweet smell.

➡ _____

30 I especially like eating her orange madeleines with a cup of tea.

➡ _____

31 Every time I see or smell madeleines, I think of my grandmother.

➡ _____

32 Let me share my grandmother's special recipe with you so that you can make orange madeleines, too.

➡ _____

33 Maybe madeleines will become a comfort food for you!

➡ _____

34 Grandma's Special Recipe: Orange Madeleines

➡ _____

35 You need: 1 cup of flour, 2/3 cup of sugar, 2 eggs, some orange peel, 1/4 cup of butter, 1/8 teaspoon of salt

➡ _____

36 1. Melt the butter and let it cool.

➡ _____

37 2. Put the eggs, sugar, and salt in a bowl and beat.

➡ _____

38 3. Add the flour to the bowl and mix.

➡ _____

39 4. Add the butter and orange peel to the mixture and mix.

➡ _____

40 5. Pour the mixture into the madeleine pan.

➡ _____

41 6. Bake in the oven for 10 to 15 minutes.

➡ _____

※ 다음 괄호 안의 단어들을 우리말에 맞도록 바르게 배열하시오.

1 (from / Letters / Readers: / Our / Comfort / Food / My)
➡ _____

2 (food / comfort / food / is / makes / that / feel / you / good / you / when / sad, / are / or / angry, / out. / stressed)
➡ _____

3 (can / it / make / also / think / you / of / moments / happy / the / from / past.)
➡ _____

4 (satisfies / it / only / not / stomach / the / also / but / heart. / the)
➡ _____

5 (foods / comfort / around / differ / world. / the)
➡ _____

6 (see / let's / comfort / what / foods / international / our / enjoy. / readers)
➡ _____

7 (from / Jessica / USA)
➡ _____

8 (comfort / my / is / food / soup. / chicken)
➡ _____

9 (the / in / USA, / eat / people / soup / this / they / when / a / cold. / have)
➡ _____

10 (I / when / was / small / a / child, / caught / I / very / a / cold. / bad)
➡ _____

11 (father / my / me / made / bowl / a / of / soup / chicken / that / so / could / I / well. / get)
➡ _____

12 (hot / the / soup / my / warmed / body, / I / and / started / slowly / to / better. / feel)
➡ _____

13 (was / it / very / tasty. / also)
➡ _____

14 (when / I / now, / catch / cold, / a / eat / I / soup. / chicken)
➡ _____

---

1 우리의 독자들로부터 온 편지: 나에게 위안이 되는 음식

2 comfort food는 여러분이 슬프거나 화가 나거나 스트레스를 받을 때 기분을 좋게 해 주는 음식이다.

3 그것은 또한 여러분에게 과거의 행복한 순간들을 생각나게 할 수 있다.

4 그것은 위뿐만 아니라 마음도 충족해 준다.

5 comfort food는 전 세계적으로 다양하다.

6 세계 여러 나라의 우리 독자들은 어떤 comfort food를 즐기는지 알아보자.

7 미국에 사는 Jessica

8 나의 comfort food는 치킨 수프야.

9 미국에서는 사람들이 감기에 걸릴 때 이 수프를 먹어.

10 나는 어린아이였을 때 매우 심한 감기에 걸렸어.

11 아빠는 내가 나을 수 있도록 치킨 수프 한 그릇을 만들어 주셨어.

12 그 뜨거운 수프는 내 몸을 따뜻하게 했고, 나는 서서히 나아지기 시작했어.

13 그것은 매우 맛있기도 했어.

14 지금도 나는 감기에 걸리면 치킨 수프를 먹어.

15 (from / Maria / Brazil)

➡ _____

16 (Brazil, / in / are / there / dishes / many / are / that / with / made / cassava, / vegetable / a / to / similar / potato. / a)

➡ _____

➡ _____

17 (love / I / chips / cassava / most. / the)

➡ _____

18 (when / once / had / I / bad / a / day / school / at / and / stressed / felt / out, / best / my / friend / me / bought / a / of / bag / chips. / cassava)

➡ _____

➡ _____

19 (I / when / to / started / eat / chips, / the / stress / my / disappeared. / suddenly)

➡ _____

20 (chip / the / of / sound / eating / made / chips / feel / me / better.)

➡ _____

21 (every / now, / time / stressed / I'm / out, / eat / I / chips. / cassava)

➡ _____

22 (I / then / good / feel / again!)

➡ _____

23 (from / Simon / France)

➡ _____

24 (have / I / comfort / many / foods, / I / but / love / the / madeleines / most.)

➡ _____

25 (madeleine / a / is / cake / small / a / looks / that / like / sea / a / shell.)

➡ _____

26 (in / people / enjoy / France / as / madeleines / an / snack. / afternoon)

➡ _____

27 (grandmother / my / makes / always / medeleines / me / for / I / when / her. / visit)

➡ _____

➡ _____

28 (taste / they / best / they / when / right / come / of / out / oven. / the)

➡ _____

15 브라질에 사는 Maria

16 브라질에는 감자와 비슷한 채소인 카사바로 만든 요리가 많아.

17 나는 카사바 칩을 좋아해.

18 한번은 내가 학교에서 안 좋은 일이 있고 스트레스를 받았을 때, 나의 가장 친한 친구가 나에게 카사바 칩 한 봉지를 사 줬어.

19 그 칩을 먹기 시작했을 때, 내 스트레스가 갑자기 사라졌어.

20 칩을 먹을 때 나는 바삭한 소리가 내 기분을 더 좋게 만들었어.

21 지금도 나는 스트레스를 받을 때마다 카사바 칩을 먹어.

22 그러면 나는 기분이 다시 좋아져!

23 프랑스에 사는 Simon

24 나는 comfort food가 많아, 하지만 가장 좋아하는 것은 마들렌이야.

25 마들렌은 조개처럼 생긴 작은 케이크야.

26 프랑스 사람들은 오후 간식으로 마들렌을 즐겨 먹어.

27 우리 할머니는 내가 찾아뵐 때는 항상 마들렌을 만들어 주셔.

28 마들렌은 오븐에서 막 나올 때 가장 맛있어.

29 (the / then / is / kitchen / with / filled / smell. / a / sweet)

➡ _____

30 (especially / I / eating / like / her / orange / with / madeleines / cup / a / tea. / of)

➡ _____

31 (time / every / see / I / or / madeleines, / smell / of / I / think / grandmother. / my)

➡ _____

32 (me / let / my / share / grandmother's / recipe / special / you / with / so / you / that / make / can / orange / too. / madeleines,)

➡ _____
_____

33 (madeleines / maybe / become / will / comfort / a / for / food / you!)

➡ _____

34 (Special / Granma's / Recipe: / Madeleines / Orange)

➡ _____

35 (need: / you / cup / 1 / flour, / of / cup / 2/3, / sugar, / of / eggs, / 2 / orange / some / peel, / cup / 1/4 / butter, / of / teaspoon / 1/8 / salt / of)

➡ _____
_____

36 (1. / the / melt / butter / let / and / cool. / it)

➡ _____

37 (2. / the / put / eggs, / and / sugar, / salt / a / in / bowl / beat. / and)

➡ _____

38 (3. / the / add / flour / to / bowl / the / mix. / and)

➡ _____

39 (4. / the / add / butter / orange / and / to / peel / the / mix. / and / mixture)

➡ _____

40 (5. / the / pour / mixture / the / into / pan. / madeleine)

➡ _____

41 (6. / in / bake / the / for / oven / to / 10 / minutes. / 15)

➡ _____

---

29 그러면 부엌은 달콤한 냄새로 가득 차.

30 나는 특히 차 한 잔과 함께 오렌지 마들렌을 먹는 것을 좋아해.

31 마들렌을 보거나 냄새 맡을 때마다 나는 할머니가 생각나.

32 너희들도 오렌지 마들렌을 만들 수 있도록 우리 할머니의 특별한 요리법을 공유할게.

33 아마도 마들렌이 너희에게도 comfort food가 될 거야!

34 할머니의 특별한 요리법: 오렌지 마들렌

35 재료: 밀가루 1컵, 설탕 2/3컵, 달걀 2개, 오렌지 껍질 조금, 버터 1/4컵, 소금 1/8티스푼

36 1. 버터를 녹여서 식힌다.

37 2. 달걀, 설탕, 소금을 그릇에 넣고 휘젓는다.

38 3. 그릇에 밀가루를 넣고 섞는다.

39 4. 반죽에 버터와 오렌지 껍질을 넣고 섞는다.

40 5. 반죽을 마들렌 팬에 붓는다.

41 6. 오븐에서 10분에서 15분 동안 굽는다.

※ 다음 우리말을 영어로 쓰시오.

1 우리의 독자들로부터 온 편지: 나에게 위안이 되는 음식

➡ _____

2 comfort food는 여러분이 슬프거나 화가 나거나 스트레스를 받을 때 기분을 좋게 해 주는 음식이다.

➡ _____

3 그것은 또한 여러분에게 과거의 행복한 순간들을 생각나게 할 수 있다.

➡ _____

4 그것은 위뿐만 아니라 마음도 충족해 준다.

➡ _____

5 comfort food는 전 세계적으로 다양하다.

➡ _____

6 세계 여러 나라의 우리 독자들은 어떤 comfort food를 즐기는지 알아보자.

➡ _____

7 미국에 사는 Jessica

➡ _____

8 나의 comfort food는 치킨 수프야.

➡ _____

9 미국에서는 사람들이 감기에 걸릴 때 이 수프를 먹어.

➡ _____

10 나는 어린아이였을 때 매우 심한 감기에 걸렸어.

➡ _____

11 아빠는 내가 나을 수 있도록 치킨 수프 한 그릇을 만들어 주셨어.

➡ _____

12 그 뜨거운 수프는 내 몸을 따뜻하게 했고, 나는 서서히 나아지기 시작했어.

➡ _____

13 그것은 매우 맛있기도 했어.

➡ _____

14 지금도 나는 감기에 걸리면 치킨 수프를 먹어.

➡ _____

15 브라질에 사는 Maria

➡ _____

16 브라질에는 감자와 비슷한 채소인 카사바로 만든 요리가 많아.

➡ _____

17 나는 카사바 칩을 좋아해.

➡ _____

18 한번은 내가 학교에서 안 좋은 일이 있고 스트레스를 받았을 때, 나의 가장 친한 친구가 나에게
카사바 칩 한 봉지를 사 줬어.

➡ _____

_____

19 그 칩을 먹기 시작했을 때, 내 스트레스가 갑자기 사라졌어.

➡ _____

20 칩을 먹을 때 나는 바삭한 소리가 내 기분을 더 좋게 만들었어.

➡ _____

21 지금도 나는 스트레스를 받을 때마다 카사바 칩을 먹어.

➡ _____

22 그러면 나는 기분이 다시 좋아져!

➡ _____

23 프랑스에 사는 Simon

➡ _____

24 나는 comfort food가 많아, 하지만 가장 좋아하는 것은 마들렌이야.

➡ _____

25 마들렌은 조개처럼 생긴 작은 케이크야.

➡ _____

26 프랑스 사람들은 오후 간식으로 마들렌을 즐겨 먹어.

➡ _____

27 우리 할머니는 내가 찾아뵐 때는 항상 마들렌을 만들어 주셔.

➡ _____

28 마들렌은 오븐에서 막 나올 때 가장 맛있어.

➡ _____

29 그러면 부엌은 달콤한 냄새로 가득 차.

➡ _____

30 나는 특히 차 한 잔과 함께 오렌지 마들렌을 먹는 것을 좋아해.

➡ _____

31 마들렌을 보거나 냄새 맡을 때마다 나는 할머니가 생각나.

➡ _____

32 너희들도 오렌지 마들렌을 만들 수 있도록 우리 할머니의 특별한 요리법을 공유할게.

➡ _____

33 아마도 마들렌이 너희에게도 comfort food가 될 거야!

➡ _____

34 할머니의 특별한 요리법: 오렌지 마들렌

➡ _____

35 재료: 밀가루 1컵, 설탕 2/3컵, 달걀 2개, 오렌지 껍질 조금, 버터 1/4컵, 소금 1/8티스푼

➡ _____

36 1. 버터를 녹여서 식힌다.

➡ _____

37 2. 달걀, 설탕, 소금을 그릇에 넣고 휘젓는다.

➡ _____

38 3. 그릇에 밀가루를 넣고 섞는다.

➡ _____

39 4. 반죽에 버터와 오렌지 껍질을 넣고 섞는다.

➡ _____

40 5. 반죽을 마들렌 팬에 붓는다.

➡ _____

41 6. 오븐에서 10분에서 15분 동안 굽는다.

➡ _____

※ 다음 우리말과 일치하도록 빈칸에 알맞은 말을 쓰시오.

Listen and Talk D

1. I like Italian food, so _____ _____ _____ go to Taste of Italy.

2. _____ the restaurant, I'd _____ _____ _____ a potato pizza.

3. _____ a drink, I'd like to _____ _____ _____ _____.

After You Read A

1. Q: _____ is _____ comfort food?

2. Jessica, _____

3. When I _____ a very _____ _____, my father _____ _____ _____ _____ _____ _____ _____ _____.

4. The hot soup warmed my body, and I slowly started to _____ _____.

5. Maria, _____

6. When I felt _____ _____, my best friend _____ _____ _____ _____ _____ _____.

7. _____ I _____ the chips, my stress _____.

8. The crisp sound of _____ chips _____ _____.

9. Simon, _____

10. My grandmother _____ madeleines _____ _____ when I visit her.

11. I especially like _____ her orange madeleines _____ tea.

12. _____ _____ I see or smell madeleines, I _____ _____ her.

Think and Write Step 2

1. _____ Comfort _____

2. My comfort food _____ _____.

3. I _____ eat it when I _____ _____.

4. _____, I didn't do _____ on a test and got _____ out.

5. I went to the store and _____ _____ _____ _____.

6. _____ _____ the sweet chocolate, I _____ _____.

7. _____ chocolate _____ me _____ _____.

※ 다음 우리말을 영어로 쓰시오.

Listen and Talk D

1. 난 이탈리아 음식을 좋아해서 Taste of Italy에 가고 싶어.
➡ _____

2. 그 식당에서 나는 감자 피자를 주문하고 싶어.
➡ _____

3. 음료로는 오렌지 주스를 주문하고 싶어.
➡ _____

After You Read A

1. Q: 너의 comfort food는 무엇이니?
➡ _____

2. Jessica, 미국
➡ _____

3. 내가 매우 심한 감기에 걸렸을 때, 아빠는 내게 치킨 수프 한 그릇을 만들어 주셨어.
➡ _____

4. 그 뜨거운 수프는 내 몸을 따뜻하게 했고, 나는 서서히 나아지기 시작했어.
➡ _____

5. Maria, 브라질
➡ _____

6. 내가 스트레스를 받았을 때, 나의 가장 친한 친구가 카사바 칩 한 봉지를 내게 사 줬어.
➡ _____

7. 칩을 먹자 내 스트레스가 사라졌어.
➡ _____

8. 칩을 먹을 때 나는 바삭하는 소리가 내 기분을 더 좋게 만들었어.
➡ _____

9. Simon, 프랑스
➡ _____

10. 우리 할머니는 내가 찾아뵐 때 마들렌을 만들어 주셔.
➡ _____

11. 나는 특히 차와 함께 할머니의 오렌지 마들렌을 먹는 것을 좋아해.
➡ _____

12. 마들렌을 보거나 냄새를 맡을 때마다 할머니를 떠올려.
➡ _____

Think and Write Step 2

1. 나의 comfort food(위로 음식)
➡ _____

2. 나의 comfort food는 초콜릿이다.
➡ _____

3. 나는 보통 그것을 기분이 좋지 않을 때 먹는다.
➡ _____

4. 최근에 나는 시험을 잘 보지 못해서 스트레스를 받았다.
➡ _____

5. 나는 가게에 가서 초콜릿을 샀다.
➡ _____

6. 달콤한 초콜릿을 먹고 난 후, 나는 기분이 좋아졌다.
➡ _____

7. 초콜릿을 먹는 것은 나를 기분 좋게 한다.
➡ _____

※ 다음 영어를 우리말로 쓰시오.

01	cause		22	expression
02	present		23	law
03	decide		24	myth
04	contact		25	include
05	explorer		26	nervous
06	factory		27	origin
07	slave		28	storm
08	flood		29	judge
09	anger		30	originate
10	century		31	produce
11	civilization		32	tool
12	suggest		33	borrow
13	advanced		34	slice
14	shortly		35	pass through
15	originally		36	come from ~
16	meaning		37	be made into ~
17	universe		38	pick up
18	trader		39	rain cats and dogs
19	design		40	keep in touch
20	experience		41	make a long face
21	justice		42	call ~ after …
			43	see eye to eye

※ 다음 우리말을 영어로 쓰시오.

01	진보한, 발전된		22	언어	
02	초래하다; 원인		23	얇게 썬 조각; 한 조각	
03	경험하다		24	제안하다	
04	화나게 하다		25	재판관, 판사; 재판하다	
05	스페인의		26	불안한	
06	빌리다		27	의미	
07	표현		28	기원, 유래	
08	공장		29	현재의	
09	접촉		30	노예	
10	홍수		31	우주, 은하계	
11	세기, 100년		32	유래하다	
12	곧, 즉시		33	원래, 본래	
13	문명		34	신화	
14	포함하다		35	~에서 오다, 유래하다	
15	탐험가		36	놀리다	
16	창조하다		37	우울한 얼굴을 하다	
17	상인, 거래자		38	거쳐 지나가다	
18	폭풍		39	행운을 빌다	
19	정의		40	몸이 안 좋은	
20	법		41	연락하다	
21	생산하다		42	전혀 ~가 아니다	
			43	~로 만들어지다	

※ 다음 영영풀이에 알맞은 단어를 <보기>에서 골라 쓴 후, 우리말 뜻을 쓰시오.

1 _____ : in a short time; soon: _____

2 _____ : to make someone angry: _____

3 _____ : happening or existing now: _____

4 _____ : a period of a hundred years: _____

5 _____ : a society that is well organized and developed: _____

6 _____ : a lot of water that covers land that is usually dry: _____

7 _____ : in the beginning, before other things happened: _____

8 _____ : someone who buys and sells goods: _____

9 _____ : all of space, including all the stars and planets: _____

10 _____ : to tell someone you think he or she should do something: _____

11 _____ : communication between people, countries either by talking or writing: _____

12 _____ : something you say, write, or do that shows what you think or feel: _____

13 _____ : the action of pressing and rubbing someone's body to help him or her relax: _____

14 _____ : someone who is owned by another person and works for them for no money: _____

15 _____ : a system of rules that a society or government develops in order to deal with crime and etc.: _____

16 _____ : to use something that belongs to someone else and that you must give back to them later: _____

보기			
law	expression	flood	present
massage	anger	century	shortly
trader	universe	slave	contact
borrow	suggest	civilization	originally

※ 다음 우리말과 일치하도록 빈칸에 알맞은 말을 쓰시오.

Listen and Talk A 1

G: Look. It's raining _____ _____ _____.

B: Raining _____ _____ _____? What does _____ _____?

G: It _____ "It's _____ _____ _____."

B: Oh. _____ _____. I have an umbrella _____ _____ _____.

Listen and Talk A 2

G: This juice is _____ _____, Suho.

B: _____ _____? _____ you _____ _____ again?

G: I said, "This juice is _____ _____." It _____ "I'll _____ _____ the juice."

B: Oh. Thanks _____ _____.

G: _____ _____.

Listen and Talk A 3

B: Everything _____ _____.

G: Yes. _____ you _____ _____ of my spaghetti?

B: No, _____. Spaghetti is _____ my cup of _____.

G: _____ your cup of _____? What _____ that _____?

B: It means "I _____ _____ _____."

G: Oh, I _____. You _____ _____ spaghetti.

Listen and Talk A 4

G: I feel _____ _____ _____.

B: _____ _____, but _____ you please _____ _____ _____?

G: I said, "I feel _____ _____ _____." It means "I _____ _____ _____." I think I _____ _____ _____.

B: Oh. _____ _____ _____ buy some medicine before you _____ on the plane? You can _____ _____ at the store _____ _____.

G: I guess I _____.

G: 봐. 고양이와 개처럼 비가 내려.
B: 고양이와 개처럼 비가 내린다고? 그게 무슨 뜻이니?
G: 그것은 "비가 아주 많이 내린다."라는 뜻이야.
B: 오, 걱정 마. 내 배낭에 우산이 있어.

G: 수호야, 이 주스는 내 위에 있어.
B: 뭐라고 했어? 다시 한 번 말해 줄래?
G: "이 주스는 내 위에 있어."라고 했어. 그것은 "내가 그 주스를 낼게."라는 뜻이야.
B: 오. 정말 고마워.
G: 천만에.

B: 모든 것이 맛있어 보여.
G: 응. 내 스파게티 좀 먹을래?
B: 괜찮아. 스파게티는 나의 차 한 잔이 아니야.
G: 네 차 한 잔이 아니라고? 그게 무슨 뜻이니?
B: 그것은 "난 무언가를 좋아하지 않아." 라는 뜻이야.
G: 오, 알겠어. 넌 스파게티를 좋아하지 않는구나.

G: 난 날씨 아래 있는 기분이야.
B: 미안하지만 다시 한 번 말해 줄래?
G: "나는 날씨 아래 있는 기분이야."라고 말했어. 그것은 "몸이 좋지 않아."라는 뜻이야. 난 감기에 걸린 것 같아.
B: 오, 비행기 타기 전에 약을 좀 사는 게 어때? 저기에 있는 가게에서 약을 살 수 있어.
G: 그래야겠다.

Listen and Talk B 1

A: Don't _____ _____ _____ _____.

B: _____ _____, but _____ _____ _____ _____ _____ _____?

A: I said, "Don't _____ _____ _____ _____."

B: _____ _____ _____ _____ _____?

A: It _____ "Don't _____ _____."

Listen and Talk B 2

M: _____ _____ _____.

W: _____ _____, but _____ _____ _____ _____ _____?

M: I said, "_____ _____ _____."

W: _____ _____ _____ _____ _____?

M: It means "_____ _____."

Listen and Talk B 3

M: I feel _____ _____ _____.

W: _____ _____, but _____ _____ _____ _____ _____ _____?

M: I said, "I feel _____ _____ _____."

W: _____ _____ _____ _____ _____?

M: It means "I _____ _____ well."

Listen and Talk C

G: Thank you for everything, Jiho. I _____ _____ _____ in Korea.

B: _____ _____. Please _____ _____ me again, Lucy.

G: I'd _____ _____, but before I do, I'd _____ _____ _____ you _____ _____ me in London.

B: Thanks. Anyway, _____'s too bad _____ you can't _____ to my soccer game tomorrow.

G: I'm sorry that I _____ _____ _____. I'll _____ _____ _____ for you.

B: _____ _____, but _____ _____ please _____ _____?

G: I said, "I'll _____ _____ _____ _____ for you." It means "I _____ _____ _____ _____ _____."

B: Oh. Thanks. _____ a nice _____.

G: Thanks. I'll _____ _____ _____.

A: 얼굴을 길쭉하게 만들지 마.
B: 미안하지만 다시 한 번 말해 줄래?
A: "얼굴을 길쭉하게 만들지 마."라고 했어.
B: 그게 무슨 뜻이니?
A: 그것은 "슬퍼하지 마."라는 뜻이야.

M: 다리를 부러뜨려.
W: 미안하지만 다시 한 번 말해 줄래?
M: "다리를 부러뜨려."라고 했어.
W: 그게 무슨 뜻이니?
M: 그것은 "행운을 빌어."라는 뜻이야.

M: 나는 날씨 아래 있는 기분이야.
W: 미안하지만 다시 한 번 말해 줄래?
M: "나는 날씨 아래 있는 기분이야."라고 했어.
W: 그게 무슨 뜻이니?
M: 그것은 "난 몸이 좋지 않아."라는 뜻이야.

G: 지호야, 모든 게 고마웠어. 한국에서 정말 좋은 시간을 보냈어.
B: 천만에. 다음에 또 와줘, Lucy.
G: 그러고 싶지만, 그 전에 난 런던으로 널 초대하고 싶어.
B: 고마워. 어쨌든, 내일 네가 내 축구 시합에 올 수 없어서 너무 안타깝다.
G: 나도 더 오래 머물 수 없어서 유감이야. 너를 위해 내 손가락을 교차할게.
B: 미안한데, 다시 한 번 말해 줄래?
G: 나는 "너를 위해 내 손가락을 교차할게."라고 말했어. 그것은 "행운을 빌게."라는 뜻이야.
B: 아, 고마워. 즐거운 여행이 되길 바랄게.
G: 고마워. 연락할게.

Review 1

G: I'll _____ _____ _____ _____ for you.

B: I'm sorry, but _____ _____ _____ _____ _____ _____?

G: I said, "I'll _____ _____ _____ _____ for you." It means "I _____ _____ _____ _____."

G: 너를 위해 내 손가락을 교차할게.
B: 미안하지만 다시 한 번 말해 줄래?
G: "너를 위해 내 손가락을 교차할게."라고 했어. 그것은 "행운을 빌게."라는 뜻이야.

Review 2

W: I _____ _____ _____ _____.

M: Excuse me, but _____ _____ _____ _____ _____ _____?

W: I said, "I _____ _____ _____ _____."

M: _____ _____ _____ _____?

W: It means "I _____ _____ _____." I think I _____ _____ _____.

M: Oh. _____ _____ _____ _____ some medicine? You can _____ _____ at the store _____ _____.

W: OK, I _____.

W: 저는 날씨 아래에 있는 기분이에요.
M: 죄송한데, 다시 한 번 말해 주시겠어요?
W: "저는 날씨 아래에 있는 기분이에요."라고 말했어요.
M: 그게 무슨 뜻인가요?
W: 그것은 "몸이 좋지 않다."라는 뜻이에요. 감기에 걸린 것 같아요.
M: 오. 약을 좀 사는 게 어때요? 저기에 있는 가게에서 약을 살 수 있어요.
W: 네, 그럴게요.

Review 3

M: Look. It's raining _____ _____ _____.

W: _____ _____ _____ _____ _____ _____ _____?

M: It's raining _____ _____ _____.

W: _____ _____ _____ _____?

M: It _____ "It's _____ _____ _____."

M: 봐요. 고양이와 개처럼 비가 내리네요.
W: 다시 한 번 말해 주시겠어요?
M: 고양이와 개처럼 비가 내려요.
W: 그게 무슨 뜻인가요?
M: 그것은 "비가 아주 많이 내린다."라는 뜻이에요.

Review 4

G: This pizza _____ _____ _____, Suho.

B: _____ _____ _____ _____ _____?

G: It means "I'll _____ _____ the pizza."

G: 수호야, 이 피자는 내 위에 있어.
B: 그게 무슨 뜻이니?
G: 그것은 "피자는 내가 살게."라는 뜻이야.

※ 다음 우리말에 맞도록 대화를 영어로 쓰시오.

Listen and Talk A 1

G: _____

B: _____

G: _____

B: _____

G: 봐. 고양이와 개처럼 비가 내려.
B: 고양이와 개처럼 비가 내린다고? 그게 무슨 뜻이니?
G: 그것은 "비가 아주 많이 내린다."라는 뜻이야.
B: 오, 걱정 마. 내 배낭에 우산이 있어.

Listen and Talk A 2

G: _____

B: _____

G: _____

B: _____

G: _____

G: 수호야, 이 주스는 내 위에 있어.
B: 뭐라고 했어? 다시 한 번 말해 줄래?
G: "이 주스는 내 위에 있어."라고 했어. 그것은 "내가 그 주스를 낼게."라는 뜻이야.
B: 오. 정말 고마워.
G: 천만에.

Listen and Talk A 3

B: _____

G: _____

B: _____

G: _____

B: _____

G: _____

B: 모든 것이 맛있어 보여.
G: 응. 내 스파게티 좀 먹을래?
B: 괜찮아. 스파게티는 나의 차 한 잔이 아니야.
G: 네 차 한 잔이 아니라고? 그게 무슨 뜻이니?
B: 그것은 "난 무언가를 좋아하지 않아." 라는 뜻이야.
G: 오, 알겠어. 넌 스파게티를 좋아하지 않는구나.

Listen and Talk A 4

G: _____

B: _____

G: _____

B: _____

G: _____

G: 난 날씨 아래 있는 기분이야.
B: 미안하지만 다시 한 번 말해 줄래?
G: "나는 날씨 아래 있는 기분이야."라고 말했어. 그것은 "몸이 좋지 않아."라는 뜻이야. 난 감기에 걸린 것 같아.
B: 오, 비행기 타기 전에 약을 좀 사는 게 어때? 저기에 있는 가게에서 약을 살 수 있어.
G: 그래야겠다.

Listen and Talk B 1

A: _____

B: _____

A: _____

B: _____

A: _____

A: 얼굴을 길쭉하게 만들지 마.
B: 미안하지만 다시 한 번 말해 줄래?
A: "얼굴을 길쭉하게 만들지 마."라고 했어.
B: 그게 무슨 뜻이니?
A: 그것은 "슬퍼하지 마."라는 뜻이야.

Listen and Talk B 2

M: _____

W: _____

M: _____

W: _____

M: _____

M: 다리를 부러뜨려.
W: 미안하지만 다시 한 번 말해 줄래?
M: "다리를 부러뜨려."라고 했어.
W: 그게 무슨 뜻이니?
M: 그것은 "행운을 빌어."라는 뜻이야.

Listen and Talk B 3

M: _____

W: _____

M: _____

W: _____

M: _____

M: 나는 날씨 아래 있는 기분이야.
W: 미안하지만 다시 한 번 말해 줄래?
M: "나는 날씨 아래 있는 기분이야."라고 했어.
W: 그게 무슨 뜻이니?
M: 그것은 "난 몸이 좋지 않아."라는 뜻이야.

Listen and Talk C

G: _____

B: _____

G: _____

B: _____

G: _____

B: _____

G: _____

B: _____

G: _____

G: 지호야, 모든 게 고마웠어. 한국에서 정말 좋은 시간을 보냈어.
B: 천만에. 다음에 또 와줘, Lucy.
G: 그러고 싶지만, 그 전에 난 런던으로 널 초대하고 싶어.
B: 고마워. 어쨌든, 내일 네가 내 축구 시합에 올 수 없어서 너무 안타깝다.
G: 나도 더 오래 머물 수 없어서 유감이야. 너를 위해 내 손가락을 교차할게.
B: 미안한데, 다시 한 번 말해 줄래?
G: 나는 "너를 위해 내 손가락을 교차할게."라고 말했어. 그것은 "행운을 빌게."라는 뜻이야.
B: 아, 고마워. 즐거운 여행이 되길 바랄게.
G: 고마워. 연락할게.

Review 1

G: _____

B: _____

G: _____

G: 너를 위해 내 손가락을 교차할게.

B: 미안하지만 다시 한 번 말해 줄래?

G: "너를 위해 내 손가락을 교차할게." 라고 했어. 그것은 "행운을 빌게."라 는 뜻이야.

Review 2

W: _____

M: _____

W: _____

M: _____

W: _____

M: _____

W: _____

W: 저는 날씨 아래에 있는 기분이에요.

M: 죄송한데, 다시 한 번 말해 주시겠어 요?

W: "저는 날씨 아래에 있는 기분이에 요."라고 말했어요.

M: 그게 무슨 뜻인가요?

W: 그것은 "몸이 좋지 않다."라는 뜻이 에요. 감기에 걸린 것 같아요.

M: 오. 약을 좀 사는 게 어때요? 저기에 있는 가게에서 약을 살 수 있어요.

W: 네, 그럴게요.

Review 3

M: _____

W: _____

M: _____

W: _____

M: _____

M: 봐요. 고양이와 개처럼 비가 내리네 요.

W: 다시 한 번 말해 주시겠어요?

M: 고양이와 개처럼 비가 내려요.

W: 그게 무슨 뜻인가요?

M: 그것은 "비가 아주 많이 내린다."라 는 뜻이에요.

Review 4

G: _____

B: _____

G: _____

G: 수호야, 이 피자는 내 위에 있어.

B: 그게 무슨 뜻이니?

G: 그것은 "피자는 내가 살게."라는 뜻 이야.

※ 다음 우리말과 일치하도록 빈칸에 알맞은 것을 골라 쓰시오.

1 English _____ of _____ _____
A. Origin   B. Words   C. Foreign

2 English has often _____ _____ from _____ cultures or
_____.
A. other   B. words   C. languages   D. borrowed

3 _____ are some _____ _____ interesting stories.
A. examples   B. with   C. here

shampoo

4 The word *shampoo* _____ _____ the Hindi word *chāmpo*,
which _____ "to _____."
A. from   B. means   C. comes   D. press

5 In India, the word _____ _____ for a _____ _____.
A. massage   B. used   C. head   D. was

6 British _____ in India _____ a bath _____ a head
massage and _____ it to Britain in the 18th century.
A. experienced   B. introduced   C. traders   D. with

7 The _____ of the word *shampoo* changed a _____ times
after it first _____ English _____ 1762.
A. entered   B. few   C. meaning   D. around

8 In the 19th _____, *shampoo* got its _____ meaning of
"_____ the _____."
A. washing   B. present   C. hair   D. century

9 _____ after that, the word began to _____ _____ _____
for a special soap for the hair.
A. used   B. shortly   C. also   D. be

robot

10 The word *robot* comes from the _____ *R.U.R.*, _____ was
_____ in 1920 _____ a Czech writer Karel Čapek.
A. written   B. play   C. by   D. which

11 In the play, robots are machines that _____ _____ _____.
A. like   B. look   C. humans

12 They _____ _____ to _____ for humans and are _____
in a factory.
A. work   B. produced   C. are   D. designed

13 It is interesting that the _____ _____ _____ the word *robot*
didn't come from Karel Čapek _____.
A. himself   B. of   C. idea   D. using

14 He originally _____ the machines in his play *labori* _____
the Latin word _____ "_____."
A. for   B. called   C. from   D. work

1 외국어에서 유래된 영어 단어

2 영어는 종종 다른 문화나 언어에서 단어를 빌려왔다.

3 여기 재미있는 이야기가 있는 몇 개의 예가 있다.

샴푸

4 *shampoo*라는 단어는 힌디어 *chāmpo*에서 왔고, '누르다'라는 의미이다.

5 인도에서 그 단어는 머리 마사지라는 의미로 쓰였다.

6 인도에 있는 영국 상인들은 머리 마사지를 함께하는 목욕을 경험했고 마사지를 18세기에 영국에 소개했다.

7 *shampoo*라는 단어의 의미는 그 단어가 1762년쯤 영어에 처음으로 들어온 이후 몇 번 바뀌었다.

8 19세기에, *shampoo*는 '머리 감기'라는 현재의 의미를 갖게 되었다.

9 그 후 얼마 지나지 않아, 그 단어는 머리에 사용하는 특별한 비누에도 쓰이기 시작했다.

로봇

10 *robot*이라는 단어는 "*R.U.R.*"에서 왔는데, 그 연극은 1920년 체코의 작가 Karel Čapek에 의해 쓰였다.

11 그 연극에서 로봇은 인간처럼 생긴 기계이다.

12 그들은 인간을 위해 일하도록 설계되고, 공장에서 생산된다.

13 *robot*이라는 단어를 사용하려는 생각이 Karel Čapek 자신에게서 나온 게 아니었다는 것이 흥미롭다.

14 그는 원래 자신의 연극에서 그 기계들을 '일'을 의미하는 라틴어에서 온 *labori*라고 불렀다.

15 _____, his brother suggested *roboti*, which means "_____
workers" _____ _____.

   A. slave   B. Czech   C. however   D. in

16 Karel Čapek liked the _____ and decided _____
the _____ *roboti*.

   A. use   B. idea   C. to   D. word

17 In 1938, the _____ was _____ a science
show on television in Britain.

   A. fiction   B. made   C. play   D. into

hurricane

18 The word *hurricane* _____ from the Spanish word *huracán*,
which _____ _____ the _____ of a Mayan god.

   A. from   B. comes   C. name   D. originates

19 In the Mayan _____ _____, Huracán is the weather god of
wind, storm, and fire, and he is one of the three _____ who
_____ humans.

   A. gods   B. myth   C. creation   D. created

20 _____, the first humans _____ the gods, _____ Huracán
_____ a great flood.

   A. so   B. however   C. caused   D. angered

21 The first _____ _____ the Mayan _____ was in
1517.

   A. civilization   B. contact   C. Spanish   D. with

22 Spanish explorers who were _____ the Caribbean
experienced a hurricane and _____ the word for it
from the people in the area.

   A. through   B. up   C. passing   D. picked

23 _____ English, one of the _____ _____ of *hurricane* was
in a play _____ Shakespeare in 1608.

   A. by   B. uses   C. early   D. in

hamburger

24 The _____ *hamburger* _____ comes _____ Hamburg,
Germany's _____ city.

   A. originally   B. word   C. second-largest   D. from

25 *Hamburger* _____ "people or _____ from Hamburg"
_____ _____.

   A. things   B. means   C. German   D. in

26 The _____ of the first hamburger is _____.

   A. clear   B. origin   C. not

27 However, it is _____ _____ the hamburger was invented
in a small town in Texas, USA, sometime _____ 1885
_____ 1904.

   A. between   B. believed   C. and   D. that

28 A cook _____ a Hamburg-style steak between two _____ of
bread, and people started to call _____ _____ a hamburger.

   A. slices   B. food   C. placed   D. such

15 하지만, 그의 형이 *roboti*를 제안했는데, *roboti*는 체코어로 '노예 근로자들'을 의미한다.

16 Karel Čapek은 그 아이디어가 마음에 들어 *roboti*라는 단어를 사용하기로 결정했다.

17 1938년에 그 연극은 영국 TV에서 공상 과학물로 만들어졌다.

태풍

18 *hurricane*이라는 단어는 스페인어 단어 *huracán*에서 왔고, 그것은 마야 신의 이름에서 유래한다.

19 마야의 창조 신화에서, Huracán은 바람, 폭풍우, 그리고 불에 관한 날씨의 신이며, 그는 인간을 창조한 세 명의 신들 중 한 명이다.

20 하지만, 최초의 인간들이 신들을 화나게 해서 Huracán은 거대한 홍수를 일으켰다.

21 스페인이 마야 문명과 했던 첫 접촉은 1517년이었다.

22 카리브 제도를 지나던 스페인 탐험가들이 허리케인을 겪었고, 그 지역 사람들로부터 그것을 의미하는 단어를 듣게 되었다.

23 영어에서 일찍이 *hurricane*을 사용한 것 중 하나는 1608년 셰익스피어에 의한 희곡에서였다.

햄버거

24 *hamburger*라는 단어는 원래 독일에서 두 번째로 큰 도시인 함부르크에서 왔다.

25 *hamburger*는 독일어로 '함부르크 출신의 사람 또는 사물'을 의미한다.

26 최초의 햄버거의 기원은 분명하지 않다.

27 하지만 햄버거는 1885년에서 1904년 사이의 언젠가 미국 텍사스에 있는 작은 마을에서 발명되었다고 믿어진다.

28 한 요리사가 빵 두 조각 사이에 함부르크 스타일의 스테이크를 넣었고, 사람들은 그런 음식을 햄버거라고 부르기 시작했다.

※ 다음 우리말과 일치하도록 빈칸에 알맞은 말을 쓰시오.

1 **English** _____ **of** _____ _____

2 English _____ _____ _____ _____ from _____ _____ or languages.

3 Here _____ some examples _____ _____ _____.

shampoo

4 The word *shampoo* _____ _____ the Hindi word *chāmpo*, _____ means "_____ _____."

5 In India, the word _____ _____ for a head massage.

6 British traders in India experienced a bath _____ _____ _____ _____ and _____ it _____ Britain in the 18th century.

7 The meaning of the word *shampoo* changed _____ _____ _____ after it first _____ English _____ 1762.

8 In the 19th century, *shampoo* got its _____ meaning of "_____ _____ _____."

9 _____ _____ _____, the word began _____ _____ _____ a special soap for the hair.

robot

10 The word *robot* comes from the play *R.U.R.*, which _____ _____ in 1920 by a _____ _____ Karel Čapek.

11 In the play, robots are machines that _____ _____ humans.

12 They _____ _____ _____ _____ _____ for humans and _____ _____ in a factory.

13 _____ is interesting that _____ _____ _____ _____ the word *robot* didn't _____ _____ Karel Čapek _____.

14 He _____ _____ the machines in his play *labori* _____ the Latin word _____ "work."

---

1 외국어에서 유래된 영어 단어

2 영어는 종종 다른 문화나 언어에서 단어를 빌려왔다.

3 여기 재미있는 이야기가 있는 몇 개의 예가 있다.

샴푸

4 *shampoo*라는 단어는 힌디어 *chāmpo*에서 왔고, '누르다'라는 의미이다.

5 인도에서 그 단어는 머리 마사지라는 의미로 쓰였다.

6 인도에 있는 영국 상인들은 머리 마사지를 함께하는 목욕을 경험했고 마사지를 18세기에 영국에 소개했다.

7 *shampoo*라는 단어의 의미는 그 단어가 1762년쯤 영어에 처음으로 들어온 이후 몇 번 바뀌었다.

8 19세기에, *shampoo*는 '머리 감기'라는 현재의 의미를 갖게 되었다.

9 그 후 얼마 지나지 않아, 그 단어는 머리에 사용하는 특별한 비누에도 쓰이기 시작했다.

로봇

10 *robot*이라는 단어는 "*R.U.R.*"에서 왔는데, 그 연극은 1920년 체코의 작가 Karel Čapek에 의해 쓰였다.

11 그 연극에서 로봇은 인간처럼 생긴 기계이다.

12 그들은 인간을 위해 일하도록 설계되고, 공장에서 생산된다.

13 *robot*이라는 단어를 사용하려는 생각이 Karel Čapek 자신에게서 나온 게 아니었다는 것이 흥미롭다.

14 그는 원래 자신의 연극에서 그 기계들을 '일'을 의미하는 라틴어에서 온 *labori*라고 불렀다.

15 _____, his brother _____ *roboti*, _____ means "slave workers" _____ _____.

16 Karel Čapek liked the idea and _____ _____ _____ the word *roboti*.

17 In 1938, the play _____ _____ _____ a science fiction show _____ _____ in Britain.

hurricane

18 The word *hurricane* _____ _____ the Spanish word *huracán*, which _____ _____ the name of a Mayan god.

19 In the Mayan _____ _____, Huracán is the weather god of wind, storm, and fire, and he is _____ _____ _____ _____ who _____ _____.

20 However, the first humans _____ the gods, _____ Huracán _____ a great _____.

21 The first _____ _____ _____ _____ the Mayan _____ was in 1517.

22 Spanish _____ who _____ _____ the Caribbean experienced a hurricane and _____ _____ the word _____ _____ from the people in the area.

23 _____ _____ _____, one of the _____ _____ of *hurricane* was in a play _____ Shakespeare in 1608.

hamburger

24 The word *hamburger* _____ _____ _____ Hamburg, Germany's _____ city.

25 *Hamburger* means "people or things _____ Hamburg" _____ _____.

26 The origin of the first hamburger _____ _____ _____.

27 However, _____ _____ _____ the hamburger was invented in a small town in Texas, USA, sometime _____ 1885 _____ 1904.

28 A cook _____ a _____ steak between _____ _____, and people started to _____ _____ a hamburger.

---

15 하지만, 그의 형이 *roboti*를 제안했는데, *roboti*는 체코어로 '노예 근로자들'을 의미한다.

16 Karel Čapek은 그 아이디어가 마음에 들어 *roboti*라는 단어를 사용하기로 결정했다.

17 1938년에 그 연극은 영국 TV에서 공상 과학물로 만들어졌다.

태풍

18 *hurricane*이라는 단어는 스페인어 단어 *huracán*에서 왔고, 그것은 마야 신의 이름에서 유래한다.

19 마야의 창조 신화에서, Huracán은 바람, 폭풍우, 그리고 불에 관한 날씨의 신이며, 그는 인간을 창조한 세 명의 신들 중 한 명이다.

20 하지만, 최초의 인간들이 신들을 화나게 해서 Huracán은 거대한 홍수를 일으켰다.

21 스페인이 마야 문명과 했던 첫 접촉은 1517년이었다.

22 카리브 제도를 지나던 스페인 탐험가들이 허리케인을 겪었고, 그 지역 사람들로부터 그것을 의미하는 단어를 듣게 되었다.

23 영어에서 일찍이 *hurricane*을 사용한 것 중 하나는 1608년 셰익스피어에 의한 희곡에서였다.

햄버거

24 *hamburger*라는 단어는 원래 독일에서 두 번째로 큰 도시인 함부르크에서 왔다.

25 *hamburger*는 독일어로 '함부르크 출신의 사람 또는 사물'을 의미한다.

26 최초의 햄버거의 기원은 분명하지 않다.

27 하지만 햄버거는 1885년에서 1904년 사이의 언젠가 미국 텍사스에 있는 작은 마을에서 발명되었다고 믿어진다.

28 한 요리사가 빵 두 조각 사이에 함부르크 스타일의 스테이크를 넣었고, 사람들은 그런 음식을 햄버거라고 부르기 시작했다.

※ 다음 문장을 우리말로 쓰시오.

1 English Words of Foreign Origin

➡ _____

2 English has often borrowed words from other cultures or languages.

➡ _____

3 Here are some examples with interesting stories.

➡ _____

shampoo 샴푸

4 The word *shampoo* comes from the Hindi word *chāmpo*, which means "to press."

➡ _____

5 In India, the word was used for a head massage.

➡ _____

6 British traders in India experienced a bath with a head massage and introduced it to Britain in the 18th century.

➡ _____

7 The meaning of the word *shampoo* changed a few times after it first entered English around 1762.

➡ _____

8 In the 19th century, *shampoo* got its present meaning of "washing the hair."

➡ _____

9 Shortly after that, the word began to be also used for a special soap for the hair.

➡ _____

robot 로봇

10 The word *robot* comes from the play *R.U.R.*, which was written in 1920 by a Czech writer Karel Čapek.

➡ _____

11 In the play, *robots* are machines that look like humans.

➡ _____

12 They are designed to work for humans and are produced in a factory.

➡ _____

13 It is interesting that the idea of using the word *robot* didn't come from Karel Čapek himself.

➡ _____

14 He originally called the machines in his play *labori* from the Latin word for "work."

➡ _____

15 However, his brother suggested *roboti*, which means "slave workers" in Czech.
➡ _____

16 Karel Čapek liked the idea and decided to use the word *roboti*.
➡ _____

17 In 1938, the play was made into a science fiction show on television in Britain.
➡ _____

hurricane 태풍

18 The word *hurricane* comes from the Spanish word *huracán*, which originates from the name of a Mayan god.
➡ _____

19 In the Mayan creation myth, Huracán is the weather god of wind, storm, and fire, and he is one of the three gods who created humans.
➡ _____
_____

20 However, the first humans angered the gods, so Huracán caused a great flood.
➡ _____

21 The first Spanish contact with the Mayan civilization was in 1517.
➡ _____

22 Spanish explorers who were passing through the Caribbean experienced a hurricane and picked up the word for it from the people in the area.
➡ _____
_____

23 In English, one of the early uses of *hurricane* was in a play by Shakespeare in 1608.
➡ _____

hamburger 햄버거

24 The word *hamburger* originally comes from Hamburg, Germany's second-largest city.
➡ _____

25 *Hamburger* means "people or things from Hamburg" in German.
➡ _____

26 The origin of the first hamburger is not clear.
➡ _____

27 However, it is believed that the hamburger was invented in a small town in Texas, USA, sometime between 1885 and 1904.
➡ _____

28 A cook placed a Hamburg-style steak between two slices of bread, and people started to call such food a hamburger.
➡ _____

※ 다음 괄호 안의 단어들을 우리말에 맞도록 바르게 배열하시오.

1 ▶ (Words / English / of / Origin / Foreign)
➡ _____

2 ▶ (has / English / borrowed / often / from / words / cultures / other / languages. / or)
➡ _____

3 ▶ (are / here / examples / some / interesting / with / stories.)
➡ _____

shampoo

4 ▶ (word / the / comes / *shampoo* / from / Hindi / the / word *chāmpo*, / means / which / press." / "to)
➡ _____

5 ▶ (India, / in / word / the / used / was / a / for / massage. / head)
➡ _____

6 ▶ (traders / British / India / in / a / experienced / bath / a / with / massage / heard / and / it / introduced / to / Britain / the / in / century. / 18th)
➡ _____
_____

7 ▶ (meaning / the / the / of / *shampoo* / word / changed / few / a / after / times / first / it / English / entered / 1762. / around)
➡ _____
_____

8 ▶ (the / in / century, / 19th *shampoo* / got / present / its / of / meaning / the / hair." / "washing)
➡ _____

9 ▶ (after / shortly / that, / word / the / to / began / be / used / also / for / special / a / soap / the / hair. / for)
➡ _____

robot

10 ▶ (word / the / comes / *robot* / from / play / the / *R.U.R.*, / was / which / in / written / 1920 / by / Czech / a / Karel / writer / Čapek.)
➡ _____
_____

---

1 외국어에서 유래된 영어 단어

2 영어는 종종 다른 문화나 언어에서 단어를 빌려왔다.

3 여기 재미있는 이야기가 있는 몇 개의 예가 있다.

샴푸

4 *shampoo*라는 단어는 힌디어 *chāmpo*에서 왔고, '누르다'라는 의미이다.

5 인도에서 그 단어는 머리 마사지라는 의미로 쓰였다.

6 인도에 있는 영국 상인들은 머리 마사지를 함께하는 목욕을 경험했고 마사지를 18세기에 영국에 소개했다.

7 *shampoo*라는 단어의 의미는 그 단어가 1762년쯤 영어에 처음으로 들어온 이후 몇 번 바뀌었다.

8 19세기에, *shampoo*는 '머리 감기'라는 현재의 의미를 갖게 되었다.

9 그 후 얼마 지나지 않아, 그 단어는 머리에 사용하는 특별한 비누에도 쓰이기 시작했다.

로봇

10 *robot*이라는 단어는 "*R.U.R.*"에서 왔는데, 그 연극은 1920년 체코의 작가 Karel Čapek에 의해 쓰였다.

11 (the / in / play, / are / robots / that / machines / like / look / humans.)

➡ _____

12 (are / they / designed / work / to / humans / for / and / produced / are / a / in / factory.)

➡ _____

13 (is / it / that / interesting / the / idea / using / of / the / *robot* / word / come / didn't / from / Karel / himself. / Čapek)

➡ _____
_____

14 (originally / he / the / called / machines / his / in / play / from / *labori* / the / word / Latin / "work." / for)

➡ _____
_____

15 (his / however, / brother / *roboti*, / suggested / means / which / workers" / "slave / Czech. / in)

➡ _____
_____

16 (Čapek / Karel / the / liked / idea / and / decided / use / to / word / the / *roboti*.)

➡ _____

17 (1938, / in / play / the / was / into / made / a / fiction / science / on / show / Britain. / in / television)

➡ _____
_____

hurricane

18 (word / the / comes / *hurricane* / from / the / word / Spanish / *huracán*, / originates / which / the / from / of / name / Mayan / a / god.)

➡ _____
_____

19 (the / in / creation / Mayan / myth, / Huracán / the / is / god / weather / wind, / of / and / storm, / fire, / he / and / is / of / one / three / the / who / gods / humans. / created)

➡ _____
_____

20 (the / however, / first / angered / humans / gods, / the / so / caused / Huracán / great / a / flood.)

➡ _____
_____

11 그 연극에서 로봇은 인간처럼 생긴 기계이다.

12 그들은 인간을 위해 일하도록 설계되고, 공장에서 생산된다.

13 *robot*이라는 단어를 사용하려는 생각이 Karel Čapek 자신에게서 나온 게 아니었다는 것이 흥미롭다.

14 그는 원래 자신의 연극에서 그 기계들을 '일'을 의미하는 라틴어에서 온 *labori*라고 불렀다.

15 하지만, 그의 형이 *roboti*를 제안했는데, *roboti*는 체코어로 '노예 근로자들'을 의미한다.

16 Karel Čapek은 그 아이디어가 마음에 들어 *roboti*라는 단어를 사용하기로 결정했다.

17 1938년에 그 연극은 영국 TV에서 공상 과학물로 만들어졌다.

태풍

18 *hurricane*이라는 단어는 스페인어 단어 *huracán*에서 왔고, 그것은 마야 신의 이름에서 유래한다.

19 마야의 창조 신화에서, Huracán은 바람, 폭풍우, 그리고 불에 관한 날씨의 신이며, 그는 인간을 창조한 세 명의 신들 중 한 명이다.

20 하지만, 최초의 인간들이 신들을 화나게 해서 Huracán은 거대한 홍수를 일으켰다.

21 (first / the / contact / Spanish / the / with / civilization / Mayan / in / was / 1517.)

⇒ _____

22 (explorers / Spanish / were / who / through / passing / the / experienced / Caribbean / hurricane / a / and / up / picked / the / for / word / from / it / people / the / area. / the / in)

⇒ _____
_____

23 (English, / in / of / one / early / the / of / uses / was / hurricane / in / play / a / Shakespeare / by / 1608. / in)

⇒ _____
_____

hamburger

24 (word / the / originally / *hamburger* / comes / Hamburg, / from / Germany's / city. / second-largest)

⇒ _____

25 (means / *hamburger* / or / "people / things / Hamburg" / from / German. / in)

⇒ _____

26 (origin / the / of / first / the / hamburger / not / clear. / is)

⇒ _____

27 (it / however, / is / that / believed / the / was / hamburger / invented / a / in / town / small / in / USA, / Texas, / between / sometime / 1904. / and / 1885)

⇒ _____
_____

28 (cook / a / placed / a / steak / Hamburg-style / two / between / of / slices / bread, / and / started / people / call / to / food / such / hamburger, / a)

⇒ _____
_____

21 스페인이 마야 문명과 했던 첫 접촉은 1517년이었다.

22 카리브 제도를 지나던 스페인 탐험가들이 허리케인을 겪었고, 그 지역 사람들로부터 그것을 의미하는 단어를 듣게 되었다.

23 영어에서 일찍이 *hurricane*을 사용한 것 중 하나는 1608년 셰익스피어에 의한 희곡에서였다.

햄버거

24 *hamburger*라는 단어는 원래 독일에서 두 번째로 큰 도시인 함부르크에서 왔다.

25 *hamburger*는 독일어로 '함부르크 출신의 사람 또는 사물'을 의미한다.

26 최초의 햄버거의 기원은 분명하지 않다.

27 하지만 햄버거는 1885년에서 1904년 사이의 언젠가 미국 텍사스에 있는 작은 마을에서 발명되었다고 믿어진다.

28 한 요리사가 빵 두 조각 사이에 함부르크 스타일의 스테이크를 넣었고, 사람들은 그런 음식을 햄버거라고 부르기 시작했다.

※ 다음 우리말을 영어로 쓰시오.

1 외국어에서 유래된 영어 단어

➡ _____

2 영어는 종종 다른 문화나 언어에서 단어를 빌려왔다.

➡ _____

3 여기 재미있는 이야기가 있는 몇 개의 예가 있다.

➡ _____

shampoo 샴푸

4 shampoo라는 단어는 힌디어 *chāmpo*에서 왔고, '누르다'라는 의미이다.

➡ _____

5 인도에서 그 단어는 머리 마사지라는 의미로 쓰였다.

➡ _____

6 인도에 있는 영국 상인들은 머리 마사지를 함께하는 목욕을 경험했고 마사지를 18세기에 영국에 소개했다.

➡ _____

_____

7 *shampoo*라는 단어의 의미는 그 단어가 1762년쯤 영어에 처음으로 들어온 이후 몇 번 바뀌었다.

➡ _____

8 19세기에, *shampoo*는 '머리 감기'라는 현재의 의미를 갖게 되었다.

➡ _____

9 그 후 얼마 지나지 않아, 그 단어는 머리에 사용하는 특별한 비누에도 쓰이기 시작했다.

➡ _____

robot 로봇

10 robot이라는 단어는 "*R.U.R.*"에서 왔는데, 그 연극은 1920년 체코의 작가 Karel Čapek에 의해 쓰였다.

➡ _____

11 그 연극에서 로봇은 인간처럼 생긴 기계이다.

➡ _____

12 그들은 인간을 위해 일하도록 설계되고, 공장에서 생산된다.

➡ _____

13 robot이라는 단어를 사용하려는 생각이 Karel Čapek 자신에게서 나온 게 아니었다는 것이 흥미롭다.

➡ _____

14 그는 원래 자신의 연극에서 그 기계들을 '일'을 의미하는 라틴어에서 온 *labori*라고 불렀다.

➡ _____

15 하지만, 그의 형이 roboti를 제안했는데, *roboti*는 체코어로 '노예 근로자들'을 의미한다.

➡ _____

16 Karel Čapek은 그 아이디어가 마음에 들어 *roboti*라는 단어를 사용하기로 결정했다.

➡ _____

17 1938년에 그 연극은 영국 TV에서 공상 과학물로 만들어졌다.

➡ _____

hurricane 태풍

18 hurricane이라는 단어는 스페인어 단어 *huracán*에서 왔고, 그것은 마야 신의 이름에서 유래한다.

➡ _____

19 마야의 창조 신화에서, Huracán은 바람, 폭풍우, 그리고 불에 관한 날씨의 신이며, 그는 인간을 창조한 세 명의 신들 중 한 명이다.

➡ _____

_____

20 하지만, 최초의 인간들이 신들을 화나게 해서 Huracán은 거대한 홍수를 일으켰다.

➡ _____

21 스페인이 마야 문명과 했던 첫 접촉은 1517년이었다.

➡ _____

22 카리브 제도를 지나던 스페인 탐험가들이 허리케인을 겪었고, 그 지역 사람들로부터 그것을 의미하는 단어를 듣게 되었다.

➡ _____

_____

23 영어에서 일찍이 *hurricane*을 사용한 것 중 하나는 1608년 셰익스피어의 희곡에서였다.

➡ _____

hamburger 햄버거

24 *hamburger*라는 단어는 원래 독일에서 두 번째로 큰 도시인 함부르크에서 왔다.

➡ _____

25 *hamburger*는 독일어로 '함부르크 출신의 사람 또는 사물'을 의미한다.

➡ _____

26 최초의 햄버거의 기원은 분명하지 않다.

➡ _____

27 하지만 햄버거는 1885년에서 1904년 사이의 언젠가 미국 텍사스에 있는 작은 마을에서 발명되었다고 믿어진다.

➡ _____

_____

28 한 요리사가 빵 두 조각 사이에 함부르크 스타일의 스테이크를 넣었고, 사람들은 그런 음식을 햄버거라고 부르기 시작했다.

➡ _____

_____

※ 다음 우리말과 일치하도록 빈칸에 알맞은 말을 쓰시오.

After You Read A

1. Online _____

2. English words _____ _____ _____ or _____

3. shampoo: It _____ _____ the Hindi word *chāmpo*, _____ means "_____ _____."

4. robot: It comes from *roboti*, _____ means "_____ _____ _____."

5. hurricane: It comes from _____ _____, *huracán*, _____ _____ _____ the name of a Mayan god.

6. hamburger: It comes from _____, _____ _____ _____ _____ _____ _____.

	1. 온라인 사전
	2. 다른 문화나 언어에서 온 영어 단어들
	3. 샴푸: 그것은 힌디어 *chāmpo*에서 왔는데, '누르다'를 의미한다.
	4. 로봇: 그것은 *roboti*에서 왔는데, *roboti*는 체코어로 '노예 근로자들'을 의미한다.
	5. 허리케인: 그것은 스페인어 *huracán*에서 왔는데, 마야 신의 이름에서 유래된다.
	6. 햄버거: 그것은 독일에서 두 번째로 큰 도시인 함부르크에서 왔다.

Around the World

1. 1. Many _____ _____ about law _____ _____ _____ .

2. Examples _____ words _____ _____ and _____ .

3. 2. _____ _____ _____ _____ _____ about music _____ come from Italian.

4. _____ _____, piano and violin _____ _____ _____ .

5. 3. Many English words for _____ come from _____ .

6. _____ _____, tomato _____ _____ *tomate* and potato comes from *patata* _____ _____ .

	1. 1. 법에 관한 많은 영어 단어들은 프랑스어에서 왔다.
	2. judge(판사)와 justice(정의)와 같은 단어들을 예로 들 수 있다.
	3. 2. 이탈리아어에서 온 음악에 관한 많은 영어 단어들이 있다.
	4. 예를 들어, piano(피아노)와 violin(바이올린) 등이 있다.
	5. 3. 채소에 관한 많은 영어 단어들은 스페인어에서 왔다.
	6. 예를 들어, tomato(토마토)는 *tomate*에서 왔고, potato(감자)는 *patata*에서 왔다.

Think and Write Step 2

1. The _____ of the _____

2. The word *sandwich* _____ _____ John Montagu, _____ was _____ _____ _____ of Sandwich.

3. He _____ _____ meat between _____ _____ _____ because he could play a card game _____ _____ _____ .

4. People _____ _____ it was a great idea and began to call _____ _____ _____ _____ _____ _____ him.

	1. 단어 sandwich의 유래
	2. 단어 sandwich는 John Montagu에게서 유래했는데, 그는 샌드위치 백작 4세였다.
	3. 그는 먹는 동안에 카드게임을 할 수 있었기 때문에 빵 두 조각 사이에 고기를 끼워서 먹는 것을 즐겼다.
	4. 사람들은 그것을 좋은 생각이라고 여겼고, 그의 이름을 따서 그런 음식을 샌드위치라고 부르기 시작했다.

※ 다음 우리말을 영어로 쓰시오.

After You Read A

1. 온라인 사전
➡ _____

2. 다른 문화나 언어에서 온 영어 단어들
➡ _____

3. 샴푸: 그것은 힌디어 chāmpo에서 왔는데, '누르다'를 의미한다.
➡ _____

4. 로봇: 그것은 roboti에서 왔는데, roboti는 체코어로 '노예 근로자들'을 의미한다.
➡ _____

5. 허리케인: 그것은 스페인어 huracán에서 왔는데, 마야 신의 이름에서 유래된다.
➡ _____

6. 햄버거: 그것은 독일에서 두 번째로 큰 도시인 함부르크에서 왔다
➡ _____

Around the World

1. 1. 법에 관한 많은 영어 단어들은 프랑스어에서 왔다.
➡ _____

2. judge(판사)와 justice(정의)와 같은 단어들을 예로 들 수 있다.
➡ _____

3. 2. 이탈리아어에서 온 음악에 관한 많은 영어 단어들이 있다.
➡ _____

4. 예를 들어, piano(피아노)와 violin(바이올린) 등이 있다
➡ _____

5. 3. 채소에 관한 많은 영어 단어들은 스페인어에서 왔다.
➡ _____

6. 예를 들어, tomato(토마토)는 tomate에서 왔고, potato(감자)는 patata에서 왔다.
➡ _____

Think and Write Step 2

1. 단어 sandwich의 유래
➡ _____

2. 단어 sandwich는 John Montagu에게서 유래했는데, 그는 샌드위치 백작 4세였다.
➡ _____

3. 그는 먹는 동안에 카드게임을 할 수 있었기 때문에 빵 두 조각 사이에 고기를 끼워서 먹는 것을 즐겼다.
➡ _____

4. 사람들은 그것을 좋은 생각이라고 여겼고, 그의 이름을 따서 그런 음식을 샌드위치라고 부르기 시작했다.
➡ _____

Step1

※ 다음 영어를 우리말로 쓰시오.

01 tight	
02 refund	
03 balance	
04 case	
05 charity	
06 comfortable	
07 receipt	
08 pocket money	
09 remaining	
10 correct	
11 budget	
12 couch	
13 divide	
14 return	
15 exchange	
16 although	
17 save	
18 donate	
19 effort	
20 lastly	
21 allowance	

22 majority	
23 medicine	
24 instead	
25 price	
26 manage	
27 work	
28 receive	
29 loose	
30 result	
31 survey	
32 recently	
33 while	
34 already	
35 get a refund	
36 would like to	
37 take care of	
38 right away	
39 use up	
40 have difficulty (in) -ing	
41 carry around	
42 on sale	
43 have money back	

※ 다음 우리말을 영어로 쓰시오.

01 환불; 환불받다

02 비록 ~이지만

03 가격

04 편안한

05 소파

06 반품하다

07 노력

08 매주의, 주간의

09 바로 잡다

10 그 대신에

11 예산

12 교환; 교환하다

13 자선 단체

14 마지막으로

15 남아 있는

16 기부하다

17 결과

18 헐렁한, 느슨한

19 영수증

20 대다수

21 지폐

22 균형, 통장의 잔액

23 용돈

24 나누다

25 받다

26 빠듯한, 꽉 조이는[딱 붙는]

27 비가 내리는

28 이미, 벌써

29 의약품

30 최근에

31 사례, 경우

32 관리하다

33 저축하다, 구하다

34 설문조사

35 즉시

36 환불받다

37 노력을 필요로 하다

38 그 자리에서, 현장에서

39 가지고 다니다

40 ~하기를 원하다, 좋아하다

41 교환받다

42 마음을 바꾸다

43 ~을 돌보다, ~을 처리하다

※ 다음 영영풀이에 알맞은 단어를 <보기>에서 골라 쓴 후, 우리말 뜻을 쓰시오.

1 _____ : not firmly fastened in place: _____

2 _____ : a substance used for treating illness: _____

3 _____ : to give money to a group that needs help: _____

4 _____ : most of the people or things in a group: _____

5 _____ : a sum of money which is returned to you: _____

6 _____ : an opinion you give someone about what they should do: _____

7 _____ : to make something right or to make it work the way it should: _____

8 _____ : an amount money that a person or company can spend: _____

9 _____ : left over after a part has been taken, used, or lost: _____

10 _____ : the amount of money that you have in your bank account: _____

11 _____ : hard work that you do when you are trying to achieve something: _____

12 _____ : the act of giving someone something and receiving something else from them: _____

13 _____ : money given by parents to a child regularly that the child can spend: _____

14 _____ : a piece of paper that shows you have paid for something: _____

15 _____ : a comfortable piece of furniture big enough for two or three people to sit on: _____

16 _____ : an organization that gives money, goods, or help to people who are poor, sick, etc.: _____

보기			
advice	correct	charity	receipt
medicine	donate	remaining	balance
budget	refund	couch	allowance
loose	majority	effort	exchange

※ 다음 우리말과 일치하도록 빈칸에 알맞은 말을 쓰시오.

Listen and Talk A 1

W: Hello. May I _____ _____?

B: Yes, please. I'd _____ _____ _____ a _____ for this watch.

W: OK. Was there anything _____ _____ it?

B: No, I just _____ my _____. Can I _____ my money _____?

W: OK. I'll _____ _____ _____ it _____ _____.

Listen and Talk A 2

W: Hello. Do you _____ _____ _____?

B: Yes. I'd _____ _____ _____ this smartphone case.

W: _____ _____. Do you have the _____ _____ you?

B: _____ _____ _____. I bought _____ three days ago.

W: Oh, then _____ _____.

Listen and Talk A 3

W: Hello. Are you _____ _____ anything _____?

B: No, I'm not. I'd _____ _____ _____ this T-shirt. It's too small.

W: Sure. What size _____ _____ _____?

B: Large, please.

W: _____ _____ _____.

B: Thank you.

Listen and Talk A 4

W: Hello. _____ can I _____ _____ _____ _____?

B: Can I _____ this black umbrella _____ a _____ color?

W: Sure. _____ color _____ you _____?

B: _____ _____ a _____ _____, please.

W: OK. _____ _____ _____.

Listen and Talk B 1

A: Hello. _____ _____ _____ _____?

B: Yes, please. _____ _____ _____ _____ this bag.

A: Sure. _____ would you like to exchange _____ _____?

B: I'd _____ _____ exchange _____ a cap.

A: OK.

A: 안녕하세요. 무엇을 도와드릴까요?
B: 네. 이 가방을 교환하고 싶어요.
A: 네. 무엇으로 교환하고 싶으세요?
B: 저는 모자로 교환하고 싶어요.
A: 알겠습니다.

Listen and Talk B 2

A: Hello. _____ _____ help you?

B: Yes, please. I'd like to _____ _____ _____ _____ this bag.

A: Sure. Do you have the _____?

B: Yes, I _____. _____ _____ _____.

A: 안녕하세요. 무엇을 도와드릴까요?
B: 네. 이 가방을 환불받고 싶어요.
A: 물론이죠. 영수증을 가지고 계시나요?
B: 네. 여기 있습니다.

Listen and Talk C

M: Hello. _____ _____ _____ _____?

G: Yes, please. I'd like to _____ _____ _____ _____ this cap.

M: Do you have the _____?

G: No, I _____. I _____ _____ _____ a gift.

M: If you don't have the receipt, then, _____ not possible _____ _____ a _____.

G: _____ _____. Then, can I _____ it _____ _____ _____?

M: Yes, you _____. What _____ _____ _____ _____ _____?

G: I _____ _____ _____ this blue bag.

M: _____ _____ _____ .... The _____ is the _____, so you can just _____ _____.

G: Thank you.

M: 안녕하세요. 도와드릴까요?
G: 네. 이 모자를 환불받고 싶어요.
M: 영수증을 가지고 있나요?
G: 아니요. 선물로 받았어요.
M: 영수증이 없으면, 환불은 가능하지 않아요.
G: 알겠어요. 그럼, 다른 것으로 교환할 수 있나요?
M: 네, 가능해요. 어떤 것을 원하시나요?
G: 이 파란색 가방을 갖고 싶어요.
M: 한번 볼게요…. 가격이 같으니까 그것을 가져가셔도 돼요.
G: 고맙습니다.

Listen and Talk D

G: I _____ this red skirt _____ _____. I like the skirt, but my sister says that the color doesn't _____ _____ _____ me. I _____ _____ I should _____ _____ _____ a different color.

B: It's _____ _____ _____ but I think it's fine.

G: 나는 지난주에 이 빨간색 치마를 샀어. 나는 치마가 마음에 드는데 내 여동생은 색깔이 나에게 잘 어울리지 않는대. 이걸 다른 색으로 교환을 해야 할지 고민이야.
B: 네가 하고 싶은 대로 하렴, 하지만 내 생각엔 괜찮은 것 같아.

Talk and Play

A: _____ _____ . I'd like to _____ this T-shirt _____ these pants.
B: OK. Is there _____ _____ _____ it?
A: I _____ _____ the color.
B: I see.

A: _____ _____ . I'd like to _____ _____ _____ this cap.
B: OK. Is there _____ _____ with it?
A: I don't like the color.
B: I see.

A: 실례합니다. 이 티셔츠를 이 바지로 교환하고 싶어요.
B: 네. 티셔츠에 무슨 문제가 있나요?
A: 색이 마음에 들지 않아요.
B: 알겠습니다.

A: 실례합니다. 저는 이 모자를 환불받고 싶어요.
B: 네. 모자에 무슨 문제가 있나요?
A: 색이 마음에 들지 않아요.
B: 알겠습니다.

Review 1

W: Hello. _____ _____ _____ _____ ?
B: Yes, please. _____ _____ _____ _____ this baseball glove.
W: OK. Was there _____ _____ _____ it?
B: No, I just _____ my _____ . Can I _____ my money _____ ?
W: OK. _____ _____ _____ .

W: 안녕하세요. 무엇을 도와드릴까요?
B: 네. 이 야구 글러브를 환불받고 싶어서요.
W: 알겠어요. 그것에 무슨 문제가 있었나요?
B: 아니요. 그냥 마음이 바뀌었어요. 제 돈을 돌려받을 수 있을까요?
W: 네. 여기 있습니다.

Review 2

M: Hello. _____ _____ _____ _____ ?
W: Yes, please. _____ _____ _____ this yellow T-shirt. It's _____ _____ _____ me.
M: Sure. What size _____ _____ _____ _____ _____ _____ ?
W: _____ size, please. Oh! Can I _____ _____ _____ red?
M: OK. _____ _____ _____ .

M: 안녕하세요. 무엇을 도와드릴까요?
W: 네. 이 노란색 티셔츠를 교환하고 싶어요. 저에게는 너무 작네요.
M: 네. 어떤 사이즈로 교환하고 싶으신가요?
W: 중간 사이즈로 주세요. 오! 빨간색 티셔츠로 바꿀 수 있을까요?
M: 네. 여기 있습니다.

Review 3

M: Hello. _____ I _____ you?
G: Yes, please. Can I _____ _____ _____ _____ this hat?
M: I'm _____ _____ _____ .
G: Then, can I _____ this hat _____ the gloves _____ there?
M: Yes, you _____ .

M: 안녕하세요. 무엇을 도와드릴까요?
G: 네. 이 모자를 환불받을 수 있을까요?
M: 죄송하지만 안 됩니다.
G: 그렇다면 이 모자를 저기에 있는 장갑으로 교환할 수 있을까요?
M: 네. 가능합니다.

Review 4

A: Hello. _____ I _____ you?
B: I'd like to _____ _____ _____ _____ this cap.
A: Sure. Do you have the _____ ?
B: Yes, I _____ . _____ _____ _____ .

A: 안녕하세요. 무엇을 도와드릴까요?
B: 네. 이 모자를 환불받고 싶어요.
A: 물론이죠. 영수증을 가지고 계시나요?
B: 네. 여기 있습니다.

※ 다음 우리말에 맞도록 대화를 영어로 쓰시오.

Listen and Talk A 1

W: _____

B: _____

W: _____

B: _____

W: _____

W: 안녕하세요. 무엇을 도와드릴까요?
B: 네, 이 손목시계를 환불받고 싶어서요.
W: 알겠습니다. 시계에 무슨 문제가 있었나요?
B: 아니요, 그냥 마음이 바뀌었어요. 돈을 돌려받을 수 있을까요?
W: 네. 지금 바로 처리해드리겠습니다.

Listen and Talk A 2

W: _____

B: _____

W: _____

B: _____

W: _____

W: 안녕하세요. 도움이 필요하신가요?
B: 네, 이 스마트폰 케이스를 환불받고 싶어요.
W: 어디 봅시다. 영수증을 가지고 계시나요?
B: 여기 있습니다. 3일 전에 구매했어요.
W: 아, 그렇다면 가능합니다.

Listen and Talk A 3

W: _____

B: _____

W: _____

B: _____

W: _____

B: _____

W: 안녕하세요. 특별히 찾으시는 것 있으세요?
B: 아니요. 저는 이 티셔츠를 교환하고 싶어서요. 너무 작아요.
W: 네. 어떤 사이즈를 원하세요?
B: 큰 사이즈로 주세요.
W: 여기 있습니다.
B: 감사합니다.

Listen and Talk A 4

W: _____

B: _____

W: _____

B: _____.

W: _____

W: 안녕하세요. 무엇을 도와드릴까요?
B: 이 검은색 우산을 다른 색으로 교환할 수 있을까요?
W: 물론이죠. 어떤 색을 원하세요?
B: 저는 노란색을 원해요.
W: 알겠습니다. 여기 있습니다.

Listen and Talk B 1

A: _____

B: _____

A: _____

B: _____

A: _____

A: 안녕하세요. 무엇을 도와드릴까요?
B: 네. 이 가방을 교환하고 싶어요.
A: 네. 무엇으로 교환하고 싶으세요?
B: 저는 모자로 교환하고 싶어요.
A: 알겠습니다.

Listen and Talk B 2

A: _____

B: _____

A: _____

B: _____

A: 안녕하세요. 무엇을 도와드릴까요?
B: 네. 이 가방을 환불받고 싶어요.
A: 물론이죠. 영수증을 가지고 계시나
　　요?
B: 네. 여기 있습니다.

Listen and Talk C

M: _____

G: _____

M: _____

G: _____

M: _____

G: _____

M: _____

G: _____

M: _____

G: _____

M: 안녕하세요. 도와드릴까요?
G: 네. 이 모자를 환불받고 싶어요.
M: 영수증을 가지고 있나요?
G: 아니요. 선물로 받았어요.
M: 영수증이 없으면, 환불은 가능하지
　　않아요.
G: 알겠어요. 그럼, 다른 것으로 교환할
　　수 있나요?
M: 네, 가능해요. 어떤 것을 원하시나
　　요?
G: 이 파란색 가방을 갖고 싶어요.
M: 한번 볼게요…. 가격이 같으니까 그
　　것을 가져가서도 돼요.
G: 고맙습니다.

Listen and Talk D

G: _____

B: _____

G: 나는 지난주에 이 빨간색 치마를 샀
　　어. 나는 치마가 마음에 드는데 내
　　여동생은 색깔이 나에게 잘 어울리
　　지 않는대. 이걸 다른 색으로 교환을
　　해야 할지 고민이야.
B: 네가 하고 싶은 대로 하렴, 하지만
　　내 생각엔 괜찮은 것 같아.

Talk and Play

A: _____

B: _____

A: _____

B: _____

A: _____

B: _____

A: _____

B: _____

Review 1

W: _____

B: _____

W: _____

B: _____

W: _____

Review 2

M: _____

W: _____

M: _____

W: _____

M: _____

Review 3

M: _____

G: _____

M: _____

G: _____

M: _____

Review 4

A: _____

B: _____

A: _____

B: _____

A: 실례합니다. 이 티셔츠를 이 바지로 교환하고 싶어요.
B: 네. 티셔츠에 무슨 문제가 있나요?
A: 색이 마음에 들지 않아요.
B: 알겠습니다.

A: 실례합니다. 저는 이 모자를 환불받고 싶어요.
B: 네. 모자에 무슨 문제가 있나요?
A: 색이 마음에 들지 않아요.
B: 알겠습니다.

W: 안녕하세요. 무엇을 도와드릴까요?
B: 네. 이 야구 글러브를 환불받고 싶어서요.
W: 알겠어요. 그것에 무슨 문제가 있었나요?
B: 아니요. 그냥 마음이 바뀌었어요. 제 돈을 돌려받을 수 있을까요?
W: 네. 여기 있습니다.

M: 안녕하세요. 무엇을 도와드릴까요?
W: 네. 이 노란색 티셔츠를 교환하고 싶어요. 저에게는 너무 작네요.
M: 네. 어떤 사이즈로 교환하고 싶으신가요?
W: 중간 사이즈로 주세요. 오! 빨간색 티셔츠로 바꿀 수 있을까요?
M: 네. 여기 있습니다.

M: 안녕하세요. 무엇을 도와드릴까요?
G: 네. 이 모자를 환불받을 수 있을까요?
M: 죄송하지만 안 됩니다.
G: 그렇다면 이 모자를 저기에 있는 장갑으로 교환할 수 있을까요?
M: 네. 가능합니다.

A: 안녕하세요. 무엇을 도와드릴까요?
B: 네. 이 모자를 환불받고 싶어요.
A: 물론이죠. 영수증을 가지고 계시나요?
B: 네. 여기 있습니다.

※ 다음 우리말과 일치하도록 빈칸에 알맞은 것을 골라 쓰시오.

1 _____ _____ **Money**
A. Dr.　　　　　　B. Ask

2 **The** _____ **Middle School** _____
A. Times　　　　　B. Green

3 _____ Spending
A. Habits　　　　　B. Teens'

4 _____ _____ are you _____ your money?
A. smart　　　　　B. with　　　　　C. how

5 These are the _____ of a _____ of 100 _____ at Green Middle School.
A. survey　　　　　B. results　　　　C. students

6 We first _____ students "Are you _____ _____ your money?"
A. with　　　　　　B. asked　　　　C. smart

7 _____ Graph 1 _____, 70% answered "No" _____ 30% answered "Yes."
A. while　　　　　B. as　　　　　C. shows

8 We then asked the students who answered "No" _____ their _____ money _____ _____.
A. biggest　　　B. is　　　C. worry　　　D. what

9 As Graph 2 shows, 60% think they don't have _____ _____ while 28% think they have _____ _____ money.
A. allowance　　B. saving　　C. enough　　D. difficulty

10 _____, 12% said they _____ money _____ things they didn't _____.
A. spent　　　B. need　　　C. lastly　　　D. on

11 Our _____ shows that the _____ of students think they are not _____ _____ their money.
A. majority　　B. survey　　C. with　　　D. smart

12 _____ money is not easy, and _____ a smart spender _____ _____.
A. takes　　B. managing　　C. effort　　D. becoming

13 Do you _____ any _____ _____?
A. money　　　B. worries　　　C. have

14 _____ _____ _____ Dr. Money.
A. with　　　　B. let's　　　　C. talk

15 _____ _____.
A. Jason　　　　B. I'm

1　Dr. Money에게 물어보세요.

2　그린 중학교 타임스

3　10대들의 소비 습관

4　당신은 돈에 관해 얼마나 현명한가?

5　이것은 Green 중학교 학생 100명의 설문 조사 결과이다.

6　우리는 먼저 학생들에게 "당신은 돈에 관하여 현명한가?"라고 물었다.

7　그래프 1이 보여 주듯이, 30%가 "예"라고 대답한 반면 70%가 "아니요"라고 답했다.

8　그 다음 우리는 "아니요"라고 대답한 학생들에게 그들의 돈에 대한 가장 큰 고민이 무엇인지 물었다.

9　그래프 2가 보여주듯이 28%가 자신들이 돈을 모으는 것에 어려움이 있다고 생각하는 반면, 60%는 충분한 용돈을 받지 못한다고 생각한다.

10　마지막으로, 12%는 필요하지 않은 것에 돈을 소비했다고 말했다.

11　우리의 설문 조사는 대다수의 학생들이 자신들이 돈에 관련하여 현명하지 못하다고 생각한다는 것을 보여준다.

12　돈을 관리하는 것은 쉽지 않고 현명한 소비자가 되는 것에는 노력이 필요하다.

13　여러분은 돈과 관련된 걱정거리가 있는가?

14　Dr. Money와 이야기해 보자.

15　저는 Jason이에요.

16 I get a _____ _____, but I _____ have _____.
A. allowance　　　B. enough　　　C. weekly　　　D. never

17 _____ Thursday, _____ of my money _____ _____.
A. gone　　　B. by　　　C. all　　　D. is

18 I don't know _____ _____ _____ this problem.
A. to　　　B. how　　　C. solve

19 Hi, _____ _____ _____.
A. Dr.　　　B. Money　　　C. I'm

20 _____ look _____ your _____ _____.
A. spending　　　B. let's　　　C. diary　　　D. at

21 You _____ _____ most of your money _____ the _____ of the week.
A. up　　　B. beginning　　　C. used　　　D. at

22 _____ my _____.
A. tip　　　B. here's

23 Don't _____ _____ all of your _____ _____.
A. around　　　B. weekly　　　C. allowance　　　D. carry

24 _____ the money _____ _____.
A. into　　　B. divide　　　C. days

25 Then _____ only the money you need _____ _____ _____.
A. for　　　B. day　　　C. each　　　D. carry

26 Hello, _____ _____.
A. Money　　　B. Dr.

27 _____ _____.
A. Steve　　　B. I'm

28 I _____ _____ _____ money.
A. difficulty　　　B. have　　　C. saving

29 For example, I've _____ _____ to go to my favorite singer's concert _____ the _____ two months.
A. last　　　B. saving　　　C, for　　　D. been

30 _____, I _____ don't have _____ _____.
A. still　　　B. however　　　C. money　　　D. enough

31 I don't know _____ _____ _____.
A. to　　　B. do　　　C. what

32 _____ _____.
A. see　　　B. let's

33 In the _____ _____ weeks, you _____ 80% of your allowance and only _____ 20%.
A. saved　　　B. few　　　C. spent　　　D. last

34 I _____ you've _____ _____ too much.
A. been　　　B. think　　　C. spending

16 저는 매주 용돈을 받지만, 절대로 충분하지 않아요.

17 목요일쯤이면 용돈이 모두 사라져요.

18 이 문제를 해결할 방법을 모르겠어요.

19 안녕하세요, Dr. Money입니다.

20 용돈 기입장을 한번 봅시다.

21 주의 초반에 용돈의 대부분을 다 썼군요.

22 이게 내 조언이에요.

23 일주일 용돈 전부를 가지고 다니지 마세요.

24 용돈을 하루 단위로 나누세요.

25 그리고 하루에 필요한 돈만 들고 다니세요.

26 안녕하세요, Dr. Money.

27 저는 Steve예요.

28 저는 돈을 모으기가 어려워요.

29 예를 들면, 저는 좋아하는 가수의 콘서트에 가려고 지난 두 달 동안 돈을 저축해 오고 있어요.

30 하지만 저는 여전히 충분한 돈을 가지고 있지 않아요.

31 어떻게 해야 할지 모르겠어요.

32 어디 봅시다.

33 지난 몇 주에 용돈의 80%를 사용하고 20%만을 저축했군요.

34 나는 Steve가 돈을 너무 많이 써 왔다고 생각해요.

35 To _____ money, you _____ to have a _____ _____.

   A. tighter   B. save   C. budget   D. need

36 _____ _____, you can _____ the 50%-40%-10% _____.

   A. follow   B. rule   C. example   D. for

37 _____ 50%, spend 40%, and _____ the _____ 10% to _____.

   A. remaining   B. donate   C. charity   D. save

38 _____ _____ the _____, you can _____ your money better.

   A. following   B. manage   C. by   D. rule

39 Then you can _____ money _____ to _____ the _____.

   A. faster   B. save   C. ticket   D. buy

40 _____ _____.

   A. Minji   B. I'm

41 I like to _____ things _____ _____.

   A. sale   B. buy   C. on

42 If something's on _____, I _____ it _____ I don't _____ it.

   A. although   B. buy   C. sale   D. need

43 _____ week, I _____ two T-shirts on _____, but I _____ have many.

   A. already   B. bought   C. last   D. sale

44 _____ things on sale is _____ if you _____ things you _____.

   A. buy   B. buying   C. need   D. good

45 In your _____, the problem is _____ you buy _____ you don't _____ need.

   A. case   B. even   C. things   D. that

46 _____ some _____.

   A. advice   B. here's

47 _____ you buy _____, ask _____, "Do I really need this?"

   A. yourself   B. before   C. something

48 Also, before you _____ _____, _____ a shopping _____.

   A. shopping   B. list   C. make   D. go

49 Don't buy _____ that aren't _____ the list even _____ they're on _____.

   A. on   B. items   C. if   D. sale

50 Then you _____ _____ things _____ the _____.

   A. spot   B. won't   C. on   D. buy

35 돈을 모으기 위해서, 더 빠듯한 예산을 세우는 것이 필요해요.

36 예를 들어, Steve는 50%-40%-10%의 규칙을 따를 수 있어요.

37 50%를 저축하고, 40%를 쓰고, 남아 있는 10%를 자선 단체에 기부하세요.

38 이 규칙을 따름으로써 돈을 더 잘 관리할 수 있어요.

39 그러면 그 티켓을 사기 위해 돈을 더 빨리 모을 수 있답니다.

40 저는 민지입니다.

41 저는 할인 판매하는 물건을 사는 것을 좋아해요.

42 어떤 물건이 할인 판매를 하면 저는 그것이 필요하지 않더라도 사요.

43 지난주에는 할인 판매하는 티셔츠 두 장을 샀지만 이미 많이 가지고 있었어요.

44 민지가 필요한 물건을 산다면 할인 판매하는 물건을 사는 것은 좋습니다.

45 민지의 경우에, 문제점은 필요하지 않은 물건도 산다는 거예요.

46 여기 몇 가지 조언이 있어요.

47 민지는 무언가를 사기 전에 "이것이 정말 필요한가?"라고 스스로에게 물어보세요.

48 또한 쇼핑하러 가기 전에 쇼핑 목록을 만드세요.

49 만약 물건들이 할인 판매 중이라고 해도 목록에 없는 물건들은 사지 마세요.

50 그러면 즉석에서 물건을 사지 않게 될 거예요.

※ 다음 우리말과 일치하도록 빈칸에 알맞은 것을 골라 쓰시오.

1 _____ Dr. _____

2 **The Green** _____ _____ _____

3 **Teens'** _____ _____

4 _____ _____ are you _____ your money?

5 These are the _____ of _____ _____ of 100 students at Green Middle School.

6 We first asked students "Are you _____ _____ your money?"

7 _____ Graph 1 _____, 70% answered "No" _____ 30% answered "Yes."

8 We then _____ the students who _____ "No" what their _____ _____ _____ is.

9 _____ Graph 2 _____, 60% _____ they don't have _____ _____ 28% think they _____ _____ _____ money.

10 _____, 12% said they _____ money _____ things they _____ _____.

11 Our survey _____ that _____ _____ of students think they are not _____ _____ their money.

12 _____ money is not easy, and _____ a smart spender _____ effort.

13 Do you have any _____ _____?

14 _____ _____ _____ Dr. Money.

15 _____ Jason.

---

1 Dr. Money에게 물어보세요.

2 그린 중학교 타임스

3 10대들의 소비 습관

4 당신은 돈에 관해 얼마나 현명한가?

5 이것은 Green 중학교 학생 100명의 설문 조사 결과이다.

6 우리는 먼저 학생들에게 "당신은 돈에 관하여 현명한가?"라고 물었다.

7 그래프 1이 보여 주듯이, 30%가 "예"라고 대답한 반면 70%가 "아니요"라고 답했다.

8 그 다음 우리는 "아니요"라고 대답한 학생들에게 그들의 돈에 대한 가장 큰 고민이 무엇인지 물었다.

9 그래프 2가 보여주듯이 28%가 자신들이 돈을 모으는 것에 어려움이 있다고 생각하는 반면, 60%는 충분한 용돈을 받지 못한다고 생각한다.

10 마지막으로, 12%는 필요하지 않은 것에 돈을 소비했다고 말했다.

11 우리의 설문 조사는 대다수의 학생들이 자신들이 돈에 관련하여 현명하지 못하다고 생각한다는 것을 보여준다.

12 돈을 관리하는 것은 쉽지 않고 현명한 소비자가 되는 것에는 노력이 필요하다.

13 여러분은 돈과 관련된 걱정거리가 있는가?

14 Dr. Money와 이야기해 보자.

15 저는 Jason이에요.

16 I get a _____ _____, but I never have _____.

17 _____ Thursday, all of my money _____ _____.

18 I don't know _____ _____ _____ this problem.

19 Hi, _____ Dr. Money.

20 Let's _____ _____ your _____ _____.

21 You _____ _____ most of your money _____ _____ _____ _____ _____ _____.

22 Here's _____ _____.

23 Don't _____ _____ all of your _____ _____.

24 _____ the money _____ days.

25 Then _____ only the money you need _____ _____ _____.

26 _____, Dr. Money.

27 _____ Steve.

28 I _____ _____ _____ money.

29 For example, _____ _____ _____ to go to my favorite singer's concert _____ _____ _____ _____ _____.

30 _____, I _____ _____ have _____ _____.

31 I don't know _____ _____ _____.

32 _____ _____.

33 _____ _____ _____ _____ _____ weeks, you spent 80% of your _____ and only _____ 20%.

34 I think _____ _____ _____ too much.

16 저는 매주 용돈을 받지만, 절대로 충분하지 않아요.

17 목요일쯤이면 용돈이 모두 사라져요.

18 이 문제를 해결할 방법을 모르겠어요.

19 안녕하세요, Dr. Money입니다.

20 용돈 기입장을 한번 봅시다.

21 주의 초반에 용돈의 대부분을 다 썼군요.

22 이게 내 조언이에요.

23 일주일 용돈 전부를 가지고 다니지 마세요.

24 용돈을 하루 단위로 나누세요.

25 그리고 하루에 필요한 돈만 들고 다니세요.

26 안녕하세요, Dr. Money.

27 저는 Steve예요.

28 저는 돈을 모으기가 어려워요.

29 예를 들면, 저는 좋아하는 가수의 콘서트에 가려고 지난 두 달 동안 돈을 저축해 오고 있어요.

30 하지만 저는 여전히 충분한 돈을 가지고 있지 않아요.

31 어떻게 해야 할지 모르겠어요.

32 어디 봅시다.

33 지난 몇 주에 용돈의 80%를 사용하고 20%만을 저축했군요.

34 나는 Steve가 돈을 너무 많이 써 왔다고 생각해요.

35 _____ _____ money, you need to _____ _____ _____ _____.

36 For example, you can _____ _____ _____ _____.

37 _____ 50%, spend 40%, and _____ _____ _____ 10% to _____.

38 _____ _____ the rule, you can _____ your money _____.

39 Then you can save money _____ _____ _____ the ticket.

40 _____ Minji.

41 I like to buy things _____ _____.

42 If something's _____ _____, I buy it _____ I don't need it.

43 Last week, I _____ two T-shirts on sale, but I _____ _____ many.

44 _____ things on sale _____ good if you buy _____ _____ _____.

45 _____ _____ _____, the problem is that you buy things you _____ _____ _____.

46 _____ some _____.

47 Before you buy something, _____ _____, "Do I really need this?"

48 Also, before you _____ _____, _____ a shopping list.

49 _____ items that aren't _____ _____ _____ even if they're on sale.

50 Then you _____ _____ things _____ _____ _____.

35	돈을 모으기 위해서, 더 빠듯한 예산을 세우는 것이 필요해요.
36	예를 들어, Steve는 50%-40%-10%의 규칙을 따를 수 있어요.
37	50%를 저축하고, 40%를 쓰고, 남아 있는 10%를 자선 단체에 기부하세요.
38	이 규칙을 따름으로써 돈을 더 잘 관리할 수 있어요.
39	그러면 그 티켓을 사기 위해 돈을 더 빨리 모을 수 있답니다.
40	저는 민지입니다.
41	저는 할인 판매하는 물건을 사는 것을 좋아해요.
42	어떤 물건이 할인 판매를 하면 저는 그것이 필요하지 않더라도 사요.
43	지난주에는 할인 판매하는 티셔츠 두 장을 샀지만 이미 많이 가지고 있었어요.
44	민지가 필요한 물건을 산다면 할인 판매하는 물건을 사는 것은 좋습니다.
45	민지의 경우에, 문제점은 필요하지 않은 물건도 산다는 거예요.
46	여기 몇 가지 조언이 있어요.
47	민지는 무언가를 사기 전에 "이것이 정말 필요한가?"라고 스스로에게 물어보세요.
48	또한 쇼핑하러 가기 전에 쇼핑 목록을 만드세요.
49	만약 물건들이 할인 판매 중이라고 해도 목록에 없는 물건들은 사지 마세요.
50	그러면 즉석에서 물건을 사지 않게 될 거예요.

※ 다음 문장을 우리말로 쓰시오.

1 ▸ Ask Dr. Money

➡ _____

2 ▸ The Green Middle School Times

➡ _____

3 ▸ Teens' Spending Habits

➡ _____

4 ▸ How smart are you with your money?

➡ _____

5 ▸ These are the results of a survey of 100 students at Green Middle School.

➡ _____

6 ▸ We first asked students "Are you smart with your money?"

➡ _____

7 ▸ As Graph 1 shows, 70% answered "No" while 30% answered "Yes."

➡ _____

8 ▸ We then asked the students who answered "No" what their biggest money worry is.

➡ _____

9 ▸ As Graph 2 shows, 60% think they don't have enough allowance while 28% think they have difficulty saving money.

➡ _____

_____

10 ▸ Lastly, 12% said they spent money on things they didn't need.

➡ _____

11 ▸ Our survey shows that the majority of students think they are not smart with their money.

➡ _____

12 ▸ Managing money is not easy, and becoming a smart spender takes effort.

➡ _____

13 ▸ Do you have any money worries?

➡ _____

14 ▸ Let's talk with Dr. Money.

➡ _____

15 ▸ I'm Jason.

➡ _____

16 I get a weekly allowance, but I never have enough.

➡ _____

17 By Thursday, all of my money is gone.

➡ _____

18 I don't know how to solve this problem.

➡ _____

19 Hi, I'm Dr. Money.

➡ _____

20 Let's look at your spending diary.

➡ _____

21 You used up most of your money at the beginning of the week.

➡ _____

22 Here's my tip.

➡ _____

23 Don't carry around all of your weekly allowance.

➡ _____

24 Divide the money into days.

➡ _____

25 Then carry only the money you need for each day.

➡ _____

26 Hello, Dr. Money.

➡ _____

27 I'm Steve.

➡ _____

28 I have difficulty saving money.

➡ _____

29 For example, I've been saving to go to my favorite singer's concert for the last two months.

➡ _____

30 However, I still don't have enough money.

➡ _____

31 I don't know what to do.

➡ _____

32 Let's see.

➡ _____

33 In the last few weeks, you spent 80% of your allowance and only saved 20%.

➡ _____

34 I think you've been spending too much.

➡ _____

35 To save money, you need to have a tighter budget.

➡ _____

36 For example, you can follow the 50%-40%-10% rule.

➡ _____

37 Save 50%, spend 40%, and donate the remaining 10% to charity.

➡ _____

38 By following the rule, you can manage your money better.

➡ _____

39 Then you can save money faster to buy the ticket.

➡ _____

40 I'm Minji.

➡ _____

41 I like to buy things on sale.   ·

➡ _____

42 If something's on sale, I buy it although I don't need it.

➡ _____

43 Last week, I bought two T-shirts on sale, but I already have many.

➡ _____

44 Buying things on sale is good if you buy things you need.

➡ _____

45 In your case, the problem is that you buy things you don't even need.

➡ _____

46 Here's some advice.

➡ _____

47 Before you buy something, ask yourself, "Do I really need this?"

➡ _____

48 Also, before you go shopping, make a shopping list.

➡ _____

49 Don't buy items that aren't on the list even if they're on sale.

➡ _____

50 Then you won't buy things on the spot.

➡ _____

※ 다음 괄호 안의 단어들을 우리말에 맞도록 바르게 배열하시오.

1 (Dr. / ask / Money)
➡ _____

2 (Green / The / School / Middle / Times)
➡ _____

3 (Spending / Teens' / Habits)
➡ _____

4 (smart / how / you / are / with / money? / your)
➡ _____

5 (are / these / results / the / a / of / survey / 100 / of / at / students / Middle / Green / School.)
➡ _____

6 (first / we / students / asked / you / "are / smart / your / with / money?")
➡ _____

7 (Graph / as / shows, / 1 / answered / 70% / while / "No" / answered / 30% / "Yes.")
➡ _____

8 (then / we / the / asked / students / answered / who / "No" / their / what / money / biggest / is. / worry)
➡ _____

9 (Graph / as / shows, / 2 / think / 60% / they / have / don't / allowance / enough / 28% / while / think / have / they / saving / difficulty / money.)
➡ _____

10 (12% / lastly, / they / said / spent / on / money / they / things / need. / didn't)
➡ _____

11 (survey / our / that / shows / the / of / majority / students / they / think / not / are / with / smart / money. / their)
➡ _____

12 (money / managing / not / is / easy, / becoming / and / smart / a / spender / effort. / takes)
➡ _____

13 (you / do / any / have / worries? / money)
➡ _____

14 (talk / let's / Dr. / with / Money.)
➡ _____

15 (Jason. / I'm)
➡ _____

1	Dr. Money에게 물어보세요.
2	그린 중학교 타임스
3	10대들의 소비 습관
4	당신은 돈에 관해 얼마나 현명한가?
5	이것은 Green 중학교 학생 100명의 설문 조사 결과이다.
6	우리는 먼저 학생들에게 "당신은 돈에 관하여 현명한가?"라고 물었다.
7	그래프 1이 보여 주듯이, 30%가 "예"라고 대답한 반면 70%가 "아니요"라고 답했다.
8	그 다음 우리는 "아니요"라고 대답한 학생들에게 그들의 돈에 대한 가장 큰 고민이 무엇인지 물었다.
9	그래프 2가 보여주듯이 28%가 자신들이 돈을 모으는 것에 어려움이 있다고 생각하는 반면, 60%는 충분한 용돈을 받지 못한다고 생각한다.
10	마지막으로, 12%는 필요하지 않은 것에 돈을 소비했다고 말했다.
11	우리의 설문 조사는 대다수의 학생들이 자신들이 돈에 관련하여 현명하지 못하다고 생각한다는 것을 보여준다.
12	돈을 관리하는 것은 쉽지 않고 현명한 소비자가 되는 것에는 노력이 필요하다.
13	여러분은 돈과 관련된 걱정거리가 있는가?
14	Dr. Money와 이야기해 보자.
15	저는 Jason이에요.

16 (get / I / weekly / a / allowance, / I / but / never / enough. / have)

➡ _____

17 (Thursday, / by / of / all / money / my / gone. / is)

➡ _____

18 (don't / I / how / know / solve / to / problem. / this)

➡ _____

19 (I'm / hi, /. Money. / Dr.)

➡ _____

20 (look / let's / your / at / diary. / spending)

➡ _____

21 (used / you / most / up / your / of / at / money / the / of / beginning / week. / the)

➡ _____

22 (my / tip. / here's)

➡ _____

23 (carry / don't / all / around / of / weekly / your / allowance.)

➡ _____

24 (the / divide / into / money / days.)

➡ _____

25 (carry / then / the / only / you / money / for / need / day. / each)

➡ _____

26 (Dr. / hello, / Money.)

➡ _____

27 (Steve. / I'm)

➡ _____

28 (have / I / saving / difficulty / money.)

➡ _____

29 (example, / for / been / I've / to / saving / to / go / my / singer's / favorite / for / concert / the / two / last / months.)

➡ _____

30 (I / however, / don't / still / have / money. / enough)

➡ _____

31 (don't / I / what / know / do. / to)

➡ _____

32 (see. / let's)

➡ _____

33 (the / in / few / last / weeks, / spent / you / of / 80% / allowance / your / and / saved / 20%. / only)

➡ _____

34 (think / I / been / you've / too / spending / much.)

➡ _____

---

16 저는 매주 용돈을 받지만, 절대로 충분하지 않아요.

17 목요일쯤이면 용돈이 모두 사라져요.

18 이 문제를 해결할 방법을 모르겠어요.

19 안녕하세요, Dr. Money입니다.

20 용돈 기입장을 한번 봅시다.

21 주의 초반에 용돈의 대부분을 다 썼군요.

22 이게 내 조언이에요.

23 일주일 용돈 전부를 가지고 다니지 마세요.

24 용돈을 하루 단위로 나누세요.

25 그리고 하루에 필요한 돈만 들고 다니세요.

26 안녕하세요, Dr. Money.

27 저는 Steve예요.

28 저는 돈을 모으기가 어려워요.

29 예를 들면, 저는 좋아하는 가수의 콘서트에 가려고 지난 두 달 동안 돈을 저축해 오고 있어요.

30 하지만 저는 여전히 충분한 돈을 가지고 있지 않아요.

31 어떻게 해야 할지 모르겠어요.

32 어디 봅시다.

33 지난 몇 주에 용돈의 80%를 사용하고 20%만을 저축했군요.

34 나는 Steve가 돈을 너무 많이 써 왔다고 생각해요.

35 (save / to / money, / need / you / have / to / tighter / budget. / a)
➡ _____

36 (example, / for / can / you / the / follow / rule. / 50%-40%-10%)
➡ _____

37 (50%, / save / 40%, / spend / and / the / donate / 10% / remaining / charity. / to)
➡ _____

38 (following / by / rule, / the / can / you / manage / money / your / better.)
➡ _____

39 (you / then / save / can / faster / money / buy / to / ticket. / the)
➡ _____

40 (Minji. / I'm)
➡ _____

41 (like / I / buy / to / on / things / sale.)
➡ _____

42 (somethiong / if / sale, / on / buy / I / although / it / I / need / don't / it.)
➡ _____

43 (week, / last / bought / I / T-shirts / two / sale, / on / I / but / have / already / many.)
➡ _____

44 (things / buying / sale / on / good / is / you / if / things / buy / need. / you)
➡ _____

45 (your / in / case, / problem / the / that / is / buy / you / things / don't / you / need. / even)
➡ _____

46 (some / here's / advice.)
➡ _____

47 (you / before / something, / buy / yourself, / ask / I / "do / need / this?" / really)
➡ _____

48 (before / also / go / you / shopping, / a / make / list. / shopping)
➡ _____

49 (buy / don't / that / items / on / aren't / the / even / list / they're / if / sale. / on)
➡ _____

50 (you / then / buy / won't / on / things / spot. / the)
➡ _____

35 돈을 모으기 위해서, 더 빠듯한 예산을 세우는 것이 필요해요.

36 예를 들어, Steve는 50%-40%-10%의 규칙을 따를 수 있어요.

37 50%를 저축하고, 40%를 쓰고, 남아 있는 10%를 자선 단체에 기부하세요.

38 이 규칙을 따름으로써 돈을 더 잘 관리할 수 있어요.

39 그러면 그 티켓을 사기 위해 돈을 더 빨리 모을 수 있답니다.

40 저는 민지입니다.

41 저는 할인 판매하는 물건을 사는 것을 좋아해요.

42 어떤 물건이 할인 판매를 하면 저는 그것이 필요하지 않더라도 사요.

43 지난주에는 할인 판매하는 티셔츠 두 장을 샀지만 이미 많이 가지고 있었어요.

44 민지가 필요한 물건을 산다면 할인 판매하는 물건을 사는 것은 좋습니다.

45 민지의 경우에, 문제점은 필요하지 않은 물건도 산다는 거예요.

46 여기 몇 가지 조언이 있어요.

47 민지는 무언가를 사기 전에 "이것이 정말 필요한가?"라고 스스로에게 물어보세요.

48 또한 쇼핑하러 가기 전에 쇼핑 목록을 만드세요.

49 만약 물건들이 할인 판매 중이라고 해도 목록에 없는 물건들은 사지 마세요.

50 그러면 즉석에서 물건을 사지 않게 될 거예요.

※ 다음 우리말을 영어로 쓰시오.

1 Dr. Money에게 물어보세요.
➡ _____

2 그린 중학교 타임스
➡ _____

3 10대들의 소비 습관
➡ _____

4 당신은 돈에 관해 얼마나 현명한가?
➡ _____

5 이것은 Green 중학교 학생 100명의 설문 조사 결과이다.
➡ _____

6 우리는 먼저 학생들에게 "당신은 돈에 관하여 현명한가?"라고 물었다.
➡ _____

7 그래프 1이 보여 주듯이, 30%가 "예"라고 대답한 반면 70%가 "아니요"라고 답했다.
➡ _____

8 그 다음 우리는 "아니요"라고 대답한 학생들에게 그들의 돈에 대한 가장 큰 고민이 무엇인지 물었다.
➡ _____

9 그래프 2가 보여주듯이 28%가 자신들이 돈을 모으는 것에 어려움이 있다고 생각하는 반면,
60%는 충분한 용돈을 받지 못한다고 생각한다.
➡ _____

_____

10 마지막으로, 12%는 필요하지 않은 것에 돈을 소비했다고 말했다.
➡ _____

11 우리의 설문 조사는 대다수의 학생들이 자신들이 돈에 관련하여 현명하지 못하다고 생각한다는
것을 보여준다.
➡ _____

12 돈을 관리하는 것은 쉽지 않고 현명한 소비자가 되는 것에는 노력이 필요하다.
➡ _____

13 여러분은 돈과 관련된 걱정거리가 있는가?
➡ _____

14 Dr. Money와 이야기해 보자.
➡ _____

15 저는 Jason이에요.
➡ _____

16 저는 매주 용돈을 받지만, 절대로 충분하지 않아요.

➡ _____

17 목요일쯤이면 용돈이 모두 사라져요.

➡ _____

18 이 문제를 해결할 방법을 모르겠어요.

➡ _____

19 안녕하세요, Dr. Money입니다.

➡ _____

20 용돈 기입장을 한번 봅시다.

➡ _____

21 주의 초반에 용돈의 대부분을 다 썼군요.

➡ _____

22 이게 내 조언이에요.

➡ _____

23 일주일 용돈 전부를 가지고 다니지 마세요.

➡ _____

24 용돈을 하루 단위로 나누세요.

➡ _____

25 그리고 하루에 필요한 돈만 들고 다니세요.

➡ _____

26 안녕하세요, Dr. Money.

➡ _____

27 저는 Steve예요.

➡ _____

28 저는 돈을 모으기가 어려워요.

➡ _____

29 예를 들면, 저는 좋아하는 가수의 콘서트에 가려고 지난 두 달 동안 돈을 저축해 오고 있어요.

➡ _____

30 하지만 저는 여전히 충분한 돈을 가지고 있지 않아요.

➡ _____

31 어떻게 해야 할지 모르겠어요.

➡ _____

32 어디 봅시다.

➡ _____

33 지난 몇 주에 용돈의 80%를 사용하고 20%만을 저축했군요.

➡ _____

34 나는 Steve가 돈을 너무 많이 써 왔다고 생각해요.

➡ _____

35 돈을 모으기 위해서, 더 빠듯한 예산을 세우는 것이 필요해요.

➡ _____

36 예를 들어, Steve는 50%-40%-10%의 규칙을 따를 수 있어요.

➡ _____

37 50%를 저축하고, 40%를 쓰고, 남아 있는 10%를 자선 단체에 기부하세요.

➡ _____

38 이 규칙을 따름으로써 돈을 더 잘 관리할 수 있어요.

➡ _____

39 그러면 그 티켓을 사기 위해 돈을 더 빨리 모을 수 있답니다.

➡ _____

40 저는 민지입니다.

➡ _____

41 저는 할인 판매하는 물건을 사는 것을 좋아해요.

➡ _____

42 어떤 물건이 할인 판매를 하면 저는 그것이 필요하지 않더라도 사요.

➡ _____

43 지난주에는 할인 판매하는 티셔츠 두 장을 샀지만 이미 많이 가지고 있었어요.

➡ _____

44 민지가 필요한 물건을 산다면 할인 판매하는 물건을 사는 것은 좋습니다.

➡ _____

45 민지의 경우에, 문제점은 필요하지 않은 물건도 산다는 거예요.

➡ _____

46 여기 몇 가지 조언이 있어요.

➡ _____

47 민지는 무언가를 사기 전에 "이것이 정말 필요한가?"라고 스스로에게 물어보세요.

➡ _____

48 또한 쇼핑하러 가기 전에 쇼핑 목록을 만드세요.

➡ _____

49 만약 물건들이 할인 판매 중이라고 해도 목록에 없는 물건들은 사지 마세요.

➡ _____

50 그러면 즉석에서 물건을 사지 않게 될 거예요.

➡ _____

※ 다음 우리말과 일치하도록 빈칸에 알맞은 말을 쓰시오.

After You Read C

1. _____ Money _____ and Dr. Money's _____

2. Jason's Worry: I _____ _____ _____, but I _____
   _____.

3. _____ _____, _____ _____ my money _____.

4. Dr. Money's Advice: _____ _____ _____ all of _____
   _____.

5. _____ the money _____ days and _____ only the money
   you _____ _____ _____ _____.

1. 십대들의 돈과 관련된 걱정거리와 Dr. Money의 조언
2. Jason의 걱정거리: 저는 매주 용돈을 받지만, 절대로 충분하지 않아요.
3. 목요일쯤이면 용돈이 모두 사라져요.
4. Dr. Money의 조언: 일주일 용돈 전부를 가지고 다니지 마세요.
5. 용돈을 하루 단위로 나누고 하루에 필요한 돈만 들고 다니세요.

Language in Use A

1. The computer I _____ _____ _____ was very _____.

2. _____ is foolish _____ _____ _____ during the _____
   _____.

3. My jeans are _____ _____, _____ I am going to _____
   them _____ _____ _____ _____.

1. 할인 중에 산 컴퓨터는 매우 값이 쌌다.
2. 우기에 캠핑을 가는 것은 어리석다.
3. 내 청바지가 너무 �꽉 끼여서 나는 그것을 더 큰 사이즈로 교환할 것이다.

Think and Write

1. My money problem is _____ I _____ _____ _____
   _____ _____.

2. One time, I _____ a smartphone case _____ _____ _____
   _____.

3. _____, I _____ _____ that I _____ _____ _____
   _____ at home.

4. I don't know _____ _____ _____ _____ _____ on the
   spot.

1. 나의 돈과 관련된 고민은 즉석에서 물건을 산다는 것이다.
2. 한번은, 나는 스마트폰 케이스가 좋아 보여서 그것을 샀다.
3. 하지만, 집에 와서는 내가 이미 케이스를 세 개 갖고 있다는 것을 발견했다.
4. 나는 즉석에서 물건을 사는 것을 어떻게 멈출 수 있는지 모르겠다.

※ 다음 우리말을 영어로 쓰시오.

After You Read C

1. 십대들의 돈과 관련된 걱정거리와 Dr. Money의 조언

   ➡ _____

2. Jason의 걱정거리: 저는 매주 용돈을 받지만, 절대로 충분하지 않아요.

   ➡ _____

3. 목요일쯤이면 용돈이 모두 사라져요.

   ➡ _____

4. Dr. Money의 조언: 일주일 용돈 전부를 가지고 다니지 마세요.

   ➡ _____

5. 용돈을 하루 단위로 나누고 하루에 필요한 돈만 들고 다니세요.

   ➡ _____

Language in Use A

1. 할인 중에 산 컴퓨터는 매우 값이 쌌다.

   ➡ _____

2. 우기에 캠핑을 가는 것은 어리석다.

   ➡ _____

3. 내 청바지가 너무 꽉 끼여서 나는 그것을 더 큰 사이즈로 교환할 것이다.

   ➡ _____

Think and Write

1. 나의 돈과 관련된 고민은 즉석에서 물건을 산다는 것이다.

   ➡ _____

2. 한번은, 나는 스마트폰 케이스가 좋아 보여서 그것을 샀다.

   ➡ _____

3. 하지만, 집에 와서는 내가 이미 케이스를 세 개 갖고 있다는 것을 발견했다.

   ➡ _____

4. 나는 즉석에서 물건을 사는 것을 어떻게 멈출 수 있는지 모르겠다.

   ➡ _____

MEMO

MEMO

MEMO

적중100 plus
1학기 전과정
영어 기출 문제집

영어 기출 문제집

적중100 plus
1학기 전과정

1학기

정답 및 해설

동아 | 윤정미

중 3

적중100

영어 기출 문제집

1학기

정답 및 해설

동아 | 윤정미

중 ③

Lesson 1

Follow Your Dream

시험대비 실력평가
p.08

| 01 ⑤ | 02 ④ | 03 ② | 04 ① |
| 05 ③ | 06 (s)table | 07 ③ | |

01 achieve: 성취하다, 달성하다 accomplish: 이루다, 성취하다, 완성하다; (목적 등을) 달성하다 / 열심히 일하면 네가 원하는 모든 것을 이룰 것이다.

02 pursue: 추구하다, 추진하다, chase: 뒤쫓다, 추적하다, 추구하다 / 건강이 회복된 덕분에 그는 자신의 연구를 지속할 수 있었다.

03 ① cause: 원인, 소금은 많은 건강 문제의 주요 원인이다. ② engineering: 공학 (기술), 엔지니어링, 이곳의 학생들은 과학과 공학을 공부하기를 싫어한다. ③ major: 중요한, 주된, 지금 세계는 2대 진영으로 양분되었다고 할 수 있다. ④ environment: 환경, 우리는 공해로부터 환경을 보호해야 한다. ⑤ bold: 용감한, 대담한, 그는 굉장히 강해 보이지만 내면은 아주 연약한 사람이에요.

04 decide on: (숙고하여 뭔가를) 고르다, (여러 가지 가능성 가운데) ~으로 결정하다 / 이 문제에 대해서는 저는 결정권이 없습니다.

05 ① in one's case: ~의 경우에, 제 경우에 학교 성적이 나쁜 것은 별 문제가 안 됐습니다. ② for a living: 생계 수단으로, 그는 생계를 위해 열심히 일해야 한다고 믿는 사람이다. ③ at all: 전혀, 그것은 나와는 전혀 무관하다. ④ in fact: 사실은, 사실, 젊은이들은 이미 새로운 나라에 살고 있다. ⑤ trial and error: 시행착오, 일반적으로 모든 업적은 시행착오를 거치게 된다.

06 stable: 안정된, 안정적인 secure: 안전한, 위험이 없는, (지위·생활·미래 등이) 안정된

07 quit: (학교, 직장 등을) 그만두다, 어떤 것을 하는 것을 멈추다

서술형 시험대비
p.09

01 (1) stable (2) major (3) inspire (4) beat

02 (1) If you want to live a happy life, follow your heart.
   (2) Children learn to use computer programs by trial and error.
   (3) I will take a chance and start my own business.

03 come true

04 (1) (s)ucceed (2) (g)oal

05 (1) living (2) for (3) all (4) make

01 (1) stable: 안정된, 안정적인 / 큰 변화나 문제없이 그대로 유지되는 (2) major: 매우 중요한, 중대한, 주된 (3) inspire: 영감을 주다, 고무하다 / 어떤 것을 성취하거나 만들고 싶게 느끼도록 만들다 (4) beat: (심장이) 고동치다, 뛰다 / 심장이 규칙적인 소리를 내고 움직이다

02 (1) follow one's heart: 마음 가는 대로 하다, follow를 추가한다. (2) trial and error: 시행착오, trial을 추가한다. (3) take a chance: 기회를 잡다, take를 추가한다.

03 come true 실현되다, 사실이 되다 / 생일의 소망이 모두 이루어지면 좋겠네요!

04 (1) 반의어 관계이다. major: 중요한, 주된 minor: 중요치 않은, 보다 중요하지 않은 fail: 실패하다 succeed: 성공하다 (2) 동의어 관계이다. encourage: 격려하다 inspire: 고무하다 aim: 목표, 목적 goal: 목표

05 (1) for a living 생계 수단으로 (2) for the first time: 처음으로 (3) not ~ at all: 전혀 ~가 아니다 (4) make a decision: 결정하다

교과서
Conversation

핵심 Check
p.10~11

1 Have you ever visited another country?
2 Have you ever been to Paris?
3 I hope you can try it sometime.

교과서 대화문 익히기

Check(√) True or False
p.12

1 F 2 T 3 F 4 T

교과서 확인학습
p.14~15

Listen and Talk A 1

Have, Spanish, before / haven't, tried it / have, I hope, can, sometime / will, For now, Spanish recipe

Listen and Talk A 2

ever, another / haven't, Have / I've been to, I hope, can, to, country sometime / to visit, interesting.

시험대비 기본평가   p.16

01 (C) → (B) → (A)

02 Have you ever visited another country?   03 ①

04 I hope that you read the book sometime.

05 How often have you been to England?

01 제주도에 가 보았는지 물어보는 질문에(C) 그렇다고 하며, 섬이 아름다웠다고 대답한다.(B) 이어서 다시 가기를 희망한다는 말을 덧붙인다(A).

02 이어지는 내용이 'No, I haven't. Have you?'라고 하고 있고 대답으로 'Yes, I've been to France.'라고 하고 있으므로 '다른 나라에 가 본 적이 있는지' 질문했음을 추론할 수 있다.

03 'I hope' 다음에 hope의 목적어를 이끄는 that이 적절하다.

04 희망을 표현할 때는 'I hope (that)+주어+동사 ~.'의 표현을 사용하여 말할 수 있다. 시간을 나타내는 부사 soon, someday, sometime 등을 문장 끝에 붙이기도 한다.

05 'Have you+과거분사 ~?'는 '~해 본 적 있어요?'라는 의미로 경험을 물을 때 사용하는 표현이다. 경험한 횟수를 물을 때는 'How often have you+과거분사 ~?'를 써서 나타낸다.

시험대비 실력평가   p.17~18

01 ④   02 ⑤   03 ②

04 I hope you become a good animal doctor someday.

05 ④   06 For now   07 ⑤   08 ②

09 (B) trial and error   (C) make a decision   10 ③

11 I've eaten[had] it once.   12 What

1 인도 카레를 먹어 봤다는 말에 인도 카레 식당에 가 보기를 바란다고 응답하는 것은 어색하다.

2 주어진 문장의 That이 가리키는 것이 앞에서 B가 하고 있는 것 (I'm doing volunteer work at the local animal house.) 을 말하므로 ⑤에 들어가는 것이 적절하다.

3 다음에 나오는 대답들로 보아 '목표'를 '이루기 위해'가 가장 적절하다.

4 I hope (that) you ~.: ~하기를 바라.

5 B의 답으로 현재완료가 나오므로 빈칸에는 경험을 묻는 현재완료가 자연스럽다.

6 for now: 우선은, 현재로는

7 'Have you ever+과거분사 ~?'는 '~을 해 본 적 있어요?'라는 의미로 경험을 물을 때 사용하는 표현이다.

8 옷을 만든다는 답으로 보아 생계를 위해 무엇을 하는지 묻는 질문이 적절하다.

9 (B) trial and error: 시행착오, (C) make a decision: 결정하다

10 (C)의 it이 주어진 글의 this book about the moon을 가리키므로 제일 먼저 나오고, 영화는 보았는지 묻고(A), 안 보았다는 답에(B), 책보다 낫다며 보기를 바라는 말로 마무리한다.(D)

11 'have+과거분사'로 '~해 본 적 있다'라는 경험을 나타낸다.

12 'How about ~?'은 '~은 어때?'라는 뜻으로 What about ~? 과 같은 뜻으로 쓰인다.

서술형 시험대비   p.19

01 Have you seen the movie

02 She likes the book better.

03 They have seen the movie.

04 Have you ever thought of becoming an animal doctor?

05 I hope you become a good animal doctor someday

06 He is doing volunteer work at the local animal house and also watching a lot of TV shows about animals.

07 should read this book about the moon

08 even, much, far, a lot, still 중 3개 이상

01 'Have you (ever)+과거분사 ~?'로 경험을 물을 수 있다.

02 유빈이는 책을 더 좋아한다고 했다.

03 Peter와 Yubin 두 사람 모두 영화를 보았다.

04 'Have you (ever)+과거분사 ~?'로 경험을 물을 수 있다.

05 '~하기를 바라, ~하면 좋겠어.'라는 뜻의 'I hope (that)+주어+(can/will)+동사 ~.'의 표현을 사용하여 희망을 표현할 수 있다.

06 소년이 하고 있는 것 두 가지를 쓰면 된다.

07 '권유, 권고'의 의미로 쓰이는 should를 추가한다.

08 비교급을 강조하는 어휘 중 3개 이상을 쓰면 된다.

Grammar

핵심 Check p.20~21

1 (1) if (2) whether

2 (1) to drink (2) to leave (3) to eat with

시험대비 기본평가 p.22

01 ③　　02 ④　　03 ④

04 (1) They want something hot to drink.

(2) Paula needs someone to talk with.

(3) There are few issues to discuss.

01 명사 뒤에서 수식하며, '미래' 의미를 갖는 것은 to부정사이다.

02 세 문장 모두 '~인지(아닌 지)' 여부를 나타내는 명사절로 접속사가 들어가는 자리이다. 문두 또는 바로 다음에 or not이 오는 경우, if는 불가능하므로, whether가 적절하다.

03 명사절 접속사 if를 찾는 문제이다. ①, ②, ③, ⑤는 모두 조건의 부사절 접속사로 쓰였다.

04 (1) something을 수식하는 말의 어순에 유의한다. something+형용사+to부정사. (2) 대화를 '함께'할 누군가이므로 with에 유의한다. (3) '~가 없다'는 내용은 There로 시작한다.

시험대비 실력평가 p.23~25

01 ④　　02 ③　　03 ⓑ, ⓕ　　04 ④

05 ③　　06 ④　　07 ④　　08 ④

09 ①　　10 ④　　11 ③　　12 ②

13 ③

14 (1) if Peter likes her (2) if she can become a teacher (3) if Sally ran in the marathon

15 ④　　16 ③　　17 ⑤

01 의문사가 없는 간접의문문을 이끄는 명사절 접속사 if는 whether와 달리 'or not'을 바로 붙여서 쓸 수 없다.

02 -thing으로 끝나는 대명사를 to부정사가 뒤에서 수식할 때는 형용사구를 to부정사 앞에 쓴다. 'something not too cold to drink'가 적절하다.

03 ⓐ 명사(주어) ⓒ 명사(목적어) ⓓ 부사(목적) ⓔ 부사(목적) ⓖ 부사(원인) collaborative research: 공동 연구

04 ask의 목적어인 명사절을 이끄는 접속사 if 또는 whether를 적절히 사용하여 영작한다.

05 'wasn't sure'처럼 불확실함을 나타내는 동사 표현의 목적어가 되는 명사절로 that절은 부적절하다. if 또는 whether를 쓰는 것이 좋으며, whether or not도 가능하다.

06 ① on은 불필요하다. on time 정시에, 제때 ② Does she have anything to eat? ③ The fox had nothing to do. ⑤ interested → interesting

07 ⓐ, ⓒ, ⓓ, ⓔ는 모두 명사적 용법으로 사용되었다.

08 그는 '아내에게 외식으로 저녁식사를 시켜줄' 돈을 가져오는 것을 잊었다. 돈이 밥을 사는 게 아니고, 돈을 가지고 소비한다는 점에서 전치사 with를 함께 쓰는 것이 좋으나, 관용적으로 쓰지 않아도 크게 문제되지는 않는다.

09 ② to play → to play with ③ to put those things → to put those things in ④ to go → to go to ⑤ to show you them → to show you (them 삭제)

10 주어 역할의 명사절을 이끄는 접속사가 필요하다. 내용상 '그 학생이 만점을 맞을지 여부는 중요하지 않다'이므로, whether가 적절하다. if는 문두에서 주어가 되는 명사절을 이끌 수 없다.

11 ① ⓐ 부사(목적) ⓑ 명사(목적어), ② ⓐ 부사(결과) ⓑ 명사(주어), ③ ⓐ 형용사(명사 수식) ⓑ 형용사(명사 수식), ④ ⓐ 명사(주어) ⓑ 부사(결과), ⑤ ⓐ 형용사(대명사 수식) ⓑ 부사(대명사 수식)

12 something great to eat이 적절하다.

13 ③ 조건의 부사절을 이끄는 접속사이다. 나머지는 모두 간접의문문의 명사절을 이끈다.

14 3인칭 전환과 시제 등에 유의하여 간접의문문을 영작한다. (3)번에서 ran을 쓰는 것에 유의한다.

15 ④만 조건의 부사절 접속사이다.

16 advice는 불가산 명사로서 단수 취급, to help가 뒤에서 수식하는 형태의 문장이 어법에 맞게 적절히 되어 있는 것을 고른다.

17 'if나 whether'가 어법상 적절히 쓰였는지 확인한다.

서술형 시험대비 p.26~27

01 (1) needs somebody to teach her Chinese

(2) was not sure whether he could pass the test

(3) got a chance to see the Northern Lights

(4) the girl if there is a bus stop nearby

02 (1) needs to train deer at 10:00

(2) toys for Santa to choose at 11:00

(3) many gifts to pack at 12:00

03 (1) to drink (2) to play with (3) to know

4 정답 및 해설

04 (1) I asked Peter if[whether] he would join our research team or not.

(2) She couldn't judge whether to accept the job offer or not.

(3) Whether you follow your heart or not matters in your life.

(4) I wasn't sure if[whether] I could succeed but I decided to try.

(5) All my classmates are wondering if it will snow tomorrow.

(6) I won first prize, which gave me a chance to think about my life.

(7) There is a hammer to nail with.

05 (1) I have many friends to help you with the project.

(2) William missed a chance to see the musical with Emma.

(3) There are many things to do to realize your dream.

(4) Does Jim have enough time to save the injured cat?

06 (1) a bed for my parents to sleep on

(2) a piece of paper for her to sign on

(3) her son some money for him to buy the shoes with

07 (1) If → Whether (2) that → if/whether

(3) to eat → to eat at/in

(4) to write → to write with

---

01 to부정사의 형용사적 용법과 접속사 if/whether가 이끄는 간접 의문문이다. 어법에 맞게 적절히 배열한다.

02 (1) 3인칭이므로 needs에 유의한다. (2) 동사가 are이므로 toys에 유의하고, to부정사의 의미상 주어로 for Santa를 쓴다. (3) many가 있으므로 gifts를 쓰고, to부정사의 수식에 유의하여 영작한다. *pack: 포장하다

03 (1) something to drink 마실 것 (2) a friend to play with 함께 놀 친구 (3) sales figures to know 알아야 할 판매액 수치 *sales figure: 매출액

04 (1) Peter가 우리 연구팀에 합류할지 여부를 묻는 것이므로 if/whether가 적절하다. (2) '일자리 제안을 받아들일지'라는 뜻으로, to부정사와 함께 쓰는 형태는 whether만 가능하다. (3) If는 문두의 명사절을 이끌 수 없다. (4) 성공할지 확신할 수 없었다는 내용이므로 if/whether가 적절하다. (5) 조건의 부사절이 아닌 명사절을 이끄는 if 문장에 미래시제 표현이 있으면, will을 써야 한다. (6) a chance to think about A: A를 생각할 기회 (7) 망치를 가지고 못을 박는 일이므로 전치사 with를 쓰는 것이 좋다. *nail: 못을 박다

05 (1) help+A(사람)+with+B(명사): A가 B를 하는 것을 돕다. (2) miss a chance: 기회를 놓치다. (3) realize one's dream: 꿈을 이루다. (4) Does로 시작하는 것에 유의한다.

06 to부정사가 명사 뒤에서 수식하는 표현들이 나오는 문장들이다. 전치사와 의미상의 주어에 유의하여 영작한다.

07 (1) If가 이끄는 명사절은 문두에서 주어 역할을 할 수 없다. Whether가 적절하다. (2) '모른다'는 동사 뒤에 that절은 부적절하다. if 또는 whether로 고친다. (3) 런던에 먹을 만한 레스토랑이 많다는 내용으로, to부정사 뒤에 장소를 나타내는 전치사 in 또는 at을 쓴다. 전치사가 없으면, 레스토랑을 먹는다는 어색한 내용이 된다. (4) 연필이나 만년필 같은 쓸 것은 write 뒤에 with를 함께 써서 명사를 수식하는 것이 적절하다.

교과서
Reading

확인문제   p.28

1 T 2 F 3 T 4 F 5 T 6 F

확인문제   p.29

1 T 2 F 3 T 4 F 5 T 6 F

확인문제   p.30

1 T 2 F 3 T 4 F 5 T 6 F

교과서 확인학습 A   p.31~33

01 Dream, Live   02 Hello

03 a photographer   04 how I found, realized

05 inspire you   06 When I was young

07 taking pictures   08 lead to a job

09 In fact, at all   10 decide on

11 looked OK

12 an engineering company 13 stable, whether

14 went on vacation   15 got a chance

16 amazing, took many pictures, dancing lights

17 For the first time, beating fast

18 entered, the pictures I took

19 won first prize   20 made me happy

21 learn more about photography

22 trial and error, part-time work

23 bold decision   24 for a living

25 wasn't sure if 26 something that

27 professional photographer

28 find a dream, realize it 29 some advice

30 follow your heart

31 what makes you happy

32 taking pictures of stars 33 work hard

34 Pursuing 35 through hard work

36 be bold

37 courage, make decisions 38 took a chance

39 truly hope

교과서 확인학습 B
p.34~36

1 Find a Dream and Live It!

2 Hello, everyone.

3 My name is David Parker, and I'm a photographer.

4 Today, I'm going to tell you how I found my dream and realized it.

5 I hope my story can inspire you.

6 When I was young, I loved stars.

7 I also liked taking pictures.

8 However, I never thought these things could lead to a job.

9 In fact, I didn't have a dream at all.

10 When I had to decide on a major in college, I chose engineering.

11 Being an engineer looked OK.

12 After college, I got a job at an engineering company.

13 It was a stable job, but I didn't know whether I really enjoyed it.

14 Everything changed when I went on vacation to Iceland one winter.

15 There I got a chance to see the Northern Lights!

16 The lights were amazing, and I took many pictures of the dancing lights in the sky.

17 For the first time in many years, I could feel my heart beating fast.

18 After I came back, I entered a photo contest with the pictures I took in Iceland.

19 Surprisingly, I won first prize, and this gave me a chance to think about my life.

20 I realized that taking pictures made me happy.

21 Suddenly, I wanted to become a good photographer, so I started to learn more about photography.

22 After years of trial and error, I got better, and I began to do some part-time work as a photographer.

23 Then one day, I made a bold decision.

24 I quit my job and decided to take pictures for a living.

25 I wasn't sure if I could succeed, but I decided to try.

26 I really wanted to do something that made me happy.

27 Now, I'm a professional photographer, and I'm happy.

28 So do you want to find a dream and realize it?

29 Here's some advice to help you.

30 First, follow your heart.

31 Think about what you like to do and what makes you happy.

32 In my case, it was taking pictures of stars.

33 Second, work hard.

34 Pursuing a dream is not easy.

35 I became a photographer through hard work.

36 Third, be bold.

37 You need courage to make decisions that will change your life.

38 I was afraid but I took a chance.

39 I truly hope you can find a dream, pursue it, and live it!

시험대비 실력평가
p.37~41

01 ① 02 ② 03 ③ 04 ⑤

05 I won first prize 06 ②, ⑤ 07 ④

08 ② 09 ①, ③, ④

10 I didn't know whether I really enjoyed it

11 ③ 12 ①, ④ 13 ⑤

14 (A) taking pictures (B) a photographer

(C) courage

15 ④ 16 ②, ⑤ 17 ② 18 ④

19 ③ 20 ②

21 (A) entered (B) if (C) professional

22 ①, ③, ④ 23 a good photographer

24 ② 25 ④

26 Think about what you like to do and what makes you happy.

27 ④ 28 in order that, may[can]

01 ⓐ lead to: ~로 이어지다, ⓑ decide on: (숙고하여 뭔가를) 고르다, (여러 가지 가능성 가운데) ~으로 결정하다

02 위 글은 '강연'이다. ① 토론, ③ (텔레비전이나 라디오에 나오는) 광고 (방송), ④ 대화, ⑤ 광고

03 '빛들은 경이로웠다'고 하면서 '수년 만에 처음으로 나는 심장

이 빠르게 뛰고 있는 것을 느낄 수 있었어요.'라고 했으므로, ③번 '흥분한'이 적절하다. ① 당황스러운, ② 겁먹은, 무서워하는, ④ 짜증이 난, ⑤ 안도하는

04 David Parker는 하늘에서 춤추는 빛들의 '그림을 많이 그린 것'이 아니라, '사진을 많이 찍었다.' ③ major in: ~을 전공하다

05 '내가 1등상을 받은 것'을 가리킨다.

06 suddenly = all of a sudden = all at once: 갑자기, ① 서둘러 ③ 빨리, ④ 서서히

07 ⓒ와 ①, ②, ③, ⑤: 관계대명사, ④ 접속사

08 앞에 나오는 내용과 상반되는 내용이 뒤에 이어지므로 However가 가장 적절하다. ① 그러므로, ③ 게다가, 더욱이, ⑤ 다시 말해서

09 ⓑ와 ①, ③, ④: 동명사, ②, ⑤: 현재분사

10 접속사 whether는 목적절을 이끌어 '~인지 아닌지'라는 의미를 나타내며 if로 바꿔 쓸 수 있다.

11 '별 사진을 찍으라.'는 것은 조언에 해당하지 않는다. '글쓴이의 경우, 하고 싶고 행복하게 하는 것이 별 사진을 찍는 거였다'고 했을 뿐이다.

12 ⓑ와 ①, ④: 동명사, ②, ③, ⑤: 현재분사

13 위 글은 '꿈을 찾아 실현하도록 도와줄 몇 가지 조언을 하는 글'이므로, 제목으로는 ⑤번 '꿈을 찾아 실현하는 법'이 적절하다.

14 David가 하고 싶었던 것은 별 '사진을 찍는 것'이었다. 그래서, 그는 '사진작가'가 되기 위해 열심히 노력했다. 그는 자신의 인생을 바꿀 결정을 하기 위해 '용기'를 필요로 했고 기회를 잡았다.

15 ④번 다음 문장의 'It'에 주목한다. 주어진 문장의 'a job at an engineering company'를 받고 있으므로 ④번이 적절하다.

16 in fact = actually = as a matter of fact: 사실은, ① 정확히, ③, ④: 특히

17 ⓑ와 ②, ⑤: 형용사적 용법, ①, ④: 명사적 용법, ③ 부사적 용법

18 ④번은 'a job at an engineering company'를 가리킨다. ② fondness: 좋아함, (~에 대한) 기호

19 at all은 not과 함께 쓰여 '전혀 ~가 아니다'라는 의미를 나타낸다. ① 어쨌든, ② 적어도, ③ not ~ in the least: 전혀 ~가 아니다, ④ 어떻게든, ⑤ 어느 정도, 약간, 다소

20 David Parker가 어떻게 그의 꿈을 실현했는지는 알 수 없다. ① He is a photographer. ③ He majored in engineering. ④ He saw them in Iceland. ⑤ He took many pictures of the dancing lights in the sky.

21 (A) 사진 경연 대회에 '참가했다'고 해야 하므로 entered가 적절하다. enter into: (논의, 처리 등을) 시작하다, (B) '성공할 수 있을지' 확신하지 못했다고 해야 하므로 if가 적절하다. 접속사 if는 목적절을 이끌어 '~인지 아닌지'라는 의미를 나타내고, that 뒤에는 확실한 내용을 나타내는 말이 와야 한다. (C) 앞부분에 직장을 그만 두고 생계 수단으로 사진을 찍기로 했

다는 말이 있으므로, '전문' 사진작가라고 하는 것이 적절하다. professional: 전문적인. amateur: 취미로 하는, 아마추어의

22 ① 주어 자리에 to부정사와 동명사 둘 다 가능, ③, ④: 목적어 자리에 to부정사와 동명사 둘 다 가능, ②, ⑤: 목적어 자리에 to부정사만 가능.

23 그는 '훌륭한 사진작가'가 되고 싶어서 사진 촬영 기술에 대해 더 배우기 시작했다.

24 이 글은 '성공할 수 있을지 확신하지 못했지만 시도한 결과, 현재 전문 사진작가가 되었다'는 내용의 글이므로, 어울리는 속담으로는 ②번 '뜻이 있는 곳에 길이 있다'가 적절하다. ① 제때의 바늘 한 번이 아홉 바느질을 던다. ③ 잘 생각해 보고 행동하라[돌다리도 두드려 보고 건너라]. ④ 사공이 많으면 배가 산으로 올라간다(어떤 일에 관여하는 사람이 너무 많으면 일을 망친다는 뜻). ⑤ 백지장도 맞들면 낫다[한 사람이 하는 것보다는 두 사람이 하는 것이 낫다].

25 여러분의 인생을 바꿀 결정을 하기 위해서는 용기가 필요하다는 말이 이어지고 있으므로, 빈칸에는 '대담한'이 적절하다. ① 침착한, 차분한, ② 참을성[인내심] 있는, ③ 후한[너그러운], ⑤ 사려 깊은

26 Think about 다음에 간접의문문의 순서로 쓰는 것이 적절하다.

27 세 번째 조언에서 '대담해지세요. 여러분의 인생을 바꿀 결정을 하기 위해서는 용기가 필요합니다.'라고 했다.

28 부사적 용법의 목적을 나타내는 to부정사는 in order that ~ may[can] ...로 고칠 수 있다.

서술형 시험대비
p.42~43

01 photography
02 (A) to quit   (B) for a living
03 I really wanted to do something that made me happy.
04 (1) 여러분의 마음을 따르세요.
   (2) 열심히 노력하세요.   (3) 대담해지세요.
05 (A) your heart   (B) what   (C) what
06 courage
07 the way how → the way 또는 how   08 major
09 (A) inspire   (B) amazing   (C) beating
10 (A) Northern Lights   (B) took many pictures
11 It   12 an unstable → a stable
13 the Northern Lights

01 훌륭한 사진작가가 되고 싶어서 '사진 촬영 기술'에 대해 더 배우기 시작했다고 하는 것이 적절하다. photography: 사진[촬영]술

02 직장을 '그만 두고' '생계 수단으로' 사진을 찍기로 결심한 것을 의미한다.

03 'really'를 'wanted' 앞에 쓰는 것이 적절하다.

7

04 세 가지 조언은 (1) Follow your heart. (2) Work hard. (3) Be bold.이다.

05 '여러분의 마음'을 따르기 위해서는, 여러분이 '무엇'을 하고 싶고 여러분을 행복하게 하는 것이 '무엇'인지 생각할 필요가 있다.

06 인생을 바꿀 결정을 하기 위해서는 '용기'가 필요하다.

07 the way how는 같이 쓸 수 없고 the way나 how만 쓰는 것이 적절하다. the way in which나 the way that도 가능하다.

08 학생이 대학에서 공부하는 전공과목, major: 전공(과목)

09 (A) 여러분에게 '영감을 주기를 바란다'고 해야 하므로 inspire가 적절하다. discourage: 낙담시키다, inspire: 영감을 주다, (B) 감정을 나타내는 동사는 감정을 유발할 때 현재분사를 쓰는 것이 적절하다. (C) 심장이 뛰어지는 것이 아니라 뛰는 것이므로 beating이 적절하다.

10 어느 겨울 아이슬란드에서 '오로라'를 보고 하늘에서 춤추는 빛들의 '사진을 많이 찍었을' 때, 그는 심장이 빠르게 뛰고 있는 것을 느낄 수 있었다.

11 가주어 'It'을 쓰는 것이 적절하다.

12 그것은 '안정적인' 직업이었지만, 난 내가 그 일을 정말로 좋아하는지는 알 수가 없었다고 해야 하므로, an unstable을 a stable로 고치는 것이 적절하다. unstable: 불안정한

13 '오로라'를 가리킨다.

영역별 핵심문제

p.45~49

01 ②   02 (c)ourage

03 (p)ursue / (a)chieve / (1) pursue (2) achieve

04 for / for   05 ④

06 Have you ever been to Canada?

07 ④   08 ⑤

09 (A) playing   (B) how   (C) to learn

10 He wants her to have a chance to learn to play the piano.   11 ⑤

12 He has the experience of visiting France.

13 other → another

14 whether she should practice running or playing

15 (1) with   (2) with/to/about/of   (3) on/in   (4) in
   (5) on   (6) with   (7) with   (8) of/about   (9) with
   (10) in

16 ②   17 to do, to take, to eat, to attend

18 ④

19 (1) if he will come back home
   (2) if he had lunch

20 ④   21 Though   22 ②   23 ④

24 (A) first prize   (B) photography

25 (A) to do   (B) happy   26 I took a chance

27 searching   28 ③   29 ⑤

---

01 <보기>와 ②번은 '실현하다'의 뜻으로 쓰였다. <보기> 그녀는 직업 가수가 되려던 야망을 결코 실현시키지 못했다. ① 그가 그렇게 아픈지 몰랐다. ② 외국에 가는 그의 꿈은 마침내 실현되었다. ③ 상황은 그들이 처음에 인식했던 것보다 더 복잡했다. ④ 그는 위험에 처해 있다는 것을 자각했다. ⑤ 이 상세한 설명은 그 장면을 사실적으로 표현하는 데 도움이 된다.

02 동의어의 관계이다. enter, come in:~에 들어가다 bravery: 용기, 용감(성), 용맹 courage: 용기

03 (1) pursue: 추구하다, 추진하다 / 무언가를 성취하기 위해 열심히 일하다 (2) achieve 성취하다, 달성하다 / 노력하여 얻다

04 for a living: 생계 수단으로 / 그들에게 생계를 위해서 무엇을 하고 있고 그들이 그것을 좋아하는지 물어보세요. for the first time: 처음으로 / 26년 만에 처음으로 허리케인이 그 도시를 강타했어!

05 제주도에 가 보았느냐는 물음에 아니라고 하면서 그 섬이 아름다우니 가 보기를 바란다고 하는 것은 어색하다.

06 'Have you (ever)+과거분사 ~?'로 경험을 물을 수 있다.

07 직업을 묻고(C), 옷을 만든다고 답하고(D), 자기 옷을 다 만들었는지 묻고(B), 다 만들었다며, 어떤 옷이 더 좋은지 묻는 질문에(A) 마지막으로 둘 다 좋다며 결정을 못 하겠다는 말로 이어지는 것이 적절하다.

08 모두 상대방은 어떤지(피아노를 칠 수 있는지) 묻고 있는데, ⑤번은 피아노를 치라고 제안하고 있다.

09 (A) enjoy의 목적어로 동명사 playing, (B) 피아노 치는 방법을 나타내는 how, (C) a chance를 수식하는 형용사적 용법의 to learn이 적절하다.

10 소년은 소녀가 피아노를 배울 기회를 갖길 바란다고 했다.

11 다른 나라로 여행할 수 있기를 바란다는 말 다음에 캐나다를 방문하고 싶다는 주어진 문장이 나오고 캐나다에 관한 책에 대해 말하는 것이 자연스러우므로 ⑤번이 적절하다.

12 소년은 프랑스에 가 보았다고 했다.

13 other는 복수명사의 앞에서 '다른'의 뜻으로 쓰이므로 another로 고쳐야 한다.

14 Jenny는 달리기를 연습할지 피아노 연주를 연습할지 결정할 수가 없다. *athlete: 운동선수(보통 육상경기)

15 to부정사가 명사를 뒤에서 수식할 때, 직접적인 목적어가 되지 않는 경우, 의미를 보조하기 위한 전치사를 쓰는 것이 좋다. 상황에 따라 쓰지 않을 수도 있다. (1) 보행 시 가지고 다닐 지팡이 (2) (~와 함께, ~에게, ~에 관해, ~에 대해) 얘기할 누군가 (3) 위에 앉을 의자 (4) 오렌지를 담을 바구니 (5) 뭔가를 위에 쓸 종이 (6) 그림 그릴 때 도구로 사용하는 붓 (7) 함께 놀 친구 (8) (~에 대해/관해) 말할 주제들 (9) 가방을 살 돈 (10) 흥미를 느낄 어떤 것

16 ㉡, ㉢, ㉤, ㉥은 모두 간접의문문을 이끄는 명사절 접속사 if이다. ㉠, ㉣은 부사절 조건문의 접속사로 쓰였다.

17 to부정사의 후치 수식을 활용하여, 각각의 명사에 적절한 동사

를 고른다. *spin class: 고정식 자전거를 이용한 헬스 운동

18 Alex가 4번 게이트로 맞게 가는지 생각하는 내용이다. 접속사 if와 '주어 he+동사' 어순이 바르게 된 것을 찾는다.

19 if를 사용하여, 간접의문문의 어순에 맞게 시제와 수에 유의하여 영작한다.

20 앞의 내용을 추가해서 설명하고 있으므로 In fact가 가장 적절하다. ① 비슷하게, ② 즉, ⑤ 그에 반해서, 그와 대조적으로

21 but을 없애고 Though나 Although로 문장을 시작할 수 있다.

22 ⓐ와 ②: (자격·기능 등이) ~로(서)(전치사), ① [보통 as … as ~로 형용사·부사 앞에서] ~와 같은 정도로(as … as ~에서, 앞의 as가 지시부사, 뒤의 as는 접속사), ③ [양태] ~처럼(접속사), ④ 예를 들면 ~처럼[같이](= such as, like), ⑤ [이유·원인] ~이므로, ~이기 때문에(접속사)

23 David Parker는 성공할 수 있을지 '확신하지 못했지만' 시도해 보기로 결심했다.

24 David Parker는 사진 경연 대회에서 '1등상'을 받았고 이것을 계기로 하여 그는 좋은 사진작가가 되기 위하여 '사진 촬영 기술'에 대해 더 배우기 시작했다. taking this opportunity: 이것을 계기로 하여

25 '내가 하고 싶고 나를 행복하게 해주었던 것'을 가리킨다.

26 take a chance: 기회를 잡다

27 spend+시간+~ing: ~하는 데 시간을 보내다

28 위 글은 박 병선 박사님을 '소개하는 글'이다. ① (신문·잡지의) 글, 기사, ② 독후감, ④ 전기, ⑤ (책·연극·영화 등에 대한) 논평[비평], 감상문

29 무엇 때문에 박 병선 박사가 해외에 있는 한국의 국보를 찾았는지는 알 수 없다. ① They respect Dr. Park Byeong-seon. ② She was a historian. ③ Because she spent her whole life searching for Korean national treasures abroad. ④ She searched for Korean national treasures abroad. accomplishment: 업적

단원별 예상문제 p.50~53

01 ③　　02 major / major
03 (1) (m)emorable　(2) (p)rofessional　(3) (g)et
04 (A) train　(B) train　(C) train(ed)
05 (C) → (B) → (A) → (D)
06 지역 동물의 집에서 자원봉사를 하고 있는 것.
07 ④　　08 recipe
09 (a) had Spanish food before　(b) tried it
10 ①　　11 ⑤　　12 ①, ⑤　　13 ④
14 (1) Mary made an appointment to meet Betty in front of the bookstore.
 (2) Daniel has several books to return to the library.

(3) Mr. Greg will buy some educational magazines to read.
(4) Sam is holding a novel to review.
15 make a decision 또는 make up my mind
16 ③　　17 looked like → looked
18 trial and error　　19 ②, ④
20 ②　　21 realize it　22 ④
23 come true 또는 become realized
24 graduation　　25 ④

01 ① 그녀는 돈이 아닌 사랑 때문에 그와 결혼하기로 결정했다. ② 어린이들을 예의 바르게 교육시키는 것은 중요하다. ③ 다음에는 변명하려고 하지 마라. ④ 그 분은 점심 식사 후 바로 돌아오실 겁니다. ⑤ 몇몇 직원들이 조기 퇴직을 자원했다.

02 major (형) 중요한, 주된 (명) 전공 (동) 전공하다 / 그녀는 20대일 때, 대표작들을 쓰기 시작했다. 나는 부모님에게 떠밀려 대학에서 의학을 전공하게 되었다.

03 (1) memorable: 기억할 만한, 인상적인 (2) professional: 전문적인, (전문) 직업의 (3) get better: (병, 상황이) 나아지다

04 (A) 기차, (B) a train of: 일련의 (C) 훈련시키다

05 자원봉사를 한다는 말에 이어 → (C)에서 좋다며 또 무엇을 하고 있는지 묻고 (else(그 외에, 그 밖에))에 유의한다.) → (B)에서 also로 추가해서 답하고 → (A)에서 '좋은 수의사가 되기를 바란다'고 말하고 → (D)에서 고마움을 표하는 순서가 자연스럽다.

06 앞 문장의 내용을 쓰면 된다.

07 지역 동물의 집에서 자원봉사를 하고 있는 것은 B이다.

08 recipe: 재료의 목록과 무엇인가를 어떻게 요리할지 알려주는 일련의 지시 사항들

09 각각 앞에 나온 내용인 (a) had Spanish food before와 (b) tried it이 생략되어 있다.

10 모두 명사를 뒤에서 수식하는 형용사적 용법인데, ①번은 부사적 용법(목적)으로 쓰였다.

11 ⑤번은 'with+목적어+분사' 형태로서 singing이 적절하다. 나머지는 모두 to부정사가 명사 뒤에서 수식하는 문장이다. ① to sleep ② to do ③ to read ④ to teach

12 ② if or not은 쓰지 않는다. or not을 삭제 또는 문장 끝에 두거나 if 대신에 whether를 쓰는 것이 적절하다. ③ tomorrow가 있으므로, 미래시제를 표현하는 will을 써야 한다. ④ last Saturday를 보아 과거시제이다. will come을 came으로 고치는 것이 적절하다.

13 when은 ⓐ와 ⓑ에 넣어도 무리가 없으나, ⓒ에는 내용상 부적절하다. 세 개의 빈칸에 모두 적절한 것은 if뿐이다. whether는 ⓑ에 적절하지 않다.

14 시제와 수의 일치에 유의하여, to부정사의 후치 수식을 어법에 맞게 활용한다. (1) 과거시제에 유의 (3) some이 있으므로 잡

9

지를 복수로 쓰는 것에 유의 (4) is를 활용해야 하기 때문에 진행시제로 쓰는 것에 유의

15 decide = make a decision = make up one's mind: 결정을 하다

16 ⓑ와 ③: (대학생의) 전공(명사), ① 주요한(형용사), ② (영국 육군, 미국 공군의) 소령(명사), ④ 대부분의, 대다수의, ⑤ (~을) 전공하다(동사)

17 look+형용사, look like+명사

18 trial and error: 시행착오

19 ⓑ와 ②, ④: [간접의문문을 이끌어] ~인지 (아닌지) (= whether), ①, ③, ⑤: (만약) ~이라면

20 이 글은 '사진 찍는 것이 자신을 행복하게 한다는 것을 깨닫고 직장을 그만 둔 다음, 전문 사진작가가 되어 지금 행복하다'는 내용의 글이므로, 주제로는 ②번 '당신을 행복하게 만드는 것을 함으로써 행복해져라'가 적절하다. ⑤ 나중에 후회하는 것보다 조심하는 것이 나으니까, 돌다리도 두드려 보고 건너라.

21 live it(= a dream) = realize it: 꿈을 실현하다

22 ④ '셋째, 대담해지세요. 여러분의 인생을 바꿀 결정을 하기 위해서는 용기가 필요합니다.'라고 언급되었다.

23 나의 꿈이 '실현되기를' 바란다고 하는 것이 적절하다. come true = become realized: 실현되다

24 graduate의 명사형인 'graduation'으로 쓰는 것이 적절하다. after graduation: 졸업 후

25 글쓴이의 브랜드 이름이 무엇인지는 대답할 수 없다. ① To become a famous fashion designer. ② Fashion design. ③ At a fashion company. ⑤ When he or she is 35.

서술형 실전문제
p.54~55

01 Yes, I have.

02 I haven't read the book, I've seen the movie

03 sometimes → sometime

04 (1) Laura asked me if I loved her.
   (2) Parker wasn't sure if he really enjoyed the job.
   (3) James wonders if he can pass the test.

05 (1) Mom wonders if Dave believes the story of the stork delivering the baby.
   (2) Dave asks Mom if there is any other way for the baby to be born.

06 ③ His camera had a flash to take a picture of the Aurora (with).　　07 any, write

08 I never thought these things could lead to a job.

09 that → whether 또는 if

10 (A) amazed　(B) for the first time

11 a dream　12 (A) Here's　(B) hard　(C) through

13 risk

---

01 빈칸 뒤에서 '그러나 책이 더 좋다'는 말이 나오므로 보았다는 응답이 적절하다.

02 but을 삭제하고 생략된 read the book를 써 준다.

03 sometimes: 때때로, 이따금 sometime: 언젠가

04 (1) 시제와 인칭에 맞게 if절이 될 때 you가 I, me가 her. love가 loved가 되는 것에 유의한다. (2) 괄호 안에 주어진 동사가 be sure인데, 내용상 의구심을 표현해야 하므로, wasn't sure가 되는 것에 유의한다. (3) mumble to oneself: 혼자 중얼거리다

05 간접의문문을 이끄는 명사절 접속사 if 뒤의 어순에 유의하여, 주어진 단어를 알맞게 배열한다. (1) delivering이 the stork를 후치 수식하는 것에 유의한다. (2) to be born의 의미상 주어가 for the baby임에 유의한다.

06 카메라에 오로라 사진을 찍을 플래시가 있었다는 문장이다. to부정사로 수식해야 한다. 전치사 with를 쓰는 것이 좋으나 생략해도 문제되지 않는다.

07 John doesn't have any pencils to write with.

08 전치사 'to'를 보충하면 된다. lead to: ~로 이어지다

09 that 뒤에는 확실한 내용을 나타내는 말이 와야 하는데, '난 내가 그 일을 정말로 좋아하는지 알 수가 없었다.'는 내용이므로 whether 또는 if로 바꾸는 것이 적절하다. 접속사 whether는 목적절을 이끌어 '~인지 아닌지'라는 의미를 나타내며 if로 바꿔 쓸 수 있다.

10 David Parker는 오로라에 '놀라' 많은 사진들을 찍었고, 수년 만에 '처음으로' 빠른 심장박동을 느낄 수 있었다. amaze: (대단히) 놀라게 하다, heart beat: 심장박동

11 '꿈'을 가리킨다.

12 (A) 주어가 'some advice'이므로 Here's가 적절하다. (B) '열심히 노력하세요.'라고 해야 하므로 hard가 적절하다. hardly: 거의 ~아니다[없다], (C) '열심히 노력해서'라고 해야 하므로 through가 적절하다. through hard work: 열심히 노력해서, though: (비록) …이긴 하지만

13 take a chance: 운에 맡기다, 기회를 잡다, take a risk: (위험할 수 있는 줄 알면서) 모험을 하다[받아들이다], take a chance와 take a risk는 둘 다 '잘 되든 안 되든 해보다'는 의미로 쓰인다.

창의사고력 서술형 문제
p.56

|모범답안|

01 (1) Have you eaten Bulgogi?
   (2) Have you had Bibimbap?
   (3) Have you tried Samgyupsal?

02 (1) whether to accept his proposal or not
   (2) if he smiled at me or laughed at me

(3) if my son will keep studying or get a job 등 if나 whether를 적절히 이용하여 어법에 맞게 쓰면 정답.

03 (A) a famous fashion designer

(B) fashion design   (C) a fashion company

(D) my own brand   (E) my first fashion show

단원별 모의고사 p.57~60

01 (1) ② (2) ⑤   02 (c)ourage

03 (g)oal   04 pollution   05 ⑤   06 ②

07 ③   08 ⑤   09 ①

10 How[What] about you?   11 ④

12 It is because she loves listening to piano music.

13 ④   14 ②   15 ①, ③, ④

16 (1) if she is going to be all right

(2) if he can move his toes

(3) if he fell by mistake

(4) if anyone will come to save him

(5) if the man is his friend, Dave

(6) if he should shoot her

17 ④ Give your daughter a spoon to eat with.

18 ①, ②, ④   19 ②   20 ③

21 happily → happy   22 ②   23 ④

01 <보기> (1) beat: (심장이) 고동치다, 기뻐서 가슴이 벅차게 두근거렸다. (2) ~에 이기다, 그가 체스에서 나를 이겼다. ① 누군가가 문을 두드리고 있었다. ② 맥박이 빠르다. ③ 누군가가 북을 치고 있었다. ④ 이런 종류의 음악은 비트가 강하다. ⑤ 우리 팀은 대량 득점으로 그들을 눌렀다.

02 courage: 용기, 두렵게 하는 어떤 것을 하는 능력

03 goal: 목표, 특히 많은 시간과 노력이 필요할 때 당신이 성취하기를 희망하는 어떤 것

04 pollution: 오염, 공기 오염은 중요한 환경 문제이다. 난 물 오염이 동물들에게 해롭다고 믿어.

05 ⑤번의 try는 '좋은지, 맛있는지 등을 보려고 먹어 보거나 해 보다'라는 뜻이다.

06 I know. I've already read it.으로 응답하는 것은 적절하다.

07 ③번 다음 문장의 your goal이 주어진 문장의 내용이므로 ③이 적절하다.

08 other를 else로 고치는 것이 적절하다.

09 여자가 목표를 이루기 위해 무엇을 하고 있는지는 알 수 없다.

10 '너는 어때?'라는 의미로 'How[What] about you?'가 적절하다.

11 (a)와 ④번은 형용사적 용법이다. ① 부사적 용법(목적) ②, ③ 명사적 용법 ⑤ 부사적 용법(형용사 수식)

12 CD를 사겠다는 말 뒤에 피아노 음악을 듣는 것을 좋아한다고 말하고 있다.

13 ④번 문장의 to catch는 부사적 용법의 '목적' 의미로 쓰였다. 나머지는 모두 형용사적 용법이다. *up-to-date 최신의

14 보기에 주어진 if는 간접의문문의 명사절을 이끄는 접속사이다. ②번을 제외한 나머지 모두 같은 역할이다. ②번은 조건의 부사절을 만드는 if가 쓰였다. *show up: 나타나다

15 ① TV를 볼 때 리모콘은 도구이다. 전치사 with가 필요하다. There is a remote controller to watch TV with.가 적절하다. ③ something to eat ④ 글쓰기에 쓰이는 종이이기 때문에 전치사 on이 필요. paper to write on이 적절하다.

16 위에 등장하는 모든 인물들의 생각은 의문사가 없는 의문문이다. 간접의문문으로 전환할 때, if 또는 whether를 사용하되, 문제의 조건에서 whether는 쓸 수 없다고 했으므로 if를 이용하여, 수와 시제에 맞춰 적절히 영작한다. 화법전환에 대한 기초 개념도 적절히 지도한다.

17 숟가락을 먹는 게 아니라, 숟가락을 가지고 먹는 것이므로 전치사 with를 쓰는 것이 적절하다.

18 접속사 whether는 목적절을 이끌어 '~인지 아닌지'라는 의미를 나타내며 if로 바꿔 쓸 수 있다. whether or not과 whether ~ or not으로 쓸 수도 있다.

19 ⓑ와 ①, ③, ⑤: 현재분사, ②, ④: 동명사, ②번의 beat: (상대, 적을) 패배시키다

20 ③번 앞 문장의 a bold decision에 주목한다. 주어진 문장의 내용을 가리키는 것이므로 ③번이 적절하다.

21 made의 목적격보어 자리이므로, happily를 형용사 happy로 고치는 것이 적절하다.

22 인생을 바꿀 결정을 하기 위해서는 용기가 필요하고, 글쓴이는 두려웠지만 기회를 잡았다'는 내용과 어울리는 속담으로는 ②번 '모험을 하지 않으면 아무것도 얻을 수 없다.'가 적절하다. ① 유유상종, ③ 안 좋은 일은 겹쳐서 일어나기 마련이다[불운은 한꺼번에 닥친다]. ④ 연습하면 익숙해진다. ⑤ 서두른다고 일이 되는 것은 아니다.

23 글쓴이가 사진작가가 되는 데 얼마나 오래 걸렸는지는 대답할 수 없다. ① I have to think about what I like to do and what makes me happy. ② No. ③ Through hard work. ⑤ Courage.

Food for the Heart

시험대비 실력평가 · p.64

01 ⑤	02 ①	03 ④	04 ④
05 ③	06 ①		

01 nap: 낮잠 / 피곤하고 졸려서 낮잠을 잤다고 하는 것이 적절하다.

02 comfort: 편안, 위로, 위안; 위로하다 / 사람들은 편안하게 사는 것을 좋아한다. 나는 그가 입은 막대한 손해를 위로해 주고 싶었다.

03 ① include: 포함하다, 서비스 사업은 다양한 비즈니스 형태를 포함한다. ② audience: 청중, 관중, 아마도 당신은 우리 청중들로부터 많은 편지를 받을 겁니다. ③ crisp: 바삭바삭한, 난 바삭바삭한 토스트에 버터를 발랐습니다. ④ melt: 녹다[녹이다], 더운 날에 햇빛은 초콜릿을 충분히 녹일 수 있다. ⑤ fix: 수리하다, 그 사람은 정말 손재주가 없어서 고칠 수 있는 게 없다. all thumbs: 일손이 아주 서툰, 재주가 없는

04 동의어 관계이다. differ: 다르다, vary: 다르다 fix: 수리하다, repair: 수리하다

05 ① similar to: ~과 비슷한, 벼룩시장은 규모만 더 크다 뿐이지 yard sale과 비슷합니다. ② stressed out: 스트레스로 지친, 학기말에 나는 스트레스로 완전히 지쳐 있었다. ③ every time: ~할 때마다, 그를 볼 때마다 그는 하품을 하고 있었다. ④ think of: ~에 대하여 생각하다, 당신이 그녀의 음악을 어떻게 생각하는지 알고 싶어요. ⑤ get well: 회복하다, 치료받으면 곧 나을 거라고 합니다.

06 take one's order: 주문을 받다, place[make] an order: 주문하다

서술형 시험대비 · p.65

01 (1) comfort (2) snack (3) recipe (4) flour

02 (1) feel (2) to go (3) but (also) (4) broke

03 (1) (d)ifference (2) (h)ealthy

04 (s)atisfaction

05 (1) The bucket is filled with sand and dirty things.
   (2) A waitress came to the table to take our order.
   (3) The tomatoes come right out of my own garden!

01 (1) comfort: 위로, 편안, 편한 느낌 (2) snack: 간식, 주된 식사 사이에 먹는 소량의 음식 (3) recipe: 조리법, 특정한 음식을 요리하기 위한 일련의 설명서 (4) flour: 밀가루, 빵과 케이크를 만드는 데 사용되는 가루

02 (1) feel better: 기분이 나아지다, 기분이 좋아지다 (2) For here or to go?: 여기에서 드시겠어요, 아니면 가져가시겠어요? (3) not only A but (also) B: A 뿐만 아니라 B도 (4) break down: 고장 나다

03 (1) '동사 - 명사' 관계이다. add: 더하다 – addition: 더하기, differ: 다르다 – difference: 차이점 (2) '명사 - 형용사' 관계이다. beauty: 아름다움 - beautiful: 아름다운, health: 건강 – healthy: 건강한

04 contentment: 만족, satisfaction: 만족, 금메달을 수상했을 때, 그녀는 비로소 만족을 찾았다.

05 (1) be filled with: ~로 가득 차다, with를 추가한다. (2) take order 주문을 받다, take를 추가한다. (3) come right out of: ~에서 바로 나오다, of를 추가한다.

[교과서] Conversation

핵심 Check · p.66~67

1 (A) What would you like to order
  (B) I'd like to order two hot dogs
2 (C) → (B) → (A)

교과서 대화문 익히기

Check(√) True or False · p.68

1 T 2 F 3 F 4 F

교과서 확인학습 · p.70~71

Listen and Talk A 1

Welcome to, What, to / want / that / for, to / For

Listen and Talk A 2

ready to / like, piece / like / here, go / go

Listen and Talk A 3

What, order / like to order / anything to / one bottle of / for here, to go / to go would, like to order / want, one / anything else / it, to go / To go

What would you like to order / I'd like to order / anything to drink / one / Is it / to go

Welcome to, What / have a, a / anything else / will that / order two bottles / Is it for here, to go / for here / comes to / Here, are

⑴ Are, ready / be all / For here / To go

⑵ would, like to / to order / anything to drink

⑶ What would you like to order / want / anything else / to go / To go

시험대비 기본평가　　　　　　　　p.72

01 Is it for here or to go?　　02 ④　　　03 ③

04 I want a hamburger.

01 'Is it for here or to go?'는 '여기에서 드시겠어요, 아니면 가져가시겠어요?'라는 뜻이다.

02 '가지고 가겠다.'라는 의미로 'It's to go.'라는 표현을 사용한다.

03 'What would you like to order?', 'May[Can] I take[have] your order?', 'Are you ready to order?' 등은 주문을 받을 때 쓰는 표현이다.

04 음식을 주문할 때 'I want+음식.'으로 표현할 수 있다.

시험대비 실력평가　　　　　　　　p.73~74

01 ④　　　　　　　　02 ②

03 What would you like to order?　　　　04 ⑤

05 ①　　　06 to go　　　　　　　07 ③

08 What would you like to order?

09 ④　　　10 ①　　　11 ①

12 Is it for here or to go?　　13 ⑤

01 다 주문했는지 묻는 말에 Yes라고 하고 주문을 하는 것은 어색하다. Yes를 No로 바꿔야 한다.

02 다음에 나오는 대답들로 보아 '여기에서 드시겠어요, 아니면 가져가시겠어요?'라고 묻는 것이 가장 적절하다.

03 주문하겠느냐고 묻는 표현으로 'May I take your order?', 'Are you ready to order?' 등으로 바꿔 쓸 수 있다.

04 소녀는 'It's for here'라고 하고 있으므로 가지고 갈 것이 아님을

알 수 있다.

05 빈칸에는 음식을 주문하는 말이 자연스럽다.

06 For here or to go?: 여기에서 드시겠어요, 아니면 가져가시겠어요?

07 주문할 준비가 되었는지 묻는 주어진 문장에 이어, (B)에서 케이크를 주문하고, (D)에서 케이크의 종류를 묻고, (A)에서 종류를 답하고, (C)에서 '여기에서 먹을 것인지 가지고 갈 것인지' 묻고, 가지고 간다며 감사를 표하는 말로 마무리한다.

08 이어지는 답으로 보아 빈칸 (A)에는 무엇을 주문할 것인지 묻는 질문이 적절하다.

09 Yes로 답하고 있으므로 의문사로 시작하는 질문은 적절하지 않다.

10 밑줄 친 문장은 무엇을 주문하겠는지 묻는 문장이다.

11 밑줄 친 (a)와 ①번은 형용사 용법으로 쓰었다. ②, ③ 명사 용법 ④, ⑤ 부사 용법

12 'Is it for here or to go?'는 '여기에서 드시겠어요, 아니면 가져가시겠어요?'라는 뜻이다.

13 B는 'It's for here'라고 말하고 있다.

서술형 시험대비　　　　　　　　　p.75

01 Would you like anything else?

02 The total comes to 12 dollars.

03 She ordered a hamburger, a chicken sandwich, one salad and two bottles of water.

04 May I take your order?

05 like

06 (B) → (A) → (C)

07 has not only food but also

08 I'd like to order Gimchi Gimbap, please.

　　I'd like Gimchi Gimbap, please.

　　I'll have Gimchi Gimbap, please.

01 의문문이므로 anything을 쓰고 -thing으로 끝나는 대명사이므로 else가 뒤에서 수식하도록 한다.

02 'come to'는 다음에 명사가 와서 '합계 ~이 되다'를 의미한다.

03 소녀가 주문한 것을 쓰면 된다.

04 주문 받을 때 쓰는 표현으로 'Are you ready to order?', 'What would you like to order?' 등으로 바꿔 쓸 수 있다.

05 Would you like ~?: ~을 원하십니까?

06 무슨 문제가 있는지 묻는 주어진 문장에 이어서, 문제를 언급하는 (B)가 나오고, 음식을 주는 (A)에 이어, 감사하는 (C)가 나오는 순서가 적절하다.

07 not only A but also B: A뿐만 아니라 B도

08 주문할 때 쓰는 표현들 중에서 3개 이상 쓰면 된다.

Grammar

핵심 Check
p.76~77

1 (1) use (2) feel
2 (1) that (2) order (3) so that

시험대비 기본평가
p.78

01 ①   02 ④   03 ④

04 (1) Let me tell you about my first love story.
   (2) Mike's father made him clean the room.
   (3) My mom had my sister buy tofu on her way home.

01 사역동사 make 뒤의 목적보어 자리에는 원형부정사를 쓴다.
02 공통으로 so가 들어가서 문장을 완성하는 것이 적절하다.
03 '목적'을 나타내는 부사절 접속사 that 외의 다른 용법으로 쓰인 that을 찾는 문제이다. ④는 '너무 ~해서 결국 …하다'라는 '결과'를 나타내는 접속사 that이다. ①, ②, ③, ⑤는 모두 '목적'의 의미로 사용되었다.
04 (1) let+목적어+원형부정사(tell) (2) make+목적어+원형부정사(clean) (3) have+목적어+원형부정사(buy) 등에 유의하여 영작한다.

시험대비 실력평가
p.79~81

01 ①   02 ④   03 ⑤   04 ③
05 ②   06 ②   07 ⑤
08 ②, ⑥, ⑦, ⑩   09 ④   10 ①
11 ④   12 ⑤   13 ①   14 ③
15 ④

16 (1) so that we may understand you
   (2) in order that he might make a living
   (3) so that Daniel could not cheat
   (4) harder in order that she could enter Harvard University

01 '사역동사 let+목적어+동사원형'이 적절하다.
02 관계대명사 that과, '사역동사 makes+목적어 you +목적보어 원형부정사 feel'을 확인한다.
03 'so that+주어+could'가 적절히 사용된 것을 찾는다.
04 ① her not be → she wouldn't be ② happiness → happy ④ so to → so as to(in order to) ⑤ for → that
05 목적보어로 동사원형을 받는 5형식의 사역동사 make를 찾는 문제이다 ⓑ to부정사가 목적보어로 쓰였다. *make a noise: 떠들다 ⓒ 4형식 동사 ⓓ 3형식 동사
06 사역동사 have, make, let 뒤의 목적보어에는 동사원형, help는

목적보어 자리에 to부정사/원형부정사 모두 가능.

07 다른 문장들은 모두 '목적'을 나타내는 두 가지 형태인데, ⑤의 두 번째 문장만 '결과'를 나타낸다. 보통, '결과'의 so (that)는 앞 문장의 끝에 콤마(쉼표)를 쓴다.
08 <보기>의 make는 5형식의 사역동사로서, 목적보어로 동사원형을 받는다. ②, ⑥, ⑦, ⑩을 제외한 나머지는 모두 다른 용례로 사용되었다. *make it: 시간 맞춰 가다
09 '유럽 여행을 갈 수 있도록 돈을 저축하고 있다.'라는 문장들로서 모두 '목적'을 나타내는데, ④는 '돈을 너무 많이 저축하고 있어서 유럽에 갈 수 있다.'라는 뜻의 '결과'를 나타낸다.
10 컴퓨터가 고장 나서 걱정하는 것은 worried이다. (B)와 (C)에는 사역동사 have와 let의 목적보어 자리이므로, 원형부정사가 적절하다.
11 해석해 보면 ④ 'Jacob은 전보다 더 열심히 공부했기 위해서 시험에 떨어졌다'라는 이상한 문장이 된다. so that을 (al)though와 같은 '양보'의 접속사로 바꾸는 것이 적절하다.
12 ① to laugh → laugh ② fixes → fix ③ going → go ④ to paint → paint
13 ② in order to that → in order that ③ be stay → be 또는 stay로 동사를 하나만 쓴다. ④ in order to → you could mix ⑤ so hard that to go → hard so that I could go
14 주어가 smell이므로 동사는 makes가 적절하다. 목적보어 자리에는 원형부정사 think of를 써야 한다.
15 'Let+목적어+원형부정사', 'so that+주어+can'에 유의한다.
16 '목적'을 나타내는 부사절 so that, in order that 뒤의 문장 구조에 유의하여, 적절히 영작한다.

서술형 시험대비
p.82~83

01 (1) in order that we could watch
   (2) What food makes you think of
   (3) slowly so that everybody could follow him
   (4) eating cassava chips made me feel better
02 (1) Eating chocolate cookies often makes Hanna feel happy.
   (2) The doctor had me wear the mask.
   (3) Sad movies always make me cry.
   (4) Mom let me play computer games.
03 (1) clean (2) to take out (3) water (4) sweep
04 (1) Write down the addresses so that you won't forget them.
   (2) Please wake me up so[in order] that I won't be late for school.
   (3) I'm saving money so that I can travel to Europe.
   (4) Comfort food can make you think of happy moments from the past.

(5) My father made me a bowl of chicken soup so[in order] that I could get well. 또는 My father made me a bowl of chicken soup in order for me to get well.

(6) The scary dog made the delivery man run away.

05 (1) You need flour and sugar so that you can make madeleines.

(2) My computer broke down, which made me feel worried.

(3) Melt the butter and let it cool.

(4) I exercise every day so that I can be healthy.

06 (1) not to be late   (2) so as not to be late

(3) in order that

07 (1) to → 삭제   (2) to → 삭제   (3) cried → cry

(4) wore → (to) wear   (5) use → to use

(6) to → 삭제   (7) help → to help   (8) to → 삭제

01 '목적'을 나타내는 부사절에 so that 대신 in order that을 쓸 수 있다. '사역동사+목적어+원형부사'에 유의한다.

02 사역동사의 목적보어 자리에 원형을 쓰는 것에 유의하여, 적절히 영작한다.

03 사역동사는 목적보어로 원형부정사를 취하지만, get은 to부정사를 취한다. *sweep: 빗자루 등으로 쓸다.

04 (1) so as that은 쓸 수 없다 (2) so order that을 so that 또는 in order that으로 고친다. (3) so which를 so that으로 바꾼다. (4) 사역동사 make는 목적보어로 원형부정사를 쓴다. (5) in order to me get well을 '목적'을 나타내는 부사절로 바꿔준다. (6) ran을 원형부정사 run으로 고친다.

06 so that과 같은 의미의 표현들을 철저히 숙지하도록 한다.

07 사역동사와 지각동사의 목적보어 자리에는 원형부정사를 쓴다. 그 외 allow, ask 등의 목적보어 자리에는 to부정사를 써야 한다.

교과서
Reading

확인문제   p.84

1 T   2 F   3 T   4 F   5 T   6 F

확인문제   p.85

1 T   2 F   3 T   4 F   5 T   6 F

확인문제   p.86

1 T   2 F   3 T   4 F   5 T   6 F

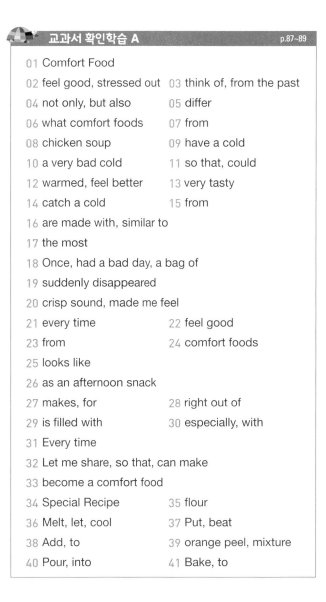

교과서 확인학습 A   p.87~89

01 Comfort Food

02 feel good, stressed out   03 think of, from the past

04 not only, but also   05 differ

06 what comfort foods   07 from

08 chicken soup   09 have a cold

10 a very bad cold   11 so that, could

12 warmed, feel better   13 very tasty

14 catch a cold   15 from

16 are made with, similar to

17 the most

18 Once, had a bad day, a bag of

19 suddenly disappeared

20 crisp sound, made me feel

21 every time   22 feel good

23 from   24 comfort foods

25 looks like

26 as an afternoon snack

27 makes, for   28 right out of

29 is filled with   30 especially, with

31 Every time

32 Let me share, so that, can make

33 become a comfort food

34 Special Recipe   35 flour

36 Melt, let, cool   37 Put, beat

38 Add, to   39 orange peel, mixture

40 Pour, into   41 Bake, to

교과서 확인학습 B   p.90~92

1 Letters from Our Readers: My Comfort Food

2 Comfort food is food that makes you feel good when you are sad, angry, or stressed out.

3 It can also make you think of happy moments from the past.

4 It satisfies not only the stomach but also the heart.

5 Comfort foods differ around the world.

6 Let's see what comfort foods our international readers enjoy.

7 Jessica from USA

8 My comfort food is chicken soup.

9 In the USA, people eat this soup when they have a cold.

10 When I was a small child, I caught a very bad cold.

11 My father made me a bowl of chicken soup so that I could get well.

15

12 The hot soup warmed my body, and I slowly started to feel better.

13 It was also very tasty.

14 Now, when I catch a cold, I eat chicken soup.

15 Maria from Brazil

16 In Brazil, there are many dishes that are made with cassava, a vegetable similar to a potato.

17 I love cassava chips the most.

18 Once when I had a bad day at school and felt stressed out, my best friend bought me a bag of cassava chips.

19 When I started to eat the chips, my stress suddenly disappeared.

20 The crisp sound of eating chips made me feel better.

21 Now, every time I'm stressed out, I eat cassava chips.

22 Then I feel good again!

23 Simon from France

24 I have many comfort foods, but I love madeleines the most.

25 A madeleine is a small cake that looks like a sea shell.

26 People in France enjoy madeleines as an afternoon snack.

27 My grandmother always makes madeleines for me when I visit her.

28 They taste best when they come right out of the oven.

29 Then the kitchen is filled with a sweet smell.

30 I especially like eating her orange madeleines with a cup of tea.

31 Every time I see or smell madeleines, I think of my grandmother.

32 Let me share my grandmother's special recipe with you so that you can make orange madeleines, too.

33 Maybe madeleines will become a comfort food for you!

34 Grandma's Special Recipe: Orange Madeleines

35 You need: 1 cup of flour, 2/3 cup of sugar, 2 eggs, some orange peel, 1/4 cup of butter, 1/8 teaspoon of salt

36 1. Melt the butter and let it cool.

37 2. Put the eggs, sugar, and salt in a bowl and beat.

38 3. Add the flour to the bowl and mix.

39 4. Add the butter and orange peel to the mixture and mix.

40 5. Pour the mixture into the madeleine pan.

41 6. Bake in the oven for 10 to 15 minutes.

시험대비 실력평가
p.93~97

01 ①, ⑤ 02 ③ 03 ⑤ 04 ③

05 ④ 06 her best friend 07 Recipe

08 ⑤ 09 ② 10 ②, ⑤

11 not tasty, but → very tasty, and 12 ④

13 ②, ⑤ 14 madeleines 15 ⑤

16 (c) → (a) → (d) → (b) 17 Ingredients

18 for 10 to 15 minutes 19 ⑤ 20 ④

21 was suddenly disappeared → suddenly disappeared

22 The crisp sound of eating chips made me feel better.

23 ①, ③, ④

24 so that I could get well 또는 in order that I could recover

25 He made her a bowl of chicken soup.

26 (A) stressed (B) think (C) around

27 ①, ④ 28 (A) heart (B) differ 29 ④

30 My grandmother always makes me madeleines

31 ⑤

01 make/let(사역동사)+목적어+동사원형, help(준사역동사)+목적어+동사원형 또는 to부정사, allow/get+목적어+to부정사

02 '세계 여러 나라의 우리 독자들은 어떤 comfort foods를 즐기는지 알아보자'고 했으므로, 뒤에 나올 내용으로는 ③번 '세계 여러 나라의 독자들이 즐기는 comfort foods'가 적절하다.

03 'comfort foods는 전 세계적으로 다양하다'고 했다. be similar to: ~와 비슷하다

04 주어진 문장의 the chips에 주목한다. ③번 앞 문장의 a bag of cassava chips를 받고 있으므로 ③번이 적절하다.

05 ⓐ와 ④: 요리, ① the dishes 설거지감[그릇들], ② 접시, ③ (식사를) 접시에 담아서 내다[up], ⑤ dish out: (흔히 많은 사람들에게 또는 많은 양을) 주다

06 Maria는 '그녀의 가장 친한 친구'가 그녀에게 사준 카사바 칩 한 봉지를 먹는 동안 스트레스가 갑자기 사라졌을 때 카사바 칩을 좋아하게 되었다.

07 recipe: 조리[요리]법 / 재료의 목록, 어떤 것을 요리하는 법을 말해 주는 지시 사항들

08 ⑤ Fry를 Bake로 고치는 것이 적절하다. Fry: 기름에 튀기다, Bake: 굽다, ⓐ Melt, ⓑ Put, ⓒ Add, ⓓ Pour

09 orange가 아니라 오렌지 껍질(orange peel)이 필요하다.

10 get well = recover = restore one's health: 병이 나아지다, ① 성장[장성]하다, ③ (안부 등에 대해 묻거나 답하는 말에서) ~하다[~하게 지내다], (탈것에) 올라타다, ④ 악화되다

11 Jessica의 아빠가 만들어 주셨던 치킨 수프는 '매우 맛있었다.'

12 Jessica가 매우 심한 감기에 걸렸을 때 그녀의 엄마가 무엇을 만들어 주었는지는 대답할 수 없다. ① It is chicken soup. ② They eat chicken soup. ③ Her father did. ⑤ She eats chicken soup. at present: 현재

13 주격 관계대명사 that이나 which가 적절하다.

14 '마들렌'을 가리킨다.

15 ⑤번에서 for me를 for you로 고치면 같은 뜻이 된다. so that ~ can(may) … = in order that ~ can(may) … = (in order/so as) for 목적격+to부정사

16 (c)의 a bowl 다음에 (a)의 the bowl이 오고, (d)의 the mixture는 (a)에서 mix한 반죽이고, (d)에서 mix한 반죽을 (b)에서 마들렌 팬에 부은 다음, 마지막으로 오븐에서 굽는 6.의 순서가 오는 것이 적절하다.

17 ingredient: (특히 요리 등의) 재료

18 10 to 15 minutes: 10분에서 15분

19 오븐을 몇 도까지 가열해야 되는지는 대답할 수 없다. ① 1 cup of flour, 2/3 cup of sugar, 2 eggs, some orange peel, 1/4 cup of butter, 1/8 teaspoon of salt, ② I need to melt the butter and let it cool. ③ I need to add the butter and orange peel to the mixture and mix. ④ For 10 to 15 minutes.

20 ⓐ with: [재료·내용물] ~으로, ⓑ similar to: ~과 비슷한

21 disappear는 수동태로 쓸 수 없는 동사이다.

22 전치사 of 뒤에 동명사 eating을 쓰고, made(사역동사)+목적어+목적격보어(동사원형)로 쓰는 것이 적절하다.

23 catch[have, get] a cold: 감기에 걸리다

24 get well = recover = restore one's health: 병이 나아지다

25 그는 그녀에게 '치킨 수프 한 그릇'을 만들어 주었다.

26 (A) '스트레스를 받을 때'라고 해야 하므로 stressed가 적절하다. stressed out 스트레스로 지친, (B) make(사역동사)+목적어+목적격보어(동사원형)이므로 think가 적절하다. (C) '전 세계적으로' 다양하다고 해야 하므로 around가 적절하다. around the world: 세계적으로, differ from ~: ~와 다르다

27 ⓐ와 ①, ④: 관계대명사, ② [반복의 대명사로서] (…의) 그것, ③ 그다지(지시부사), ⑤ 저것(지시대명사)

28 comfort foods는 위뿐만 아니라 '마음'도 충족시켜 주는 음식이고, 전 세계적으로 '다양하다.' satisfy hunger: 공복을 채우다, 허기를 만족시키다

29 위 글은 마들렌이 Simon의 가장 좋아하는 comfort food가 된 경위를 설명하는 글이므로, 제목으로는 ④번 'Simon의 comfort food는 무엇인가?'가 적절하다.

30 for를 없애고 '간접목적어+직접목적어'의 순서로 바꿔서 4형식

으로 고치는 것이 적절하다.

31 Simon의 할머니의 마들렌을 만드는 특별한 요리법이 무엇인지는 대답할 수 없다. ① He loves madeleines the most. ② It looks like a sea shell. ③ They enjoy them when they eat an afternoon snack. ④ With a cup of tea.

서술형 시험대비 p.98~99

01 She always makes madeleines for him.

02 Every time I see or smell madeleines, I think of my grandmother.

03 (A) a sea shell   (B) an afternoon snack

04 (A) Melt   (B) beat

05 what comfort foods our international readers enjoy

06 It satisfies the heart as well as the stomach.

07 (A) the heart   (B) happy moments

08 for me to get well

09 A bowl of chicken soup 또는 The hot soup

10 (A) Chicken soup   (B) feel better

11 she bought → her best friend bought her

12 (A) a potato   (B) dishes

13 (A) bought   (B) better

---

01 Simon의 할머니는 Simon이 찾아뵐 때는 항상 마들렌을 만들어 주신다.

02 every time: ~할 때마다

03 마들렌은 '조개'와 매우 비슷한 모양을 가진 작은 케이크이고, 프랑스 사람들은 '오후 간식'으로 그것을 즐겨 먹는다.

04 (1) 버터를 '녹여서' 식힌다. (2) 달걀, 설탕, 소금을 그릇에 넣고 '휘젓는다.'

05 see의 목적어가 되는 간접의문문(의문사+주어+동사)의 순서로 쓰는 것이 적절하다.

06 not only A but also B = B as well as A: A뿐만 아니라 B도

07 comfort food는 여러분이 슬프거나 화가 나거나 스트레스를 받을 때 기분을 좋게 해줄 뿐만 아니라 여러분에게 과거의 '행복한 순간들'을 생각나게 할 수 있기 때문에 '마음'도 충족해 줄 수 있다.

08 so that+주어+동사: ~하도록(목적), 의미상의 주어 for me 다음에 to부정사를 사용하여 고치는 것이 적절하다.

09 'a bowl of chicken soup' 또는 'The hot soup'를 가리킨다.

10 '치킨 수프'가 Jessica의 comfort food이다. 그 뜨거운 수프가 그녀의 몸을 따뜻하게 하고 그녀는 서서히 '나아지기' 시작하기 때문에, 그녀는 감기에 걸리면 치킨 수프를 먹는다.

11 한번은 그녀가 학교에서 안 좋은 일이 있고 스트레스를 받았을 때, '그녀의 가장 친한 친구'가 그녀에게 카사바 칩 한 봉지를 사

17

쥤다.

12 카사바는 '감자'와 비슷한 채소이고, 브라질에는 카사바로 만든 '요리'가 많다.

13 학교에서 안 좋은 일이 있고 스트레스를 받았을 때, 그녀의 가장 친한 친구가 그녀에게 '사준' 카사바 칩 한 봉지를 먹음으로써 그녀는 그렇게 할 수 있었다. 그녀가 그 칩을 먹기 시작했을 때, 그녀의 스트레스가 갑자기 사라졌고 칩을 먹을 때 나는 바삭한 소리가 그녀의 기분을 '더 좋게' 만들었다.

영역별 핵심문제
p.101~105

01 ② 02 as well

03 (d)isappear / (m)elt / (1) disappear (2) melt

04 tasty / salty

05 (A) with (B) not (C) but 06 ④

07 ⑤ 08 Will that be all? 09 To go

10 (A) to order (B) to go 11 ①

12 B ordered two doughnuts and one orange juice.

13 William join his reading club

14 review the math textbook

15 (1) dance (2) to go (3) to perform (4) come
(5) to open (6) singing (7) melt

16 ③ 17 ①, ⑤

18 so that he could avoid being scolded

19 so that we can understand our language better

20 ③ 21 Comfort food

22 ④ 23 ④

24 whenever / each time / when, always

25 ⑤ 26 ⑤ 27 ③

28 a side dish → an afternoon snack 또는 a small cake

29 ② 30 ⑤

01 ① 더 이상 둘러대지 않고 단도직입적으로 말할게. ② 계란들을 휘젓고, 나머지 재료들에 첨가해라. ③ 우박이 창문을 두드려 댔다. ④ 그녀를 보았을 때 그는 심장이 멎는 것 같았다. ⑤ 일본은 절대 한국을 이길 수 없을 것 같은데. hailstone: 우박

02 not only A but also B = not only A but B as well, 그의 직업은 재미있을 뿐 아니라 보수도 매우 좋다.

03 (1) disappear: 사라지다, 보거나 찾을 수 없게 되다 / PC가 사라질 거라고 말하는 사람은 별로 없다. (2) melt: 녹다, 액체가 되다. 얼음은 여름이 시작하면서부터 녹아내리기 시작했다.

04 명사에 -y를 붙여 형용사가 되는 어휘들이다. • 그 케이크는 언제나 달고 맛있습니다. • 점심에 너무 짠 음식을 먹었나 봐.

05 be filled with ~: ~로 가득 차다, not only A but also B: A 뿐만 아니라 B도

06 'No, thank you.'가 적절하다.

07 주문하시겠느냐는 질문에 이어, 주문을 하고(D), 마실 것을 원하는지 묻고(B), 우유를 주문하고(C), 그것이 다인지 묻는 질문에(A) 그렇다고 답하는 주어진 문장으로 이어지는 것이 적절하다.

08 all이 대명사로 쓰였다.

09 'to go'는 'take out'과 같이 '가져가겠다'라는 의미이다.

10 (A) 'would like' 다음에 to부정사, (B) for here or to go?: 여기에서 드시겠어요, 아니면 가져가시겠어요?

11 주문하시겠느냐는 말 다음에 그렇다고 말하고 주문하는 말이 나오는 것이 자연스러우므로 ①번이 적절하다.

12 B는 도넛 두 개와 오렌지 주스 하나를 주문했다.

13 William이 Henry에게 John과 함께 독서 클럽에 가입할 것을 요청하고, Henry가 허락해 주는 내용이다.

14 선생님이 Elizabeth의 수학 성적에 놀라서, 당장 교과서를 복습하도록 권유하는 내용이다.

15 사역동사와 지각동사의 목적보어 자리에는 동사원형을 쓰는 것에 유의한다. 지각동사는 동사원형 대신 현재분사도 가능하다. want, expect, ask 등의 동사는 목적보어 자리에 to부정사를 쓰는 것이 적절하다.

16 so that 뒤에는 절을 써야 한다. for him to win을 he could win으로 고치는 것이 적절하다.

17 ② 사역동사 let 뒤의 목적보어 자리에 원형부정사를 써야 한다. ③ 'let+목적어+동사원형'은 틀린 곳이 없으나, don't가 부적절하다. 주어가 3인칭 단수이기 때문에 doesn't 또는 didn't로 고쳐야 한다. 일선 학교에서 이렇게 핵심 어법사항은 맞게 하고, 다른 기본적인 부분을 틀리게 하는 문장이 나오는 경우가 있으니, 주의하도록 한다. ④ 사역동사 had가 있으므로 to를 삭제한다.

18 Jim은 부모님께 혼나는 것을 피하려고 헤드폰을 썼다. *scold: 혼내다, 꾸짖다

19 우리는 우리말을 더 잘 이해하기 위해 한자를 배운다.

20 Jane의 아버지가 chicken soup를 만든 것은 딸인 Jane이 회복하도록 하는 이유이다. 의미상 주어를 따로 표시하지 않고 so as to get well이 되면, Jane의 아버지 자신이 회복하기 위해 만들었다는 내용이 되므로 의미가 달라진다.

21 'Comfort food'를 가리킨다.

22 이 글은 'comfort food는 슬프거나 화가 나거나 스트레스를 받을 때 기분을 좋게 해 주는 음식이고, 과거의 행복한 순간들을 생각나게 할 수 있다'는 내용의 글이므로, 주제로는 ④번 'comfort food는 마음에 영양분을 준다.'가 적절하다.

23 ⓐ와 ①, ②, ③, ④: 동명사, ⑤ 현재분사

24 every time = whenever = each time = when ~, always: ~할 때마다

25 카사바 칩을 먹을 때 나는 바삭한 소리가 Maria의 기분을 '더 좋게' 만들었다. nervous: 불안해[초조해/두려워] 하는

26 프랑스 사람들은 오후 '간식으로' 마들렌을 즐겨 먹는다고 해야

하므로, as가 적절하다. as: (자격·기능 등이) ~로(서)

27 ③번 다음 문장의 Then에 주목한다. 주어진 문장의 내용을 받고 있으므로 ③번이 적절하다.

28 마들렌은 프랑스 사람들이 즐겨 먹는 '오후 간식(또는 작은 케이크)'이다. side dish: (샐러드와 같이, 주 요리에 곁들이는) 곁들임 요리, 반찬

29 위 글은 '에세이(수필)'이다. ① (신문·잡지의) 글, 기사, ③ 독후감, ④ (책·연극·영화 등에 대한) 논평[비평], 감상문, ⑤ 요약, 개요

30 글쓴이가 얼마나 자주 comfort food를 사는지는 알 수 없다. ① It is chocolate. ② When the writer feels bad. ③ Because the writer didn't do well on a test. ④ The writer went to the store and bought some chocolate. / The writer bought some chocolate and ate it.

단원별 예상문제
p.106~109

01 ③　　　02 but / but
03 (1) (s)tressed out　(2) (s)imilar　(3) filled
04 ②　　　05 (B) → (D) → (C) → (A)　　06 ③
07 I'd like to order two bottles of water.
08 order
09 Would you like anything to drink? 또는 Would you like to order anything to drink?
10 ③　　　11 ①
12 Eating chocolate makes David feel better.
13 (1) Damon had Morgan check the script.
　(2) Damon shouted, "Let me know if you're ready."
　(3) Andy made the actors keep standing.
　(4) Mary helped Scarlet (to) focus on her acting.
　(5) Fred's wealth made Damon decide to join the movie.
14 ①　　　15 (A) from　(B) better　(C) tasty
16 ③
17 ⓐ two-thirds　ⓑ one-fourth 또는 a fourth 또는 one quarter 또는 a quarter　ⓒ one-eighth
18 the butter　19 ③　　　20 is → are　21 ④
22 A madeleine is a small cake that looks like a sea shell.
23 visit to → visit　　　24 ①

01 ① 그의 연설은 청중의 눈물을 자아냈다. ② 좀 더 분명하게 설명해 주시겠습니까? ③ 이제부터 주문을 받을 수 있어요. ④ 습관은 나라마다 다르다. ⑤ 이 소년이 앉을 자리 좀 만들어 주시겠어요?

02 not only A but also: A 뿐만 아니라 B도. 그녀는 엄하기만 한 것이 아니라, 굉장히 마음이 따뜻하기도 합니다. not A but

B: A가 아니라 B, 그는 선생님이 아니라 의사이다.

03 (1) stressed out: 스트레스로 지친 (2) similar to: ~과 비슷한 (3) be filled with: ~로 가득 차다

04 ② fog의 형용사형은 foggy이다.

05 주문하시겠느냐는 말에 이어 → (B)에서 주문을 하고 → (D)에서 다른 주문이 있는지 묻고 → (C)에서 추가해서 주문하고 → (A)에서 그것이 전부인지 묻고 다음에 아니라면서 다시 추가하는 순서가 자연스럽다.

06 대화에서 함께 온 사람에 대해 소녀가 she라고만 할 뿐 누구인지는 알 수 없다.

07 'I'd like to order ~'를 이용하고 물 두 병은 'two bottles of water'로 나타낸다.

08 '식당에서 음식이나 음료를 요구하다'라는 의미로 '주문하다'가 적절하다. order: 주문하다

09 Would you like (to order) anything to drink?를 이용하여 나타낸다.

10 지각동사 hear 뒤의 목적보어 자리에는 원형부정사 또는 현재분사를 쓰는 것이 적절하다.

11 ①은 '너무 ~해서 …하다'라는 의미의 '결과'를 나타내는 상관접속사 so ~ that이다. 나머지는 모두 '목적'의 'so that'이다.

12 내용상 '초콜릿을 먹는 것이 David을 더욱 기분 좋게 만든다.'는 것이므로, 동명사 주어, 사역동사, 원형부정사 등을 활용해서 적절히 영작한다.

13 5형식의 사역동사 활용에 유의하여, 주어진 단어들을 정리한다.

14 모두 '목적'을 나타내는 부사절 접속사 'so that'인데, ①번만 '결과'의 의미로 쓰였다.

15 (A) '미국에 사는' Jessica라고 해야 하므로 From이 적절하다. from: ~ 출신의[에서 온], (B) 서서히 '나아지기' 시작했다고 해야 하므로 better가 적절하다. (C) very 다음에는 '형용사'를 쓰는 것이 적절하므로 tasty가 적절하다.

16 ③ Jessica의 '아빠'가 Jessica에게 치킨 수프를 만들어 주셨다. ⑤ at present: 현재

17 분자는 기수, 분모는 서수로 쓰고, 분자를 먼저 읽고 분모를 나중에 읽는다. 그리고 분자가 2 이상이면 분모에 복수형 어미 -s를 붙인다. ⓑ one 대신 a를 쓰는 경우에는 보통 하이픈을 긋지 않는다.

18 '버터'를 가리킨다.

19 ⓔ의 the mixture는 2번과 3번에서 섞은 달걀, 설탕, 소금, 밀가루 반죽이고, 그 다음 순서로 4번에서 ⓔ의 반죽에 버터와 오렌지 껍질을 넣고 섞으라고 되어 있다.

20 주격 관계대명사 that의 선행사가 many dishes이기 때문에, 동사를 are로 고치는 것이 적절하다.

21 ⓑ와 ①, ②, ③, ⑤: 옛날 (언젠가), 한번은, 일찍이 (formerly)(부사), ④ 한 번[일단] ~하면(접속사)

22 look like: ~처럼 보이다

19

23 visit은 타동사이므로, 전치사 없이 바로 목적어를 가지는 것이 적절하다.

24 ⓒ와 ①: 곧, 바로, 즉시, ② 오른쪽의, ③ (도덕·사회 통념상) 옳은, ④ 권리[권한], ⑤ (특정한 상황·사람·사물에) 맞는[알맞은]

명사: ~처럼 보이다, (B) 뒤에 형용사가 있으므로 taste가 적절하다. taste+형용사: 맛이 ~하다, ~한 맛이 나다, (C) 'let(사역동사)+목적어+목적격보어(동사원형)'이므로 share가 적절하다.

11 'Then'은 '마들렌이 오븐에서 막 나올 때'를 가리킨다.

12 마들렌을 보거나 냄새 맡을 때마다 Simon은 할머니가 생각난다.

01 stressed out

02 He bought a house to live in with his mom[mother].

03 is full of

04 ③ Speak very clearly so that they can understand you.

05 ④ There was a big fire, so the officers made[let] everyone leave.

06 (1) so that it could cool her body
   (2) let my sister wear   (3) in order to give

07 that are   08 Thanks to

09 (A) Cassava chips   (B) crisp sound

10 (A) looks like   (B) taste   (C) share

11 When they come right out of the oven

12 Every time he sees or smells madeleines, he thinks of her.

01 '삶의 어려움 때문에 매우 긴장되고 불안한'을 나타내는 말은 'stressed out'이다. stressed out: 스트레스로 지친

02 (a)의 'to eat'은 앞에 나온 명사를 수식하는 to부정사의 형용사적 용법이다. 집에서 사는 것이므로 전치사 in을 빠뜨리지 않도록 주의한다.

03 be filled with = be full of: ~으로 가득 차다

04 ③ 문맥상 목적을 나타내므로 in that을 so that이나 in order that으로 고쳐야 한다.

05 사역동사 두 개를 같이 썼으므로, made 또는 let 둘 중 한 개만 남긴다. stubborn: 완고한, 고집센

06 <보기>의 단어들을 사용하고, 중복 없이 문맥에 맞게 영작해야 하므로, '목적'의 의미를 표현할 때, 'so that 부사절'과 'in order to 부사구'를 어디에 쓰는 것이 좋을지 결정한다. 허락을 나타내는 사역동사 let도 (2)번 문장에 들어가야 한다.

07 주격 관계대명사 that과 be동사인 are를 함께 생략할 수 있다.

08 'Because of'도 가능하다. thanks to: ~ 덕분에

09 '카사바 칩'은 Maria의 comfort food이다. 그녀가 카사바 칩을 먹을 때 스트레스가 갑자기 사라지고 기분이 다시 좋아진다. 게다가, 칩을 먹을 때 나는 '바삭한 소리'가 그녀의 기분을 더 좋게 만든다.

10 (A) 뒤에 명사가 있으므로 looks like가 적절하다. look like+

|모범답안|

01 (1) What would you like to order?
   (2) Are you ready to order?
   (3) May I take your order?

02 (1) Tim let Sam and Paula shake hands with each other.
   (2) Sam had Tim introduce Paula to him.
   (3) Tim made Sam and Paula end their fight.

03 (A) chocolate   (B) feel bad   (C) didn't do well
   (D) some chocolate   (E) felt better

02 사역동사와 목적보어 자리의 동사원형을 적절히 사용해 내용에 알맞게 구성한다.

01 discomfort   02 (f)ix

03 (b)eat   04 ①   05 ⑤   06 ③

07 (S)tir   08 Dessert   09 ④   10 ①

11 It's for here   12 Yes → No

13 ③   14 ②

15 ⓐ allowed   ⓑ to use   ⓒ played   (A) so that
   ⓓ stay   ⓔ feel

16 ⑤

17 (1) sweep the playground
   (2) to put the can into the recycle bin
   (3) had Kathy pick up a can
   (4) to throw away an empty bottle
   (5) (to) sort the garbage

18 Comfort food is food that makes you feel good when you are sad, angry, or stressed out.

19 Comfort food satisfies the heart as well as the stomach.

20 which is 또는 that is

21 my best friend bought a bag of cassava chips for me

22 ②   23 ④   24 is full of   25 ③

01 appear: 나타나다 – disappear: 사라지다 : comfort: 위로, 위안 – discomfort: 불쾌, 불안

02 fix: 수리하다. 고장 난 것을 고치다

03 beat: 휘젓다, 섞다. 포크나 주방 기계로 신속하게 함께 섞다

04 take an order: 주문을 받다. 저, 여기 음식 주문하려고 하는데요. take a nap: 낮잠을 자다. 나는 오후에는 대개 낮잠을 자요.

05 lately: 최근에, 얼마 전에 recently: 최근에 / 이 부채들은 요즘 관광객들에게 대단히 인기가 있습니다.

06 bake: 굽다, 오븐에서 건열을 이용하여 음식을 조리하다

07 beat: 휘젓다, (휘저어) 섞다 stir: 젓다, (저어 가며) 섞다[넣다]. 밀가루와 우유를 (저어 가며) 함께 섞어라..

08 '식사의 끝에 먹는 과일이나 푸딩같은 달콤한 것'은 '디저트'이다. dessert: 디저트

09 B는 도넛 두 개와 오렌지 주스 하나를 주문하고 있다.

10 place를 take로 고치는 것이 적절하다. take an order: 주문을 받다, place[make] an order: 주문하다

11 'for here'는 '여기(매장)에서 먹겠다'라는 의미이다. It's를 앞에 붙여 쓰면 된다.

12 그것이 전부인지를 묻는 M의 말에 물 두 병을 주문하고 있으므로 Yes를 No로 고치는 것이 적절하다.

13 ① what he passed → that he could pass ② so와 that 사이에 hard가 들어가면 '너무나 열심히 공부해서 결국'이라는 뜻이 된다. ④, ⑤ 둘 다 앞뒤가 안맞는 문장이다.

14 ②번은 4형식 동사로서 '만들어 주다'의 의미이며, ②번을 제외한 나머지는 모두 목적보어 자리에 동사원형을 취하는 5형식의 사역동사 make가 쓰였다.

15 ⓐ when 부사절이 과거시제이므로 과거동사 allowed가 적절하다. ⓑ 'allow+목적어' 뒤에는 to부정사 ⓒ 탁구는 스포츠이므로 played(시제는 과거) ⓓ 조동사 could 뒤에 동사원형 ⓔ 사역동사 made의 목적보어 자리이므로 원형부정사 (A) so that 대신 in order that을 써도 좋다.

16 (가)+(C): Willy는 다른 사람들도 마들렌을 만들 수 있도록 그의 할머니의 요리법을 공유하고 싶었다. (나)+(D): 내 여자친구는 스트레스를 받을 때, 다시 기분이 좋아지도록 종종 카사바 칩을 먹는다. (다)+(A): Trump 씨는 감옥에 가지 않기 위해서 모든 빚을 갚았다. (라)+(B): Carla는 뮤지컬을 보기 위해서 극장까지 택시를 탔다.

17 각 인물에 맞게 5형식 문장을 구성한다. have, make는 목적보어 자리에 동사원형을, ask, get은 to부정사를 활용하여 표현한다. *sweep the ground: 운동장을 빗질로 쓸다 *sort the garbage: 분리수거하다

18 주격 관계대명사 that이 선행사인 food를 수식하도록 배열하는 것이 적절하다.

19 comfort food는 위뿐만 아니라 마음도 충족해 준다. B, not A: A가 아니라 B

20 '주격 관계대명사+be동사'인 'which is' 또는 'that is'가 생략되어 있다.

21 buy는 for를 사용하여 3형식으로 고친다.

22 위 글은 Maria의 스트레스를 사라지게 하고 기분이 다시 좋아지게 만드는 음식에 대한 글이므로, 제목으로는 'Maria의 comfort food는 무엇인가?'가 적절하다.

23 ⓐ make는 for를 사용하여 3형식으로 고친다. ⓑ share A with B: (A를 B와) 함께 쓰다, 공유하다

24 be filled with = be full of: ~로 가득 차다

25 마들렌은 '오븐에서 막 나올 때' 가장 맛있다.

Lesson 3

Stories of English Words and Expressions

시험대비 실력평가
p.120

01 ⑤	02 universe	03 ⑤	04 ①
05 ④	06 ①		

01 동의어 관계이다. source: 근원, origin: 기원, determine: 결정하다, decide: 결심하다

02 '항성과 행성을 포함한 모든 공간'은 'universe(우주, 은하계)'가 적절하다. 그는 우주 기원의 새로운 개념을 발표했다.

03 ① present: 현재의. 우리의 현재 상황은 어렵지만, 우리는 최선을 다할 것이다. ② suggest: 제안하다. 선생님은 우리가 매일 신문을 읽어야 한다고 제안하셨다. ③ justice: 정의. 만약 당신이 좋은 판사가 되기를 원한다면 남을 공정하게 판단하시오. ④ civilization: 문명. 잉카 제국은 매우 발달된 문명이었다. ⑤ myth: 신화. 여느 대단한 신화나 전설처럼 여전히 한 가지 의문점이 남아 있다. legend: 전설

04 origin: 기원, 유래 / 햄버거의 유래는 분명하지 않다.

05 ① originate from: ~에서 비롯되다, 그 영화의 제목은 라틴어 표현에서 유래되었다. ② keep in touch: 연락하다, 나는 너와 계속 연락을 하고 싶지만 방법을 모르겠어. ③ introduce: 소개하다, 새로운 사람들을 소개해 줄 수 있습니다. ④ produce: 생산하다, destroy: 파괴하다, 저희는 그 모델을 더 이상 생산하지 않습니다. ⑤ call ~ after …: …을 본떠 ~의 이름을 부르다, 그들은 첫딸 이름을 아기의 할머니 이름을 따서 지었다.

06 cup of tea: [부정어와 함께; one's ~] 기호[취미]에 맞는 사람[물건], 공포영화는 정말 내 취향이 아니다. break a leg: 행운을 빌다, 그 배우는 나에게 행운을 빈다고 말했다.

서술형 시험대비
p.121

01 (1) flood (2) slave (3) suggest (4) borrow

02 (1) Italian (2) suggestion

03 (1) weather (2) pulling (3) picks (4) passing

04 (1) The teacher was angered by the student's rudeness.
(2) Have you ever experienced cultural differences?

---

(3) If you want to turn on the computer, press this red button.
(4) He passed the exam for entering a law school.

01 (1) flood: 홍수, 평상시 마른 땅을 뒤덮는 많은 물 (2) slave: 노예, 돈을 받지 않고 다른 사람에게 소유되어 그들을 위하여 일하는 사람 (3) suggest: 제안하다, 무엇을 해야 하는지를 누군가에게 말하다 (4) borrow: 빌리다, 누군가에게 속한 것을 사용하고 나중에 되돌려 주어야만 하다

02 (1) '나라 이름 – 형용사/언어'의 관계이다. China 중국 – Chinese 중국의; 중국어, Italy: 이탈리아 – Italian: 이탈리아의; 이탈리아어 (2) '동사 - 명사' 관계이다. decide: 결심하다 – decision: 결심, suggest 제안하다 – suggestion 제안

03 (1) under the weather: 몸이 안 좋은 (2) pull one's leg: 놀리다 (3) pick up: ~을 익히게 되다 (4) pass through: 거쳐 지나가다

04 (1) anger: 화나게 하다, 수동태가 적절하므로 was를 추가한다. (2) experience: 경험하다, 현재완료가 적절하므로 have를 추가한다. (3) press: 누르다, on을 추가한다. turn on: 켜다 (4) law: 법, law를 추가한다. law school: 법학 대학원

교과서

Conversation

핵심 Check
p.122~123

1 What does that mean
2 (D) → (B) → (C) → (A)

교과서 대화문 익히기

Check(√) True or False
p.124~125

1 F 2 T 3 T 4 F 5 T 6 F 7 T 8 F

교과서 확인학습
p.127~129

Listen and Talk A 1

cats and dogs / cats and dogs, that mean / means, a lot / worry

Listen and Talk A 2

on me / Excuse me, Can, say that / on me, pay for / a lot / You're welcome

Listen and Talk A 3

delicious / Would, like some / not, tea / Not, tea / don't like something / see

Listen and Talk A 4

under the weather / Excuse me, can, say that again / under the weather, don't feel well / Why don't you, get, get / should

Listen and Talk B 1

make a long face / Excuse me, can you please say that again / make a long face / What does that mean / feel sad

Listen and Talk B 2

Break a leg / Excuse me, can you please say that again / Break a leg / What does that mean / Good luck

Listen and Talk B 3

under the weather / Excuse me, can you please say that again / under the weather / What does that mean

Listen and Talk C

had a great time / My pleasure, come visit / love to, like to invite / it, that, come / longer, keep my fingers crossed / Excuse me, can you, say that again / keep my fingers crossed, wish you good luck / Have, trip / keep in touch

Review 1

keep my fingers crossed / can you please say that again / keep my fingers crossed, wish you good luck

Review 2

feel under the weather / can you please say that again / feel under the weather / What does that mean / don't feel well / Why don't you buy / will

Review 3

cats and dogs / Can you say that again / cats and dogs / What does that mean / a lot

Review 4

is on me / What does that mean / pay for

시험대비 기본평가　　　　　　　　　p.130

01 It's raining cats and dogs.　　　　02 ④

03 ③　　　　　　04 Can you say that again?

01 'It's raining cats and dogs.'는 '비가 아주 많이 내린다.'라는 뜻이다.

02 'What does that mean?'은 '그게 무슨 뜻이니?'라는 뜻으로 상대방이 한 말의 의미를 설명해 달라고 요청할 때 쓰는 표현이

다.

03 'That's alright.'은 상대방이 'I'm sorry.'로 미안함을 표한 것에 대한 답으로 쓰는 표현이다.

04 'Can you say that again?'은 반복해서 말해 줄 것을 요청할 때 쓰는 표현이다.

시험대비 실력평가　　　　　　　　　p.131~132

01 ④　　　　　　　　02 ②

03 I don't like something.

04 What does that mean?

05 ⑤　　　　06 ⑤　　　07 Don't feel sad.

08 ③　　　　09 ④

10 can you please say that again　　　11 ②

12 I wish you good luck.　　13 ⑤

01 무슨 뜻인지 묻는 말에 했던 말을 반복하는 것은 어색하다. A와 B를 서로 바꿔야 한다.

02 다음에 나오는 말들로 보아 B는 스파게티를 안 좋아하므로 ② 번이 가장 적절하다.

03 뒤에 이어서 소녀가 'You don't like spaghetti.'라고 하고 있으므로 좋아하지 않는다고 했음을 알 수 있다.

04 What does that mean?: 상대방이 한 말의 의미를 설명해 달라고 요청할 때 쓰는 표현이다.

05 소녀가 'Oh, I see.'라고 하고 있으므로 이해했음을 알 수 있다.

06 빈칸 다음에서 앞에서 한 말을 다시 하고 있으므로 빈칸에는 다시 한 번 반복해서 말해 줄 것을 요청하는 말이 자연스럽다.

07 Don't make a long face. = Don't feel sad.: 슬퍼하지 마.

08 반복해서 설명해 줄 것을 요청하는 주어진 문장에 이어, (C)에서 다시 한 번 말해 주고, (B)에서 한 말의 의미를 설명해 달라고 요청하고, (A)에서 설명해 주고, (D)에서 '약을 좀 사라'고 제안한 후, 그렇게 하겠다는 말로 마무리한다.

09 'You can say that again.'은 동의할 때 쓰는 말로 적절하지 않다.

10 이어지는 말로 보아 빈칸 (B)에는 다시 한 번 반복해서 말해줄 것을 요청하는 질문이 적절하다.

11 '즐거운 여행이 되길 바란다'는 말에 고맙다며 '연락하겠다.'라고 하는 말이 적절하다.

12 I wish you good luck.은 행운을 비는 표현이다.

13 밑줄 친 문장은 다시 말해 줄 것을 요청할 때 쓰는 표현이다.

서술형 시험대비　　　　　　　　　p.133

01 (D) → (B) → (C) → (A)

02 Please come visit me again

23

03 It's because she can't stay longer. 또는 It's because she has to leave now.

04 I don't feel well.

05 Because she has a cold.

06 They are at the airport.

07 This pizza is on me   08 for

01 축구 시합에 올 수 없어서 너무 안타깝다는 문장에 이어서, 유감이라며 행운을 빈다는 (D)가 나오고, 다시 말해줄 것을 요청하는 (B)가 나오고, 다시 말해주는 (C)가 나오고, 고맙다며 즐거운 여행이 되길 바라는 (A)에 이어, 고맙다며 연락하겠다고 하는 순서가 적절하다.

02 'come visit'는 'come and visit' 또는 'come to visit'으로도 쓸 수 있다.

03 Lucy는 '더 오래 머물 수 없어서 유감이야.'라고 하고 있고 마지막에 '즐거운 여행이 되길 바랄게.'라고 하고 있으므로 헤어지면서 하는 대화임을 알 수 있다.

04 'I feel under the weather.'의 뜻인 'I don't feel well.'을 쓰면 된다.

05 소녀는 'I think I have a cold.'라고 말하고 있다.

06 소년이 '비행기 타기 전에 약을 좀 사는 게 어때?'라고 하는 것으로 보아 공항에 있다는 것을 추측할 수 있다.

07 '~ is on me'는 '내가 내겠다.'라는 의미이다.

08 'pay for'는 '~에 대한 값을 지불하다'라는 뜻이다.

교과서
Grammar

핵심 Check
p.134~135

1 (1) which (2) which

2 (1) that (2) that

시험대비 기본평가
p.136

01 (1) that → which (2) it → 삭제, 또는 which → and
(3) which → who (4) and → 생략, 또는 which → it

02 ③   03 ②

04 It is thought that the origin of the first hamburger is not clear.

01 (1) 콤마가 있는 계속적 용법의 관계대명사 자리이므로 that이 아닌 which가 적절하다. (2) 관계대명사가 있을 때는 관계대명사가 대신 받는 주어 또는 목적어 자리는 생략된다. 그러므로 it을 생략하는 게 적절하다. 단, which 대신 접속사 and를 쓸 경

우에는 it을 생략하지 않는다. (3) 인간을 창조한 신들이 선행사이므로 관계대명사는 who가 적절하다. (4) 접속사 and가 있을 때에는 which로 바꾸지 않고, 대명사 it을 그대로 쓰는 것이 적절하다. and를 생략하고 관계대명사절을 쓰는 것도 좋다.

02 ③번을 포함 모두 가주어-진주어 구문의 It으로 시작했다. 그러나 다른 것은 진주어절을 이끄는 접속사 that이지만, ③은 명사 book을 수식하는 지시형용사 that이다. 동명사 reading이 진주어로 쓰였다.

03 계속적 용법의 관계대명사로서, 선행사는 작품명인 Sunflowers이다. which가 적절하다.

04 원래 문장에서의 that절이 think의 목적어로 쓰였으므로, 주어로 바꿔 수동태로 만들면 That the origin of the first hamburger is not clear is thought.가 된다. 진주어로 하는 것이 조건이므로, 가주어 It으로 시작하면, 정답과 같이 되는데, 이 때 일반인 주어 people을 수동태에서 by people로 표시할 필요는 없다.

시험대비 실력평가
p.137~139

01 ⓐ have → has ⓑ who → which,
ⓒ which → and 또는 such food 생략,
ⓔ which → who

02 ②

03 it is true that Mat cheated on the exam

04 ④   05 ①   06 ⑤   07 ④

08 My friends know Jasmine, who has no math problems that can't be solved.

09 ⑤   10 ⑤

11 It is important that they (should) learn many words of foreign origin.   12 ②

13 I want to visit the British Museum, which is in London.

14 ④   15 ①

16 It is surprising that the pizza was made by Jane, who is only 7.

17 ②, ③, ⑤

01 ⓐ 선행사가 the Louvre이므로 관계대명사 뒤의 동사는 단수 취급 ⓑ 선행사가 사람이 아니므로 which가 적절. ⓒ 관계대명사 뒤에는 불완전한 절이다. 목적어를 생략하거나, which를 접속사 and로 수정해야 한다. ⓔ 사람이 선행사이다.

02 ②번의 that은 It ~ that 강조구문으로 쓰였다. 나머지는 모두 가주어 It과 진주어 명사절의 접속사 that이다.

03 동사의 시제 cheated에 유의하여, 가주어 it과 that절을 활용해서 글자 수에 맞게 영작한다.

04 내용상 기술자에게 노트북의 수리를 맡겼고, '그 기술자가 노트북을 수리한 것'이 '비용이 들게 하다'라는 의미의 동사 cost의

주어가 되는 선행사이므로, 관계대명사 which가 적절하다.

05 영작하면, 'It is interesting that the idea of using the word *robot* didn't come from the author himself.'이다.

06 ⑤번은 'It ~ that' 강조구문이다. 나머지는 모두 가주어 It과 진주어 명사절을 이끄는 접속사 that이 쓰였다.

07 ④번은 가주어 It과 진주어 명사절을 이끄는 접속사 that이 쓰였다. 나머지는 모두 'It ~ that' 강조구문이다.

08 계속적 관계대명사 who까지는 어렵지 않은데 has no math problems that can't be solved에 유의해야 한다.

09 내용상 '올림픽이 서울에서 개최된' 1988년을 선행사로 받는 관계대명사이므로, 관계대명사 앞에 in이 있어야 한다. Seoul 앞의 in과는 무관하다. which를 in which 또는 관계부사 when으로 바꿔야 한다.

10 빈칸은 모두 관계사가 들어가는 자리이다. 선행사는 각각 (A) a girl, (B) a button, (C) 1517이다. 1517은 연도이고, 뒤에 완전한 절이므로 관계부사 when 또는 in which가 적절하다.

11 명사절 접속사 that과 주어 they를 활용하여 영작한다. 내용상 당위의 should가 필요한데, 생략 가능하기 때문에 쓰지 않아도 된다.

12 ①, ③은 앞 문장 전체가 선행사이므로, ④번은 불필요한 of를 삭제하고, 계속적 용법의 관계대명사 which가 적절하다. ⑤번은 동사의 수의 일치가 틀렸다. ① that → which, ③ who → which, ④ of which → which, ⑤ come → comes

13 문맥상 방문을 원하는 곳과 위치에 대한 설명을 해야 하므로, 대영박물관 뒤에 which is in London을 쓴다.

14 ④번을 제외한 모든 문장에는 진주어 명사절을 이끄는 접속사 that이 쓰였고, 다른 단어로 대체 불가능하다. ④에는 'It ~ that' 강조구문이 쓰였고, 강조되는 명사의 성격에 따라 that을 who/which로, 부사(구/절)이 강조될 때는 when/where로 대체 가능하다. ④는 where로 대체할 수 있다.

15 옳은 문장은 ⑥ 1개이다. ⓐ that → which 또는 and it, ⓑ were → was, ⓒ which → that ⓓ who → which, ⓔ and who → who 또는 and he

16 진주어 접속사 that과 '계속적' 용법의 관계대명사 who를 사용하여, 문맥에 맞게 배열한다.

17 ② 앞 문장 전체가 선행사이므로, 관계대명사는 that이 아닌 which가 적절하다. ③ 사람이 선행사이므로 who를 써야 한다. ⑤ 가주어-진주어 구문이라면 that 뒤가 완전한 절이 되어야 한다. 강조구문이 될 수도 없는 잘못된 문장이다.

서술형 시험대비
p.140~141

01 amazing that an old lady who can't remember anything sings along

02 (1) Mom said, "I feel under the weather," which means "I don't feel well."

(2) Emma is a coffee trader, who buys and sells coffee.

(3) I learned the expression, "This is on me," which refers to "I'll pay for this."

03 (1) of → for (2) for → of (3) what → that
(4) of → for (5) excited → exciting

04 It is interesting that some animals such as beavers can use tools.

05 (1) which → it[that] 또는 but 삭제
(2) which → and 또는 such food 삭제
(3) who → which
(4) that → which
(5) it → and it, 또는 it → which

06 It is true that many English words came from different peoples.

07 (1) Robot comes from roboti , which means 'slave workers' in Czech.

(2) Most people in the temple stop working every three hours, who pray to their god.

(3) Hamburger comes from Hamburg, which is the second-largest city in Germany.

(4) Amy uses shampoo every day to wash her dog, which[who] doesn't like it.

(5) Wendy received a massage from her aunt, but it didn't make her feel better.

(6) The castle looked quite modern, though[but] it was built in the 8th century.

(7) Maria loves Spanish food, which actually is not Spanish but Mayan.

---

01 '어떤 것도 기억 못하는 할머니가 자신의 어린 시절 노래를 따라 부르는 것은 놀랍다'는 내용이다. 가주어-진주어 구문을 활용하여, 주어진 단어들을 적절히 배열한다.

02 (1), (3)과 (2)의 차이는 '선행사가 사람인지 아닌지'이다. (2)는 선행사가 사람이다. *refer to:~을 지칭하다, 언급하다

03 (1), (2), (4) to부정사구가 진주어로 쓰인 가주어-진주어 구문이다. 일반적으로 '의미상 주어'는 to부정사 앞에 'for+목적격'으로 쓰지만, 사람의 성품이나 성질에 관한 형용사가 있을 경우 'of+목적격'으로 써야 한다. (3) what 대신 가주어-진주어 구문의 접속사 that을 써야 한다. (5) 주어가 사람이 아니라 that절이므로 excited가 아닌, exciting을 써야 한다.

04 가주어-진주어 형식이므로 It is interesting으로 시작해서 that절을 이끄는 것이 핵심이 되는 영작 문제이다. some animals such as beavers의 어순과 글자 수에 유의한다.

05 (1) 앞 문장 전체가 선행사이므로 접속사 but을 삭제하거나, 앞 문장 전체를 받는 대명사로 바꾸는 것이 적절하다. (2) 관계대명사 which를 쓰면, such food를 없애야 한다. 아니면, which를 접속사 and로 바꿔도 어법상 맞다. (3) 선행사가 요가 동작이므로

which가 적절하다. (4) 앞 문장 전체가 선행사이고, 콤마가 있으므로 that을 which로 해야 한다. (5) 접속사가 없으므로 and를 넣어 주거나 it을 관계대명사 which로 바꿔야 한다.

06 가주어-진주어 형태로 적절하게 배열하되, peoples의 형태에 유의하도록 한다. people은 a people, peoples와 같은 형태로 쓰면 국민, 민족의 의미가 있다.

07 접속사와 대명사는 계속적 용법의 관계대명사로 바꿀 수 있다. (4)의 dog은 관점에 따라 which, who 둘 다 가능하므로 어느 것을 써도 틀리지 않으며, (6)의 접속사 though도 내용상 but으로 써도 괜찮다.

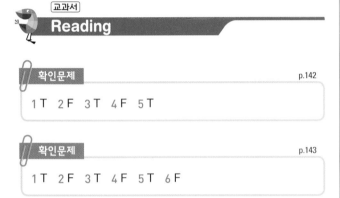

Reading

확인문제　　　　　　　　　　p.142

1 T　2 F　3 T　4 F　5 T

확인문제　　　　　　　　　　p.143

1 T　2 F　3 T　4 F　5 T　6 F

교과서 확인학습 A　　　　　　p.144~145

01 Foreign Origin
02 borrowed words, other cultures
03 with interesting stories
04 from, to press　　　05 was used
06 with a head massage　07 a few times, entered
08 present, washing the hair
09 Shortly after that, to be also used
10 was written　　　　11 look like
12 are designed, are produced
13 the idea of using, himself
14 from, for　　　　　15 However, in Czech
16 to use　　　　　　17 was made into
18 originates from
19 creation myth, gods, created
20 angered, so, caused　21 Spanish contact with
22 passing through, picked up, for it
23 In English, uses, by
24 originally, second-largest
25 in German　　　　26 is not clear
27 it is believed that, between, and
28 placed, Hamburg-style, two slices of bread, such food

교과서 확인학습 B　　　　　　p.146~147

1 English Words of Foreign Origin
2 English has often borrowed words from other cultures or languages.
3 Here are some examples with interesting stories.
4 The word *shampoo* comes from the Hindi word *chāmpo*, which means "to press."
5 In India, the word was used for a head massage.
6 British traders in India experienced a bath with a head massage and introduced it to Britain in the 18th century.
7 The meaning of the word *shampoo* changed a few times after it first entered English around 1762.
8 In the 19th century, *shampoo* got its present meaning of "washing the hair."
9 Shortly after that, the word began to be also used for a special soap for the hair.
10 The word *robot* comes from the play *R.U.R.*, which was written in 1920 by a Czech writer Karel Čapek.
11 In the play, robots are machines that look like humans.
12 They are designed to work for humans and are produced in a factory.
13 It is interesting that the idea of using the word *robot* didn't come from Karel Čapek himself.
14 He originally called the machines in his play *labori* from the Latin word for "work."
15 However, his brother suggested *roboti*, which means "slave workers" in Czech.
16 Karel Čapek liked the idea and decided to use the word *roboti*.
17 In 1938, the play was made into a science fiction show on television in Britain.
18 The word *hurricane* comes from the Spanish word *huracán*, which originates from the name of a Mayan god.
19 In the Mayan creation myth, Huracán is the weather god of wind, storm, and fire, and he is one of the three gods who created humans.
20 However, the first humans angered the gods, so Huracán caused a great flood.
21 The first Spanish contact with the Mayan civilization was in 1517.
22 Spanish explorers who were passing through the Caribbean experienced a hurricane and picked up the word for it from the people in the area.

23 In English, one of the early uses of *hurricane* was in a play by Shakespeare in 1608.

24 The word *hamburger* originally comes from Hamburg, Germany's second-largest city.

25 *Hamburger* means "people or things from Hamburg" in German.

26 The origin of the first hamburger is not clear.

27 However, it is believed that the hamburger was invented in a small town in Texas, USA, sometime between 1885 and 1904.

28 A cook placed a Hamburg-style steak between two slices of bread, and people started to call such food a hamburger.

시험대비 실력평가
p.148~151

01 ⑤　　02 and it　　03 ①　　04 ④

05 (A) Hamburg　(B) *hamburger*　(C) Hamburg

06 robots are machines that look like humans

07 ⑤　　08 They were called *labori*.　09 ②

10 (A) weather　(B) great flood

11 the Caribbean　　12 ②, ⑤

13 *chāmpo*　14 ③　　15 ②　　16 ①

17 ④　　18 It's the name of a Mayan god.

19 (A) so　(B) were　(C) was　　20 ⑤

21 Germany's second-largest city　　22 ①

01 ⓐ from: (출처, 기원) ~에서 온, ⓑ introduce A to B: B에게 A를 소개하다

02 which는 *chāmpo*를 선행사로 하는 관계대명사로 계속적 용법으로 쓰였다. 계속적 용법의 관계대명사는 '접속사+대명사'로 바꿔 쓸 수 있다.

03 영어가 다른 문화나 언어에게 '빌려준' 많은 단어를 가지고 있는 것이 아니라, 영어가 종종 다른 문화나 언어에서 단어를 '빌려왔다'고 되어 있다. ② originate in/from: ~에서 유래하다

04 ④ two slices of bread: 빵 두 조각, ② lump: (보통 특정한 형태가 없는) 덩어리, a lump of sugar(각설탕 한 개), ③ (초콜릿·비누 등 막대기같이 생긴 것을 가리켜) 바[막대/개], a bar of chocolate/soap(초콜릿/비누 한 개)

05 '함부르크'는 독일에서 두 번째로 큰 도시의 이름이고, *hamburger*라는 단어는 독일어로 '함부르크' 출신의 사람 또는 사물을 의미한다.

06 look like: …처럼 보이다

07 ⓑ와 ⑤: 가주어, ① 가목적어, ② [사정·상황을 막연히 가리키는] 비인칭 주어, ③ 문장의 어떤 부분을 강조할 때 쓰는 대명사, ④ 그것(앞에 이미 언급되었거나 현재 이야기되고 있는 사

물·동물을 가리킴)

08 *labori*라고 불렸다.

09 ③번의 the gods는 ①번에서 언급한 the three gods를 가리키며, 그 사이의 '매년 허리케인이 카리브 제도 근처의 많은 지역에 해를 끼친다.'는 ②번 문장은 전체 글의 흐름에서 벗어난다.

10 마야의 창조 신화에 따르면, '날씨'의 신이며 인간을 창조한 세 명의 신들 중 한 명인 Huracán은 최초의 인간들이 신들을 화나게 했기 때문에 '거대한 홍수'를 일으켰다.

11 '카리브 제도'를 가리킨다.

12 ⓐ와 ②, ⑤: 경험 용법(ever, never, once, twice, how many times, before, often 등과 함께 쓰임,), ① 결과 용법, ③ 계속 용법, ④ 완료 용법

13 the word는 '*chāmpo*'를 가리킨다.

14 '이 글은 다른 문화나 언어에서 유래된 영어 단어 중 *shampoo*라는 단어의 기원과 의미 변화에 관한 내용이므로, 제목으로는 ③번 '*shampoo*라는 단어에 대한 재미있는 이야기를 소개해 드리겠습니다.'가 적절하다.

15 ⓐ word for ~: ~에 해당하는 단어, ~을 의미하는 단어, ⓑ in: 언어, 재료 등을 나타냄, in Czech: 체코어로

16 (A)와 ①: 동격 관계, ② [성질·상태] ~의, ~을 지닌, ③ [재료] ~으로 (만든), ~으로 (된), ④ [분리·박탈] ~을, ⑤ [기원·출처] ~으로부터, ~의

17 *labori*라는 단어가 얼마나 오래 사용되었는지는 알 수 없다. ① In the play *R.U.R.* ② It indicated a machine that looked like a human. indicate: 가리키다, 지칭하다 ③ A Czech writer Karel Čapek used it. ⑤ It means "work" in Latin.

18 스페인어 단어 *huracán*의 기원은 마야 신의 이름이다.

19 (A) 최초의 인간들이 신들을 '화나게 해서' Huracán은 거대한 홍수를 일으켰다고 해야 하므로 so가 적절하다. (B) 선행사가 Spanish explorers이므로 were가 적절하다. (C) 'one of the+복수 명사'에서 주어가 단수(one)이므로 동사는 was가 적절하다.

20 ⑤는 'a hurricane'을 가리킨다.

21 second-largest: 두 번째로 큰

22 이 글은 '*hamburger*라는 단어와 햄버거라는 음식이 만들어지게 된 기원'을 소개하는 글이므로, 주제로는 ①번 '*hamburger*라는 단어와 최초의 햄버거의 기원'이 적절하다.

서술형 시험대비
p.152~153

01 Spanish　02 one of the early uses of hurricane

03 (A) Huracán　(B) *huracán*　(C) *hurricane*

04 (A) first hamburger　(B)Hamburg-style steak

05 (A) borrowed　(B) massage　(C) times

06 did not change at all → changed a few times

07 (A) to press　(B) head massage

08 which a Czech writer Karel Čapek wrote in 1920

09 using the word *robot*

10 (A) *labori*　(B) *roboti*　(C) science fiction show

01 Spanish: 스페인의(형용사); 스페인어(명사)

02 one of the+복수 명사: ~ 중의 하나

03 (1) 마야어에서: 마야의 창조 신화에서 마야의 신 'Huracán'은 날씨의 신이다. (2) 스페인어에서: 스페인어 단어 'huracán'은 스페인 탐험가들이 카리브 제도를 지나는 동안 그들이 겪었던 허리케인을 의미하는 단어를 그 지역 사람들로부터 듣게 되었다. (3) 영어에서: 'hurricane'이라는 단어는 huracán이라는 단어에서 왔고, 1608년 셰익스피어에 의해 그의 희곡에서 사용되었다.

04 1885년에서 1904년 사이의 언젠가 미국 텍사스에 있는 작은 마을에서 한 요리사가 빵 두 조각 사이에 '함부르크 스타일의 스테이크'를 넣어 '최초의 햄버거'를 발명했다.

05 (A) 다른 문화나 언어에서 단어를 '빌려왔다'고 해야 하므로 borrowed가 적절하다. borrow: 빌리다, lend: 빌려주다, (B) 머리 '마사지'라고 해야 하므로 massage가 적절하다. message: 메시지[메일/문자], (C) '몇 번' 바뀌었다고 해야 하므로 times가 적절하다. a few times: 몇 번, a few hours: 몇 시간

06 *shampoo*라는 단어의 의미는 그 단어가 1762년쯤 영어에 처음으로 들어온 이후 '몇 번 바뀌었다.'

07 힌디어 *chāmpo*는 '누르다'를 의미하고, 인도에서는 그 단어를 '머리 마사지'라는 의미로 썼다.

08 계속적 용법의 관계대명사는 목적격이라도 생략할 수 없다.

09 '*robot*이라는 단어를 사용하는 것'을 가리킨다. 동격 관계의 전치사 of 다음에 나오는 'using the word *robot*'을 가리킨다.

10 (1) 1920년, "*R.U.R.*"이라는 연극에서 체코의 작가 Karel Čapek이 인간처럼 생긴 기계를 '*labori*'라고 불렀다. (2) Karel의 형이 *labori* 대신 '*roboti*'를 사용할 것을 제안했다. (3) 1938년에 "*R.U.R.*"이라는 연극은 영국 TV에서 '공상 과학물'로 만들어졌다.

영역별 핵심문제　　　　　　p.155~159

01 ①　　　　02 picked up　03 trader / originally

04 (l)aw / (o)rigin / (1) law　(2) origin

05 (A) Vietnamese　(B) French　(C) Irish　06 ⑤

07 Will you have some of my spaghetti? /

Do you want (to have) some of my spaghetti?

08 ③　　　　09 It's raining a lot.

10 Because he has an umbrella in his backpack.

11 ④　　　　12 The girl will pay for the juice.

13 ④　　14 ④　　15 ①　　16 ④

17 ③　　18 ①　　19 ⑤

20 My father made a family motto, which would remind us the love between family members that had never been thought of before.

21 ④　　22 was used　23 ③　　24 ②

25 (A) interesting　(B) to use　(C) into

26 ③　　27 ④

01 ① 넌 그런 아이디어가 언제 생각났니? ② 이 훌륭한 전통은 어디에서 유래됐을까? ③ 요가는 인도에서 유래했다. ④ 많은 모래 폭풍은 몽골에서 유래된다. ⑤ 스팸 메일의 발원지가 어느 국가인가?

02 '의도하지 않고 새로운 기술을 배우거나 버릇을 시작하다'라는 의미로 'pick up(~을 익히게 되다)'이 적절하다.

03 (1) 주어로 명사가 나오는 것이 적절하다. 동사에 er을 붙여 명사가 된 어휘인데, 동사가 e로 끝나므로 r만 붙인다. trader: 상인, 거래자. 그 상인은 제조업자로부터 직접 제품을 구매했다. (2) 문장 구성상 부사가 적절하다. originally: 원래, 본래 / 명사 origin에 al을 붙여 형용사가 되고 거기에 ly를 붙여 부사가 된 어휘이다. 내 가족은 원래 멕시코에서 왔다.

04 (1) law: 법, 사회나 정부가 범죄 등을 다루기 위해 개발한 규칙의 체계. 누구나 법 앞에 평등하다. (2) origin: 기원, 유래, 무엇인가의 시작, 근거 또는 근원. 토성 고리의 기원은 아직도 알려지지 않았다. Saturn: 토성

05 Vietnam - Vietnamese, France - French, Ireland - Irish 각 나라와 그 나라의 형용사형이나 언어, 사람으로 쓰이는 어휘이다.

06 모든 것이 맛있어 보인다는 말에 이어, 그렇다면 스파게티를 좀 먹겠는지 묻고(D), 괜찮다며 스파게티는 'not my cup of tea'라고 하자(B), 그게 무슨 뜻인지 묻고(C), 의미를 설명해 주고(A), 알겠다고 답하며 주어진 문장으로 이어지는 것이 적절하다.

07 Would you like ~? = Will you have ~? = Do you want (to have) ~?

08 약을 좀 사는 게 어떠냐는 말에 '너는 그렇게 해야 한다.'고 대답하는 것은 어색하다. 'I guess I should.'가 적절하다.

09 'It's raining cats and dogs.'는 'It's raining a lot.'과 같은 의미이다.

10 소년이 소녀에게 '걱정 마.'라고 한 이유는 배낭에 우산이 있기 때문이다.

11 다시 한 번 말해 달라는 말에, 다시 한 번 말해 주고 나서 그 의미를 설명하는 것이 자연스러우므로 ④번이 적절하다.

12 첫 문장에서 소녀가 'This juice is on me, Suho.'라고 하고 있다.

13 소녀가 'This juice is on me, Suho.'라고 말하고 있는 것으로

보아 주스를 마셨음을 짐작할 수 있다.

14 ① that → who ② what → which[that] ③ which → who ⑤ what → which[that]

15 의문사절은 that절처럼 가주어-진주어 구문의 주어로 쓸 수 있다. ①번의 that은 불필요하므로, 삭제해야 한다.

16 ① 선행사가 있으므로 what 대신 that 또는 which가 적절하다 ② it 불필요 ③ which 뒤에 동사 is 필요 ⑤ and 불필요

17 ① and 불필요 ② it 불필요 ④ 내용상 which를 명사절을 이끄는 접속사 that으로 고치는 것이 적절하다 ⑤ knows는 단수 동사이다. 주어가 all of whom이므로 복수동사가 적절하다.

18 ①번의 that은 'It ~ that' 강조구문의 that이다. 나머지는 모두 가주어-진주어 구문에서 진주어 역할을 하는 명사절 접속사 that으로 사용되었다.

19 <보기>의 which는 '계속적 용법'의 관계대명사로 사용되었다. ⑤번의 which는 의문형용사로서 '어느'라는 뜻이다. 나머지는 모두 관계대명사로 사용되었다.

20 본문에 나온 표현만으로 계속적, 제한적 관계대명사를 모두 사용해야 하기 때문에, 보충 설명이 필요한 두 번째 문장을 계속적 용법의 'which'로 연결하고, 수동태 형태의 세 번째 문장을 제한적 용법의 'that'으로 연결하는 것이 적절하다. *family motto: 가훈

21 buy and sell → buys and sells

22 인도에서 그 단어는 머리 마사지라는 의미로 '쓰였다'고 해야 하므로 수동태로 쓰는 것이 적절하다.

23 ③ Shortly는 '곧, 얼마 안 있어'라는 뜻이다.

24 이 글은 shampoo라는 단어의 기원과 의미 변화에 관한 내용이므로, 주제로는 ②번 'shampoo라는 단어의 기원과 의미'가 적절하다.

25 (A) 감정을 나타내는 동사는 감정을 유발할 때 현재분사를 쓰는 것이 적절하므로 interesting이 적절하다. (B) decide는 목적어로 to부정사를 취하므로 to use가 적절하다. (C) 공상 과학물에 의해 만들어진 것이 아니라, '공상 과학물로 만들어지게 된', 즉 '공상 과학물이 된' 것이므로 into가 적절하다. be made into ~: ~이 …으로 만들어지다

26 ⓐ와 ③: 강조의 의미, ①, ⑤: 관용어구, by oneself: 홀로(alone), for oneself: 혼자 힘으로, ②, ④: 재귀적 용법(주어와 목적어가 같은 경우)

27 The word *roboti* means "slave workers" in Czech.

단원별 예상문제
p.160~163

01 ②   02 ③
03 experience(d) / experience
04 (1) (s)lice   (2) slaves   (3) flood
05 Why don't you buy   06 get   07 ④
08 I'm in trouble.   09 We ate a lot.

10 ④   11 (1) ⓑ (2) ⓐ (3) ⓑ (4) ⓐ (5) ⓑ
12 ⑤
13 It was foolish of the donkey to deceive its master.
14 빵 두 조각 사이에 함부르크 스타일의 스테이크를 넣은 음식
15 ④   16 (A) Hamburg   (B) Hamburg-style
17 ⓐ are designed   ⓑ are produced
18 (A) ②, ③, ⑤   (B) ①, ④   19 (A) *labori*   (B) *roboti*
20 ①   21 ②, ⑤
22 a bath with a head massage   23 ②
24 (A) between two slices of bread
    (B) a card game

01 ②번은 반의어 관계이다. 나머지는 모두 동의어 관계이다. include: 포함하다, exclude: 제외하다 ① trader: 상인, 거래자, merchant: 상인 ③ present: 현재의, current: 현재의 ④ suggest: 제안하다, propose: 제안하다 ⑤ design: 설계하다, devise: 고안하다

02 ① be in hot water: 곤경에 처하다, 그는 차를 훔쳐서 법적 곤경에 처했다. ② pig out: 돼지 같이 먹다, 내가 좋아하는 요리들을 엄마가 만들어 놔서 엄청 먹었어. ③ a piece of cake: 식은 죽 먹기, 그 코스가 점수 따기 쉽다는 얘길 들었어. ④ keep fingers crossed: 행운을 빌다, 새로 하는 사업이 잘 되길 빌어. ⑤ see eye to eye: 의견을 같이하다, 그들은 서로 뜻이 맞지 않는다.

03 experience: 경험하다(동); 경험(명). 우리는 홍수 때문에 힘든 시기를 경험했다. 헤밍웨이는 후에 이탈리아에서의 그의 경험에 대해 썼다.

04 (1) slice: 얇게 썬 조각, 한 조각 (2) slave: 노예 (3) flood: 홍수

05 'Why don't you ~?'는 '권유'하는 표현으로 'How about ~?', 'What about ~?', 'What do you say to ~?' 등으로 바꿔 쓸 수 있다.

06 get on: 타다, get: 얻다, 입수하다, 사다

07 소녀가 비행기에 탄 후, 무엇을 할 것인지는 알 수 없다.

08 'I'm in hot water.'는 '나 지금 곤경에 빠졌어.'라는 의미로 'I'm in trouble.'을 의미한다고 할 수 있다.

09 'We pigged out.'은 '엄청 많이 먹었어요.'라는 의미로 'We ate a lot.'을 의미한다고 할 수 있다.

10 관계대명사는 접속사와 대명사 역할이므로, 뒤에 불완전한 절이 온다. ④번의 it을 삭제하는 것이 적절하다.

11 (1), (3), (5)는 'It ~ that' 강조 구문이고 (2), (4)는 접속사 that이 이끄는 진주어 명사절이 쓰였다.

12 ⑤번의 선행사는 fire가 아니라 '앞 문장 전체'이다. Jim은 불을 두려워하지 않았고, 그것(Jim이 불을 두려워하지 않음)이 그가 소방관이 되는 것을 가능하게 했다.

13 가주어-진주어 형태로 배열할 때, to부정사가 진주어가 된다. 의미상 주어가 당나귀이므로 전치사 for를 넣기 쉬운데, foolish로 보아 of를 추가하는 것이 적절하다.

14 그런 음식은 '한 요리사가 빵 두 조각 사이에 함부르크 스타일의 스테이크를 넣은 음식'을 가리킨다.

15 최초의 햄버거의 기원은 분명하지 않다.

16 *hamburger*는 독일어로 '함부르크' 출신의 사람 또는 사물을 의미하는데, 이 음식은 빵 두 조각 사이에 '함부르크 스타일'의 스테이크를 넣어 만들었기 때문이다.

17 robots는 설계되거나 생산되는 것이므로 수동태(ⓐ are designed, ⓑ are produced)로 쓰는 것이 적절하다.

18 (A)와 ②, ③, ⑤: 관계대명사, (B)와 ①, ④: 접속사

19 "*R.U.R.*"이라는 연극에서 인간처럼 생긴 기계들이 원래 *labori*라고 불렸지만, *roboti*로 변경되었다.

20 주어진 문장의 the word에 주목한다. ①번 앞 문장의 *chāmpo*를 가리키므로 ①번이 적절하다.

21 ⓐ와 ②, ⑤: ~에서 유래하다, come from = derive from = be derived from도 같은 뜻이다. ④ come up with: ~을 생각해 내다

22 '머리 마사지를 함께하는 목욕'을 가리킨다.

23 after: ~을 따라서

24 단어 *sandwich*는 샌드위치 백작 4세에게서 유래했는데, 그는 먹는 동안에 '카드 게임'을 하기 위하여 '빵 두 조각 사이에' 고기를 끼워서 먹는 것을 즐겼기 때문이다.

🦉 **서술형 실전문제** p.164~165

01 Excuse me

02 She invites him to London.

03 He is seeing off Lucy.

04 which means she wishes you good luck

05 it is believed that the hamburger was invented in a small town in Texas, USA.

06 entered into → entered

07 the word *chāmpo*

08 (A) a head massage   (B) washing the hair
   (C) a special soap for the hair

09 *roboti → labori, labori → roboti*

10 (A) Latin   (B) slave workers

01 '누군가를 짜증나게 할지도 모를 어떤 것을 하거나 말하기 전에 사용되는' 말은 'Excuse me.'이다.

02 'I'd like to invite you to visit me in London.(난 런던으로 널 초대하고 싶어.)'이라고 Lucy는 지호를 런던으로 초대하고 있다.

03 지호는 Lucy를 배웅하고 있다. see off: ~를 배웅[전송]하다

---

04 계속적 용법의 관계대명사 which로 시작하여, 선행사에 맞게 단수동사 means와, 화법에 맞춰서 she wishes you good luck을 알맞게 배열한다.

05 가주어-진주어 표현과 우리말의 '믿어진다'에 알맞게 It is believed로 시작하여, 기본 어순에 적절하게 배열한다.

06 enter(~에 들어가다[오다])는 타동사이기 때문에, 전치사 없이 바로 목적어를 쓰는 것이 적절하다. enter into: (논의·처리 등을) 시작하다

07 인도에서 사람들은 '*chāmpo*라는 단어'를 머리 마사지라는 의미로 썼다.

08 (1) 18세기에, 인도에서 '머리 마사지'(*chāmpo*)를 함께하는 목욕을 경험했던 영국 상인들이 그것을 영국에 소개했다. (2) 19세기에, *shampoo*는 '머리 감기'라는 현재의 의미를 갖게 되었다. (3) 그 후 얼마 지나지 않아, 그 단어는 '머리에 사용하는 특별한 비누'에도 쓰이기 시작했다.

09 "*R.U.R.*"라는 연극에서 Karel Čapek은 인간처럼 생긴 기계들을 '*labori*'라고 불렀지만, 그의 형은 그것들을 '*roboti*'로 부를 것을 제안했다.

10 *labori*는 '라틴어'로 일을 의미하고, *roboti*는 체코어로 '노예 근로자들'을 의미한다.

🐇 **창의사고력 서술형 문제** p.166

|모범답안|

01 (1) Do you know what the expression "He hit the ceiling again" means? It means "He was angry again."

(2) Do you know what the expression "He pulled my leg" means? It means "He made fun of me."

(3) Do you know what the expression "It's a piece of cake" means? It means "It's very easy."

02 (A) the 4th Earl of Sandwich
   (B) between two slices of bread
   (C) play a card game   (D) eating
   (E) a sandwich

🎯 **단원별 모의고사** p.167~172

01 borrow   02 century   03 ⑤   04 (c)ause

05 (p)ress   06 civilization   07 ①

08 weather   09 ④

10 He suggests to her that she buy some medicine.

11 Have a nice trip.

12 He asks Lucy to come visit him again.

13 She asks Jiho to visit her in London.
14 (1) The fox tried to eat the grapes, which were too high.
　　(2) The grapes were so high for the fox, who considered them sour.
15 ①
16 (1) I watched the movie *Frozen 2*, which is the second episode of *Frozen*.
　　(2) It was surprising that Taeyeon sang its Korean version OST.
17 ⑤
18 (1) The octopus artist has many hands, which helps her draw at once.
　　(2) One of the musical geniuses is Mozart, who wrote a symphony at the age of eight.
19 British traders　　　　20 ③
21 (A) washing the hair　(B) a special soap
22 ④　　　　23 ③　　　　24 ②　　　　25 ③
26 ⓑ exclude → include　　27 origin　　28 ②
29 (A) Mayan　(B) a hurricane　(C) picked up
30 Dictionary　　　　　　31 originates from

01 special: 특별한 – general: 일반적인, lend: 빌려주다 – borrow: 빌리다
02 '백년의 기간'은 'century(세기, 100년)'가 적절하다. 그 성은 8세기 중반에 지어졌다.
03 law: 법, expression: 표현, 그녀를 사랑하지 말라는 법은 없다. 그는 그녀에게 사랑의 표시로 장미꽃을 보냈다. rare: 드문, row: 열, 줄, raw: 날 것의, 가공하지 않은, low: 낮은, invention: 발명, creation: 창조, depression: 불경기, 불황, impression: (사람·사물로부터 받는) 인상[느낌]
04 cause: 초래하다 – 어떤 일이 일어나도록 만들다
05 press: 누르다 – 어떤 것을 강하게 밀다
06 civilization: 문명 – 잘 정돈되고 발전된 사회 / 동양 사회는 서양 문명을 받아들이지 않았다.
07 do yoga: 요가를 하다. 나는 일주일에 두 번 요가를 한다. pick up: ~을 익히게 되다. 나는 이 책에서 몇몇 유용한 영어 표현을 익혔다.
08 '특정한 시간에 한 지역의 대기의 상태'를 나타내는 말은 '날씨'이다.
09 dose를 get이나 buy로 고치는 것이 적절하다. dose: 투약하다, 복용시키다
10 소년은 소녀에게 가게에서 약을 살 것을 제안하고 있다. suggest에 이끌리는 that절에서는 '(should+)동사원형'을 사용하는 것에 주의한다.
11 지호가 Lucy를 배웅하고 있는 것이므로 '즐거운 여행이 되길 바랄게.'라고 하는 것이 적절하다.
12 지호는 Lucy에게 다음에 또 와 달라고 하고 있다.

13 Lucy는 지호에게 런던으로 초대하고 싶다고 하고 있다.
14 접속사와 대명사를 사용해서 다시 쓰면, (1) The fox tried to eat the grapes, but they were too high. (2) The grapes were so high for the fox, and it considered them sour. 가 된다. but they = which, and he = who로 쓰였다.
15 주어진 문장은 '계속적' 용법의 관계대명사이다. ③, ④번은 전치사의 목적어 역할(한정적 용법), ②, ⑤번은 의문사로 쓰인 which이다.
16 내용을 정확히 이해하고, 조건에 맞게 질문에 답하도록 한다. (1) 관계대명사의 계속적 용법을 활용한다. (2) 주어진 조건에 its와 the Korean version OST의 사용과 가주어-진주어 형식을 반드시 사용하도록 했음에 유의하여 영작한다.
17 ⑤번만 강조구문이고, 나머지는 모두 접속사 that이다.
18 관계대명사 계속적 용법의 영작이다. (1) which 뒤의 동사의 수의 일치 helps에 유의, (2) who 뒤의 동사의 시제 일치 wrote에 유의하여 주어진 단어들을 적절히 배열한다.
19 인도에서 머리 마사지를 함께하는 목욕을 경험한 '영국 상인'들이 그것을 18세기에 영국에 소개했다.
20 ⓐ와 ③: 약 ~, ~쯤(부사), ① 사방에(서)(부사), ② (건너편에[에서/으로]) 돌아(전치사), ④ 이리저리, 여기저기(부사), ⑤ ~ 둘레에, ~ 주위에(전치사)
21 *shampoo*라는 단어의 원래 의미는 '누르다'였지만, 19세기 이후, 그것은 '머리 감기' 뿐만 아니라 머리에 사용하는 '특별한 비누'에도 쓰여 왔다.
22 ④번 다음 문장의 However에 주목한다. 주어진 문장의 내용과 상반되는 내용을 뒤에 이끌고 있으므로 ④번이 적절하다.
23 ⓐ와 ③, ⑤: 부사적 용법, ①, ②, ④: 명사적 용법
24 이 글은 *hurricane*이라는 단어의 기원에 관한 내용이므로, 제목으로는 ②번 '*hurricane*이라는 단어의 기원'이 적절하다.
25 ③ Huracán은 '지진'이 아니라 '홍수'를 일으켰다.
26 judge(판사)와 justice(정의)와 같은 단어들을 예로 들 수 있다(포함한다)고 해야 하기 때문에, include로 고치는 것이 적절하다. include: 포함하다, exclude: 제외[배제]하다
27 위 글의 내용은 다른 언어에서 '유래된' 몇 영어 단어에 대한 것이다.
28 앞에 나오는 내용과 상반되는 내용이 뒤에 이어지므로 However가 가장 적절하다. ① 게다가, 더욱이, ③ 그러므로, ⑤ 비슷하게, 유사하게, 마찬가지로
29 (1) '마야의' 창조 신화에서, 날씨의 신인 Huracán은 최초의 인간들이 그들의 창조주인 신들을 화나게 했기 때문에 거대한 홍수를 일으켰다. (2) 1517년에 스페인 탐험가들이 카리브 제도를 지나는 동안 '허리케인'을 겪었고 그 지역 사람들로부터 그것을 의미하는 단어를 '듣게 되었다'(pick up: 정보를 듣게/알게 되다/배우다).
30 '사전'이 적절하다.
31 originate from: ~에서 비롯되다

Be a Smart Spender

01 ⑤   02 budget   03 ②   04 ①

05 ④   06 ③

01 반의어 관계이다. easy: 쉬운, difficult: 어려운, true: 진실 인, false 거짓인

02 '개인이나 회사가 쓸 수 있는 금액'은 'budget(예산)'이 적절하 다. 그 예산의 적은 일부만이 책에 쓰인다.

03 ① on the spot: 즉각, 즉석에서. 그는 차를 보고 즉석에서 사 기로 결정했다. ② change one's mind: 마음을 바꾸다. 그 가 마음을 바꿀 가능성은 전혀 없다. ③ take care of: 돌보 다, 처리하다. 제가 처리해야 할 일이 몇 가지 있어요. ④ have difficulty (in) -ing: ~하는 데 어려움을 겪다. 이번 주까지 생 산을 완료해야 한다는 당신의 의견을 이해하기가 어렵습니다. ⑤ get a refund: 환불받다. 나는 이 티켓을 환불받으려고 노력 중이다.

04 receipt: 영수증. 내가 뭔가를 20일 전에 샀는데, 영수증이 없 어.

05 ① result: 결과. 그 투표 결과는 오늘 밤에 발표될 것이다. ② refund: 환불. 그 점원은 내 돈을 환불해줄 것이다. ③ loose: 헐렁한. 이 바지는 나에게 조금 헐렁하다. ④ Efforts: 노력. 평 화를 지키려던 노력들은 실패했다. ⑤ donate: 기부하다. 그는 아프리카에 있는 학교에 돈을 기부했다.

06 on sale: 할인 중인, 판매되는. 그 셔츠는 40퍼센트까지 할인 판매중이다. take effort: 노력을 필요로 하다. 그것은 시간과 노력이 필요할 것입니다. expansion: 팽창, 신장, hide: 숨기 다

01 (1) correct (2) effort (3) remaining (4) majority

02 (1) loose (2) advice

03 (1) effort (2) (t)ight (3) (r)eceived (4) exchange

04 (1) Mike has difficulty using his new camera.

   (2) I have saved my allowance to buy a hat.

   (3) Justin played the guitar on the spot.

   (4) It is easy to check your bank balance on the Internet.

01 (1) correct: 바로 잡다. 무엇인가를 제대로 되도록 하거나 원래 의 방식대로 작동하게 만들다 (2) effort: 노력, 어떤 것을 이루 려고 애쓸 때 하는 힘든 일 (3) remaining: 남아 있는, 일부가 제거되거나 사용되거나 분실된 후에 남아 있는 (4) majority: 대다수. 한 그룹 내의 대부분의 사람이나 물건

02 (1) '반의어'의 관계이다. same: 같은, different: 다른, loose: 느슨한, tight: 꽉 조이는[딱 붙는] (2) '동사 - 명사' 관계이 다. donate: 기부하다 – donation: 기부, advise: 충고하다 – advice: 충고

03 (1) make an effort: 노력하다 (2) tight: 빠듯한 (3) receive: 받다 (4) exchange: 교환하다

04 (1) have difficulty (in) -ing: ~ 하는 데 어려움을 겪다. 'have difficulty (in)' 다음에 동명사가 적절하므로 using을 추가한다. (2) allowance: 용돈. 'pocket money'도 '용돈'이 라는 뜻이지만 한 단어이므로 allowance를 추가한다. (3) on the spot 즉각, 즉석에서. spot을 추가한다. (4) balance: 잔 액. 가주어 it을 추가한다.

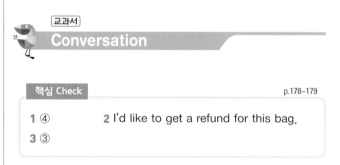

교과서

Conversation

1 ④   2 I'd like to get a refund for this bag.

3 ③

교과서 대화문 익히기

1 T   2 F   3 T   4 F   5 T   6 F   7 F   8 T

교과서 확인학습 p.183~185

Listen and Talk A 1

help you / refund / wrong / get, back / take care of

Listen and Talk A 2

need some help / return / Let's see, receipt / Here it is, it / it's possible

Listen and Talk A 3

looking for, special / exchange / would you like / Here you are

Listen and Talk A 4

What, do for you / for / What, would, like / I'd like, one / Here you are

Listen and Talk B 1

May I help you / I'd like to / What, it for / it for

Listen and Talk B 2

May I / get a refund for / receipt / do, Here it is

Listen and Talk C

May I help you / get a refund for / receipt / don't, it as / it's, to get / I see, exchange, for something else / can, would you like to get / want to get / Let me see, take it

Listen and Talk D

look good on, if, exchange it for / up to

Talk and Play

Excuse me, exchange, for / anything wrong
Excuse me, get a refund for / anything wrong

Review 1

May I help you / I'd like to return / anything wrong with / have, back / Here's your money

Review 2

Can I help you / I'd like to exchange / would you like to exchange it for / have it in / Here you are

Review 3

get a refund for / afraid you can't / exchange, for / can

Review 4

get a refund for / receipt / do, Here it is

시험대비 기본평가   p.186

01 ③   02 Can I have my money back?

03 ③   04 May I help you?

01 이어지는 대화에서 돈을 되돌려 받고 있으므로 환불을 요청하는 표현이 적절하다.

02 'get one's money back'은 '돈을 돌려받다'라는 뜻이다.

03 '어떤 것의 대가를 지불했음을 보여주는 종이 조각'은 'receipt(영수증)'이다.

04 'Do you need some help?'는 'May I help you?'로 바꿔 쓸 수 있다.

시험대비 실력평가   p.187~188

01 ④   02 ③

03 can I exchange it for something else?

04 it's not possible to get a refund

---

05 ⑤   06 ②, ④   07 ①   08 ②

09 ③   10 ④   11 ⑤

12 He wants to exchange the black umbrella for a yellow one[umbrella].

13 umbrella

01 영수증이 있는지 묻는 말에 교환하고 싶다고 말하는 것은 어색하다. A와 B를 서로 바꿔야 한다.

02 다음에 나오는 말들로 보아 상점에서 일어난 대화로 M이 점원으로 보이므로 ③번이 가장 적절하다.

03 뒤에서 G가 모자를 가방과 교환하고 있으므로 교환을 요청하는 표현이 적절하다. exchange A for B: A를 B로 바꾸다

04 get a refund: 환불받다

05 대화의 마지막 부분에서 M이 'you can just take it(this blue bag).'라고 하고 있다.

06 'Here it is.'와 'Here you are.'는 모두 '여기 있습니다.'라는 의미이다.

07 (a)에는 의문문이므로 anything, (b)에는 'Are you ~?'로 묻고 있으므로 'I'm not', (c)에는 change는 '바꾸다'라는 뜻이고, exchange는 '교환하다'라는 뜻이므로 exchange가 적절하다.

08 상점에서 손님을 응대하는 주어진 글에 이어, (B)에서 교환하고 싶다고 말하며 작다고 이유를 말하자, (C)에서 어떤 사이즈로 교환하고 싶은지 묻고, (A)에서 사이즈를 말하며 빨간색으로 바꿀 수 있는지 묻고, (D)에서 그렇다며 물건을 건네줄 때 쓰는 'Here you are.'로 마무리한다.

09 A가 'What would you like to exchange ~?'라고 묻고 있으므로 교환하고 싶다는 말을 했음을 추론할 수 있다.

10 exchange A for B: A를 B로 바꾸다

11 밑줄 친 문장은 환불을 요청할 때 쓰는 표현이다.

12 소년은 'Can I exchange ~?'라고 말하고 있다.

13 one은 부정대명사로 앞에 나온 'umbrella'를 대신해서 쓰이고 있다.

서술형 시험대비   p.189

01 (D) → (C) → (A) → (B)

02 Is it possible for me to get a refund for this cap?

03 It's because she doesn't have the receipt since she received it as a gift.

04 She finally gets a blue bag.

05 If you don't have the receipt, then, it's not possible to get a refund.

06 Here you are.

07 It's because the T-shirt is too small.

08 Are you looking for anything special?

09 refund

33

01 영수증이 없으면, 환불은 가능하지 않다는 문장에 이어서, 알았다며 교환은 가능한지 묻는 (D)가 나오고, 가능하다며 어떤 것을 원하는지 묻는 (C)가 나오고, 원하는 것을 말하는 (A)가 나오고, 가격이 같으니까 가져가셔도 된다는 (B)에 이어, 고맙다고 말하는 순서가 적절하다.

02 밑줄 친 (a)는 환불을 요청하는 표현이다. it을 가주어로 하여 가능한지를 묻는 표현으로 쓸 수 있다.

03 소녀는 모자를 선물로 받았기 때문에 영수증이 없다.

04 마지막 부분에서 'so you can just take it(blue bag)'이라고 하고 있다.

05 it을 가주어로 쓴다.

06 'Here you are.'는 '여기 있습니다.'라는 뜻이다.

07 소년은 셔츠가 너무 작아서 교환하고 싶다고 말하고 있다.

08 look for: 찾다 anything은 형용사가 뒤에서 수식하므로 anything special로 써야 하는 것에 주의한다.

09 '반환되는 돈의 총액'은 'refund(환불금)'이다.

교과서
Grammar

핵심 Check   p.190~191

1 (1) since (2) for

2 (1) Let's decide what to eat for lunch.

(2) She doesn't know how to ride a bike.

시험대비 기본평가
p.192

01 (1) where to go (2) which book to choose

(3) what to buy for her

(4) how I should[can] get to

02 (1) Marie has been playing computer games for four hours.

(2) Susan and her friends have been watching a drama for two hours.

03 how to use / how I can[should] use 04 ②

01 '의문사+to부정사'는 '의문사+주어+should[can/could]+동사원형'의 형태로 바꿔 쓸 수 있다.

02 (1) 주어가 3인칭 단수이므로 have been은 has been으로, 현재완료진행시제이므로 play는 playing으로 쓰는 것에 유의한다. (2) have been watching에 유의하여 배열한다.

03 '의문사+to부정사'는 '의문사+주어+should[can/could]+동사원형'의 형태로 바꿔 쓸 수 있다. '~를 사용하는 법'은 'how to use'이며, 절로 바꾸면 'how 주어 can[should] use'가 된

다.

04 현재완료진행시제는 '동작'을 대상으로 한다. '상태'를 나타내는 know, have 등의 동사는 쓸 수 없다. have been knowing → have known

시험대비 실력평가
p.193~195

01 ③　　　　　02 has been solving the puzzle since

03 (1) when to visit the palace

(2) which color to use

04 ①　　　　　05 that → what 또는 which　06 ②

07 ③　　　　08 ③　　　　09 ②　　　　10 ②

11 ⓓ when → where　　　12 ⑤

13 ③　　　　　14 ⑤

15 (1) has been traveling (2) has been learning

(3) has been taking (4) has been listening

(5) have been painting

16 ⑤

17 (1) who[whom] to invite (2) when to visit

(3) when to stop (4) who[whom] to meet

(5) which way to choose (6) what dress to wear

01 '과거형+현재진행형'은 현재완료진행시제로 표현한다. 'has been composing'이 적절하다.

02 과거에 시작된 일이 현재에도 진행되고 있을 때, 현재완료진행시제로 표현한다. 동사는 'has been solving'이, 전치사는 '~이래로'를 나타내는 since가 적절하다.

03 '의문사+주어+should[can/could]+동사원형'의 형태는 '의문사+to부정사'로 바꿔 쓸 수 있다. 의문문이 '의문사+to부정사구'로 바뀌었으므로 주절에 맞게 물음표는 쓰지 않는다. (2) 문장에서의 which는 의문형용사로 사용되었다.

04 (1) 어느 것을 사야 할지 (2) 어떻게 고칠지 (3) 어디에서 숙박해야 할지 등에 적절한 의문사를 찾는다.

05 그의 아내를 위해 무엇을 살지 물어보는 것이므로 의문대명사 what 또는 which가 적절하다.

06 '의문사+to부정사'는 '의문사+주어+should[can/could]+동사원형'의 형태로 바꿔 쓸 수 있다.

07 주어진 단어를 활용하여 영작하면, Let her know when to start the meeting.이 된다.

08 ① visiting → visited ② see → seen ④ since → for ⑤ '먹어 본 적이 있다'라는 경험을 표현하는 글은 완료진행형으로 쓸 수 없다. has been eating → has eaten

09 의문대명사 which와 to부정사가 결합해서 명사구를 만들 때, which는 내용상 to부정사의 목적어 역할을 한다. 그러므로 the oven은 불필요하다. which를 의문부사 how나 when 등으로 바꾸는 것이 적절하다.

10 ① '아침부터 앉아 있었다'는 내용이므로 'has sat' 또는 'has

been sitting'이 적절하다. ③ '가지고 있다'는 상태를 나타내는 동사 have는 현재완료진행형으로 쓸 수 없다. ④ 직업을 잃는 것도 상태이므로 현재완료진행형으로 쓸 수 없다. ⑤ 'have been making' 또는 'have made'가 적절하다.

11 'Peter의 사무실이 어떻겠는가?'라는 A의 대답으로 미뤄 보아, 흐름상 ④는 '어디에서 과자를 만들지 모르겠다'는 내용이다. when을 where로 바꾸는 것이 적절하다.

12 <보기>는 현재완료시제의 용법들 중 '경험'이며, ① 결과 ② 완료 ③ 계속 ④ 결과로 사용되었다. ⑤는 '시장으로 두 번 선출되었다'는 내용으로 <보기>와 같은 '경험' 용법이다.

13 a. what should → what she should b. why to come은 쓸 수 없다. d. where to going → where to go

14 현재완료시제의 '계속' 용법, 또는 현재완료진행시제가 적절하다.

15 (1) 청소년 원정대의 여행 (2) 외국어 학습 (3) 약 복용 (4) 라디오 청취 (5) 벽화 그리기 등 각각의 내용에 적절하게 동사를 선택하여, 주어의 수에 맞게 has/have 등을 활용하여 현재완료진행시제를 쓴다. *expedition: 원정대

16 현재완료진행시제는 과거에 시작한 일이 현재까지 진행되고 있음을 의미하며, ⑤는 '15분 전까지'라는 명백한 과거시제 표현이기 때문에 부적절하다.

17 'whom to'는 'who to'로도 쓸 수 있다. 우리말에 맞게 적절한 의문사와 to부정사를 쓰도록 한다.

서술형 시험대비 p.196~197

01 (1) The runners have been working out in the gym for over eight hours.
(2) Grace has been chewing a gum after lunch for 30 minutes.
(3) Patrick has been composing online since he first bought a computer.

02 which, how to drink

03 (1) has been writing an email for 5 hours
(2) has been learning Chinese for 2 years
(3) has been practicing playing the cello for 4 months

04 (1) Mason told me how to use my laptop.
(2) Can you teach me how to play the piano?

05 (1) decide which novel to read
(2) tell us when to visit your office
(3) know where to park my car
(4) teach her how to play the violin

06 (1) look after his mom three years ago / looking after
(2) watch birds an hour ago / watching birds

07 Aiden has been doing his daughter's homework for five hours.

08 (A) which club to join   (B) where to apply
(C) when you will apply

01 현재완료진행시제에 맞게 각 단어를 적절히 활용한다.

02 둘 중 어느 것을 마실지는 'which to drink'이고, 어떻게 마실지는 'how to drink'이다. and로 연결해서 빈칸의 개수를 맞게 하려면 'which and how to drink'가 적절하다.

03 전치사 for를 꼭 사용해야 하기 때문에, 기간 계산에 유의한다. (1) 아침 7시에서 정오까지이므로 '5시간 동안' (2) 2017년 5월부터 2019년 5월이므로 '2년 동안' (3) 4달 전에 시작했으므로 '4개월 간'이 적절하다. 또한, practice는 동명사를 목적어로 취하므로 playing 형태에도 유의해야 한다.

04 '노트북을 사용하는 방법'은 'how to use my laptop'이다. '피아노를 어떻게 연주하는지'도 '피아노 연주 방법'과 같다. 'how to play the piano'를 쓴다.

05 (1) '두 가지 소설을 모두 읽고 싶은데, 어느 소설을 읽을지 결정할 수 없다' (2) '몇 시에 당신의 사무실을 방문해야 할지 모르므로 말해 달라' (3) '어디에 주차할지 모르겠다' (4) '바이올린 연주 방법을 가르쳐 달라' 등의 내용에 맞게 의문사와 동사들을 활용하여 영작한다.

06 현재완료진행시제는 '과거에 시작된 일'을 '현재에도 계속 하고 있는 것'이므로, '과거 시작 시점'과 '현재 상태'의 두 문장으로 나눌 수 있다. 시작 시점에 ago가 함께 쓰이는 것에 유의한다.

07 5시간 전에 집에 도착한 딸 Emma가, 집에 도착하자마자 아버지에게 숙제를 부탁했고, Emma 대신 숙제를 시작한 아버지 'Aiden이 5시간 동안 딸의 숙제를 하고 있는 중'이므로, 현재완료진행시제를 활용하여 영작한다.

08 (A) 클럽을 선택하는 것이므로 의문형용사 which와 to부정사를 사용해서 which club to join (B) 의문부사 where를 사용 (C) 'when to apply'라고 하면, 빈칸 개수도 안 맞고 will을 쓸 수 없다. when you will apply가 적절하다.

교과서 Reading

확인문제 p.198

1 T 2 F 3 T 4 F 5 T 6 F

확인문제 p.199

1 T 2 F 3 T 4 F 5 T 6 F

확인문제 p.200

1 T 2 F 3 T 4 F 5 T 6 F

01 Ask
02 Times
03 Spending Habits
04 How smart
05 a survey
06 smart with
07 As, while
08 biggest money worry
09 As, enough allowance, have difficulty saving
10 Lastly, spent, on
11 the majority, smart with
12 Managing, becoming
13 money worries
14 talk with
15 I'm
16 weekly allowance, enough
17 is gone
18 how to solve
19 I'm
20 spending diary
21 used up, at the beginning
22 my tip
23 carry around
24 Divide, into
25 carry, for each day
26 Hello
27 I'm
28 have difficulty saving
29 I've been saving, for the last two months
30 However, still don't
31 what to do
32 Let's see
33 In the last few
34 you've been spending
35 have a tighter budget
36 the 50%-40%-10% rule
37 donate the remaining
38 By following, manage, better
39 faster to buy
40 I'm
41 on sale
42 although
43 already have
44 things you need
45 In your case, don't even need
46 Here's
47 ask yourself
48 go shopping
49 on the list
50 on the spot

1 Ask Dr. Money
2 The Green Middle School Times
3 Teens' Spending Habits
4 How smart are you with your money?
5 These are the results of a survey of 100 students at Green Middle School.
6 We first asked students "Are you smart with your money?"
7 As Graph 1 shows, 70% answered "No" while 30% answered "Yes."
8 We then asked the students who answered "No" what their biggest money worry is.

9 As Graph 2 shows, 60% think they don't have enough allowance while 28% think they have difficulty saving money.
10 Lastly, 12% said they spent money on things they didn't need.
11 Our survey shows that the majority of students think they are not smart with their money.
12 Managing money is not easy, and becoming a smart spender takes effort.
13 Do you have any money worries?
14 Let's talk with Dr. Money.
15 I'm Jason.
16 I get a weekly allowance, but I never have enough.
17 By Thursday, all of my money is gone.
18 I don't know how to solve this problem.
19 Hi, I'm Dr. Money.
20 Let's look at your spending diary.
21 You used up most of your money at the beginning of the week.
22 Here's my tip.
23 Don't carry around all of your weekly allowance.
24 Divide the money into days.
25 Then carry only the money you need for each day.
26 Hello, Dr. Money.
27 I'm Steve.
28 I have difficulty saving money.
29 For example, I've been saving to go to my favorite singer's concert for the last two months.
30 However, I still don't have enough money.
31 I don't know what to do.
32 Let's see.
33 In the last few weeks, you spent 80% of your allowance and only saved 20%.
34 I think you've been spending too much.
35 To save money, you need to have a tighter budget.
36 For example, you can follow the 50%-40%-10% rule.
37 Save 50%, spend 40%, and donate the remaining 10% to charity.
38 By following the rule, you can manage your money better.
39 Then you can save money faster to buy the ticket.
40 I'm Minji.
41 I like to buy things on sale.
42 If something's on sale, I buy it although I don't need it.
43 Last week, I bought two T-shirts on sale, but I already have many.

44 Buying things on sale is good if you buy things you need.

45 In your case, the problem is that you buy things you don't even need.

46 Here's some advice.

47 Before you buy something, ask yourself, "Do I really need this?"

48 Also, before you go shopping, make a shopping list.

49 Don't buy items that aren't on the list even if they're on sale.

50 Then you won't buy things on the spot.

시험대비 실력평가   p.207~211

01 ⑤   02 ②   03 Seventy(70)

04 ①

05 50%를 저축하고, 40%를 쓰고, 남아 있는 10%를 자선 단체에 기부하는 것

06 (A) 20   (B) 50   07 ④   08 ②

09 ②   10 ②   11 ③   12 five

13 ④   14 ②   15 ③

16 (A) 80   (B) 40   17 ①, ③, ⑤

18 items that aren't on the list

19 (A) on sale   (B) a shopping list

20 (A) is gone   (B) most   (C) Divide

21 By Thursday, all of my money is gone.

22 ③   23 the negative

24 60% thinks → 60% think
   28% thinks → 28% think

25 ④   26 ④

27 ⓐ 100 students at Green Middle School
   ⓑ the students who answered "No"

28 three-fifths

01 ⓐ with: [관계·입장] ~에 관해서[대해서], ~에 있어서는, ~의 경우는, ⓑ spend+돈+on: ~에 돈을 쓰다

02 ② 위 글은 '(신문·잡지의) 글, 기사'이다. ① 수필, ③ 요약, 개요, ④ (책·연극·영화 등에 대한) 논평[비평], 감상문, ⑤ 독후감

03 학생 100명에게 설문 조사한 중에 70%가 "아니요"라고 답했기 때문에, '70명'에 해당한다.

04 ① 앞의 내용의 예가 나오고 있으므로 For example이 가장 적절하다. ② 게다가, 더욱이, ③ 그러므로, ⑤ 즉[말하자면]

05 다음에 이어지는 문장의 내용을 쓰는 것이 적절하다.

06 Dr. Money는 Steve에게 용돈의 '20%'에서 '50%'로 저축률을 늘리라고 충고한다.

07 ④번 다음 문장의 내용은 Dr. Money의 조언을 구체적으로 설

명하는 것이므로 ④번이 적절하다.

08 이 글은 '목요일쯤이면 용돈의 대부분을 다 쓰고 용돈이 절대로 충분하지 않다고 말하고 있는 Jason에게 용돈을 하루 단위로 나누라는 조언을 하는 내용'의 글이므로, 제목으로는 ②번 '용돈이 절대로 충분하지 않다고요? 용돈을 하루 단위로 나누세요.'가 적절하다. ① broke: 빈털터리의

09 '화요일'이 아니라 '목요일쯤'이면 용돈이 모두 사라진다.

10 (A)의 then asked가 (B)의 first asked보다 뒤에 나와야 하고, (C)의 60%가 (A)의 the students 중의 60%를 가리키므로 (A) 다음에 (C)가 와야 한다. 그러므로 (B)-(A)-(C)의 순서가 적절하다.

11 ⓐ와 ③: ~와 같이, ~처럼(접속사), ① ~이므로, ~인 까닭에 (접속사), ② ~처럼(전치사), ④ ~하고 있을 때(접속사), ⑤ 보통 as ... as ~로 형용사·부사 앞에서] ~와 같은 정도로 (as ... as ~에서, 앞의 as가 지시부사, 뒤의 as는 접속사)

12 충분한 용돈을 받지 못한다고 생각하는 학생들의 퍼센트(60%)가 필요하지 않은 것에 돈을 소비했다고 말한 학생들의 퍼센트 (12%)보다 '5배' 더 크다. five times: 5배

13 '더 빠듯한 예산'을 세우는 것이 필요하다고 하는 것이 적절하다. ① loose: 느슨한, ② deposit: (은행에의) 예금, 예금액

14 위 글은 '용돈의 80%를 사용하고 20%만을 저축해 온 Steve에게 돈을 모으기 위해서 더 빠듯한 예산을 세워 50%를 저축하고, 40%를 쓰고, 남아 있는 10%를 자선 단체에 기부하라고 조언하는 내용'의 글이므로, 주제로는 ②번 '돈을 모으기 위해서, 50%-40%-10%의 규칙을 따르기'가 적절하다.

15 이 글은 '돈을 모으기 위해서, 더 빠듯한 예산을 세우는 것이 필요하다'는 내용의 글이므로, 어울리는 속담으로는 '티끌 모아 태산'이 적절하다. ③을 제외한 나머지: 티끌 모아 태산, ③ 소탐대실; 한 푼 아끼려다 열 냥 잃는다, 적은 금액을 절약하려고 그 때문에 큰돈을 잃는 것은 어리석다는 것을 뜻하는 속담.

16 Dr. Money는 Steve에게 용돈의 '80%'에서 '40%'로 소비를 줄이라고 충고한다.

17 ⓐ와 ①, ③, ⑤: 재귀적 용법(주어와 목적어가 같음), ②, ④: 강조 용법(주어, 목적어, 보어와 동격일 때, 생략 가능)

18 '목록에 없는 물건들'을 가리킨다.

19 (A) 민지의 돈에 대한 고민: 어떤 물건이 '할인 판매를 하면' 저는 그것이 필요하지 않더라도 사요. 지난주에는 할인 판매하는 티셔츠 두 장을 샀지만 이미 많이 가지고 있었어요. (B) ◼의 조언: 쇼핑하러 가기 전에 '쇼핑 목록'을 만드세요. 목록에 없는 물건들은 사지 마세요.

20 (A) disappear는 수동태로 쓸 수 없으므로 is gone이 적절하다. (B) 용돈의 '대부분'이라고 해야 하므로 most가 적절하다. almost: 거의 (C) 용돈을 하루 단위로 '나누라'고 해야 하므로 Divide가 적절하다. add: (수·양을) 합하다[더하다]

21 바로 앞 문장의 내용인 '목요일쯤이면 용돈이 모두 사라져요.'를 가리킨다.

22 Jason은 이 문제를 해결할 방법을 모르겠다고 했으므로, '무엇을 해야 할지 알지만 실천하지 않는 것이 문제'라는 ③번이 옳지 않다.

23 answer in the negative: '아니오'라고 대답하다, 부정[거절]하다, answer in the affirmative: 긍정하다(say yes)

24 60%와 28% 뒤에 of the students who answered "No"가 각각 생략되어 있으므로, 60%와 28%를 복수 취급하는 것이 적절하다.

25 "아니요"라고 대답한 학생들 중의 '28%'가 자신들이 돈을 모으는 것에 어려움이 있다고 생각한다고 했으므로, 'More than one third'를 'Less than 30%'로 고치는 것이 적절하다. ③ three-fifths: 5분의 3

26 ④번의 save는 '구하다'는 뜻이 아니라, '(돈을) 모으다, 저축하다'라는 뜻임, rescue: 구출하다, 구조하다, ① outcome: 결과, ② whereas: 반면에(두 가지 사실을 비교·대조할 때 씀), ③ 용돈, ⑤ finally: (여러 개를 언급할 때) 마지막으로

27 ⓐ는 'Green 중학교 학생 100명', ⓑ ""아니요"라고 대답한 학생들'을 가리킨다.

28 60% = three-fifths: 5분의 3

서술형 시험대비 p.212~213

01 (A) As (B) who (C) Lastly
02 trouble[a hard time/a problem]
03 Forty-two 또는 42
04 (A) smart (B) money worries
05 I should[can]
06 Then carry only the money you need for each day
07 (A) never have enough (B) Divide
08 To save money, you need to have a tighter budget. 또는 You need to have a tighter budget to save money.
09 ① 2,000원 ② 5,000원 ③ 8,000원
　 ④ 4,000원 ⑤ 0원 ⑥ 1,000원
10 (A) ask herself (B) make a shopping
11 (A) should not (B) even if (C) if

01 (A) 그래프 1이 '보여 주듯이'라고 해야 하므로 As가 적절하다. as: ~와 같이, ~처럼(접속사), since: ~부터[이후], ~ 때문에, (B) 선행사(사람)가 있으므로 관계대명사 who를 쓰는 것이 적절하다. (C) '마지막으로'라고 해야 하므로 Lastly가 적절하다. at last: 마침내, lastly: 마지막으로

02 have difficulty/trouble/a hard time/a problem ~ing: ~하는 데 어려움을 겪다

03 "아니요"라고 대답한 학생들(70명)의 60%가 충분한 용돈을 받지 못한다고 생각하는 것이므로, 70명×0.6 = 42명

04 Green 중학교 학생 100명 중 70명은 '현명한' 방법으로 돈을 쓰지 못하고, 충분한 용돈을 받지 못하는 것, 돈을 모으는 것에 어려움이 있는 것, 필요하지 않은 것에 돈을 소비하는 것과 같은 '돈에 대한 고민들'을 가지고 있다.

05 의문사+to부정사 = 의문사+주어+should[can]+동사원형

06 the money와 you need 사이에 목적격 관계대명사가 생략되어 있음.

07 Jason의 돈에 대한 고민: 저는 매주 용돈을 받지만, '절대로 충분하지 않아요.' 목요일쯤이면 용돈이 모두 사라져요. Dr. Money의 조언: 일주일 용돈 전부를 가지고 다지지 마세요. 용돈을 하루 단위로 '나누세요.' 그리고 하루에 필요한 돈만 들고 다니세요.

08 have a tighter budget: 더 빠듯한 예산을 세우다

09 ① 용돈의 20%, ② 용돈의 50%, ③ 용돈의 80%, ④ 용돈의 40%, ⑤ 0%, ⑥ 용돈의 10%

10 (A) 무언가를 사기 전: "이것이 정말 필요한가?"라고 '스스로에게 물어보아야' 한다. (B) 쇼핑하러 가기 전: '쇼핑 목록을 만들어야' 한다.

11 '비록' 물건들이 할인 판매 중이라고 해도 '만약' 그것이 쇼핑 목록에 없다면 사지 '말아야 한다.'고 해야 하므로 (A) should not (B) even if (C) if가 적절하다.

영역별 핵심문제 p.215~219

01 ①
02 (c)harity / (e)xchange / (1) charity (2) exchange
03 on sale 04 spender / allowance
05 (A) (d)ifficulty (B) (f)oolish (C) (t)ight 06 ④
07 I'd like to get a refund for this baseball glove.
08 Here you are., Here it is. 09 ②
10 Excuse me.
11 Because he doesn't like the color.
12 Is there anything wrong with it?
13 ⑤ 14 ③
15 has been studying wild animals in Africa for 11 years
16 ④
17 (A) has been trying to be (B) since 18 ③, ④
19 (1) has been taking pictures of himself
　 (2) has been watching birds
20 ① 21 ⑤ 22 ③
23 ①, ②, ⑤ 24 Twenty-eight(28) 25 ④
26 ③ 27 Divide the money into days.
28 once 29 shopping
30 something that is on sale
31 Here are some tips.
32 Because she buys things she doesn't even need.

01 ①번은 '잔액'이라는 의미로 쓰였고 <보기>와 나머지는 모두 '균형'이라는 뜻으로 쓰였다. <보기> 우리의 내부를 자세히 들여다보면 완벽한 균형을 찾을 수 있다. ① 인터넷으로 예금 잔액 조회가 가능하다. ② 일과 놀이에 있어 균형을 유지할 필요가 있다. ③ 운동선수는 훌륭한 균형 감각이 필요하다. ④ 그 순간에 그가 균형을 잃고 넘어졌다. ⑤ 그 강타의 충격으로 Jack이 휘청거리며 균형을 잃었다.

02 (1) charity: 자선 단체. 가난하거나 아픈 사람에게 돈, 물품 또는 도움을 주는 단체. 그는 세상을 떠난 아내를 추모하여 그 자선 단체를 설립했다. (2) exchange: 교환. 누군가에게 무엇인가를 주고 그들로부터 다른 어떤 것을 받는 행위. 포로 교환은 오늘 오전에 이뤄졌다.

03 '특히 상점이나 가게에서 살 수 있는'이라는 의미로 'on sale(할인 중인, 판매되는)'이 적절하다.

04 (1) 보어로 형용사의 수식을 받는 명사가 나오는 것이 적절하다. 동사에 er을 붙여 명사가 된 어휘이다. spender: 돈을 쓰는 사람. 다음에 크게 한 턱 내세요. (2) 문장 구성상 목적어로 관사가 앞에 있으므로 명사가 적절하다. allowance: 용돈. 동사 allow에 -ance를 붙여 명사가 된 어휘이다. 나는 부모님에게서 용돈을 받는다.

05 (A) have difficulty (in) -ing ~하는 데 어려움을 겪다 (B) foolish: 어리석은 (C) tight: 꼭 조이는[딱 붙는], 빠듯한

06 (D)의 무엇을 도와줄지 묻는 말에 이어, (B)에서 야구 글러브를 환불받고 싶다고 말하고, (A)에서 무슨 문제가 있는지 묻고, (C)에서 아니라며 마음이 바뀌었다고 한 후, 알았다며 돈을 돌려주는 주어진 문장으로 이어지는 것이 적절하다.

07 return 대신에 'get a refund for'를 쓸 수 있다.

08 Here's your money. = Here you are. = Here it is.

09 'I'm afraid'는 유감스러운 내용을 말할 때 예의상 덧붙이는 표현이므로 그 다음에 긍정의 내용이 나오는 것은 어울리지 않는다. 'I'm afraid you can't.'가 적절하다.

10 '(1) 누군가를 불쾌하게 할지도 모르는 것을 하거나 말하기 전에, 또는 누군가의 주의를 끌기 위해, (2) 잠시 동안 장소를 떠날 때' 사용되는 표현은 'Excuse me.(실례합니다.)'이다.

11 소년은 '색이 마음에 들지 않아요.'라고 하고 있다.

12 'Is there'로 '있다'는 것을 나타내고 'anything wrong'으로 '잘못된 것 = 문제'를 나타낸다. wrong이 뒤에서 anything을 수식하는 것에 유의한다.

13 소년이 티셔츠를 바지로 교환하려는 것으로 보아 두 사람은 상점에서 대화를 나누고 있음을 짐작할 수 있다.

14 ① why+to부정사 형태는 쓸 수 없다. ② when 뒤에 주어가 나오면 to부정사를 쓸 필요가 없다. 문맥상 when도 좋지 않다. when they를 what으로 바꾸는 것이 적절하다. ④ starting → start. ⑤ using → use *photocopier: 복사기

15 과거의 시작 시점부터 현재까지 지속되는 것은 현재완료진행시제로 표현하며, 기간은 전치사 for를 이용한다.

16 언제 시작할지 알려달라는 말이므로, 'when to start'를 'when I should start'로, 'let me know'를 'tell me'로 전환한 문장이 가장 적절하다.

17 배우가 된 이후로 지금까지 최고의 여배우가 되기 위해 노력해 오고 있다는 말로 보아 'try to be' 표현을 활용하여, 현재완료진행시제로 쓴다. '~한 이래로'는 since가 적절하다.

18 ③ 자동사 fall은 have been fell로 쓸 수 없으므로 'I have fallen'으로 쓰면 적절하다. ④ 강당이 덥게 느껴지는 '상태'이므로, 진행형은 부적절하다. 'has felt' 또는 feels가 적절하다.

19 주어진 문장들에 공통으로 '~ 이후로, ~ 동안'의 표현이 있으므로, 현재완료진행시제를 쓰는 것이 적절하다. be동사를 시제와 인칭에 맞게 'has been V-ing'로 쓴다. (1) 준수는 점심시간 이후로 한 시간 동안 꽃밭에서 자기 사진을 찍고 있다. (2) 영수는 세 시 이후로 30분 동안 새들을 관찰하고 있다.

20 영작하면, 'Let her know when to leave.'이다.

21 대화의 답이 노란색 제품이 훨씬 더 냄새가 좋다고 했으므로, 선택의문사 which가 쓰인 ⑤번이 적절하다. ①은 모양에 관한 질문이므로 부적절하고, ②도 향수 냄새를 맡는 법을 묻고 있으므로, 답이 될 수 없다.

22 현재완료진행시제는 과거에 시작한 일이 현재까지 진행되고 있음을 의미하며, '동작의 진행'을 나타내기 때문에 상태 표현 동사에 사용할 수 없다. ③ own은 '소유하고 있다'라는 뜻으로, 진행형으로 쓰지 않는다. *relative: 친척

23 ⓐ와 ①, ②, ⑤: 동명사, ③, ④: 현재분사

24 '28%'의 학생들이 자신들이 돈을 모으는 것에 어려움이 있다고 생각한다.

25 평균적으로, 학생들이 1주일에 용돈을 얼마나 받는지는 알 수 없다. on average: 평균적으로 ① 30 students are smart spenders. ② 70 students aren't smart with their money. ③ They think they are not smart with their money. ⑤ No, it takes effort to become a smart spender.

26 ⓐ by+때: '~쯤에는', '~까지는'(완료), ⓑ at the beginning of the week: 주의 초반에

27 divide A into B: A를 B로 나누다

28 Jason은 매주 용돈을 받으므로, 일주일에 '한번'이라고 하는 것이 적절하다.

29 go ~ing: ~하러 가다

30 '할인 판매를 하는 물건'을 가리킨다.

31 tip은 셀 수 있는 명사이므로 some 다음에 복수 형태로 써야 하고, Here 다음의 동사도 are로 바꾸는 것이 적절하다.

32 조언의 내용 중 'In your case, the problem is that ~'에서, 민지의 문제점이 '필요하지 않은 물건도 사는 것'임을 알 수 있고, 그런 이유로 민지는 비록 할인 판매하는 물건을 사지만 현명한 소비자가 아니다.

01 ②   02 ④   03 back / back

04 (1) (A)lthough (2) (n)ative (3) (r)ecently

05 ④   06 If I cannot get a refund for this hat

07 if 또는 whether

08 Because her sister says that the color doesn't look good on her.

09 ②   10 ③

11 To return the smartphone case.

12 ③   13 ⑤   14 ①, ④

15 ⓐ risen → rising   ⓑ what → how

    ⓒ which → how   ⓓ since → for

    ⓔ has been having → has had

16 allowance   17 ⑤

18 More than → Less than   19 ②   20 ②, ⑤

21 ③   22 to buy → buying   23 ②

---

01 ②번은 반의어 관계이다. 나머지는 모두 동의어 관계이다. divide: 나누다, combine: ~을 결합시키다 ① recently: 최근에, lately: 최근에 ③ pocket money: 용돈, allowance: 용돈 ④ result: 결과, outcome: 결과 ⑤ paper money: 지폐, bill: 지폐

02 ① medicine: 의약품. 우리는 의사들이 여러분의 건강을 유지할 수 있도록 해주는 데 기여하는 의약품을 제조합니다. ② work: 작동하다. 그 기계는 스스로 작동한다. ③ case: 사례. 그것은 미국에서의 첫 광우병 발병 사례였다. ④ carry around: 가지고 다니다. 동전이 너무 많으면 갖고 다니기가 아주 무거워요. ⑤ be gone: 사라지다. 그들이 간 뒤에 돈이 없어진 것을 알았다.

03 • have money back: 돈을 돌려받다. 그것이 실패하면 돈은 돌려받을 수 있다. • get back: (특히 자기 집이나 머무르고 있는 곳으로) 돌아오다[가다]. 너 지난밤에 몇 시에 돌아왔니?

04 (1) although: 비록 ~일지라도 (2) native: 토착민, 현지인 (3) recently: 최근에

05 빈칸 다음에 '죄송하지만 안 됩니다.'라고 하고 있고, 대화의 뒷부분에서 '그렇다면 이 모자를 저기에 있는 장갑과 교환할 수 있을까요?'라는 말로 보아 '환불'을 요청했음을 추론할 수 있다.

06 이 대화에서 Then(그렇다면)은 '환불이 안 된다면'이라는 뜻이다.

07 'I wonder.'와 'Should I exchange it for a different color?'라는 두 문장을 간접의문문으로 연결한 것으로 의문사가 없으므로 if나 whether를 이용하여 연결해야 한다.

08 소녀는 '여동생이 색깔이 그녀에게 잘 어울리지 않는다'고 해서 다른 색으로 교환할지 고민이라고 하고 있다.

09 스마트폰 케이스를 환불받고 싶다는 말에, '잠시만요.(가만있자.)'라고 한 후, 영수증을 가지고 있는지 묻는 것이 자연스러우

므로 ②번이 적절하다. 다른 곳은 모두 어울리지 않음을 확인한다.

10 소년이 왜 반품하려고 하는지는 알 수 없다.

11 소년은 smartphone case를 반품하기 위해 상점을 방문하고 있다.

12 각각 (A) '어디에서 묵을지' (B) '어떻게 갈지' (C) '무엇을 할지' 등의 내용이므로, 그에 적절한 의문사를 선택한다.

13 모든 지문에 현재완료진행시제가 쓰였다. ⑤번 문장은 시제 자체에는 문제가 없으나, 'during the summer vacation'이 '명백한 과거 시점'을 지칭하므로, '과거에 시작된 일이 지금도 진행되고 있다'는 의미의 현재완료진행시제로 표현할 수 없다. during을 since로 바꾸면, '지난 여름방학 이후로 Trump의 아들들이 포커 게임을 해오고 있는 중이다'가 된다.

14 의문사의 종류가 다른 두 개를 찾는 문제이다. '의문사+to부정사' 표현에서는 주로 의문대명사와 의문부사가 쓰이는데, 내용상 ①, ④번에는 의문대명사 which 또는 what을 써야 하고, 나머지는 모두 의문부사가 적절하다. ② how to play ③ where[when] to beg for money ⑤ when, where 모두 가능.

15 ⓐ 기름 가격이 2년간 꾸준히 상승해오고 있다. 능동의 현재완료진행이므로 risen을 rising으로 고친다. ⓑ '깊은 바다에서 어떻게 수영할지'이므로 how ⓒ '젓가락을 써 본 적이 없으므로 면을 어떻게 먹을지'가 적절하다. ⓓ 랩 가사같은 소리를 '15분간' 외치고 있으므로 since를 for로 고친다. (단, '15분전부터'라는 말도 가능하기 때문에, 그럴 경우 뒤에 ago를 추가하면 되는데, 골라서 고치는 문제이므로 since를 수정) ⓔ '소유'를 나타내는 have는 진행형을 쓸 수 없다. 현재완료시제로도 충분히 표현 가능.

16 allowance: 용돈, (특정 목적을 위한) 비용, 어떤 사람에게 필요한 물건들을 사는 것을 돕기 위해 대체로 규칙적으로 주어지는 돈

17 (A)와 ⑤: [반대·비교·대조를 나타내어] 그런데, 한편(으로는), ①, ②, ③: ~하는 동안, 하는 사이, ④: ~하는 한

18 필요하지 않은 것에 돈을 소비했다고 말한 학생들은 '돈에 관하여 현명하지 않다'고 말한 70명 중의 12%로 8.4명에 해당하기 때문에, '10명 미만'으로 고치는 것이 적절하다.

19 ②번 다음 문장의 For example에 주목한다. 주어진 문장의 a tighter budget의 예에 해당하므로 ②번이 적절하다.

20 (A)와 ②, ⑤: 계속 용법, ① 경험 용법, ③ 결과 용법, ④ 완료 용법

21 Steve가 용돈의 80%를 무엇에 썼는지는 대답할 수 없다. ① To go to his favorite singer's concert. ② No. ④ He needs to have a tighter budget. ⑤ She advises him to follow the 50%-40%-10% rule.

22 즉석에서 물건을 사는 것을 그만두는 방법을 모른다고 해야 하

므로 buying으로 고치는 것이 적절하다. stop+~ing: ~을 그만두다, stop+to부정사: ~하기 위해 멈추다

23 위 글은 자신의 '소비' 습관의 문제점에 관한 조언을 구하는 글이다.

서술형 실전문제
p.224~225

01 received 02 She takes the blue bag.

03 Because the price of the blue bag is the same as that of the cap.

04 (1) What has Brian been watching since nine o'clock?

 (2) She has been teaching French in a middle school in Incheon for five years.

05 (1) what he should do next

 (2) how she can get to the subway station

 (3) where he should park his luxury car

 (4) how she could move the toy

06 minority → majority 07 It

08 Twelve(12) 09 I still don't have enough money

10 saving → spending

11 (A) saving money (B)50%-40%-10%

01 '누군가가 어떤 것을 당신에게 주거나 보내준 후에 그것을 갖다'는 'receive'이다.

02 소녀는 모자 대신에 파란색 가방을 가져간다.

03 소녀는 모자와 파란색 가방의 가격이 같기 때문에 파란색 가방을 가져갈 수 있다. that을 사용하라고 했으므로 'that of the cap'으로 표현해야 함에 주의한다.

04 현재완료진행형을 적절히 사용한다. (1) 의문문이므로 의문사 what을 문두에 놓고, has와 주어 Brian을 도치하는 점에 유의한다.(2) 인천의 한 중학교: a middle school in Incheon

05 '의문사+to부정사'는 '의문사+주어+should[can/could]+동사원형'의 형태로 바꿔 쓸 수 있다. can의 경우, 시제에 맞게 can과 could를 구분하며, (2)는 현재, (4)는 과거이다.

06 '대다수'의 학생들이 자신들이 돈에 관련하여 현명하지 못하다고 생각한다. minority: 소수

07 가주어 'It'을 쓰는 것이 적절하다.

08 '12%'의 학생들이 필요하지 않은 것에 돈을 소비한다.

09 still을 보충하면 된다. still은 부정의 조동사 앞에 쓴다.

10 용돈의 80%를 사용하고 20%만을 저축했기 때문에, '돈을 너무 많이 써 왔다고 생각한다.'로 고치는 것이 적절하다.

11 Steve의 돈에 대한 고민: 저는 좋아하는 가수의 콘서트에 가기 위한 '돈을 모으기가' 어려워요. 저는 더 많은 돈을 모을 필요가 있어요. Dr. Money의 조언: 더 빠듯한 예산을 세우는 것이 필요해요. '50%-40%-10%'의 규칙을 따르세요. 50%를 저축하고, 40%를 쓰고, 남아 있는 10%를 자선 단체에 기부하세요.

창의사고력 서술형 문제
p.226

|모범답안|

01 (1) Is it possible to get a refund for

 (2) Is it OK to get a refund for

02 (1) Alex has been teaching his students how to solve the cube puzzle for five years.

 (2) Alex has been teaching English to the middle school students for 15 years.

 (3) Alex has been teaching Esther to solve the cube puzzle for a year.

 (4) Esther has been learning English from Alex for a year.

03 (A) money prob (B) on the spot (C) nice
 (D) had three cases

단원별 모의고사
p.227~231

01 (o)utcome 02 advice

03 allowance 또는 pocket money 04 ④

05 difficulty 06 on the spot 07 ⑤

08 ③ 09 ④ 10 as

11 The price is the same, so you can just take it.

12 (1) how to handle (2) has been biting

 (3) which foot to put out

13 ④

14 (1) has been watching the films directed by Bong for four

 (2) has been working at a store owned by Butler for

15 (1) Wilson has been learning how to fix the photocopier since this morning.

 (2) Susan's friends have been carrying those heavy bags for three hours.

16 ②

17 Jack has been working at the department store since last month.

18 ① 19 isn't → aren't

20 what their biggest money worry is

21 No, they aren't.

22 ⑤ 23 ② 24 ④번 → remaining

25 ⑤

26 (A) although (B) advice (C) even if

27 on the spot 28 ③

01 동의어 관계이다. lastly: 마지막으로 – finally: 마지막으로, result 결과 – outcome 결과

02 '누군가에게 무엇을 해야 할지 말해 주는 의견'은 'advice(충고)'가 적절하다. 부모님의 충고를 들어라.

03 allowance: 용돈. 부모에 의해 아이에게 규칙적으로 주어지는 아이가 쓸 수 있는 돈. 그녀는 용돈을 모아 노트북을 샀다.

04 on sale: 할인 중인, 판매되는. 아이스크림이 반값에 팔리고 있다. remaining: 남아 있는. Jack은 남은 주스를 마셨다.

05 have difficulty (in) -ing: ~하는 데 어려움을 겪다. 나는 영어로 의사소통하는 데 어려움을 겪었다.

06 on the spot: 즉각, 즉석에서. 그는 그 차를 보고 즉석에서 사기로 결정했다.

07 빈칸 다음에 '그렇다면 이 모자를 저기에 있는 장갑으로 교환할 수 있을까요?'라고 하고 있으므로, 환불 요청에 대해 거절했음을 추론할 수 있다.

08 ©의 change를 exchange로 고치는 것이 적절하다.

09 교환을 요청하는 말에, 가능하다며 어떤 것을 원하는지 묻는 것이 자연스러우므로 ④번이 적절하다.

10 as는 전치사로 '~로서'의 의미이다. as a gift: 선물로

11 so는 여기서 결과를 나타내는 접속사이다.

12 (1) 어떻게 처리할지 'how to handle', (2) 5분 전부터 물어뜯고 있는 것은 현재완료진행시제로 표현한다. (3) 어느 발을 내밀지 'which foot to put out' *governor: 통치자, 원님

13 ④ 의문대명사 what은 to부정사 뒤에 목적어를 쓰지 않는다. what이 목적어 역할을 하기 때문이다. how로 고치는 것이 적절하다.

14 조건을 충족시키면서 10 단어를 넘지 않도록 하고, 명사를 뒤에서 꾸미는 분사의 어법에도 유의한다. (1) 지난 토요일에 시청을 시작해서 오늘이 화요일이므로 기간은 4일이다. (2) 글자 수에 유의하여 마지막에 for가 오도록 영작한다.

15 (1) 어떻게 수리하는지: how to fix, 오늘 아침부터: since this morning (2) 저 무거운 가방들: those heavy bags

16 <보기>는 현재완료의 용법 중 '계속'이며, 과거에 시작된 일이 현재에도 지속되고 있음을 나타낸다. ②는 '건물 내부의 모든 방들에 대한 점검을 끝냈다'는 내용으로, '완료' 용법이며, 나머지는 모두 '계속' 용법이다.

17 '지난달 이후로'는 since last month를 쓴다.

18 ①번 다음 문장의 some advice에 주목한다. 주어진 문장은 the problem에 대한 조언이므로 ①번이 적절하다.

19 주격 관계대명사 that의 선행사가 items이기 때문에, aren't로 고치는 것이 적절하다.

20 asked의 직접목적어가 되도록, 간접의문문의 순서로 쓰는 것이 적절하다.

21 설문 조사에 따르면, 대다수의 학생들은 현명한 소비자가 아니다.

22 필요하지 않은 것에 돈을 소비한 학생들의 퍼센트(12%)는 충분한 용돈을 받지 못한다고 생각하는 학생들의 퍼센트(60%)의 '5분의 1'이다. ① 3분의 1, ② 3분의 2, ③ 4분의 1, ④ 4분의 3, ⑤ 5분의 1

23 앞에 나오는 내용과 상반되는 내용이 뒤에 이어지므로

However가 가장 적절하다. ① 게다가, 더욱이, ③ 따라서, 그러므로, ⑤ 비슷하게

24 ④ remaining 남아 있는, ① have difficulty –ing: ~하는 데 어려움이 있다, ② '현재완료진행시제'로 써서 과거부터 현재까지 돈을 저축해 오고 있다는 의미를 나타냄. ③ '현재완료진행시제'로 써서 과거부터 현재까지 돈을 너무 많이 써 오고 있다는 의미를 나타냄. ⑤ by ~ing: ~함으로써

25 50%-40%-10%의 규칙은 50%를 '저축하고', 40%를 '쓰고', 남아 있는 10%를 자선 단체에 기부하는 것을 의미한다.

26 (A) 뒤에 '주어+동사'가 있으므로 although가 적절하다. 'although+주어+동사', 'in spite of' 뒤에는 '주어+동사'가 올 수 없다. (B) advice: 셀 수 없는 명사이다. (C) '비록 물건들이 할인 판매 중이라고 해도'라고 해야 하므로 even if가 적절하다. even if: ~라고 할지라도, as if: 마치 ~인 것처럼

27 on the spot: 즉각, 즉석에서

28 민지가 필요한 물건을 산다면 할인 판매하는 물건을 사는 것은 좋지만, 필요하지 않은 물건도 사기 때문에 현명한 소비자가 아니다.

교과서 파헤치기

Lesson 1

단어 TEST Step 1   p.02

01 공학 (기술), 엔지니어링   02 졸업하다
03 용감한, 대담한   04 기회
05 알다, 깨닫다, 실현하다[달성하다]   06 목표
07 입장하다, 참가하다   08 따르다, 뒤를 잇다
09 성취하다, 달성하다
10 (심장이) 고동치다, 뛰다   11 시간제 근무의
12 환경, 상황, 분위기
13 (직장·학교 등을) 그만두다, (하던 일을) 그만두다
14 자원하다, 봉사하다   15 회사
16 (특정 직업을) 훈련하다   17 ~인지 아닌지
18 대학(교)   19 공기 오염   20 안정된, 안정적인
21 (상을) 타다, 이기다   22 추구하다, 좇다
23 결정, 결심   24 엔지니어, 기술자   25 성공하다
26 영감을 주다, 고무하다
27 기억할 만한, 인상적인
28 전문적인, (전문) 직업의   29 이끌다
30 중요한, 주된; 전공, 전공하다
31 (특정) 지역의, 현지의   32 용기
33 사진 촬영술   34 놀랍게도   35 사실은
36 (병이나 상황이) 나아지다   37 생계 수단으로
38 실현되다, 사실이 되다   39 ~의 경우에
40 전혀 ~가 아니다   41 처음으로
42 기분 내키는 대로 하다   43 결정하다

단어 TEST Step 2   p.03

01 college   02 decision   03 follow
04 goal   05 courage   06 surprisingly
07 achieve   08 beat   09 bold
10 environment   11 chance   12 succeed
13 professional   14 volunteer   15 company
16 air pollution   17 whether   18 pursue
19 engineer   20 win   21 graduate
22 inspire   23 local   24 major
25 part-time   26 lead   27 memorable
28 photography   29 quit   30 realize
31 stable   32 engineering   33 train
34 designer   35 not ~ at all   36 in fact
37 decide on   38 make a decision
39 come true   40 take a chance   41 get better
42 in one's case   43 for the first time

단어 TEST Step 3   p.04

1 achieve, 성취하다, 달성하다   2 quit, (하던 일을) 그만두다
3 contest, 대회   4 bold, 용감한, 대담한   5 major, 전공
6 beat, (심장이) 고동치다, 뛰다   7 stable, 안정된, 안정적인
8 realize, 실현하다[달성하다]   9 graduate, 졸업하다
10 goal, 목표   11 inspire, 영감을 주다
12 pursue, 추구하다, 추진하다
13 train, (특정 직업을) 훈련하다   14 courage, 용기
15 trial and error, 시행착오   16 designer, 디자이너

대화문 TEST Step 1   p.05~06

Listen and Talk A 1

Have, had Spanish, before / haven't, Have, tried it / have, I hope, can, sometime / will, For now, Spanish recipe

Listen and Talk A 2

Have, ever visited another / haven't, Have / I've been to, I hope, can, to another country sometime / to visit, looks, interesting

Listen and Talk A 3

should / already read it / did, How about, Have you also seen / haven't / even better than, I hope, soon

Listen and Talk A 4

listening to / too, enjoy playing the / can play the / How about you / never learned how to play / fun, I hope, chance to learn

Listen and Talk C

about training / do, all kinds of / Have, ever thought, becoming / have, to become / are you doing to achieve, goal / doing volunteer work / else, doing / also watching / great, I hope, someday

Review 1

have, tried, before / haven't / How about, Have, tried / eaten, once, delicious

Review 2

favorite, Have, read it / haven't, seen, How about, Have, seen, too / have, more, I hope, sometime / will

대화문 TEST Step 2   p.07~08

Listen and Talk A 1

G: Have you ever had Spanish food before?
B: No, I haven't. Have you tried it?
G: Yes, I have. I hope you can try it sometime. It's really good.
B: I will. For now, I'll just buy this Spanish recipe book.

Listen and Talk A 2

B: Have you ever visited another country?

G: No, I haven't. Have you?

B: Yes, I've been to France. I hope you can travel to another country sometime.

G: Yes, I really want to visit Canada. Look! This book about Canada looks very interesting.

Listen and Talk A 3

G: You should read this book about the moon. It's really interesting.

B: I know. I've already read it.

G: You did? How about the movie? Have you also seen the movie about the book?

B: No, I haven't.

G: Well, it's even better than the book. I hope you can see the movie soon.

Listen and Talk A 4

G: I'm going to buy this CD. I love listening to piano music.

B: Me, too. I also enjoy playing the piano.

G: Really? So you can play the piano?

B: Yes. How about you?

G: Well, I've never learned how to play.

B: It's fun. I hope you'll have a chance to learn.

Listen and Talk C

B: I really liked your book about training dogs.

W: Thank you. Do you like dogs?

B: Yes, I do. I love all kinds of animals.

W: Have you ever thought of becoming an animal doctor?

B: Yes, I have. I really want to become an animal doctor.

W: What are you doing to achieve your goal?

B: I'm doing volunteer work at the local animal house.

W: That's good. What else are you doing?

B: I'm also watching a lot of TV shows about animals.

W: You're doing great! I hope you become a good animal doctor someday.

B: Thank you.

Review 1

G: Mike, have you tried Bulgogi before?

B: No, I haven't.

G: How about Bibimbap? Have you tried that?

B: Yes, I've eaten it once. It was really delicious.

Review 2

G: My favorite book is *Charlie and the Chocolate Factory*. Have you read it, Peter?

B: No, I haven't, but I've seen the movie. How about you, Yubin? Have you seen the movie, too?

G: Yes, I have. But I like the book more. I hope you can read it sometime.

B: OK, I will.

본문 TEST Step 1   p.09~11

01 Find, Dream, Live   02 Hello, everyone

03 My name, I'm, photographer

04 going, how, found, realized

05 hope, inspire you   06 When I was young

07 also, taking pictures

08 never thought, lead to

09 In fact, at all

10 decide on, chose engineering

11 Being, looked OK

12 college, job, engineering company

13 stable, but, whether, enjoyed

14 changed, went on vacation

15 got, chance, see

16 amazing, took, pictures, lights

17 For, year, beating fast

18 back, entered, with, took

19 won, prize, chance, think

20 realized, made me happy

21 become, so, learn more

22 trial, error, better, part-time

23 one, made, bold decision

24 quit, decided, for, living

25 wasn't sure, succeed, try

26 something that made, happy

27 professional photographer, happy

28 find, dream, realize it

29 some advice to help

30 follow your heart

31 what makes you happy

32 case, taking, stars   33 work hard

34 Pursuing, dream, easy   35 through hard work

36 be bold

37 courage, make decisions, life

38 afraid but, took, chance

39 truly hope, find, pursue

01 Find, Dream, Live   02 Hello
03 a photographer
04 going to, how I found, realized
05 hope, inspire you   06 When I was young
07 liked taking pictures
08 never thought, lead to a job
09 In fact, at all
10 decide on, college, engineering
11 Being, looked OK
12 After college, an engineering company
13 stable, whether
14 when, went on vacation   15 got a chance
16 amazing, took many pictures, dancing lights
17 For the first time, years, beating fast
18 came back, entered, the pictures I took
19 won first prize, chance to think
20 realized, made me happy
21 Suddenly, learn more about photography
22 trial and error, got better, part-time work
23 one day, bold decision
24 decided to, for a living
25 wasn't sure if, succeed, to try
26 something that, happy
27 professional photographer
28 find a dream, realize it
29 some advice to help
30 follow your heart
31 what makes you happy
32 case, taking pictures of stars
33 work hard   34 Pursuing, easy
35 through hard work
36 be bold
37 courage, make decisions, life
38 afraid, took a chance
39 truly hope

1 꿈을 찾고 실현하세요!
2 여러분, 안녕하세요.
3 나의 이름은 David Parker이고, 나는 사진작가입니다.
4 오늘 나는 어떻게 내가 꿈을 찾아서 실현했는지 이야기하려고 해요.
5 나의 이야기가 여러분에게 영감을 주기를 바라요.
6 나는 어렸을 때 별을 사랑했어요.
7 나는 또한 사진 찍는 것을 좋아했어요.

8 하지만 나는 이것들이 직업과 연관될 수 있다고 전혀 생각하지 못했어요.
9 사실 나는 아예 꿈이 없었어요.
10 내가 대학에서 전공을 정해야 했을 때, 나는 공학을 선택했어요.
11 엔지니어가 되는 것이 괜찮아 보였거든요.
12 대학 졸업 후 저는 엔지니어링 회사에 취직했어요.
13 그것은 안정적인 직업이었지만, 난 내가 그 일을 정말로 좋아하는지는 알 수가 없었어요.
14 어느 겨울, 내가 아이슬란드로 휴가를 갔을 때 모든 것이 바뀌었어요.
15 그곳에서 나는 오로라를 볼 수 있는 기회가 있었죠.
16 빛들은 경이로웠고 나는 하늘에서 춤추는 빛들의 사진을 많이 찍었어요.
17 수년 만에 처음으로 나는 심장이 빠르게 뛰고 있는 것을 느낄 수 있었어요.
18 나는 돌아와서 아이슬란드에서 찍은 사진으로 사진 경연 대회에 참가했어요.
19 놀랍게도 나는 1등상을 받았고, 이 일은 나에게 인생을 생각해 볼 기회를 주었어요.
20 나는 사진 찍는 것이 나를 행복하게 한다는 것을 깨달았어요.
21 갑자기 나는 좋은 사진작가가 되고 싶어서 사진 촬영 기술에 대해 더 배우기 시작했어요.
22 몇 년의 시행착오 끝에 나는 더 나아졌고 사진작가로 시간제 근무일을 하기 시작했어요.
23 그러던 어느 날 나는 대담한 결심을 했어요.
24 나는 직장을 그만 두고 생계 수단으로 사진을 찍기로 했어요.
25 나는 내가 성공할 수 있을지 확신하지 못했지만 시도해 보기로 결심했어요.
26 나는 나를 행복하게 만드는 무언가를 정말로 하고 싶었어요.
27 지금, 나는 전문 사진작가이고, 나는 행복합니다.
28 그렇다면 여러분은 꿈을 찾아 실현하고 싶은가요?
29 여기 여러분을 도와줄 몇 가지 조언이 있습니다.
30 첫째, 여러분의 마음을 따르세요.
31 여러분이 무엇을 하고 싶고 여러분을 행복하게 하는 것이 무엇인지 생각해 보세요.
32 나의 경우에 그것은 별 사진을 찍는 거였어요.
33 둘째, 열심히 노력하세요.
34 꿈을 추구하는 것은 쉽지 않아요.
35 나는 열심히 노력해 사진작가가 되었어요.
36 셋째, 대담해지세요.
37 여러분의 인생을 바꿀 결정을 하기 위해서는 용기가 필요합니다.
38 나는 두려웠지만 기회를 잡았어요.
39 나는 여러분이 꿈을 찾고, 꿈을 추구하고, 꿈을 실현하길 진심으로 바랍니다!

1 Find a Dream and Live It!

2 Hello, everyone.

3 My name is David Parker, and I'm a photographer.

4 Today, I'm going to tell you how I found my dream and realized it.

5 I hope my story can inspire you.

6 When I was young, I loved stars.

7 I also liked taking pictures.

8 However, I never thought these things could lead to a job.

9 In fact, I didn't have a dream at all.

10 When I had to decide on a major in college, I chose engineering.

11 Being an engineer looked OK.

12 After college, I got a job at an engineering company.

13 It was a stable job, but I didn't know whether I really enjoyed it.

14 Everything changed when I went on vacation to Iceland one winter.

15 There I got a chance to see the Northern Lights!

16 The lights were amazing, and I took many pictures of the dancing lights in the sky.

17 For the first time in many years, I could feel my heart beating fast.

18 After I came back, I entered a photo contest with the pictures I took in Iceland.

19 Surprisingly, I won first prize, and this gave me a chance to think about my life.

20 I realized that taking pictures made me happy.

21 Suddenly, I wanted to become a good photographer, so I started to learn more about photography.

22 After years of trial and error, I got better, and I began to do some part-time work as a photographer.

23 Then one day, I made a bold decision.

24 I quit my job and decided to take pictures for a living.

25 I wasn't sure if I could succeed, but I decided to try.

26 I really wanted to do something that made me happy.

27 Now, I'm a professional photographer, and I'm happy.

28 So do you want to find a dream and realize it?

29 Here's some advice to help you.

30 First, follow your heart.

31 Think about what you like to do and what makes you happy.

32 In my case, it was taking pictures of stars.

33 Second, work hard.

34 Pursuing a dream is not easy.

35 I became a photographer through hard work.

36 Third, be bold.

37 You need courage to make decisions that will change your life.

38 I was afraid but I took a chance.

39 I truly hope you can find a dream, pursue it, and live it!

Team Project Step 3

1. respect

2. a historian

3. chose, spent her whole life searching, abroad

After You Read B

1. Advice

2. Follow, heart

3. what you like to do, what makes you happy

4. hard

5. Pursuing, is

6. bold

7. courage to make decisions

Think and Write

1. to become a famous fashion designer

2. are, to do to realize my dream

3. design school, study fashion design

4. after I graduate, work at

5. When, own brand

6. hold my first fashion show

7. hope, will come true

Team Project Step 3

1. We respect Dr. Park Byeong-seon.

2. She was a historian.

3. We chose her because she spent her whole life searching for Korean national treasures abroad.

After You Read B

1. David Parker's Advice

2. 1. Follow your heart.

3. Think about what you like to do, what makes you happy

4. 2. Work hard.

5. Pursuing a dream is not easy.

6. 3. Be bold.

7. You need courage to make decisions that will change your life.

Think and Write

1. My dream is to become a famous fashion designer.

2. There are many things to do to realize my dream.

3. First, I'll go to design school and study fashion design.

4. Then, after I graduate, I'll work at a fashion company.

5. When I'm 30, I'll start my own brand.

6. When I'm 35, I'll hold my first fashion show.

7. I hope my dream will come true.

Lesson 2

단어 TEST Step 1   p.26

01 수리하다	02 갑자기	03 바삭바삭한
04 다르다	05 다행스럽게도	06 포함시키다
07 더하다	08 청중, 관중	09 사발
10 맛있는	11 사라지다	12 아마도
13 특히	14 순간	15 낮잠
16 한 번	17 분명하게	18 위로, 위안
19 섞다, 혼합하다	20 차게 하다	21 주문하다; 주문
22 버섯	23 위, 복부, 배	
24 껍질; 껍질을 벗기다[깎다]		25 조리법
26 만족하게 하다	27 쏟아 붓다	28 혼합물, 반죽
29 양, 수량, 분량	30 최근에	31 ~하는 동안
32 녹이다	33 밀가루	
34 따뜻하게 하다; 따뜻한		35 ~ 한 그릇
36 ~과 비슷한	37 고장 나다	38 회복하다
39 ~하기 위하여	40 ~로 가득 차다	
41 기분이 나아지다, 기분이 좋아지다		42 ~하기를 원하다
43 A 뿐만 아니라 B도		

단어 TEST Step 2   p.27

01 add	02 maybe	03 audience
04 bowl	05 mix	06 comfort
07 differ	08 melt	09 mushroom
10 cool	11 nap	12 beat
13 disappear	14 especially	15 tasty
16 fix	17 flour	18 mixture
19 fortunately	20 laptop	21 suddenly
22 moment	23 once	24 crisp
25 order	26 include	27 stomach
28 peel	29 recipe	30 satisfy
31 taste	32 pour	33 quantity
34 recently	35 get well	36 be filled with ~
37 take an order	38 similar to ~	39 do one's best
40 stressed out	41 so that 주어 can ~	
42 break down	43 not only A but (also) B	

단어 TEST Step 3   p.28

1 melt, 녹이다   2 comfort, 위로, 위안, 편안   3 peel, 껍질

4 fix, 수리하다   5 crisp, 바삭바삭한   6 bake, 굽다

7 laptop, 휴대용 컴퓨터   8 disappear, 사라지다

9 bowl, 사발   10 recipe, 조리법   11 order, 주문하다

12 flour, 밀가루   13 snack, 간식   14 beat, 휘젓다, 섞다
15 satisfy, 만족하게 하다   16 audience, 청중, 관중

Listen and Talk A 1

Welcome to, What, to / want to order / that, all / for here, to go / For here

Listen and Talk A 2

ready to order / like, piece, cake / What kind, like / here, go / go

Listen and Talk A 3

What, like to order / like to order / anything to drink / one bottle of / for here, to go / to go

Listen and Talk A 4

would, like to order / want, one / Would, like anything else / it, to go / To go

Listen and Talk B

What would you like to order / I'd like to order / anything to drink / one / Is it, to go / for here, to go

Listen and Talk C

Welcome to, What, like to order / have a, a / anything else / will that / order two bottles of / Is it for here, to go / for here / comes to / Here, are

Review

(1) Are, ready to / like / be all / For here / To go

(2) would, like to / like to order / anything to drink / be all

(3) What would you like to order / want / Would, like anything else / for here, to go / To go

Listen and Talk A 1

W: Welcome to Italian Food. What would you like to order?
B: I want to order a mushroom pizza.
W: Will that be all?
B: Yes.
W: Is the order for here or to go?
B: For here, please.

Listen and Talk A 2

W: Hello. Are you ready to order?
B: Yes, please. I'd like a piece of cake.
W: What kind of cake would you like?
B: Chocolate cake, please.
W: For here or to go?

B: To go, please. Thank you.

Listen and Talk A 3

W: Hello. What would you like to order?
B: I'd like to order Manduguk.
W: Would you like anything to drink?
B: Yes, one bottle of water, please.
W: Is it for here or to go?
B: It's to go, please.

Listen and Talk A 4

W: Hello. What would you like to order?
B: I want a hot dog and one milk, please.
W: Would you like anything else?
B: No, thank you.
W: Will it be for here or to go?
B: To go, please. Thank you.

Listen and Talk B

A: Hello. What would you like to order?
B: I'd like to order two hot dogs.
A: Would you like anything to drink?
B: Yes, one orange juice, please.
A: Is it for here or to go?
B: It's for here, please. / B: It's to go, please.

Listen and Talk C

M: Welcome to Sandwich Place. What would you like to order?
G: I'd like to have a hamburger, and she'll have a chicken sandwich.
M: Would you like anything else?
G: One salad, please.
M: OK, then will that be all?
G: No, I'd like to order two bottles of water.
M: Is it for here or to go?
G: It's for here, please.
M: The total comes to 12 dollars.
G: OK. Here you are.

Review

(1) M: Hello. Are you ready to order?
    G: Yes, please. I'd like a chicken salad.
    M: Will that be all?
    G: Yes.
    M: For here or to go?
    G: To go, please.

(2) W: Hello. What would you like to order?
    B: I'd like to order a sandwich.
    W: Would you like anything to drink?
    B: Yes. One milk, please.
    W: Will that be all?
    B: Yes. Thank you.

(3) W: Hello. What would you like to order?

B: I want Gimchi Gimbap, please.

W: Would you like anything else?

B: No, thank you.

W: Is it for here or to go?

B: To go, please.

본문 TEST Step 1
p.33~35

01 Letters, Readers, Comfort

02 feel good, stressed out

03 make, think, moments, past

04 not only, but also   05 differ around

06 Let's, what, international readers

07 from USA   08 My, chicken soup

09 when, have, cold   10 caught, bad cold

11 bowl, so that, could

12 warmed, slowly, feel better

13 also very tasty

14 catch, cold, soup   15 from Brazil

16 made with, similar to   17 chips the most

18 Once, bad, stressed, bag

19 When, started, suddenly disappeared

20 crisp sound, made, feel

21 every time, stressed out   22 Then, feel good

23 from France   24 have many, but, most

25 looks like, sea shell

26 in, as, afternoon snack

27 makes, for, when, visit   28 taste, right out, oven

29 filled with, smell

30 especially, eating, with

31 Every time, think of   32 Let, share, so that

33 Maybe, become, for

34 Grandma's Special Recipe

35 flour, peel, salt   36 Melt, let, cool

37 Put, bowl, beat   38 Add, to, mix

39 Add, peel, mixture, mix

40 Pour, mixture into   41 Bake, for, to

본문 TEST Step 2
p.36~38

01 Letters, Readers, Comfort Food

02 makes you feel good, stressed out

03 can also, think of, from the past

04 not only, but also   05 differ around

06 Let's, what comfort foods

07 from USA

---

08 chicken soup   09 when, have a cold

10 caught a very bad cold

11 a bowl of, so that, could get well

12 warmed, feel better   13 very tasty

14 catch a cold   15 from Brazil

16 there are, are made with, similar to

17 the most

18 Once, had a bad day, stressed out, a bag of

19 suddenly disappeared

20 crisp sound of eating, made me feel

21 every time, stressed out

22 feel good   23 from

24 comfort foods, the most

25 looks like, sea shell

26 as an afternoon snack

27 always makes, for   28 right out of

29 is filled with, smell

30 especially like eating, with

31 Every time, think of

32 Let me share, so that, can make

33 become a comfort food

34 Special Recipe   35 flour, peel, cup of

36 Melt, let, cool   37 Put, bowl, beat

38 Add, to, mix

39 Add, orange peel, mixture

40 Pour, into   41 Bake, for, to, minutes

본문 TEST Step 3
p.39~41

1 우리의 독자들로부터 온 편지: 나에게 위안이 되는 음식

2 comfort food는 여러분이 슬프거나 화가 나거나 스트레스를 받을 때 기분을 좋게 해 주는 음식이다.

3 그것은 또한 여러분에게 과거의 행복한 순간들을 생각나게 할 수 있다.

4 그것은 위뿐만 아니라 마음도 충족해 준다.

5 comfort food는 전 세계적으로 다양하다.

6 세계 여러 나라의 우리 독자들은 어떤 comfort food를 즐기는지 알아보자.

7 미국에 사는 Jessica

8 나의 comfort food는 치킨 수프야.

9 미국에서는 사람들이 감기에 걸릴 때 이 수프를 먹어.

10 나는 어린아이였을 때 매우 심한 감기에 걸렸어.

11 아빠는 내가 나을 수 있도록 치킨 수프 한 그릇을 만들어 주셨어.

12 그 뜨거운 수프는 내 몸을 따뜻하게 했고, 나는 서서히 나아지기 시작했어.

13 그것은 매우 맛있기도 했어.

14 지금도 나는 감기에 걸리면 치킨 수프를 먹어.

15 브라질에 사는 Maria

16 브라질에는 감자와 비슷한 채소인 카사바로 만든 요리가 많아.

17 나는 카사바 칩을 좋아해.

18 한번은 내가 학교에서 안 좋은 일이 있고 스트레스를 받았을 때, 나의 가장 친한 친구가 나에게 카사바 칩 한 봉지를 사 줬어.

19 그 칩을 먹기 시작했을 때, 내 스트레스가 갑자기 사라졌어.

20 칩을 먹을 때 나는 바삭한 소리가 내 기분을 더 좋게 만들었어.

21 지금도 나는 스트레스를 받을 때마다 카사바 칩을 먹어.

22 그러면 나는 기분이 다시 좋아져!

23 프랑스에 사는 Simon

24 나는 comfort food가 많아. 하지만 가장 좋아하는 것은 마들렌이야.

25 마들렌은 조개처럼 생긴 작은 케이크야.

26 프랑스 사람들은 오후 간식으로 마들렌을 즐겨 먹어.

27 우리 할머니는 내가 찾아뵐 때는 항상 마들렌을 만들어 주셔.

28 마들렌은 오븐에서 막 나올 때 가장 맛있어.

29 그러면 부엌은 달콤한 냄새로 가득 차.

30 나는 특히 차 한 잔과 함께 오렌지 마들렌을 먹는 것을 좋아해.

31 마들렌을 보거나 냄새 맡을 때마다 나는 할머니가 생각나.

32 너희들도 오렌지 마들렌을 만들 수 있도록 우리 할머니의 특별한 요리법을 공유할게.

33 아마도 마들렌이 너희에게도 comfort food가 될 거야!

34 할머니의 특별한 요리법: 오렌지 마들렌

35 재료: 밀가루 1컵, 설탕 2/3컵, 달걀 2개, 오렌지 껍질 조금, 버터 1/4컵, 소금 1/8티스푼

36 1. 버터를 녹여서 식힌다.

37 2. 달걀, 설탕, 소금을 그릇에 넣고 휘젓는다.

38 3. 그릇에 밀가루를 넣고 섞는다.

39 4. 반죽에 버터와 오렌지 껍질을 넣고 섞는다.

40 5. 반죽을 마들렌 팬에 붓는다.

41 6. 오븐에서 10분에서 15분 동안 굽는다.

본문 TEST Step 4 - Step 5   p.42~47

1 Letters from Our Readers: My Comfort Food

2 Comfort food is food that makes you feel good when you are sad, angry, or stressed out.

3 It can also make you think of happy moments from the past.

4 It satisfies not only the stomach but also the heart.

5 Comfort foods differ around the world.

6 Let's see what comfort foods our international readers enjoy.

7 Jessica from USA

8 My comfort food is chicken soup.

9 In the USA, people eat this soup when they have a cold.

10 When I was a small child, I caught a very bad cold.

11 My father made me a bowl of chicken soup so that I could get well.

12 The hot soup warmed my body, and I slowly started to feel better.

13 It was also very tasty.

14 Now, when I catch a cold, I eat chicken soup.

15 Maria from Brazil

16 In Brazil, there are many dishes that are made with cassava, a vegetable similar to a potato.

17 I love cassava chips the most.

18 Once when I had a bad day at school and felt stressed out, my best friend bought me a bag of cassava chips.

19 When I started to eat the chips, my stress suddenly disappeared.

20 The crisp sound of eating chips made me feel better.

21 Now, every time I'm stressed out, I eat cassava chips.

22 Then I feel good again!

23 Simon from France

24 I have many comfort foods, but I love madeleines the most.

25 A madeleine is a small cake that looks like a sea shell.

26 People in France enjoy madeleines as an afternoon snack.

27 My grandmother always makes madeleines for me when I visit her.

28 They taste best when they come right out of the oven.

29 Then the kitchen is filled with a sweet smell.

30 I especially like eating her orange madeleines with a cup of tea.

31 Every time I see or smell madeleines, I think of my grandmother.

32 Let me share my grandmother's special recipe with you so that you can make orange madeleines, too.

33 Maybe madeleines will become a comfort food for you!

34 Grandma's Special Recipe: Orange Madeleines

35 You need: 1 cup of flour, 2/3 cup of sugar, 2 eggs, some orange peel, 1/4 cup of butter, 1/8 teaspoon of salt

36 1. Melt the butter and let it cool.

37 2. Put the eggs, sugar, and salt in a bowl and beat.

38 3. Add the flour to the bowl and mix.

39 4. Add the butter and orange peel to the mixture and mix.

40 5. Pour the mixture into the madeleine pan.

41 6. Bake in the oven for 10 to 15 minutes.

구석구석지문 TEST Step 1

p.48

Listen and Talk D

1. I'd like to

2. At, like to order

3. For, order an orange juice

After You Read A

1. What, your

2. USA

3. caught, bad cold, made me a bowl of chichken soup

4. feel better

5. Brazil

6. stressed out, bought me a bag of cassava chips

7. When, ate, disappeared

8. eating, made me feel better

9. France

10. makes, for me

11. eating, with

12. Every time, think of

Think and Write Step 2

1. My, Food

2. is chocolate

3. usually, feel bad

4. Recently, well, stressed

5. bought some chocolate

6. After eating, felt better

7. Eating, makes, feel good

구석구석지문 TEST Step 2

p.49

Listen and Talk D

1. I like Italian food, so I'd like to go to Taste of Italy.

2. At the restaurant, I'd like to order a potato pizza.

3. For a drink, I'd like to order an orange juice.

After You Read A

1. Q: What is your comfort food?

2. Jessica, USA

3. When I caught a very bad cold, my father made me a bowl of chicken soup.

4. The hot soup warmed my body, and I slowly started to feel better.

5. Maria, Brazil

6. When I felt stressed out, my best friend bought me a bag of cassava chips.

7. When I ate the chips, my stress disappeared.

8. The crisp sound of eating chips made me feel better.

9. Simon, France

10. My grandmother makes madeleines for me when I visit her.

11. I especially like eating her orange madeleines with tea.

12. Every time I see or smell madeleines, I think of her.

Think and Write Step 2

1. My Comfort Food

2. My comfort food is chocolate.

3. I usually eat it when I feel bad.

4. Recently, I didn't do well on a test and got stressed out.

5. I went to the store and bought some chocolate.

6. After eating the sweet chocolate, I felt better.

7. Eating chocolate makes me feel good.

51

10 suggest, 제안하다　11 contact, 접촉

12 expression, 표현　13 massage, 마사지

14 slave, 노예　15 law, 법　16 borrow, 빌리다

단어 TEST Step 1　　p.50

01 초래하다; 원인　02 현재의　03 결심하다

04 접촉　05 탐험가　06 공장

07 노예　08 홍수　09 화나게 하다

10 세기, 100년　11 문명　12 제안하다

13 진보한, 발전된　14 곧, 즉시　15 원래, 본래

16 의미　17 우주, 은하계　18 상인, 거래자

19 설계하다　20 경험하다　21 정의

22 표현　23 법　24 신화

25 포함하다　26 불안한　27 기원, 유래

28 폭풍　29 재판관, 판사; 재판하다

30 유래하다　31 생산하다　32 도구

33 빌리다　34 얇게 썬 조각; 한 조각

35 거쳐 지나가다　36 ~에서 오다, 유래하다

37 ~로 만들어지다　38 ~을 익히게 되다

39 비가 세차게 내리다　40 연락하다

41 우울한 얼굴을 하다

42 …을 본떠 ~의 이름을 부르다　43 의견을 같이하다

단어 TEST Step 2　　p.51

01 advanced　02 cause　03 experience

04 anger　05 Spanish　06 borrow

07 expression　08 factory　09 contact

10 flood　11 century　12 shortly

13 civilization　14 include　15 explorer

16 create　17 trader　18 storm

19 justice　20 law　21 produce

22 language　23 slice　24 suggest

25 judge　26 nervous　27 meaning

28 origin　29 present　30 slave

31 universe　32 originate　33 originally

34 myth　35 come from ~　36 pull one's leg

37 make a long face　38 pass through

39 break a leg　40 under the weather

41 keep in touch　42 not ~ at all　43 be made into ~

단어 TEST Step 3　　p.52

1 shortly, 곧, 즉시　2 anger, 화나게 하다

3 present, 현재의　4 century, 세기, 100년

5 civilization, 문명　6 flood, 홍수　7 originally, 원래

8 trader, 무역업자　9 universe, 우주, 은하계

대화문 TEST Step 1　　p.53~55

Listen and Talk A 1

cats and dogs / cats and dogs, that mean / means, raining a lot / Don't worry, in my backpack

Listen and Talk A 2

on me / Excuse me, Can, say that / on me, means, pay for / a lot / You're welcome

Listen and Talk A 3

looks delicious / Would, like some / thanks, not, tea / Not, tea, does, mean / don't like something / see, don't like

Listen and Talk A 4

under the weather / Excuse me, can, say that again / under the weather, don't feel well, have a cold / Why don't you, get, get medicine, over there / should

Listen and Talk B 1

make a long face / Excuse me, can you please say that again / make a long face / What does that mean / means, feel sad

Listen and Talk B 2

Break a leg / Excuse me, can you please say that again / Break a leg / What does that mean / Good luck

Listen and Talk B 3

under the weather / Excuse me, can you please say that again / under the weather / What does that mean / don't feel

Listen and Talk C

had a great time / My pleasure, come visit / love to, like to invite, to visit / it, that, come / can't say longer, keep my fingers crossed / Excuse me, can you, say that again / keep my fingers crossed, wish you good luck / Have, trip / keep in touch

Review 1

keep my fingers crossed / can you please say that again / keep my fingers crossed, wish you good luck

Review 2

feel under the weather / can you please say that again / feel under the weather / What does that mean / don't feel well, have a cold / Why don't you buy, get medicine, over there / will cats and dogs / Can you say that again / cats and dogs / What does that mean / means, raining a lot

Review 4

is on me / What does that mean / pay for

대화문 TEST Step 2   p.56~58

Listen and Talk A 1

G: Look. It's raining cats and dogs.

B: Raining cats and dogs? What does that mean?

G: It means "It's raining a lot."

B: Oh. Don't worry. I have an umbrella in my backpack.

Listen and Talk A 2

G: This juice is on me, Suho.

B: Excuse me? Can you say that again?

G: I said, "This juice is on me." It means "I'll pay for the juice."

B: Oh. Thanks a lot.

G: You're welcome.

Listen and Talk A 3

B: Everything looks delicious.

G: Yes. Would you like some of my spaghetti?

B: No, thanks. Spaghetti is not my cup of tea.

G: Not your cup of tea? What does that mean?

B: It means "I don't like something."

G: Oh, I see. You don't like spaghetti.

Listen and Talk A 4

G: I feel under the weather.

B: Excuse me, but can you please say that again?

G: I said, "I feel under the weather." It means "I don't feel well." I think I have a cold.

B: Oh. Why don't you buy some medicine before you get on the plane? You can get medicine at the store over there.

G: I guess I should.

Listen and Talk B 1

A: Don't make a long face.

B: Excuse me, but can you please say that again?

A: I said, "Don't make a long face."

B: What does that mean?

A: It means "Don't feel sad."

Listen and Talk B 2

M: Break a leg.

W: Excuse me, but can you please say that again?

M: I said, "Break a leg."

W: What does that mean?

M: It means "Good luck."

Listen and Talk B 3

M: It means "Good luck."

W: Excuse me, but can you please say that again?

M: I said, "I feel under the weather."

W: What does that mean?

M: It means "I don't feel well."

Listen and Talk C

G: Thank you for everything, Jiho. I had a great time in Korea.

B: My pleasure. Please come visit me again, Lucy.

G: I'd love to, but before I do, I'd like to invite you to visit me in London.

B: Thanks. Anyway, it's too bad that you can't come to my soccer game tomorrow.

G: I'm sorry that I can't stay longer. I'll keep my fingers crossed for you.

B: Excuse me, but can you please say that again?

G: I said, "I'll keep my fingers crossed for you." It means "I wish you good luck."

B: Oh. Thanks. Have a nice trip.

G: Thanks. I'll keep in touch.

Review 1

G: I'll keep my fingers crossed for you.

B: I'm sorry, but can you please say that again?

G: I said, "I'll keep my fingers crossed for you." It means "I wish you good luck."

Review 2

W: I feel under the weather.

M: Excuse me, but can you please say that again?

W: I said, "I feel under the weather."

M: What does that mean?

W: It means "I don't feel well." I think I have a cold.

M: Oh. Why don't you buy some medicine? You can get medicine at the store over there.

W: OK, I will.

Review 3

M: Look. It's raining cats and dogs.

W: Can you say that again?

M: It's raining cats and dogs.

W: What does that mean?

M: It means "It's raining a lot."

Review 4

G: This pizza is on me, Suho.

B: What does that mean?

G: It means "I'll pay for the pizza."

01 Words, Foreign Origin
02 borrowed words, other, languages
03 Here, examples with
04 comes from, means, press
05 was used, head massage
06 traders, experienced, with, introduced
07 meaning, few, entered, around
08 century, present, washing, hair
09 Shortly, be also used
10 play, which, written, by   11 look like humans
12 are designed, work, produced
13 idea of using, himself
14 called, from, for work
15 However, salve, in Czech
16 idea, to use, word   17 play, made into, fiction
18 comes, originates from, name
19 creation myth, gods, created
20 However, angered, so, caused
21 Spanish contact with, civilization
22 passing through, picked up
23 In, early uses, by
24 word, originally, from, second-largest
25 means, things, in German
26 origin, not clear
27 believed that, between, and
28 placed, slices, such food

01 Words, Foreign Origin
02 has often borrowed words, other cultures
03 are, with interesting stories
04 comes from, which, to press
05 was used
06 with a head massage, introduced, to
07 a few times, entered, around
08 present, washing the hair
09 Shortly after that, to be also used for
10 was written, Czech writer
11 look like
12 are designed to work, are produced
13 It, the idea of using, come from, himself
14 originally called, from, for
15 However, suggested, which, in Czech
16 decided to use
17 was made into, on television

18 comes from, originates from
19 creation myth, one of the three gods, created humans
20 angered, so, caused, flood
21 Spanish contact with, civilization
22 explorers, were passing through, picked up, for it
23 In English, early uses, by
24 originally comes from, second-largest
25 from, in German   26 is not clear
27 it is believed that, between, and
28 placed, Hamburg-style, two slices of bread, call such food

1 외국어에서 유래된 영어 단어
2 영어는 종종 다른 문화나 언어에서 단어를 빌려왔다.
3 여기 재미있는 이야기가 있는 몇 개의 예가 있다.
4 *shampoo*라는 단어는 힌디어 chāmpo에서 왔고, '누르다'라는 의미이다.
5 인도에서 그 단어는 머리 마사지라는 의미로 쓰였다.
6 인도에 있는 영국 상인들은 머리 마사지를 함께하는 목욕을 경험했고 마사지를 18세기에 영국에 소개했다.
7 *shampoo*라는 단어의 의미는 그 단어가 1762년쯤 영어에 처음으로 들어온 이후 몇 번 바뀌었다.
8 19세기에, *shampoo*는 '머리 감기'라는 현재의 의미를 갖게 되었다.
9 그 후 얼마 지나지 않아, 그 단어는 머리에 사용하는 특별한 비누에도 쓰이기 시작했다.
10 robot이라는 단어는 "*R.U.R.*"에서 왔는데, 그 연극은 1920년 체코의 작가 Karel Čapek에 의해 쓰였다.
11 그 연극에서 로봇은 인간처럼 생긴 기계이다.
12 그들은 인간을 위해 일하도록 설계되고, 공장에서 생산된다.
13 robot이라는 단어를 사용하려는 생각이 Karel Čapek 자신에게서 나온 게 아니었다는 것이 흥미롭다.
14 그는 원래 자신의 연극에서 그 기계들을 '일'을 의미하는 라틴어에서 온 *labori*라고 불렀다.
15 하지만, 그의 형이 *roboti*를 제안했는데, *roboti*는 체코어로 '노예 근로자들'을 의미한다.
16 Karel Čapek은 그 아이디어가 마음에 들어 roboti라는 단어를 사용하기로 결정했다.
17 1938년에 그 연극은 영국 TV에서 공상 과학물로 만들어졌다.
18 hurricane이라는 단어는 스페인어 단어 huracán에서 왔고, 그것은 마야 신의 이름에서 유래한다.
19 마야의 창조 신화에서, Huracán은 바람, 폭풍우, 그리고 불에 관한 날씨의 신이며, 그는 인간을 창조한 세 명의 신들 중 한 명이다.

20 하지만, 최초의 인간들이 신들을 화나게 해서 Huracán은 거대한 홍수를 일으켰다.

21 스페인이 마야 문명과 했던 첫 접촉은 1517년이었다.

22 카리브 제도를 지나던 스페인 탐험가들이 허리케인을 겪었고, 그 지역 사람들로부터 그것을 의미하는 단어를 듣게 되었다.

23 영어에서 일찍이 *hurricane*을 사용한 것 중 하나는 1608년 셰익스피어의 희곡에서였다.

24 *hamburger*라는 단어는 원래 독일에서 두 번째로 큰 도시인 함부르크에서 왔다.

25 *hamburger*는 독일어로 '함부르크 출신의 사람 또는 사물'을 의미한다.

26 최초의 햄버거의 기원은 분명하지 않다.

27 하지만 햄버거는 1885년에서 1904년 사이의 언젠가 미국 텍사스에 있는 작은 마을에서 발명되었다고 믿어진다.

28 한 요리사가 빵 두 조각 사이에 함부르크 스타일의 스테이크를 넣었고, 사람들은 그런 음식을 햄버거라고 부르기 시작했다.

본문 TEST Step 4-Step 5
p.65~69

1 English Words of Foreign Origin

2 English has often borrowed words from other cultures or languages.

3 Here are some examples with interesting stories.

4 The word *shampoo* comes from the Hindi word *chāmpo*, which means "to press."

5 In India, the word was used for a head massage.

6 British traders in India experienced a bath with a head massage and introduced it to Britain in the 18th century.

7 The meaning of the word *shampoo* changed a few times after it first entered English around 1762.

8 In the 19th century, *shampoo* got its present meaning of "washing the hair."

9 Shortly after that, the word began to be also used for a special soap for the hair.

10 The word *robot* comes from the play *R.U.R.*, which was written in 1920 by a Czech writer Karel Čapek.

11 In the play, robots are machines that look like humans.

12 They are designed to work for humans and are produced in a factory.

13 It is interesting that the idea of using the word *robot* didn't come from Karel Čapek himself.

14 He originally called the machines in his play *labori* from the Latin word for "work."

15 However, his brother suggested *roboti*, which

means "slave workers" in Czech.

16 Karel Čapek liked the idea and decided to use the word *roboti*.

17 In 1938, the play was made into a science fiction show on television in Britain.

18 The word *hurricane* comes from the Spanish word *huracán*, which originates from the name of a Mayan god.

19 In the Mayan creation myth, Huracán is the weather god of wind, storm, and fire, and he is one of the three gods who created humans.

20 However, the first humans angered the gods, so Huracán caused a great flood.

21 The first Spanish contact with the Mayan civilization was in 1517.

22 Spanish explorers who were passing through the Caribbean experienced a hurricane and picked up the word for it from the people in the area.

23 In English, one of the early uses of *hurricane* was in a play by Shakespeare in 1608.

24 The word *hamburger* originally comes from Hamburg, Germany's second-largest city.

25 *Hamburger* means "people or things from Hamburg" in German.

26 The origin of the first hamburger is not clear.

27 However, it is believed that the hamburger was invented in a small town in Texas, USA, sometime between 1885 and 1904.

28 A cook placed a Hamburg-style steak between two slices of bread, and people started to call such food a hamburger.

구석구석지문 TEST Step 1
p.70

After You Read A

1. Dictionary

2. from other cultures, languages

3. comes from, which, to press

4. which, slave workers, in Czech

5. Spanish word, which originates from

6. Hamburg, the second-largest city in Germany

Around the World

1. English words, come from French

2. include, like judge, justice

3. There are many English words, that

4. For example, come from Italian

5. vegetables, Spanish

6. For example, comes from, in Spanish

Think and Write Step 2

1. Origin, Word *Sandwich*

2. comes from, who, the 4th Earl

3. enjoyed eating, two slices of bread, while he was eating

4. thought that, such food a sandwich after

구석구석지문 TEST Step 2 p.71

After You Read A

1. Online Dictionary

2. English words from other cultures or languages

3. shampoo: It comes from the Hindi word *chāmpo*, which means "to press."

4. robot: It comes from *roboti*, which means "slave workers" in Czech.

5. hurricane: It comes from Spanish word, *huracán*, which originates from the name of a Mayan god.

6. hamburger: It comes from Hamburg, the second-largest city in Germany.

Around the World

1. 1. Many English words about law come from French.

2. Examples include words like judge and justice.

3. 2. There are many English words about music that come from Italian.

4. For example, piano and violin come from Italian.

5. 3. Many English words for vegetables come from Spanish.

6. For example, tomato comes from *tomate* and potato comes from *patata* in Spani

Think and Write Step 2

1. The Origin of the Word *Sandwich*

2. The word sandwich comes from John Montagu, who was the 4th Earl of Sandwich.

3. He enjoyed eating meat between two slices of bread because he could play a card game while he was eating.

4. People thought that it was a great idea and began to call such food a sandwich after him.

Lesson 4

단어 TEST Step 1 p.72

01 빠듯한, 꽉 조이는[딱 붙는]	02 환불; 환불받다
03 균형, 통장의 잔액 04 사례, 경우	05 자선 단체
06 편안한 07 영수증	08 용돈
09 남아 있는 10 바로 잡다	11 예산
12 소파 13 나누다	14 반품하다
15 교환; 교환하다 16 비록 ~이지만	17 저축하다, 구하다
18 기부하다 19 노력	20 마지막으로
21 용돈 22 대다수	23 의약품
24 그 대신에 25 가격, 가치	26 관리하다
27 작동하다 28 받다	29 헐렁한, 느슨한
30 결과 31 설문조사	32 최근에
33 ~하는 동안, ~하는 반면에	34 이미, 벌써
35 환불받다 36 ~하기를 원하다, 좋아하다	
37 ~을 돌보다, ~을 처리하다	38 즉시
39 다 쓰다, 완전히 소모하다	
40 ~하는 데 어려움을 겪다	41 가지고 다니다
42 할인 중인, 판매되는	43 돈을 돌려받다

단어 TEST Step 2 p.73

01 refund	02 although	03 price
04 comfortable	05 couch	06 return
07 effort	08 weekly	09 correct
10 instead	11 budget	12 exchange
13 charity	14 lastly	15 remaining
16 donate	17 result	18 loose
19 receipt	20 majority	21 paper money
22 balance	23 allowance, pocket money	
24 divide	25 receive	26 tight
27 rainy	28 already	29 medicine
30 recently	31 case	32 manage
33 save	34 survey	35 right away
36 get a refund	37 take effort	38 on the spot
39 carry around	40 would like to	
41 get an exchange		
42 change one's mind		43 take care of ~

단어 TEST Step 3 p.74

1 loose, 느슨한 2 medicine, 의약품 3 donate, 기부하다

4 majority, 대다수 5 refund, 환불 6 advice, 충고

7 correct, 바로 잡다 8 budget, 예산

9 remaining, 남아 있는　10 balance, 잔액

11 effort, 노력　12 exchange, 교환

13 allowance, 용돈　14 receipt, 영수증

15 couch, 소파　16 charity, 자선 단체

대화문 TEST Step 1　p.75~77

Listen and Talk A 1
help you / like to get, refund / wrong with / changed, mind, get, back / take care of, right away

Listen and Talk A 2
need some help / like to return / Let's see, receipt with / Here it is, it / it's possible

Listen and Talk A 3
looking for, special / like to exchange / would you like / Here you are

Listen and Talk A 4
What, do for you / exchange, for, different / What, would, like / I'd like, yellow one / Here you are

Listen and Talk B 1
May I help you / I'd like to exchange / What, it for / like to, it for

Listen and Talk B 2
May I / get a refund for / receipt / do, Here it is

Listen and Talk C
May I help you / get a refund for / receipt / don't, received, it as / it's, to get, refund / I see, exchange, for something else / can, would you like to get / want to get / Let me see, price, same, take it

Listen and Talk D
bought, last week, look good on, wonder if, exchange it for / up to you

Talk and Play
Excuse me, exchange, for / anything wrong with / don't like

Excuse me, get a refund for / anything wrong

Review 1
May I help you / I'd like to return / anything wrong with / changed, mind, have, back / Here's your money

Review 2
Can I help you / I'd like to exchange / too small for / would you like to exchange it for / Medium, have it in / Here you are

Review 3
May, help / get a refund for / afraid you can't / exchange, for, over / can

대화문 TEST Step 2　p.78~80

Review 4
May, help / get a refund for / receipt / do, Here it is

Listen and Talk A 1
W: Hello. May I help you?

B: Yes, please. I'd like to get a refund for this watch.

W: OK. Was there anything wrong with it?

B: No, I just changed my mind. Can I get my money back?

W: OK. I'll take care of it right away.

Listen and Talk A 2
W: Hello. Do you need some help?

B: Yes. I'd like to return this smartphone case.

W: Let's see. Do you have the receipt with you?

B: Here it is. I bought it three days ago.

W: Oh, then it's possible.

Listen and Talk A 3
W: Hello. Are you looking for anything special?

B: No, I'm not. I'd like to exchange this T-shirt. It's too small.

W: Sure. What size would you like?

B: Large, please.

W: Here you are.

B: Thank you.

Listen and Talk A 4
W: Hello. What can I do for you?

B: Can I exchange this black umbrella for a different color?

W: Sure. What color would you like?

B: I'd like a yellow one, please..

W: OK. Here you are.

Listen and Talk B 1
A: Hello. May I help you?

B: Yes, please. I'd like to exchange this bag.

A: Sure. What would you like to exchange it for?

B: I'd like to exchange it for a cap.

A: OK.

Listen and Talk B 2
A: Hello. May I help you?

B: Yes, please. I'd like to get a refund for this bag.

A: Sure. Do you have the receipt?

B: Yes, I do. Here it is.

Listen and Talk C
M: Hello. May I help you?

G: Yes, please. I'd like to get a refund for this cap.

57

M: Do you have the receipt?

_: No, I don't. I received it as a gift.

M: If you don't have the receipt, then, it's not possible to get a refund.

G: I see. Then, can I exchange it for something else?

M: Yes, you can. What would you like to get?

G: I want to get this blue bag.

M: Let me see .... The price is the same, so you can just take it.

G: Thank you.

Listen and Talk D

G: I bought this red skirt last week. I like the skirt, but my sister says that the color doesn't look good on me. I wonder if I should exchange it for a different color.

B: It's up to you but I think it's fine.

Talk and Play

A: Excuse me. I'd like to exchange this T-shirt for these pants.

B: OK. Is there anything wrong with it?

A: I don't like the color.

B: I see.

A: Excuse me. I'd like to get a refund for this cap.

B: OK. Is there anything wrong with it?

A: I don't like the color.

B: I see.

Review 1

W: Hello. May I help you?

B: Yes, please. I'd like to return this baseball glove.

W: OK. Was there anything wrong with it?

B: No, I just changed my mind. Can I have my money back?

W: OK. Here's your money.

Review 2

M: Hello. Can I help you?

W: Yes, please. I'd like to exchange this yellow T-shirt. It's too small for me.

M: Sure. What size would you like to exchange it for?

W: Medium size, please. Oh! Can I have it in red?

M: OK. Here you are.

Review 3

M: Hello. May I help you?

G: Yes, please. Can I get a refund for this hat?

M: I'm afraid you can't.

G: Then, can I exchange this hat for the gloves over there?

M: Yes, you can.

Review 4

A: Hello. May I help you?

B: I'd like to get a refund for this cap.

A: Sure. Do you have the receipt?

B: Yes, I do. Here it is.

본문 TEST Step 1   p.81~83

01 Ask Dr.

02 Green, Times

03 Teens', Habits

04 How smart, with

05 results, survey, students

06 asked, smart with

07 As, shows, while

08 what, biggest, worry is

09 enough allowance, difficulty saving

10 Lastly, spent, on, need

11 survey, majority, smart with

12 Managing, becoming, takes effort

13 have, money worries

14 Let's talk with

15 I'm Jason

16 weekly allowance, never, enough

17 By, all, is gone

18 how to solve

19 I'm Dr. Money

20 Let's, at, spending diary

21 used up, at, beginning

22 Here's, tip

23 carry around, weekly allowance

24 Divide, into days

25 carry, for each day

26 Dr. Money

27 I'm Steve

28 have difficulty saving

29 been saving, for, last

30 However, still, enough money

31 what to do

32 Let's see

33 last few, spent, saved

34 think, been spending

35 save, need, tighter budget

36 For example, follow, rule

37 save, donate, remaining, charity

38 By following, rule, manage

39 save, faster, buy, ticket

40 I'm Minji

41 buy, on sale

42 sale, buy, although, need

43 Last, bought, sale, already

44 Buying, good, buy, need

45 case, that, things, even

46 Here's, advice

47 Before, something, yourself

48 go shopping, make, list

49 items, on, if, sale

50 won't buy, on, spot

01 Ask, Money
02 Middle School Times
03 Spending Habits
04 How smart, with
05 results, a survey
06 smart with
07 As, shows, while
08 asked, answered, biggest money worry
09 As, shows, think, enough allowance while, have difficulty saving
10 Lastly, spent, on, didn't need
11 shows, the majority, smart with
12 Managing, becoming, takes
13 money worries
14 Let's talk with
15 I'm
16 weekly allowance, enough
17 By, is gone
18 how to solve
19 I'm
20 look at, spending diary
21 used up, at the beginning of the week
22 my tip
23 carry around, weekly allowance
24 Divide, into
25 carry, for each day
26 Hello
27 I'm
28 have difficulty saving
29 I've been saving, for the last two months
30 However, still don't, enough money
31 what to do
32 Let's see
33 In the last few, allowance, saved
34 you've been spending
35 To save, have a tighter budget
36 follow the 50%-40%-10% rule
37 Save, donate the remaining, charity
38 By following, manage, better
39 faster to buy
40 I'm
41 on sale
42 on sale, although
43 bought, already have
44 Buying, is, things you need
45 In your case, don't even need
46 Here's, advice
47 ask yourself
48 go shopping, make
49 Don't buy, on the list
50 won't buy, on the spot

1 Dr. Money에게 물어보세요.
2 그린 중학교 타임스
3 10대들의 소비 습관
4 당신은 돈에 관해 얼마나 현명한가?
5 이것은 Green 중학교 학생 100명의 설문 조사 결과이다.
6 우리는 먼저 학생들에게 "당신은 돈에 관하여 현명한가?"라고 물었다.
7 그래프 1이 보여 주듯이, 30%가 "예"라고 대답한 반면 70%가 "아니요"라고 답했다.
8 그 다음 우리는 "아니요"라고 대답한 학생들에게 그들의 돈에 대한 가장 큰 고민이 무엇인지 물었다.
9 그래프 2가 보여주듯이 28%가 자신들이 돈을 모으는 것에 어려움이 있다고 생각하는 반면, 60%는 충분한 용돈을 받지 못한다고 생각한다.
10 마지막으로, 12%는 필요하지 않은 것에 돈을 소비했다고 말했다.
11 우리의 설문 조사는 대다수의 학생들이 자신들이 돈에 관련하여 현명하지 못하다고 생각한다는 것을 보여준다.
12 돈을 관리하는 것은 쉽지 않고 현명한 소비자가 되는 것에는 노력이 필요하다.
13 여러분은 돈과 관련된 걱정거리가 있는가?
14 Dr. Money와 이야기해 보자.
15 저는 Jason이에요.
16 저는 매주 용돈을 받지만, 절대로 충분하지 않아요.
17 목요일쯤이면 용돈이 모두 사라져요.
18 이 문제를 해결할 방법을 모르겠어요.
19 안녕하세요, Dr. Money입니다.
20 용돈 기입장을 한번 봅시다.
21 주의 초반에 용돈의 대부분을 다 썼군요.
22 이게 내 조언이에요.
23 일주일 용돈 전부를 가지고 다니지 마세요.
24 용돈을 하루 단위로 나누세요..
25 그리고 하루에 필요한 돈만 들고 다니세요.
26 안녕하세요, Dr. Money.
27 저는 Steve예요.
28 저는 돈을 모으기가 어려워요.
29 예를 들면, 저는 좋아하는 가수의 콘서트에 가려고 지난 두 달 동안 돈을 저축해 오고 있어요.
30 하지만 저는 여전히 충분한 돈을 가지고 있지 않아요.
31 어떻게 해야 할지 모르겠어요.
32 어디 봅시다.
33 지난 몇 주에 용돈의 80%를 사용하고 20%만을 저축했군요.
34 나는 Steve가 돈을 너무 많이 써 왔다고 생각해요.
35 돈을 모으기 위해서, 더 빠듯한 예산을 세우는 것이 필요해요.
36 예를 들어, Steve는 50%-40%-10%의 규칙을 따를 수 있어요.
37 50%를 저축하고, 40%를 쓰고, 남아 있는 10%를 자선 단체에 기부하세요.
38 이 규칙을 따름으로써 돈을 더 잘 관리할 수 있어요.
39 그러면 그 티켓을 사기 위해 돈을 더 빨리 모을 수 있답니다.
40 저는 민지입니다.
41 저는 할인 판매하는 물건을 사는 것을 좋아해요.
42 어떤 물건이 할인 판매를 하면 저는 그것이 필요하지 않더라도 사요.

43 지난주에는 할인 판매하는 티셔츠 두 장을 샀지만 이미 많이 가지고 있었어요.

44 민지가 필요한 물건을 산다면 할인 판매하는 물건을 사는 것은 좋습니다.

45 민지의 경우에, 문제점은 필요하지 않은 물건도 산다는 거예요.

46 여기 몇 가지 조언이 있어요.

47 민지는 무언가를 사기 전에 "이것이 정말 필요한가?"라고 스스로에게 물어보세요.

48 또한 쇼핑하러 가기 전에 쇼핑 목록을 만드세요.

49 만약 물건들이 할인 판매 중이라고 해도 목록에 없는 물건들은 사지 마세요.

50 그러면 즉석에서 물건을 사지 않게 될 거예요.

본문 TEST Step 4 · Step 5 p.90~95

1 Ask Dr. Money

2 The Green Middle School Times

3 Teens' Spending Habits

4 How smart are you with your money?

5 These are the results of a survey of 100 students at Green Middle School.

6 We first asked students "Are you smart with your money?"

7 As Graph 1 shows, 70% answered "No" while 30% answered "Yes."

8 We then asked the students who answered "No" what their biggest money worry is.

9 As Graph 2 shows, 60% think they don't have enough allowance while 28% think they have difficulty saving money.

10 Lastly, 12% said they spent money on things they didn't need.

11 Our survey shows that the majority of students think they are not smart with their money.

12 Managing money is not easy, and becoming a smart spender takes effort.

13 Do you have any money worries?

14 Let's talk with Dr. Money.

15 I'm Jason.

16 I get a weekly allowance, but I never have enough.

17 By Thursday, all of my money is gone.

18 I don't know how to solve this problem.

19 Hi, I'm Dr. Money.

20 Let's look at your spending diary.

21 You used up most of your money at the beginning of the week.

22 Here's my tip.

23 Don't carry around all of your weekly allowance.

24 Divide the money into days.

25 Then carry only the money you need for each day.

26 Hello, Dr. Money.

27 I'm Steve.

28 I have difficulty saving money.

29 For example, I've been saving to go to my favorite singer's concert for the last two months.

30 However, I still don't have enough money.

31 I don't know what to do.

32 Let's see.

33 In the last few weeks, you spent 80% of your allowance and only saved 20%.

34 I think you've been spending too much.

35 To save money, you need to have a tighter budget.

36 For example, you can follow the 50%-40%-10% rule.

37 Save 50%, spend 40%, and donate the remaining 10% to charity.

38 By following the rule, you can manage your money better.

39 Then you can save money faster to buy the ticket.

40 I'm Minji.

41 I like to buy things on sale.

42 If something's on sale, I buy it although I don't need it.

43 Last week, I bought two T-shirts on sale, but I already have many.

44 Buying things on sale is good if you buy things you need.

45 In your case, the problem is that you buy things you don't even need.

46 Here's some advice.

47 Before you buy something, ask yourself, "Do I really need this?"

48 Also, before you go shopping, make a shopping list.

49 Don't buy items that aren't on the list even if they're on sale.

50 Then you won't buy things on the spot.

After You Read C

1. Teens', Worries, Advice
2. get an allowance, never have enough
3. By Thursday, all of, is gone
4. Don't carry around, weekly allowance
5. Divide, into, carry, need for each day

Language in Use A

1. bought on sale, cheap
2. It, to go camping, rainy reason
3. too light, so, exchange, for a bigger size

Think and Write

1. that, buy things on the spot
2. bought, because it looked nice
3. However, found out, already had three cases
4. how to stop buying things

After You Read C

1. Teens' Money Worries and Dr. Money's Advice
2. Jason's Worry: I get an allowance, but I never have enough.
3. By Thursday, all of my money is gone.
4. Dr. Money's Advice: Don't carry around all of weekly allowance.
5. Divide the money into days and carry only the money you need for each day.

Language in Use A

1. The computer I bought on sale was very cheap.
2. It is foolish to go camping during the rainy reason.
3. My jeans are too light, so I am going to exchange them for a bigger size.

Think and Write

1. My money problem is that I buy things on the spot.
2. One time, I bought a smartphone case because it looked nice.
3. However, I found out that I already had three cases at home.
4. I don't know how to stop buying things on the spot.

MEMO

MEMO

MEMO

적중 100 plus

1학기 전과정

영어 기출 문제집

정답 및 해설

동아 | 윤정미

적중 1○○ + 특별부록

Plan B

우리학교 최신기출

동아 · 윤정미 교과서를 배우는

학교 시험문제 분석 · 모음 · 해설집

전국단위 학교 시험문제 수집 및 분석
출제 빈도가 높은 문제 위주로 선별
문제 풀이에 필요한 상세한 해설

동아 · 윤정미

◎ 선택형 문항의 답안은 컴퓨터용 수정 싸인펜을
사용하여 OMR 답안지에 바르게 표기하시오.
◎ 서술형 문제는 답을 답안지에 반드시 검정
볼펜으로 쓰시오.
◎ 총 29문항 100점 만점입니다. 문항별 배점
은 각 문항에 표시되어 있습니다.

[인천 ㅇㅇ중]

1. 다음 빈칸에 공통으로 들어갈 말로 가장 적절한 것
은?   (2점)

• I hope you can _____ your dream.
• I didn't _____ that there was a problem.

① realize   ② pursue   ③ decide
④ succeed   ⑤ achieve

[전북 ㅇㅇ중]

2. 다음 설명이 의미하는 단어를 쓰시오.   (3점)

• the main subject that a college student
  studies

답: _____

[경북 ㅇㅇ중]

3. 다음 중 짝지어진 대화가 자연스럽지 <u>않은</u> 것은? (3점)

① A: Have you ever tried Spanish food?
   B: Yes, I have. It's my favorite food.
② A: Have you run a marathon before?
   B: No, I haven't. I want to try it sometimes.
③ A: Have you seen the movie before?
   B: Yes, I have. I hope I can see the movie
   soon.
④ A: Have you thought of becoming a teacher?
   B: Yes, I have. I really want to be an
   English teacher.
⑤ A: Have you ever been to Jeju-do?
   B: No, I've never been there. I hope I can
   visit there someday.

[광주 ㅇㅇ중]

4. 다음 대화의 빈칸 (A)에 들어갈 가장 알맞은 말은?
                                                          (3점)

B. Have you ever visited another country?
G: No, I haven't. Have you?
B: Yes, I've been to France. (A)_____
G: Yes, I really want to visit Canada. Look!
   This book about Canada looks very
   interesting.

① Did you go to another country then?
② I hope you can travel to another country
   sometime.
③ Have you ever seen that movie?
④ Did you see that movie sometime?
⑤ Have you been to America?

[경북 ㅇㅇ중]

5. 다음은 두 사람이 번갈아가며 나눈 대화이다. 내용
의 흐름이 자연스럽도록 (A)~(D)를 순서대로 바르게
배열한 것은?   (4점)

W: I'm going to buy this CD. I love listening
   to piano music.
(A) Really? So you can play the piano?
(B) Well, I've never learned how to play.
(C) Yes. How about you?
(D) Me, too. I also enjoy playing the piano.
M: It's fun. I hope you'll have a chance to
   learn.
                                        M: Man, W: Woman

① (B)-(C)-(A)-(D)   ② (B)-(D)-(C)-(A)
③ (D)-(A)-(C)-(B)   ④ (D)-(C)-(A)-(B)
⑤ (C)-(A)-(B)-(D)

[6~7] 다음 대화를 읽고 물음에 답하시오.

A: I really liked your book about training dogs.

B: Thank you. Do you like dogs?

A: Yes, I do. I love all kinds of animals.

B: Have you ever thought of becoming an animal doctor?

A: Yes, I have. I really want to become an animal doctor.

B: What are you doing to achieve your goal?

A: I'm doing volunteer work at the local animal house.

B: That's good. What else are you doing?

A: I'm also watching a lot of TV shows about animals.

B: You're doing great! I hope you become a good animal doctor someday.

A: Thank you.

6. 위 대화의 두 사람의 관계로 가장 적절한 것은? (3점)

① 배우 - 관객
② 작가 - 독자
③ 의사 - 환자
④ 엄마 - 아들
⑤ 점원 - 손님

7. 위 대화를 읽고 알 수 있는 사실로 알맞은 것은? (3점)

① A는 동물 훈련사가 되고 싶어 한다.
② B는 언젠가 A가 책을 쓰기를 희망한다.
③ A는 지역 요양원에서 봉사활동을 하고 있다.
④ A는 동물에 관한 TV 프로그램을 많이 본다.
⑤ A는 모든 동물들 중 개를 제일 좋아한다.

8. 다음 대화의 밑줄 친 ⓐ~ⓔ 중, 흐름상 어색한 것은? (3점)

A: You should read this book about the moon. ⓐIt's really interesting.

B: ⓑI know. I've already read it.

A: You did? ⓒDo you know there is a movie about the book? Have you watched it?

B: ⓓNo, I haven't.

A: ⓔWhy don't you read the book first?

① ⓐ   ② ⓑ   ③ ⓒ   ④ ⓓ   ⑤ ⓔ

9. 대화의 빈칸에 들어갈 말로 알맞은 것은? (4점)

A: _____
B: Yes, I have. I saw a beautiful view from the mountains.

① Have you ever found mushrooms in the field?
② What did you see from the mountain?
③ Have you ever tried scuba diving?
④ Were you going to see a beautiful view?
⑤ Have you ever been to Canada?

10. 'W'의 말에 이어질 대화가 자연스럽게 이루어지도록 (A)~(C)를 바르게 배열한 것은? (3점)

W: Have you ever visited another country?
(A) Yes, I've been to France. I hope you can travel to another country sometime.
(B) Yes, I really want to visit Canada.
(C) No, I haven't. Have you?

① (A)-(C)-(B)   ② (A)-(B)-(C)   ③ (B)-(A)-(C)
④ (C)-(A)-(B)   ⑤ (C)-(B)-(A)

[11~12] 다음 대화를 읽고 물음에 답하시오.

B: I really liked your book about training dogs.

W: Thank you. Do you like dogs?

B: Yes, I do. I love all kinds of animals.

W: (A)Have you ever thought of becoming an animal doctor?

B: Yes, I have. I really want to become an animal doctor.

W: What are you doing to achieve your goal?

B: I'm doing volunteer work at the local animal house.

W: That's good. What else are you doing?

B: I'm also watching a lot of TV shows about animals.

W: You're doing great! I hope you become a good animal doctor someday.

B: Thank you.

*B: boy, W: woman

---

11. 위 대화의 밑줄 친 (A)의 의도로 가장 알맞은 것은? (3점)

① 이유 묻기   ② 경험 묻기

③ 동의 구하기   ④ 희망 표현하기

⑤ 설명 요청하기

12. 위 대화의 내용과 일치하는 것은? (4점)

① The boy is talking to an animal doctor.

② The boy's goal is to be an animal trainer.

③ The woman's book is about training dogs.

④ The boy is watching TV shows about volunteer work.

⑤ The woman hopes the boy will be a good writer someday.

13. 다음 주어진 우리말과 같은 뜻이 되도록 영작할 때 〈보기〉의 단어들 중 빈칸에 들어갈 단어의 순서가 다섯 번째인 것은? (4점)

• 그 케이크를 자를 칼이 없다.

→ There is _____.

〈보기〉

with / knife / no / the / to / cut / cake

---

① the   ② cake   ③ with

④ no   ⑤ cut

14. 다음 중 어법상 바르지 않은 문장은? (4점)

① I have a lot of homework to do.

② Can you bring me anything eat?

③ I need somebody to teach me Chinese.

④ Sue wonders if Jake will come to the party.

⑤ Do you know whether there is a bank in this building?

15. 다음 밑줄 친 부분의 성격이 다른 것은? (3점)

① They wondered if he joined the club.

② He wants to know if she likes flowers.

③ We don't know if she will come tomorrow.

④ She asked me if I would be free on Sunday.

⑤ I will move to a new house if I get the money.

16. 다음 문장의 빈칸에 들어갈 말로 적절한 것을 모두 쓰시오. (정답 2개) (5점)

• Sue is wondering _____ there's a pizza shop at the airport.

→ Sue는 공항에 피자 가게가 있는지 궁금해 하고 있다.

→ _____

[17~18] 다음 글을 읽고 물음에 답하시오.

After I came back, I entered a photo contest with the pictures I took in Iceland.

(A) Surprisingly, I won first prize, and this gave me a chance to think about my life. I realized that taking pictures made me happy.
(B) After years of trial and error, I got better, and I began to do some part-time work as a photographer.
(C) Suddenly, I wanted to become a good photographer, so I started to learn more about photography.

Then one day, I made a bold decision. I quit my job and decided to take pictures for a living. I wasn't sure ⓐif I could succeed, but I decided to try. I really wanted to do something that made me happy. Now, I'm a professional photographer, and I'm happy.

17. 위 글의 흐름에 맞게 (A)~(C)를 바르게 나열한
것은? (4점)
① (A)-(B)-(C)   ② (A)-(C)-(B)
③ (B)-(A)-(C)   ④ (B)-(C)-(A)
⑤ (C)-(B)-(A)

18. 밑줄 친 ⓐ와 쓰임이 다른 하나는? (4점)
① I will see if the children are at home now.
② They asked us if we were invited to the party.
③ My mom wants to know if Aciel is still in Korea.
④ I doubt if he will listen to the advice, but I'll give it a try.
⑤ I will get the job if the interview is easy.

[19~20] 다음 글을 읽고 물음에 답하시오.

Hello, everyone. My name is David Parker, and I'm a photographer. Today, I'm going to tell you how I found my dream and ⓐrealized it. I hope my story can ⓑinspire you.
When I was young, I loved stars. I also liked taking pictures. However, I never thought these things could lead to a job. In fact, I didn't have a dream at all.
When I had to decide on a ⓒmajor in college, I chose engineering. Being an engineer looked OK. After college, I got a job at an engineering company. It was a ⓓstable job, but I didn't know whether I really enjoyed it.
Everything changed when I went on vacation to Iceland one winter. There I got a chance to see the Northern Lights. The lights were amazing, and I took many pictures of the dancing lights in the sky. For the first time in many years, I could feel my heart ⓔbeating fast.

19. 위 글의 ⓐ~ⓔ 중 우리말 뜻이 문맥에 맞지 않는
것은? (3점)
① ⓐ-깨달았다   ② ⓑ-영감을 주다
③ ⓒ-전공과목   ④ ⓓ-안정된
⑤ ⓔ-뛰는

20. 위 글의 내용과 일치하는 것은? (4점)
① David Parker is going to talk about photography.
② He wanted to be a photographer when he was young.
③ He studied engineering in college.
④ He was satisfied with the engineering job.
⑤ When he saw the Northern Lights, he had a heart problem.

[21~23] 다음 글을 읽고 물음에 답하시오.

Hello, everyone. My name is David Parker, and I'm a photographer. Today, I'm going to tell you how I found my dream and realized it. I hope my story can inspire you.

(A) When I was young, I loved stars. I also liked taking pictures. However, I never thought these things could lead to a job. In fact, I didn't have a dream at all.

(B) Everything changed when I went on vacation to Iceland one winter. There I got a chance ⓐsee the Northern Lights. The lights were amazing, and I took many pictures of the dancing lights in the sky. For the first time in many years, I could feel my heart ⓑbeating fast.

(C) When I ⓒhave to decide on a major in college, I chose engineering. ⓓBeing an engineer looked OK. After college, I got a job at an engineering company. It was a stable job, but I didn't know ⓔwhether I really enjoyed it.

21. 위 글의 (A)~(C) 순서가 의미상 자연스러운 것은? (3점)

① (A)-(C)-(B)
② (A)-(B)-(C)
③ (B)-(A)-(C)
④ (B)-(C)-(A)
⑤ (C)-(A)-(B)

22. 위 글의 ⓐ~ⓔ 중, 쓰임이 옳은 것을 모두 고르면? (3점)

① ⓐ, ⓑ
② ⓐ, ⓓ
③ ⓑ, ⓓ
④ ⓑ, ⓓ, ⓔ
⑤ ⓒ, ⓓ, ⓔ

23. 위 글의 내용과 일치하지 않는 것은? (정답 2개) (4점)

① David Parker, who is a photographer, is going to tell how he found his dream and realized it.

② David thought his hobby of taking pictures could lead to a job.

③ David majored in engineering in college because working as an engineer looked exciting.

④ David wasn't sure if he really enjoyed being an engineer.

⑤ It was a very exciting experiences to David to take pictures of the Northern Lights.

24. 다음 글의 빈칸 (A), (B), (C)에 들어갈 알맞은 말을 <보기>에서 고를 때 순서대로 배열한 것은? (4점)

Do you want to find a dream and realize it? Here's some advice to help you.

First, (A)_____. Think about what you like to do and what makes you happy. In my case, it was taking pictures of stars.

Second, (B)_____. Pursuing a dream is not easy. I became a photographer through hard work.

Third, (C)_____. You need courage to make decisions that will change your life. I was afraid but I took a chance. I truly hope you can find a dream, pursue it, and live it.

<보기>
ⓐ work hard ⓑ follow your heart
ⓒ be bold

① ⓐ-ⓑ-ⓒ
② ⓑ-ⓐ-ⓒ
③ ⓑ-ⓒ-ⓐ
④ ⓒ-ⓐ-ⓑ
⑤ ⓒ-ⓑ-ⓐ

[25~29] 다음 글을 읽고 물음에 답하시오.

Hello, everyone. My name is David Parker, and I'm photographer. Today, I'm going to tell you how I found my dream and realized it. I hope my story can inspire you.

When I was young, I loved stars. I also liked taking pictures. (가)_____, I never thought ⓐthat these things could lead me to a job. In fact, I didn't have a dream at all. When I had to decide on a major in college, I chose engineering. Being an engineer looked OK. After college, I got a job at an engineering company. It was a stable job, but I didn't know ⓑthat I really enjoyed it.

(A) Then one day, I made a bold decision. I quit my job and decided to take pictures for a living. I wasn't sure whether I could succeed, but I decided to try. I really wanted to do something ⓒthat made me happy. Now, I'm a professional photographer, and I'm happy.

(B) After I came back, I entered a photo contest with the pictures ⓓthat I took in Iceland. Surprisingly, I won first prize, and this gave me a chance to think about my life. I realized ⓔthat taking pictures made me happy. Suddenly, I wanted to become a good photographer, so I started to learn more about photography. After years of trial and error, I got better, and I began to do some part-time work as photographer.

(C) Everything changed when I went on vacation to Iceland one winter. There I got a chance to see the Northern Lights. The lights were amazing, and I took many pictures of the dancing lights in the sky. For the first time in many years, I could feel my heart beating fast.

25. 위 글의 (가)에 들어갈 말로 알맞은 말은?　(3점)
① After
② However
③ Therefore
④ In addition
⑤ For example

26. 위 글의 밑줄 친 ⓐ~ⓔ 중 단어의 쓰임새가 어색한 것은?　(4점)
① ⓐ　② ⓑ　③ ⓒ　④ ⓓ　⑤ ⓔ

27. 위 글의 흐름에 맞게 (A)~(C)를 바르게 배열한 것은?　(3점)
① (A)-(B)-(C)　② (A)-(C)-(B)
③ (C)-(A)-(B)　④ (C)-(B)-(A)
⑤ (B)-(A)-(C)

28. 위 글의 종류로 알맞은 것은?　(4점)
① 연설문　② 기행문
③ 독후감　④ 소설
⑤ 조사보고서

29. 위 글의 내용과 일치하지 않는 것은?　(3점)
① David is a photographer.
② David didn't have a dream when he was young.
③ David studied engineering in college.
④ David won first prize in a photo contest.
⑤ David went on a business trip to Iceland.

◎ 선택형 문항의 답안은 컴퓨터용 수정 싸인펜을 사용하여 OMR 답안지에 바르게 표기하시오.
◎ 서술형 문제는 답을 답안지에 반드시 검정 볼펜으로 쓰시오.
◎ 총 28문항 100점 만점입니다. 문항별 배점은 각 문항에 표시되어 있습니다.

[송파구 ○○중]

1. 다음 영영풀이에서 설명되지 <u>않은</u> 단어는?　　(3점)

- to show someone the way
- to achieve something that you want
- to work hard in order to achieve something
- to tell someone you think he (or she) should do something

① inspire　　② lead　　③ suggest
④ realize　　⑤ pursue

[경북 ○○중]

2. 다음 중 짝지어진 단어의 관계가 나머지와 <u>다른</u> 것은?　　(2점)

① rain – rainy　　② snow – snowy
③ loud – loudly　　④ sleep – sleepy
⑤ health – healthy

[경남 ○○중]

3. 다음 중 자연스럽지 <u>않은</u> 대화를 고르면?　　(3점)

① A: I really liked your book about training dogs.
　 B: Thank you.

② A: Have you ever thought of becoming an animal doctor?
　 B: Yes, I do. I like raising dogs.

③ A: What are you doing to achieve your goals?
　 B: I am doing volunteer work.

④ A: Do you like dogs?
　 B: Yes, I do. I love all kinds of dogs.

⑤ A: I hope you can travel to another country sometime.
　 B: Yes, I really want to.

[충남 ○○중]

4. 대화의 빈칸에 들어갈 말로 알맞은 것은?　　(3점)

A: Have you ever had Spanish food before?
B: _____ Have you tried it?
A: Yes, I have. I hope you can try it sometime. It's really good.
B: I will. For now, I'll just buy this Spanish recipe book.

① Yes, I do.　　　　② Yes, I have.
③ No, I don't.　　　④ No, I haven't.
⑤ No, I didn't.

[광주 ○○중]

5. 다음 대화의 내용과 일치하는 것은?　　(4점)

B: I really liked your book about training dogs.
W: Thank you. Do you like dogs?
B: Yes, I do. I love all kinds of animals.
W: Have you ever thought of becoming an animal doctor?
B: Yes, I have. I really want to become an animal doctor.
W: What are you doing to achieve your goal?
B: I'm doing volunteer work at the local animal house.
W: That's good. What else are you doing?
B: I'm also watching a lot of TV shows about animals.
W: You're doing great! I hope you become a good animal doctor someday.
B: Thank you.

① 남자는 모든 종류의 동물과 식물을 좋아한다.
② 남자는 수의사가 되고 싶어 한다.
③ 남자는 요양원에서 봉사활동을 한다.
④ 남자는 방송국에서 근무한다.
⑤ 여자는 남자의 꿈을 바꾸려고 한다.

[6~7] 다음 대화를 읽고 물음에 답하시오.

B: I really liked your book about training dogs.

W: Thank you. Do you like dogs?

B: Yes, I do. I love all kinds of animals.

W: Have you ever thought of becoming an animal doctor?

(A) What are you doing to achieve your goal?

(B) Yes, I have. I really want to become an animal doctor.

(C) That's good. What else are you doing?

(D) I'm doing volunteer work at the local animal house.

B: I'm also watching a lot of TV shows about animals.

W: You're doing great! I hope you become a good animal doctor someday.

B: Thank you.

6. 위 대화의 흐름에 알맞게 (A)~(D)를 나열한 것은?
(4점)

① (A)-(D)-(C)-(B) ② (B)-(A)-(D)-(C)

③ (B)-(C)-(A)-(D) ④ (D)-(B)-(A)-(C)

⑤ (D)-(A)-(B)-(C)

7. 위 대화의 내용과 일치하지 않는 것은? (4점)

① W는 개 훈련에 관한 책을 썼다.

② B는 장래에 수의사가 되기 바란다.

③ B는 모든 종류의 동물을 좋아한다.

④ B는 동물에 관한 영화를 많이 관람하고 있다.

⑤ W는 B가 좋은 수의사가 되기를 희망한다.

8. 대화의 (A)~(E) 중 흐름상 어색한 것은? (4점)

G: (A)You should read this book about the moon. It's really interesting.

B: I know. (B)I've never read it.

G: You did? How about the movie? (C)Have you also seen the movie about the book?

B: (D)No, I haven't.

G: (E)Well, it's even better than the book.

① (A)   ② (B)   ③ (C)   ④ (D)   ⑤ (E)

9. 다음 대화의 빈칸에 들어갈 내용으로 가장 적절한 것은? (3점)

A: Have you ever visited another country?

B: No, I haven't. Have you?

A: Yes, I _____ France. I hope you can travel to another country sometime.

B: Yes, I really want to visit. Canada. Look! This book about Canada looks very interesting.

① went to   ② have been to

③ have gone to   ④ haven't visited

⑤ haven't been to

10. 다음은 민호의 생각이다. 민호가 생각하는 것을 영어로 가장 바르게 옮긴 문장은? (4점)

• Minho: Did I turn off TV?

① Minho isn't sure whether he turns off TV.

② If Minho turns off TV, he isn't sure.

③ Minho isn't sure if he turned off TV.

④ Minho is sure that he is going to turn off TV.

⑤ Minho turned off TV whether he isn't sure.

11. 다음 Dialogue 속 주어진 모든 문장을 (HERE)에 넣을 때 올바른 순서로 배열한 것은? (4점)

M: I really liked your book about training dogs.
W: Thank you. Do you like dogs?
M: Yes, I do. I love all kinds of animals.
W: Have you ever thought of becoming an animal doctor?
　　　　　　(HERE)
W: You're doing great! I hope you become a good animal doctor someday.
M: Thank you.

<Dialogue>
ⓐ I'm also watching a lot of TV shows about animals.
ⓑ What are you doing to achieve your goal?
ⓒ I'm doing volunteer work at the local animal house.
ⓓ Yes, I have. I really want to become an animal doctor.
ⓔ That's good. What else are you doing?

① ⓐ-ⓒ-ⓑ-ⓔ-ⓓ　　② ⓑ-ⓓ-ⓐ-ⓔ-ⓒ
③ ⓑ-ⓔ-ⓐ-ⓒ-ⓓ　　④ ⓓ-ⓑ-ⓒ-ⓔ-ⓐ
⑤ ⓓ-ⓔ-ⓐ-ⓒ-ⓑ

12. 다음 대화의 빈칸에 들어갈 알맞은 말은? (3점)

A: _____
B: Yes, I have. The island was beautiful.

① How was your trip to Jejudo?
② Have you ever been to Jejudo?
③ Did you enjoy your trip to Jejudo?
④ Do you have any plan to visit Jejudo?
⑤ Are you going to visit Jejudo this summer?

13. 다음 빈칸에 들어갈 말로 알맞은 것은? (3점)

• I wonder _____ she'll come to see me on my birthday.

① what　　② that　　③ if
④ why　　⑤ which

14. 다음 중 어법상 옳은 문장은? (4점)

① He needs somebody to talk.
② They have no house to live in.
③ I want something to cold drink.
④ Please give me a chance to explaining.
⑤ Do you want delicious anything to eat?

15. 다음 빈칸에 들어갈 말로 가장 적절한 것을 쓰시오. (5점)

• 나는 앉을 의자 하나가 필요하다.
= I need a chair _____.

→ _____

16. 다음 중 어법상 어색한 것은? (4점)

① I want to know if she is home now.
② I wonder if the restaurant is open on Sunday.
③ Mike asked Susan whether she was angry.
④ Jane isn't sure whether he locked the door.
⑤ He is wondering if it rains tomorrow.

[17~18] 다음 글을 읽고 물음에 답하시오.

Hello, everyone. My name is David Parker, and I'm a photographer. Today, I'm going to tell you how I found my dream and realized it. I hope my story can inspire you.

When I was young, I loved stars. I also liked taking pictures. However, I never thought these things could lead to a job. In fact, I didn't have a dream at all.

When I had to decide on a major in college, I chose engineering. Being an engineer looked OK. After college, I got a job at an engineering company. It was a stable job, but I didn't know (A)if I really enjoyed it.

Everything changed when I went on vacation to Iceland one winter. There I got a chance to see the Northern Lights. The lights were amazing, and I took many pictures of the dancing lights in the sky. For the first time in many years, I could feel my heart beating.

17. 위 글의 David Parker에 관한 내용과 일치하는 것은? (4점)

① He is telling the audience about his hobbies.

② He wanted to be an astronaut when he was a child.

③ He decided to become a photographer when he was in college.

④ He was fully satisfied with his first job because it was stable.

⑤ Taking pictures of the Northern Lights made him feel his heart beating.

18. 밑줄 친 (A)if와 쓰임이 다른 것은? (3점)

① I wonder if Mom is sick.

② Mike will be upset if he hears the news.

③ They will find out if he is telling the truth.

④ I'm not sure if you could help the children.

⑤ Kate asked him if he wanted to join her club.

19. 다음 글의 흐름으로 보아 주어진 문장이 들어가기에 가장 적절한 곳은? (4점)

Then one day, I made a bold decision.

After I came back, I entered a photo contest with the pictures I took in Iceland. (A) Surprisingly, I won first prize, and this gave me a chance to think about my life. I realized that taking pictures made me happy. (B) Suddenly, I wanted to become a good photographer, so I started to learn more about photography. (C) After years of trial and error, I got better, and I began to do some part-time work as a photographer. (D) I quit my job and decided to take pictures for a living. I wasn't sure if I could succeed, but I decided to try. (E) I really wanted to do something that made me happy. Now, I'm a professional photographer, and I'm happy.

① (A)　② (B)　③ (C)　④ (D)　⑤ (E)

20. 글의 흐름상 빈칸에 들어갈 적절한 말은? (4점)

Do you want to find a dream and realize it? Here's some advice to help you.

First, follow your heart. Think about what you like to do and what makes you happy. In my case, it was taking pictures of stars.

Second, work hard. Pursuing a dream is not easy. I became a photographer through hard work.

Third, be bold. You need _____ to make decisions that will change your life. I was afraid but I took a chance.

① pain　② chance　③ comfort

④ courage　⑤ patience

[21~22] 다음 글을 읽고 물음에 답하시오.

After I came back, ⓐI entered a photo contest with the pictures I take in Iceland. Surprisingly, I won first prize, and this gave me a chance to think about my life. ⓑI realized taking pictures made me happy. Suddenly, I wanted to become a good photographer, so I started to learn more about photography. ⓒAfter years of trial and error, I got better, and I began doing some part-time work as a photographer.

Then one day, I made a bold decision. I quit my job and decided to take pictures for a living. ⓓI wasn't sure that I could succeed, but I decided to try. ⓔI really wanted to do something made me happy.

So do you want to find a dream and realize it? Here's some advice to help you.

First, follow your heart. Think about what you like to do and what makes you happy. (A)

Second, work hard. (B) Pursuing a dream is not easy. (C) I became a photographer through hard work.

Third, be bold. You need to courage to make decisions that will change your life. (D) I was afraid but I took a chance. (E)

[23~24] 다음 글을 읽고 물음에 답하시오.

When I was young, I loved stars. I also liked taking pictures. However, I never thought these things could lead to a job. (A)_____ fact, I didn't have a dream at all. When I had to decide on a major in college, I chose engineering. Being an engineer looked OK. After college, I got a job at an engineering company. It was a stable job, but I didn't know whether I really enjoyed it.

Everything changed when I went on vacation to Iceland one winter. There I got a chance to see the Northern Lights. The lights were amazing, and I took many pictures of the dancing lights in the sky. (B)_____ the first time in many years, I could feel my heart beating fast.

23. 위 글의 빈칸 (A), (B)에 들어갈 말이 순서대로 바르게 짝지어진 것은?　　　　　　(4점)

① At - On　　　　② In - On

③ In - For　　　　④ On - For

⑤ On - From

21. 위 글의 밑줄 친 ⓐ~ⓔ 중, 어법과 의미가 <u>모두</u> 옳은 것은?　　　　　　(3점)

① ⓐ, ⓑ　　　② ⓐ, ⓓ　　　③ ⓑ, ⓒ

④ ⓒ, ⓔ　　　⑤ ⓓ, ⓔ

24. 위 글의 내용과 일치하지 <u>않는</u> 것은?　　(3점)

① The writer liked stars when he was young.

② The writer enjoyed taking photos in his childhood.

③ The writer majored in engineering in college.

④ The writer was satisfied with his job as an engineer.

⑤ The writer took pictures of the Northern Lights in Iceland.

22. 위 글의 흐름으로 보아 주어진 문장이 들어가기에 가장 적절한 곳은?　　　　　　(4점)

In my case, it was taking pictures of starts.

① (A)　② (B)　③ (C)　④ (D)　⑤ (E)

[25~28] 다음 글을 읽고 물음에 답하시오.

Hello, everyone. My name is David Parker, and I'm a photographer. Today, I'm going to tell you ⓐhow did I find my dream and realized it. I hope my story can inspire you. When I was young, I loved stars. I also liked taking pictures. However, I never thought these things could lead (A)_____ a job. In fact, I didn't have a dream at all.

When I had to decide (B)_____ a major in college, I chose engineering. ⓑBe an engineer looked OK. After college, I got a job at an engineering company. It was a stable job, but I didn't know whether I really enjoyed it.

Everything changed when I went (C)_____ vacation to Iceland one winter. There I got a chance to see the Northern Lights. The lights were amazing, and I took many pictures of the ⓒdancing lights in the sky. For the first time in many years, I could feel my heart ⓓto beat fast.

After I came back, I entered a photo contest with the pictures ⓔI took in Iceland. Surprisingly, I won first prize, and this gave me a chance to think about my life. I realized that taking pictures made me happy. Suddenly, I wanted to become a good photographer, so I started to learn more about photography. After years of trial and error, I got better, and I began to do some part-time work as a photographer.

Then one day, I made a bold decision. I quit my job and decided to take pictures for a living. I wasn't sure ⓕif I could succeed, but I decided to try. I really wanted to do something that made me happy. Now, I'm a professional photographer, and I'm happy.

25. 위 글의 빈칸 (A), (B), (C)에 들어갈 말로 바르게 짝지어진 것은? (4점)

	(A)	(B)	(C)
①	to	in	on
②	at	on	for
③	on	to	for
④	on	for	on
⑤	to	on	on

26. 위 글의 ⓐ~ⓔ 중, 어법상 옳은 것을 있는 대로 모두 고른 것은? (4점)

① ⓐ, ⓓ 　 ② ⓑ, ⓒ 　 ③ ⓒ, ⓔ

④ ⓐ, ⓒ, ⓓ 　 ⑤ ⓑ, ⓒ, ⓔ

27. 위 글의 밑줄 친 ⓕ와 쓰임이 다른 것은? (3점)

① I will go on a picnic if it doesn't rain tomorrow.

② Steven is asking the woman if she can help him.

③ I am not sure if they will allow us to park there.

④ I don't know if I should buy a new pair of shoes.

⑤ Sue is wondering if there's a pizza shop at the airport.

28. 위 글의 David Parker에 대한 설명으로 바른 것은? (3점)

① He really enjoyed his first job.

② He had a dream when he was young.

③ He majored in photography in college and became a photographer.

④ He became a professional photographer after he went through trial and error.

⑤ He quit his job because he was sure that he could succeed as a photographer.

◎ 선택형 문항의 답안은 컴퓨터용 수정 싸인펜을 사용하여 OMR 답안지에 바르게 표기하시오.
◎ 서술형 문제는 답을 답안지에 반드시 검정 볼펜으로 쓰시오.
◎ 총 27문항 100점 만점입니다. 문항별 배점은 각 문항에 표시되어 있습니다.

[경북 ○○중]

1. 다음 중 밑줄 친 부분의 우리말 뜻이 알맞지 <u>않은</u> 것은?　(3점)

① Dad threw away the apple <u>peel</u>. (껍질)
② The taste of noodles <u>differs</u> from country to country. (다르다)
③ <u>Add</u> the flour to the bowl and mix. (첨가하다)
④ <u>Pour</u> the mixture into the madeleine pan. (붓다)
⑤ The result of the exam didn't <u>satisfy</u> her parents. (실망시키다)

[경북 ○○중]

2. 다음 빈칸에 공통으로 들어갈 말로 가장 알맞은 것은?　(4점)

• It's not easy to _____ him in a race.
• Please _____ egg whites with a 1/2 cup of sugar.

① beat　　② pour　　③ bake
④ melt　　⑤ crisp

[전북 ○○중]

3. 다음 대화가 이루어지고 있는 장소로 알맞은 곳은?　(3점)

A: Hello. What would you like to order?
B: I want a hot dog and one milk, please.
A: Would you like anything else?
B: No, thank you.
A: Will it be for here or to go?
B: To go, please. Thank you.

① 커피숍　　② 슈퍼마켓　　③ 음악 학원
④ 요리 학원　　⑤ 패스트푸드점

[양천구 ○○중]

4. 다음 대화의 내용을 두 문장으로 요약하고자 한다. 빈칸 (A), (B)에 들어갈 단어로 가장 적절한 것은?　(4점)

Maria: Simon, what is your comfort food?
Simon: I have many comfort foods, but I love madeleines the most.
Maria: What is that?
Simon: A madeleine is a small cake that looks like a sea shell. People in France enjoy madeleines as an afternoon snack.
Maria: Oh, I see. Why do you like madeleines the most?
Simon: My grandmother always makes madeleines for me when I visit her. They taste best when they come right out of the oven. Then the kitchen is filled with a sweet smell. I especially like eating her orange madeleines with a cup of tea. Every time I see or smell madeleines, I think of my grandmother.

↓

Simon's comfort food is a madeleine, which is a (A)_____ cake that looks like a sea shell. He likes madeleines the most because they (B)_____ him of his grandmother.

	(A)	(B)
①	tiny	cook
②	big	think
③	big	review
④	small	advise
⑤	small	remind

5. 다음 대화의 빈칸에 들어갈 말로 알맞은 것은? (3점)

A: Are you ready to _____?
B: Yes. I'll have a hamburger and a coke.

① order　　　② try　　　③ pay
④ cook　　　⑤ pour

6. 다음 음식을 주문하는 상황의 대화 중 어색한 것은? (4점)

① W: Hello, are you ready to order?
　　B: Yes, please. I'd like a piece of cake.
② W: Would you like anything to drink?
　　B: No, thank you.
③ W: Would you like anything else?
　　B: Yes, please. That's all.
④ W: Will it be for here or to go?
　　B: To go, please. Thank you.
⑤ W: The total comes to 12 dollars.
　　B: OK. Here you are.

7. 다음 중 짝지어진 대화가 어색한 것은? (3점)

① A: This is on me.
　　B: Excuse me? Can you say that again?
② A: Can I have a drink?
　　B: Sure. What drink do you prefer?
③ A: Is it for here or to go?
　　B: It's for here, please.
④ A: What do you do for a living?
　　B: My dream is to become a chef.
⑤ A: Would you like anything else?
　　B: No, thank you.

8. 다음 대화에 관해 바르게 설명하고 있는 사람은? (3점)

M: Welcome to Sandwich Place. What would you like to order?
G: I'd like to have a hamburger, and my friend will have a chicken sandwich.
M: Would you like anything else?
G: One salad, please.
M: OK, then will that be all?
G: No, I'd like to order two bottles of water.
M: The total comes to 12 dollars.
G: OK. Here you are.

① 은서: M은 음식을 주문하고 있어.
② 영신: G는 샐러드 두 개를 주문했어.
③ 영훈: G는 자신의 음식만 주문했어.
④ 동영: G는 물 두 병을 주문했어.
⑤ 채령: 치킨 샌드위치와 햄버거의 가격은 12달러야.

9. 다음 대화가 자연스럽도록 (A)~(E)를 바르게 배열하면? (4점)

Hello. What would you like to order?
(A) It's to go, please.
(B) I want a hot dog.
(C) Is it for here or to go?
(D) One bottle of water, please.
(E) Would you like anything to drink?

① (B)-(E)-(D)-(C)-(A)
② (B)-(C)-(D)-(E)-(A)
③ (B)-(D)-(C)-(A)-(E)
④ (D)-(C)-(A)-(E)-(B)
⑤ (D)-(E)-(B)-(C)-(A)

[10~11] 다음 대화를 읽고 물음에 답하시오.

Staff: Welcome to Sandwich Place.
_____

Sujin: I'd like to have a hamburger, and she'll have a chicken sandwich.
Staff: Would you like anything else?
Sujin: One salad, please.
Staff: OK, then will that be all?
Sujin: No, I'd like to order two bottles of water.
Staff: The total comes to 12 dollars.
Sujin: OK. Here you are.

10. 위 대화의 내용과 일치하는 것은? (3점)

① Sandwich Place에서는 햄버거를 팔지 않는다.
② Sujin은 추가 주문 없이 한 번에 주문했다.
③ 음료수를 포함한 음식의 가격의 합계는 $12이다.
④ 치킨 샌드위치는 Sujin을 위한 것이다.
⑤ Sujin은 햄버거와 샌드위치 1개씩, 그리고 물 2병을 주문했다.

11. 위 대화의 빈칸에 들어갈 수 있는 표현이 <u>아닌</u> 것은? (4점)

① What would you like to order?
② May I take your order?
③ What would you like to have?
④ Would you like anything to drink?
⑤ Are you ready to order?

12. 다음 주어진 우리말과 같도록 2가지 문장을 쓰시오. (5점)

• 그녀는 아름다울 뿐만 아니라 현명하기도 하다.
(beautiful과 clever을 사용할 것.)

(1) She is _____ .
(2) She is _____ .

13. 다음 중 어법상 옳은 것은? (3점)

① Rinda had her brother fixed her computer.
② Mr. Yoo let she wear his shirt.
③ She will not only dance but also sing.
④ Tom did his best as that his team could win.
⑤ I'm saving money so that can I travel to Europe.

14. 다음 문장 중 어법상 옳은 것으로만 묶인 것은? (4점)

(A) They asked me help him to carry the heavy box.
(B) He had us to clean our classroom.
(C) We felt the house shake.
(D) Let me show you my room.
(E) Plants makes the air clean.

① (A), (C)   ② (B), (C)
③ (B), (D)   ④ (C), (D)
⑤ (D), (E)

15. 다음 문장을 우리말로 해석하시오. (5점)

(1) My father was so busy that he couldn't call me.
(2) Did you give up your job so that you could take care of your mother?

정답: (1) _____
　　　(2) _____

[16~19] 다음 글을 읽고 물음에 답하시오.

Jessica's Comfort Food

My comfort food is chicken soup. In the USA, people eat this soup when they have a cold. (A) When I was a small child, I caught a very bad cold. ⓐMy father made me a bowl of chicken soup so that I could get well. (B) It was also very tasty. (C) Now, when I catch a cold, I eat chicken soup.

Maria's Comfort Food

In Brazil, there are many dishes that are made with cassava, a vegetable similar to a potato. I love cassava chips the most. (D) Once when I had a bad day at school and felt stressed out, my best friend bought me a bag of cassava chips. (E) When I started to eat the chips, my stress suddenly ⓑdisappeared. The crisp sound of eating chips made me feel better. Now, every time I'm stressed out, I eat cassava chips. Then I feel good again!

16. 위 글의 내용을 바르게 이해한 것은? (4점)

① 닭고기 수프는 몸에 좋지만 맛이 없다.

② Maria는 친구가 만들어 준 카사바를 먹었다.

③ 미국 사람들은 감기에 걸리면 닭고기 수프를 먹는다.

④ 브라질에는 감자와 카사바로 함께 만든 음식이 많다.

⑤ Maria가 카사바 칩을 먹을 때 아무 소리도 나지 않았다.

17. 위 글의 흐름으로 보아 주어진 문장이 들어가기에 가장 적절한 곳은? (4점)

It warmed my body, and I slowly started to feel better.

① (A)　② (B)　③ (C)　④ (D)　⑤ (E)

18. 위 글의 밑줄 친 ⓐ와 그 의미가 같은 것은? (3점)

① My father made a bowl of chicken soup me

② My father made of me a bowl of chicken soup

③ My father made a bowl of chicken soup of me

④ My father made a bowl of chicken soup for me

⑤ My father made a bowl of chicken soup to me

19. 위 글의 밑줄 친 ⓑ에 쓰인 disappear의 영영풀이로 알맞은 것은? (4점)

① to become impossible to see or find

② to be different from something else

③ to mix food together quickly using a fork or a kitchen tool

④ to make someone happy by doing what he or she wants

⑤ to tell someone you think he or she should do something

20. 다음 글의 흐름과 관련이 없는 문장은? (4점)

Comfort food is food that makes you feel good when you are sad, angry or stressed out. ⓐIt can also make you think of happy moments from the past. ⓑIt satisfies not only the stomach but also the heart. ⓒSometimes, spicy food makes you have a stomach ache. ⓓComfort foods differ around the world. ⓔLet's see what comfort foods our international readers enjoy.

① ⓐ　② ⓑ　③ ⓒ　④ ⓓ　⑤ ⓔ

[21~22] 다음 글을 읽고, 물음에 답하시오.

Letters from Our Readers: My Comfort Food
Comfort food is food @that makes you feel good when you are sad, angry, or stressed out. ⓑIt can also make you think of happy moments from the past. It satisfies not only the stomach but also the heart. Comfort foods ⓒdiffer around the world. Let's see what comfort foods our international readers enjoy.

Jessica From USA

My comfort food is chicken soup. In the USA, people eat this soup when they have a cold. When I was a small child, I caught a very bad cold. My father made me a bowl of chicken soup so that I could get well. The hot soup warmed my body, and I slowly started ⓓto feel better. ⓔIt was also very tasty. Now, when I catch a cold, I eat chicken soup.

21. 위 글의 내용과 일치하지 않는 것은? (3점)

① Jessica's comfort food is chicken soup.
② Comfort food satisfies the heart as well as the stomach.
③ When you are sad, comfort food makes you feel good.
④ People in the USA eat chicken soup when they catch a cold.
⑤ The chicken soup was not delicious, but it made Jessica feel better.

22. 위 글의 밑줄 친 @~ⓔ에 관해 올바르게 설명하고 있는 사람은? (4점)

① 진수: @는 목적격 관계대명사이다.
② 철민: ⓑ가 가리키는 것은 comfort food이다.
③ 진명: ⓒ는 different로 바꾸어야 어법에 맞는 문장이 된다.
④ 민영: ⓓ는 어법에 맞지 않게 사용되었다.
⑤ 규철: ⓔ가 가리키는 것은 a bad cold이다.

[23~24] 다음 글을 읽고, 물음에 답하시오.

Simon from France

I have many comfort foods, but I love madeleines the most. A madeleine is a small cake that looks (A)_____ a sea shell. People in France enjoy madeleines as an afternoon snack. My grandmother always makes madeleines for me when I visit her. They taste best when they come right out of the oven. Then the kitchen is filled (B)_____ a sweet smell. I especially like eating her orange madeleines with a cup (C)_____ tea. Every time I see or smell madeleines, I think of my grandmother.
Let me share my grandmother's special recipe with you so that you can make orange madeleines, too. Maybe madeleines will become a comfort food for you!

23. 위 글의 빈칸 (A)~(C)에 들어갈 말이 순서대로 바르게 짝지어진 것은? (4점)

① at - with - for
② for - of - with
③ like - of - with
④ for - with - at
⑤ like - with - of

24. 위 글의 내용과 일치하지 않는 것은? (4점)

① Simon이 가장 좋아하는 comfort food는 마들렌이다.
② 프랑스 사람들은 오후 간식으로 마들렌을 즐겨 먹는다.
③ 할머니는 Simon이 방문하면 마들렌을 만들어 주신다.
④ 마들렌은 오븐에서 막 나올 때 가장 맛이 좋다.
⑤ Simon은 할머니의 마들렌 요리법을 모른다.

[25~26] 다음 글을 읽고 물음에 답하시오.

Jessica from USA

My comfort food is chicken soup. In the USA, people eat this soup when they have a cold. When I was a small child, I caught a very bad cold. ⓐMy father made me a bowl of chicken soup so that I could get well. The hot soup warmed my body, and I slowly started to feel better. It was also very tasty. Now, when I catch a cold, I eat chicken soup.

Maria from Brazil

In Brazil, there are many dishes that are made with cassava, a vegetable similar to a potato. I love cassava chips the most. ⓑOnce when I had a bad day at school and felt stressed out, my best friend bought me a bag of cassava chips. When I started to eat the chips, my stress suddenly disappeared. ⓒThe crisp sound of eating chips made me feel better. Now, every time I'm stressed out, I eat cassava chips. Then I feel good again!

Simon from France

I have many comfort foods, but I love madeleines the most. A madeleine is a small cake that looks like a sea shell. People in France enjoy madeleines as an afternoon snack. My grandmother always makes madeleines for me when I visit her. They taste best when they come right out of the oven. ⓓThen the kitchen is filled with a sweet smell. I especially like eating her orange madeleines with a cup of tea. Every time I see or smell madeleines, I think of my grandmother. ⓔLet me share my grandmother's special recipe with you so that you can make orange madeleines, too. Maybe madeleines will become a comfort food for you!

25. 위 글의 내용과 일치하는 것은?   (4점)

① Jessica makes chicken soup when his father catches a cold.
② Cassava chips are the only kind of food that you can make with cassava.
③ Madeleines taste best when they are cool enough.
④ Seeing madeleines makes Simon think of his grandmother.
⑤ Maria usually eats cassava chips when her stress is all gone.

26. 위 글의 ⓐ~ⓔ를 해석한 것이 자연스럽지 않은 것은?   (3점)

① ⓐ 아빠는 건강을 회복하기 위해 내게 치킨 수프를 만들게 하셨다.
② ⓑ 언젠가 학교에서 힘든 날을 보내고 스트레스를 받았을 때
③ ⓒ 칩을 먹는 바삭거리는 소리가 나를 기분 좋게 해 주었다.
④ ⓓ 그 때 주방이 달콤한 냄새로 가득 찬다.
⑤ ⓔ 너희들도 오렌지 마들렌을 만들 수 있도록 내가 할머니의 특별 레시피를 공유할게.

27. 다음 글의 ⓐ~ⓔ 중 흐름상 가장 어색한 문장을 고른 것은?   (4점)

ⓐYesterday my computer broke down, so I couldn't do my homework. ⓑI felt worried because of it. ⓒFortunately, my brother let me use his laptop. ⓓI like shopping on the Internet. ⓔWhile I was doing my homework, Mom had Dad fix my computer.

① ⓐ   ② ⓑ   ③ ⓒ   ④ ⓓ   ⑤ ⓔ

◎ 선택형 문항의 답안은 컴퓨터용 수정 싸인펜을 사용하여 OMR 답안지에 바르게 표기하시오.
◎ 서술형 문제는 답을 답안지에 반드시 검정 볼펜으로 쓰시오.
◎ 총 26문항 100점 만점입니다. 문항별 배점은 각 문항에 표시되어 있습니다.

[대구 ○○중]

1. 다음 빈칸에 공통으로 들어갈 말로 가장 적절한 것은? (4점)

• I'm so sorry, I _____ a mistake.
• Julie _____ Mijin water the plants in the garden.
• My best friend _____ me this doll for my birthday present.

① got   ② had   ③ gave
④ made   ⑤ helped

[광주 ○○중]

2. 다음 중 영어 단어와 그 영영풀이가 바르게 연결된 것은? (4점)

① flour: a powder used for making bread and cakes
② appear: to become impossible to see or find
③ melt: to mix food together using a kitchen tool
④ comfort: a feeling of being worried and tired
⑤ quality: an amount that you can measure or count

[부산 ○○중]

3. 다음 중 대화가 <u>어색한</u> 것은? (3점)

① A: You should read this book about the moon. It's really interesting.
   B: I know. I've already read it.
② A: I'm not feeling well. I think I have a cold.
   B: That's too bad. I hope you feel better soon.
③ A: Would you like anything else?
   B: Yes. One milk. please.
④ A: Are you ready to order?
   B: Yes, please. I'd like a piece of cake.
⑤ A: What would you like to order?
   B: No, thank you. I want a spinach pizza.

[경북 ○○중]

4. 다음 주어진 말에 이어질 대화의 순서가 가장 적절한 것은? (4점)

Hello. Are you ready to order?

(A) Yes, one bottle of water, please.
(B) Yes, please. I want to have a hot dog.
(C) It's to go, please.
(D) Would you like anything do drink?
(E) Is it for here or to go?

① (A)→(D)→(E)→(B)→(C)
② (A)→(E)→(D)→(C)→(B)
③ (B)→(D)→(A)→(E)→(C)
④ (B)→(D)→(E)→(A)→(C)
⑤ (D)→(C)→(B)→(A)→(E)

[충남 ○○중]

5. 다음 대화의 빈칸에 들어갈 말로 알맞은 것은? (3점)

A: Welcome to Italian Food.
   _____
B: I want to order a mushroom pizza.

① What's your favorite food?
② Can I have the menu, please?
③ What would you like to order?
④ Would you like anything to drink?
⑤ Have you tried Italian food before?

6. 다음 대화 내용을 제대로 이해하고 있는 사람은? (4점)

A: Welcome to Sandwich Place. What would you like to order?
B: I'd like to have a hamburger, and my friend will have a chicken sandwich.
A: Would you like anything else?
B: One salad, please.
A: OK, then will that be all?
B: No, I'd like to order two bottles of water.
A: Is it for here or to go?
B: It's for here, please.
A: The total comes to 12 dollars.
B: OK. Here you are.

① Diego: A and B are talking in a restaurant.
② Maria: B is ordering food only for herself.
③ Jamie: A is a customer and B is a clerk.
④ Sandra: B will take food to her house with her friend.
⑤ Yujin: B will get more order from A after this conversation.

7. 다음 대화의 빈칸에 들어갈 말로 알맞은 것은? (4점)

A: Hello. Are you ready to order?
B: Yes, please. I'd like a piece of cake.
A: What kind of cake would you like?
B: Chocolate cake, please.
A: _____
B: To go, please. Thank you.

① Will that be all?
② For here or to go?
③ Will you pay in cash?
④ Where are you going?
⑤ Would you like anything else?

8. 다음 중 자연스러운 대화가 되도록 (A)~(E)를 바르게 배열한 것은? (4점)

W: Welcome to Dessert World. May I take your order?

(A) For here, please.
(B) Is it for here or to go?
(C) Yes, please. I'd like to order a hot dog.
(D) Would you like anything to drink?
(E) Yes, an orange juice, please.

① (A)-(D)-(C)-(B)-(E)
② (C)-(D)-(E)-(B)-(A)
③ (C)-(B)-(A)-(E)-(D)
④ (E)-(B)-(C)-(A)-(D)
⑤ (E)-(D)-(C)-(B)-(A)

9. 다음 중 짝지어진 대화가 <u>어색한</u> 것은? (3점)

① A: What kind of cake would you like to have?
   B: Chocolate cake, please.
② A: What would you like to order?
   B: I want to get a mushroom pizza.
③ A: Is the order for here or to go?
   B: For here, please.
④ A: Would you like anything else?
   B: I don't like them at all.
⑤ A: Will that be all?
   B: No, I'd like one chicken salad, too.

[10~11] 다음 대화를 읽고 물음에 답하시오.

Man: Welcome to Sandwich Place.
　　　(A)＿＿＿＿＿＿＿＿＿＿＿＿＿＿＿
Somi: I'd like to have a hamburger, and she'll have a chicken sandwich.
Man: Would you like anything else?
Somi: One salad, please.
Man: OK, then will that be all?
Somi: No, I'd like to order two bottles of water.
Man: Is it for here or to go?
Somi: It's for here, please.
Man: The total comes to 12 dollars.
Somi: OK. Here you are.

10. 위 대화의 빈칸 (A)에 들어갈 말로 <u>어색한</u> 것은?

(4점)

① May I take your order?
② Are you ready to order?
③ What do you want to order?
④ What would you like to order?
⑤ What do you usually have for lunch?

11. 위 대화의 내용과 일치하는 것은? (4점)
① Somi is taking the man's order.
② Somi wants to eat at the restaurant.
③ Somi works at a fast food restaurant.
④ The man is ordering the food and drinks.
⑤ Somi will pay 12 dollars only for the drinks.

12. 다음 〈보기〉에서 어법상 올바른 문장의 총 개수는?

(4점)

＜보기＞
(A) Help me to solve this problem.
(B) Mom had my brother cleaned his room.
(C) Sad movies make me crying all the time.
(D) My parents never let me to play online games all day.
(E) My teacher has us wash our hands before lunch time.

① 1개　② 2개　③ 3개　④ 4개　⑤ 5개

13. 다음 중 영어 문장을 우리말로 <u>잘못</u> 옮긴 것은?

(3점)

① She came early to get a better seat at the musical.
= 그녀는 더 나은 뮤지컬 좌석을 얻기 위해 일찍 왔다.

② Put the milk in the refrigerator so that it won't spoil.
= 우유가 상하지 않도록 냉장고에 넣어라.

③ I was too tired to focus on studying.
= 나는 공부에 집중해서 너무 피곤했다.

④ Be quiet so that I can concentrate on my work.
= 내 일에 집중할 수 있도록 조용히 해 줘.

⑤ He got up early in order to see the sunrise.
= 그는 일출을 보기 위해 일찍 일어났다.

14. 다음 중 어법상 옳지 <u>않은</u> 것은? (4점)

① The box was heavy so that I couldn't move it.
② He speaks so clearly that everyone could understand him.
③ Please write down the address so that you won't forget it.
④ Mom parked the car under a tree so that it won't get too hot.
⑤ I lowered my voice so that no one could hear our conversation.

[15~19] 다음 글을 읽고 물음에 답하시오.

<Maria from Brazil>

In Brazil, there are many dishes that ⓐare made with cassava, a vegetable similar to a potato, I love cassava chips the most. Once when I had a bad day at school and felt stressed out, my best friend bought me a bag of cassava chips. When I started ⓑto eat the chips, my stress suddenly disappeared. The crisp sound of eating chips made me ⓒfeel better. Now, every time I'm stressed out, I eat cassava chips. Then (A)_____.

<Simon from France>

I have many comfort foods, but I love madeleines the most. A madeleine is a small cake that looks like a sea shell. People in France enjoy madeleines as an afternoon snack. My grandmother always makes madeleines for me when I visit her. They taste best when they come right out of the oven. Then the kitchen ⓓis filled with a sweet smell. I especially like eating her orange madeleines with a cup of tea. Every time I see or smell madeleines, I think of my grandmother.

Let me ⓔsharing my grandmother's special recipe with you so that you can make orange madeleines, too. Maybe madeleines will become a comfort food for you!

---

16. 위 글의 밑줄 친 ⓐ~ⓔ 중 어법상 어색한 것은?

(3점)

① ⓐ   ② ⓑ   ③ ⓒ   ④ ⓓ   ⑤ ⓔ

17. 위 글의 주제로 가장 적절한 것은?   (4점)

① Madeleines
② Chicken Soup
③ Comfort Food
④ Homemade Food
⑤ Food Around the World

18. 위 글의 내용과 일치하는 것은?   (4점)

① A madeleine is made with a sea shell.
② Simon makes his grandmother madeleines when he visits her.
③ The French always eat madeleines for breakfast.
④ Simon thinks of his grandmother whenever he smells madeleines.
⑤ Madeleines taste best before they are baked in the oven.

15. 위 글의 빈칸 (A)에 들어갈 말로 가장 적절한 것은?   (4점)

① I am sad!
② I run to school!
③ I feel good again!
④ I won't eat it again!
⑤ I become stressed out!

19. 위 글에서 답을 찾을 수 <u>없는</u> 질문은?   (4점)

① What is Maria's comfort food?
② How much is a bag of cassava chips?
③ What happened when Maria started to eat the chips?
④ What is Simon's favorite comfort food?
⑤ When do madeleines taste best?

[20~22] 다음 글을 읽고 물음에 답하시오.

Jessica from USA

My comfort food is chicken soup. In the USA, people eat this soup when they have a cold. When I was a small child, I caught a very bad cold. My father (A)내가 나을 수 있도록 치킨 수프 한 그릇을 나에게 만들어 주셨지. The hot soup warmed my body, and I slowly started to feel better. It was also very ⓐ[taste / tasty]. Now, when I catch a cold, I eat chicken soup.

Maria from Brazil

In Brazil, there are many dishes that are made with cassava, a vegetable similar to a potato. I love cassava chips the most. Once when I had a bad day at school and felt stressed out, my best friend bought me a bag of cassava chips. When I started to eat the chips, my stress suddenly ⓑdisappear. The crisp sound of eating chips made me feel better. Now, ⓒ_____ I'm stressed out, I eat cassava chips. Then I feel good again!

Simon from France

I have many comfort foods, but I love madeleines the most. A madeleine is a small cake that looks like a sea shell. People in France enjoy madeleines as an afternoon snack. My grandmother always makes madeleines for me when I visit her. They taste best when they come right out of the oven. Then the kitchen ⓓis filled ( ) a sweet smell. I especially like ⓔeat her orange madeleines with a cup of tea. Every time I see or smell madeleines, I think of my grandmother.

Let me share my grandmother's special recipe with you so that you can make orange madeleines, too. Maybe madeleines will become a comfort food for you!

---

20. 위 글의 내용으로 알 수 있는 것은? (4점)

① Jessica's father was a professional chef.
② American people enjoy eating chicken soup when it is cold.
③ There are a lot of vegetables similar to a potato in Brazil.
④ Maria felt stressed out and had a bad day because of her best friend.
⑤ A madeleine is the food that makes Simon think of his grandmother.

21. 위 글의 밑줄 친 (A)의 우리말과 같은 뜻이 되도록 〈보기〉의 단어를 한 번씩 모두 사용하여 영작하시오. (5점)

<보기>
could / for / chicken / bowl / so / well of / get / a / me / soup / that / I / made

→ _____

22. 위 글의 ⓐ~ⓔ에 대한 설명으로 어색한 것은? (4점)

① ⓐ: 둘 중 알맞은 단어는 tasty이다.
② ⓑ: disappear의 바른 형태는 was disappeared이다.
③ ⓒ: 빈칸에 알맞은 단어는 '~할 때마다'를 뜻하는 whenever이다.
④ ⓓ: '~로 가득 차다'의 의미로 빈칸에 알맞은 단어는 with이다.
⑤ ⓔ: eat의 바른 형태는 to eat이다.

[23~24] 다음 글을 읽고 물음에 답하시오.

Jessica from USA

My comfort food is chicken soup. In the USA, people eat this soup when they have a cold. When I was a small child. I caught a very bad cold. My father made me a bowl of chicken soup so that I could get well. The hot soup warmed my body, and I slowly started to feel (A)[better / worse]. It was also very tasty. Now, when I catch a cold, I eat chicken soup.

Maria from Brazil

In Brazil, there are many dishes are made with cassava, a vegetable similar to a potato. I love cassava chips the (B)[most / least]. Once when I had a bad day at school and felt stressed out, my best friend bought me a bag of cassava chips. When I started to eat the chips, my stress suddenly (C)[appeared / disappeared]. The crisp sound of eating chips made me feel better. Now, every time I'm stressed out, I eat cassava chips. Then I feel good again!

---

23. 위 글의 (A), (B), (C)에 알맞은 말을 차례대로 나열한 것은? (4점)

	(A)	(B)	(C)
①	better	most	appeared
②	better	least	disappeared
③	better	most	disappeared
④	worse	least	appeared
⑤	worse	most	appeared

24. 위 글의 내용과 일치하는 것은? (4점)

① Jessica's uncle made a bowl of chicken soup for her.

② When Jessica has a cold, she eats fried chicken.

③ Many dishes in the USA are made with cassava.

④ Maria's best friend made her cassava chips.

⑤ Maria eats cassava chips when she is stressed out.

[25~26] 다음 글을 읽고 물음에 답하시오.

Simon from France

I have many comfort foods, but I love madeleines the most. A madeleine is a small cake that looks like a sea shell. People in France enjoy madeleines ⓐ_____ an afternoon snack. My grandmother always makes madeleines for me when I visit her. They taste best when they come right out ⓑ_____ the oven. Then the kitchen is filled ⓒ_____ a sweet smell. I especially like eating her orange madeleines with a cup of tea. Every time I see or smell madeleines, I think ⓑ_____ my grandmother.

Let me (A)_____ my grandmother's special recipe with you so that you can make orange madeleines, too. Maybe madeleines will become a comfort food for you!

---

25. 위 글의 빈칸 ⓐ~ⓒ에 들어갈 단어가 순서대로 바르게 짝지어진 것은? (4점)

① as - at - of

② as - of - with

③ of - as - with

④ after - of - as

⑤ with - of - about

26. 위 글의 빈칸 (A)에 들어갈 말로 가장 적절한 것은? (4점)

① stop   ② need   ③ share

④ catch   ⑤ differ

◎ 선택형 문항의 답안은 컴퓨터용 수정 싸인펜을 사용하여 OMR 답안지에 바르게 표기하시오.
◎ 서술형 문제는 답을 답안지에 반드시 검정 볼펜으로 쓰시오.
◎ 총 26문항 100점 만점입니다. 문항별 배점은 각 문항에 표시되어 있습니다.

[송파구 ○○중]

1. 다음 짝지어진 의미가 서로 같지 <u>않은</u> 것은?   (4점)

① • This juice is on me.
  • I'll pay for the juice.

② • Don't make a long face.
  • Don't feel sad.

③ • It's raining cats and dogs.
  • It's raining a lot.

④ • I feel under the weather.
  • I don't feel well.

⑤ • Spaghetti is not my cup of tea.
  • I like spaghetti.

[인천 ○○중]

2. 다음 밑줄 친 부분의 우리말 번역이 <u>어색한</u> 것은?
(3점)

① Yoga <u>came from</u> India. (유래했다)

② Kimchi is a <u>healthy</u> Korean food. (건강에 좋은)

③ I <u>picked up</u> some money on the street. (주웠다)

④ The travelers <u>passed through</u> the desert. (멀리 돌아서 지나갔다)

⑤ The Mayan <u>civilization</u> in Central America was very advanced. (문명)

[경기 ○○중]

3. 다음 대화의 빈칸에 들어갈 말로 가장 알맞은 것은?
(4점)

A: Break a leg.
B: Excuse me? Can you say that again?
A: I said, "Break a leg."
B: What does that mean?
A: It means "＿＿＿＿＿＿＿＿＿＿＿＿"

① Good luck.   ② Don't feel sad.
③ I'll pay for this.   ④ I don't feel well.
⑤ It's raining a lot.

[경기 ○○중]

4. 주어진 말에 이어질 대화의 순서가 가장 적절한 것은?
(4점)

Everything looks delicious.

(A) That means "I don't like something."
(B) Yes. Would you like some of my spaghetti?
(C) Oh, I see. You don't like spaghetti.
(D) No, thanks. Spaghetti is not my cup of tea.
(E) Not your cup of tea? What exactly do you mean?

① (A)-(D)-(E)-(B)-(C)   ② (A)-(E)-(D)-(C)-(B)
③ (B)-(D)-(A)-(E)-(C)   ④ (B)-(D)-(E)-(A)-(C)
⑤ (D)-(C)-(B)-(A)-(E)

[성북구 ○○중]

5. 다음 그림 속 밑줄 친 문장을 옳게 영작한 것은? (3점)

점심은 내가 살게.

① What will we eat for lunch?
② Lunch is on me.
③ Let's have lunch with me.
④ Let's go out for lunch.
⑤ I'm going to have lunch.

[6~7] 다음 대화를 읽고 물음에 답하시오.

Lucy: Thank you for everything, Jiho. ⓐI had a great time in Korea.

Jiho: My pleasure. Please come visit me again, Lucy.

Lucy: ⓑI'd love to, but before I do, I'd like to invite you to visit me in London.

Jiho: Thanks. Anyway, ⓒit's too bad that you can't come to my soccer game tomorrow.

Lucy: I'm sorry that I can't stay longer. I'll keep my fingers crossed for you.

Jiho: Excuse me, ⓓwhat do that mean?

Lucy: It means "I wish you good luck."

Jiho: Oh. Thanks. Have a nice trip.

Lucy: Thanks. ⓔI'll keep in touch.

B: Everything looks delicious.

G: Yes. Would you like some of my spaghetti?

B: No, thanks. Spaghetti is not my cup of tea.

G: Not your cup of tea? What does that mean?

B: It means "(B)_____."

G: Oh, I see. You don't like spaghetti.

① (A) This juice is on me
　 (B) I don't like something

② (A) I feel under the weather
　 (B) I like to eat something

③ (A) It's raining cats and dogs
　 (B) I feel so good

④ (A) This juice looks delicious
　 (B) I need to take some medicine

⑤ (A) I want to drink this juice
　 (B) I want to have a cup of tea

6. 위 대화의 ⓐ~ⓔ 중 어법상 옳지 <u>않은</u> 것은?　(4점)

① ⓐ　② ⓑ　③ ⓒ　④ ⓓ　⑤ ⓔ

7. 위 대화의 내용과 일치하는 것은?　(3점)

① Jiho는 런던에 살고 있다.

② Jiho는 Lucy에게 행운을 빌어줬다.

③ Lucy는 Jiho의 축구 시합에 갈 수 없다.

④ Jiho는 내일 런던에서 축구 시합이 있다.

⑤ Lucy는 한국에서 더 이상 머물고 싶지 않았다.

8. 다음 대화의 흐름상 빈칸 (A), (B)에 들어갈 표현이 순서대로 바르게 짝지어진 것은?　(4점)

G: (A)_____, Suho.

B: Excuse me? Can you say that again?

G: I said, "(A)_____." It means "I'll pay for the juice."

B: Oh. Thanks a lot.

G: You're welcome.

9. 다음 대화의 내용과 일치하는 것은?　(4점)

Jane: Thank you for everything, Jiho. I had a great time in Korea.

Jiho: My pleasure. Please come visit me again, Jane.

Jane: I'd love to, but before I do, I'd like to invite you to visit me in London.

Jiho: Thanks. Anyway, it's too bad that you can't come to my soccer game tomorrow.

Jane: I'm sorry that I can't stay longer. I'll keep my fingers crossed for you.

Jiho: Excuse me, but can you please say that again?

Jane: I said, "I'll keep my fingers crossed for you." It means "I wish you good luck."

Jiho: Oh. Thanks. Have a nice trip.

Jane: Thanks. I'll keep in touch.

① Jane은 한국을 떠나려고 한다.

② Jane은 한국에서 힘든 시간을 보냈다.

③ Jiho는 런던에 더 이상 머물 수 없다.

④ Jiho는 내일 열릴 축구경기에 갈 수 없다.

⑤ Jiho는 Jane에게 행운을 빌어준다.

[10~11] 다음 대화를 읽고 물음에 답하시오.

> B: Everything looks delicious.
> G: Yes. Would you like some of my spaghetti?
> B: No, thanks. Spaghetti is not my cup of tea.
> G: Not your cup of tea? What does that mean?
> B: It means "(A)_____"
> G: Oh, I see. You don't like spaghetti.

10. 위 대화를 읽고 알 수 <u>없는</u> 것은?　　　(4점)

① 남자와 여자는 스파게티에 관해 이야기하고 있다.

② 여자는 남자에게 자신의 스파게티를 맛보라고 제안했다.

③ 여자는 남자의 의도를 한 번에 이해하지 못했다.

④ 남자는 평소에 차를 마시며 휴식을 취한다.

⑤ 남자는 여자의 스파게티를 먹어보라는 제안을 거절했다.

11. 위 대화의 빈칸 (A)에 들어갈 말로 가장 자연스러운 것은?　　　(3점)

① I don't feel well.

② I agree with you.

③ I wish you good luck.

④ I can't understand it.

⑤ I don't like something.

12. 다음 빈칸에 알맞은 말을 쓰시오.　　　(5점)

> • The word *shampoo* comes from the Hindi word *chāmpo*, _____ means "to press."

→ _____

13. 다음 중 어법상 바르지 <u>않은</u> 것은?　　　(4점)

① This is the Eiffel Tower, which is in Paris.

② This is King Sejong, that invented *Hangeul*.

③ He's not sure if he can pass the test or not.

④ She's wondering whether she should go or stay.

⑤ Mom doesn't know whether or not I have a dream.

14. 다음 우리말 문장을 영어로 바르게 옮긴 것은? (4점)

> • 까마귀들이 매우 영리하다는 것은 흥미롭다.

① It is interesting that crows are very smart.

② That was true crows are very smart.

③ It is not surprising that crows are very smart.

④ This is strange what crows are very smart.

⑤ What was not true that crows are very smart.

15. 다음 주어진 우리말과 의미가 같도록 괄호 안의 단어들을 바르게 배열했을 때, 7번째로 올 단어는?　　　(4점)

> • 그가 매운 음식을 잘 먹는다는 것은 확실하다.
> (eat, certain, spicy food, it, well, that, can, is, he)

① eat　　② spicy　　③ that

④ can　　⑤ well

[16~17] 다음 글을 읽고 물음에 답하시오.

English has often borrowed words from other cultures or languages. Here are some examples with interesting stories.

shampoo

The word *shampoo* comes from the Hindi word *chāmpo*, which means "to press." In India, the word (A)[used / was used] for a head massage. British traders in India experienced a bath with a head massage and (B)[introduced / was introduced] it to Britain in the 18th century.

The meaning of the word *shampoo* changed a few times after it first entered English around 1762. In the 19th century, *shampoo* got its present meaning of "washing the hair." Shortly after that, the word began to be also used for a special soap for the hair.

robot

The word *robot* comes from the play *R.U.R.*, which was written in 1920 by a Czech writer Karel Čapek. In the play, robots are machines that look like humans. They (C)[designed / are designed] to work for humans and are produced in a factory.

It is interesting that the idea of using the word *robot* didn't come from Karel Čapek himself. He originally called the machines in his play *labori* from the Latin word for "work." However, his brother suggested *roboti*, which means "slave workers" in Czech. Karel Čapek liked the idea and decided to use the word *roboti*. In 1938, the play was made into a science fiction show on television in Britain.

16. 위 글의 내용과 일치하지 <u>않는</u> 것은? (4점)

① 희곡 'R.U.R.'에서 로봇들은 공장에서 생산된다.

② 영어에는 다른 문화나 언어에서 빌려온 단어들이 있다.

③ *roboti*는 '일(work)'을 의미하는 라틴어 단어에서 유래되었다.

④ 희곡 'R.U.R.'은 영국 TV에서 공상 과학물로 만들어졌다.

⑤ 18세기에는 *shampoo*라는 단어가 '머리 감기'라는 의미가 아니었다.

17. 위 글의 괄호 (A), (B), (C) 안에서 문맥에 맞는 낱말로 가장 적절한 것은? (4점)

	(A)	(B)	(C)
①	used	was introduced	designed
②	was used	was introduced	are designed
③	used	introduced	designed
④	was used	introduced	are designed
⑤	was used	was introduced	designed

18. 다음 글의 빈칸 (A)에 들어갈 문장으로 가장 적절한 것은? (4점)

The word *hamburger* originally comes from Hamburg, Germany's second-largest city. *Hamburger* means "people or things from Hamburg" in German. The origin of the first hamburger is not clear. However, (A)_____ _____ in a small town in Texas, USA, sometime between 1885 and 1904. A cook placed a Hamburg-style steak between two slices of bread, and people started to call such food a hamburger.

① it believes the hamburger was invented

② it believes that the hamburger was invented

③ it is believed that the hamburger was invented

④ it is believing that the hamburger was invented

⑤ it believed that the hamburger was invented

[19~20] 다음 글을 읽고 물음에 답하시오.

The word *hurricane* comes from the ⓐSpanish word *huracán*, which comes from the name of a Mayan god. In the Mayan ⓑcreation myth, Huracán is the weather god of wind, storm, and fire, and he is one of the three gods who created humans. However, the first humans ⓒangered the gods, so Huracán caused a great flood.

The first Spanish contact with the Mayan civilization was in 1517. Spanish explorers who were ⓓpassing through the Caribbean experienced a hurricane and ⓔpicked out the word for it from the people in the area. 영어에서 *hurricane*이 초기에 사용된 예 하나는 1608년에 셰익스피어가 쓴 희곡에서였다.

19. 위 글에서 밑줄 친 ⓐ~ⓔ 중에서 문맥상 낱말의 쓰임이 적절하지 <u>않은</u> 것은?　　(4점)

① ⓐ　　② ⓑ　　③ ⓒ　　④ ⓓ　　⑤ ⓔ

20. 위 글의 밑줄 친 우리말을 영작할 때, 다음 〈보기〉에서 필요한 단어만 골라 빈칸을 올바르게 완성한 것을 고르면?　　(4점)

| 〈보기〉 is / a / at / 1608 / by / was / in / play / Shakespeare / in |

In English, one of the early uses of *hurricane* _____.

① in play at 1608 was at a Shakespeare
② was in a play by Shakespeare in 1608
③ is in a play by Shakespeare at 1608
④ was at 1608 by Shakespeare in a play
⑤ is a play by Shakespeare in 1608

21. (A)~(E) 중 아래 문장이 들어가기에 가장 적절한 곳은?　　(4점)

He originally called the machines in his play *labori* from the Latin word for "work."

(A) It is interesting that the idea of using the word *robot* didn't come from Karel Čapek himself. (B) However, his brother suggested *roboti*, which means "slave workers" in Czech. (C) Karel Čapek liked the idea and decided to use the word *roboti*. (D) In 1938, the play was made into a science fiction show on television in Britain. (E)

① (A)　② (B)　③ (C)　④ (D)　⑤ (E)

[22~23] 다음 글을 읽고 물음에 답하시오.

The word *hamburger* originally comes from Hamburg, Germany's second-largest <u>city</u>. *Hamburger* means "<u>people</u> or things from Hamburg" in German.

The <u>origin</u> of the first hamburger is not <u>clear</u>. However, it is believed that the hamburger was invented in a small town in Texas, USA, sometime between 1885 and 1904.

A cook placed a Hamburg-style steak between two slices of bread, and people started to call <u>such</u> food a hamburger.

22. 위 글의 밑줄 친 단어 중 다음 영영풀이에 해당하는 것은?　　(4점)

the beginning, cause, or source of something

① city　　　② people　　　③ origin
④ clear　　　⑤ such

23. 위 글의 내용과 일치하는 것은?　　(4점)

① 함부르크는 독일에서 가장 큰 도시이다.
② 햄버거가 발명된 시기는 분명하지 않다.
③ 햄버거는 함부르크에서 처음 만들어졌다.
④ 미국의 텍사스 사람들이 햄버거를 즐겨 먹었다.
⑤ 햄버거라는 이름은 요리를 처음 만든 요리사가 지었다.

[24~26] 다음 글을 읽고 물음에 답하시오.

(A)_____ Here are some examples with interesting stories.

shampoo

The word *shampoo* comes from the Hindi word *chāmpo*, which means "to press." In India, ⓐit was used for a head massage. British traders in India experienced a bath with a head massage and introduced ⓑit to Britain in the 18th century.

The meaning of the word *shampoo* changed a few times after ⓒit first entered English around 1762. In the 19th century, *shampoo* got its present meaning of "washing the hair." Shortly after that, it began to be also used for a special soap for the hair.

robot

The word *robot* comes from the play *R.U.R.*, which was written in 1920 by a Czech writer Karel Čapek. In the play, robots are machines that look like humans. ⓓThey are designed to work for humans and are produced in a factory.

It is interesting that the idea of using the word *robot* didn't come from Karel Čapek himself. He originally called the machines in his play *labori* from the Latin word for "work." However, his brother suggested *roboti*, which means "slave workers" in Czech. Karel Čapek liked the idea and decided to use ⓔit. In 1938, the play was made into a science fiction show on television in Britain.

24. 위 글의 빈칸 (A)에 들어갈 내용으로 가장 적절한 것은? (3점)
① The English word *shampoo* originated from India.
② Some English words have come from other countries.
③ There are lots of English words with African origin.
④ Historically, English has borrowed words from Czech.
⑤ The meanings of some English words have changed a lot.

25. 위 글의 밑줄 친 ⓐ~ⓔ가 가리키는 대상이 적절하지 <u>않은</u> 것은? (4점)
① ⓐ the word *chāmpo*
② ⓑ a bath with a head massage
③ ⓒ the word *shampoo*
④ ⓓ the robots in the play *R.U.R.*
⑤ ⓔ the word *labori*

26. 위 글을 읽고 알 수 있는 내용으로 적절하지 <u>않은</u> 것은? (4점)
① 단어 *shampoo*는 인도에 있던 영국 무역상을 통해 영국으로 소개되었을 것이다.
② 현대 영어에서 단어 *shampoo*는 '머리를 감다'라는 동사뿐만 아니라 '머리를 감는 용도의 비누'라는 명사의 의미로도 쓰인다.
③ 단어 robot은 1920년에 쓰여진 체코의 한 연극에 나오는 단어 *roboti*에서 유래되었다.
④ Karel Čapek은 자신의 연극에 나오는 기계의 이름으로 '노예 노동자'보다 '일'이라는 의미를 더 선호했을 것이다.
⑤ 연극 R.U.R.이 영국의 TV쇼로 만들어지면서 단어 robot이 영국에 소개되었을 것이다.

◎ 선택형 문항의 답안은 컴퓨터용 수정 싸인펜을
사용하여 OMR 답안지에 바르게 표기하시오.
◎ 서술형 문제는 답을 답안지에 반드시 검정
볼펜으로 쓰시오.
◎ 총 26문항 100점 만점입니다. 문항별 배점
은 각 문항에 표시되어 있습니다.

[충남 ○○중]

1. 다음 영어 표현과 그 뜻을 연결한 것으로 가장 적절
한 것은? (4점)

① Break a leg. – Watch out.

② You're pulling my leg. – It's very easy.

③ I'm in hot water. – I'll pay for hot water.

④ I feel under the weather. – I don't feel well.

⑤ Don't make a long face. – Don't be nervous.

[용산구 ○○중]

2. 다음 각 단어의 영영풀이가 <u>어색한</u> 것은? (4점)

① originally – in the beginning

② century – a period of ten years

③ press – to push something with your finger

④ hurricane – a storm with very strong fast winds

⑤ shampoo – a liquid soap used for washing hair

[성북구 ○○중]

3. 다음 빈칸 (A)에 공통으로 들어갈 표현으로 적절한
것은? (3점)

Girl: (A)_____ Can you buy some medicine for me?
Boy: Excuse me. What did you say?
Girl: I said (A)_____. It means "I don't feel well."

① I'm in hot water.

② I am on cloud nine.

③ It's not my cup of tea.

④ I feel under the weather.

⑤ It's raining cats and dogs.

[인천 ○○중]

4. 다음 대화의 밑줄 친 'I'll keep in touch.'가 의미하
는 바로 가장 적절한 것은? (4점)

G: Thank you for everything, Jiho. I had a great time in Korea.
B: My pleasure. Please come visit me again, Lucy.
G: I'd love to, but before I do, I'd like to invite you to visit me in London.
B: Thanks. Anyway, it's too bad that you can't come to my soccer game tomorrow.
G: I'm sorry that I can't stay longer. I'll keep my fingers crossed for you.
B: Excuse me, but can you please say that again?
G: I said, "I'll keep my fingers crossed for you." It means "I wish you good luck."
B: Oh, Thanks. Have a nice trip.
G: Thanks. <u>I'll keep in touch</u>.

① Watch out.

② Don't be nervous.

③ You and I agree.

④ I wish you good luck.

⑤ I'll call you or write to you.

[전북 ○○중]

5. 다음 대화의 빈칸 ⓐ에 들어갈 알맞은 것은? (4점)

A: Dinner is on me.
B: Excuse me, but what does that mean?
A: ⓐ_____

① I said, "Dinner is on me."

② Let's have dinner together.

③ It means "I'll pay for dinner."

④ I'd like to eat Spanish food.

⑤ I'm sorry, but I already ate dinner.

[6~7] 다음 대화를 읽고 물음에 답하시오.

Lucy: Thank you for everything, Jiho, I had a great time in Korea.

Jiho: My pleasure. Please come visit me again, Lucy.

Lucy: I'd love to, but before I do, I'd like to invite you to visit me in London.

Jiho: Thanks. Anyway, it's too bad that you can't come to my soccer game tomorrow.

Lucy: I'm sorry that can't stay longer. I'll keep my fingers crossed for you.

Jiho: _____

Lucy: I said, "I'll keep my fingers crossed for you." It means "I wish you good luck."

Jiho: Oh. Thanks. Have a nice trip.

Lucy: Thanks. I'll keep in touch.

6. 위 대화의 빈칸에 들어갈 말로 알맞지 <u>않은</u> 것은? (4점)

① What did you say?

② Can you repeat that?

③ Why do you think so?

④ Excuse me? I beg you pardon?

⑤ Can you please say that again?

7. 위 대화의 내용과 일치하지 <u>않는</u> 것은? (4점)

① Jiho는 내일 축구 시합이 있다.

② Lucy는 한국에서 즐거운 시간을 보냈다.

③ Jiho와 Lucy는 계속 연락하고 지낼 것이다.

④ Jiho는 Lucy에게 런던에 가기로 손가락을 걸고 약속했다.

⑤ "I'll keep my fingers crossed for you."는 행운을 빈다는 뜻이다.

8. 다음 대화의 빈칸에 들어갈 말로 가장 적절한 것은?

(4점)

A: I feel under the weather.

B: Excuse me, but can you please say that again?

A: I said, "I feel under the weather." It means "_____" I think I have a cold.

B: Oh. Why don't you buy some medicine before you get on the plane? You can get medicine at the store over there.

A: I guess I should.

① Good luck.　　　　② Don't feel sad.

③ I don't feel well.　　④ It's raining a lot.

⑤ Don't be nervous.

9. 다음 대화의 빈칸에 들어갈 표현으로 가장 적절한 것은? (4점)

W: Thank you for everything, Jiho. I had a great time in Korea.

M: My pleasure. Please come visit me again, Lucy.

W: I'd love to, but before I do, I'd like to invite you to visit me in London.

M: Thanks. Anyway, it's too bad that you can't come to my soccer game tomorrow.

W: I'm sorry that I can't study longer. Break a leg.

M: Excuse me, but can you please say that again?

W: I said, "Break a leg." It means "_____"

M: Oh. Thanks. Have a nice trip.

W: Thanks. I'll keep in touch.

① Good luck.　　　　② Take it easy.

③ Don't feel sad.　　④ Let me think about it.

⑤ I'm worried about you.

10. 다음 대화를 읽고 빈칸에 들어갈 알맞은 표현을
    고르면?   (4점)

Linda: Everything looks delicious.
Minsu: Yes. Would you like some of my
       spaghetti?
Linda: No, thanks. Spaghetti is not my cup of
       tea.
Minsu: Not your cup of tea? What does that
       mean?
Linda: It means "_____"
Minsu: Oh, I see. What would you like to
       eat?

① I don't feel well.
② I ate it like a bird.
③ I don't like something.
④ I make it easy for you.
⑤ I'll pay for the spaghetti.

11. 다음 중 어법상 올바른 문장은?   (4점)

① My uncle, which lives in Cheongju, is an
  English teacher.
② Ron is my friend, that I study with in the
  same class.
③ My father, whose is a scientist, is now in
  China.
④ Julia lost her ring, which were very
  expensive.
⑤ She lied to her mom, which made her angry.

12. 다음 <보기>와 같이 문장을 바꿔 쓸 때 빈칸에 들
    어갈 말로 가장 적절한 것은?   (3점)

<보기>
• That he lost the race was shocking.
→ _____ was shocking that he lost the
  race.

① It   ② This   ③ That
④ What   ⑤ Which

13. 다음 두 문장을 관계대명사의 계속적 용법으로 바
    르게 연결한 것은?   (4점)

A: I am reading a book about Paris.
+
B: I visited Paris two years ago.

① I am reading a book about Paris, that I
  visited two years ago.
② I am reading a book about Paris, which I
  visited two years ago.
③ I am reading a book about Paris, who I
  visited two years ago.
④ I am reading a book about Paris that I
  visited two years before.
⑤ I am reading a book about Paris that I
  visited two years before.

14. 다음 글 (A)를 읽고 who나 which를 활용하여 글
    (B)의 빈칸 ⓐ와 ⓑ를 완성하시오.   (5점)

(A)
(Mona Lisa)
Leonardo da Vinci painted it.
(the Eiffel Tower)
Gustave Eiffel designed and built it.

(B)
I want to see the Mona Lisa, ⓐ_____
_____. I also want to visit the Eiffel
Tower, ⓑ_____.

ⓐ _____

ⓑ _____

[15~17] 다음 글을 읽고 물음에 답하시오.

The word *hurricane* comes from the Spanish word *huracán*, which ⓐoriginates from the name of a Mayan god. In the Mayan creation myth, Huracán is the weather god of wind, storm, and fire, and he is one of the three gods who created humans. However, the first humans ⓑangered the gods, so Huracán caused a great flood.

The first Spanish contact (A)_____ the Mayan civilization was in 1517. Spanish explorers who were ⓒpassing through the Caribbean experienced a hurricane and picked (B)_____ the word for it from the people in the area. In English, one of the early uses of *hurricane* was in a play by Shakespeare in 1608.

The word *hamburger* originally comes from Hamburg, Germany's second-largest city. *Hamburger* means "people or things from Hamburg" ⓓin German.

The origin of the first hamburger is not clear, However, it is believed that the hamburger ⓔwas invented in a small town in Texas, USA, sometime between 1885 and 1904. A cook placed a Hamburg-style steak between two slices of bread, and people started to call such food a hamburger.

15. 위 글의 문맥상 ⓐ~ⓔ 중 우리말 의미가 옳지 **않**은 것은? (3점)

① ⓐ originates from: ~에서 유래한다

② ⓑ angered: 화나게 했다

③ ⓒ passing through: ~을 통과해 지나가는

④ ⓓ in German: 독일인들은

⑤ ⓔ was invented: 발명되었다

16. 위 글의 내용과 일치하는 것은? (4점)

① *hurricane*은 독일어 단어에서 왔다.

② 스페인과 마야 문명과의 첫 접촉은 1608년이었다.

③ hurricane은 셰익스피어의 희곡에서 쓰이기도 했다.

④ *Hamburg*는 독일에서 가장 큰 도시이다.

⑤ 한 요리사가 자기가 만든 음식을 *hamburger*라고 이름 붙였다.

17. 위 글의 빈칸 (A), (B)에 들어갈 말로 바르게 짝지어진 것은? (4점)

① in - from

② in - up

③ with - up

④ with - to

⑤ from - to

18. 다음 글의 빈칸에 들어갈 표현으로 알맞은 것은? (4점)

The word *shampoo* comes from the Hindi word *chāmpo*. In India, the word was used for a head massage. British traders in India experienced a bath with a head massage and introduced it to Britain in the 18th century. _____ after it first entered English. In the 19th century, *shampoo* got its present meaning of "washing the hair." Shortly after that, the word began to be also used for a special soap for the hair.

① The meaning of the word *shampoo* changed a few times

② The word *shampoo* started to be used for a special soap for the hair

③ British traders enjoyed the bath with a head massage

④ The meaning of the word *shampoo* has not changed at all

⑤ The word *shampoo* originated from the Hindi word *chāmpo*

[19~20] 다음 글을 읽고 물음에 답하시오.

---

shampoo

The word *shampoo* comes from the Hindi word *chāmpo*, which means "to press." In India, the word was used for a head massage. British traders in India experienced a bath with a head massage and introduced it to Britain in the 18th century.

The meaning of the word *shampoo* changed a few times after it first entered English around 1762. In the 19th century, *shampoo* got its present meaning of "washing the hair." Shortly after that, the word began to be also used for a special soap for the hair.

robot

The word *robot* comes from the play *R.U.R.* and it was written in 1920 by a Czech writer Karel Čapek. In the play, robots are machines that look like humans. They are designed to work for humans and are produced in a factory.

(A)_____ is interesting (B)_____ the idea of using the word *robot* didn't come from Karel Čapek himself. He originally called the machines in his play *labori* from the Latin word for "work." However, his brother suggested *roboti*, and it means "slave workers" in Czech. Karel Čapek liked the idea and decided to use the word *roboti*.

---

19. 위 글의 빈칸 (A), (B)에 들어갈 것으로 가장 알맞게 짝지어진 것은? (4점)

	(A)	(B)
①	It	that
②	It	what
③	It	why
④	That	what
⑤	That	why

20. 위 글의 내용과 일치하는 것은? (4점)

① 샴푸라는 단어는 '머리 감다'라는 힌디어 *chāmpo* 에서 유래된다.

② 18세기 영국에서는 두피 마사지가 큰 유행이었다.

③ 19세기에 샴푸라는 단어는 '머리 감기'라는 뜻을 갖게 되었다.

④ 희곡 *R.U.R.*의 로봇들은 인간과는 다르게 생겼다.

⑤ *roboti*라는 단어는 라틴어에서 유래된다.

[21~22] 다음 글을 읽고 물음에 답하시오.

The word *hurricane* (A)_____ the Spanish word *huracán*, which (A)_____ the name of a Mayan god. In the Mayan creation myth, Huracán is the weather god of wind, storm, and fire, and he is ⓐone of the three gods who created humans. However, the first humans angered the gods, so Huracán ⓑcaused a great flood. The first Spanish contact with the Mayan civilization was in 1517. Spanish explorers ⓒwho were passing through the Caribbean experienced a hurricane and ⓓpicked up the word for it from the people in the area. In English, ⓔone of the early uses of *hurricane* was in a play by Shakespeare in 1608.

---

21. 위 글의 (A)에 공통으로 들어갈 수 있는 표현으로 적절한 것은? (3점)

① differs from   ② suffers from

③ escapes from   ④ recovers from

⑤ originates from

22. 밑줄 친 ⓐ~ⓔ의 의미로 어색한 것은? (4점)

① ⓐ - 인간을 창조한 세 명의 신들 중 한 명

② ⓑ - 거대한 태풍을 일으켰다

③ ⓒ - 카리브 해를 통과하고 있던

④ ⓓ - 그것을 가리키는 단어를 알게 되었다

⑤ ⓔ - 'hurricane'이 초기에 사용된 예 중 하나

[23~24] 다음 글을 읽고 물음에 답하시오.

---
hurricane

(A)The word *hurricane* comes from the Spanish word *huracán*, which originates from the name of a Mayan god. (B)In the Mayan creation myth, Huracán is the weather god of wind, storm, and fire, and he is one of the three gods who created humans. (C)However, the first humans angered the gods, so Huracán caused a great flood. (D)The first Spanish contact with the Mayan civilization was in 1517. (E)Spanish explorers experienced a hurricane in the Caribbean. Then, they picked up the word for it from the people in the area. In English, one of the early uses of *hurricane* was in a play by Shakespeare in 1608.

---

23. 위 글의 문장 (A)~(E)에 대한 우리말 해석이 정확한 것은? (4점)

① (A): hurricane이라는 단어는 스페인어 단어인 *huracán*에서 왔는데, 그것은 신을 섬기는 제사의 이름에서 유래한다.

② (B): 마야의 창조 신화에서 *huracán*은 바람, 폭풍우, 그리고 물을 다스리는 날씨의 신이다.

③ (C): 하지만 최초의 인간들이 그 신들을 화나게 했고, 그래서 Huracán은 인간에게 지독한 가뭄을 내렸다.

④ (D): 스페인이 마야 문명을 처음 공격했던 것은 1517년이었다.

⑤ (E): 카리브해에서 스페인 탐험가들이 허리케인을 겪었다.

24. 위 글을 참고하여 다음 A의 질문에 대한 B의 답변으로 적절한 것을 고르면? (4점)

A: Who is Huracán in the Mayan creation myth?

B: _____
---

① It was in 1517.

② It comes from the Spanish word *huracán*.

③ It was in a play by Shakespeare in 1608.

④ He is the weather god of wind, storm, and fire.

⑤ Spanish explorers experienced a hurricane and picked up the word for it.

[25~26] 다음 글을 읽고 물음에 답하시오.

The word *robot* comes from the play *R.U.R.*, which ⓐwere written in 1920 by a Czech writer Karel Čapek. In the play, robots are machines that look like humans. They are designed to work for humans and ⓑproduce in a factory.

(A)It is interesting that the idea of using the word *robot* didn't come from Karel Čapek himself. He originally called the machines in his play *labori* from the Latin word for "work." However, his brother suggested *roboti*, ⓒthat means "slave workers" in Czech. Karel Čapek liked the idea and decided ⓓusing the word *roboti*. In 1938, the play ⓔwas made into a science fiction show on television in Britain.

---

25. 밑줄 친 ⓐ~ⓔ 중, 어법상 옳은 것은? (4점)

① ⓐ   ② ⓑ   ③ ⓒ   ④ ⓓ   ⑤ ⓔ

26. 위 글의 (A)의 that과 쓰임이 같은 것은? (3점)

① It was a flower that my mother gave me.

② It was yesterday that Tom broke the window.

③ It was Sumi that he met on the street last Sunday.

④ It is true that Ms. Smith will come back next week.

⑤ It is in the morning that I enjoy swimming with my sister.

◎ 선택형 문항의 답안은 컴퓨터용 수정 싸인펜을 사용하여 OMR 답안지에 바르게 표기하시오.
◎ 서술형 문제는 답을 답안지에 반드시 검정 볼펜으로 쓰시오.
◎ 총 28문항 100점 만점입니다. 문항별 배점은 각 문항에 표시되어 있습니다.

[경북 ○○중]

1. 다음 짝지어진 두 단어의 관계가 나머지와 다른 것은?
(3점)

① buy – sell   ② true – false
③ smart – foolish   ④ sick – healthy
⑤ easy – different

[경북 ○○중]

2. 다음 두 사람의 관계로 적절한 것은?   (3점)

W: Hello. Do you need some help?
B: Yes. I'd like to return this smartphone case.
W: Let's see. Do you have the receipt with you?
B: Here it is. I bought it three days ago.
W: Oh, then it's possible.

① cook – guest   ② mother – son
③ doctor – nurse   ④ clerk – customer
⑤ teacher – student

[부산 ○○중]

3. 대화의 빈칸에 들어갈 가장 알맞은 말은?   (4점)

A: Hello. I'd like to exchange this T-shirt for these pants.
B: Is there anything wrong with it?
A: _____
B: I see.

① It is broken.
② No, I love it.
③ I don't like the color.
④ I want my money back.
⑤ I want to get a refund.

[경북 ○○중]

4. 다음 중 의도하는 바가 나머지 넷과 다른 것은? (4점)

① Excuse me?
② May I help you?
③ I beg your pardon?
④ Can you repeat that?
⑤ Could you say that again?

[경북 ○○중]

5. 다음 빈칸에 들어갈 말로 어색한 것은?   (4점)

A: Excuse me. I'd like to get a refund for this shirt.
B: OK. Is there anything wrong with it?
A: _____
B: I see.

① It's too tight.
② I like the color.
③ I changed my mind.
④ It's too small for me.
⑤ It's very uncomfortable.

[인천 ○○중]

6. 다음 빈칸에 공통으로 들어갈 말로 알맞은 것은? (3점)

• Before you go shopping, make a shopping list. Don't buy items that aren't _____ the list even if they're _____ sale. Then you won't buy things _____ the spot.

① on   ② in   ③ at
④ off   ⑤ into

7. 다음 짝지어진 대화 중 <u>어색한</u> 것은?　　　　(3점)

① A: How do I know when to submit the report?

　　B: It is written on the board.

② A: Do you know where to buy a Nintendo Switch?

　　B: Sorry. I don't know.

③ A: I've done cleaning the floor. Tell me how to do it.

　　B: Why don't you empty the trash can first?

④ A: What are you looking for?

　　B: My earphones. I don't know where to find it.

⑤ A: What's wrong?

　　B: I got lost. Can you tell me how to get to Shinmok Middle School?

8. 다음 대화를 읽고 질문에 답할 수 <u>없는</u> 것은?　(4점)

Man: Hello. May I help you?

Lucy: Yes, please. I'd like to get a refund for this cap.

Man: Do you have the receipt?

Lucy: No, I don't. I received it as a gift.

Man: If you don't have the receipt, then, it's not possible to get a refund.

Lucy: I see. Then, can I exchange it for something else?

Man: Yes, you can. What would you like to get?

Lucy: I want to get this blue bag.

Man: The price is the same, so you can just take it.

Lucy: Thank you.

① What is Lucy doing?

② When did Lucy buy the cap?

③ Why can't Lucy get a refund?

④ Is it allowed to exchange the cap for something else?

⑤ Does Lucy have the receipt?

9. 다음 대화를 읽고 <u>어색한</u> 부분끼리 짝지어진 것은?

(4점)

M: The jeans I bought on sale ⓐ<u>was</u> very cheap, but I need to ⓑ<u>exchange</u> them for a smaller size.

W: What's the problem?

M: It's too ⓒ<u>tight</u> and I want a different color.

W: The real problem is your spending habit. You already have many jeans. It's not ⓓ<u>smart</u> to buy more jeans.

M: That's true. It's not ⓔ<u>easy</u> to become a smart spender but, I changed my mind. I'll follow your advice and ⓕ<u>return</u> them tomorrow.

① ⓐ, ⓑ　　　② ⓐ, ⓒ　　　③ ⓑ, ⓒ

④ ⓓ, ⓕ　　　⑤ ⓔ, ⓕ

10. 다음 두 문장의 의미가 모두 드러나도록 한 문장으로 바꾼 것은?　　　　(4점)

• She started to do her homework two hours ago.

• She is still doing her homework.

① She did her homework two hours ago.

② She has started to do her homework two hours ago.

③ She is going to do her homework for two hours.

④ She has doing her homework two hours ago.

⑤ She has been doing her homework for two hours.

[11~12] 다음 대화를 읽고 물음에 답하시오.

> A: Hello. May I help you?
> B: Yes, please. I'd like to get a refund for this cap.
> A: Do you have a receipt?
> B: No, I don't. I received it as a gift.
> A: If you don't have the receipt, then it's not possible to get a refund.
> B: I see. Then, can I exchange it for something else?
> A: Yes, you can. What would you like to get?
> B: I want to get this blue bag.
> A: Let me see.... The price is the same, so you just can take it.
> B: Thank you.

11. 위 대화에서 두 사람의 관계로 알맞은 것은? (3점)

① clerk - customer
② writer - reader
③ friend - friend
④ doctor - patient
⑤ teacher - student

12. 위 대화 다음에 아래와 같이 문자 메시지를 작성할 때, 빈칸 (A)~(C)에 각각 들어갈 단어로 가장 적절한 것은? (4점)

> Mom: Did you get a(n) (A)_____ for the cap?
> → No, I couldn't. Instead, I (B)_____ it for a (C)_____.

	(A)	(B)	(C)
①	refund	exchange	blue bag
②	refund	exchanged	blue cap
③	refund	exchanged	blue bag
④	exchange	refund	blue cap
⑤	exchange	refunded	blue cap

13. 다음 중 어법상 바르게 쓰인 문장은? (3점)

① How long did they been reading books?
② I have learning Chinese since last month.
③ It has been snowed since last night.
④ She has been watched TV for three hours.
⑤ He has been talking on the phone for an hour.

14. 다음 중 두 문장의 의미가 서로 같지 <u>않은</u> 것은? (3점)

① When I feel stressed, I run.
= When I'm stressed out, I run.
② The bags are full of potatoes.
= The bags are filled with potatoes.
③ It has been raining for two hours.
= It began raining two hours ago, but it isn't raining now.
④ John ran hard to win the race.
= John ran hard so that he could win the race.
⑤ Bibimbap is healthy as well as delicious.
= Bibimbap is not only delicious but also healthy.

15. 다음 문장의 빈칸에 들어가는 의문사를 각각 쓰시오. (6점)

> • She taught me _____ to use this machine, but it's still difficult to use.
> • We haven't decided _____ to travel, maybe Canada or France?
> • Can you tell me _____ to go to school? This week, or next week?

→ _____ _____ _____

[16~18] 다음 글을 읽고 물음에 답하시오.

Q: Hello, Dr. Money. I'm Steve. I have difficulty saving money. For example, I've been saving ⓐto go to my favorite singer's concert for the last two months. (A)_____, I still don't have enough money. I don't know what ⓑto do.

A: Let's see. In the last few weeks, you spent 80% of your allowance and only ⓒsaved 20%. I think you've been ⓓspend too much. To save money, you need to have a tighter budget. (B)_____, you can follow the 50%-40%-10% rule. Save 50%, spend 40%, and donate the remaining 10% to charity. By ⓔfollowing the rule, you can manage your money better. Then you can save money faster to buy the ticket.

16. 위 글의 빈칸 (A)와 (B)에 들어갈 말이 순서대로 바르게 짝지어진 것은?　　　　(4점)

	(A)	(B)
①	However	For example
②	Therefore	For instance
③	Similarly	In other words
④	Furthermore	Even though
⑤	In fact	On the other hand

17. 위 글의 밑줄 친 ⓐ~ⓔ 중, 어법상 어색한 것은?　　　　(3점)

① ⓐ　　② ⓑ　　③ ⓒ　　④ ⓓ　　⑤ ⓔ

18. 위 글의 내용과 일치하는 것은?　　　　(3점)

① Steve는 돈을 모으는 데 어려움이 없다.
② Steve는 콘서트 표를 살 돈을 모두 모았다.
③ Steve는 용돈의 대부분을 저축했다.
④ Dr. Money는 Steve가 충분히 저축하고 있다고 생각한다.
⑤ 50%-40%-10% 규칙은 50%를 저축하고, 40%를 소비하고, 10%를 기부하는 것을 말한다.

[19~20] 다음 글을 읽고 물음에 답하시오.

<Teens' Spending Habits>

How smart are you with your money? These are the results of a survey of 100 students at Green Middle School.

We first asked students "Are you smart with your money?" As Graph 1 shows, 70% answered "No" while 30% answered "Yes." We then asked the students who answered "No" what their biggest money worry is. As Graph 2 shows, 60% think they don't have enough allowance while 28% think they have (A)_____ saving money. Lastly, 12% said they spent money on things they didn't need.

Our survey shows that the majority of students think they are not smart with their money. Managing money is not easy, and becoming a smart spender takes effort.

19. 위 글의 내용과 일치하지 않는 것은?　　　　(4점)

① To be a smart spender takes effort.
② The second question was asked of 70 students.
③ The survey asked 100 students at Green Middle School about their spending habits.
④ Graph 1 shows that the majority of students think they are not smart with their money.
⑤ We can see that most of the students think they get enough allowance from Graph 2.

20. 문맥상 (A)에 들어갈 수 없는 것은?　　　　(3점)

① trouble　　　　　② difficulty
③ difference　　　　④ a problem
⑤ a hard time

[21~24] 다음 글을 읽고 물음에 답하시오.

Q: I'm Jason. I get a weekly allowance, but I never have enough. By Thursday, all of my money is gone. ⓐI don't know what I should do.

A: Hi, I'm Dr. Money. Let's look at your spending diary. ⓑYou used up most of your money at the beginning of the week. Here's my tip. Don't carry around all of your weekly allowance. Divide the money into days and carry only the money you need for each day.

Q: Hello, Dr. Money. I'm Steve. It is not easy to save money. ⓒFor example, I've been saved my allowance to go to my favorite singer's concert for the last two months. However, I still don't have enough money.

A: Let's see. In the last few weeks, you spent 80% of your allowance and only saved 20%. I think you spend too much. To save money, you need to have a tighter budget. For example, you can follow the 50%-40%-10% rule. ⓓSave 50%, spend 40%, and donate the remaining 10% to charity. By following the rule, you can manage your money better. ⓔThen you can save money faster to buy the ticket.

Q: I'm Minji. I like to buy things on sale. ⒶIf something's on sale, I buy it Ⓑalthough I don't need it. Last week, I bought two T-shirts on sale, but I already have many.

A: Buying things on sale is good Ⓒif you buy things you need. In your case, the problem is Ⓓif you buy things you don't even need. Here's some advice. Before you buy something, ask yourself, "Do I really need this?" Also, when you go shopping, make a shopping list Ⓔeven if they're on sale. Then you won't buy things on the spot.

---

21. 위 글의 밑줄 친 ⓐ~ⓔ 중 어법상 옳지 <u>않은</u> 것은? (4점)

① ⓐ ② ⓑ ③ ⓒ ④ ⓓ ⑤ ⓔ

22. 위 글에 쓰인 어휘의 영영풀이가 <u>아닌</u> 것은? (3점)

① being offered at a reduced price
② a sum of money which is returned to you
③ to give money to a group that needs help
④ in the exact place where something is happening
⑤ money given by parents to a child regularly so that the child can spend

23. 위 글의 밑줄 친 Ⓐ~Ⓔ 중 문맥상 <u>어색한</u> 것은? (3점)

① Ⓐ ② Ⓑ ③ Ⓒ ④ Ⓓ ⑤ Ⓔ

24. 위 글의 내용과 일치하지 <u>않는</u> 것은? (4점)

	Problem	Advice
Jason	① I think my allowance is not enough.	② Write a spending diary and check how you spend your money.
Steve	③ Saving money is not easy.	④ Manage your money within a strict budget.
Minji	I cannot help buying things on sale.	⑤ Make a shopping list and be careful not to buy things you don't really need.

*cannot help ~ing: ~하지 않을 수 없다

[25~26] 다음 글을 읽고 물음에 답하시오.

How smart are you with your money? These are the results of a survey of 100 students at Green Middle School.

We first asked students "Are you smart with your money?" As Graph 1 shows, 70% answered "No" while 30% answered "Yes." We then asked the students (A)_____ answered "No" what their biggest money worry is. As Graph 2 shows, 60% think they don't have enough allowance while 28% think they have difficulty saving money. Lastly, 12% said they spent money on things they didn't need.

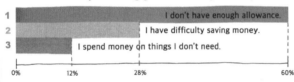

Our survey shows that the (B)_____ of students think they are not smart with their money. Managing money is not easy, and becoming a smart spender takes effort.

25. 위 글의 빈칸 (A), (B)에 들어갈 단어로 알맞게 짝지어진 것은? (4점)

	(A)	(B)
①	who	some
②	who	majority
③	which	rest
④	which	majority
⑤	which	rest

26. 위 글의 내용과 일치하는 것은? (4점)

① 위의 설문은 중학생 대상이었다.

② 70%의 학생들은 돈 관리를 잘하고 있다.

③ 과반수의 학생들은 본인의 용돈에 만족해한다.

④ 28%의 학생들이 저금을 하고 있다.

⑤ 12%의 학생들이 꼭 필요한 곳에 용돈을 쓰고 있다.

[27~28] 다음 글을 읽고 물음에 답하시오.

Q: I'm Jason. I get a weekly allowance, but I never have enough. By Thursday, all of my money is gone. I don't know how to solve this problem.

A: Hi, I'm Dr. Money. Let's look at your spending diary. You used _____ most of your money _____ the beginning of the week. Here's my tip. Don't carry _____ all of your weekly allowance. Divide the money _____ days. Then carry only the money you need for each day.

27. 다음 중 빈칸 어디에도 들어갈 수 없는 것은? (3점)

① at   ② up   ③ of

④ into   ⑤ around

28. By which day of the week is Jason's allowance all gone? (3점)

① Monday   ② Tuesday

③ Wednesday   ④ Thursday

⑤ Friday

◎ 선택형 문항의 답안은 컴퓨터용 수정 싸인펜을 사용하여 OMR 답안지에 바르게 표기하시오.
◎ 서술형 문제는 답을 답안지에 반드시 검정 볼펜으로 쓰시오.
◎ 총 27문항 100점 만점입니다. 문항별 배점은 각 문항에 표시되어 있습니다.

[송파구 ㅇㅇ중]

1. 다음 중 단어의 영어 설명으로 옳은 것은?   (4점)

① budget: a sum of money which is returned to you
② refund: the money you have in your bank account
③ balance: money given by parents to a child regularly
④ change: an amount of money that a person or company can spend
⑤ receipt: a piece of paper that shows you have paid for something

[부산 ㅇㅇ중]

2. 다음 두 단어의 관계가 나머지와 다른 것은?   (3점)
① easy - difficult   ② loose - tight
③ same - similar   ④ smart - foolish
⑤ cheap - expensive

[대전 ㅇㅇ중]

3. 다음 대화를 읽고 대답할 수 있는 질문은?   (4점)

Clerk: Hello. May I help you?
Girl: Yes, please. I'd like to get a refund for this cap.
Clerk: Do you have the receipt?
Girl: No, I don't. I received it as a gift.
Clerk: If you don't have the receipt, then, it's not possible to get a refund.
Girl: I see. Then, can I exchange it for something else?
Clerk: Yes, you can. What would you like to get?
Girl: I want to get this blue bag.
Clerk: Let me see .... The price is the same, so you can just take it.
Girl: Thank you.

① How much is the cap?
② What color is the cap?
③ When did the girl get the gift?
④ Why did the girl go to the shop?
⑤ Why did the girl buy the blue bag?

[충남 ㅇㅇ중]

4. 다음 중 의도가 가장 다른 하나는?   (4점)
① I'd like to return this.
② I'd like to get a refund.
③ Can I get my money back?
④ Do you have the receipt with you?
⑤ Is it possible to get my payment back?

[강북구 ㅇㅇ중]

5. 다음 대화의 내용과 일치하는 것은?   (3점)

Man: Hello. May I help you?
Girl: Yes, please, I'd like to get a refund for this cap.
Man: Do you have the receipt?
Girl: No, I don't. I received it as a gift.
Man: If you don't have the receipt, then, it's not possible to get a refund.
Girl: I see. Then, can I exchange it for something else?
Man: Yes, you can. What would you like to get?
Girl: I want to get this blue bag.
Man: Let me see .... The price is the same, so you can just take it.
Girl: Thank you.

① The girl will get a refund for her cap.
② The man wants to get a gift.
③ The man is interested in fashion.
④ The man needs the girl's money.
⑤ The girl will take a blue bag.

6. 다음 대화의 빈칸에 들어갈 말로 가장 적절한 것은? (3점)

Woman: Hello. What can I do for you?
IU: I don't like this color.
_____
Woman: Let's see. Do you have the receipt?
IU: Here it is. I bought it a day ago.
Woman: Oh, then it's possible. Which one do you like?
IU: I like a silver one.
Woman: Here you are.
IU: Thank you.

① May I help you?
② I'll take care of it.
③ Could I get my money back?
④ Would you like to get a refund?
⑤ I'd like to exchange this smartphone.

7. 다음 대화의 흐름이 가장 자연스러운 것은? (4점)

① A: Do you need some help?
   B: Yes, please. I'd like to return this smartphone case.

② A: What kind of cake would you like?
   B: I need some chocolate and flour to make a cake.

③ A: Have you seen three movies in one day?
   B: I can't go to see a movie with you this week.

④ A: Would you like some of my spaghetti?
   B: Yes, please. Spaghetti is not my cup of tea.

⑤ A: Can I exchange this black umbrella for a different color?
   B: I hope you can enjoy this rainy season.

[8~9] 다음 대화를 읽고 물음에 답하시오.

Man: Hello. May I help you?
Girl: Yes, please. I received this cap as a gift. Can I get a refund for it?
Man: (A)_____
     If you don't have the receipt, then, it's not possible to get a refund.
Girl: I see. Then, can I exchange it for something else?
Man: Yes, you can. What would you like to get?
Girl: I want to get this blue bag.
Man: Let me see .... The price is the same, so you can just take it.
Girl: Thank you.

8. 위 대화의 빈칸 (A)에 들어갈 가장 적절한 말은? (3점)
① OK. Here it is.
② Do you have the receipt?
③ Do you want to exchange?
④ Can I get my money back?
⑤ What would you like to get?

9. 위 대화의 내용상 다음 빈칸에 들어갈 수 없는 것은? (4점)

Girl은 _____.

① 모자를 선물 받았다.
② 가방을 돈을 주고 샀다.
③ 결국 환불을 받지 못했다.
④ 모자와 가방의 가격이 동일했다.
⑤ 모자를 환불받기 위해 가게를 찾았다.

10. 다음 (A)에 들어갈 말로 적절하지 <u>않은</u> 것은? (4점)

> W: Hello. Do you need some help?
> B: Yes. (A)_____
> W: Let's see. Do you have the receipt with you?
> B: Here it is. I bought it three days ago.
> W: Oh, then it's possible.

① Can I return this watch?

② I'd like to return this watch.

③ I wonder if I can return this watch.

④ Is it possible to get a refund for this watch?

⑤ Would you like to get a refund for this watch?

11. 다음 중 빈칸에 가장 <u>부적절한</u> 말은? (3점)

> A: May I help you?
> B: Yes. I'd like to exchange this.
> _____

① It's too big.

② It's my favorite.

③ It doesn't fit me.

④ I don't like the color.

⑤ I just changed my mind.

12. 다음 중 어법상 옳은 문장은? (4점)

① It has been raining heavily since last night.

② Jessica has been sick last Sunday.

③ She has been watching TV since two hours.

④ I have been playing soccer all day yesterday.

⑤ Jason and Andy has been reading books for three hours.

13. 다음 중 어법상 올바른 문장의 개수는 <u>모두</u> 몇 개인가? (4점)

> • How long have you been waiting for the bus?
> • The museum has been building in 2019.
> • My father was been working in a bank.
> • She has been teaching English for 3 years.
> • People is said that he was born in Peru.
> • It was the book that he gave me for my birthday.
> • He has been feeling sick since yesterday.

① 2개 ② 3개 ③ 4개 ④ 5개 ⑤ 6개

14. 다음 (A)와 (B)의 의미가 같도록 빈칸에 알맞은 말을 쓰시오. (5점)

> (A) Can you tell me when I should return the book?
> = (B) Can you tell me _____ the book?

→ _____

15. 어법상 옳은 것만을 <u>모두</u> 고른 것은? (4점)

> (A) I want to learn to what swim.
> (B) I asked him where to go shopping.
> (C) Jane has been feeling sick last night.
> (D) I have been watch TV for 2 hours.
> (E) He has been teaching English since 2010.

① (A), (C) ② (B), (E) ③ (B), (C)

④ (A), (C), (D) ⑤ (B), (D), (E)

[16~18] 다음 글을 읽고 물음에 답하시오.

Do you have any money worries? Let's talk with Dr. Money.

Q: I'm Jason. I get a weekly allowance, but I never have enough. By Thursday, all of my money is gone. I don't know how to solve this problem.

A: Hi, I'm Dr. Money. Let's look at your spending diary. You used up most of your money at the beginning of the week. Here's my tip. Don't carry around all of your weekly allowance. Divide the money into days. (A)_____

Q: Hello, Dr. Money. I'm Steve. Saving money is hard for me. For example, I've been saving to go to my favorite singer's concert for the last two months. However, I still don't have enough money.

A: Let's see. In the last few weeks, you spent 80% of your allowance and only saved 20%. I think you've been spending too much. To save money, you need to have a ⓐ_____ budget. For example, you can follow the 50%-40%-10% rule. Save 50%, spend 40%, and donate the remaining 10% to charity. By following the rule, you can manage your money better. Then you can save money faster to buy the ticket.

16. 위 글의 (A)에 들어갈 Dr. Money의 조언으로 가장 적절한 것은?　　　　　　　(3점)

① Ask your parents for more allowance.

② Take two-day allowance and spend it all.

③ Carry only the money you need for each day.

④ Take out money from your savings and spend it.

⑤ Go out without money and ask friends to buy you snacks.

17. 위 글의 ⓐ에 들어갈 말로 적절한 것은?　(4점)

① faster　　　② tighter　　　③ cleaner

④ closer　　　⑤ easier

18. 위 글을 읽고 추측할 수 <u>없는</u> 것은?　(4점)

① On Friday, Jason usually has no money left.

② Jason usually carries all his money when he gets his allowance.

③ Steve's been spending most of his allowance.

④ Steve needs to save 30% more to go to the concert.

⑤ Steve plans to ask his parents to buy him the ticket.

19. 다음 글에서 전체적인 흐름과 <u>관계없는</u> 문장은?
　　　　　　　　　　　　　　　　(4점)

Q. I'm Minji. I like to buy things on sale. If something's on sale, I buy it although I don't need it. ⓐLast week, I bought two T-shirts on sale, but I already have many.

A. Buying things on sale is good if you buy things you need. ⓑIn your case, the problem is that you buy things you don't even need. Here's some advice. ⓒBefore you buy something, ask yourself, "Do I really need this?" ⓓHowever, you shouldn't miss 'Buy One and Get Another One For Free.' Also, before you go shopping, make a shopping list. ⓔDon't buy items that aren't on the list even if they're on sale. Then you won't buy things on the spot.

① ⓐ　　② ⓑ　　③ ⓒ　　④ ⓓ　　⑤ ⓔ

[20~21] 다음 글을 읽고 물음에 답하시오.

Q: Hello, Dr. Money. I'm Steve. I have difficulty saving money. For example, I ⓐ<u>have been saving</u> to go to my favorite singer's concert for the last two months. However, I still don't have enough money. I don't know what to do.

A: Let's see. In the last few weeks, you spent 80% of your allowance and only saved 20%. I think you've been spending too much. ⓑ<u>To save money</u>, you need to have a tighter budget. ⓒ<u>For example</u>, you can follow the 50%-40%-10% rule. Save 50%, spend 40%, and donate the remaining 10% to charity. ⓓ<u>By following</u> the rule, you can manage your money ⓔ<u>better</u>. Then you can save money faster to buy the ticket.

20. 위 글의 내용과 일치하는 것은?   (3점)

① Steve does not have trouble with saving money.

② Steve has gone to concert twice for 2 months.

③ Steve spent only 20 percent of his allowance.

④ Dr. Money thinks Steve has followed the rule.

⑤ It is useful to manage money under the rule.

21. 위 글의 밑줄 친 ⓐ~ⓔ에 대한 설명 중 옳지 <u>않은</u> 것은?   (4점)

① ⓐ: 과거에서 시작된 일이 현재까지 영향을 미치기 때문에 have saved로 바꿔야 한다.

② ⓑ: to 부정사의 부사적 용법으로 '~하기 위해서'로 해석된다.

③ ⓒ: '예를 들어'라는 뜻으로 For instance로 바꿀 수 있다.

④ ⓓ: 전치사 By 뒤의 following은 동명사로, '~하면서' 또는 '~함으로써'라고 해석할 수 있다.

⑤ ⓔ: 원형은 well이고 최상급은 best이다.

[22~23] 다음 글을 읽고 물음에 답하시오.

Minji: I'm Minji. I like to buy things (A)_____. If something's (A)_____, I buy it (B)_____ I don't need it. Last week, I bought two T-shirts (A)_____, but I already have many.

Dr. Money: Buying things (A)_____ is good if you buy things you need. In your case, the problem is that you buy things you don't even need. Here's some advice. Before you buy something, ask yourself, "Do I really need this?" Also, before you go shopping, make a shopping list. Don't buy items that aren't on the list even if they're (A)_____. Then you won't buy things (C)_____.

22. 위 글의 (A)~(C)에 들어갈 표현으로 가장 알맞은 것은?   (4점)

	(A)	(B)	(C)
①	on sale	although	on the spot
②	on sale	if	in the spot
③	for sale	although	in the spot
④	for sale	although	on the spot
⑤	for sale	if	in the spot

23. 위 글의 Dr. Money의 충고가 <u>아닌</u> 것은?   (3점)

① 즉석에서 물건을 구매하지 않는다.

② 할인 물건이라고 다 구매하지는 않는다.

③ 쇼핑을 하기 전에 쇼핑 목록을 작성한다.

④ 쇼핑 목록에 없더라도 할인 물건은 구매한다.

⑤ 구매를 하기 전에 정말 필요한 물건인지 생각해 본다.

[24~25] 다음 글을 읽고 물음에 답하시오.

[Q] Hello, Dr. Money. I'm Steve. I have difficulty saving money. (A)_____, I've been saving to go to my favorite singer's concert for the last two months. (B)_____, I still don't have enough money. I don't know what to do.

[A] Let's see. In the last few weeks, you spent 80% of your allowance and only saved 20%. I think you've been spending too much. To save money, you need to have a tighter budget. For example, you can follow the 50%-40%-10% rule. Save 50%, spend 40%, and donate the remaining 10% to charity. By following the rule, you can manage your money better. Then you can save money faster to buy the ticket.

24. 위 글의 빈칸 (A)와 (B)에 들어갈 말로 알맞은 것은? (4점)

	(A)	(B)
①	For example	However
②	Therefore	Otherwise
③	Therefore	However
④	However	For example
⑤	For example	Therefore

25. 위 글을 참고하여 Steve가 50%-40%-10% 법칙을 따를 경우 아래 빈칸 (A)~(C)에 들어가기에 알맞은 것은? (4점)

Steve's monthly allowance: ₩150,000	
saving	₩(A)_____
(B)_____	₩60,000
donating	₩(C)_____

	(A)	(B)	(C)
①	70,000	donating	10,000
②	70,000	sending	1,5000
③	75,000	donating	50,000
④	75,000	spending	15,000
⑤	85,000	spending	10,000

[26~27] 다음 글을 읽고 물음에 답하시오.

Q: I'm Minji. I like to buy things ⓐon sale. If something's on sale, I buy it ⓑalthough I don't need it. Last week, I bought two T-shirts on sale, but I already have many.

A:

(A) Also, before you go shopping, make a shopping list. Don't buy items that aren't on the list ⓒeven if they're on sale. Then you won't buy things ⓓon the spot.

(B) Buying things on sale is good if you buy things you need. ⓔIn your case the problem is that you buy things you don't even need.

(C) Here's some advice. Before you buy something, ask yourself, "Do I really need this?"

26. 위 글의 밑줄 친 ⓐ~ⓔ의 우리말 의미가 <u>어색한</u> 것은? (3점)

① ⓐ: 할인 판매 중인　② ⓑ: 비록 ~일지라도

③ ⓒ: 만약 ~라면　④ ⓓ: 즉석에서

⑤ ⓔ: 너의 경우에

27. 위 글의 흐름에 맞게 (A)~(C)를 바르게 배열한 것은? (4점)

① (A)-(C)-(B)　② (B)-(A)-(C)

③ (B)-(C)-(A)　④ (C)-(A)-(B)

⑤ (C)-(B)-(A)

정답 및 해설

Lesson 1 (중간)

01 ①	02 major	03 ③	04 ②	05 ③	06 ②
07 ④	08 ⑤	09 ⑤	10 ④	11 ②	12 ③	13 ①
14 ②	15 ⑤	16 if, whether		17 ②	18 ⑤
19 ①	20 ③	21 ①	22 ④	23 ②, ③	24 ②
25 ②	26 ②	27 ④	28 ①	29 ⑤	

01 realize: 실현하다, (목표 등을) 이루다, 깨닫다, 알아차리다, 인식하다

02 '대학생이 공부하는 주요 과목'은 'major(전공)'이다.

03 영화를 보았다고 답한 후에 곧 보기를 바란다는 것은 어색하다.

04 '난 캐나다에 정말 가고 싶어.'라는 바람을 표하는 것으로 보아 '언젠가 다른 나라를 여행해 보기를 바라.'가 적절하다.

05 피아노 음악 듣는 걸 좋아한다는 말에 이어 (D) 자기도 좋아한다고 말하자 (A) 정말이냐며 피아노를 칠 수 있는지 묻고 (C) 그렇다면 상대방은 어떤지 묻자 (B) 배운 적 없다고 답한다.

06 'I really liked your book about training dogs.'로 보아 '작가 - 독자'의 관계가 가장 적절하다.

07 'I'm also watching a lot of TV shows about animals.'라고 했다.

08 이미 책을 읽었다고 했는데 책을 먼저 읽으라고 하는 것은 어색하다.

09 '산에서 멋진 광경을 보았다'라는 말로 보아 ⑤번이 적절하다. ②번은 의문사로 질문을 했기 때문에 적절하지 않다.

10 다른 나라 방문 경험을 묻는 말에 (C) 없다며 있는지 반문하자 (A) 프랑스를 방문했다고 답하며 다른 나라에 방문해 보기를 희망하자 (B) 캐나다 방문을 희망하는 말로 대답한다.

11 'Have you ever ~?'는 '경험'을 묻는 표현이다.

12 'I really liked your book about training dogs.'라고 했다.

13 영작하면 'no knife to cut the cake with'이다.

14 'to eat'이 anything을 수식하도록 해야 한다.

15 ⑤번은 '조건절'을 이끌고 나머지는 '명사절'을 이끈다.

16 동사의 목적절을 이끄는 접속사로 whether와 if가 적절

17 사진 경연 대회에 참가했다는 것에 이어 (A) 1등 상을 받고 (C) 사진작가가 되고 싶어지고 (B) 몇 년의 시행착오 끝에 사진작가로 일하게 되는 순서가 자연스럽다.

18 ⑤번은 '조건절'을 이끌고 있지만 ⓐ와 나머지는 '명사절'을 이끈다.

19 ⓐ는 '깨달았다'가 아니라 '실현했다'의 뜻이다.

20 'When I had to decide on a major in college, I chose engineering.'라고 했다.

21 (A)에서 어렸을 때 이야기를 하고 (C) 대학에서 전공으로 공학을 선택하고 취직했으나 정말로 좋아하는지는 알 수가 없었지만 (B) 사진을 찍으며 심장이 빠르게 뛰고 있는 것을 느낄 수 있었다는 순서가 적절하다.

22 ⓐ see → to see ⓒ have to → had to

23 'I never thought these things could lead to a job.', 'Being an engineer looked OK.'라고 했다.

24 (A) 좋아하는 것을 생각하라고 했으므로 ⓑ,
(B) 열심히 노력해서 사진작가가 됐다고 했으므로 ⓐ,
(C) 용기가 필요하다고 했으므로 ⓒ가 적절하다.

25 서로 상반되는 내용이 이어지므로 'However'가 적절하다.

26 동사의 목적어로 that절이 나올 경우 '단정적인 사실'이 나온다. 내용상 '단정적인 사실'이 아니므로 'whether' 나 'if'가 적절하다.

27 (C) 아이슬란드로 휴가를 가서 오로라의 사진을 찍으며 심장이 빠르게 뛰는 것을 느끼고 (B) 돌아와서 찍은 사진으로 사진 경연 대회에 참가해서 상을 받고 (A) 대담한 결심을 하고 직장을 그만두고 생계 수단으로 사진을 찍기로 했다는 순서가 자연스럽다.

28 'I'm going to tell you how I found my dream and realized it.'라고 했다.

29 'Everything changed when I went on vacation to Iceland one winter.'라고 했다.

Lesson 1 (중간)

01 ①	02 ③	03 ②	04 ④	05 ②	06 ②	07 ④
08 ②	09 ②	10 ③	11 ④	12 ②	13 ③	14 ②
15 to sit on[in]	16 ⑤	17 ⑤	18 ②	19 ④	20 ④
21 ③	22 ①	23 ③	24 ④	25 ⑤	26 ③	27 ①
28 ④						

01 순서대로 lead, realize, pursue, suggest의 영영풀이이다.

02 ③번은 '형용사-부사'이지만 나머지는 '명사-형용사'이다.

03 'Have you ever ~?'로 경험을 물었으므로 'Yes, I do.'가 아니라 'Yes, I have.'로 답해야 한다.

04 Have you ever ~?'로 물었으므로 'Yes, I have.'나 'No, I haven't.'로 답해야 한다. 뒤에서 'I hope you can try it sometime.'이라고 했으므로 'No, I haven't.'가 적절하다.

05 'I really want to become an animal doctor.'라고 했다.

06 수의사가 되는 것을 생각해 봤는지 묻자 (B) 그렇다며 수의사가 되고 싶다고 하고 (A) 목표를 이루기 위해 하고 있는 것을 묻자 (D) 자원봉사라고 답하고 (C) 또 무엇을 하는지 묻자 also로 추가해서 답하는 순서가 적절하다.

07 동물에 관한 '영화'가 아니라 'TV shows'를 많이 관람하고 있다.

08 앞에서 'I know.'라고 했으므로 'I've already read it.'이 자연스럽다.

09 'Yes'로 답했으므로 '가 본 적이 있다'라는 ②번이 적절하다.

10 TV를 껐는지 아닌지 확신할 수 없다는 내용의 ③번이 적절하다.

11 경험을 묻는 질문에 ⓓ 있다고 답하고 ⓑ 목표를 이루기 위해 무엇을 하는지 묻자 ⓒ 자원봉사를 하고 있다고 답하고 ⓔ 또 무엇을 하는지 묻자 ⓐ also로 추가해서 답하는 순서가 자연스럽다.

12 'Yes, I have.'로 답하고 있으므로 경험을 묻는 ②번이 적절하다.

13 '~인지 아닌지'의 의미로 명사절을 이끄는 if가 적절하다.

14 ① talk → talk to[with]
③ to cold drink → cold to drink
④ explaining → explain
⑤ delicious anything → anything delicious

15 의자 위에 앉는 것이므로 전치사 on이나 in을 써야 한다. 수식받는 명사가 전치사의 목적어일 경우 전치사를 생략하면 안 된다.

16 '조건'의 부사절과는 달리 '명사절'을 이끄는 if의 경우 미래는 미래시제로 써야 한다. rains → will rain

17 '빛들의 사진을 많이 찍었어요. 수년 만에 처음으로 나는 심장이 빠르게 뛰고 있는 것을 느낄 수 있었어요.'라고 했다.

18 ②번은 '조건절'을 이끌지만 (A)와 나머지는 '명사절'을 이끈다.

19 '대담한 결심을 했다'는 주어진 글에 이어 그 결심의 내용이 나오는 (D)가 적절하다.

20 앞에서 'be bold'라고 했으므로 courage가 적절하다.

21 ⓐ take → took ⓓ that → if ⓔ made → that made

22 주어진 문장의 it이 가리키는 것이 (A) 앞 문장의 'what you like to do and what makes you happy'이므로 (A)가 적절하다.

23 (A) in fact: 사실은, 사실상
(B) for the first time: 처음으로

24 'It was a stable job, but I didn't know whether I really enjoyed it.'이라고 했다.

25 (A) lead to: ~로 이어지다
(B) decide on: (숙고하여 뭔가를) 고르다
(C) go on vacation to: ~로 휴가를 가다

26 ⓐ did I find → I found ⓑ Be → Being
ⓓ to beat → beat[beating]

27 ①은 '조건절'을 이끌고 ⓕ와 나머지는 '명사절'을 이끈다.

28 'After years of trial and error, I got better, and I began to do some part-time work as a photographer.'라고 한 후 'Now, I'm a professional photographer, and I'm happy.'라고 했다.

Lesson 2 (중간)

01 ⑤ 02 ① 03 ⑤ 04 ⑤ 05 ① 06 ③ 07 ④

08 ④ 09 ① 10 ③ 11 ④

12 (1) She is not only beautiful but also clever.
　　(2) She is clever as well as beautiful.

13 ③ 14 ④

15 (1) 나의 아버지는 너무 바빠서 나에게 전화를 할 수 없었다. (2) 너는 엄마를 돌보기 위해 너의 일을 포기했니?

16 ③ 17 ② 18 ④ 19 ① 20 ③ 21 ⑤ 22 ②

23 ⑤ 24 ⑤ 25 ④ 26 ① 27 ④

01 satisfy: 만족시키다, 충족하다

02 beat: (게임·시합에서) 이기다, 휘젓다, 잘 섞다

03 'hot dog와 milk'를 주문하고 가져오겠다는 것으로 보아 ⑤번이 적절하다.

04 'A madeleine is a small cake that looks like a sea

shell.'이라고 했고 'Every time I see or smell madeleines, I think of my grandmother.'라고 했다. remind: ~에게 생각나게 하다

05 B가 주문하고 있으므로 '주문하다'를 의미하는 order가 적절하다.

06 더 필요한 것은 없는지 묻는 질문에 '있다(Yes)'고 답한 후에 '그게 전부예요.'라고 말하는 것은 어색하다.

07 직업이 무엇인지 묻고 있는데 꿈이 요리사가 되는 것이라고 답하는 것은 어색하다.

08 G가 'I'd like to order two bottles of water.'라고 했다.

09 주문하겠느냐고 묻자 (B) 핫도그를 주문하고 (E) 마실 것을 묻자 (D) 물 한 병으로 답하고 (C) 여기서 먹을 것인지 갖고 갈 것인지 묻자 (A) 가져갈 것이라고 답한다.

10 Staff가 'The total comes to 12 dollars.'라고 했다.

11 음식을 주문했는데 ④번은 마실 것이 필요한지 묻고 있다.

12 not only A but also B = B as well as A: A뿐만 아니라 B도. 이때 A와 B는 문법적으로 같은 것이 나와야 한다.

13 ① fixed → fix ② she → her ④ as → so
⑤ can I → I can

14 (A) help → to help (B) to clean → clean
(E) makes → make

15 (1) so+형/부+that ...: 너무 ~해서 …하다
(2) so that: ~하기 위해

16 'My comfort food is chicken soup. In the USA, people eat this soup when they have a cold.'라고 했다.

17 주어진 문장의 It이 가리키는 것이 (B) 앞 문장의 'a bowl of chicken soup'이므로 (B)가 적절하다.

18 수여동사로 쓰인 make는 간접목적어를 직접목적어 뒤로 보낼 때 전치사 for를 사용한다.

19 disappear(사라지다): 보거나 찾는 것이 불가능하게 되다

20 Comfort food(마음에 위안이 되는 음식)에 관한 글에서 '매운 음식은 복통을 일으킬 수 있다'라는 것은 흐름상 어색하다.

21 'It was also very tasty.'라고 했다.

22 ⓐ는 주격 관계대명사이다.
ⓒ differ는 그 자체로 맞다.
ⓓ는 어법에 맞다.
ⓔ가 가리키는 것은 a bowl of chicken soup이다.

23 (A) look like+명사: ~처럼 보이다

(B) be filled with: ~로 가득 차다
(C) a cup of tea: 한 잔의 차

24 'Let me share my grandmother's special recipe with you so that you can make orange madeleines, too.'라고 했다.

25 'Every time I see or smell madeleines, I think of my grandmother.'라고 했다.

26 ⓐ 아빠는 내가 나을 수 있도록 치킨 수프 한 그릇을 만들어 주셨다.

27 컴퓨터가 고장이 나서 숙제를 할 수 없었는데 동생이 빌려줘서 숙제를 했고 그동안 엄마는 아빠가 컴퓨터를 고치도록 하셨다는 내용에서 '인터넷으로 쇼핑하는 것을 좋아한다.'라는 ⓓ는 어색하다.

Lesson 2 (중간)

> **01** ④ **02** ① **03** ⑤ **04** ③ **05** ③ **06** ① **07** ②
> **08** ② **09** ④ **10** ⑤ **11** ② **12** ② **13** ③ **14** ①
> **15** ③ **16** ⑤ **17** ③ **18** ④ **19** ② **20** ⑤
> **21** made a bowl of chicken soup for me so that I could get well
> **22** ② **23** ③ **24** ⑤ **25** ② **26** ③

01 • make a mistake: 실수하다
• …을 (~에게) 하게 하다(사역동사)
• 만들다

02 ② appear → disappear ③ melt → beat
④ worried and tired → relaxed
⑤ quality → quantity

03 주문하겠느냐는 물음에 괜찮다고 하고서 피자를 달라고 하는 것은 어색하다.

04 주문하겠느냐는 물음에 (B) 핫도그를 주문하고 (D) 마실 것을 묻자 (A) 물 한 병을 주문하고 (E) 여기서 먹을지 가져갈지를 묻자 (C) 가져갈 거라고 답한다.

05 피자를 주문하고 있으므로 주문하겠느냐는 질문이 어울린다.

06 음식을 주문 받고 있으므로 ①번이 적절하다.

07 가져가겠다는 답으로 보아 여기서 먹을지 가져갈지를 묻는 것이 자연스럽다.

08 주문하겠는지 묻자 (C) 핫도그를 주문하고 (D) 마실 것을 묻자 (E) 오렌지 주스를 주문하고 (B) 여기서 먹을지 가져갈지를 묻자 (A) 여기서 먹겠다고 답하는 순서이다.

09 더 주문할 것이 없는지 묻는 질문에 그것들 다 좋아하지 않

는다고 하는 것은 어색하다.

10 ⑤번은 점심으로 보통 무엇을 먹는지 묻는 것이다.

11 Somi가 'It's for here, please.'라고 했다.

12 사역동사의 목적격보어로 동사원형을 쓴다.
(B) cleaned → clean (C) crying → cry
(D) to play → play

13 too ~ to …: 너무 ~해서 …할 수 없다

14 so that ~은 '~하도록'이라는 뜻으로 목적의 의미를 나타내는 접속사이다. heavy so → so heavy

15 카사바 칩을 먹기 시작하자 내 스트레스가 갑자기 사라졌다고 하면서 칩을 먹을 때 나는 바삭하는 소리가 내 기분을 더 좋게 만들었다고 했으므로 '기분이 다시 좋아져!'가 적절하다.

16 사역동사 Let 다음에 목적격보어로 동사원형인 share가 나와야 한다.

17 Maria와 Simon이 본인들에게 위안이 되는 음식 (Comfort Food)에 대해 말하고 있다.

18 'Every time I see or smell madeleines, I think of my grandmother.'라고 했다.

19 카사바 칩 한 봉지의 가격은 알 수 없다.

20 'Every time I see or smell madeleines, I think of my grandmother.'라고 했다.

21 so that ~ 구문을 이용한다.

22 disappear는 자동사이므로 수동태의 형태로 쓸 수 없다. disappeared가 적절하다.

23 (A) 뜨거운 수프는 몸을 따뜻하게 했고, 서서히 '나아지기' 시작했다.
(B) 카사바 칩을 먹기 시작하자 스트레스가 갑자기 사라졌으므로 '가장' 좋아한다.
(C) 칩을 먹을 때 나는 바삭하는 소리가 내 기분을 더 좋게 만들었으므로 스트레스가 갑자기 '사라졌다'.

24 'every time I'm stressed out, I eat cassava chips'라고 했다.

25 ⓐ as: ~로서
ⓑ out of: ~의 밖으로, ~에서 think of: ~을 생각하다 [머리에 떠올리다]
ⓒ be filled with: ~로 가득 차다

26 '아마도 마들렌이 너희에게도 comfort food가 될 거야!'라는 말로 보아 share가 적절하다.

Lesson 3 (기말)

01 ⑤	02 ④	03 ①	04 ④	05 ②	06 ④	07 ③
08 ①	09 ①	10 ④	11 ⑤	12 which		13 ②
14 ①	15 ①	16 ③	17 ④	18 ①	19 ⑤	20 ②
21 ②	22 ③	23 ②	24 ②	25 ⑤	26 ④	

01 'is not my cup of tea'는 '좋아하지 않는다'라는 의미이다.

02 pass through: 통과하다

03 Break a leg. = Good luck.

04 '맛있어 보인다'에 이어 (B) 스파게티를 권하고 (D) 안 좋아한다(not my cup of tea)고 말하자 (E) 무슨 뜻인지 묻고 (A) 안 좋아한다는 말이라고 설명하고 (C) 이해하는 순서이다.

05 Lunch is on me. = I will pay for lunch.

06 ⓓ what does that mean?

07 'it's too bad that you can't come to my soccer game tomorrow'라고 했다.

08 (A) I'll pay for the juice. = This juice is on me.
(B) not my cup of tea = don't like something

09 'Please come visit me again, Jane.', 'Have a nice trip.' 등을 통해 ①번이 답임을 알 수 있다.

10 'not my cup of tea'는 '좋아하지 않는다'라는 의미일 뿐이다.

11 'You don't like spaghetti.'라고 이해하는 것으로 보아 'I don't like something.'이 적절하다.

12 앞에 콤마(,)가 있고 선행사가 *chāmpo*이므로 which가 맞다.

13 that은 계속적 용법의 관계대명사로 쓰이지 않는다.

14 It을 가주어로 쓰고 that절을 진주어로 쓴다.

15 바르게 배열하면 'It is certain that he can eat spicy food well.'이 된다.

16 'his brother suggested *roboti*, which means "slave workers" in Czech'라고 했다.

17 (A) 단어가 사용된 것이므로 수동태
(B) 소개한 것이므로 능동태
(C) They가 robots를 가리키므로 설계되는 수동태가 적절하다.

18 It이 가주어이고 that이 진주어절로 수동태 'is believed'로 써야 한다.

19 picked out(선택하다, 가려내다)이 아니라 picked up ((정보를) 듣게 되다, 알게 되다)이 적절하다.

20 과거 시제이며 '셰익스피어가 쓴 희곡'을 'a play by

Shakespeare'로 나타낸다.

21 주어진 문장의 He가 (B) 앞 문장의 Karel Čapek이므로 (B)가 적절하다.

22 '무언가의 시작, 원인 또는 근원'을 가리키는 말은 'origin' 이다.

23 'it is believed that the hamburger was invented in a small town in Texas, USA, sometime between 1885 and 1904'라고 했으므로 분명하지 않다.

24 shampoo와 robot의 예를 통해 다른 나라에서 들어온 영어 단어에 대해 말하고 있으므로 ②번이 적절하다.

25 ⓔ의 it은 Karel Čapek의 형이 제안한 *roboti*를 가리킨다.

26 'his brother suggested roboti, which means "slave workers" in Czech. Karel Čapek liked the idea and decided to use it.'이라고 했다.

Lesson 3 (기말)

> **01** ④ **02** ② **03** ④ **04** ⑤ **05** ③ **06** ③ **07** ④
> **08** ③ **09** ① **10** ③ **11** ⑤ **12** ① **13** ②
> **14** ⓐ which Leonardo da Vinci painted
>   ⓑ which Gustave Eiffel designed and built
> **15** ④ **16** ③ **17** ④ **18** ① **19** ① **20** ③ **21** ⑤
> **22** ② **23** ⑤ **24** ④ **25** ⑤ **26** ④

01 ① Break a leg. = Good luck.
  ② You're pulling my leg. = You're kidding.
  ③ in hot water = in trouble
  ⑤ Don't make a long face. = Don't feel sad.

02 century – a period of a hundred years

03 I feel under the weather. = I don't feel well.

04 keep in touch: 연락하다

05 '~ is on me.'는 'I'll pay for ~.'라는 의미이다.

06 모두 '(반복) 설명을 요청'하는 표현인데 ③번은 '왜 그렇게 생각하니?'라고 묻는 것이다.

07 손가락을 걸고 약속하지는 않았다.

08 뒤에서 'I think I have a cold.'라고 한 것으로 보아 ③번이 적절하다.

09 Break a leg. = Good luck.

10 ~ is not my cup of tea. = I don't like ~.

11 ① which → who ② that → whom
  ③ whose → who ④ were → was

12 진주어로 that절이 나와 있으므로 가주어 It이 적절하다.

13 두 문장에 공통으로 있는 Paris를 선행사로 하고 계속적 용법의 관계대명사 which를 이용하여 콤마(,)와 함께 쓴다.

14 콤마(,)가 있으므로 계속적 용법의 관계대명사 which를 이용하여 쓴다.

15 in German: 독일어로

16 'In English, one of the early uses of *hurricane* was in a play by Shakespeare in 1608.'라고 했다.

17 (A) contact with: ~와의 접촉
  (B) pick up: (정보를) 듣게 되다, 알게 되다

18 뒤에서 *shampoo*의 의미가 변한 것을 설명하고 있으므로 ①번이 적절하다.

19 (A)에는 가주어로 It이, (B)에는 진주어절을 이끄는 that이 적절하다.

20 'In the 19th century, *shampoo* got its present meaning of "washing the hair."'라고 했다.

21 '~에서 유래하다'라는 의미의 'originates from'이 적절하다.

22 flood: 홍수

23 explorer: 탐험가

24 'In the Mayan creation myth, Huracán is the weather god of wind, storm, and fire'라고 했다.

25 ⓐ were → was ⓑ produce → are produced
  ⓒ that → which ⓓ using → to use

26 (A) 문장의 that과 ④는 진주어이지만 나머지는 'It is[was] ~ that' 강조 용법의 that이다. (①은 관계대명사로 볼 수도 있음.)

Lesson 4 (기말)

> **01** ⑤ **02** ④ **03** ③ **04** ② **05** ② **06** ① **07** ③
> **08** ② **09** ② **10** ⑤ **11** ① **12** ③ **13** ⑤ **14** ③
> **15** how, where, when **16** ① **17** ④ **18** ⑤ **19** ⑤
> **20** ③ **21** ③ **22** ② **23** ④ **24** ② **25** ② **26** ①
> **27** ③ **28** ④

01 반의어의 관계이지만 ⑤번은 반의어가 아니다. easy – difficult가 되면 반의어 관계이다.

02 반품하겠다고 하며, 영수증을 확인하고 있으므로 ④번이 적절하다.

03 무엇이 잘못되었는지 묻고 있으므로 그에 맞는 대답인 ③번이 적절하다.

04 ②번은 도움을 주겠다는 의도이지만 나머지는 '반복을 요

청'하는 것이다.

05 무엇이 잘못되었는지 묻고 있으므로 문제에 대해 대답해야 하는데 ②번은 좋아한다고 답하고 있다.

06 on the list: 목록에 on sale: 할인 판매 중인 on the spot: 즉석에서, 그 자리에서

07 마루 청소를 끝냈다고 하면서 방법을 묻는 것은 어색하다.

08 Lucy가 모자를 산 것이 아니라 선물로 받았다.

09 ⓐ The jeans가 주어이므로 were가 맞다. ⓒ 더 작은 사이즈로 교환할 필요가 있다고 했으므로 'large'가 적절하다.

10 두 시간 전에 숙제를 시작해서 아직 하고 있으므로 현재완료진행시제로 나타낸다.

11 환불하겠다고 하며, 영수증을 확인하고 있으므로 ①번이 적절하다.

12 환불 요청을 했으나 안 되었고 대신 파란 가방으로 교환했으므로 ③번이 적절하다.

13 ① did → have ② learning → learned
③ snowed → snowing ④ watched → watching

14 ③ but it isn't → and it is

15 순서대로 • how, • where, • when이 들어간다.

16 (A) 상반되는 내용이 나오고 있으므로 However, (B) 예를 들고 있으므로 For example이 적절하다.

17 you've been에 이어지는 spending이 적절하다.

18 'Save 50%, spend 40%, and donate the remaining 10% to charity.'라고 했다.

19 '60% think they don't have enough allowance'라고 했다.

20 have difficulty[trouble/a problem/a hard time] -ing: ~하는 데 어려움이 있다

21 I've been saved → I've been saving

22 각각 ① on sale ② refund ③ donate ④ on the spot ⑤ allowance이다.

23 ⓓ는 if가 아닌 that이 나와야 한다.

24 'Divide the money into days and carry only the money you need for each day.'라고 했다.

25 (A) the students를 선행사로 하는 주격 관계대명사가 필요하다. (B) "당신은 돈에 관하여 현명한가?"라는 질문에 70%가 "아니요"라고 답했으므로 'majority(대다수)'가 적절하다.

26 'These are the results of survey of 100 students at Green Middle School.'이라고 했다.

27 순서대로 up, at, around, into가 들어간다.

28 'By Thursday, all of my money is gone.'이라고 했

다.

Lesson 4 (기말)

01 각각 ① refund ② balance ③ allowance ④ budget 이다.

02 모두 '반의어'인데 ③번은 '반의어'가 아니다.

03 'I'd like to get a refund for this cap.'라고 했다.

04 모두 '환불을 요청'하는 표현인데 ④번은 영수증을 갖고 왔느냐는 질문이다.

05 'The price is the same, so you can just take it.'이라고 했다.

06 색깔이 싫다고 은색으로 바꿔가고 있으므로 ⑤번이 적절하다.

07 도움이 필요한지 묻는 말에 스마트폰 케이스를 반품하고 싶다고 하고 있다.

08 빈칸 다음에 '영수증이 없으면 환불 받을 수 없다'고 말하고 있으므로 ②번이 적절하다.

09 가방을 돈을 주고 산 것이 아니라 선물로 받은 모자와 교환했다.

10 ⑤번은 환불받고 싶은지 묻는 질문이지만 나머지는 반품하거나 환불받고 싶다는 표현이다.

11 ②번은 교환하려는 이유로 부적절하다.

12 ② last Sunday → since last Sunday
③ since → for
④ have been playing → played
⑤ has → have

13 순서대로 • 맞음 • has been building → was built
• was → has • 맞음 • People → It • 맞음 • 맞음

14 의문사+주어+should+동사원형 = 의문사+to부정사

15 (A) to what → how to
(C) last night → since last night
(D) watch → watching

16 앞에서 '용돈을 하루 단위로 나누라'고 했으므로 '하루에 필요한 돈만 들고 다니라'고 하는 것이 적절하다.

17 앞에서 '너무 많이 써 왔다'고 했으므로 '더 빠듯한 예산을 세우라'고 하는 것이 적절하다.

18 Steve가 부모님께 티켓을 사달라고 요청할 계획이라는 언급은 없다.

19 필요없는 것은 사지 말라는 충고에서 '그래도 하나 사면 하나를 무료로 받는 것을 놓치지 말라'고 하는 것은 어색하다.

20 'By following the rule, you can manage your money better.'라고 했다.

21 ⓐ는 현재도 진행되고 있는 것으로 고칠 필요 없다.

22 (A) on sale: 할인 판매 중인 for sale: 팔려고 내놓은
(B) '필요하지 않은데도' 산다는 문맥이 적절하다.
(C) on the spot: 즉석에서

23 '쇼핑 목록에 없으면 할인 물건이라도 구매하지 마라'고 했다.

24 (A) 예를 들고 있으므로 For example, (B) 상반되는 내용이 이어지므로 However가 적절하다.

25 (A) 150,000 X 50% = 75,000
(B) 150,000 X 40% = 60,000(spending)
(C) 150,000 X 10% = 15,000

26 even if: (비록) ~일지라도, (설사) ~이라고 할지라도

27 (B) 필요하지 않은 물건도 산다는 문제를 지적하고 (C) 조언을 하며 (A) Also로 추가로 조언하는 순서가 적절하다.

적중 1○○ + 특별부록

Plan B

우리학교
최신기출

동아 · 윤정미 교과서를 배우는

학교 시험문제 분석 · 모음 · 해설집

전국단위 학교 시험문제 수집 및 분석
출제 빈도가 높은 문제 위주로 선별
문제 풀이에 필요한 상세한 해설

중3-1
영어

동아 · 윤정미

값 6,000원

53370
9 791133 716036
ISBN 979-11-337-1603-6